JOURNAL FOR THE STUDY OF THE NEW TESTAMENT
SUPPLEMENT SERIES
3

Editors
Ernst Bammel
Anthony Hanson
David Hill
Max Wilcox

Editorial Secretary
Bruce D Chilton

Department of Biblical Studies
The University of Sheffield
Sheffield S10 2TN
England

STUDIA BIBLICA 1978

III.   Papers on Paul and Other
New Testament Authors

SIXTH INTERNATIONAL CONGRESS ON
BIBLICAL STUDIES

Oxford 3-7 April 1978

Edited by E. A. Livingstone

**Journal for the Study of the New Testament
Supplement Series, 3**

Sheffield
1980

ISSN 0143-5108
ISBN 0 905774 27 2

Published by
JSOT Press
Department of Biblical Studies
The University of Sheffield
Sheffield S10 2TN

Artwork by University of Sheffield
Printing Unit
Printed in Great Britain by
Redwood Burn Limited Trowbridge and Esher
1980

Contents

Prefaces

EDITOR'S PREFACE

The Sixth International Congress on Biblical Studies met in Oxford from 3 to 7 April 1978, under the direction of the Rev. Dr H.F.D. Sparks and the Rev. Dr G.B. Caird. After the invitations to the Congress had been sent out, the publishers of the *Journal for the Study of the Old Testament* kindly offered to issue the proceedings, and these volumes contain the majority of the papers which speakers were willing to have included. It is my pleasant duty to thank those who spoke at the Congress, and especially those whose papers were offered for publication, since it is upon the speakers that the value of any such congress primarily depends.

15 St. Giles,   E.A. Livingstone
Oxford

GENERAL EDITORS' PREFACE

Studia Biblica 1978: III is the third of three volumes devoted to the proceedings of the Sixth International Congress on Biblical Studies held in the Examinations Schools of the University of Oxford from April 3rd to 7th, 1978. The first volume, on Old Testament and related subjects, was published by JSOT Press in June, 1979 as volume 11 in the Supplement Series of the *Journal for the Study of the Old Testament*, and the second, on the Gospels, in May, 1980 as volume 2 in the present Series. This collection of the three volumes of *Studia Biblica 1978* forms the sequel to *Studia Evangelica,* the successive volumes of which have presented papers from previous Congresses, and have been published by the Berlin Academy in their series *Texte und Untersuchungen zur Geschichte der altchristlichen Literatur.* The change of title from *Studia Evangelica* to *Studia Biblica* reflects the broadened scope of the papers read.

At the 1978 Congress more than 470 participants from many countries gathered to hear and discuss the 170 lectures, papers and communications scheduled and skilfully organised by Miss Elizabeth Livingstone. The General Editors of the Supplement Series of the *Journal for the Study of the New Testament* are pleased to be able to make available to a wider audience, as well as to participants themselves, the greater part of the proceedings. One report of the Congress, in the *Catholic Biblical Quarterly* for July, 1978, commented: "Since the only disappointment of the Congress was that it was humanly impossible to hear all the major papers, not to mention the countless *deliciae* of the short reports, the published proceedings will be eagerly anticipated".

A word about the format of the published papers is in order. Readers of papers were asked to take the responsibility of preparing their papers according to the conventions of the *Journal of Theological Studies,* with the exception of the use of Arabic rather than Roman numerals for reference to Biblical chapters. In the case of those papers which were prepared according to some other system of conventions no endeavour has been made to enforce a rigid adherence to the *JTS* style. The General Editors are, however, deeply grateful to the Editors of the *Journal for the Study of the Old Testament,* David J.A. Clines, Philip R. Davies, and David M. Gunn, for their labour in preparing authors' type-scripts for reproduction in a format that is in each case internally consistent and intelligible. Any minor blemishes remain the authors' responsibility.

Ernst Bammel
Anthony Hanson
David Hill
Max Wilcox

October, 1980

Inhalt und Funktion des Urchristlichen Osterglaubens

H.-W. Bartsch,
6302 Lich 1,
Hungenerstr. 51,
W. Germany.

Es wird heute in der Neutestamentlichen Forschung beider
Konfessionen zwar nicht mehr einhellig angenommen, dass der
urchristliche Glaube seinen Ansatz im Glauben an den
auferstandenen Christus hat, die Rückführung des urchristlichen
Glaubens auf den "historischen Jesus" wird zunehmend verstreten.
Dennoch dürfen wir mit der Annahme, dass der urchristliche
Glaube Ostern entstand, einsetzen, da unsere Untersuchung über
die in 1. Kor 15,3-7 von Paulus zitierte Tradition eben diese
Annahme bestätigen wird. Die ersten Christen glaubten an den
Κύριος 'Ιησοῦς Χριστός, weil er ihnen als solcher erschienen
war und nicht wegen einer Autorität, die der vorösterliche
Jesus von Nazareth erworben hatte und die sich über seinen Tod
hinüberrettete /1/. Wenn wir diese von der formgeschichtlichen
Forschung erarbeitete Position einnehmen, muss sich aber die
Frage stellen, was dieser Glaube inhaltlich besagte. Wir
können uns nicht damit zufrieden geben, dass er die Realität
der Auferstehung bezeugt; denn welchen sachlichen Inhalt sollte
der Glaube an einen Auferstandenen haben? Inwiefern ist mit
Jesu Auferstehung der Tod besiegt, wie Paulus es 1. Kor 15,54
schreibt? Diese Frage hat die neutestamentliche Forschung
bisher kaum berührt. Sie ist aber gerade darum in jüngster
Zeit wesentlich geworden, da die Aussage von Jesu Auferstehung
als urchristliches Glaubensbekenntnis mehr und mehr jeden
Inhaltes entleert wurde. Wozu brauchten die ersten Christen
die Aussage über Jesu Auferstehen, wenn sie nur "die Sache
Jesu" weitergehen lassen wollten? Warum gaben sie ihm die
Titel Kyrios und Christus, wenn nur seine Sache, die
Verkündigung des kommenden Gotesreiches, weitergehen sollte.
Es hätte genügt, ihn als Prophet wie den Täufer zu
verehren, als Rabbi, wie es später Rabbi Aqiba gegenüber
geschah. Wir haben darum allen Grund zu fragen, welcher
spezifische Inhalt sich mit der Aussage 1. Kor 15,4f verbindet,
dass Christus ἐγήγερται τῇ ημέρα τῇ τρίτῃ...καὶ ὅτι ὤφθη Κηφᾷ.

*Die zuerst von U. Wilckens (Der Ursprung der Uberlieferung
der Erscheinungen des Auferstandenen, in : "Dogma und
Denkstrukturen", 1963, S. 56ff) vorgetragene These, es handle
sich um eine Legitimationsformel für Petrus und die anderen
Zeugen, die dann von R. Pesch (Zur Entstehung des Glaubens an
die Auferstehung Jesu, ThQu 1973, S. 2Olff) dahin weiter
entwickelt ist, dass diese Legitimationsformel keinerlei
inhaltliche Bedeutung habe, überzeugt darum nicht, weil sich
kein Text findet, der nachweist, dass eine derartige
Legitimationsformel weiter Verwendung fand. Sollte diese
Annahme zutreffen, müsste die frühe Christenheit bis in die
zweite Generation die Träger der Autorität derart qualifizieren.
Sie tut es aber nicht; denn - wie zu zeigen sein wird -
diese Wendung ὤφθη + Dativ (es ist besser, nicht gleich von
einer Formel zu sprechen) begegnet in der Apg keineswegs als
solche, sondern Lukas verwendet sie in seinem Werk in völlig
anderer Funktion.*

Es ist danach aber auch darum zu fragen, weil die
Kontinuität christlichen Glaubens von der Urchristenheit bis zur
Gegenwart festgehalten wird. Mag sich der christliche Glaube
in der Geschichte gewandelt haben, mögen verschiedene
konfessionelle Ausprägungen festzustellen sein, so ist allen
christlichen Konfessionen und Denominationen der Anspruch
dennoch gemeinsam, Nachfolger des Glaubens der ersten Christen
zu sein. Die Annahme, dass die jeweilige konfessionelle
Aussage mit dem urchristlichen Glauben in ungebrochener
Kontinuität steht, lässt sich aber nur als zutreffend erweisen,
wenn dieser urchristliche Glaube inhaltlich bestimmt ist, wenn
diese Annahme nicht als unbegründetes Postulat erscheinen soll.
Wir können uns auch nicht mit der vom Ökumenischen Rat 1948
beschlossenen Formulierung begnügen, die als bindendes Element
für alle Kirchen aussagt: "Der Ökumenische Rat der Kirchen ist
eine Gemeinschaft von Kirchen, die unseren Herrn Jesus Christus
als Gott und Heiland anerkennen." Gewiss geht diese Aussage
auf den urchristlichen Osterglauben zurück und versucht, ihn
derart inhaltlich zu bestimmen. Gerade wenn man diese Formel
inhaltlich akzeptiert, ist es aber notwendig, sie exakt auf den
Ansatz des Glaubens zurückzuführen. Wir haben zu fragen,
inwiefern die älteste urchristliche Tradition 1. Kor 15,3-5 zu
der inhaltlichen Aussage führt, die der ÖRK als die allen
Kirchen gemeinsame Basis nennt.

Damit haben wir bereits die Annahme als gegeben genannt,
dass 1. Kor 15,3-5 die älteste urchristliche Tradition bietet,
die uns den Ansatz des urchristlichen Glaubens wiedergibt.

Auch diese Annahme bedarf jetzt keiner näheren Begründung, zumal
sie - abgesehen von unterschiedlicher Abgrenzung der Tradition -
bis heute Überzeugung der überwiegenden Mehrheit in der
neutestamentlichen Forschung ist. Wir gehen davon aus, dass
der folgende Text das Minimum einer einheitlich von Paulus
zitierten Überlieferung bietet: = (ὅτι) Χριστὸς ἀπέθανεν ὑπὲρ
τῶν ἁμαρτιῶν ἡμῶν, κατὰ τὰς γραφάς, καὶ
(ὅτι) ἐτάφη, καὶ
(ὅτι) ἐγήγερται τῇ ἡμέρᾳ τῇ τρίτῃ κατὰ τὰς γραφάς, καὶ
(ὅτι) ὤφθη Κηφᾷ, εἶτα τοῖς δώδεκα /2/
Ob die folgenden parallelen Aussagen über das Erscheinen des
Christus der gleichen oder anderer Tradition entstammen, braucht
zunächst nicht zu interressieren, da es allein darum geht, dass
die Urchistenheit ihren Glauben als Glaube an die Auferstehung
Christi und an sein Erscheinen bezeugt. Es kann offen bleiben,
ob Paulus verschiedene Traditionen miteinander verbindet, die
vielleicht sogar miteinander konkurrierten, oder ob er die
älteste Tradition von dem Erscheinen des Christus vor Kephas/
Simon durch Überlieferung erweitert, die in anderen Gemeinden
als Grundlage der Verkündigung dient. Die Gleichförmigkeit der
Aussagen das wiederholte ὤφθη + Dativ, könnte auch von Paulus
selbst gebildet sein, um die Einheit der in allen Gemeinden
grundlegenden Predigt (V.11) zu unterstreichen /3/.

*Die Annahme, dass Paulus durch eigene Redaktion die ihm bekannte
Tradition wesentlich bestimmt hat, ist zwar in der Exegese kaum
vertreten worden, da das Bemühen um eine Analyse
unterschiedlicher Traditionen vorherrscht. Dennoch erscheint
es berechtigt, eine solche Redaktion des Paulus zu erwägen, da
er selbst das Ziel seiner Argumentation, die Übereinstimmung
der urchristlichen Predigt und des urchristlichen Glaubens in
allen Gemeinden nennt. Deutlich ist der Eingriff des Paulus in
die von ihm weitergegebene Tradition lediglich V.6:* ἔπειτα ὤφθη
ἐπάνω πεντακοσίοις ἀδελφοῖς ἐφάπαξ, ἐξ ὧν οἱ πλείονες μένουσιν
ἕως ἄρτι, τινὲς δὲ ἐκοιμήθησαν. *Die Hinzufügung des zweiten
Teil des Satzes ist von der Argumentation des Paulus her
verständlich, während der vorhergehende Hauptsatz besser zu
einer Gemeindetradition zu rechnen ist, in der auf die
Erscheinung vor Kephas, vor dem Gremium der Jünger die vor der
Gemeinde folgt, die in den 500 Brüdern repräsentiert ist.*

Dass am Anfang der Überlieferung die Erscheinung vor
Kephas/Simon stand, wird nicht nur durch die Parallelle Lk 24,
34 nahegelegt, die die gleiche Aussage in etwas abgewandelter
und jüngerer Form bietet: ὄντως ἠγέρθη ὁ κύριος καὶ ὤφθη Σίμωνι

/4/. Es zeigt sich auch darin, dass Simon Petrus seine
vorrangige Position in der Überlieferung auch nach dem Übergang
der Gemeindeleitung auf Jakobus (Apg 12,17; 15,13; 21,18)
behält, in den Jüngerlisten ausnahmslos an erster Stelle
genannt wird und im NT wie in der apokryphen Tradition Briefe
und ein Evangelium zugeschrieben erhält. Seine in der
Erscheinung gründende apostolische Autorität ist also niemals
infrage gestellt worden.

Die für die Bestimmung des Ansatzes urchristlichen
Glaubens entscheidende Frage ist nunmehr, welche argumentative
Folge der Doppelsatz hat: (Χριστὸς) ἐγήγερται τῇ ἡμέρᾳ τῇ
τρίτῃ... καὶ ὤφθη Κηφᾷ. Zweifellos hat der Doppelsatz eine
chronologische Folge nennen wollen: Nach der Auferstehung am
dritten Tage ist der Christus dem Kephas erschienen. Es ist
aber nicht ebenso eindeutig, dass diese chronologische Folge
auch die argumentative einschliesst: Die Auferstehung des
Christus wurde durch seine Erscheinung bestätigt, unterstrichen.
Dass die Überlieferung derartig argumentiert, kann aus der
Parallele entnommen werden, die vorausgeht: Er ist gestorben
und wurde begraben, d.h. Das Begrabenwerden bestätigt die
Realität des Sterbens. Diese Parallele ist jedoch nur
beweiskräftig, wenn sie zum Ansatz der Überlieferung gehört.
Lk 24, 34 zeigt jedoch, dass die Doppelaussage über die
Auferstehung und Erscheinung auch selbständig tradiert wurde.
Sie zeigt darüber hinaus, dass in der Entwicklung dieser
Aussage der Aorist vom zweiten Glied, der Erscheinung auf das
erste, auf die Auferstehung übertragen wurde. So darf
geschlossen werden, dass am Anfang die Erscheinung als das ein-
malige Geschehen ausgesagt wurde, von dem her der Glaube an
das im Perfekt ausgedrückte Auferstandensein des Christus
erschlossen wurde. Der Glaube an den auferstandenen Christus
ist danach in der dem Kephas und anderen Jüngern widerfahrenen
Erscheinung begründet /5/.

*Dass der Glaube an den auferstandenen Christus ohne jedes den
Glauben begründende Ereignis entstanden sei, dass er wie R.
PESCH a.a.o. annimmt, in dem durch den historischen Jesus
vermittelten Glauben an seine Messianität gründet, ist eine
unwahrscheinliche Annahme, die den ersten Christen innerhalb
weniger Tage Reflexionen zumutet, die nur in der Gegenwart am
Schreibtisch möglich sind. H. vCAMPENHAUSEN: Der Ablauf der
Osterereignisse und das leere Grab, 3.Aufl.1963 sieht darum im
Auffinden des leeren Grabes das den Glauben begründende
Ereignis. Jedoch bleibt auch bei dieser Annahme eine
entsprechend folgernde Reflexion für die Jünger notwendig, die*

*keineswegs zwingend war, wie die relativ späte Legende Jh 20,
llff zeigt. Diese Annahme CAMPENHAUSENs hat darum wenig
Anhänger gefunden.*

Steht darum argumentativ für den Anfang des urchristlichen
Osterglaubens die Aussage ὤφθη Κηφᾷ an erster Stelle der
Überlieferung, so drängt sich die Frage auf, was die ersten
Christen damit sagen wollen, welchen Vorstellungsgehalt sie mit
dieser Aussage verbinden.

*Die Schwierigkeit, diese Frage zu beantworten, darf daran
gezeigt werden, dass J. SCHNIEWIND 1937 auf die Frage eines
Studenten, wie diese Erscheinung geschehen sei, antwortete, es
liesse sich dies nicht genau sagen, auf jeden Fall aber sei es
nicht so gewesen, dass der Auferstandene den Jüngern wie vorher
alltäglich begegnet sei, und sie hätten darauf nur so reagiert,
als sei Christus eine Zeitlang fort gewesen: "Schön, dass du
wieder da bist." Die Erscheinung sei also mehr als eine
alltägliche Begegnung gewesen. Es geht darum, dieses "mehr"
näher zu bestimmen.*

Für die inhaltliche Bestimmung der Wendung bietet sich
zuerst die NT Konkordanz an. Welche Bedeutung hat sie an
anderen Stellen des NTs? Dabei ergibt sich jedoch schon auf
den ersten Blick, dass es einerseits nur wenige Stellen gibt,
die ihrerseits wenig Aussagewert haben. Paulus selbst
verwendet die Wendung nicht wieder, vielmehr nennt er die ihm
zuteil gewordene Erscheinung Gl 1,15f und 1.Kor 9,1 mit anderen
Vokabeln. Ebenso fehlt die Wendung in allen nachösterlichen
Erscheinungsberichten sowohl bei Mth, Lk und Jh wie in dem an
Mk 16,8 angehängten Sammelbericht. Lk 24,34 - eben die alte
Tradition - ist die einzige synoptische Parallele zu 1.Kor 15,5.

Das Vorkommen der Wendung in der joh. Apokalypse (11,19;
12,1.3) zeigt lediglich - wie auch der Christushymnus 1.Tim
3,16 ὤφθη ἀγγέλοις - dass sie in apokalyptischem Kontext
begegnet, der für sie inhaltlich bestimmend sein kann. Dass
die Wendung bei den Synoptikern nur Mk 9,4 Par begegnet, hat
zu Spekulationen darüber geführt /6/, ob hier ein ursprünglicher
Osterbericht vorliegt, ohne dass jedoch gewertet wurde,
dass in der Verklärungsperikope nicht Christus erscheint,
sondern Moses und Elia den Jüngern und dem verklärten Jesus.

Weiter kann demgegenüber der relativ häufige Gebrauch
führen, den Lukas in seinem Doppelwerk von der Wendung macht.
Ordnen wir seinen Gebrauch chronologisch nach den Ereignissen,

für die Lukas die Wendung benutzt, so ergibt sich folgendes
Bild: Apg 7,2 (Abraham), 7,26.30 (Moses); Lk 1,11 (Zacharias);
22,43 (Gethsemane); Lk 24,34/Apg 13,31 (Christus den Jüngern);
Apg 2,3 (Pfingsten); 9,17/26,16 (Christus dem Paulus); 16,9
(der Mann von Mazdeonien dem Paulus). Bei dieser Verwendung
fällt einerseits auf, dass Lukas in der Parallele zu Mk 9,4 die
Wendung abwandelt zum Partizip und andererseits, dass er in der
Stephanusrede die Wendung bewusst aus der LXX übernimmt, sodass
angenommen werden darf, dass er aus der LXX auch ihre
Bedeutung übernimmt. Es kann sich also lohnen, das Vorkommen
der Wendung in der LXX zu überprüfen.

Der Gebrauch von ὤφθη in der LXX.

Mit Gn 12,7 beginnend bis zu den Königs - und
Chronikbüchern wird ὤφθη + Dativ fast ausschliesslich für das
Erscheinen Gottes, seines Engels oder seiner Doxa gebraucht
/7/. Die Wendung wird von 3 Rg 11,9 an, wo sie zum letzten
Mal zu finden ist - nach der historischen Chronologie der
Ereignisse, nicht der Literatur, die für die LXX Übersetzer
uninteressant war -, nicht wieder verwandt. Keine prophetische
Vision wird mit ihr berichtet. Schon diese Begrenzung
erscheint bedeutsam. Sie wird es umso mehr, als auch innerhalb
des Zeitraums von Abraham bis Salomo Differenzierungen im
Gebrauch festzustellen sind. Dafür gehen wir die einzelnen
Stellen durch.

1. Abraham, Isaak und Jakob

Gn 12,7: Καὶ ὤφθη κύριος τῷ Αβραμ καὶ εἶπεν αὐτῷ Τῷ σπέρματί
σου δώσω τὴν γῆν ταύτην. καὶ ᾠκοδόμησεν ἐκεῖ Αβραμ
θυσιαστήριον κυρίῳ τῷ ὀφθέντι αὐτῳ.

Die Wendung wird im gleichen Wortlaut Gn 17,1; 18,1
wiederholt. Gn 22,14 wird der Name des Berges יִרְאֶה יְהוָה =
Κύριος εἶδεν in der im masoretischen Text gleich lautenden
ätiologischen Begründung mit Κύριος ὤφθη wiedergegeben.

Gn 26,2 wiederholt sich die Erscheinung Gottes von Gn 12,7
für Isaak: ὤφθη δὲ αὐτῷ κύριος καὶ εἶπεν....(3) σοὶ γὰρ καὶ τῷ
σπέρματί σου δώσω πᾶσαν τὴν γῆν ταύτην καὶ στήσω τὸν ὅρκον μου,
ὅν ὤμοσα Αβραμ τῷ πατρί σου. Ausdrücklich wird hier für Isaak
die gleiche Gotteserscheinung berichtet, die Abraham gegeben
war. Die kultätiologische Bedeutung, die die Erscheinung Gn
12,7 hat, hat eine weitere Erscheinung vor Isaak Gn 26,24 /8/.

Während der Traum Jakobs Gn 28,10ff in Bethel/Luz nicht

mit unserer Wendung erzählt wird, obwohl er dieselbe
Verheissung enthält, wie sie Abraham und Isaak gegeben wurde,
wird zunächst dieser Traum durch das Partizip ὀφθείς Gn 31,13;
35,1 qualifiziert, um danach eindeutig wiederholt zu werden,
verbunden mit kultätiologischer Bedeutung, wie sie bereits dem
Traum beigegeben ist. Gn 35,9: ᾽Ὤφθη δὲ ὁ θεὸς Ιακωβ ἔτι ἐν
λουζα.... und die Landverheissung wird unter Bezugnahme auf
Abraham ebenfalls wiederholt. Gn 48,3 berichtet Jakob dies im
gleichen Wortlaut seinem Sohn Joseph.

Ex 6,3 wird die Bedeutung der Wendung zusammenfassend für
die drei Erzväter genannt: ᾽Εγω κύριος· καὶ ὤφθην πρὸς Αβρααμ
καὶ Ισαακ καὶ Ιακωβ, θεὸς ὢν αὐτῶν, καὶ τὸ ὄνομά μου κύριος οὐκ
ἐδήλωσα αὐτοῖς. Für die Priesterschrift beginnt hier zwar ein
neuer Abschnitt mit der Offenbarung des Jahwenamens, für die
LXX Übersetzer ist dies von geringerer Bedeutung als die vorher
berichtete neue Erscheinung eines Engels Jahwes nach den 430
Jahren der Sklaverei.

2. Moses und Israel in der Wüste.

Während die Zeit in Ägypten, jene 430 Jahre ohne eine
Erscheinung Gottes des Herrn blieben, setzt die Befreiung
Israels aus der Sklaverei mit einer Erscheinung ein.
Ausdrücklich wird diese Erscheinung in Beziehung zu denen
gesetzt, die die Erzväter erfuhren.
Ex 3,2: ὤφθη δὲ αὐτῷ (Μωυσης) ἄγγελος κυρίου ἐν φλόγι πυρὸς ἐκ
τοῦ βάτου.....(6) καὶ εἶπεν αὐτῷ Εγω ειμι ὁ θεὸς τοῦ
πατρός σου, θεὸς Αβρααμ καὶ θεὸς Ισαακ καὶ θεὸς Ιακωβ.
Die oben zitierte Stelle Ex 6,3 stellt nochmals sicher, dass
das jetzt beginnende Handeln Gottes an seinem Volk Israel
wieder aufnimmt, was den Erzvätern mit dem Erscheinen des Herrn
gegeben war.

Es folgen während des ganzen Wüstenzuges Erscheinungen der
Doxa Jahwes vor Moses und Aaron und vor dem ganzen Volk. Sie
unterscheiden sich jedoch nicht nur dadurch, dass niemals
wieder wie Gn 12,7 einfach berichtet wird ὤφθη κύριος, sondern
es ist immer die δόξα κυρίου, deren Erscheinen zu berichten
ist. Jedoch auch dieses Erscheinen kann nicht so angenommen
werden, wie dies Abraham möglich war. Es gilt jetzt, was Ex
33, 18ff Moses als Antwort auf seinen Wunsch erfährt, Gott zu
schauen: Kein Mensch kann leben, der Gott geschaut hat.
Entsprechend ist auch die Erscheinung der Doxa Jahwes entweder
von der Wolke verhüllt, oder sie wird mit zur Erde gebeugtem

Angesicht empfangen.

Ex 16,10: καὶ ἡ δόξα κυρίου ὤφθη ἐν νεφέλῃ. Ebenso ist
der Wortlaut Num 14.10. Wird dagegen wie Num 16.19 im
Zusammenhang mit dem Aufruhr Kohras das Erscheinen des Herrn
ohne diesen Zusatz berichtet, so bedeutet dies den Tod, dem das
Volk nur durch die Fürbitte von Moses und Aaron entgeht,
während die "Rotte Korah" von der Erde verschlungen wird.
Dasselbe wiederholt sich unmittelbar darauf, als das Volk wegen
des Todes dieser Sippe gegen Moses und Aaron murrt. Zunächst
bedeckt die Wolke das Zelt des Heiligtums und erst darauf
heisst es Num 17,7 (LXX; MT 16,42): καὶ ὤφθη ἡ δόξα κυρίου.

Andererseits kann dieses Nichtsehen bei einer Erscheinung
auch durch das Herabbeugen zur Erde, also von dem Empfänger der
Erscheinung bewirkt werden.

Num 20,6: καὶ ἦλθεν Μωσῆς καὶ Ααρων ἀπὸ προσώπου τῆς
συναγωγῆς ἐπὶ τὴν θύραν τῆς σκηνῆς τοῦ μαρτυρίου
καὶ ἔπεσαν ἐπὶ πρόσωπον, καὶ ὤφθη ἡ δόξα κυρίου
πρὸς αὐτούς. Sinngemäss ebenso ist die Erscheinung
vor dem Volk Lev 9,23f berichtet.

Wie sehr die LXX Übersetzer daran interessiert sind, kein
direktes Sehen der Doxa Jahwes berichten zu müssen, zeigt sich
Num 14,10, wo nach dem MT dies Fall ist. Sie fügen die
Verhüllung einfach ein: καὶ ἡ δόξα κυρίου ὤφθη ἐν νεφέλῃ ἐπὶ
τῆς σκηνῆς τοῦ μαρτυρίου ἐν πᾶσι τοῖς υἱοῖς Ισραηλ.

Nicht mehr zur Wüstenzeit Israels, aber auch noch nicht zur
Königszeit gehören zwei Erscheinungen eines Engels Jahwes, die
im Richterbuch berichtet sind, und beide Gestalten,die eine
Erscheinung erfahren, ragen in ihrer Bedeutung für Israel unter
den anderen des Richterbuches hervor, es sind Gideon und Simson.
Die Berufung Gideons durch den Engel des Herrn gleicht bis in
den Wortlaut der des Moses, während die Erscheinung vor der
Frau des Manoah, der Mutter des Simson der gleicht, die Gn 18,1
dem Abraham einen Sohn verheisst. In beiden Fällen wird ein
Sohn der bis dahin Unfruchtbaren verheissen. Insofern dürfen
diese beiden Erscheinungen im Zusammenhang der vorausgegangenen
gesehen werden.

Jdc 6,12: καὶ ὤφθη αὐτω ὁ ἄγγελος κυρίου καὶ εἶπεν πρὸς αὐτὸν
Κύριος μετὰ σοῦ, δύνατος τῇ ἰσχύι (ἰσχυρος τῶν
δυνάμεων = B).

Zu bemerken ist, dass der Alexandrinus statt ὤφθη αὐτῷ liest
εὗρεν αὐτόν. Obwohl diese LA keinerlei Anspruch auf
Ursprünglichkeit erheben kann, zeigt sie doch die Unsicherheit
der Abschreiber, in diesem Zusammenhang, angesichts der
wechselnden Haltung Israels eine Erscheinung zu berichten.
Allerdings ist Jdc 13,3 textkritisch ohne eine derartige
Variante.

Es folgt auf die Erscheinung und Berufung des Gideon wie
bei der Berufung des Moses das Zögern des Berufenen und die
Bitte um Zeichen, dass es wirklich Jahwe ist, der Gideon beruft.

Jdc 13,3: καὶ ὤφθη ἄγγελος κυρίου πρὸς τὴν γυναῖκα καὶ εἶπεν
πρὸς αὐτήν und es folgt die Verheissung eines Sohnes, der - wie
später der Täufer - als Nasiräer aufwachsen soll.

Diese beiden Erscheinungen sind jedoch Ausnahmen, vor
allem weil sie nicht wie für die Erzväter oder die Wüstenzeit
eine dauernde Gegenwart Jahwes bezeugen, sondern nur vorüber-
gehende Episoden der Richterzeit einleiten. Jedoch ist
besonders bei der Erscheinung, die die Geburt des Simson
ankündigt, deutlich, dass erst diese Einleitung der Simson-
Sagen zusammen mit dem Schluss Jdc 16,4-30 den Sagen ihre
theologische Bedeutung geben und die Einfügung in das
deuteronomistische Geschichtswerk begründen.

3. Die Königszeit

Nur einmal wird II. Chr. 3,1 im Rückblick die Begegnung
Davids mit dem Engel Jahwes 2. Rg 24,17f als eine Erscheinung
bezeichnet, obwohl sie auch I. Chr. 21,18 nicht als direkte
Begegnung berichtet ist. II. Chr. 3,1: καὶ ἤρξατο Σαλωμων τοῦ
οἰκοδομεῖν τὸν οἶκον κυρίου ἐν Ιερουσαλημ ἐν ὄρει τοῦ Αμορια,
οὗ ὤφθη κύριος Δαυιδ τῷ πατρὶ αὐτοῦ. Es ist jedoch deutlich,
dass es dabei nicht eigentlich um die Erscheinung vor David
geht, sondern die Legitimierung des Tempelbaus ist der Sinn
dieser Verwendung der für eine Erscheinung Jahwes typischen
Wendung. Der Sprachgebrauch ist durch die für Salomo
berichteten Erscheinungen bestimmt. Bedeutsamer für die
Interpretation der LXX Übersetzer ist die unterschiedliche
Übersetzung, die sie dem 2 RG 22 und Ps 17 (MT 18) überlieferten
Psalm Davids geben. Obwohl kaum ein Paralleltext im AT so
wortgetreu gleichlautend überliefert ist, übersetzen die LXX
Übersetzer Vll unterschiedlich. 2. Rg 22,11: καὶ ἐπεκάθισεν
ἐπὶ χερουβιν καὶ ἐπετάσθη, καὶ ὤφθη ἐπὶ πτερύγων. Obwohl der
MT wörtlich genau derselbe ist, lautet die LXX Version von Ps

17, 11 anders: καὶ ἐπέβη ἐπὶ χερουβιν καὶ ἐπετάσθη, ἐπετάσθη
ἐπὶ πτερύγων ἀνέμων. Man wird für den Unterschied kaum die
mögliche textkritische Variante verantwortlich machen können,
dass die Übersetzer 2.Rg 22,11 wajjera᾽ lasen und darum
übersetzten ὤφθη, während sie Ps 17,11 wajjere᾽ lasen und
korrekt mit ἐπετασθη ubersetzten. Haben sie doch die
vorhergehende Vokabel wajjaᶜop ebenfalls - und zwar an beiden
Stellen mit ἐπετάσθη übersetzt. Eher kann angenommen werden,
dass die Übersetzung des gleichen Textes an den verschiedenen
Stellen unabhängig voneinander, vielleicht durch verschiedene
Übersetzer erfolgte. Dann ist aber das Interesse der
Übersetzer erkennbar, im Munde Davids das Zeugnis von einem
Erscheinen Jahwes zu bringen. Dieses Interesse bestand für das
Psalmbuch nicht, das dem Gebrauch durch jeden Beter offen stand.
Was David aussagen konnte, durfte der Beter nicht wiederholen.
Für ihn muss die Schilderung Ps 17,8-16 eine Theophanie bleiben,
wie sie vom Berge Sinai berichtet wird, ohne dass sie die
Qualität gewinnt, die ὤφθη ihr gibt. Für die beiden
Erscheinungen Jahwes vor Salomo begegnet wieder der Sprach-
gebrauch der Genesis, d.h. es wird direkt und ohne Einschränkung
das Erscheinen Jahwes bezeugt.

3.Rg 3,5 (= 2.Chr. 1,7): καὶ ὤφθη κύριος (2.Chr = ὁ θεὸς) τῷ
Σαλωμων ἐν ὕπνῳ (- 2.Chr.): τὴν νύκτα. Es folgt die Bitte
Salomos und die Verheissung Gottes, ihm Weisheit und langes
Leben zu geben.

3.Rg 9,2 (2.Chr. 7,12 mit den gleichen Varianten): καὶ ὤφθη
κύριος τῷ Σαλωμων δεύτερον, καθὼς ὤφθη ἐν Γαβαων. Hier gibt
Jahwe nach dem Tempelbau die Verheissung, dass er in diesem
Haus seinen Namen wohnen lassen will und Salomos Herrschaft auf
ewig festigen, wenn er Gottes Satzungen hält. Das Ende der
Erscheinungen, begründet in dem Zorn Gottes erfolgt aufgrund
der Abgötterei Salomos zu einem orientalischen Herrschertum mit
den fremden Kulten.

3.Rg 11,9 (ohne Parrallele in den Chronikbüchern): ὠργίσθη
κύριος ἐπὶ Σαλωμων, ὅτι ἐξέκλινεν καρδίαν αὐτοῦ ἀπὸ κυρίου
θεοῦ Ισραηλ τοῦ ὀφθέντος αὐτῷ δίς.

Das Partizip ὀφθείς nimmt hier wie auch Gen 12,7; 31,13;
35,1; Jdc 6,26 eindeutig die Erscheinungen auf, die vorher
berichtet sind. Sie gewinnen dadurch die besondere Qualität,
als mit ihnen die Zuwendung Jahwes zu Salomo und seinem Volk
zum Ausdruck gebracht ist.

Folgerungen

Überblickt man das Vorkommen von ὤφθη + Dativ in der LXX, das für den historisierenden Blick der Übersetzer mit Salomo zuende geht, so wird deutlich, dass sie in der Vokabel nicht einfach eine Verbform von ὁρᾶν sehen, sondern sie mit einer besonderen Aussage verbinden, die nur für diese drei Epochen möglich ist, für die Zeit der Erzväter Abraham, Isaak und Jakob, für die Zeit des Wüstenzuges und für die Zeit der Könige David/ Salomo. Es sind die Zeiten der Heilsgegenwart Gottes bei seinem Volk und deren Vätern. Dass die LXX Übersetzer eben diese Bedeutung in der Vokabel sahen, wird dadurch bestätigt, dass zu ihrer Zeit unter der Herrschaft der Seleukiden und dann der Römer die Erzväterzeit ebenso wie die Zeit des Wüstenzuges und des davidischen Königtums messianischen Charakter gewannen. Es sind die Heilszeiten, deren Wiederkommen man erwartete.

Einen indirekten Beleg dafür bietet die Entwicklung der griechischen Bibelübersetzung in späterer Zeit. Einerseits fällt in späterer Zeit die Scheu vor der Benutzung der Vokabel, Tob 12,22 heisst es von Tobit und seinem Sohn: καὶ ἐξομολογοῦντο... ὡς ὤφθη αὐτοῖς ὁ ἄγγελος κυρίου. *Im 1. Makkabäerbuch kann die Vokabel sogar völlig unspezifisch - tatsächlich jetzt nur eine Form des Verbums* ὁρᾶν *gebraucht werden (4,69:9; 6,43; 9,27) und ebenso 2. Makk 3,25.*
Am deutlichsten ist der Wandel aber dort, wo wir den älteren LXX Text mit jüngeren Abwandlungen vergleichen können. Dafür bietet Dan 8,1 in der Doppelfassung die Möglichkeit, LXX:
Ἔτους τρίτου βασιλεύοντος Βαλτασαρ ὅρασις, ἣν εἶδον ἐγὼ Δανιηλ
Theod.; Ἐν ἔτει τρίτω τῆς βασιλείας Βαλτασαρ ὅρασις ὤφθη πρός με, ἐγὼ Δανιηλ. *Dass die LXX Übersetzer hier bewusst vorgegangen sind, zeigt sich daran, dass sie das gleiche Verbum und die gleiche Form die sie sonst mit* ὤφθη *übersetzen, hier anders wiedergeben, während sich Theodotion exakt an den Wortlaut des MT hält.*

Diese Bedeutung von ὤφθη wird an einer Stelle durch unterschiedliche Übersetzung innerhalb der LXX Handschriften besonders deutlich. Jer 31,3 lautet nach dem MT, wie die Luther Übersetzung korrekt wiedergibt: "Der Herr ist mir erschienen von Ferne: Ich habe dich je und je geliebt...." Damit ist der Satz als ein Ausspruch des Propheten auf ihn selbst bezogen verstanden: Ihm ist der Herr erschienen, um dadurch das folgende Wort mit besonderer Autorität zu versehen, die das V2 einleitende: so spricht der Herr, nicht nur wieder aufnimmt,

sondern verstärkt. Die LXX Übersetzer haben jedoch - aufgrund
einer anderen Vorlage? - den Satz auf das vorher genannte in
der Wüste, wandernde Israel bezogen und übersetzen: κύριος
πόρρωθεν ὤφθη αὐτῷ Ἀγάπησιν αἰωνίαν ἠγάπησά σε κτλ.

Sinaiticus und Alexandrinus wandeln aber auch diesen Text,
der sich durchaus in das Geschichtsbild auch der LXX einfügt,
ab und lesen: κύριος πόρρωθην ὀφθήσεται αὐτῷ κτλ. Aus dem
Rückblick auf die Wüstenzeit wird nunmehr eine eschatologische
Verheissung, deren Erfüllung noch aussteht. In jedem Fall
jedoch haben die LXX Übersetzer nicht schreiben können, dass
dem Propheten eine Erscheinung Jahwes gegeben wurde, wie sie
einst die Erzväter und die Wüstengeneration erlebten.

*Die eschatologische Verheissung des Erscheinens Jahwes bzw
seiner Doxa.*

Wie die Abwandlung von Jer 31 (LXX 38),3 durch S und A
das Erscheinen Jahwes mit ὀφθήσεται verheisst, so kündigt
Moses dem Volk in der Wüste die Erscheinung Jahwes an Lev 9,4:
ὅτι σήμερον κύριος ὀφθήσεται ἐν ὑμῖν. Er ordnet darum
Opfer an und wiederholt die Ankündigung V6. Sie findet nach
der Ausführung der Opfer und der Heiligung des Volkes ihre
Verwirklichung, die 9,23 mit der bekannten Wendung berichtet
wird. Eine andere Ankündigung der Erscheinung findet sich Ex.
16,7. Dort wird dem murrenden Volk verheissen: καὶ πρωῒ ὄψεσθε
τὴν δόξαν κυρίου κτλ. Die Erfüllung wird V10 ebenfalls mit der
gleichen Wendung berichtet. Diese Korrespondenz zwischen der
futurischen Verheissung und der Aorist Wendung für die
Erfüllung ist darum bedeutsam, weil wir die beiden futurischen
Wendungen ὀφθήσεται und ὄψονται bzw ὄψεσθε in den
eschatologischen Verheissungen der Propheten und der Psalmen
finden. Es geht für uns dabei nicht um eine Analyse des jeweils
zugrunde liegenden MT, um die literarkritische Feststellung
seiner Entstehung, sondern es geht allein um die griechische
Übersetzung, wie sie zZt der Urchristenheit die Erwartung im
jüdischen Volk bestimmte. Sie finden wir in der LXX
Übersetzung.

Beide Verbformen finden sich nebeneinander in gegenseitiger
Korrespondenz Jes 40,5 in dem grösseren eschatologischen
Zusammenhang, der, wie wir für die LXX festhalten müssen, keine
zeitgeschichtliche Interpretation erlaubt, sondern Verheissung
für ausstehende Zukunft ist: καὶ ὀφθήσεται ἡ δόξα κυρίου, καὶ
ὄψεται πᾶσα σὰρξ τὸ σωτήριον τοῦ θεοῦ. In einem gleichen
eschatologischen Zusammenhang steht Jes 60, 2f:...ἐπὶ δὲ σὲ
φανήσεται κύριος, καὶ ἡ δόξα αὐτοῦ ἐπὶ σὲ ὀφθήσεται (3) καὶ
πορεύσονται βασιλεῖς τῷ φωτί σου καὶ ἔθνη τῇ λαμπρότητί σου.

Ps 101, 17: ὅτι οἰκοδομήσει κύριος τὴν Σιων / καὶ ὀφθήσεται
ἐν τῇ δόξῃ αὐτοῦ. Auch für diese Wendung und ihre Bedeutung
haben die LXX Übersetzer manchmal den MT korrigiert, um sie
eindeutiger zu bringen. So lautet Ps 84,8 im MT /9/: Sie (die
im Hause des Herrn Wohnenden) wandern von Kraft zu Kraft bis
sie Gott schauen in Zion. Diesem Pilgerlied haben die LXX
Übersetzer erst die eschatologische Wendung gegeben, indem sie
den Text abänderten: πορεύσονται ἐκ δυνάμεως εἰς δύναμιν /
ὀφθήσεται ὁ θεὸς τῶν θεῶν ἐν Σιων.

Noch häufiger begegnet in eschatologischen Verheissungen
die zweite Jes 40,5 genannte Verbform. Sie kann in der 2.
pers. pl. absolut stehen: Jes 66,14: καὶ ὄψεσθε, καὶ χαρήσεται
ὑμῶν ἡ καρδία. In der 3. pers. pl. ist dagegen immer die
ökumenische Weite des Endgeschehens im Blick: Jes 66, 18:
ἔρχομαι συναγαγεῖν πάντα τὰ ἔθνη καὶ τὰς γλώσσας, καὶ ἥξουσιν
καὶ ὄψονται τὴν δόξαν μου. Um die Breite des Vorkommens zu
zeigen, seien noch folgende Stellen angegeben: Jes 49,7; 52,8;
10; Ez 39,21; Jo 3,1; Mi 7,9. 15. 16; Hab 3,10 /10/, Sach 9,5;
10,7; Mal 1,5; 3,18.

Dass dieser Sprachgebrauch der LXX der apokalyptischen
Erwartung zZt Jesu und der Urchristenheit entspricht, dass die
Übersetzer bewusst diese Erwartung damit wiedergeben wollen,
findet eine Bestätigung in dem allerdings nur teilweise im
Griechischen rekonstruierbaren Sprachgebrauch der
nachbiblischen Apokalypsen.

Im Henochbuch ist eine Differenzierung festzustellen,
durch die prophetische Visionen von ihrer Interpretation
unterschieden werden. Der Seher gibt an (Hen 39,4): Hier
schaute ich ein anderes Gesicht. Dies entspricht dem
Sprachgebrauch, den wir Dan 8,1 in der LXX sahen: ὅρασις, ἣν
εἶδον κτλ. In gleicher Weise ist auch in den Schriftpropheten
von ihren Gesichten die Rede. Vgl. auch Hen 39,6. 10; 40,1
u.ö. In der Interpretation durch den Engel heisst es dann
aber...."wenn der Auserwählte vor dem Herrn der Geister
erscheinen wird". (Hen 52,9, vgl 69,29) Die verschiedenen
Übersetzungen des ursprünglich griechischen IV Esra 7,33
variieren für die entsprechende Wendung, die H. Gunkel
übersetzt: Der Höchste erscheint auf dem Richterthron.
Während die lateinische Übersetzung revelabitur liest und auch
die syrische diese Bedeutung ergibt, lesen die äthiopischen
und arabischen Übersetzungen entsprechend Gunkels deutscher
Übertragung. Das griechische Original könnte gelesen haben
καὶ ὀφθήσεται ὁ ὕψιστος ἐπὶ τοῦ θρόνου τῆς κρίσεως /11/.

Ähnlich verhält es sich mit IV Esra 13,32 (Gunkel): "...dann
wird mein Sohn erscheinen, den du als Mann, der emporsteigt,
gesehen hast." Auch hier könnte das griechische Original
gelesen haben: καὶ τότε ὀφθήσεται ὁ υἱός μου κτλ. Während wir
bisher nur das griechische Original rekonstruieren konnten,
haben wir für die andere futurische Verheissung Hen 100, 4 den
Beleg im griechischen Original: ὁ ὕψιστος ἐγερθήσεται ἐν ἡμέρᾳ
κρίσεως. .....(6) τότε ὀφόνται οἱ φρόνιμοι τῶν ἀνθρώπων καὶ
κατανοήσουσιν οἱ υἱοὶ τῆς γῆς ἐπὶ τοὺς λόγους τούτους.

     Es ist daraus zu entnehmen, dass von den atlichen Propheten
her sich zZt der nachbiblischen Apokalypsen, also über die Zeit
Jesu und des Urchristentums hinaus, der Sprachgebrauch erhalten
hat, dass das erwartete Kommen der Heilszeit als ein Erscheinen
Gottes bzw seines Messias (= seines Sohnes) verheissen wird.
Korrespondiert aber, wie wir feststellten, diese Verheissung mit
der als ὤφθη κύριος bzw ἄγγελος oder δόξα κυρίου bezeichneten
Erfüllung, dann ist der Schluss berechtigt, dass für die ersten
Christen, die Autoren der Überlieferung von 1.Kor 15,3-5 der
Satz Χριστὸς ὤφθη Κηφᾷ die Erfüllung der prophetischen
Verheissungen, wie sie vor allem in Deutero- und Tritojesaja,
aber auch in den Psalmen zu finden sind, bezeugen sollte.

     Rechnen wir zu den Verheissungen, die das Erscheinen des
Herrn in seiner Doxa ankündigen, auch diejenigen, die wie Js
66,18 verheissen ὄφονται τὴν δόξαν μου, (vgl die übrigen
Stellen) dann gewinnt die These E. LOHMEYERs in "Galiläa und
Jerusalem" FRLANT Heft 52, 1936, S.10ff, die Vokabel ὄψεσθε sei
terminus technicus für die Verheissung der Parusie Mk 14,28//16,
7 und Mk 14,62 Wahrscheinlichkeit. Wir haben den von ihm zur
Begründung herangezogenen Stellen des NTs und Test Zeb 9,8
weitere aus den AT-Verheissungen in der LXX Fassung hinzugefügt.
Diese These, von HvCAMPENHAUSEN (Ablauf der Osterereignisse,
S.48 Anm 193) als "bare Willkür" zurückgewiesen, hat W. MARXSEN:
Der Evangelist Markus, FRLANT Heft 49, 1956, S.73ff mE fruchtbar
dahin weitergeführt, dass zZt des Markus, also beim Beginn des
jüdischen Aufstandes 66-70 nChr, die Parusie mit Mk 16,7 in
Gaiiläa verheissen wird. Es wird damit also nicht die
Jüngerflucht - die "Legende der Kritik" - von Mk 14,51 zur
Voraussetzung genommen, sondern es wird unter Voraussetzung der
Ersterscheinung vor Petrus, der darum besonders genannt wird,
die vollendende Parusie-Erscheinung in Galiläa verheissen.

     Für den Inhalt des urchristlichen Osterglaubens ergibt sich
danach, dass jene Erscheinung vor Petrus für die ersten Christen
entsprechend den prophetischen Verheissungen die Heilsgegenwart

Gottes wiederbrachte, wie sie den Erzvätern, dem Volk Israel in
der Wüste und zzt des Königtums David/Salomos gegeben war.
Die Heilszeit bricht mit der Erscheinung des Christus an.

Der Gebrauch von ὤφθη im lukanischen Doppelwerk

Wir haben oben bereits die Stellen aufgelistet, an denen Lukas
in seinem Doppelwerk die Wendung ὤφθη + Dativ verwendet. Und
ebenfalls hatte uns seine Bezugnahme auf die LXX in Apg 7, der
Stephanusrede, darauf gewiesen, dass er die Bedeutung dieser
Wendung der LXX entnommen hat. Wir können von daher nunmehr
überprüfen, in wiefern, und evtl in welcher Abwandlung er jenen
urchristlichen Glauben weiterführt, dass mit dem Erscheinen
des Christus jene Heilszeit beginnt, wie sie den Vorvätern
gegeben war.

Es sind für ihn nur zwei Heilszeiten, auf die er Bezug
nimmt, die des Abraham, dh der Erzväter, die er mit Apg 7,2
exemplarisch nennt, die des Wüstenzuges, die er 7,26.30 mit der
Erscheinung vor Moses ebenso exemplarisch nennt, während er die
Königszeit ausdrücklich ausnimmt, da für ihn der Tempelbau
selbst als dem Jahwe-Glauben unangemessen diese Zeit
disqualifiziert.

Er führt diese Linie der Heilsereignisse dann aber weiter.
Sie beginnt neu mit dem Anfang seines Evangeliums, dem
Erscheinen des Gabriel vor Zacharias, die Lukas wörtlich nach
Ex 3,2, dem Erscheinen vor Moses berichtet: (Lk 1,11) ὤφθη δὲ
αὐτῷ ἄγγελος κυρίου. Nehmen wir die Parallele Jdc 6,12; 13,3
hinzu, so ergibt sich auch für die Weiterführung der lukanischen
Erzählung die Parallele, dass der Zweifel des Zacharias dem
des Gideon ebenso entspricht wie dem des Moses, und dass die
Geburt eines Sohnes durch die Unfruchtbare verheissen wird wie
der Frau das Manoah und der Sara (Gen 18,1ff). Dies ist aber
verbunden mit der eschatologischen Verheissung, dass den
"Vielen" diese Geburt eschatologische Freude bringen wird
(V14ff).

*Lk 22,43f erfordert zunächst die textkritische Überlegung,
ob diese Szene von dem Erscheinen des Engels vor Jesus in
Gethsemane nach den Codices P75 ABTW als ausserkanonische
Überlieferung, die nachträglich hier eingefügt ist, zu streichen
ist, oder ob sie mit S* DKLXΔ*ΘΠ*Ψ als zum ursprünglichen Text
zugehörig anzusehen ist. (Wir haben die zahlreichen Minuskeln,
die für die Zugehörigkeit sprechen, nicht aufgeführt.) Ebenso
sprechen zahlreichen KVV-Zitate für die Ursprünglichkeit,*

wie die Tilgung durch Marcion den Grund fur das nachträgliche
Auslassen nennen könnte, das eindeutig für eine Reihe von
Codices wie den Sinaiticus nachzuweisen ist: Die Szene
widersprach dem inzwischen herrschenden Bild von Jesus, dem
Sohn Gottes. Zudem ist die Szene gerade mit dem Erscheinen
des Engels Zeichen für Verwurzelung nicht nur im AT, sondern
Jesus erfährt dasselbe, was Abraham, Isaak und Jakob und Moses
erfuhren. Diese Einbettung des Leidens Jesu in die Tradition
des ATs wird für Marcion Grund für die Tilgung gewesen sein.

Lk. 22, 43: ὤφθη δὲ αὐτῷ ἄγγελος ἀπ'οὐρανοῦ ἐνισχύων αὐτόν.
Wiederum nimmt Lukas die atliche Tradition von Erscheinungen
auf /12/, um damit das folgende Geschehen in seinem
eschatologischen Charakter zu qualifizieren. Zwar hat er 9,31
in der Verklärungsperikope die Wendung aus der Mk/Mt Parallele
durch das Partizip ersetzt und damit in ihrer Bedeutung
abgeschwächt, aber vor dem entscheidenden eschatologischen
Geschehen übernimmt er aus der Uberlieferung /13/ diese Wendung,
um damit Jesus als den Träger und Vermittler der Heilsgegenwart
Gottes zu qualifizieren. Wie Moses für Lukas aufgrund der ihm
gegebenen Erscheinung (Apg 7,30 = Ex 3,2) seinen hebräischen
Brüdern diese Heilsgagenwart vermittelt (Apg 7,26), so
vermittelt Jesus für ihn aufgrund dieser Erscheinung des Engels
Gottes seinen Jüngern mit seinem Erscheinen (Lk. 24,34) diese
Heilsgegenwart Gottes.

Lk. 24,34//Apg 13,31 ubernimmt Lukas die urchristliche
Überlieferung und wandelt sie nur dahin ab, daB er entsprechend
der gewandelten Vorstellung den entscheidenden Akt Gottes in
dem Erwecktwerden des Kyrios bezeugt. Der Aorist Passiv ἠγέρθη
entspricht der Wendung Apg 3,15; 4, 10; 5,30; 13,30; Rm 10,9:
ὁ θεὸς ἤγειρεν αὐτὸν ἐκ νεκρῶν /14/.

Apg 2,3 wird das Pfingstgeschehen ausser durch die übrigen
apokalyptischen Züge auch durch die Vokabel ὤφθη als Heilsereignis
qualifiziert. Ap 9,17//26,16 ordnet Lukas entsprechend
1.Kor 15,8 die Berufung des Paulus durch den ihm erscheinenden
Christus der Erscheinung vor Petrus als gleichwertig zu.

Apg 16,9: καὶ ὅραμα διὰ τῆς νυκτὸς τῷ Παυλω ὤφθη, ἀνὴρ
Μακεδών τις κτλ. ist gegenüber den anderen Stellen
unterschiedlich konstruiert. Es lässt sich auch nicht
inhaltlich mit ihnen parallel stellen, weil es weder ein
Engel Gottes ist, der Paulus nach Mazedonien ruft, noch eine
andere himmlische Erscheinung. Erst nachträglich qualifiziert
Lukas diese Erscheinung als den Ruf Gottes. Es darf daraus jedoch
entnommen werden, dass Lukas diesen Übergang von Kleinasien nach
Griechenland als einen das Heilsgeschehen weiterführenden Schritt
qualifizieren wollte /15/.

Apg 26,15b-16: ὁ δὲ κύριος εἶπεν, Ἐγώ εἰμι Ἰησοῦς ὃν σὺ διώκεις (16) ἀλλὰ ἀνάστηθι καὶ στῆθι ἐπὶ τοὺς πόδας σου· εἰς τοῦτο γὰρ ὤφθην σοι, προχειρίσασθαί σε ὑπηρέτην καὶ μάρτυρα ὧν τε εἶδές με ὧν τε ὀφθήσομαί σοι. Es folgt eine ausführliche Weisung für die Mission. Dieser abschliessende Bericht über die Berufung des Paulus trägt eindeutig die Züge lukanischer Darstellung /16/, darum muss die vordringliche Frage des Exegeten darauf gerichtet sein, was der Leser aus dieser Darstellung erfahren soll. Ist dies vor allem die inhaltliche Füllung des Missionsauftrags, Juden und Heiden die Augen zu öffnen, sie aus der Dunkelheit ins Licht, aus der Macht des Satans zu Gott zu führen, dass sie Vergebung der Sünden und das Erbe mit den Heiligen durch den Glauben an den Erschienenen empfangen, dann sind die beiden Aussagen ὤφθην σοι und ὀφθήσομαι σοι die beiden Ereignisse, die diese Epoche der Mission begrenzen. Sie beginnt mit dem Erscheinen des Christus und sie endet mit dem verheissenen, die Erwartungen erfüllenden Erscheinen in der Parusie /17/.

Lukas nimmt also die urchristliche Überlieferung inhaltlich abgewandelt auf. Die Erscheinung vor Petrus und den Aposteln bis zu der vor Paulus hat ihre Bedeutung nicht mehr zuerst darin, dass das Kommen des Gottesreiches mit dem Erscheinen des Messias begann, sondern einerseits ist das Handeln Gottes in dem Auferwecken des Gekreuzigten in den Mittelpunkt getreten und andererseits qualifiziert ὤφθη den Missionsauftrag, und die Verheissung der noch ausstehenden Parusie-Erscheinung wird mit ὀφθήσομαι entsprechend den AT-Propheten wieder aufgenommen.

Die Funktion des urchristlichen Glaubens an die Erscheinung des Christus.

Befinden wir uns bei der Analyse von 1.Kor 15,5 als Zeugnis des urchristlichen Glaubens auf relativ sicherem Boden, da die Belege aus der LXX als zeitgeschichtliche Parallele für die jüdische Erwartung unsere Argumentation stützen, so kann dies nicht für die Frage nach der Funktion dieses Glaubens gelten. Da wir davon ausgehen dürfen, dass der urchristliche Glaube die verheissene Heilsgegenwart Gottes als mit dem Erscheinen des Christus verwirklicht annahm, kann es für die Frage nach der Funktion dieses Glaubens nur darum gehen, einen Neuansatz zu versuchen, der zur Diskussion gestellt wird. Wir beschränken uns dafür zunächst auf das Bekenntnis 1.Kor 12,3: Κύριος Ἰησοῦς und fragen nach dem Zusammenhang dieses ältesten urchristlichen Bekenntnisses mit dem 1.Kor 15,3-5 bezeugten Glauben. Dabei muss uns die Tatsache leiten, dass die ersten Christen, die dieses

Bekenntnis formuliert haben, ausnahmslos Juden waren, für die
es unmöglich war, neben dem einen Kyrios einen anderen zu
bekennen und sei dieser auch der Christus. Es muss also
die Möglichkeit einer Übertragung des Kyrios-Titels auf den
Auferstandenen gegeben haben, ohne dass die ersten Christen,
die sich weiter als zur Synagoge zugehörig verstanden, dadurch
in Konflikt mit dem jüdischen Bekenntnis Dt 6,4 gerieten.

*Dass dieser Konflikt später entstand und zur Trennung der
Christen vom Judentum führte, lässt sich an der Entwicklung der
Perikope vom grossen Gebot Mk 12,28-34 innerhalb der Synoptiker
bezeugen. Vor allem zeigen die Parallelen, dass weder Mt 22,37
noch Lk 10,27 in der Antwort an den Schriftgelehrten wie Mk 12,
29 im Munde Jesu das Bekenntnis aus Dt 6,4 zitiert wird:
ἄκουε 'Ισραήλ, κύριος ὁ θεὸς ἡμῶν κύριος εἷς ἐστιν. Dass Mt/Lk
bewusst ändern, zeigt in der Einleitung die Hinzufügung, dass der
Schriftgelehrte - bei Mt ein Pharisaer, bei Lu ein
Gesetzeslehrer - seine Frage stellt, um Jesus zu versuchen.
Vor allem aber tilgen beide die ganze zweite Hälfte des
Lehrgesprächs, das bei ihnen erst zum Streitgespräch wird.
In keiner anderen Perikope findet sich eine Anerkennung des
Schriftgelehrten, wie sie Mk 12,34 bezeugt ist: οὐ μακρὰν εἶ ἀπὸ
τῆς Βασιλείας τοῦ θεοῦ. (vgl. zur literarischen Analyse
R. BULTMANN: Geschichte der snopt.Tradition, 3.Aufl. 1958, S.21
und M. DIBELIUS: Die Formgeschichte des Evangeliums, 3.Aufl.
1959, S.160).*

*Dieser tiefgreifende Eingriff in die Uberlieferung lässt sich
nur von daher verstehen, dass der Widerspruch zwischen dem
jüdischen Bekenntnis und dem ontologisch verstandenen Kyrios-
Titel fur Jesus unerträglich wurde. Die entschlossene Trennung
vom Judentum zeigt sich an kaum einer Stelle so deutlich wie
in der Tilgung eines Gesprächs Jesu mit einem Schriftgelehrten,
das ihre ursprüngliche Nähe bezeugte.*

Bedenken wir den zeitgeschichtlichen Kontext fur die
Entstehung des Kyrios-Titels innerhalb der Urchristenheit, dann
werden uns die Analysen fraglich /18/, die von vorneherein
eine kultische Bedeutung dieses Titels annehmen, ihm damit von
vorneherein ontologische Bedeutung beimessen. Und ebenso wenig
wahrscheinlich erscheint eine ungebrochene kontinuierliche
Entwicklung von einer Höflichkeitsanrede für Jesus zu dem Titel
Kyrios, dem Gottespradikat /19/, die schrittweise aufgrund der
Vollmacht erfolgte, die Jesus als irdischer Mensch bewiesen
hatte, auch wenn hinzugefügt wird, dass seine "Erhöhung" der

letzte Grund für den entscheidenden Schritt gewesen ist /20/.
Auch wenn anzunehmen ist, dass Jesus als Kyrios angeredet werden
konnte, ohne dass dies mehr als die Höflichkeitsantede war (zB
Mk 7,28; 11,3), so war offensichtlich die am meisten
gebräuchliche Anrede für ihn διδάσκαλε, die manchmal auch
noch in der hebräischen Form ραββει begegnet. Es ist aber
anzunehmen, dass für die ersten Christen mit der Bildung ihres
Bekenntnisses zum Kyrios Jesus auch diese Höflichkeitsanrede
die Qualität des Prädikats Adonaj erhielt.

*Der 1.Kor 16,22 erhaltene Gebetsruf "Maranatha" bildet für
diese Behauptung keinen Gegenbeweis; denn in diesem Gebetsruf
ist der aramäisch angerufene Herr selbstverständlich ebenso
qualifiziert. Die Übersetzung der Rufes Apoc 22,20 beweist
dies.*

In der LXX finden sich einige Stellen, die uns zumindest
den Weg erkennen lassen können, der von 1.Kor 15.3-5 Χριστος...
ὤφθη Κηφᾷ zu ὁ κύριος ... ὤφθη Σίμωνι Lk 24,34 führte.

Thr 4,20 ist das hebräische *Messias JHWH* handschriftlich
unterschiedlich als Χριστὸς κύριος oder χριστὸς κυρίου
wiedergegeben. Diese Differenz wird auf das für beide Formen
gleiche Kürzel Κυ zurückgehen während dieselbe Variante Ps Sal
17,32 bereits als christliche Korrektur gesehen werden kann,
die ihrem Christus den Kyrios Titel beilegte /21/. Das ist von
daher verständlich, dass die Christen die an dieser Stelle
gegebene eschatologische Verheissung erfüllt sahen. Jedoch ist
diese Übersetzung sicher nicht in den LXX Texten der Synagoge
möglich, da der Begriff "der Gesalbte des Herrn" für den König
festgelegt ist (1.Sam 24,7.11 u.ö.) und zuerst Jes 45,1
messianische Bedeutung gewinnt, wo Kyros so bezeichnet wird.

Dass die frühe Christenheit diese Tradition kannte und auch
benutzte, lassen Lk 2,11 und 2,26 erkennen. Während in der
Ankündigung der Geburt Jesu an die Hirten nur einige
altlateinische Übersetzungen, sowie das Diatessaron und
syrische Übersetzungen statt Χριστὸς κύριος den Genitiv κυρίου
lesen, spricht V26 Simeon eindeutig vom Χριστὸς κυρίου.

Zeigt sich damit jedoch lediglich an literarischen Spuren,
wie der Weg zum absoluten Gebrauch des Kyrios-Titels gegangen
sein kann, so können wir doch von dem Inhalt des urchristlichen
Osterglaubens her die Übertragung des Kyrios-Titels in seiner
funktionalen Bedeutung verstehen. Wenn wir feststellen können,

dass des Erscheinen eines Engels des Herrn bzw seiner Doxa
gleichbedeutend ist mit dem Erscheinen des Herrn, dass zB Manoah
Jdc 13,22 nach der Erscheinung des Engels sich fürchtet, weil
er Gott gesehen hat, so wird es verständlich, dass für die
ersten Christen ebenso die Gleichsetzung von einem Erscheinen
des Christus Gottes mit einem Erscheinen des Kyrios nahe lag.

Der Titel Χριστὸς θεοῦ *begegnet nur Lk 9,20 in Abwandlung des*
absoluten Χριστός *in der Mk Parallele (8,29) und der*
Erweiterung Mt 16,16 ὁ χριστὸς ὁ υἱὸς τοῦ θεοῦ ζῶντος. *Da*
dieser Titel nicht wieder begegnet, vielmehr in der späteren
Entwicklung die Bezeichnung als Gott auf Christus selbst
übertragen wird (2.Pe 1,1), darf angenommen werden, dass Lk 9,20
alte Überlieferung wiedergibt.

        Damit ist der Kyrios-Titel zunächst nur in funkkionaler
Bedeutung gebraucht worden, seine Übertragung auf Jesus als
den Christus ist die erste Funktion des urchristlichen
Osterglaubens, die angenommen werden darf. Es spricht nicht
dagegen, dass diese funktionale Bedeutung bald durch die
ontologische verdrängt wurde, wie dies notwendig mit dem
Übergang in den hellenistischen Sprachbereich geschah. Es muss
sogar angenommen werden, dass auch in der ältesten uns
erreichbaren Überlieferung 1.Kor 12,3 dieses Bekenntnis für
die korinthischen Adressaten bereits ontologische Bedeutung
hatte, und Paulus musste dies hinnehmen. Damit ist aber
keineswegs die Überlegung widerlegt, die ursprünglich, d.h.
im zweisprachigen jüdischen Bereich, wo dies Bekenntnis
entstand und von Paulus angenommen wurde, eben diese
funktionale Bedeutung vom Inhalt des urchristlichen
Osterglaubens her nahe legt.

/1/   vgl dazu die Darstellungen des Lebens Jesu von M. Dibelius
(1939), G. Bornkamm (1956), H. Braun (1969), H.-W. Bartsch (1970)
und anderen. Stets ist der urchristliche Glaube einsetzend mit
dem Osterglauben Ansatz für die Analyse der urchristlichen
Überlieferung.
/2/   Das ὅτι - recitativum ist eingeklammert,weil es eventuell
von Paulus im Anschluss, an den Einleitungssatz selbständig
eingefügt ist. Dies wird jedoch nicht allgemein angenommen.
Den angegebenen Umfang der Überlieferung nehmen an H. GRASS:
Ostergeschehen und Osterberichte, 2.erw.Aufl.1952,

HvCAMPENHAUSEN: Der Ablauf der Osterereignsse und das leere
Grab, 3.Aufl.1966, während E.BAMMEL: Herkunft und Funktion der
Traditionselemente in 1.Kor 15,1-11, Theol.Ztschr.Basel 1955,
S.401ff bereits in diesem Text unterschiedliche
Überlieferungselemente sieht, wie auch U. WILCKENS: Der Ursprung
der Überlieferung der Erscheinungen des Auferstendenen, in:
Dogma und Denkstrukturen, 1963, S.56ff. Die Erkenntnis, dass
Paulus hier Überlieferung zitiert, findet sich zuerst bei
J.W. STRAATMANN: De realiteit van's Heeren opstanding uit de
dooden, 1862. Seit A. SEEBERG: Der Katechismus der
Urchristenheit, 1903 (Neuaufl.1974) hat sie sich für die
neutestamentliche Exegese durchgesetzt.
/3/   vgl. die Literatur bei H. CONZELMANN: Der erste Brief
an die Korinther, 1969, S.294f und S.300, zu V6: H.-W. BARTSCH:
Die Argumentation des Paulus in 1.Cor 15,3-11, ZNW 1964, S.261-
274. Die von Bultmann beanstandete "fatale Argumentation"
des Paulus (Kerygma und Mythos I,5. Aufl. S.44f), die
Auferstehung in V6 durch Zeugen erweisen zu wollen, ist als
eine Fehldeutung dieses Satzes erwiesen, so auch CONZELMANN
a.a.O.z.St.
/4/   vgl. dazu R. PESCH: Zur Entstehung des Glaubens an die
Auferstehung Jesu, ThQu 1973, S.212f.
/5/   Die nüchterne Analyse von M. DIBERLIUS: Jesus, Göschen Bd.
1130, 1939 (1966) S.120ff ist noch immer unwiderlegt. Danach
gab es für den Glauben an die Auferstehung Jesu zwar gewisse
Vorbedingungen im pharisäischen Glauben: "Aber die ntlichen
Berichte zeigen, ...dass etwas eingetreten sein muss, was binnen
kurzem einen völligen Umschlag der Stimmung der Jünger
bervorrief .... Dieses "etwas" ist der historische Kern des
Osterglaubens." Wir versuchen, dieses "Etwas" näher zu
bestimmen.
/6/   zuletzt W. SCHMITHASS: Der Markusschluss, die
Verklärungsgeschichte und die Aussendung der Zwölf, ZThK 1972,
S.379-411. Diese Konstruktion ist nur möglich, weil
W. MICHAELIS; Die Erscheinungen des Auferstandenen, 1944 und
ThWtbNT V, S.331ff die Erscheinungen Gottes lediglich als
"Wortoffenbarungen" interpretiert. Gerade weil das Sehen
Gottes Ex 33,20 mit dem Tode bedroht ist, kommt dem ὤφθη
besondere Bedeutung des ὤφθη garnicht erwogen wird.
/7/   Es ist willkürlich und nur in einem theologischen Postulat
begründet, wenn W. MICHAELIS; Die Erscheinungen des
Auferstandenen, 1944 und ThWtbNT V, S.331ff die Erscheinungen
Gottes lediglich als "Wortoffenbarungen" interpretiert. Gerade
weil das Sehen Gottes Ex 33,20 mit dem Tode bedroht ist, kommt
aber dem ὤφθη besondere Bedeutung zu.

/8/ vgl. dazu die instruktive Studie von R. RENDTORFF: Die
Offenbarungsvorstellungen im Alten Israel, in: Offenbarung als
Geschichte (hgb.W. PANNENBERG), 2.Aufl.1963, S.21ff. Der hier
verwendete Begriff von Offenbarung darf allerdings infrage,
gestelt werden, da es gerade bei der Kultätiologie mehr um die
Vergewisserung der Gegenwart Gottes geht, die mehr als eine
Offenbaruug ist.
/9/ Die textkritische Schwierigkeit des MT weist auf die
Problematik, vgl. A. WEISER: Die Psalmen ATD 14/15,1966, S.385.
/10/ Auch hier haben die LXX Übersetzer in den Text
eingegriffen. MT: "Die Berge sehen dich und erbeben ..." LXX:
ὄψονταί σε καὶ ὠδινήσουσιν λαοί - Es geht den LXX Übersetzern
nicht um das kosmische Ereignis, sondern um die Völker, die
Ökumene. Vgl. dazu K. ELLIGER: Das Buch der zwölf kleinen
Propheten ATD 25,1967, S.52f.
/11/ Die verschiedenen Übersetzungen sind entnommen aus:
Die Esra Apokalypse (IV. Esra erster Teil, die Überlieferung
hgb von B. VIOLET, 1910, S-140ff, die deutsche Übersetzung
von H. GUNKEL in E. KAUTZSCH: Die Apokryphen und Pseudepigraphen
des Alten Testaments. II, 1900, S.331ff. Die Rekonstruktion
des griechischen Textes unterscheidet sich von der, die
A. HILGENFELD: Messias Judaeorum, 1869 S.64ff gibt, der anstatt
ὤφθη hier ἀποκαλυφθήσεται setzt.
/12/ Darauf verweist auch E. KLOSTERMANN: HdbNT 5,1929, S.217,
vgl. die Literatur bei W. GRUNDMANN: Das Evangelium nach Lukas,
2.Aufl.1963, S.410.
/13/ Es kann sich dabei durchaus um ursprünglich selbständige
Überlieferung handeln, wie B.M. METZGER: A Textual Commentary on
the Greek NT, 1971, S.177 annimmt, nur wird sie durch Lukas und
nicht durch einen Interpolator eingefügt wein.
/14/ B. RIGAUX: Dieu l'a ressuscité, 1973 setzt in seinen
Überlegungen bei diesem Stadium ein, ohne jedoch die
vorhergehende urchristliche Vorstellung zu berücksichtigen.
/15/ Dass mit dem "Gesicht" die Tradition des AT über
"enthüllende Traumgesichte" aufgenommen wird (H. CONZELMANN:
HdbNT 7,1963, S.90), kennzeichnet lediglich die Vorstellungswelt.
Wesentlicher ist, wie Lukas dieses "Gesicht" von anderen
unterscheidet. Damit in Zussammenhang darf auch das hier
beginnende viel diskutierte "Wir" gesehen werden. Es mag ebenso
wie ὤφθη den entscheidenden Schritt kennzeichnen.
/16/ vgl die Belege bei H. CONZELMANN a.a.O. z.St. und
E. HAENCHEN, Apostelgeschichte z.St.
/17/ Dass die Verheissung ὀφθήσομαί σοι Paulus als Empfänger
"himmlischer Gesichte" charakterisieren will (so E. HAENCHEN,
a.a.O. S.617) ist schon darum nicht möglich, weil kein weiteres

Gesicht geschildert wird. Es wird damit aber auch die
spezifische Bedeutung des Verbums verkannt. Die von
M. DIBELIUS: Aufsätze zur Apg 1951, S.83 vorgeschlagene Tilgung
des σου und Korrektur des ὀφθήσομαι in ὀφθήσεται, die auch
HAENCHENs Interpretation zugrunde liegt, ist bei Beachtung
dieser spezifischen Bedeutung der Verbform nicht notwendig.
Sie nimmt der Aussage das ihr eigene Gewicht.

/18/ W. BOUSSETs grundlegendes Werk "Kyrios Christos" 1913,
Neuaufl.1967, das bis in die Gegenwart die Interpretation
bestimmt, setzt faktisch mit einem bereits gewandelten
Kyrios-Titel ein, wenn er den Kyrios als den in der Gemeinde
gegenwärtigen Herrn im Unterschied zum eschatologischen Christus
bezeichnet. Am Anfang der Urchristenheit steht nicht der
Gottesdienst, sondern das gemeinsame Leben mit den Mahlen.

/19/ Ph. VIELHAUER: Ev.Theol.1965, S.24ff weist darauf hin,
dass in jüdischen LXX Handschriften das Tetragramm unübersetzt
bleibt, es geht uns aber um christliche Handschriften, wie
auch Paulus sie benutzte.

/20/ so F. HAHN: Christologische Hoheitstitel, FRLANT Heft 83,
S.95f.

/21/ Diese Annahme entnehme ich der LXX Ausgabe hgb. A. RAHLFS,
II, 1935, S.764 (Fussnote zu Thr 4,20) und S.488 (Fussnote zu
Ps Sal 17,32). Zu vermerken ist noch, dass Ps Sal 18, tit. und
18,5.7. eindeutig Χριστὸς κυρίου zu lesen ist, eine Bestätigung
für die christl.Korrektur in 17,32, da nur dort die
eschatologische Ausrichtung eindeutig ist.

The Georgian Version of the Book of Revelation

Rev. Dr. J.N. Birdsall,
Reader in New Testament Studies and Textual
 Criticism,
University of Birmingham,
Birmingham, England.

In Professor Metzger's recently published *Early Versions
of the New Testament* there appears a summary of the work of
Professor Molitor upon the Georgian version of the book of
Revelation, stating that "the translation must have been rather
free, for the Georgian rendering shows traces of influence from
the Philoxenian Syriac version and the Armenian version of that
book" /1/. It has so fallen out that although I have had a
long-standing interest in the text of Revelation and of the
Georgian text of it in particular, it is only by the stimulus
of these remarks of Metzger that I have been brought to look
into the matter and to examine the views of Molitor, which I
have long considered to be gravely erroneous, highly improbable
on historical grounds alone. It is a pity that Metzger should
have canonized such opinions by putting them without previous
critical appraisal into the very valuable collection of
information to which his reputation will give an undeserved
status of fact. Although it is probably shutting the stable
door after the horse has bolted, I shall endeavour in this
paper to give a summary of research in progress and to show why
Molitor's view cannot be entertained.

The Georgian version of Revelation and its most ancient
manuscripts have been known to Western scholarship since at
least 1928 when R.P. Blake outlined the data in a note attached
to the well-known article on "The Caesarean Text of the Gospel
of Mark" /12/. The same information is also to be found in
Michael Tarhnisvili's adaptation of the work of Korneli
Kekelidze, under the title *Geschichte der kirchlichen
georgischen Literatur* /3/. At length, in 1961 an edition
appeared, prepared by Ilia Imnaisvili /4/. It is based upon
three manuscripts, two now in the collections of the Institute
of Manuscripts at Tbilisi, and one at St Catherine's monastery

on Mt Sinai /5/. The two Tbilisi manuscripts are of the tenth
century, one expressly dated in AD 978, while the Sinai
manuscript is of the twelfth century. There are other
manuscripts of the same version, but they date from the eight-
eenth and nineteenth centuries.

Imnaišvili's edition is primarily concerned with the
linguistic data of the version. He gives a brief introduction
about the origin of Revelation, for which his authority is
Engels, an account of the Greek commentators, relying upon the
work of Josef Schmid /6/, an account of the manuscripts, their
dating and colophons, giving the rest of his study to the
language. He gives only the briefest résumé about the text of
his edition, and no information about the principles of its
establishment. He gives no stemma, but it is clear from a
study of his text and its apparatus criticus that he is
following the three manuscripts mentioned: yet in a number of
places he has amended the text, going completely against the
agreement of the manuscripts, whereas on close examination
their text reveals a quite specific form of text, well known to
us in the Greek tradition.

The version meets us, in all three manuscripts, in the
following form: first, a continuous text of Revelation is
found; then a commentary upon the text repeated in lemmata,
which is ascribed to Andreas of Cappadocian Caesarea. The two
older manuscripts have this as total content, while the Sinai
manuscript adds two spiritual colloquies of Dorotheus of Gaza.
The dated Tbilisi ms. and the Sinai ms. each contain a colophon,
not identical in wording, but both asking our prayers for
Euthymius, the translator of the book. This identifies the
work as that ascribed to Euthymius the Athonite in the Life of
John and Euthymius /8/, the founders of Iberon monastery on Mt
Athos. This is available to us in the Latin of Paul Peeters /
/9/, and in an abbreviated English version by David Lang /10/.
In a list of the translations from Greek made by Euthymius are
named the Apocalypse of St John the Divine with St Andrew of
Crete's commentary /11/ (showing the very common confusion of
the Andrews of Crete and Caesarea, which frequently meets us in
Greek manuscripts). John the father of Euthymius was a court
official of David, king of Western Georgia in the tenth century.
David was vassal of the Greek emperor, and noble children were
given as hostages to ensure his good conduct. Amongst these
was Euthymius. His father in due course left the world and
became a monk in Tao-klarjetia in Western Georgia. He at length
used his contacts in the Byzantine court to have his son restored

to him, and took him with him into the monastic life, first on
the Bithynian Olympus and later on Athos. It is evident from
the story that when his father received him back, the boy had
forgotten his mother tongue, while his Greek was good. His
father taught him Georgian all over again, but he never attained
fluency in it, until, as the hagiographer tells, the
intervention of the Blessed Virgin availed to grant it to him.
To the problems which are the ground of the story may be due
the fact, on which one of his successors in translation from
Greek comments, that he paraphrased, sometimes abbreviating,
sometimes expanding /12/. It is due to him that the story of
Barlaam and Joasaph was translated into Greek, while there is
a vast body of Georgian literature rendered from Greek by him.
It is the truth of the attribution to him of the translation of
Revelation, in a work written in the succeeding generation, that
Molitor calls in question.

     Molitor is a scholar to whom the Western student of
Georgian owes much. His Georgian glossary to the published
parts of the Georgian New Testament /13/ is an indispensable
tool for all stages of study and expertise. As editions by
native Georgians appeared, not furnished with a translation into
a Western language, he undertook to make good the lack by
publishing a Latin version in *Oriens Christianus*. In the brief
remarks associated with the translation of the continuous text
in Imnaisvili's edition, he has given the view of the origin
of the version, to which reference has already been made /14/.
He tells us that in translating, doubts arise whether we have
a word for word translation of a Greek original, and later,
speaks of a clearly traceable Syriac-Armenian influence upon
the text. In the conclusion of his work, he asks "But is it a
direct translation (Originaluebertragung) from the Greek? This
appears more than doubtful" /15/. As the basis of this last
remark, he has presented a collation of the version with a
Syriac and an Armenian text and a list of sixty seven cases
where either Syriac, Armenian or both Syriac and Armenian
influence is said to be visible. In examining his work and
attempting to understand its method doubts at once arise. He
never refers to the Greek text. Then, the Syriac used is the
version considered to be Philoxenian, found in a single
manuscript. Another version of which several manuscripts are
known, sometimes thought to be Harklean, has no use made of
it /16/. As to the Armenian, Molitor has limited himself to
the edition of the Bible by the Mekhitarist scholar Zohrabian:
the materials amassed by Conybeare and by Murad /17/ are not
used by him. This is a serious fault on his part, since the

text published by Zohrabian is the work of Nerses of Lampron
in the twelfth century /18/. This is both later than the
Georgian manuscripts with which we are dealing, and, furthermore,
like the Georgian version, was based on the commentary of A
Andreas of Caesarea, which Nerses translated at the same time.
In this case, Molitor is comparing the Georgian with a version
which is later in date, and which because of its base, must
necessarily have many textual features in common with the
Georgian. It is true that Nerses' text was a revision of an
older Armenian version by the text contained in the Andreas
commentary: it could then have some readings with which the
Georgian has affinity. But there is no mention of this and no
attempt on Molitor's part to distinguish the two components of
the Armenian text.

Earlier than the work of both Imnaišvili and Molitor,
there appeared the crown of the lifework of Josef Schmid upon
the Greek text of the Revelation /19/. Two of its three volumes
are devoted to the commentary of Andreas: and the third to a
discussion of the ancient recensions, and the establishment of
the original text. Here then we have to hand a valuable tool
for the study of any version, and expecially of one which is
linked with the Andreas commentary. Imnaišvili knew it, but
made only perfunctory use of it, while Molitor never refers to
it. I consider, however, that we shall be justified to make it
the basis of any analysis of the text of the Georgain version,
traditionally a translation linked with that of the Andreas
commentary.

It is difficult to be certain of the implications of
Molitor's words of which the gist has been given above. Does
he imply that the work of Euthymius was made from an Armenian
base, or even from a Syriac? or that he was revising an earlier
version in Georgian? or that he consulted Armenian and Syriac
versions in making his translation? We shall try to deal with
these three possibilities. Was he revising an earlier version?
We know of no such version. Conybeare, in his study of the
Armenian was able to demonstrate the existence of an early
version from newly discovered manuscripts and from quotations.
Due to the painstaking cataloguing of the collections in
Georgia, and elsewhere, there are now no major resources in
Georgian which we do not know, and there are no manuscripts of
Revelation but those edited by Imnaišvili or mentioned by him.
Nor are quotations known. Blake points out that Revelation was
never canonized in the Georgian church /20/, which fact is

emphasised by the appearance of Euthymius' work in manuscripts
which are not biblical in content. Was the translator then
consulting Armenian or Syriac versions in his work? This is
highly unlikely. Even if his family knew Armenian, as they
might have done in Western Georgia /21/, he had even lost his
mother tongue, let alone a second language. A knowledge of
Syriac in Byzantium at this period would have been a rare
accomplishment, and we may feel sure that his biographer would
have commented upon it. It would be anachronistic to suggest
a scientific desire to consult other versions. In any case,
the Syrians and Armenians were monophysite heretics, and
consultation of their work would have been undesirable even if
it had been possible.

Was the translation then made from Armenian or Syriac
(perhaps by someone other than Euthymius, if Molitor would
accept my arguments)? In attempting to answer this question,
I submit that it is methodologically unsound to start by a
comparison with Armenian or Syriac versions, even if we were
to use all available materials. We must start with the
tradition, namely that Euthymius translated Revelation and the
commentary of Andreas. This, as we have seen, appears to be
specifically corroborated by the manuscripts themselves in the
colophons. A detailed investigation may help us to corroborate
it even more. We must first determine whether the continuous
text is identical with that found in the lemmata of the
commentary, since, if it were not, there might be some *prima
facie* case for the suggestion that the continuous text is not
the work of Euthymius. Should the text be identical in both
its unbroken form and in the lemmata, we can ask the most telling
question, namely, is that text one which could have been found
in a Greek manuscript with the Andreas commentary which, *ex
hypothesi,* will have been the exemplar of the translator? These
are the essential primary questions, and in the light of the
answers which the data give, we can proceed to examine the
sixty-seven readings adduced by Molitor.

The format of the three manuscripts is unknown in the Greek
tradition of the Andreas commentary. Here we meet with various
arrangements: a central continuous text surrounded by by a
marginal commentary: or a commentary divided by the text given
in lemmata: or various excerpted or abbreviated forms of which
Schmid has written. But a continuous text without commentary
followed by a lemmatized commentary is, it would seem, unknown.
We might then find that the Georgian continuous text differs
from the text of the lemmata, and thus derived from a source

other than the Andreas commentary tradition. However,
examination shows that this is not so: while there are minor
variations between the continuous text and the lemmata, they
are essentially the same. I have found throughout the book
only thirteen places where the two differ in a particular related
to the differentiation of major text-types /22/.

In proceeding to investigate whether the text is one that
could be found in a Greek exemplar of the tenth century, it may
be well to remind ourselves of the analyses of Schmid. He
found four text-types in Revelation, two anciently attested and
two relatively more recent in attestation. The two former are
respectively those known in the uncials A and C and the
commentary of Oecumenius, on the one hand, and in the Codex
Sinaiticus, the Chester Beatty papyrus of Revelation (p.47) and
the quotations of Origen, on the other. The "younger" texts
are those found in manuscripts of the Andreas commentary, on the
one hand, and the text attested in most minuscules, the "Koine"
text. These are referred to as the *An* and the *K* texts. There
are a few minuscules which contain mixed texts derived from
these two types. Many *An* manuscripts have a text basically *An*
but contaminated by *K*. Schmid deliberately left out of account
the ancient versions: his critics have suggested that as in
other parts of the New Testament, the versions and certain
minuscules may prove upon examination to reveal traces of a
further text-type or types (a sort of "Caesarean" phenomenon,
so to say). Some exploratory work has been done on this by one
of my own pupils /23/, but for the time being we must work with
Schmid's categories. We shall find that we not only must, but
also can be content to do so.

The continuous text of the Georgian version, basically
identical as it is with the lemmata of the commentary, should
prove to belong to the *An* type, although it might be
contaminated with *K* readings or be one of the definable later
mixed texts. To test this a full collation of the version has
been made against the Greek text, and the variant readings
revealed have been primarily compared with the lists given by
Schmid of the distinctive readings of the four text-types, with
the following results. There are thirty-nine readings common
to *An* and *K:* and thirty-six distinctive of *An* /24/: but the
overwhelming number of readings which the collation reveals are
K readings, one hundred and fifty-two in total /25/. It would
appear then from this that the base of the Georgian version is
an *An* text heavily contaminated by *K* readings. Readings not
found in Schmid's lists have been analyzed in the first ten

chapters of Revelation; they number ninety-seven. Out of these,
thirty-seven have Greek attestation, usually drawn from both
the *An* and the *K* streams. Twenty-one have support only from
versions, ranging from the Latin to the Bohairic. Thirty-nine
are peculiar to this version, sixteen of which clearly belong
to the category of the idiom of the language or to various
aspects of the style of the translator. The other twenty-three
may well be explicable under these heads. This analysis of the
readings of minor attestation is necessarily provisional: any
student of the problems inherent in the textual definition of
an ancient version will be aware that many readings in which
versions apparently coincide may arise independently and
fortuitously. But as this evidence grows, the conclusion of
the primary analysis by major text-type is confirmed. The
version has a Greek text at base, an *An* text heavily contaminated
by the *K* text. It is interesting that Blake, who had examined
the Tbilisi manuscripts, said in 1928 that the version "is
connected with the Greek branch of the tradition and not with
the Oriental" /26/, and Molitor and Metzger might have been
wise to note this judgement.

The evidence does not lead to a pinpointing of the
affiliation of the Georgian within the *An* tradition: it seems
to coincide precisely neither with any sub-group of that
tradition nor with one of the mixed texts. Yet this is not
surprising when we reflect that very few manuscripts of
Revelation antedate the two Tbilisi manuscripts. Greek
manuscripts of the *An* text-type known to us may be descendants
of those from which Euthymius took his text or be more distantly
related: but none will be ancestors of the direct line! Indeed,
it is not too much to say that this version is one of the
earliest extant witnesses to the *An* text, and when analyzed
will be more important than Nerses' Armenian (which Schmid
considered important enough to cite occasionally), antedating it
as it does by two clear centuries.

We must now turn to the evidence alleged by Molitor. Before
doing so we may remind ourselves of one reason why versions in
different languages may fortuitously coincide in renderings.
This will be so if the literary form of one language has been
influenced by the other: this is a case which meets us when we
deal with interrelations of Armenian and Georgian. One of the
routes by which the Christian faith came to the Georgians lay
through Armenia, and Armenian Christianity was a major factor
in the formation of the Georgian literary language. There are,
as is well known, loan words, calques of Armenian syntax and

word-formation. A style was thus created which went back to the
form of the Armenian language, but could be found, once
established as the approved style, in documents which were
original compositions or translated from sources other than
Armenian. Euthymius did not create a new style - as Blake
reminds, us, basing himself on a suggestion of Marr, in
Euthymius' day "the old traditions were too strong" /27/ - so
that he produced in his Biblical work a kind of analogy to the
English Revised Version where many of the Hebraisms of the
Authorized Version were retained. When he came to do new work,
untranslated before, the power of the old literary language
would still be paramount, and thus, even in his original work
Armenian locutions would still have their place. Since behind
the early Armenian tradition lies the literature of the Syriac
church, Syriacisms are to be found in Armenian style and through
it, in literary Georgian.

No study of Euthymius as translator has yet been made: this
no doubt rests on the fact that of his vast output little has
yet been edited, apart from Biblical recensions for which he
was responsible. In connection with the question under our
consideration, I have made some study of his translation of the
Apophthegmata Patrum /28/. Because of the dissimilarities of
the subject matter and the style of the originals, the data thus
derived cannot be widely used, but it is a useful auxiliary to
set by the side of the evidence from earlier Georgian works,
of the way in which Euthymius would be likely to translate a
Greek text.

A further criterion to be applied to the material is
that where the text of Revelation presents us with obscurities,
or with solecisms, as it frequently does, independent translators
may well coincide in their resolution of these.

I have analyzed the cases adduced by Molitor /29/ into the
following categories. Twenty-one are found as variant readings
of the *An*-tradition in the margin of Schmid's edition, seven
of these being major text-typical readings of which we have
already taken account /30/. Twelve cases may be accounted for
by Euthymian style as we know it from the *Apophthegmata* - nine
of these are the substitution of preterite forms of the verb
"to say" for the historic present, a feature which is regular
in the *Apophthegmata* /31/. Eight cases are explicable as
inherited Biblical phraseology: such as "inhabitants of the
earth" for "inhabitants (or, dwellers) upon the earth" /32/;
"he that hath ears" for "he that hath an ear" /33/; the stock

phrase "the sea and the dry land" for "the sea and the earth"
/34/. Stylistic changes, including the removal of solecisms,
account for nineteen cases; six of these are the addition of the
copula to nominal sentences /35/. There are further cases of
this not shared with Armenian or Syriac which show this to be a
feature of the translator's method. Four are paraphrases or
interpretative translations /36/, of which also other instances
are known, to which Molitor does not refer. There are several
attractions of case, in places where Revelation, following its
own syntax, gives an anacoluthon. In the six remaining cases,
I find that four present "no case to answer" /37/, and two are
questions of vocabulary. In the latter sub-category, one word
("one another", as it would be in English) /38/ is rare, but
is known elsewhere. Its derivation might be a calque of Syriac:
but it was current in the time of Euthymius and is used in his
biography. Was that then translated from Syriac?

The other case is the translation of the Greek *phiale* "bowl"
in chapter fifteen and elsewhere. The Georgian here used
lanknaki which appears to mean a flat dish, and this is so,
Molitor believes, in the vocabulary of the Syriac and Armenian
traditions /39/. For various reasons, I cannot see the
difficulty here. For one thing, whatever may be true of *phiale*,
a saucer shaped container is quite a possible interpretation,
and in the context, easier to pour from, even for angels
expecially since a shower of afflictions is the desired
objective. Again, the question of vocabulary does not seem to
favour the derivation of this translation from Syriac to Armeni
Armenian. Syriac *zakuran*, to judge from the thesaurus, can
cover shapes of vessel in the liturgical context, from chalice
to paten. The Armenian *skavarak* renders *trublion* in one passage
of Matthew and *poterion* in another. The Greek *paropis,* on the
other hand, is rendered by *tast*. But the interpretation is in
itself not unfeasible, as we have suggested, and might have bé
been widely held. Perhaps ancient earthenware technology, and
the representations of iconographers can help us to explain it,
but time has lacked to go to them on this point.

Thus, but two tests, we find that the Georgian version of
Revelation is what it is said to be: a translation from the
Greek. Both the positive evidence of collation with the Greek
tradition, and the negative evidence drawn from an examination
of the alleged evidence of translation from Armenian and Syriac
sources (or whatever the hypothesis may be presumed to be),
show that this is so. The latter data in fact emphasise the
truth of the ascription to Euthymius of a style of translation

bordering upon paraphrase, indicated by Ephrem Mcire /40/. The
sanctity of a scriptural text had kept this tendency in check
in the case under review: when we look at the translation of
the Andreas commentary (a study which lies outside the primary
object of this paper) we see this style in a fuller manifestation.
Both text and commentary in their Georgian dress are of
importance for our fuller knowledge of the text of Revelation
itself, and for the increase of information about Euthymius'
techniques of translation and traditions of interpretation. The
commentary may prove of further significance in the textual
criticism of the work of Andreas, and thus, the first, the
fifth and the tenth centuries of the Christian era will receive
illumination from it.

        In conclusion I would add that I regret that it should be
necessary to unveil grave faults in the work of a veteran
scholar to whom we all owe much. But to allow an erroneous
opinion to remain uncorrected, now given such prestige as the
bibliographical exhaustiveness of Metzger will provide, would
in my view hamper the progress of those very researches which
it has been the concern of Professor Molitor to promote.

NOTES

/1/   Oxford, 1977, p.197.
/2/   *Harvard Theological Review XXI*, p.287, n.7.
/3/   *Citta del Vaticano (Studi e testi 185)* 1955, pp.131,135.
/4/   *Works of the department of Old Georgian Language no.7:*
Iovanes gamochadeba da misi t'argmaneba (The Revelation of John
and its interpretation).
/5/   G. Garitte, *Catalogue des manuscrits géorgiens littéraires*
du Mont Sinai (CSCO 165), Louvain, 1956, pp.258-262. (Codex 85.)
/6/   *Studien zur Geschichte der griechischen Apokalypse-Textes*,
Muenchen, 1955.
/7/   Three striking examples of this are the removal of the
following variants:
    (a)   επλυναν : επλατυναν (7.14).
    (b)   the anacoluthon ει τις εχει αιχμαλωσιαν υπαγει ει τις εν
           μαχαιρα δει αυτον αποκτανθηναι (13.10)
    (c)   αγιων : εθνων (15.3)
/8/   Most recently edited by Ilia Abuladze, *Monuments of Old*
Georgian Hagiographical Literature. vol 2, Tbidlisi, 1967,
pp.38-100.
/9/   *Histoires monastiques géorgiennes. (Analecta Bollandiana.*

XXXVI -XXXVII. 1917-1919), Bruxelles, 1922, pp.8-68.
/10/ *Lives and legends of the Georgian saints*, London, 1956, 1976, pp.154-165.
/11/ Abuladze pp.62f.; Peeters pp.34f.; Lang p.162.
/12/ Ephrem Mcire, quoted by Tarhnisvili, *op.cit.* p.130.
/13/ *Glossarium ibericum in quattuor evangelia, etc. (CSCO subsidia vols. 20,21,23,25)*, Louvain, 1962-65.
/14/ *Oriens Christianus 50* (1966), pp.1-12; 51 (1967) pp.1-28; 52 (1968) pp.1-21.
/15/ *Oriens christianus 52*, p.21.
/16/ For bibliographical details reference may be made to Metzger *op.cit.*, pp.67f.
/17/ *ibid.*, pp.168f.
/18/ Schmid, *op.cit.*, pp.99-114; Conybeare, *The Armenian Version of Revelation*, London, 1907, pp.62ff., 137.
/19/ n.6 *supra*.
/20/ *Loc.cit.*
/21/ P. Peeters. *Le trefonds oriental de l'hagiographie byzantine*, Bruxelles, 1950, pp.162f.
/22/ Viz. 1:15; 1:18; 3.17; 6.5; 9.6; 9.12/13; 16:3; 16.13; 16.18; 18.6; 19:17; 22.8; 22.12.
/23/ Raphaelle Collins. "Some variant readings of the Apocalypse" (Minor dissertation for the degree of M.A.: University of Birmingham, 1971) [Unpublished.]
/24/ Amongst the typical *An* readings are the following:

   2.22 ϵργων αυτης: ϵργων αυτων
   9.12 ϵτι: *om.*
  13.6 την σκηνην αυτου: + και
  18.14 ϵυρησουσιν: ϵυρησϵις
  19.9 του γαμου: *om.*
  19.17 το δϵιπνον το μϵγα του θϵου: το δϵιπνον του μϵγαλου
        θϵου
  22.3,5 ϵτι: ϵκϵι

/25/ Amongst the typical *K* readings are the following:

   1.5 λυσαντι : λουσαντι
   2.20 την γυναικα: + σου
   4.8 αγιος
   6.1,5,7 + και ιδϵ; in verss seqq. *om.* και ϵιδον
   7.14 ϵπλυναν: ϵπλατυναν
  11.13 ωρα: ημϵρα
  13.10 ϵι τις ϵχϵι αιχμαλωσιαν υπαγϵι ϵι τις ϵν μαχαιρα δϵι
        αυτον αποκτανθηναι *sic*
  14.8 ἤ: *om.*
  15.3 βασιλϵυς των ϵθνων
  16.16 Αρμαγϵδων : μαγϵδων
  18.2 ϵπϵσϵν 2°: *om.*

19.15   ρομφαια: + διστομος
20.2   σατανας: + ο πλανων την οικουμενην ολην
21.6   γεγοναν: γεγονα
ibid.   ειμι: *om.*
21.9   την γυναικα την νυμφην του αρνιου *hoc ordine*
22.14   πλυνοντες τας στολας αυτων: ποιουντας τας εντολας
         αυτον (*K An*).

/26/   *Loc.cit.*
/27/   R.P. Blake, "Georgian Theological Literature", *Journal of Theological Studies 26,* (1924), pp.50-64. See p.55. (This article, based on the first edition of Kekelidze's History of Georgian Literature, is a very valuable introduction to the subject, which benefits from Blake's expert acquaintance with the language and the literature of Georgia).
/28/   *Old Georgian translations of documents of the middle ages: I. The translation by Euthymius the Athonite of an ancient recension of the Georgian Patericon,* edited by M. Dvali, Tbilisi, 1966. I understand from private correspondence that Father Bernard Outtier of Solesmes has also made some preliminary study of the style of Euthymius as shown in this document.
/29/   Molitor gives his attestation in three lists, namely Syriac, Syro-Armenian, and Armenian: I refer to these in the following footnotes as S, SA, and A, followed by a numeral.
/30/   The seven are S2,S5,S22,SA3,A12,A16,A17: the rest are S2 (another point), S8,S17,S19,S21,S23,S27,SA8,SA10,SA11,SA18, SA19,A3,A9.
/31/   The nine are S6-12, SA13,SA17: the others are S4,A16,A18.
/32/   S3,S15,S16,A8: the form can be paralleled in Jeremiah and Psalms, to give the instances I have checked.
/33/   SA1: this seems clearly to be due to the influence of the form found in the gospels e.g. Matt. 10:27; Mk. 4:9.
/34/   A6.
/35/   S18, S23,S29,SA15,SA16,A10. We may compare 8:13 where ουαι is rendered *vae ars* (woe is) without any coincidence with another version.
/36/   E.g. *gnome* at 17:13/17 is rendered *nebay,* which means "will" (SA 12) this in fact is the meaning of *gnome* in the context. The Georgian rendering can be paralleled in the Pauline corpus at Philemon 14 in mss. of the older recensions. There too it is an accurate translation.
/37/   S20,S26,S28 and SA5 (where the variant readings in the context do not tally in the three versions).
/38/   S14. See Abuladze *Dzvel k'art'uli enis lek'sikoni,* Tbilisi, 1973, p.149 s.v. *ert'manert'i.*
/39/   The information here is collected from *Thesaurus Syriacus*

ed. R. Payne Smith, Oxford, 1879, 1891; *Concordance of the Old and New Testaments* (of the Armenian Bible), Jerusalem, 1895.
/40/   N. 12, *supra.*

This lecture has also been published in Le Muséon vol.91 (Louvain 1978) pp.355-366. While that edition was already in the press and too late for any addition to be made, I learnt of the death of Professor Molitor on July 24, 1978. I accordingly wish to add here that I knew him personally and had visited him twice in his home. On the second occasion I stayed for some days as the guest of his sister and himself. I was deeply impressed by the quality of his priestly life and moved by his simple humanity. He was very happy, at home in his native Rhineland, from which he had been absent for many years of his life. He leaves behind, not only the reputation of a pioneer *géorgisant,* but the memory of a minister of Christ whom one was the better for having known.

A tribute upon his seventieth birthday appeared in <u>Bedi Kartlisa</u> (révue de kartvélologie) vol.32 (Paris 1974) with a full bibliography. An obituary is to be found in <u>Oriens Christianus</u> vol.62 (Wiesbaden 1978) and an abbreviated form of this with a continuation of his bibliography in <u>Bedi Kartlisa</u> vol.37 (Paris 1979).

A Contextual Interpretation of Galatians 3:27

Oscar S. Brooks,
William Jewell College,
Liberty,
Missouri, 64068,
U.S.A.

Although the epistle to Galatians is somewhat brief,
approximately two-fifths of it is given over to a defence of
Paul's apostleship. Yet the theological importance of the
writing is not measured by its verse content. Various studies
have been made of its destination, its relation to Acts 11 and
15, and the specific identity of Paul's opponents, as well as
its doctrines. The phrase "justification by faith" immediately
calls to mind the Epistle to the Galatians and Luther's
interpretation of it /1/. Many a beginning Greek student has
enjoyed the Apostle's abrupt style and pugnacious tone as he
defends his position and takes the offensive against his
opponents.

Baptism is the Epistle to the Galatians, the concern of
this paper, has also been studied. Standard works on baptism
in the New Testament recognize Galatians 3:27. Flemington /2/,
Beasley-Murray /3/, and Schnackenburg /4/ have all included
this text in their study as well as those who have dealt with
Pauline Theology: Ridderbos /5/, Whiteley /6/, and others. Some,
however, do not give this text its deserved attention.

The idea of baptism in Galatians centers on ἐβαπτίσθητε
and ἐνεδύσασθε in 3:27, but simply to exegete a single verse
or the few adjoining verses is not enough. The need to set
the verse against the major themes of the epistle was recognized
by Augustin Grail in "Le Baptême dans l'Épître aux Galates" /7/.
This paper follows a similar method but emphasizes different
themes and comes to different conclusions.

The method here is (1) to make a brief survey of the
epistle with attention to the argument in chapters 3 and 4, (2)
to emphasize the development of thought in 3:23-4:7 by noting

specific themes and concepts, and (3) to draw the appropriate
conclusions.

I

    The epistle is very conveniently divided into three units
of two chapters each. The first two chapters are
autobiographically written to argue against those who challenge
Paul's apostolic credentials (1:12) and the completeness of
his Gospel (1:8f.). In relating autobiographical material
Paul shows that his mission to the gentiles was sanctioned by
the Jerusalem church without an imposition of the rite of
circumcision (2:3, 7-10). His account of his confrontation
with Peter in Antioch provides Paul with the opportunity to
contrast righteousness by works of law and "righteousness
through faith in Jesus Christ" (2:16). The Apostle reaches
the climax of his autobiographical material when he testifies
to his intimate association with Christ:

    I have been crucified with Christ: it is no longer I
    who live, but Christ who lives in me: and the life
    I now live in the flesh, I live by faith in the Son
    of God who loved me and gave himself for me (2:20).

    Already in the first two chapters Paul has identified the
problem of circumcision, the theme of faith-righteousness,
and the intimate association of the believer with Christ.

    Having given his own testimony in 2:20, Paul opens the
second section of his epistle (chs. 3-4) by evoking a response
from his readers regarding their own salvation experience: "Did
you receive the spirit by works of the law or by hearing with
faith?" (3:2). This question states the thesis of Paul's
argument in this section: God's blessing does not come by works
of law but through hearing with faith. This thesis had been
challenged by Paul's opponents so he takes the occasion to
verify it again.

    Here Paul must convince the Galatian Christians that they
have been legitimately included in God's design of salvation.
The new believers must experience a sense of belonging. They
must have a new identity, a new history. They must be
incorporated into something. They must be brought into
continuity with all that has gone on before. This was to be
no easy matter to accomplish, yet it was essential to the
spiritual well-being of the convert. Paul's opponents had a

ready answer: circumcision, the law. This would immediately
incorporate them into the entire Jewish religious history.
They would belong to Moses and to Abraham. Paul will not
concede!

For Paul the law was a curse (3:10). Hebrew scripture
itself did not support dependence on the law (3:11). The law
came in because of transgression as a custodian until the
promised heir came (3:24).

If Paul rejected the law for his Galatian believers, what
could he say to them regarding their religious history? They
were legitimate sons of Abraham because they were men of
faith (3:7). Paul offers the interpretation that God's promise
to Abraham "in thee shall all the nations of the earth be
blessed" was God's preaching the gospel to Abraham. So the
believers are, even without circumcision, a part of the
religious heritage beginning with Abraham. Now the promised
blessing is none other than Christ, Abraham's offspring, who
has already brought the believers to sonship in God (3:26).
They have received adoption as sons (4:5).

By this argumentation Paul is reassuring the Galatians
that they belong to the religious history beginning with Abraham
and are legitimately included in it.

This new association with God through Christ is free from
any Jewish obligation imposed by the law and at the same time
it frees the gentile believer from his prior religious
commitment to what are described as elemental spirits (4:3)
and beings that are "no gods" (4:8). This reminds the readers
that they are neither in bondage to gentile errors or Jewish
requirements, but rather they are men of faith and freedom in
Christ. They are not slaves but free.

The third section of the epistle is hortatory, encouraging
the Galatians to develop a life-style commensurate with the
new spiritual freedom they have been granted in Christ (chs. 5-6).

II

This brief survey has shown that while the debate is
joined at the point of the law the vital issue is how a gentile
believer is included in the religious continuity from Abraham
to Christ. It is the matter of what standing, status, or

ritual incorporates the believer into the history of salvation.
At the personal level, the question is one of identity and
belonging.

Paul addresses this problem in the crucial section of
3:23-4:7. Here several concepts will be examined. First,
there is the sonship of the believer. Beginning in 3:23, the
era before Christ and the era since Christ are contrasted.
Previously, man was under the custodianship of the law. This
places man in a subjugated relationship. Then when Christ came,
the era of faith, man had the possibility of becoming a son of
God through faith. This raises his status and brings him into
fulfilment with the primal promise to Abraham (Gen. 12:7; 15:5ff.),
as well as the prophetic promise of Hosea (1:10) taken over by
Paul in Rom. 9:26. By using the idea of sonship, Paul is
drawing the Galatian believers into an intimate relation to
God assuring them of their place in his divine economy. This
assurance is without the law, but emphatically related to
Christ: "for in Christ Jesus you are all sons of God, through
faith" (3:26). This sentence is further amplified and the
relation of Jesus to the believers' sonship is more deliberately
articulated:

But when the time had fully come, God sent forth his
Son, born of a woman, born under the law to redeem those
who were under the law, so that we might receive
adoption as sons (4:4-5).

Here the new relation of sonship between God and man is
related to God's redemptive plan in Christ /8/. There could
be no doubt for the reader on what grounds he experienced this
new relation; Christ set forth by God at the right time has
redeemed the believer from his enslavement.

This brings out the second idea to be noted, the former
estate of the believer. Paul uses several analogies at this
point. He says that the believer was formally under a
custodian, the law (3:23f.). This reference is to the sequence
of the period of the law followed by the new era of faith in
Christ. So also Paul is likening the minor who is an heir to a
slave (4:1). It is the intention here to identify the gentile
aspect of the believers' former estate when they were enslaved
to their own religious beliefs (elemental spirits) and
superstitions (4:8) /9/.

    The third idea in this section is "redeem". Christ
"redeemed us from the curse of the law" (3:13; cf. 4:4).
This continues Paul's imagery of custodian, minor heir, and
slave. Something must effect the change from the former
estate to the new status. Christ did it in the role of
redeemer. At this point it is fitting to see in this term
the manumission of slaves, the setting free to a new status /10/.
Christ is what God did to bring about man's new relationship
to himself.

    The fourth idea is freedom or oneness that results from
this new era of redemption: "There is neither Jew nor Greek,
there is neither slave nor free, there is neither male nor
female: you are all one..." (3:28). This statement should be
read with the idea of heirship and sonship in mind. The
Galatian believers are not to think of rank and status, or
whether some are more worthy than others; rather they are to
look upon themselves and one another as equals, heirs of the
same Lord, so having a bond of unity that transcends all marks
of rank and status. This is both freedom from the former
religious and social schemes and at the same time an assurance
of belonging to one another because they belong to Christ.

    This brings out the fifth item to be noted, intimacy with
Christ. This idea is already present in the concept of
redemption. The redeemed enjoys a certain degree of association
with the redeemer or else the transaction would not take place,
but this intimate association with Christ is heightened when
Paul asserts: "and because you are sons, God has sent the
spirit of His Son into your hearts, crying "Abba Father!" (4:6).
"The word *Abba* is one of the Aramaic expressions of the primitive
church that passed over the gentile usage" /11/. Jeremias has
shown that in Mark 14:36 this word is from the historical
Jesus /12/. When Jesus used it he was declaring an intimacy
with God of a superlative nature. Jesus taught his disciples
to address God as Father (Mt. 6:9), and offered them an intimate
relation to him: "so that you may be sons of your father"
(Mt. 5:45). Paul has taken up this primitive concept and
asserts that the spirit of the Son is in the believer's heart
assuring him of his relation to God in the very same manner
as Jesus' relation to God. Paul recalls this intimate Aramaic
address to God, already known by the Galatians, as the most
weighty evidence possible that they are children of God /13/.
That is to say, the understanding of the intimate relation
between Christ and the believer should begin with this verse.

In further describing this intimacy, Paul uses his
favourite phrase "in Christ" (3:26, 28). This phrase has long
since been exegeted to mean that the believer has come into an
intimate, profound, association with Christ /14/. Perhaps the
best interpretation is Paul's own statement quoted above: "It
is no longer I who live, but Christ who lives in me" (2:20).
Modern terminology may understand Paul's personal intimacy as
well as that attributed to the believer along the lines of one's
attaining a new self understanding, a new direction, destiny, or
mission.

The sixth element in this paragraph to be noted should be
understood from the previous discussion of intimacy with Christ.
Paul reminds the Galatian believers that "they have put on
Christ" (3:27). Since a similar statement is made apart from
any reference to baptism, "put on the Lord Jesus Christ"
(Rom. 13:12), its basic meaning is not dependent upon its
proximity to baptism in Galatians.

"Put on" means literally "to dress" or "to clothe"; thus
one wears something. When used in a figurative sense, as it
is here, it means that one exemplifies or is known by the
characteristic, virtue, or trait that he puts on. So in
Col. 3:12 Paul introduces a long paragraph of admonitions by
saying "put on ...". He wishes his readers to exemplify the
qualities of the virtues he lists: Be like this! This idea of
putting on is extended to the entire personality in Eph. 4:24
where the Christian is admonished to "put on the new Man, the
one created similar to God". This statement is saying "put on
Christ". Likewise Col. 3:10 calls for a putting on of the new
nature in the likeness of its creator. Again this is a reference
to the new understanding of life which Christ brings. The idea
of putting on Christ is not a novel phrase to the baptismal
passage in Galatians. In fact, it is a normative idea in Paul's
thought and it is clearly articulated in the references where
he insists that the believer has become a new creation. What
Paul wishes to stress is that the believer has become like
Christ in that he embodies the very characteristics and
likeness of him /15/.

This fits into the larger context where the main issue is
sonship, the believers' relation to God. The believer has
received adoption through Christ's redemption, he can address
God as "Abba", in Christ he is a son of God. "To put on Christ"
is another way of saying the believer has been brought into the

same relation with God that Christ enjoys. Paul is saying,
"you have put on a sonship like Christ's".

The final item to be noted is "baptized into Christ".
Oepke /16/, Schnackenburg /17/, and others reject the mystical
reading of this phrase in the sense of being immersed into
Christ. "Baptized" here is simply a reference to the rite
practised by the Christian community from primitive times /18/.
This rite undoubtedly involved water and initiated the believer
into the Christian circle /19/. The exact mode is not central
to the understanding at this point. The phrases βαπτίζειν εἰς
and βαπτίζειν εἰς τὸ ὄνομα do not carry different meanings.
"To be baptized into Christ" conveys the same significance as
"to be baptized in the name of Christ". In either case Christ
is what makes the baptism different from other water rituals /20/.
One is baptized with reference to Christ. Schnackenburg uses
the analogy of the "baptism of John" in Acts 19:3-5, and the
"baptism of Moses" in I Cor. 10:2 to interpret that the person's
name is the reference to whom the one being baptized is
related /21/. When the *name* is stressed, τὸ ὄνομα,
interpretation is aided by reference to pagan documents where
the word refers to ownership and authority /22/. As Deissman
observed long ago, "*to baptize into the name of the Lord, ...*
constitutes the *belonging* to God ... /23/".   References in
Rabbinic writing use "name" in such phrases as "in virtue of
the name", "on the basis of the name", and "with appeal to the
name". An example: a slave undergoes the bath "in the name
of a free man /24/". That is, he attains the status of a free
man. Applying the Greek and Rabbinic background to baptism,
a possible paraphrase could well be: "baptized into the power
and ownership of Christ". This accords well with the
following phrase already discussed; "to put on Christ".

Recalling that "to put on" is interpreted as putting on
sonship, and baptism is into the power and ownership, it is easy
to say that each of the two foci of the sentence complements
and amplifies the other. Oepke says that "to put on Christ"
is a heightened form of "to be baptized into Christ". The
above interpretation of this single sentence with "to baptize"
and "to put on" warrants this conclusion. When Paul writes:
"for as many of you as were baptized into Christ, have put on
Christ", he is saying: "You were baptized into Christ's
ownership. You have been intimately associated with him,
through him you are sons of God".

III

Before drawing together the results of this study of a
Pauline baptismal text, a caution or two is in order. First,
there is often the tendency on the part of an interpreter to
over-exegete, read into the text more than is there. This is
done because the interpreter is a third party to a correspondence
between two parties who are involved with the issue. So the
modern interpreter seeks to enter a dialogue that has been fixed
in time. Paul knew perfectly well how much or how little to
elaborate a point for the understanding of the Galatians.
Modern interpreters try to measure the meaning with precision
beyond their abilities, and so run the risk of over-interpreting.

Secondly, one may approach this text as if it were Paul's
definitive statement on baptism. This should not be done.
The intention of Paul here is to argue another point, and
baptism is merely a reference that helps support the main issue.

Thirdly, it is the temptation of modern interpreters to
give numerous cross-references to Paul's other writings in
explaining a single text. This article has used this method,
but with restraint. It must be remembered that the Galatian
readers did not have this privilege. They depended solely on
this epistle and their prior understanding of the Christian
message as delivered by Paul. A corollary to this is the way
modern exegetes begin with more obvious baptismal passages in
Paul and move to the more obscure. This will produce an effect
quite different from interpreting each baptismal text
independently. This study has tried to emphasize the contextual
interpretation of a single baptismal text /25/.

What are the results? First, the baptismal text is in a
context where the author is trying to assure the Galatians of
their salvation without capitulating to the Jewish law. More
specifically he is describing how their relation to God is
established. The key idea is sonship in reference to God.
This sonship is based on the believers' intimate association
with Christ. The believers are "in Christ" and "have put on
Christ".

In this context Paul uses the term "baptism". The
believers "have been baptized into Christ". This is obviously
not a statement that seeks to explain the meaning of baptism,
rather to support the basic meaning of the context. So baptism

should be interpreted from the context, not the context from baptism. What can be said about the meaning of baptism? It was, when practised among the Galatians, a rite that identified their relationship to God in Christ. This is as much as can legitimately be interpreted. That is the way Paul has used it. Any more is to go beyond the bounds of the text. Admittedly this method constrains itself to the immediate context; but, if applied to other Pauline texts, this method of constraint may produce fresh insight into the nature of baptism in the Pauline churches.

NOTES

/1/   T.W. Manson, "The Problem of the Epistle to the Galatians", *Studies in the Gospels and Epistles,* ed. Matthew Black (Manchester: University Press, 1962), p.168.
/2/   W.F. Flemington, *The New Testament Doctrine of Baptism* (London: S.P.C.K., 1953).
/3/   G.R. Beasley-Murray, *Baptism in The New Testament* (London: Macmillan, 1963).
/4/   Rudolf Schnackenburg, *Baptism in the Thought of St. Paul,* trans. G.R. Beasley-Murray (Oxford: Basil Blackwell, 1964).
/5/   Herman Ridderbos, *Paul: An Outline of His Theology,* trans. John Richard De Witt (Grand Rapids: William B. Eerdmans, 1975), pp.406-414.
/6/   D.E.H. Whiteley, *The Theology of St. Paul,* (Oxford: Basil Blackwell, 1964), pp.166-174.
/7/   Augustin Grail, "Le Baptême dans L'Épître aux Galates", *Revue Biblique,* LVIII (1951), pp.503-520.
/8/   Ridderbos, *op. cit.,* p.197, stresses that the various salvation terms find expression in the "concept adoption of sons".
/9/   Ernest De Witt Burton, *A Critical and Exegetical Commentary on the Epistle to the Galatians* (Edinburgh: T. & T. Clark, 1921), p.518.
/10/   *Cf.* Adolf Deissmann, *Light from the Ancient East,* trans. Lionel R.M. Strachen (New York: Harper and Brothers, n.d.), pp.318-330, for the classical treatment of manumission.
/11/   C.H. Dodd, *The Epistle of Paul to the Romans,* (London: Hodder and Stoughton, 1932), p.129, commenting on Rom. 8:16.
/12/   Joachim Jeremias, *The Central Message of the New Testament* (New York: Charles Scribner's Sons, 1965), pp.17ff.
/13/   Dodd, *loc. cit.*

/14/   Adolf Deissmann, *Paul*, trans. William E. Wilson (London: Hodder and Stoughton, 1926), ch.6; James S. Stewart, *A Man In Christ* (New York: Harper and Brothers, n.d.), ch.4; W.D. Davies, *Paul and Rabbinic Judaism* (London: S.P.C.K., 1955), ch.5.

/15/   Cf. William F. Arndt and F. Wilbur Gingrich, *A Greek-English Lexicon of the New Testament* (Chicago: University of Chicago Press, 1957), p.263, for meaning of ἐνδύω. An insight into the figurative use of this word is found in Athenaeus, a third century A.D. Greek writer, in Book XII, 537 of his *Deipnosophiste* where he relates a story from Ephippus about Alexander the Great how he would dress himself in the holy garments of various deities - Ammon, Artemis, Hermes - claiming to himself their qualities. Paul's thought is far superior. He in no way is suggesting that one should take on the garments or symbols of Christ. Rather they have become associated with Christ. For Athenaeus' story *cf.* Athenaeus, *Deipnosophiste*, Loeb Classical Library. Eng. trans. by Charles Burton Gulick (Cambridge: Harvard University Press, 1963), Vol.V, pp.429ff.

/16/   Albrecht Oepke, *TDNT*, I, p.539.

/17/   Schnackenburg, *op. cit.*, pp.21ff.

/18/   Oepke, *loc. cit.*

/19/   I.H. Marshall, "The Meaning of the Verb 'to baptize'", *Evangelical Quarterly*, XLV (July-September, 1973), p.131.

/20/   Oepke, *loc. cit.*

/21/   Schnackenburg, *op. cit.*, p.23.

/22/   Hans Bietenhard, *TDNT*, V, p.245.

/23/   G. Adolf Deissman, *Bible Studies*, trans. Alexander Grieve (2nd edn.; Edinburgh: T. & T. Clark, 1903), p.147; James Hope Moulton and George Milligan, *The Vocabulary of the Greek New Testament* (London: Hodder and Stoughton, 1930), ὄνομα (5).

/24/   Beitenhard, *op. cit.*, p.268.

/25/   William E. Hull, "Baptism in the New Testament: a Hermeneutical Critique", *Review and Expositor*, LXV (Winter, 1968), 3-12, elaborates the point made in this paragraph.

The Identity of ἐγώ in Romans 7:7-25

David H. Campbell,
Department of Theology,
Durham University.

The identity of the "ego" in Rom.7:7-25 has long been a
matter of dispute among exegetes. Modern interpretation has
tended to fall into two categories, that which, following
W.G. Kümmel and others /1/, sees here a portrayal of "man under
law" in a general sense; and that which, following E. Stauffer
and others /2/, views the passage as a depiction of the flow
of salvation history. The traditional interpretation, held
by Augustine and the Reformers, i.e. that Paul is, at least in
vv.14-25, speaking of present Christian experience, has been
largely set aside, though one or two recent studies have
proposed its revival /3/. After an exhaustive survey of the
history of interpretation, O. Kuss concluded that the
obscurities in the passages were such that the exegetical
battle over it would have no end /4/. We hope to show, however,
that the evidence may prove such passimism unfounded.

Romans, as James Dunn points out /5/, is a carefully planned
letter. It is therefore rather unlikely, *ceteris paribus,* that
here in the midst of a sustained and coherent exposition of the
Christian life (Rom. 5-8), we have a portrait of the unbeliever
practically unequalled in terms of depth and vividness anywhere
in Paul's writings. Perhaps the most serious error one could
commit in attempting to make sense of Rom. 7 is to isolate it
from its natural context. In Rom. 5 Paul commences his description of Christian experience. Having declared at 5:21 that
"grace will rule through righteousness to eternal life through
Jesus Christ our Lord", Paul must now make clear how this comes
to fruition in the Christian life, and so must come to grips
with those factors which remain stumbling blocks to the
attainment of Christian maturity. This he does in Rom. 6,7 and
8. In ch. 6 the topic is dying to sin and the flesh through
slavery to righteousness; in ch. 7 the flesh, sin and God's Law;
and in ch. 8 the flesh, sin and God's Spirit /6/. These are not
three separate battles, but rather one conflict described from
three different perspectives. Hence, it is important for our

understanding of the identity of the speaker in Rom. 7 to
determine what Rom. 6 and 8 have to say about Christian existance.

Rom. 6 deals with our death to sin. It is, to be sure,
peppered profusely with past tenses; against this, however, we
note the string of imperatives starting with λογίζεσθε in
v.11 /7/, by which Paul - very much in the present tense -
exhorts his readers to put sin to death in their lives. In v.14
we are told, "sin will have no lordship over you", yet in v.12
Paul has said, "Do not allow sin to rule in your mortal bodies".
We find the same phenomenon in ch.8 which, like ch.6, begins
with an affirmation that deliverance from sin is already
accomplished - yet only a few verses further on, we find the
indicative, "we are debtors, brethren, to live not according
to the flesh but according to the Spirit" (v.12), followed by two
open conditionals indicating the possibility of living in either
fashion. Indeed, it is hard to see why Paul would have bothered
to outline the alternatives in 8:5-12 at all unless both options
were in some sense actual possibilities for his hearers.

In addition to this, we may note the following points:

(i)   We assume that δεδικαίωται ἀπὸ τῆς ἁμαρτίας (6:7)
is to be understood with reference to Paul's teaching on
justification, rather than being an implication of actual
empirical freedom from sin - which would imply that Paul
believed in sinlessness, a supposition which seems highly
unlikely in view of the parenetical content of his letters /8/;

(ii)   Paul's use of the phrase διὰ τὴν ἀσθενείαν τῆς
σαρκὸς ὑμῶν (6:19), which undoubtedly refers to the present
experience of Christians, must shed some light on the temporal
reference of σάρξ in ch.7, and links with 8:26, where the
Spirit is said to aid our ἀσθενεία (and where Paul is again
speaking unquestionably of redeemed man) /9/;

(iii)   The concept of δουλεία τῷ θεῷ in 6:17-23 (once
again describing the present experience of Christians) links
closely with 7:25b, δουλεύω νόμῳ θεοῦ. This would appear to
suggest grounds for a present reference of 7:25b, a phrase
which, in the opinion of many interpreters, is a summation of
vv.14-25 as a whole;

(iv)   7:24-25a seem to suggest *in nuce* what Paul
expands upon at 8:18ff, which latter passage refers to a future
deliverance from δουλεία τῆς φθορᾶς and from ἀσθενεία - a

deliverance which will prove finally decisive in our struggle against these *still-potent* forces. Packer points out that the thought of "deliverance from the body" is the same in 7:24 as in 8:23 /10/;

(v) Rom.8:10 also suggests the Christian's continued vulnerability to sin and the flesh. Thus Cranfield: "We take the reference to be then to the fact that the Christian must still submit to death as the wage of sin, because he is a sinner" /11/. Rom.8:11 is thus probably a reference to the resurrection, not to some present experience of sanctification or perfection /12/;

(vi) The absence of any reference to the Spirit in ch.7 is satisfactorily accounted for if we realise that Paul is focussing here on the relationship of the Christian to God's holy and righteous Law. There is, for that matter, no reference to the Spirit in ch.6, yet no one seems to think that this precludes a description of Christian experience there. If, instead of erecting an artificial and arbitrary barrier between Rom.7 and Rom.8, we were to allow Paul's narrative to flow naturally, the solution to the question would come in short order at 8:4, where Spirit and Law are brought together;

(vii) The understanding that 7:1-6 indicates an absolute freedom from the Law cannot be accepted without hesitation /13/, particularly when the Apostle is at such pains in our own text to defend the goodness and (evidently) eternal value of the same Law. It is an unfortunate datum of modern exegesis of this chapter that arguments rejecting a present reference should start with the (unproven) assumption that the Law is a hostile power, or at least one belonging to the old aeon. Exegetes appear, at least on this score, to follow each other in a circular dance - rarely, if ever, questioning the "choreography"!

We now come to the question of the use of the first person in the section as a whole. The *Stilform* theory of Kümmel, while at first sight attractive, presents certain difficulties. It avoids, to be sure, most objections, but only in the sense that its vagueness equally precludes the affording of any satisfactory answers. How, Dunn asks, can Rom.7 denote "everyman" - except for Paul /14/? Even in 1 Cor.13, the use of the first person, while certainly rhetorical, clearly has both personal and temporal reference, viz. the present Christian experience of Paul and the Corinthians. And Rom.7,

on any view, has a greater element of *personal* vividness and
specificity than does 1 Cor.13. Indeed, Dunn notes, in all
the Pauline "ego" passages cited by Kümmel, Paul is himself
included in the subject reference, except for one or two cases
involving imaginary objectors /15/. Longenecker points out
that Kümmel's Rabbinic examples are late (second century) and
have a similarly imaginary and even conjured character /16/.
Without some personal and temporal aspect, statements such as
ἔζων and ἀπέθανον, not to mention the dramatic cry of v.24,
become meaningless and unreal. Packer notes that if Paul
(even though expressing a general truth) excludes himself, the
whole tenor of the passage becomes theatrical and artificial;
the existential anguish of vv.15ff and v.24 are too real to
exclude personal involvement /17/. It is also not to be
discounted that Paul, knowing the delicacy of what he is about
to say, prefers to put the whole matter within a personal
perspective, much as might any preacher sensitive to the
feelings of his listeners. This implies the realisation,
however, that the preacher fully shares the weaknesses of the
people.

The considerations thus far adduced weigh not only against
the rhetorical-general approach but also against one seeing
here a portrayal of salvation history. For it is central to
the position of the latter that introduction of any personal
or biographical element into the passage is incompatible with
any view of the account as describing something which occurred
several millenia in the past; such an interpretation, if it
is at all valid, must be seen in relation to the outworking of
this salvation history in the life of the Apostle and his
readers.

We must also note that the use of the present tense in
vv.14-25, when linked with the concurrent use of the first
person singular and the extraordinarily vivid exclamations
of the passage, point to an experience which is both real and
present to the speaker /18/. In v.15, for instance, it is
surely more reasonable to assume that the speaker is confronted
with a dilemma with which he is fully familiar but somehow
cannot resolve, than to suppose that the whole is seen only
"through the eyes of faith", the "Unbegreiflichkeit"
representing the contrast between past action and present
comprehension thereof, an interpretation which surely has
little contextual evidence to commend itself /19/. We may
also refer in passing to the description of the speaker in

these verses as one who delights in God's Law and in willing
the good /20/, and that he does so κατα τον εσω ανθρωπον (7:22),
an expression used elsewhere in Paul (cf. 2 Cor.4:16 for the
closest parallel) to refer to the Christian believer /21/.
Finally, it should be pointed out that the natural interpretation
of αυτὸς ἐγώ in v.25b is that it is a simple assertion of
man's unity (and hence responsibility before God) over against
any possible suggestion of dualism Paul's readers might
otherwise have drawn from the context. There does not seem to
be any objective grammatical or contextual support for
translating the phrase "I myself, without Christ" /22/. In
addition to this, we may record Dunn's observation that νοῦς
here must refer to the mind renewed by the Spirit, for Paul
nowhere speaks of the natural mind /23/; Cranfield suggests
that the idea here should be linked with the ἀνακαίνωσις τοῦ
νοός of Rom.12:2 - the mind "being renewed by" God's Spirit /24/.

     Why then the past tense in vv.7-13? In light of the
strong case made by Lyonnet /25/, it cannot now be denied that
the Paradise account was in some sense in the Apostle's mind,
although the direct citation of the Mosaic commandment and
the fact that he could scarcely have used the word νομος
(particularly after having written vv.1-6) point also to a
reminiscence of Sinai. The most likely conclusion (taking
Kümmel's various objections into account) is that Paul is
thinking here of the whole sorry experience of the human race,
commencing (and being determined) in Paradise, and coming to a
further important juncture at Sinai; we must see the latter
reference, however, in the larger perspective of the history
of the human race in Adam. We have thus a natural resumption
of 5:12ff, where sin and death are linked to the Fall and
Adam's disobedience to the commandment. The fact that Paul
appears to make little of the transition at v.14 /26/ and that
ἤδειν (v.7) implies continuing experience /27/ leads to the
recognition that the continuity of experience is such that
vv.7-13 become simultaneously the experience of Paul himself
as of every "man-in-Adam", an experience which, though
certainly characteristic of pre-Christian existence, becomes
tangible in the fullest sense in our present Christian life
where the battle against sin is for the first time truly joined.
This is why, as Bengel long ago noted, no dramatic break can
be postulated at v.14; and in this sense, the whole passage,
vv.7-25, is a description of present Christian experience. The
past tenses of vv.7-13 are ingressive, and are explicated with
reference to continuing experience by the present tenses of

vv.14-25. As with anyone else recounting an illustration from his own experience, Paul quite naturally begins in the past; after all, our entire experience *is* past, except for the ever-fleeting present moment. Just because Paul speaks in the past tense, however, does not mean he is speaking of his *non-Christian* past; indeed, the close connection between the two sections of our passage /28/ points to the opposite conclusion.

May we in closing note that if Rom.7 is taken as expressive of Christian experience, we do not thereby devalue the deliverance wrought in Christ. We merely assert the seriousness of the battle in which we are engaged: a battle, however, destined to be won - which is understood clearly as long as we hold Rom.6-8 closely together. Thus we can declare with the Apostle, "Wretched man that I am - who will rescue me from this body of death? Thanks be to God, through Jesus Christ our Lord!"

NOTES

/1/ Cf. W.G. Kümmel, *Röm 7 und die Bekehrung des Paulus* (1929), reprinted in *Röm 7 und das Bild des Menschen im NT* (München: Chr. Kaiser Verlag, 1974). Other proponents of this position include P. Althaus, K. Kertelge, C.L. Mitton, and H.W. Schmidt.

/2/ Cf. E. Stauffer, art. "ἐγώ", *TDNT* II, pp.343-362. Other proponents of this view include P. Benoit, F.-J. Leenhardt, and S. Lyonnet.

/3/ Cf. A. Nygren, *Commentary on Romans*, tr. C.C. Rasmussen (London: SCM, 1952); C.E.B. Cranfield, *The Epistle to the Romans* (I.C.C.), I. (Edinburgh: T. and T. Clark, 1979); J.D.G. Dunn, "Rom. 7:14-25 in the Theology of St. Paul", *TZ* 31.5 (1975), pp.257-273; J.I. Packer, "The 'wretched man' in Romans 7", *Studia Evangelica II* (Berlin: Akademie Verlag, 1964), pp.621-627; and some others.

/4/ Cf. O. Kuss, *Der Römerbrief* (Regensburg, 1959) II, pp.462-485.

/5/ Dunn, p.260.

/6/ Cf. Dunn, *loc.cit.*

/7/ On the imperatival nature of λογίζεσθε, cf. Cranfield, p.315.

/8/ Cf. Cranfield, p.311 n.1.

/9/   Cranfield notes, "What is meant is the incomprehension, insensitiveness, insincerity and proneness to self-deception, which characterize the fallen human nature even of Christians..." (p.326 n.1).

/10/   Packer, p.626; cf. Cranfield, pp.365-366, who also notes that ταλαίπωρος (7:24) can indicate distress, affliction, suffering, "without in any way implying hopelessness" (p.366).

/11/   Cranfield, p.389.

/12/   Cf. *op.cit.*, p.391.

/13/   Cf., for instance, Cranfield on Rom.7:1-6 (pp.331-340); also his article "St. Paul and the Law", *SJT* 17 (1964), pp.43-68, especially under section (9).

/14/   Dunn, p.260.

/15/   *Ibid.*, p.261.

/16/   Richard N. Longenecker, *Paul: Apostle of Liberty* (1964; r.p. Grand Rapids: Baker, 1976), p.88.

/17/   Packer, p.623.

/18/   Cranfield, quoting Calvin, argues that the only natural way to understand the present tense here is that Paul "is depicting in his own person the character and extent of the weakness of believers" - though Calvin sees the description of the believer beginning at v.15 (p.356).

/19/   Mitton's suggestion that we have here an example of the "historical present" is undermined by his own admission that such a phenomenon is otherwise unexampled in Paul; cf. his article "Romans vii - Reconsidered (part 2)", *ET* 65 (1953-54), pp.99-103.

/20/   Cf. Cranfield, p.346; Packer, p.625.

/21/   Cf. Dunn, p.262; Cranfield, p.363.

/22/   J. Kürzinger cites Bauer in support of this contention, but admits, noting Kuss' observation that this meaning cannot be derived from the wording itself (but rather must come from the context), that the issue is far from clear; cf. "Der Schlüssel zum Verständnis von Röm 7", *BZ* 7 (1963), p.272. Packer notes that Bauer can give no parallel usage (p.625). Cranfield comments, "The words ... would seem to be best explained neither as emphasizing that Paul is speaking of himself nor that the sentence is stating what is true apart from Christ's intervention, but rather as underlining the full personal involvement of the Christian as the subject of both statements" (p.369 n.4). Leenhardt admits that the phrase as a whole is an embarrassment to his position, "car l'homme qui s'exprime plus haut approuvait la loi de Dieu, mais il ne pouvait pas certes dire qu'il en était l'esclave, ce qu'il supposerait qu'il lui obéisse" (cf. his commentary, *Épître de saint Paul aux Romains* (Neuchatel: Delachaux et Niestlé, 1957), p.112.

/23/ Dunn, p.263.

/24/ Cranfield, p.363.

/25/ Cf. his articles, "L'histoire du salut selon le chapitre VII de l'épître aux Romains", *Biblica* 43 (1962), pp.117-151; "Tu ne convoiteras pas (Rom.7:7)", *Neotestamentica et Patristica (Novum Testamentum Supplements,* 6) (Leiden: Brill, 1962), pp.157-166; and "Quaestiones ad Rom 7:7-13", *VD* 40 (1962), pp.163-183.

/26/ Cf. Dunn, p.261; Althaus,"Zur Auslegung von Röm 7:14ff: Antwort an Anders Nygren", *TLZ* 77 (1952), col. 477, cites Bengel, "hoc versu 14 nec particula 'enim' ullum omnino, nedum res ipsa tam grandem patitur saltum fieri ab uno statu in alterum".

/27/ Cf. Dunn, p.261; Cranfield, p.348; C.K. Barrett, *A Commentary on the Epistle to the Romans* (New York: Harper and Row, 1957), p.142.

/28/ Most commentators, regardless of viewpoint, agree that vv.7-13 and vv.14-25 must be held fairly closely together; cf., for instance, Althaus, col. 477; Dunn, p.262; Kümmel, pp.89-90; and K. Stalder, *Das Werk des Geistes in der Heiligung bei Paulus* (Zürich: Evangelische Verlag, 1962), who notes that v.14 is in fact the "Ausgangspunkt" of v.7, the place where the foolishness of the question of v.7 is brought to light (p.290).

Salvation for Jews and Gentiles: Krister Stendahl and Paul's Letter to the Romans

Dr. W.S. Campbell,
Head of Religious Studies,
Westhill College,
Selly Oak,
Birmingham, 29.
ENGLAND.

In his recent stimulating and provocative study, *Paul Among Jews and Gentiles* /1/, Krister Stendahl has highlighted what I consider to be some of the most significant factors for the interpretation of Paul's letter to the Romans. Having researched in this area, I find myself very much in accord with the main emphases of his interpretation, i.e. that the focus in Romans is really the relation between Jews and Gentiles, that chs. 9-11 are the climax of Paul's argument and that the justification of the individual is not the centre of Paulinism /2/. In relation to the latter it seems to me that justification in Paul is essentially the determining principle in his discussion of the constitution and continuity of the people of God. I was delighted to find in Stendahl a concern to treat Jews as Jews and not merely as stereotypes for wrong attitudes towards God /3/. How refreshing also to find Paul portrayed as a lively missionary, concerning himself with what we might call living theological issues.

I wish to concentrate in this paper on one of the most interesting and provocative views which Stendahl has proposed. This is the view that Paul comes to the point where he sees Christianity is on its way to becoming a Gentile church. Simultaneously, according to Stendahl, he sees that God has mysterious and special plans for the salvation of Israel /4/. The question which I wish to dispute with Stendahl is whether it is correct to maintain, as he does, that Paul in Rom. 11 reveals a mystery which affirms a God-willed co-existence between Judaism and Christianity in which the missionary urge to convert Israel is held in check. I will investigate Paul's statements in Rom. 11 concerning the salvation of the Jews in

order to determine whether in this chapter there is one way
of salvation or two.

    In ch.11:1, Paul begins by repudiating the suggestion that
God might have cast off his people. Those who had suggested
such a possibility we discover later to be Roman Gentile
Christians who in their own self-conscious conceit imagine that
God has rejected the Jews /5/. The first proof that God has
not cast off his people is Paul himself. He is an example of a
believing Jew - an indication that God has not forgotten the
special place of Israel "whom He foreknew", as Paul reminds the
Romans (v.2).

    The second proof that Paul offers is that of the believing
remnant (vv.2-5). The faithfulness of God is such that he has
always preserved a remnant that has remained faithful throughout
the vicissitudes of Israel's history. As in Old Testament times
"so too at this present time there is a remnant, chosen by
grace". (v.5). We note how Paul carefully stresses that it
is an election of grace, not of works, thus indicating that his
theology of the remnant is closely related to his discussion of
faith and works in chs.3-4. Paul sees this remnant as
representing the whole nation of Israel, the first fruits of
the harvest which is 'all Israel' - a saving remnant (11:16) /6/.

    In v.11, in a sort of midrash on the 'jealousy' motif
based on Deut.32:16.f /7/, Paul refutes what seems to have been
a current view among Gentile Christians in Rome and possibly
elsewhere i.e. that the Jews as a whole had stumbled because
it was God's will that they should fall - the present hardening
was God's final judgement upon Israel and salvation was now
open only to the Gentiles. A main aim of Paul in Romans is
to show that the salvation of Gentiles and the salvation of
Israel are not two distinct and mutually exclusive entities /8/.
On the contrary when Israel stumbled, God's intention was to
bring the gospel to the Gentiles. Moreover the salvation of
the Gentiles is understood by Paul as a means of winning the
Jewish people to salvation. Already in 10:19 Paul sees
Deut.32:21 as offering guidance on how the salvation of the
Gentiles would lead to the salvation of Israel. So Paul in
evangelising the Gentiles is magnifying his ministry and thereby
working indirectly for the salvation of the Jews /9/. Here he
seems to see a parallel between his own ministry and that of
Christ whom he describes in 15:8 as becoming a servant to the
circumcised and also to the Gentiles /10/.

It seems strange that in v.14 Paul speaks of saving only some of his fellow Jews by making them jealous. Munck says that this is by no means due to Paul's humility and that τυνες does not necessarily mean a small number but "an indefinite number which the context must further define, i.e. a not inconsiderable number" /11/. Munck considers that there are three periods in question here - "first, that already described in which Israel apart from this remnant was unbelieving, while the Gentiles received the gospel: next the period now beginning, when the great results of the mission among the Gentiles begin to make an impression on Israel, so that the tide turns, and an indefinite but not inconsiderable number are won for Christ: and lastly, the decisive and final period when God intervenes and saves the whole of Isarel" /12/.

It seems to me that Munck is wrong in seeing three distinct periods. He himself states that Paul sees no decisive difference between the first and second periods nor does Paul feel himself to be separated from the third period i.e. the salvation of all Israel, as something he cannot take part in and prepare for /13/. Even the arrival of the fullness of salvation mentioned in 11:25ff. is not an entirely new phase in *Heilsgeschichte*, as it makes use of that jealousy in the Jews which Paul believes is even now in the present the decisive means of breaking down Israel's obduracy and for changing the destiny of the people. It would seem therefore that in Paul's mind there is no absolute distinction between his present evangelistic activity in winning the Gentiles and thereby making the Jews jealous, and the expected salvation of Israel after the fullness of the Gentiles has come in. The same verb παραζηλῶσαι is used in vv.11 and 14 which suggests that Paul's winning of some Jews and the total effect of believing Gentiles on the Jews is one and the same process.

This goes against Stendahl's view of a God-willed separate existence for unbelieving Jews /14/. W.D. Davies has outlined two possible approaches to Rom.11:25-27, Paul's famous passage setting forth the mystery that all Israel will be saved. These verses can be taken as a construction of Paul's peculiar thinking about the end - a special mystery here proclaimed by Paul (11:25), which we should not expect to find in his own previous writings. Alternatively, they can be taken as part of a tradition of early Christian eschatology on which Paul drew, even though he contributed his own emphasis. The first approach comes to concentrate on the theology of Paul, the second more on his christology /15/.

Stendahl points out that Paul does not say, "When the time
of God's kingdom, the consummation, comes Israel will accept
Jesus as Messiah"! He says only, "The time will come when all
Israel will be saved". Stendahl finds it stunning that Paul
writes the whole section of Rom.10:17-11:36 without using the
name of Jesus Christ, the concluding doxology being the only
such doxology in Paul's writings without any christological
element /16/. But, as Davies notes /17/, Stendahl does not
discuss the meaning of ὁ ρυόμενος (v.26). This could certainly
mean Christ, the Deliverer. On the other hand those who
believe there is a special way of salvation for the Jews can
interpret it to mean God himself. The reference to "my covenant
with them" in 11:27 would on this interpretation mean the
eternal covenant between Yahweh and Israel as distinct from
the new covenant referred to in I Cor.11:25 and II Cor.3:6
which fulfilled the hope of Jer.31:33 and which embraces both
Jews and Gentiles in the church. This would mean that the
whole process of Israel's salvation at the limit of history
will be the work of God; this view of the future does not bring
Israel into connection with the Christ of the new covenant for
Gentiles at all /18/. This interpretation would support
Stendahl's thesis that "it dawns on Paul that the Jesus
movement is to be a Gentile movement - God being allowed to
establish Israel in his own time and way" /19/.

In opposition to Stendahl however, it seems preferable to
take the more christological understanding of Rom.11:25-27.
As in I Thess.1:10 the deliverer is Christ /20/. This passage
is not to be considered in isolation from its context as the
γαρ with which it commences would indicate /21/. The whole of
ch.11 must be seen in the light of the Jewish or Jewish
Christian eschatology which Paul had inherited but which had
been radically revised by him through his understanding of
Christ and his reflection upon his missionary activity. Even
the concluding doxology, although it does not mention the name
of Christ, is implicitly christological and, as Barrett has
pointed out,is a carefully constructed conclusion emphasizing
the solidarity of Jews and Gentiles in the ultimate purpose
of God /22/.

It is a risk to place too much significance on the argument
from silence. Although the name of Christ is not specifically
mentioned, Paul at two important points in ch.11 uses what must

be broadly termed a christologically based argument. This is
what was known to the rabbis as the *Kal Wachomer* type of
argument, i.e. arguing 'a minore ad majus'. In 11:24, Paul
writes "for if you (Gentiles) have been cut from what is by
nature a wild olive tree, and grafted, contrary to nature into
a cultivated tree, *how much more* will these natural branches
be grafted back into their own olive" /23/. The same argument
has already been used in 11:12 - "now if their trespass means
riches for the world and their failure means riches for the
Gentiles, *how much more* will their full inclusion mean". Paul
has previously used this type of argument in Rom.5:9-10 -
"Since, therefore, we are now justified by his blood, *much more*
shall we be saved by him from the wrath of God. For if while
we were enemies we were reconciled to God by the death of his
Son, *much more,* now that we are reconciled, shall we be saved
by his life".   Here as also in Rom.5:15-17 and II Cor.3:7-11
the argument is basically a christo-centric one. It is on the
basis of what God has done in the Christ event and what he
himself has already experienced of the outworking of that event
that Paul expects his 'much more'.

    Having considered therefore what is written in Rom.11
concerning the salvation of the remnant, or of Paul himself, or
of the outcome of his Gentile mission in making some of the Jews
jealous - hence leading them to faith - it would appear that
no distinction can be drawn between the salvation enjoyed in
Christ and that which is being sought or hoped for, for Israel
in the future. It seems highly questionable therefore whether
there is, as Stendahl claims, a special way of salvation for
Israel and whether there is a God willed co-existence which
places a curb upon the missionary urge to convert Israel /24/.
That Paul expected the salvation of Israel only after the
'fullness of the Gentiles' does not necessarily mean that it
had to be brought about by a different process. In opposition
to Stendahl's view that Paul no longer regards it as a direct
task to challenge Israel, Davies rightly questions whether Paul
would ever have given up trying to present the claims of Christ
wherever he encountered a Jew /25/. But he draws a distinction
between an approach to individuals and one to the nation as a
whole. I do not find this a meaningful distinction.

    Another factor which may tell against Stendahl's thesis
is that it is doubtful whether Christianity did in fact exist
as a distinct separate religious movement prior to A.D. 70 /26/.
It follows from this that if Christianity is still in some

sense part of Judaism in the late fifties, since Paul still
hopes for the salvation of all Israel then he would be unlikely
to encourage a cessation of mission or to envisage a separate
existence for the church over against Israel. 'The new Israel'
is a post-Pauline concept /27/. It was only after the Bar
Kochba revolt in the Second Century that the church began to
describe itself in this way.

A possible interpretation of ch.10:12-21 is that although
Israel has heard the gospel (10:19), they have not as yet truly
understood (10:3) /28/, and when Paul claims that "there is no
distinction between Jew and Greek; the same Lord is Lord of all
and bestows his riches upon all who call upon him", he intends
in fact to include Israel and his question "How shall they hear
without a preacher ?" may have some reference to preaching the
gospel to the Jews and possibly to his forthcoming visit to
Jerusalem. Paul could indeed have avoided the dangerous visit
to Jerusalem and he need not have taken such a large company
with him had he not regarded the collection visit as "fraught
with eschatological meaning" /29/.

Rom.9-11 is then Paul's argument for a church of Jews and
Gentiles as the consummation of God's eschatological purpose
now coming to fruition. He sees the pride and anti-Judaism of
Gentile Christians as a threat both to the unity of the church
and to the future salvation of Israel. He seeks to thwart any
break away of the Christian community from its Jewish roots /30/.
Both in his carefully planned and painfully executed collection
project and in his letter to the Romans, Paul's aim is to bring
about unity and harmony throughout the church so that the
eschatological work of God may proceed unhindered /31/. Paul's
theology is thoroughly christological and so for him there can
only be one way of salvation for both Jews and Gentiles /32/.

NOTES

/1/   British edition S.C.M. (1977).
/2/   On the state of the current debate on what constitutes the
centre of Pauline theology see W.D. Davies, 'Paul and the People
of Israel', New Testament Studies, xxiv (1977) pp.15-16, 33 n.1,
and Stendahl, op. cit., pp.129ff.
/3/   Op. cit. pp.5,95 and 133. The interpretation of Rom.9-11
has been vitiated by the tendency to see the Jew in these

chapters as a type of the adherent of works-righteousness of ch.4. Some Lutheran scholars have shown a marked tendency in this respect e.g. E. Käsemann, 'Paul and Israel', *New Testament Questions of Today*, (London 1969) pp.183ff.

/4/   *Op. cit.*, p.4. Cf. also Stendahl's foreword to J. Munck's book *Christ and Israel*, (Philadelphia 1967).

/5/   O. Glombitza describes the Roman Christians as 'geschichtlos' because they have erected their own view of the gospel and of history into a sort of 'Heilsegoismus'. 'Welche Sorge treibt den Apostel Paulus zu den Sätzen Röm.11:25f.?' *Novum Testamentum*, vii (1964) pp.312f. See also T.W. Manson, 'Romans', *Peake's Commentary on the Bible*, Ed. M. Black and H.H. Rowley, (London 1962), p.949.

/6/   Cf. C. Müller, *Gottes Gerechtigkeit und Gottes Volk: Eine Untersuchung zu Römer 9-11*, (Göttingen 1964) pp.45-46, and E. Flesseman-van Leer, 'Jew and Gentile: Some Considerations Suggested by Dr. Hay's Reply', Canadian Journal of Theology, iii (1957) p.238. Cf. also Munck *op. cit.*, pp.110f.

/7/   A.T. Hanson, *Studies in Paul's Technique and Theology*, (London 1974) p.167.

/8/   H.W. Bartsch,*Antijudaismus im Neuen Testament*, hrsg. von W.P. Eckert, N. Levinson, M. Stöhr (Munich 1967) p.35.

/9/   According to Munck Paul is convinced that "Israel is still the chief goal of God's will to salvation", *op. cit.*, p.123.

/10/ Although Munck's view of Paul's apostleship and eschatology has (rightly) been disputed, e.g. W.D. Davies in his review of *Paulus und die Heilsgeschichte* in New Testament Studies, ii, (1955) pp.60f., Munck's writings have inspired much of the recent interest in Romans 9-11.

/11/ *Op. cit.*, pp.123ff.

/12/ *Op. cit.*, p.124.

/13/ "Even though he himself will not experience it since his task is to be done when the fulness of the Gentiles has been achieved". *op. cit.*, p.124.

/14/ *Op. cit.*, p.4.

/15/ *Op. cit.*, p.24.

/16/ *Op. cit.*, p.4.

/17/ *Op. cit.*, p.25 n.3.

/18/ W.D. Davies, *op. cit.*, p.26.

/19/ *Op. cit.*, p.132.

/20/ Davies, *op. cit.*, p.27.

/21/ E. Käsemann, *An die Römer*, (Tübingen, 1973) p.301.

/22/ *A Commentary on the Epistle to the Romans*, Black's New Testament Commentaries, (London, 1957) p.222.

/23/ Rom.11:17-24 is a midrash based on Jer.11:16-19, cf.

Hanson, *op. cit.*, pp.120f. and 167.

/24/ *Op. cit.*, p.4.

/25/ *Op. cit.*, p.26 n.4.

/26/ Davies, *op. cit.*, pp.19f.

/27/ Cf. P. Richardson, *Israel in the Apostolic Church*, SNTS Monograph Series (Cambridge, 1969). Richardson claims that Paul refused to take the term 'Israel' and to fill it with a solely Christian content - "The obvious feature of the olive tree figure, sometimes overlooked, is that a pruned Israel retains its place in God's activity". (p.129).

/28/ Since Paul is not attempting to prove Israel's guilt, it is better to follow Zahn's understanding of the verse as meaning "Has Israel not first (of all peoples) become acquainted with the gospel?" This avoids the problem of ascribing to Israel a purely intellectual comprehension of the gospel and fits in better with the discussion in ch.11. Surprisingly Munck follows Kühl on this verse rather than Zahn, *op. cit.*, pp.99f.

/29/ Cf. F.F. Bruce, *New Testament History*, (London, 1969) p.335 and Munck, *op. cit.*, pp.9f. See also his discussion of Karl Holl's thesis in *Paul and the Salvation of Mankind*, pp.287f.

/30/ Davies' thorough and illuminating study of Paul's attitude to Israel highlights this aspect of Pauline theology. See especially pp.16f.

/31/ H.W. Bartsch, *op. cit.*, pp.36f.

/32/ Contra C. Plag, *Israels Wege zum Heil*, (Stuttgart, 1969).

Christ the End of the Law: Romans 10:4

Rev. Dr. W.S. Campbell,
3 Goldfinch Close,
Bournville,
Birmingham B30 1XD.
ENGLAND.

If there is any one good reason for choosing to speak about
this verse, it is because there is such widespread disagreement
about its meaning. As C.F.D. Moule says, "It is one of the most
hotly debated passages in the Pauline epistles" /1/. An
unfortunate feature of this verse is that its interpretation
tends to be determined more by the understanding of Pauline
theology that one brings to it than by what the text actually
says.

We draw attention first of all to the wider context in
which the verse is set i.e. the letter to the Romans. This is
extremely significant because Paul's attitude to the Jews and
to the Law is so much more conciliatory in Romans than in
Galatians /2/. Moreover, since Romans is the later and more
thorough document wherever there is a divergence of view, I
consider it advisable to put more weight on Romans than
Galatians. As W.D. Davies says, "Paul's criticisms of the Law
were not uniformly negative - they fluctuated with the
conditions which he faced. For example, in Romans he abandoned
the unqualified dismissal of the Law expressed in Galatians"/3/.

We should also note that this letter includes such
favourable references to the Law as 7:12, "So the Law is holy,
and the commandment is holy and just and good", and 13:10,
"Love is the fulfilling of the Law", and 8:3-4, "God sent his
son ... in order that the just requirement of the Law might be
fulfilled in us". The more immediate context i.e. ch.10 also
supports a positive understanding of the Law /4/. What Barth
says of 10:6f. can be extended to cover the entire chapter -
"All that we read ... is one invitation to participate in the
Law's fulfilment" /5/. Ch.10 presupposes the situation

outlined by Paul at the end of ch.9; despite the fact that the
gospel has been taken to the Jews, the majority of them are
still unbelieving - the mission to the Jews has met with only
slight success. Paul is here simply describing and assessing
this contemporary situation. As at the beginning of chs.9 and
11, he speaks sadly and with deep concern for his unbelieving
brethren. His diagnosis is that though it must be granted that
they have a zeal for God, it is in fact unenlightened.

This ignorance can also be described in terms of the Law
and of righteousness. The Jews sought to achieve righteousness
by way of the Law, i.e. by using the Law as a means to legal
righteousness, but they did not succeed in fulfilling the Law
and so failed to find righteousness /6/. Bring has drawn our
attention to the fact that Law and righteousness are virtually
synonymous here /7/ - a strong indication of Paul's positive
intention concerning the Law in this section. It is also
noteworthy that the description of Jewish unbelief as failure
to fulfil the Law is the opposite of what Paul claims for
believers in 8:4, where it is said that the just requirement of
the Law is fulfilled in those who walk according to the Spirit
/8/. They missed the goal of the Law - true righteousness,
because they sought a righteousness of their own achievement and
did not submit to God's righteousness (as revealed in Jesus
Christ) (10:3). This is the dark background of Jewish unbelief
which is presupposed in 10:4. This verse marks the beginning
of Paul's exposition of Christ as the τέλος of the Law, rather
than a continuation of what the Law and self-righteous Jews
could not do /9/. M.J. Suggs suggests that by identification
of Christ-Wisdom-Torah in 10:6-10, Paul sought to resolve the
tension between Gospel and Law and thereby rescue his gospel
from the stigma of absolute opposition to the Law /10/.

This leads us to the problem of the interpretation of
τέλος in 10:4. The basic issue in the text is whether τέλος
has the temporal sense of 'end' or 'cessation' /11/, or whether
it has the final sense of 'goal' or 'outcome' /12/, or possibly
combines both these meanings /13/. The contrasts between faith
and works in 9:30-31, between God's righteousness and a
righteousness of our own (10:3), and the righteousness of the
Law and the righteousness out of faith (10:5-6), have been
regarded as ample evidence for the temporal sense and Christ is
thus considered as the end of the Law as a means to
righteousness /14/. This is the meaning preferred by the New
English Bible which gets rid of the ambiguity of 'end' (which

could be used both in the sense of termination or of goal), and
translates "For Christ ends the Law", thereby actually
strengthening the negative emphasis of the verse by using a
verb instead of the Greek noun, whereas with strange
inconsistency, the same word is translated 'end' in 6:21-22.
We feel that this translation does less than justice to the
original text. "Paul is not saying that Christ destroyed or
ended the Law (τελευτή) or that He is the 'cul-de-sac'
(τελευτᾶν) thereof" /15/. If this is what Paul says, it means
that he allows that prior to Christ the achievement of
righteousness by works was a perfectly valid activity. It
would also mean that Christ is the end of a false principle
which, as a matter of historical fact, He was not, since
law-righteousness continued to be the aim of the Jews /16/. Our
modern distinction which regards the Old Testament as 'The Law'
(in a legalistic sense) in contrast to the New Testament as
The Gospel' tends to encourage such a view, particularly
evident among Lutherans /17/. It is most unlikely however,
that Paul, who argued so strongly in Rom.4 that Abraham was
justified by faith, would allow that anyone at any time could
be justified by works of law ("... by such shall no flesh be
justified". 3:20).

    This problem is often overcome by the argument that Paul
is not thinking of the Old Testament use of the Law, but
rather of the legalistic use by the Judaism of his own time.
He is not so much criticizing the Law as what the Jews were
doing with the Law /18/. If we bear in mind the fact that the
Greek language which Paul used had no word-group to denote
legalism, legalist or legalistic /19/, then we can appreciate
the great problem Paul faced when he sought to distinguish
between a good Law and the bad use of it by the Jews. There
is no doubt that this fact helps us to clarify some texts
where Paul's language concerning the Law is rather ambiguous,
but it is doubtful if it is of any help in this text. The
εἰς δικαιοσύνην is best understood as expressing purpose so
that we should translate the verse "For Christ is the
completion of the Law that everyone who has faith may be
justified" /20/. But what law is intended here? We do not
regard the Law in this section as the Old Testament law
misused /21/, or as the Mosaic law which is only part of the
total revelation of God, or even as a reference to the promises
contained in the Law but "as the Law in its fulness as a
revelation of God's promises and righteous demands which were
fulfilled in Christ and therefore reached their end in Him"/22/.

That this interpretation of the Law is justified is confirmed
by the fact, which we have already noted, that in ch.9:30-32
Law and righteousness were virtually interchangeable and also
that in 10:6-8 not only is the Law quoted but Christ himself
is understood by Paul to stand in the place of 'this commandment'
in Deut.30:11 /23/. Karl Barth gives a useful interpretation
of τέλος in this verse when he understands it as ἀνακεφαλαίωσις-
the sum or totality of all that the Law stood for - as expressed
in the rabbinic concept of the 'kelal' /24/. If we interpret
law in this verse in its fullest sense and bear in mind the
normal Jewish revulsion against any suggestion that the Law
should be abolished, it is unlikely that the statement here
means simply that Christ is the termination of the Law /25/.

If there is any suggestion of termination in the verse,
this negative sense cannot be primary, as Du Plessis suggests
/26/, but at best secondary. This is more in accord with the
normal meaning of New Testament τέλος according to Du Plessis'
own investigation. Du Plessis found that "the New Testament
revealed a unique use of the word τέλος. In this application
the creative appropriation of New Testament writers manifested
itself conspicuously; τέλος received at their hands its
messianic and eschatological connotation and this motif
provided the fundamental theme of New Testament kerygma" /27/.
For the New Testament writers Christ himself determined the
meaning of τέλος and all the separate uses of the word were
determined by a christological basis /28/. When we consider
the messianic and christological emphases surrounding the word
τέλος these are more likely to have fulfilment rather than
abrogation as their primary sense. The investigation of
secular and biblical uses of τέλος by Flückiger supports this
interpretation. He found that at every place in biblical Greek
where τέλος can be translated by 'end' (*Ende*), the basic meaning
of 'goal' (*Ziel*) is also in the background /29/. Another
factor gives additional evidence that the primary meaning of
τέλος in v.4 is goal or completion. The διώκων in 9:31 means
striving after a goal (cf. Phil.3:12,14). The Jews were
running or striving after a goal but did not achieve it. This
goal of righteousness is, in 10:4, declared to be Christ /30/.
Bring gives as meaning for τέλος "the winning post in a race,
the completion of a task, the climax of a matter" /31/.

If we accept the final sense of τέλος as fulfilment or
completion, as primary in 10:4, it may be allowed that the
secondary sense of end or termination may also be included. As

Leenhardt suggests "Christ puts an end to the Law because the
Law finds in Him its goal and its crown" /32/. In any case it
is not a static abrogation of the Law that Paul intends by the
word τέλος because τέλος itself is a dynamic concept embodying
the idea of one phase ending, coinciding with the inception of
another. Christ as the τέλος of the Law is not so much
abrogation of the Law, but "an act of transition, of
transformation of its (the Law's) servitude from death to
life" /33/. Moreover, the final sense of τέλος fits in better
with εἰς δικαιοσύνην and also gives a better understanding of
the γάρ at the beginning of vv.4 and 5.

The context of 9:30 f. shows that Paul is not attacking
the Jews but simply outlining their failure to find salvation.
In view of this we think it more fitting that Paul in 10:3,
instead of proceeding to contrast the way of Christ with the
error of the Jews should proceed instead to explain that because
the Jews did not understand the real meaning of the Law (9:31)
they could not appreciate Christ as the positive fulfilment of
that Law. We conclude then that the γάρ in 10:4 means a
continuation of the argument in 10:3 and that it refers to
Christ not to emphasize the distance of the Jews from salvation
but to so present Christ in Jewish terms /34/ as the completion
of their revelation, that their failure to recognize Him
becomes all the more surprising. By virtue of the fact that
Christ has fulfilled the Law, life and righteousness are now
freely available for the people of the Law, and likewise on the
same terms, to those without the Law /35/. The immediate
context is in keeping with this interpretation of 10:4 as is
also the contents of chs.9-11 when viewed as the climax of an
argument extending throughout chs.1-11 and having its practical
application in chs.14-15 /36/.

Despite traditional exegesis, even 10:5-6 is not to be
seen as conflicting with this interpretation. The γάρ in v.5
and the δέ in v.6 have traditionally been regarded as plainly
denoting a contrast between law-righteousness and the
righteousness of faith, and as such were basic to the argument
for the temporal sense of τέλος in v.4. But neither of these
words need necessarily mean that this contrast is intended. If
it is correct to maintain that v.4 sets out not what men cannot
do, but what Christ has done, i.e. His fulfilment of the Law,
then the γάρ of v.5 may be regarded as introducing the
explanation of *how* Christ is the goal of the Law /37/. He is
the completion of the Law by virtue of the fact that He lived

it and practised it/38/.

It may legitimately be argued that Christ is not
necessarily intended by the words from Lev.18:5, "the man who
practises the righteousness which is based on the Law shall
live by it". Ridderbos holds that "What Paul means to say is
this, that he who strives after the righteousness that is by
the Law is then bound to the word of Moses, that is, to do
what the Law demands. ... In that sense it can be said that
Moses (or the Law itself) defines the righteousness that is of
the Law. This is not an appeal to Moses in support of 'a
false position', but a binding of this position to its own
point of departure; he who seeks righteousness in the Law faces,
as appears from the Law itself, the requirement of doing" /39/.
It should be noted however that Ridderbos' view does not
necessarily rule out the interpretation of 10:4 advocated in
this paper, despite his opposition to it.

Again the δέ of v.6 is only an insurmountable obstacle
to our argument if taken as adversative as is normally done.
But this is not necessarily the only possibility and it is
quite legitimate to interpret it as having only a transitional
or explanatory function /40/ and so vv.6 f. as well as v.5 may
be properly understood as a continuation of v.4 of Christ as the
goal of the Law.

This interpretation avoids the problem which we would
otherwise have of holding that Paul in v.5 quotes Moses
(Lev.18:5) as an example of the wrong kind of righteousness -
law-righteousness, whereas in v.6 he quotes Deut.30:12 f. (also
from Moses) in support of faith-righteousness. Given Paul's
view of the Old Testament, it is unlikely as Bring asserts,
that Paul himself could set scripture against scripture in the
course of his own argument /41/. Instead of setting out a
contrast between law-righteousness (v.5) and faith-righteousness
(v.6), Paul intends both quotations to support his claim that
the righteousness now realised in Christ is that to which
Moses also pointed. The righteousness ἐκ τοῦ νόμου (v.5) is
thus seen to be equivalent to the righteousness to which the
Old Testament witnesses i.e. the righteousness of faith (and
not law-righteousness).

Although it is not feasible within the scope of this paper
to deal with the remainder of ch.10, it is fair to assert that
several factors, namely the Neofiti Targum, our increasing

knowledge of Paul's use of the Old Testament /42/, and of
Palestinian Judaism, along with a greater awareness of the
particularity of the Pauline letters, are combining to point
towards a fuller understanding of the development of Paul's
argument in Rom.10. In view of this a fresh look at the
interpretation of v.4 was considered necessary and will, it
is hoped, prove relevant for the understanding of the entire
chapter /43/.

NOTES

/1/   "Obligation in the Ethic of Paul" in *Christian History
and Interpretation: Studies Presented to John Knox,* Ed.
W.R. Farmer, C.F.D. Moule, R.R. Niebuhr, (Cambridge 1967), p.401.
/2/   Cf. C.E.B. Cranfield, "St. Paul and the Law", *SJT* xvii,
(1964) pp.43 ff., and W.D. Davies, "Paul and the People of
Israel", *NTS,* xxiv, (1977), pp.12 ff.
/3/   *Op.cit.* p.19.
/4/   Ch.10 is not merely a recapitulation from another angle
of what has already been stated in ch.9. Ch.10 has a
transitional function - between the emphasis upon God's freedom
in relation to Israel in ch.9 and that upon his commitment to
Israel in ch.11; cf. J. Munck, *Christ and Israel,* (Philadelphia
1967), p.78.
/5/   *A Shorter Commentary on Romans,* (London 1959), p.127.
/6/   It is not the activity of doing the Law that is wrong but
that this leads to the wrong end. Paul's fundamental critique
of the Law is that following the Law does not result in being
found in Christ. Cf. E.P. Sanders, *Paul and Palestinian
Judaism,* (London 1977), pp.550-1.
/7/   "Paul and the Old Testament: A Study of the Ideas of
Election, Faith and Law in Paul with Special Reference to
Rom.9:30-10:21". *Studia Theologica,* xxv, (1971), p.46.
/8/   Cf. F.F. Bruce, *The Epistle of Paul to the Romans,*
(London 1963), p.198.
/9/   Cf. A.J. Bandstra, *The Law and the Elements of the World,*
(Kampen 1964), p.104. This interpretation is based on a
comparison between Rom.10:4 f. and Phil.2:7 f. first proposed
by Schlatter. Cf. also Munck, *op.cit.* pp.88-9.
/10/ "The Word is Near You: Rom.10:6-10 within the Purpose
of the Letter", in *Christian History and Interpretation,
op.cit.* p.311.
/11/ This view with minor variations is held (among others) by
Sanday and Headlam, *The Epistle to the Romans,* ICC, (Edinburgh

1902), p.284; Gutbrod, *Theological Dictionary of the New Testament*, trans. by G.W. Bromiley, vol. iv, pp.1068 f.; Lietzmann, *An die Römer*, (Tübingen 1928), p.96; Bultmann, "Christus, des Gesetzes Ende", in *Glauben und Verstehen*, ii, (Tübingen 1952), p.48; E. Bammel, "Νόμος Χριστοῦ", *Studia Evangelica*, iii, (1964), pp.123 f.; and Käsemann, *An Die Römer*, (Tübingen 1973), p.270.

/12/ In general support of this view we find - K. Barth, *The Doctrine of God. Church Dogmatics*, II(2), (Edinburgh 1957), p.245; M. Barth, *Jesus, Paulus und die Juden*, (Zurich 1957), pp.60 f.; H.W. Bartsch, "The Concept of Faith in Paul's Letter to the Romans", *Biblical Research*, xiii, (1968), pp.51-2; R. Bring, *Christus und das Gesetz*, (Leiden 1969), pp.35-72; C.E.B. Cranfield, *op.cit.* pp.48-53; Flückiger, "Christus, des Gesetzes τέλος ", *Theologische Literaturzeitung*, x, (1954), pp.153-4.

/13/ Others allow that both emphases are legitimate while differing as to which is primary, cf. Du Plessis, ΤΕΛΕΙΟΣ: *The Idea of Perfection in the New Testament*, (Kampen 1959), pp.142 f.; C.F.D. Moule, *op. cit.* pp.401 f. and "Fulfilment-Words in the New Testament: Use and Abuse", New Testament Studies xiv, (1967/68), pp.301 f.; and C.K. Barrett, "The Interpretation of the Old Testament in the New", *The Cambridge History of the Bible*, I, pp.408 f.

/14/ Cf. Sanday and Headlam, who hold that the "principle of work righteousness" was brought to an end by Christ, *op. cit.* pp.283 f.

/15/ Du Plessis, *op. cit.* p.142.

/16/ Cf. Barrett, *A Commentary on the Epistle to the Romans*, (London 1957), p.198.

/17/ Luther never intended to drive a wedge between the Old Testament and the New - his lectures on Genesis show that he considered the chief content of the O.T. to be the promise that Christ would come. Cf. Bring, *op. cit.* p.23.

/18/ Cf. H.N. Ridderbos, *Romeinen*, (Kampen 1959), p.233, as quoted by Du Plessis *op. cit.* p.123.

/19/ Cf. Cranfield, *op. cit.* p.55, and Moule, *op. cit.* pp.389 f.

/20/ Cf. Bring's translation of this verse, *op. cit.* p.45.

/21/ Cf. Du Plessis's view - "The primary sense is a negative one: termination of the profound fallacy that the fulfilment of the Law is a method of redemption at all". (*op. cit.* p.142).

/22/ Cf. Bandstra, *op. cit.* p.106.

/23/ Cf. Bandstra, *op. cit.* p.106; Bring, *op. cit.* p.49. Lietzmann notes that Paul has substituted the personified 'righteousness' for the original phrase in Deuteronomy 'this

commandment'; *op. cit.* p.96.
/24/ *The Doctrine of God, Church Dogmatics,* II(2), p.245.
/25/ Cf. Moule, "If anything is superseded, it is not Torah
as such but a temporary covenant; and thus the finality,
paradoxically, is the beginning of a new era". "Fulfilment
Words in the New Testament". *op. cit.* p.302.
/26/ *Op. cit.* p.242.
/27/ *Ibid.*
/28/ *Ibid.* See also p.135.
/29/ *Op. cit.* p.154.
/30/ Cf. Bring, *Christus und das Gesetz,* pp. 35 f., "Paul and
the Old Testament" p.47, n.22; Flückiger, *op. cit.* pp.154-6;
and Moule, *op. cit.* pp.301 f. Contra, cf. Käsemann, *op. cit.*
p.370.
/31/ "Paul and the Old Testament", *op. cit.* p.47.
/32/ *The Epistle to the Romans,* (London, 1961), p.266.
/33/ Cf. Du Plessis, *op. cit.* p.142. See also the remainder
of this section "Christ, Conversion of the Law", (pp.142-6).
/34/ Paul's apologetic intention i.e. not to give needless
offence to Jews or Jewish Christians in Jerusalem, but to make
his position as palatable as possible, is rightly noted by
Suggs (*op. cit.* p.298), though he tends to put too much stress
on Romans as a 'brief' to Jerusalem rather than to Rome.
/35/ Cf. R. Bring, "The Message to the Gentiles", *Studia
Theologica,* xix, (1965), pp.36-7.
/36/ This view of Romans, the outcome of my Ph.D. thesis
presented to the University of Edinburgh, 1972, is summarized
in a lecture given at the Fifth International Congress of
Biblical Studies, Oxford 1973, which is still awaiting
publication in the next issue of *Studia Evangelica.* See also
my article, "Why Did Paul Write Romans?", *The Expository Times,*
lxxxv, (1974), pp.264-269.
/37/ Cf. Cranfield, *op. cit.* p.49.
/38/ Bandstra, *op. cit.* p.104.
/39/ *Paul. An Outline of His Theology.* Trans. by J.R. De Witt,
(London 1977), p.156.
/40/ Cf. Bandstra, *op. cit.* p.104, n.133.
/41/ *Op. cit.* p.49., Suggs, *op. cit.* p.301.
/42/ Cf. A.T. Hanson, *Studies in Paul's Technique and Theology,*
(London 1974), pp.136 f., and M. Black, "The Christological Use
of the Old Testament in the New Testament". *NTS,* xviii, (1971),
pp.1-14.
/43/ Stuhlmacher advocates a reconsideration of the relationship
between Law and Gospel in Paul's theology. "Das Ende des
Gesetzes". *ZTK,* lxvii, (1970), pp.14 f.

The Ultimate Restoration of all Mankind: 1 Corinthians 15:22

William V. Crockett,
University of Glasgow.

In 1 Corinthians 15:22 Paul writes, "For as in Adam all die, so also in Christ all shall be made alive". The concern of this paper centers on the two seemingly parallel occurrences of πάντες. If the whole human family dies in Adam, can it then be said that this same human family will also be restored to life in Christ? In short, are the 'all' who are in Christ identical with the 'all' who are in Adam?

Before dealing specifically with this question, it is well to recognize that while Paul uses the word πάντες in 1 Corinthians 15:22, in what might be called its parallel passage (Romans 5:19), Paul employs a different term - οἱ πολλοί (the many). Romans 5:19 reads: "For as through the one man's disobedience the many were made sinners, even so through the obedience of the one the many will be made righteous". Paul's use of οἱ πολλοί could suggest that the sense of 5:19b is exclusive, reading as follows: "through the obedience of one, many (but not all) will be made righteous". But this is almost certainly not the intended meaning. While it would not be correct to say that πολλοί is identical with πάντες, nevertheless, in the present passage πολλοί is used in its Hebraic inclusive sense. As C.K. Barrett points out, "in Old Testament usage 'many' often means not 'many contrasted with all' but 'many contrasted with one or some'" /1/. There is then an inclusive sense of the whole.

That this inclusive sense of πολλοί should be understood here is made clear by the preceding verses 12-18. For example, through Adam in verse 12 death comes to πάντας men; the same death in verse 15a comes to οἱ πολλοί. Through Christ in verse 15b the gift (of life) comes to τοὺς πολλοῦς; the same life in verse 18 comes to παντας men /2/. It is concluded then that in 5:19 οἱ πολλοί is best understood in the Hebraic inclusive sense - 'all' were made sinners- 'all' will be made

righteous. There is thus no meaningful difference with respect
to the inclusiveness of Romans 5:19 and 1 Corinthians 15:22.
The former declares that through the obedience of Christ all
will be made righteous; the latter that through his resurrection
all will be made alive. The question earlier posed then
remains: If the whole human family dies in Adam, will it also
be restored to life in Christ?

It is recognized at the outset that the natural sense of
1 Corinthians 15:22 is that ultimately the whole human family
will be raised: "For as in Adam all die, so also in Christ all
shall be made alive". It is more probable, however, that Paul
meant that only those who belonged to Christ would be made
alive.

Robertson and Plummer, who also hold to a restrictive
understanding of this verse, suggest that a proper paraphrase
would be as follows: "As it is in Adam that all who die
die, so it is in Christ that all who are made alive are made
alive" /3/. The tautology "all who are made alive are made alive",
however, does not clarify the position that only believers will
be made alive since the 'all' who die may still be the 'all' who
are made alive. Moreover, it is highly unlikely that Paul had
in mind a resurrection or 'quickening' of both the righteous
and the wicked dead (which Robertson and Plummer rightly note
is "not the same as saying that all will be saved" /4/). While
it may be that Paul does suggest a resurrection of the wicked -
albeit to judgement - in 1 Corinthians 6:2; 11:32; Romans 2:5
(cf. Acts 24:15 and John 5:29), such a resurrection is not an
issue in 1 Corinthians 15:22. The 'all' Paul had in mind
included only those who belonged to Christ. The following
three reasons point to this conclusion.

First, as Hans Conzelmann rightly finds, the whole of
chapter 15 has only believers in mind /5/. This being the
case, Paul's intent would be to assure his fellow believers
that they 'all' shall indeed be made alive. Furthermore,
Conzelmann's point gains added force when it is remembered
that in this same chapter some Corinthians, while affirming
the resurrection of Christ, nevertheless, were denying the
resurrection of Christians (verses 12,13). Paul argues against
this in verses 12-19 saying that if there were no resurrection
of the dead for Christians, then Christ also is not raised,
and those who have hoped in Christ are to be most pitied. "But
in fact Christ has been raised from the dead", exclaims Paul in

verse 20, and is the first fruits of those (brethren - cf. verse 6) who have fallen asleep. Through him, then, has come the certainty of resurrection for Christians (verse 21). Therefore, just as certain as it is that in Adam all die, so also in Christ shall all (Christians) be made alive in the resurrection (verse 22).

If it is granted that the above reconstruction represents Paul's thought in this passage, then the 'all' who are made alive are the ones who belong to Christ.

The second reason which suggests that the 'all' in verse 22b refers to believers is that just as ἐν τῷ Ἀδὰμ πάντες means 'all who are in Adam', so too ἐν τῷ χριστῷ πάντες means 'all who are in Christ'. In this way the understanding would be that only those who are 'in Christ' will be restored to life. Against this, however, it might be argued that the meaning intended is that just as all die as a *result* of Adam's sin, so too will all be made alive as a *result* of Christ's resurrection. But this is unlikely because (a) such a rendering does not take seriously the formula ἐν χριστῷ which implies a solidarity with Christ, and further designates a new organism which now exists alongside the other organism - ἐν Ἀδὰμ /6/, (b) it cannot be assumed at the outset that all die solely as a result of Adam's sin, as if he *alone* were responsible for our demise /7/, and therefore it also cannot be assumed that all rise solely as a result of Christ's resurrection, and (c) even if it were assumed in 22b that all are made alive as a result of Christ's resurrection, the question still remains open as to whether the πάντες is totally inclusive. It may not be. Indeed the reverse may be preferable, for as Hans-Alwin Wilcke argues, it is not the two πάντες that are set parallel by the ὥσπερ-οὕτως (as - so), but rather the results of the deaths of both Adam and Christ /8/.

It is better to conclude then that the ἐν in verse 22 points to those who belong to Adam and to those who belong to Christ.

The third reason suggesting that the 'all' to be restored to life refers exclusively to believers is that while it may be unclear in verses 21 and 22 as to who will or will not be included in the resurrection, verse 23 on the other hand does specify a particular group: "those who are Christ's" (cf. 1 Corinthians 3:23; Galatians 5:24).

In reference to this last point, however, it might be added
that Lietzmann /9/, Weiss /10/, and others have suggested that
τὸ τέλος in verse 24 is best translated 'the rest' (rather than
the more common 'the end'). On this view, verses 22 - 24a
would read as follows:

> For as in Adam all die, so also in Christ shall all
> be made alive. But each in his own order (τάγματι):
> Christ the first fruits, after that those who are
> Christ's at his coming, then (comes) the rest (τέλος).

Here τελος would refer to a third τάγμα - the rest of
mankind. Such a rendering, of course, would point to the
ultimate restoration of all mankind. But as Allo /11/, Davies
/12/, Héring /13/, and Wilcke /14/ have convincingly shown,
apart from the fact that the phrase εἶτα τὸ τέλος is used as
part of a series, there is no further evidence to suggest that
τὸ τέλος should be understood in any other manner than its
familiar sense - 'the end' /15/.

While it cannot be concluded from 1 Corinthians 15:22
that all humanity will one day be restored to life, it is
important to note that the reverse is equally true. The fact
that Paul's present concern is with those who are 'in Christ'
does not mean that the rest of mankind will not one day
themselves be found 'in Christ'. This, in fact, may be the
case, but such a conclusion cannot be derived from the above
text /16/.

NOTES

/1/   C.K. Barrett, *A Commentary on the Epistle to the Romans*
(London: 1957), p.114. Cf. W.D. Davies, *Paul and Rabbinic
Judaism* (London:²1955), p.57.
/2/   Cf. Ernest Best, *One Body in Christ* (London: 1955), p.37.
/3/   Archibald Robertson and Alfred Plummer, *A Critical and
Exegetical Commentary on the First Epistle of St. Paul to the
Corinthians* (Edinburgh:²1914), p.353.
/4/   *Ibid.*
/5/   Hans Conzelmann, *A Commentary on the First Epistle to
the Corinthians* (Philadelphia: 1975), p.268, n.49.
/6/   Cf. Best, *op. cit.*, pp.26-29; A.S. Peake, 'The
Quintessence of Paulinism', *BJRL* iv (1917-18), pp.303-11;
Robin Scroggs, *The Last Adam: A Study in Pauline Anthropology*

(London: 1966), pp.87-88, 100ff.

/7/   See C.E.B. Cranfield, *A Critical and Exegetical Commentary on the Epistle to the Romans*, Vol. i (Edinburgh: 1975), pp.275-79 who discusses ἥμαρτον as referring to "men's sinning in their own persons but as a result of their corrupt nature inherited from Adam".

/8/   Hans-Alwin Wilcke, 'Das Problem eines messianischen Zwischenreichs bei Paulus', *AThANT* li (1967), pp.69-75; cited by Conzelmann, *op. cit.*

/9/   Hans Leitzmann, *An die Korinther*, revised W.G. Kummel (Tübingen:⁴1949), p.80.

/10/ Johannes Weiss, *Der erste Korintherbrief* (Göttingen: 10 1925), p.358.

/11/ E.B. Allo, *Saint Paul: Première Épître aux Corinthiens* (Paris: 1956), pp.406-8.

/12/ Davies, *op. cit.*, pp.293-94.

/13/ Jean Héring, *The First Epistle of Saint Paul to the Corinthians* (London: ²1962), pp.165-67.

/14/ Wilcke, *op. cit.*, pp.85-101.

/15/ It is generally accepted that the two examples where τὸ τέλος can be construed to mean 'the rest' (LXX, Isa. 19:15 and Aristotle, *De Generatione Animalium* 1:18) are at best ambiguous and obscure. And although it does not affect the conclusion of this paper, it is also extremely unlikely that το τέλος should be considered an adverb meaning 'finally' (as in Karl Barth, *The Resurrection of the Dead* (New York: 1933), p.171 and F.C. Berkitt, *JTS* xvii (1916), pp.384-85.

/16/ A more complete presentation would include discussion of 1 Corinthians 15:28c ("that God may be everything to everyone"). It is believed that the emphasis is on God's sovereignty, and in view of verses 24-28b, it would seem that final restoration of all humanity is not foremost in Paul's mind.

New Testament Text and Old Testament Context in Heb.12.3

Rev. Dr. Paul Ellingworth,
Translation Consultant,
United Bible Societies,
56 Craigton Road,
Aberdeen,   AB1 7UN.

Ἀναλογίσασθε γὰρ τὸν τοιαύτην ὑπομεμενηκότα ὑπὸ τῶν ἁμαρτωλῶν εἰς ἑαυτὸν ἀντιλογίαν, ἵνα μὴ κάμητε ταῖς ψυχαῖς ὑμῶν ἐκλυόμενοι.

"Consider him who endured from sinners such hostility against himself, so that you may not grow weary or faint-hearted" (RSV).

Current discussion of this verse may be summed up by saying that textual critics have generally abdicated their responsibility in favour of exegetes, while exegetes, lacking firm guidance on the textual evidence, have failed to reach a common mind.

The main textual problem /1/ is whether to read a singular εἰς ἑαυτόν or εἰς αὐτόν, with Tischendorf and most modern editions, or a plural εἰς ἑαυτούς or εἰς αὐτούς with Westcott and Hort /2/. There is agreement that the weight of external evidence is on the side of the plural. Zuntz goes so far as to describe it as "the old recoverable reading by the consensus of all the ancient witnesses and of most versions" - a judgement which does not prevent him from opting from the singular /3/. The UBS text committee recognised that "external evidence strongly favors" the plural, but among its members only Wikgren drew the conclusion that the plural was to be preferred, as being both "the qualitatively best supported and the more difficult (though meaningful) reading, and the one more likely to be altered" /4/.

Perhaps paradoxically, the difficulty which inhibits most textual critics from adopting the internally and externally preferable plural reading is not in itself textual but exegetical; namely, the difficulty of knowing what εἰς ἑαυτούς or εἰς αὐτούς could mean in this context. Riggenbach's judgement that the plural is "schlechterdings sinnlos" is quoted or

paraphrased both by textual critics like Zuntz ("the attempts
at making sense of it only prove its absurdity" /5/), and by
most commentators, including Bruce, who re-examines the
evidence in detail /6/, and Michel, who does not /7/.

Translations take one of three main lines. Probably the
largest group, from AV to the Traduction Oecuménique de la
Bible, adopts the singular reading explicitly (so among others
RSV, Knox, Phillips, *Die Gute Nachricht*). A sizeable second
group, including the Jerusalem Bible, NEB, TEV, NIV and common
language translations in several European languages, follow
the example of the Sahidic and Armenian in not translating the
words explicitly at all. In the case of the ancient versions,
this is sometimes understood as presupposing an otherwise
unattested Greek text lacking the phrase; the phrase has also
been conjectured on other grounds to be a gloss /8/. It would
seem more likely that translations, both ancient and modern,
omit the words because the singular reading is largely
pleonastic /9/; these versions may therefore be taken to imply
a singular reading. NEB, for example, has: "Think of him who
submitted to such opposition from sinners". To add "against
himself" would harm the style without improving the sense; but
to add "against themselves" would be a different matter. There
remains a small and heterogeneous third group of translations
which explicitly adopt a plural reading. Apart from marginal
renderings (e.g. in ARV and the Jerusalem Bible), the plural is
represented by the English RV and Goodspeed (with Westcott and
Hort), the translation accompanying Montefiore's commentary /10/,
and the Jehovah's Witnesses' New World Translation.

The main purpose of this note is to suggest that sense can
be made of the plural if, and only if, it is seen as a verbal
allusion to the LXX of Num. 17.3 (16.38 in EVV). The negative
side of this proposal ("only if") is easily stated. Arguments
for a plural reading unsupported by a reference to Num. 17.3
are so strained as to be self-defeating. Theodoret's
construction ἀθτιλογίσασθε ... εἰς ἑαυτούς is clearly forced,
like the Bohairic construction ἀντιλογίαν εἰς ἑαυτούς /11/.
The psychologising interpretation of von Soden, followed by
Inge and others /12/, is also beside the point: that in
contradicting Christ, the sinners were contradicting their
true or better selves.

Conversely, it is unnecessarily difficult to find a
reference to Num. 17.3 while adopting a singular reading; yet

this is done implicitly by Nestle-Aland, and in detail by
Buchanan /13/. If Bruce can argue that the LXX τῶν ἁμαρτωλῶν
τούτων ἐν ταῖς ψυχαῖς αὐτῶν "would scarcely have suggested to
our author the locution τῶν ἁμαρτωλῶν εἰς ἑαυτούς", the
argument from εἰς ἑαυτόν to the LXX plural is correspondingly
weaker /14/.

What, then, is the evidence for an allusion to Num. 17.3?
The question may be approached on three levels: firstly, and
most directly, by comparison of the texts in question;
secondly, and most generally, by enquiring into the antecedent
probability of such an allusion; and thirdly, at an intermediate
level, by examining the use of related Old Testament passages
in Heb.

On the first level, it is enough to note that Bruce
somewhat understates the extent of the parallel, which includes
ταῖς ψυχαῖς ὑμῶν in Heb. 12.3b, cf. ταῖς ψυχαῖς αὐτῶν in Num.
17.3. (As if by compensation, however, Bruce notes a parallel
to the thought of Heb. 6.6, ἀνασταυροῦντας ἑαυτοῖς τὸν υἱὸν τοῦ
θεοῦ, especially if ἑαυτοῖς is understood as a dative of
disadvantage: "crucifying the Son of God to their own hurt").

On the level of antecedent possibilities, each reader's
pre-conceptions tend to tip the balance for or against
recognising a given allusion. What, in the present instance,
Moffatt considered "far-fetched" /15/ appears to Montefiore as
"likely", since the thought of the author of Heb. "is so steeped
in the Old Testament" /16/. However, legitimate
preconceptions are those which are open to revision in the
light of fuller evidence, and I have argued elsewhere /17/ that
there is cumulative evidence in Heb. for a coherent though
selective use, not of isolated Septuagintal words or phrases,
but of entire passages - a use which goes far beyond the range
of explicit quotation and historical reference.

It is however on the third, intermediate level that the
matter must ultimately be decided. What is the evidence for
Heb.'s use of related passages in Num. or elsewhere? What, so
to speak, are the stepping-stones by which one may safely pass
from the situation of the writer of Heb. to the apostasy and
destruction of Korah, Dathan, Abiram and their 250 followers?

Heb.'s interest in this part of Num. is amply attested.
The long quotation from Ps. 94 in Heb. 3.7-11 refers back to

events described in Ex. 17.1-7 (Moses striking the rock at
Massah and Meribah), probably combined, as in Dt. 33.8, with
the similar episode described in Num. 20.1-13. The latter
passage concludes with a reference to the ὕδωρ ἀντιλογίας
(Hebrew "Meribah") which is used as a set phrase in Num. 27.14,
Dt. 32.51, 33.8 and Ps. 80.7. It is significant in this
connection that the key word ἀντιλογία is used in Jude 11 in
an explicit reference to Korah.

Hofius has shown /18/ how frequent are the points of
contact between the exposition of ψ 95 in Heb. 3.12-4.11, and
the LXX of Num., especially chapter 14. Several of these
allusions are recognised by editions and translations of
Heb. /19/, though the nearest approach to a quotation from
Num. in this passage is in the historical reference to "the
sinners" ὧν τὰ κῶλα ἔπεσεν ἐν τῇ ἐρήμῳ (Heb. 3.17, cf. Num.
14.29,32).

The wider context of this incident includes the previous
quotation in Heb., in which Moses is said to have been "faithful
in all (God's) house" (Heb. 3.5, cf. 3.2, Num. 12.7). Num.
also contains detailed accounts of sacrifices offered daily
(καθ' ἡμέραν), either indefinitely (4.16) or over a fixed
period (7.11, cf. vv. 12.89). The same phrase is used in
Heb. 7.27, 10.11 to contrast Old Testament sacrifices with
the ἐφάπαξ of the cross. Most of the cult objects to which
Heb. 9.1-5 makes summary reference are described in Num. as
fully as anywhere else in the Pentateuch /20/. Heb. appears to
reflect Num.'s concern to distinguish between mere error or
weakness on the one hand (Heb. 5.2), and deliberate sin on the
other /21/. Later in Num., the story of Balaam (linked with
Korah in Jude) reaches its climax in an oracle to which Heb. 8.2
makes an unquestioned allusion - the σκηναί, ἃς ἔπηξεν κύριος of
Num. 24.6 become in Heb. 8.2 a single true tabernacle /22/.

If, with these points of contact in mind, we return to the
apostasy of Korah and his company, the thematic parallels with
Heb. become clearer. Both texts are concerned with the danger
that part of God's people will be destroyed (compare, e.g., Num.
17.6 with Heb. 6.4-6, and the thrice repeated μή τις of Heb.
12.15f.). In both, sin, like law, is conceived predominantly
in cultic terms. Because the author of Heb. is a Christian, his
perspective is reversed by comparison with that of the Old
Testament. In Num., the apostasy of Korah consists in his
assuming the priesthood without authorisation (Num. 17.5, cf.

3.10, Heb. 5.4) and leading unlawful worship, while the apostasy
which the writer of Heb. fears is probably that of rejecting
Christ in favour of the institutions of the old covenant. The
cultic *tertium comparationis* is however firm. Moreover, the sin
of Korah and his allies, like that of Nadab and Abihu elsewhere
in Num., is that of kindling πῦρ ἀλλότριον (17.1, cf. 3.4,
26.61). The punishment of both groups was appropriately to be
consumed by a fire which did come from the Lord (Lev. 10.2,
Num. 16.35). It is perhaps no coincidence that Heb. 12 ends
by describing God as πῦρ καταναλίσκον, though the immediate
allusion here is to another part of the Pentateuch /23/.

   To read Heb. 12.3 as an allusion, primarily to the sin of
Korah, with ἀντιλογία as a subordinate reference to Israel's
rebellion /24/ at Meribah, would therefore not be a leap in
the dark, but a recognition of one further reference to a part
of the Septuagint which is known beyond reasonable doubt to
underlie several other passages in Heb. If the text is read
in this way, other details fall into place. Ἀναλογίσασθε may
mean "consider and compare" the reader's possible future
sufferings, not only with the shame of Christ's crucifixion
(v.2), but with what Riggenbach finely called "der gesamte
Widerstreit gegen seine Person bis hin zu dessen höchster
Dokumentierung in der Kreuzigung" /25/. Riggenbach does not
say so, but the rebellion could indeed reach back, for the
author of Heb., to the time before the incarnation, Christ being
even then the κύριος against whom Korah's rebellion was
directed. τὸν ὑπομεμενηκότα, it is true, is something short
of an explicit reference to Christ, but such a reference is
virtually demanded by the emphatic Ἰησοῦν of v. 2, and would
give greater force to the perfect /26/. The reason for the
article τῶν ἁμαρτωλῶν /27/ becomes apparent: reference is
specifically to "the sinners" who spoke and acted against the
Lord in ancient as in recent times. The rejection of Christ,
one might say, is Massah and Meribah, the ὕδωρ ἀντιλογίας, all
over again.

   What, then, do the texts in question mean? How are they
to be translated? (Translation is often the acid test of
exegesis). Num. 17.3 itself is somewhat unclear: the most
probable identification of participants would lead to the
translation: "They (Korah, Dathan and Abiram) have sanctified
the censers of these (250) sinners at the cost of their (the
sinners') lives". As for Heb. 12.3, an expanded translation
might run:

"Compare, then your situation with that of Christ, who
throughout our people's history endured opposition similar
to what you endure; notably when 'the sinners', led astray by
Korah and his friends, brought about their own destruction.
If you will stand firm in the same way, you will not perish
because your souls, like theirs, have grown weary in their
long pilgrimage to the promised land /28/".

NOTES

/1/   The argument of this note is not significantly affected
by whether or not ἐκλελυμένοι is read for ἐκλυόμενοι with
p^{13,46} D* 1739.
/2/   The textual evidence is most conveniently presented in
the UBS Greek New Testament (3rd edition, 1975).
/3/   G. Zuntz, *The Text of the Epistles* (London, 1953), 120.
/4/   B.M. Metzger, *A Textual Commentary on the Greek New
Testament* (London and New York, 1971), 675.
/5/   E. Riggenbach, *Der Brief an die Hebräer* (Leipzig, 1913),
391; Zuntz, *loc. cit.*
/6/   F.F. Bruce, *Commentary on the Epistle to the Hebrews*
(London, 1965), 345 n.5, 355.
/7/   O. Michel, *Der Brief an die Hebräer* (Gottingen, 7th
edition 1975), 437 n. 1, describes the singular reading as "wohl
allein sinngemäss".
/8/   J. Moffatt, *The Epistle to the Hebrews* (Edinburgh, 1924),
198, quoting A.B. Davidson; similarly C. Spicq, *L'Epître aux
Hébreux* (Paris, 1952), vol. I, 429f.
/9/   Spicq, *loc. cit.*
/10/   Montefiore diverges at this point from the British and
Foreign Bible Society's Greek-English diglot, on which his
commentary is generally based.
/11/   G.W. Horner, *The Coptic Version of the New Testament in
the Northern Dialect* ... (Oxford, 1898-1905), vol. 3, 541;
cf. Riggenbach, *loc. cit.*
/12/   Referred to by Riggenbach and Bruce, *loc. cit.*
/13/   G.W. Buchanan, *To the Hebrews* (New York, 1972), 210,
cf. 180.
/14/   *Op. cit.*, 345 n. 5 (346).
/15/   *Loc cit.*
/16/   H.W. Montefiore, *A Commentary on the Epistle to the
Hebrews* (London, 1964), 216.

/17/   *The Old Testament in Hebrews: exegesis, method and hermeneutics*. Unpublished Ph.D. thesis, Aberdeen 1977.

/18/   O. Hofius, *Katapausis* (Tübingen, 1970), 117-39.

/19/   E.g., the UBS Greek text lists 17 references to Num., including Num. 14.1-35 cf. Heb. 3.16-8; Num. 14.21-3 cf. Heb. 3.11; Num. 14.22f. cf. Heb. 3.18; Num. 14.29 cf. Heb. 3.17.

/20/   Note especially the references to Aaron's rod in Num. 17.

/21/   Ἀκούσιος and ἀκουσίως Num. 15.24-9, 35.11,15, cf. ἑκουσίως Heb. 10.26.

/22/   There is evidence of Heb.'s interest in the context of this allusion.

/23/   Dt. 4.24 or 9.3.

/24/   On the meaning of ἀντιλογία, see especially Riggenbach, Michel and Bruce *ad loc.*, with further references; also J.H. Moulton and G. Milligan, *The Vocabulary of the Greek Testament* (London, 1929), *s.v.*

/25/   *Loc. cit.;* similarly Spicq, *op. cit.*, and *L'Epître aux Hébreux* (Sources Bibliques, Paris, 1977), 200, referring explicitly to the incarnate life of Jesus.

/26/   Moffatt, *loc. cit.*, strangely dismisses ὑπομεμενηκότα as "another aoristic perfect like κεκάθικεν" in Heb. 12.2. In fact, κεκάθικεν itself is a normal durative perfect, corresponding to the κάθου ... ἕως ... of ψ 109.1 = Heb. 1.13.

/27/   Cf. τοῖς ἁμαρτήσασιν in Heb. 3.17.

/28/   W.F. Arndt and F.W. Gingrich, *A Greek-English Lexicon of the New Testament* (Chicago and Cambridge, 1957), *s.v.* κάμνω "be hopelessly sick, waste away ... or even ... die". It is perhaps surprising that A.T. Hanson, *Christ in the Old Testament* (London, 1965), 48-82, in a detailed survey of Heb., does not relate Heb. 12.3 to the theme of the pre-existent activity of Christ in the Old Testament.

Controversy in the New Testament

Rev. J.C. Fenton,
Christ Church,
Oxford.

People sometimes talk as though the time when the apostles
were alive had been a time when the church was free from
controversy. To what extent was this so? And if it were the
case that there was controversy among the first Christians,
what would be the implications?

I

There are passages in the New Testament itself that lead
one to think that the time of the apostles was a time when
Christians were united in holding one common apostolic faith.
This idea is to be found, not only in the reference in Jude to
the faith which was once for all delivered to the saints
(verse 3), but also in the statement in Ephesians that the
mystery of Christ ... *has now been revealed to his holy
apostles and prophets by the Spirit* (3:4f); the suggestion is
that the time of the apostles was a time when revelation was
received, and, one might think, they received it together and
held it as a common faith. The picture in Acts is of the
church as united: the company of those who believed were of one
heart and soul (4:32); and the D-text adds: *and there was no
such thing as a quarrel* (διάκρισις) *among them.* As the story
in Acts unfolds, differences of opinion arise from time to time
among the believers, but they are always dealt with immediately
and effectively; and, in any case, there are not many of them.

From passages such as these it would be easy to conclude,
and indeed many people have concluded, that the earliest days
of Christianity were harmonious.

That point of view is supported by a particular habit or
device that is comparatively common among New Testament
writers: namely, the predicting of disagreement among believers
as an event to come in the future; division and error are part

of the drama of the last days, and writers warn their readers to
be on the alert and expect this to be the case. The conclusion
one might draw would be that there had been no such divisions
or disagreements up to the time of writing: they would be a new
phenomenon, belonging to a new stage in the process by which
this age would be succeeded by the age to come.

Thus, for example, Paul says to the Ephesian elders, in
Acts:

> *I know that after my departure fierce wolves will come in
> among you, not sparing the flock; and from among your own
> selves will arise men speaking perverse things, to draw
> away the disciples after them* (20:29f).

The reader might draw the conclusion from this that there had
been no *fierce wolves* who had come into the congregation during
Paul's ministry, and that no one had arisen among them to speak
perverse things or *draw away disciples* as long as Paul himself
was alive and present.

Similarly it is said in I Timothy that

> *The Spirit expressly says that in later times some will
> depart from the faith by giving heed to deceitful spirits
> and doctrines of demons* (4:1).

Satan will be more active as his end approaches; and one of
the forms of his activity will be the propagation of false
doctrine. If there is to be more of that in the future, it
could be argued that there had been less of it in the past.

Again, in 2 Timothy:

> *But understand this, that in the last days there will
> come times of stress .... As Janues and Jambras opposed
> Moses, so these men also oppose the truth* (3:1;9).

False teaching will be part of the troubles of the last days.

In I John, this belief is made the basis of an argument
aimed at showing that Christians are living in the end-time:

> *Children, it is the last hour; and as you have heard that
> antichrist is coming, so now many antichrists have come;*

therefore (ὅθεν) *we know that it is the last hour*
(2:18).

The antichrists are those who hold a different doctrine from
the author; their appearance on the stage of history shows what
time it is: the final hour has now come at last. One might
reason as follows: If false teachers are evidence for the
arrival of the end, there can have been no false teachers in
the time before that; otherwise, how could it be known from the
appearance of false teachers that the end had come. (If it is
said, When the shadow reaches this point, it is evening; it is
implied that the shadow will not reach this point until it is
evening).

The same idea is found in Jude:

But you must remember, beloved, the predictions of the
apostles of our Lord Jesus Christ; they said to you,
"In the last days there will be scoffers, following
their own ungodly passions" (verses 17f).

It was almost certainly this passage in Jude that gave the
author of 2 Peter the idea for writing his work: he would supply
the source for Jude, and provide the very quotation that Jude
would seem to have made; here then is the apostle making that
prediction in 2 Peter:

First of all you must understand this, that scoffers
will come in the last days with scoffing, following
their own passions and saying, "Where is the promise of
his coming? ..." (3:3).

This strong emphasis on the prediction of doctrinal
controversy as a feature of the last days has the effect,
whether it was intended or whether it was not intended, of
making one think that in the beginning things were different;
they did not disagree among themselves then.

If the New Testament could lead to the conclusion that the
early church was free from controversy, then the writers who
were not included in the Canon, or who came later, can be
quoted to this effect even more. They seem to have looked back
on the time of the apostles as a golden age, in which truth
was revealed, and all was light.

Thus, to give two examples, the impression one derives
from the First Epistle of Clement (42-44) is that the apostles
had their instructions from Christ, so that they could act with
complete wisdom; they had authority and foresight to appoint
bishops, and not only bishops, but bishops' successors. They
knew what to do, and they did it.

Similarly, in Irenaeus:

*The Church although scattered through the whole world
even to the ends of the earth has received the faith
from the Apostles and from their disciples .... Since
the Church has received this preaching and this faith,
as we have said, although she is scattered through the
whole world, she preserves it carefully, as one household:
and the whole Church alike believes in these things, as
having one soul and heart [?Acts 4:32] in unison preaching
these beliefs, and teaches and hands them on as having
one mouth (Against Heresies I.x.1-2; Tr. H. Bettenson, in
The Early Christian Fathers (Oxford 1969) p.92).*

The implication of this passage is that the apostolic age was
the time when the faith was received by the apostles, and that
subsequent ages preserve and teach that self-same faith.

Thus both the New Testament itself, partly in some of its
direct statements, and partly through the device of predictions
of heresy, and the writings of the Fathers, encourage us to hold
the view that it was not until later that the church ran into
controversy. There was, one would think, no controversy as
long as the apostles were alive.

II

This was certainly not so, and there is ample evidence to
prove it. The questions to be raised are: What place did
controversy hold in the period when the New Testament books
were being written? How important was controversy as a factor
in the production of Christian writing during the first hundred
years after Easter? To what extent were Christians at that
time people who disagreed with one another over what they
believed? If disagreement was characteristic of Christians
at that time, why was it so? And are there any implications
to be drawn from this subject?

III

Certainly some of the New Testament writings were composed because their authors wanted to oppose teachers and doctrines that were, in their view, dangerous and false. These doctrines were held by people who hoped they too were Christians, and by teachers who believed that they too were expounding the one true gospel. It would be a serious mistake to draw the conclusion that, because the New Testament writers called these people false teachers, or anti-christs, this was how they thought about themselves; it was the last thing they would have called themselves; on the contrary, it was exactly that they themselves would have called the New Testament authors. It is necessary to see the sectarians as they saw themselves, which was not as sectarians, but as those who were right, and belonged to the true church. "Heretic" is not usually a self-designation.

The simplest method would be to take the books of the New Testament in the order in which they are now placed in the canon; here is a first list of works written to refute the teaching of people who believed themselves to be Christians.

The two letters to the Corinthians (however many they were originally); in both of them Paul deals with varieties of Christian faith and ethics that he himself regarded as pernicious; though those who held them believed them to be the truth, the real and liberating knowledge.

Secondly, the letter to the Galatians, on the assumption that those who were bewitching them (cf. 3:1) were Christian believers of one sort or another and not, on the older view, unbelieving Jews from the local synagogues. Paul's arguments about his apostleship, his relationship with the Jerusalem church and with Peter at Antioch, seem to imply that the dispute in Galatia was a dispute among Christians, and not between Christians and Jews.

Third, the letter to the Colossians, which could never have been written in the way it is, if there had not been a Colossian heresy.

Similarly, the second letter to the Thessalonians, whether it is by Paul or not, is largely concerned with the repudiation of a doctrine that claims to be Pauline, that the day of the Lord has come. Paul, if it is Paul, or another in his name,

disowns teaching that is being put about as Paul's, and that
no doubt is genuinely believed by some to be what Paul meant,
or what he implied.

The letter of James, on one view, presupposes a party
which taught that a man could be saved by faith without works
and appealed to Paul as the authority for this doctrine; the
author of the letter chooses the pseudonym James because he
knows that there were actual differences of opinion between
the historical James and the historical Paul; and he writes as
if he were that James in order to answer these latter-day
Paulinists.

The second letter of Peter, like 2 Thessalonians, is an
answer to those who say, *"Where is the promise of his coming?
For ever since the fathers fell asleep, all things have
continued as they were from the beginning of creation"* (3:4).
They are probably gnostics of some kind, but they thought of
themselves as genuine Christians.

The three letters of John have for their background the
controversy over the nature of the incarnation, and arise out
of the schism that has developed between those who hold
different doctrines.

Finally, the letter of Jude seems to be written against
gnostic libertines, who, it is said, had gained admission into
the church (verse 4).

There are eleven New Testament writings in this first
group. In each instance it is possible to make out a case that
controversy was the immediate cause of writing. Not one of
these books would have been recognizably the same as it is
now, or would even have existed, if there had not been
disagreement between the Christians involved.

IV

There is a second group of New Testament books, in which
the importance of polemics is less obvious at first, but on
closer examination it is realized that this factor is present.

First, the letter to the Romans, when it is seen as what
Paul thinks it necessary for him to say to believers in Rome,
in order to recommend himself to them as an apostle, and win

their approval in preparation for his intended visit to the city and the mission in the West that he has planned. The content and, above all, the manner of Romans are evidence for the existence of considerable conflicts over the faith and practice of believers in Rome at the time of writing; or, at the least, they are evidence that Paul believed that he must write in this way, and not simply inform them of the date when his boat was due at Puteoli.

Ephesians, on the hypothesis that it is not by Paul, shows us somebody appealing to his authority against people whose Christology and Ecclesiology were, in the writer's view, inadequate; mere *winds of doctrine* expressing the cunning of men and their craftiness in deceitful wiles (4:14).

It is difficult to know what to say about Philippians, partly because we do not know whether it is a single letter, or composite, but even more, because we do not know who the people are who are mentioned: *Some indeed preach Christ from envy and rivalry* (1:15); *Look out for the dogs* (3:2); *Many live as enemies of the cross of Christ* (3:18) - are these unbelievers, or believers? If believers, then Philippians belongs within this group. Moreover, the theme of unity running through the letter implies that the situation to which he was writing involved discord and divisions.

The Pastoral Epistles belong in this group, on any view of their authorship: false teachers who are mentioned in each of these letters regard themselves as within the church, and teach a *different doctrine* (I Tim.1:3)

One theory about the letter to the Hebrews is that it was written as part of the controversy over sin after baptism and the question of the possibility of second repentance; it is an attack on the notion that there is any hope for those who have been initiated and then fallen into sin. This implies that there were those who held this position and practised some form of re-admission of sinners to the congregation. The controversy continued for more than a century, and Hebrews was appealed to by the rigorists, because it expressed their view.

Finally, we must include Revelation in this list: John knows people in the seven churches who are to be opposed: Nicolaitans, the synagogue of Satan, Balaamites and Jezebelites; people, perhaps, who adopted a different attitude on the question

of Church and State from that of John himself; people who
wanted to practise some accommodation with the Empire, and
did not go all the way with John in identifying the Emperor
with the beast.   They could have quoted Paul in Romans, and
the Pastorals and I Peter if they were in existence at that
time.   The Apocalypse has certainly had its opponents in the
history of the church; it probably belongs to controversy from
the first.

In this second group we have a further eight New Testament
books.   Controversy plays some part in their production, but
perhaps not such an important part as in the first eleven; and
it is not as obvious at first that these eight are polemical,
as it was with the eleven in the first group.

V

There is a third and final group in which controversy has
played some part, but it is much more difficult to show that
it has.

Take Matthew first.   Matthew is not simply an enlarged
version of Mark; it is an edited version, and the editing is
evidence for a different theology; Matthew disagreed with Mark,
and corrected him.   This can be seen in the matter of Jesus
and the law of Moses, for example.   A reader of Mark could
easily form the impression that Jesus had come to abolish the
law.   In Mark, the first public appearance of Jesus after the
baptism is in a synagogue, and the story has a double theme:
Jesus brings new teaching to the people, and power which is
effective over unclean spirits.   The man with the unclean
spirit speaks both for the demons and for Judaism as a
whole when he says to Jesus, *You have come to destroy*
(ἀπολέσαι) *us* (1:24); the whole .congregation says, *What is
this?   A new teaching!   With authority he commands even the
unclean spirits and they obey him* (1:27).   Mark's theology is
that Jesus has come to abolish the law, and to destroy the
destroyers of the earth.   Matthew's is different, and he
replaces the story of Jesus in the synagogue at Capernaum with
the Sermon on the Mount, in which, by contrast, Jesus says:

> *Think not that I have come to abolish* (καταλῦσαι)
> *the law and the prophets; I have not come to abolish
> them but to fulfil them* (5:17).

There has been a difference of opinion between Mark and
Matthew on the Lord and the law, and it shows all the way
through Matthew's gospel, whenever the subject comes up.
Professor R.H. Lightfoot used to say that he supposed that
when Matthew had finished writing his gospel, he tore up his
copy of Mark and threw it into the waste paper basket, because
there would be no further use for it. Perhaps he tore it up
for another reason also - the reason for which he had replaced
Mark : he regarded Mark as a dangerous libertine; similarly,
Mark, if he ever read Matthew, must have thought of him as a
pedantic legalist.

The case is the same with Luke. The differences between
Luke and Mark are partly due to differences between the
theologies of their authors. Those who think that Luke used
Matthew as well as Mark say that the differences between Luke
and Matthew are also the result of different theological
standpoints. Neither Luke nor Matthew wrote their gospels
simply because they had more material than Mark; they
had another motive: they did not agree with Mark; they wanted
to give a different impression. They wrote different gospels,
because they believed different gospels.

It is more clear that this is so in the case of John's
gospel. It is another, more radical attempt to re-write the
gospel, and it claims the authority of an unnamed disciple who
is superior to Peter and has greater insight and understanding
because he, unlike the others, is *the disciple whom Jesus
loved* (21:20 etc.); behind the formulation of that description
there must lie bitter controversy and wide disagreement.

Finally, we can include Acts in this group; the differences
between Acts and the Pauline letters are the result of an
attempt to present Paul in a different light from that in which
his later followers were presenting him; it is the result of
controversy, and it is an attempt to heal a breach.

In this third group we have four New Testament books:
controversy is not apparent on the surface, but it has to be
pre-supposed in order to account for the evident differences in
the writings themselves. If there had been no disagreements,
there would have been only one gospel which all would have
accepted.

But there is one book that we might add to this group of
four, and it is Mark. The problem here is that we have nothing

earlier of the same kind with which to compare it. What we
must do, instead, is ask, Why was the book written in this way?
It is possible to return answers of this sort: He wrote his
gospel in this way, because he wanted to refute people who held
these beliefs. This has been studied in connexion with the
emphasis on the suffering of the Son of man and of his followers,
which is so characteristic of Mark; with the Marcan secrecy
theme - another peculiarity of the book; and with the tradition
of the miracles in Mark. In each case, polemical motives can
be postulated; and if we follow those who lead us in this
direction, then the third group contains, not four, but five
books of the New Testament.

VI

The three books of the New Testament in the production of
which, as far as one can see, controversy between Christians
played no part are I Thessalonians, Philemon and I Peter. In
I Thessalonians, the background is controversy with the Jews;
in I Peter, conflict with Gentile persecutors; and in Philemon
a matter between Paul and Philemon himself, though Paul goes
some way towards enlarging the scope of the problem by
addressing the letter, not to Philemon alone, but to Apphia and
Archippus and *the church in your house* (verse 2); he is making
the matter as public as he can (see also perhaps Col. 4:17).
It may be important, however, that there are some books in the
New Testament that are not the result of controversy, as we
shall see later.

VII

There is a great deal of room for differences of opinion
in these matters with which we have been dealing; but to
summarize the point, we could say that in the view of the New
Testament that is being advocated here twenty-four out of the
twenty-seven New Testament books are to varying degrees the
the result of controversy among Christians; that is to say,
eight-ninths of the canon is polemical; or, to put it another
way, eighty-nine per cent of the New Testament is the result
of Christian disagreement.

Sometimes, the disagreements became extremely bitter; at
least that is how it seems to us, who are accustomed to more
irenic and ecumenical discussion between people who hold
different opinions on matters of faith and morals. Paul, for

example, calls his opponents in Corinth servants of Satan
(2 Cor. 11:15); the author of 2 Peter borrows from Jude a list
that includes most of the evil characters in the Old Testament,
to which he adds the dog turning back to his own vomit, and
the sow wallowing in the muck (2:22); the writer of I John
calls the schismatics anti-christs, false prophets, men of the
world, that is, of the devil (2:18; 4:1-6); the person who
uses the pseudonym Jude ransacks the Old Testament and other
literature to find things to say against the gnostics of his
time; and John calls his opponents Jezebelites, Balaamites,
Satanists (Rev. 2 and 3). It is a world to which most of us
are happy not to belong, though anyone who has had the
misfortune to be brought up in Liverpool in the 1930's, or in
Northern Ireland today, will recognize it.

VIII

When this subject is under discussion, there is one
objection that is frequently made, and it is as follows: You
cannot use the New Testament as evidence to show what Christians
of the first century were like, because as evidence it is only
partial, and has passed through a process of selection. Just
as the communications media report only crimes and disasters,
but tell us nothing about law-abiding citizens and average
fine weather, so it is only the controversies of the Christians
that became literature, not their agreements. Rows are news:
peace is not. We should not therefore conclude that Christians
of the first century were contentious, solely from the evidence
of contentions that we have in the New Testament. The number
who were of *one heart and soul* (Acts 4:32) may have exceeded
by far those who were involved in polemics and schisms.

Is the answer to this objection something along these
lines? - We thought that there were three New Testament books
that were written without polemical intent: viz. I Thessalonians,
Philemon and I Peter. Their existence answers the point of
the objector. If these books could be written without
controversy among Christians, then why not more? Had all
early Christian literature been polemical, the case would have
been different. Then, the objector would have been able to
put his point as follows: All Christian writing of this period
is the result of rows: i.e. no rows - no books, because only
rows produce books. Books are evidence of rows, therefore all
you can deduce from the books is the existence of the rows,
but not the extent of them; they cannot point to the non-rows.

As long as we can show him some writing that was not polemical,
he cannot take this line. We can, moreover, ask him: If only
eleven per cent of the New Testament is the result of peace,
why is this percentage so low? (It would, of course, be lower
still, if the reckoning were made by pages, instead of books).

IX

The drift of the argument is that the first Christians
(so far as the evidence shows) were contentious and polemical
people, frequently involved in disputes and controversies;
and the question that this raises is, why was this so? What
was it that made them such? There are two points.

The first is that Christianity began in controversy, so
it is not surprising that it continued as it had started.
It began in the controversies that Jesus provoked in Galilean
synagogues with Pharisees and teachers of the law. It is not
at all surprising that this saying is attributed to Jesus: *Do
not think that I have come to bring peace on earth; I have not
come to bring peace, but a sword* (Matt. 10:34). He is seen
here, (or, perhaps, he saw himself) as a divisive person, who
caused separations in families, and made friends into enemies;
he invited people, it was thought, to follow him against the
stream. The dispute that Jesus initiated, and that issued
in his death, was ably kept alive by Paul until the sixties;
when he writes 2 Corinthians he has already had the thirty-nine
lashes in the synagogue for misbehaviour five times, and one
stoning (2 Cor.11:24). By the time of Paul's death in the
mid-sixties, Christians must have become accustomed to living
by differences of opinion. Some of these differences were
between Christians and Jews; some between Christians and the
mob; others between Christians and the Roman authorities.
There is, perhaps, a carry-over effect: those who take faith
for their guide are inevitably bound in the end to differ among
themselves; hence the conflicts between Judaizers and Paulinists,
Paul and the Gnostics; John and the Docetists; and so on.

This leads on to the other reason why Christians were, and
still are, contentious. It is part of a general principle,
formulated after observing University affairs by a former
colleague in Durham (Professor I.G. Simmons): "The mutual
contentiousness of those involved in any specific academic
discipline is inversely related to the hardness of the data of
that discipline". Theology is a soft-data discipline; it has

no facts. It has to do with faith, that is, with opinions.
Hence the high reading of mutual contentiousness among its
professors.

Finally, three modest conclusions.

1. If it is sometimes the case that New Testament writings
come from contexts and backgrounds that involved controversy,
it is necessary to reconstruct the controversy in order to
understand the writing in question in its original sense.
Further, it is necessary to make allowances for the fact that
the writing was a weapon used between Christians in controversy,
when assessing its value, or putting it to some other use.
In cases of difference of opinion between those who are
believers, there is usually truth on both sides: the ultimate
winner of the controversy wins at the expense of the truth
held by the loser. To be canonized is a pyrrhic victory.

2. The repeated exhortations in the New Testament to be *of
one mind* (Phil.2:2), to *be at peace with one another* (Mark 9:50),
not to pass judgement on one another (Rom.14:13) etc., begin
to make new sense when it is realized that the people to whom
they were addressed were of many minds, and did not live at
peace with one another, and did judge each other; they were
rife with *disputes over opinions* (Rom.14:1): concerning food
and drink; observance or non-observance of calendars; the law
and the gospel; mercy and judgement, and many other things too.
As long as we thought that there were no controversies in the
age of the apostles, we could not make sense of these
exhortations to unity. Once it is realized how disputatious
they were, we see how appropriate such exhortations were also.

3. If it is a phantasy that the time of the apostles was a
golden age, free from bitter controversy, it will be a good
thing to get rid of it, and at the same time to jettison
unnecessary guilt-feelings that we are worse than our fathers.
We are certainly no better: but it is a help to know that we
are much the same. If it is right to look back to the early
church, and to model ourselves on it, it would not be apostolic,
in that sense, to have a unified and fixed theology, to which
all members assented.

The human condition may be such that truth can only exist
alongside error, in the church no less than elsewhere; it may

have to be argued for repeatedly, and repeatedly fought over.
Archbishop Trench made the point over a century ago:

> *It has been already remarked ... and assuredly is very*
> *well worthy of notice, that the two Churches which are*
> *spiritually in the most sunken condition of all, that,*
> *namely, of Sardis and this of Laodicea, are also the*
> *two in which alone there are no traces of adversaries*
> *from without, or of hinderers to the truth from within ....*
> *It was not good for the Sardian and Laodicean Churches*
> *to be without this necessity of doing earnest battle for*
> *the truth .... In a world of imperfections like ours, it*
> *argued no healthy spiritual life that there should have*
> *been none there to call the truth into question and*
> *debate (The Epistles to the Seven Churches in Asia*
> (London, 1861), pp.206-8).

To sum up: No controversies, no truth. No contentions
among Christians, only one-ninth of the New Testament. There
may therefore be additional reasons to that given by Paul why
there must be factions (αἱρέσεις) *among you* (I Cor. 11:19).

'Like Newborn Babes' — The Image of the Child in 1 Peter 2:2-3

Rev. Dr. J. Francis,
Department of Religion,
Sunderland Polytechnic,
73 Hillcrest,
Middle Herrington,
Sunderland, Tyne and Wear,
ENGLAND.

The purpose of this note is to examine the image of the child at 1 Peter 2:2-3 with reference not so much to its component parts but to the relationship of the various parts to one another within the presentation as a whole. Discussion of the image takes us straight to the heart of the debate on 1 Peter itself; whether it is a genuine letter or is but a baptismal homily incorporated within a later epistolary framework. While it is not possible here to enter that debate afresh beyond noting such elements as are necessary for the understanding of the passage in question, suffice it to say that for many the baptismal homily theory has not proved convincing, or at least if such a document does lie beneath the letter it has been thoroughly worked over and integrated into the writer's purpose. That purpose seems to be an exhortation to stand fast in a time of trial and opposition, and such baptismal elements as are present within the letter (3:19ff) form part of a spiritual exhortation that is derived from the significance of the Christian, and hence baptismal, life as a whole. It is in this context that we should understand the exhortation to "put off" the ways of falsehood with which the child image is introduced, for it is an example of the wider New Testament practice of applying typically baptismal language to the wider implications of faith /1/.

This view of 1 Peter is further confirmed by the non-applicability to the child image of the similar sounding Rabbinic description of the proselyte as a newborn child /2/. Despite certain points of similarity between the two contexts e.g. exhortation to turn one's back upon the past, to regard one's former life and its habits as over and done with (1:18 cf 2:1 ἀποθέμενοι οὖν) the Rabbinic phrase fails as an explanation

of the image here at two important points. Firstly the Rabbinic
comparison of the proselyte with a newborn child remains
purely at the level of a comparison. Thus he is likened to a
newborn child but is not declared actually to be one /3/. To
this extent the comparison involved in ὡς at 1 Peter 2:2 goes
beyond that of the Rabbinic phrase. Secondly, and this may
partly explain the reason for the Rabbinic description
remaining purely at the level of a comparison for all the
profound legal and moral implications that are derived from
it, the idea of divine regeneration which is of course contained
in ἀρτιγέννητα is avoided by normative Judaism which preferred
to express the divine activity in terms of creation /4/. So
there is no indication that for the Rabbis the proselyte is
thought of as being divinely begotten in baptism or rendered
a child in this sense, but this is precisely the thought that
is implied in ἀρτιγέννητα. Consequently the particle ὡς is not
simply a comparison of longing for milk "just as newborn babes
do" as if it were a matter simply of illustrative example, but
marks the actual ground of the appeal since they are indeed
God's very children, begotten by Him through baptism and faith
in the gospel.

     Equally in the interpretation of the image recourse need
not necessarily be made to the initiation rites of the Mystery
Cults, despite the similarity of Sallust's description of the
initiate as being "fed on milk as though being reborn", and
the fact that the readers living in Asia Minor would no doubt
be familiar with such customs. The imagery of milk and of
feeding/nourishing is widespread in the Ancient World and is
found equally in Jewish sources as a description of Torah
learning /5/. Again the nourishment on which the babes feed,
although it is full of eschatological hope, is not thought of
as so often in the Mystery rites as a divine drug that mediates
salvation in a quasi-magical fashion. More particularly with
reference to the adjective ἀρτιγέννητα we cannot give an over
precise interpretation of the writer's use of νῦν and ἄρτι /6/,
and the description in any case is closely related both to the
λογικὸν ἄδολον γάλα around which the image as a whole revolves
and to the writer's exhortation that this is what should be
sought after and desired (ἐπιποθήσατε).

     If then neither of these contexts prove wholly satisfactory
for the interpretation of the image how then should we
understand the writer's intention in using it at this point?
E.G. Selwyn /7/ in his commentary on 1 Peter remarks that "the

purpose of the adjective (i.e. ἀρτιγέννητα) is to make the
passage more vivid" while J.N.D. Kelly /8/ suggests at this
point that in βρέφη the writer "carries one stage further the
picture of rebirth he has already used in 1:3, 1:23". May it
not however be equally possible, and this we shall now argue,
that the writer in his concern for his readers' continued
fidelity to the gospel (expressed in τὸ λογικὸν ἄδολον γάλα
ἐπιποθήσατε) has in fact combined two distinct though not
unrelated ideas, that of regeneration through the word with
obedient understanding of the word. This would mean that we
have here really a composite image whereby the writer has
underpinned a description of his readers as babes who are
nourished on the gospel with the separate idea of the readers
as those who are begotten of God through believing acceptance
of the gospel.

(a) the phrase ὡς ἀρτιγέννητα βρέφη is in reality tautologous
since βρέφος itself means a newly born babe or infant. Thus
one is lead to enquire what the function of the adjective is in
relation to the noun where it seems to do more than simply
confirm the image as a whole but to contribute directly to it
from its previous association with the gospel/word of God in
1:23 and possibly 1:3.

(b) elsewhere in the New Testament the image of the child and
the notion of supernatural begetting are not necessarily
connected and this suggests that they can move in separate
circles of thought; James 1:18, Titus 3:5, John 3:5ff *passim*,
contrast Gal.4:6, Rom.8:15-16. Apart from 1 Peter 2:2 it is
only perhaps at John 1:12-13 and 1 John 3:9-10 that they are
brought together though again it is not clear how much of the
frequent idea of heavenly birth in the Johannine literature is
developed from early gospel tradition concerning the child and
entering or receiving the Kingdom (cf Matt.18:3, Mark 10:15,
Luke 18:17). This link between the child and heavenly begetting
is of course to be distinguished from the description of the
pupil-teacher relationship in terms of a child being begotten
by its father. The latter is frequent in Judaism /9/ and
underlies for example Paul's description of his readers as his
children whom he has fathered or nursed in the gospel
(1 Cor.4:15, Gal.4:19, 1 Thess.2:11 cf Philem.10, 2 Cor.6:13,
Mark 10:24, John 13:33 and possibly 1 John 2:1, 12, 18). (This
clearly is not the background to our particular passage
(ἀρτιγέννητα) in view of 1:3, 23 which involves heavenly
begetting and the fact anyway that the writer had not himself

evangelised his readers (1:12).)

(c) so far as the description of the readers as βρέφη is
concerned, given the wide background to child/feeding imagery
in the Ancient World, the description of the Qumran covenanters
as babes is noteworthy (1 QH.7:20ff), not least because of the
several points of resemblance between 1 Peter (especially 2:4ff)
and Qumran. Thus the Teacher (presumably) says:

> Thou hast made me a father to sons of grace,
> and as a foster-father to men of marvel;
> They have opened their mouths like little babes ...
> like a child playing in the lap of its nurse" /10/.

While clearly this imagery owes something to the Jewish
description of the teacher as a father/nurse in relation to his
pupil whom he begets and feeds as his child (cf 1 QH.3:1ff. if
such refers to the Teacher's founding of the community), the
description of the covenanters as babes who feed upon milk is
instructive in view of their declared intention to be the
righteous remnant of Israel, God's holy and obedient people.
Also instructive is the Targum to Is.28:9 which translates
"To whom will he teach knowledge?... them that are weaned from
the milk and drawn from the breasts" by "To whom was the Law
given and who was commanded to understand wisdom? Was it not
the house of Israel who were beloved above all nations and
cherished above all kingdoms? (Cf 2:9ff). This follows a
development in the Old Testament itself of seeing Israel as
God's child which is fed and nourished by Him (Jer.31:20,
Hos.11:1, Ps.103:13, Is.1:2, 30:1ff, 66:10-13). This general
casting of Israel in the role of a child fits well with the
writer's view of his readers as God's chosen and obedient
people who sojourn through this life in the knowledge of the
gospel /11/ (1:1, 1:13ff, 2:4ff, 2:11, 4:17). Therefore βρέφη
and their longing for milk would be a further explication of
the readers as "children of obedience" at 1:14 in fulfilment
of their calling as God's Israel.

(d) the thrust of the image as a whole and generally the
content of the letter is toward faith in and fidelity to the
gospel. It is this common denominator that links the
regeneration cycle of ideas to the child cycle of ideas. At
1:23 regeneration is explicitly linked to the gospel as God's
word and after Scriptural support is taken up in ἀρτιγέννητα -
ἐν αὐτῷ αὐξήθητε, harking back to ἀναγεγεννήμενοι ἐκ σπορᾶς

ἀφθάρτου (1:23). Regeneration in relation to the gospel may
also underly 1:3 since it is of the essence of the writer's
purpose to emphasise the message as one of hope, God having
vindicated Christ after his suffering (1:11). Thus the readers
are begotten to a lively hope on the basis of such a gospel as
this. Equally however they are also thought of as God's chosen
and holy people who should be obedient to His word in the
course of their earthly pilgrimage (1:2, 1:13ff, 2:4ff, 2:11ff)
Thus parallel to the imagery of regeneration through the word
(1:23) is the imagery of being God's Israel purified through
obedience to the truth (1:22). The two cycles of ideas meet in
the child image of 2:2 around the common theme of adherence
to the gospel, confirmed in the content of the milk as being
both the word about Christ (1:25) and even Christ himself (2:3
κύριος and the play on χρηστός, together with the ambiguous
ἐν αὐτῷ rather than δι'αὐτοῦ).

By way of conclusion we may briefly ask what purpose this
combination of imagery serves for the writer in his epistolary
task. A possible answer may be suggested from elements drawn
from the remainder of the image in the description of the milk
by which the babes are nourished, linking that to the summary
of the gospel which he appears to give in 1:11 as "the
sufferings and subsequent glories of Christ" /12/.

(a) the milk nourishment is described firstly as λογικόν, and
while several explanations of the word have been given it would
seem to mean more than just spiritual as opposed to literal or
actual milk /13/. Rather it may recall at least in part the
mention of God's word or λόγος in 1:22-25 so that while the
A.V. translation "milk of the Word" seems slightly redundant in
view of the close association between gospel and Christ already
present in γάλα, λογικόν may be thought to mean spiritual in
the sense of describing the enduring purpose of God and His
word and this in turn recalls the content of that word as
Christ's vindication after his sufferings (1:11). Consequently
this milk is indeed true nourishment for God's people who have
been called by Him, and as begotten by this word they are born
into that life that has an enduring quality in contrast to the
vain customs which marked the life into which they had been
humanly born (1:18 cf 4:4) /14/. This word is also thereby
germinally present within them assuring them even now of the
promised fulfilment of God's purpose 1:3ff).

(b) the milk nourishment is also described as ἄδολον which

recalls the mention of δόλον in 2:1. Thus it is related
directly to the readers' Christian life rather than being simply
either a polemic against "impure" nourishment or a recollection
of the possible sinlessness of the infant (ἀναμαρτήτων νηπίων
Hermas *Mand*. 2:1 *Sim*. 9:29). The injunction to sinlessness and
the description of the milk as being pure, however, take us back
to the understanding of the gospel at 1:11 as Christ's sufferings
and subsequent glories. The writer lays great emphasis on the
sinless nature of Christ's sufferings (2:19ff, 3:18ff, 4:12ff).
Thus as Christ was vindicated by God after sinless suffering
so those who are nourished by that gospel must likewise endure
as God's holy people both sinlessly and patiently.

The purpose therefore of the writer in thus combining
regeneration and child imagery in relation to the gospel on
which they are nourished and by which they grow is to relate as
closely as possible understanding and experience. As God's
people obedient to His word it is seen to inform their very
life at its root. As both the assurance of God's victory in a
time of adversity and the call to patient endurance of that
adversity it is not only the word by which they live but which
lives in them enabling them through its true nourishment both
to endure and to grow toward the fulfilment of God's purpose.

NOTES

/1/   This then would give the aorist participle ἀποθέμενοι
(2:1) its full meaning, as being not simply a present request
but a reminder of what the decisiveness of baptism should mean.
/2/   Yeb.22a, 48b, 62a; Strack-Billerbeck *Kommentar zum Neuen
Testament aus Talmud und Midrasch* ii p.420ff.
/3/   E. Sjöbert "Wiedergeburt und Neuschöpfung im
palästinischen Judentum" *Stud. Theol*. 4. (1950), 44-85.
/4/   There are of course occasional references to divine
begetting in the Old Testament e.g. Deut. 32:18, Ps.2:7, Ezek.
16:8ff but this way of describing the divine activity was
increasingly avoided by Judaism. (The reading at 1QSa2:11 in
the Qumran scrolls remains uncertain). See T.D.N.T. 'γεννάω' I
pp.668-9 (Buchsel); R. Brown *St. John's Gospel* New York 1966
p.138ff; C.K. Barrett *The Gospel According to St. John* London
1965, p.171ff.
At Deut.32:18 the link between heavenly birth and God as the
Rock is interesting in relation to the linked imagery in 1
Peter 2:2ff between regeneration and stone(s).

/5/   C.G. Montefiore and H. Loewe *A Rabbinic Anthology* London
1938 p.163ff, 171ff; *T.D.N.T.* 'γάλα' I pp.645-647 (Schlier).
/6/   P. Tachau *'Einst' und Jetzt' im Neuen Testament*
Göttingen 1972, p.16ff.
/7/   E.G. Selwyn *The First Epistle of St. Peter* 2nd edit.
London 1964, p.154.
/8/   J.N.D. Kelly *The Epistles of Peter and Jude* London, 1969,
p.84.
/9/   b. Sanh. 19b cf. 99b "he who teaches the son of his
neighbour the Torah, Scripture ascribes it to him as if he had
begotten him" so fulfilling the command "be fruitful and
multiply".
/10/   G. Vermes' translation *The Dead Sea Scrolls in English*
(Pelican) 1966, p.174.
/11/   See P. Richardson *Israel in the Apostolic Church*
Cambridge, 1969 p.171ff; J.H. Elliott *The Elect and the Holy*
Leiden 1966.
/12/   In distinction from 4:13 it seems preferable to refer
1:11 to a description of the suffering and victory of Christ
himself as foretold by Old Testament prophecy. See Kelly
op. cit. p.58ff.
/13/   *T.D.N.T.* 'λογικός' IV p.142ff (Kittel); R. Reitzenstein
Die Hellenistischen Mysterienreligionen Leipzig 1927 p.328ff;
R. Perdelwitz "Die Mysterienreligionen und das Problem des 1
Petrusbrief" *Religionsgeschichtliche Versuche und Vorarbeiten*
xi (3 heft) Geissen 1911-12, p.65ff; F.J. Hort *The First
Epistle of Peter* (1.1-2.17) London 1898 *ad. loc.* See also
C.F.D. Moule "Sanctuary and Sacrifice in the Church of the New
Testament" *J.T.S.* n.s.1 (1950) 29-41 esp. pp.34-35; W. Grundmann
"Die 'ΝΗΠΙΟΙ' in der urchristlichen Paränese" *N.T.S.* 5 (1958-59)
188-205 esp. pp.188-190.
/14/   See W.C. van Unnik "The critique of paganism in 1 Peter
1:18" in *Neotestamentica et Semitica* Studies in honour of
Matthew Black, Edinburgh 1969, pp.129-142.

Wisdom, Power and Wellbeing

A Set of Biblical Parameters for Man and their Use in the
New Testament to undergird Jesus' and the Christian's Humanity

James M. Gibbs,
The Queen's College,
Somerset Road,
Birmingham, B15 2QH.
ENGLAND.

A model which is both ancient and pervasive, being found
in the Old Testament, the intertestamental writings and the
New Testament, defines the true, God-intended humanity as
having wisdom, power and wellbeing, and as having these three
elements only through total dependence upon God who gives these
gifts. In our presentation of data concerned with this model,
we shall first define what is encompassed by 'wisdom', 'power'
and 'wellbeing'. Secondly we shall present OT, intertestamental,
and some NT passages (the latter from *Luke-Acts, John* and
1 John) which we believe reflect this pattern, after which we
shall comment on them. Thirdly, we shall indicate some further
background on Passover expectations and the Wisdom model among
the Jews, and fourthly, we shall examine at greater length the
use of the model of the wise, powerful and wellborn humanity
as used by Paul in *1 Corinthians*, by Mark and by Matthew to
undergird the nature of Jesus' and the Christians' humanity.

I. Defining the Parameters

The present writer's field is the NT, and it is here (and
initially in *1 Corinthians*) that he first encountered the use
of the three-fold paradigm of 'wise', 'powerful' and 'wellborn'
being applied extensively to individuals and groups, either to
Jesus as embodying wisdom, power and wellbeing, or to various
individuals or groups within the Christian community as being
(or not being) wise, powerful and wellborn, as in *1 Cor.* 1.26.

1 Cor. 1.26-31 begins by reminding the Corinthians that they formerly were not 'wise' (σοφοί), 'powerful' (δυνατοί) or 'wellborn' (εὐγενεῖς), and it ends by explicitly citing a version of *Jer.* 9.24 (MT *v.* 23), 'Let him who boasts boast in the Lord'. Since *Jer.* 9.23 (MT *v.* 22) speaks of the wise man, the mighty man and the rich man, it seems obvious that Paul has *Jer.* 9.23-24 in mind throughout *1 Cor.* 1.26-31, but has readily substituted 'wellborn' for 'riches' in alluding to *Jer.* 9.23 in *1 Cor.* 1.26.

Thus in searching for OT and intertestamental passages that might reflect this three-parameter model for humanity, it was with the recognition that the whole pattern might be applied to individuals or to groups within a community (with each group representing one facet) or to a community as a whole. It was also to be expected that 'wellbeing' might be related to 'riches' or interchangeable with it in at least some passages. Since Paul speaks of Christ crucified as both the 'Wisdom of God' and the 'Power of God' (*1 Cor.* 1.24), one might find passages where the motifs of wisdom and power appear to be interwoven.

The present author lacks the time, competence and resources for undertaking a careful form-critical study and suggested history of the use of the wise, powerful, wellborn motifs, and this we leave to others. My own concern is more to move backwards from the NT phenomena to see what underpinning can be found in earlier writings. However, at least by hindsight, working definitions can be given of what is meant by 'wisdom', 'power' and 'wellbeing' or 'riches' that will enable others to see if there is coherent logic in the attempted detection of these three elements in the passages presented below /1/.

Wisdom: This motif is concerned with the will of God, its nature (e.g. mercy), knowledge of it (wisdom, understanding) or departure from it (ignorance, sinfulness, iniquity). One also finds figures representing wisdom among men, whether true or false: prophets, judges, etc.

Power: Here we find might or power, symbols for them (either symbols of God's power such as wind, tumult and lightning, or symbols of human power such as chariots, warriors and fortresses), acts of might (e.g. sitting in the seas) or persons of might (e.g. mighty men or men of war).

Wellbeing: Here are encompassed elements that make for wellbeing, such as bread and water, riches, honour, good paternity or choice of spouse, imperishability, long life, a right relationship with God (one of dependent faith), and God as the life-maker. We also encounter here the false alternatives to true wellbeing: a claim to be God, a worshipping of lifeless idols, perishability, the withdrawal of sustenance, and the cutting off by God of the life of transgressors.

From the above we may note that under each aspect there are positive and negative elements, with the negative elements involving a departure from dependence on God for wisdom (i.e. following one's own will rather than God's), for power (e.g. chariots), and for wellbeing (e.g. claiming to be self-sufficient or depending on idols), or else they involve man in his finitude as contrasted with God.

II. Passages Reflecting the Parameters

With the above in mind, we shall list passages apparently structured on the paradigm /2/, indicating, where convenient, portions pertaining to the respective elements (* = riches; # = riches combined with wellbeing motif).

	Wisdom	Power	Wellbeing/Riches
1. *Gen* 41.39-45 (Joseph)	39	40-41 43b-44	42-43#, 45
2. *Deut* 6.5	5a heart (*lēbāb*)	5c might ($m^e\,'\bar{o}d$)	5b being (*nepeš*)
3. *1 Kings* 3.9-13[3]	9, 12	11b, 13b	11a#, 13a#
4. *2 Chron* 1.10-12	10, 12a	11b, 12c	11a#, 12b#
5. *Ps* 1.2-3 (?)	2	3ab	3c
6 *Ps* 139	1-6	7-12	13-18
7 *Isa* 3.1-3 (4-7?)	2b, 3b, 4, 7a	2a, 3a, 5a, 6b, 7c	1, 5b, 6a, 7b
8. *Isa* 55.1-11	6-9	10-11	1-5
9. *Isa* 58.1-11	1-2, 6a	3b-4a, 6b	3a, 7

	Wisdom	Power	Wellbeing/Riches
10. *Jer* 9.23-24 (MT 22-23)	23a, 24	23b	23c*
11. *Jer* 10.3-10 (*vs* idols)	7-8	3-6	9-10
12. *Jer* 10.11-16 (*vs* idols)	12ab, 14a	12a, 13	11, 14b-16
13. *Jer* 51.15-19 (= 10.12-16 with minor variations)			
14. *Ezek* 28.2-10[4]	3-5[5], 7	2c, 8	2b, 9-10
15. *Hosea* 10.13-16	13a	13b-14a	14b-15
16. *Obad* 8-10	8	9	10
17. *Micah* 5.10-14	12	10-11	13-14
18. *Micah* 6.8	8b	8a	8c (ṣn [hiph.][6])
19. *Zech* 9.2-3	2b	3a	3bc-4*
20. *I Esdras* (3 Ezra) 3.17b-4.32[7]	3.17b-24	4.1-12	4.13-32#
21. *Tobit* 4.13-19[8] (?)	14b-19	14a	13
22. *Wisdom* 1.1-15 (?)	4-11	1-3	12-15
23. *Wisdom* 7.22b-8.8 (the figure of Wisdom)	7.22b-23; 8.4a, 7-8	7.24-25, 27-28, 30-8.1, 4a, 5c-6	7.26, 29; 8.2-3, 5*
24. *Sir* 10.24	24b judge	24c ruler	24a nobleman
25. *Baruch* 3.14[9] (within the summons to Israel of 3.9-4.4)			
26. *IQS* 1.11-13*[10] (concerning conditions of entry into the community)			
27. *IQS* 11.15b-22 (Benediction[11])	15b-16a, 17b 17d-18a, 18c-19a, 22b	16b, 17c 18b 19b-20a[12], 20b	16c-17a 21-22a

Luke-Acts Passages

	Wisdom	Power	Wellbeing/Riches
Luke 1.51-53	51b	51a, 52	53
Acts 6.5, 8, 10 (Stephen)	10 (wisdom)	5b (Spirit), 8 (power), 10 (Spirit)	5b (faith), 8 (grace)

	Wisdom	Power	Wellbeing/Riches

See also *Luke* 2.40 (Jesus); 2.52 (Jesus)[13]; 10.27[14]; *Acts* 6.3
(choosing the Seven).

Johannine Passages

	Wisdom	Power	Wellbeing/Riches
John 16.8-11	8b (righteous-ness)	8c (judgment)	8a (sin)
	10 (righteous-ness)[15]	11 (judgment)	9 (believe not)
1 John 2.12-14[16]	13a, 14b	13b, 14c	12, 14a

Johannine passages.

We shall begin our comments by looking at *1 John* 2.12-14.
In verses 12 and 14a wellbeing is expressed in terms of the new
status characterized by forgiveness of sins and the Father-child
relationship. That they 'have known the Father' is apparently
the basis for their being called τεκνία (*v.* 12) and παιδία
(*v.* 14a), 'little children'. Regarding those who are called
'fathers', it was the function of a father to teach his
children, as Joseph speaks of God having made him a father to
Pharaoh, *Gen.* 45.8. Thus *1 John* 2.13a, 14b simply say the
fathers 'have known him who is from the beginning' without
specifying anything more narrowly or explicitly, and thereby
encompassing the whole knowledge of God.

In 2.13b and 14c the power motif is expressed in terms of
'having conquered' and 'being strong', as one might expect.
The noteworthy point is that this combat motif is connected
with νεανίσκοι, 'young men', which appears to be a quasi-
technical term for a Christian initiate in at least *Mark,
Matthew* and *1 John* /17/. A combat imagery associated with
Christian initiation, in which the anointing of the baptismal
candidate with oil is likened to the gladiator's anointing
before a fight, is spoken of by Ambrose of Milan, Cyril of
Jerusalem and Chrysostom of Constantinople (all fourth century)
/18/.

When we further note the renouncing of the world (*1 John*
2.15) and the references to anointing in 2.20 and 27, it
appears likely that at least *1 John* 2.15-29 is a portion of a

a baptismal homily /19/, one which, as we have seen, involves
the motifs of wisdom, power and wellbeing. This connection of
the three parameters with initiation into the community and as
the marks of those within the community is strikingly parallel
to *1 QS* 1.11-13 (No. 26 above).

The passage in *1 John* enables us to see more readily that
John 16.8-11 indeed relates to our triad (although in point of
fact the latter passage was detected long before the *1 John* one
because of its parallels to the justice - mercy (= love) -
faith form of the triad as used in *Matthew*, as we shall see
below.   ·

   The linking of wisdom and power. Among the passages we
have examined, some clearly deal with three separate aspects,
those we have called 'wisdom', 'power' and 'wellbeing' (or
'riches'). But there have also been several passages, as we
expected, where the wisdom and power aspects have clearly been
in parallel to each other, with identical things being spoken
of each, as in *Isa*. 3.1-3; *Jer*. 10.12 and 51.15. The following
are a random selection of some further passages which conjoin
wisdom and power without any clearly defined aspects of
wellbeing in the passages as well: *Job* 12.13: 'with him (= God)
are wisdom and might'; 12.16: 'with him are strength and
wisdom'; 26.12: 'by his power he stilled the sea, by his
understanding he smote Rahab'; 26.2-3: 'him who has no power ...
him who has no wisdom'; *Isa*. 10.13: 'By the strength of my hand
I have done it, and by my wisdom, for I have understanding'.
We would suggest that this phenomenon is easy to understand in
terms of the prophetic conviction that God's word does not
return to him empty (40.8; 55.11; *Jer*. 12.25; cf. the divine
fiat in *Gen*. 1). Thus we may conclude that there is ample
precedent for Paul's speaking of Christ crucified as being
both 'the Power of God and the Wisdom of God' (*1 Cor*. 1.24).

   Personified Wisdom as all-embracing. We may note that
Wisdom itself, as in *Wisd*. 7.22-8.8 (No. 23 above), comes to
encompass within itself wisdom, power and wellbeing. Without
pressing the point, we would suggest that this may be at least
part of what may lie behind Matthew's apparent christological
model of Jesus as the Torah incarnate (i.e., Wisdom incarnate)
who embodies and enfleshes the total demand of *Mic*. 6.8 (cf.
Matt. 23.23) in word, will and deed. It also suggests that
1 Cor. 1.30 should be rendered as 'He is the source of your
life in Christ Jesus, whom God made to be to us Wisdom:

righteousness and sanctification and redemption', i.e. with
the last three items in apposition to wisdom. This spreading
of wisdom across all three of our parameters may also help to
explain why, as we shall see when we look at *1 Corinthians,* it
is that Paul can associate himself as an apostle above all with
bringing love as God's wisdom and yet can present the apostles,
including himself, as the ones who embody the true wisdom,
power and wellbeing (*1 Cor.* 4.10).

Further comments on individual passages. It is possible
that not all of the passages we have given (e.g. *Mic.* 6.8) were
initially thought of in terms of wisdom, power and wellbeing
(or riches), but some of them (including *Mic.* 6.8) were
subsequently used as such by at least one or more NT writers.

Passages from the eighth century BC which are taken up in
the NT appear to include *Isa.* 3.3 (reflected in the 'wise
masterbuilder' /20/ of *1 Cor.* 3.10) and *Mic.* 6.8 (taken up in
Matt. 23.23 as defining the deep things of Torah). *Jer.* 9.23-24,
a seventh century BC passage, is taken up in *Bar.* 3.9-37 /21/
and in *1 Cor.* 1.26-31.

We have suggested that the three notes of *Deut.* 6.5 (part
of the Shema) are related respectively to wisdom, wellbeing
and power, with *lēbāb*, 'heart', being taken in terms of will,
nepes being taken in the sense of 'living being' so that it
corresponds to wellbeing, and *mᵉʾōd*, 'might', naturally being
power. We have seen that Luke 10.37, apparently working from
the four-note form of this passage as found in Mark 12.29-30
(with its two equivalents for *lēbāb*, namely, καρδία, 'heart',
and διανοία, 'mind'), has changed the last three prepositions
presumably in order to conform the passage to a wellbeing -
power - wisdom sequence, with 'out of all thy heart' in the
opening phrase being used to stand for the whole person.

We have seen a number of passages where wellbeing has
been expressed in terms of riches, and *1 Esdras* 4.13-32, on
women as being strongest, has shown us the overt combining of
the elements of riches ('gold and silver') and wellbeing
(giving birth to all men).

Septuagintal Greek. If we look at the LXX to see how our
relevant Hebrew words have been rendered in these particular
passages, and then examine Hatch and Redpath, *Concordance to
the Septuagint* /22/, to see what Hebrew forms the various

Greek words have rendered, we may make the following cursory observations.

The Hebrew vocabulary used for the wisdom motif in the passages we have examined are translated in the LXX in those passages by such words as σοφία (used in the LXX nearly exclusively for ḥokmāh), σύνεσις (used over half the time for $t^e b\hat{u}n\bar{a}h$, but with a number of occurrences for $da^c at$, ḥokmāh and $madda^c$), γνῶσις (used predominantly for $da^c at$, and only for $da^c at$ among the Hebrew words we have noted), ἐπιστήμη (used approximately equally for $t^e b\hat{u}n\bar{a}h$ and $da^c at$, with its three occurrences for ḥokmāh confined to Ezekiel), and φρόνησις (used roughly equally for $t^e b\hat{u}n\bar{a}h$ and ḥokmāh).

Of the three (or four) words for power we have identified, $m^{e c}od$ is translated by δύναμις, $g^e b\hat{u}rah$ and $kō^a h$ by ἰσχύς, and hayil, supposedly used for 'wealth in Ezek. 28.4 f. and Zech. 9.4, is translated in all these occurrences by δύναμις.

Of the three other words particularly associated with wellbeing in terms of wealth or honour, $^c\bar{o}ser$ is rendered in all our passages by πλοῦτος, $n^e k\bar{a}s\hat{i}m$ by χρήματα, and $k\bar{a}b\hat{o}d$ by δόξα.

Concluding remarks. From the foregoing passages we may conclude that the model of wise - powerful - wellborn (or rich) appears to be pervasive and continuous from at least the eighth century BC onwards /23/. As we expected, we have seen the model applied to individuals, groups within society and whole peoples, as, for example, in its application to new members and the whole community at Qumran (1 QS 1.11-13) and in the Johannine community (1 John 2.12-14). Thus it can be used effectively to relate individuals to a community and vice versa.

The overall theme is one of dependence upon God alone, and when this dependence is lacking, then either there is indicated a lack of the three elements or there is a declaration by God that he will withdraw them.

III. Background on Passover and Wisdom /24/

Before we look at the use of the wise-powerful-wellborn model in Paul, Mark and Matthew we need to look at expectations

centred on Passover and to highlight certain aspects of the
Wisdom model among the Jews in order to enhance our
understanding of the NT writings to which we shall then turn.

The Passover Nexus

By the first century AD a number of motifs were centred
on the season of Passover. Four relevant OT passages occur in
Jewish lectionary usage either on the feast itself or in
Sabbath readings at this season in the triennial lectionary
used by synagogues under Palestinian influence /25/. The first
three passages are *Gen*. 1.1-2.3, *Exod*. 11.1-12.28, and *Micah*
6.8, which speaks of man as called to justice, mercy and faith
/26/.

Gen. 1 speaks of man's creation as the image of God and as
called to be his vice-regent (1.26-28). *Exod*. 11.1-12.28
recounts the redemption of Israel, whom God elected to be his
Son (*Exod*. 4.22-23, J). Israel's calling as Son of God was to
be the true humanity by showing forth God's will, character and
work through total dependence and obedience. As Robin Scroggs
has shown (*The Last Adam* (Oxford, 1966), in the first century
AD Adam was coming to be viewed as the first patriarch of
Israel. The close connection between the ultimate destiny of
Israel and Adam is shown in the second century BC by Dan. 7.13 ff.,
where the glorified 'one like unto a son of man' refers to the
righteous remnant of Israel at the End-time /27/. This
interpretation is reinforced by the Damascus Document (*CD* 3.12-21),
which says that the righteous remnant shall have the 'glory of
Adam' in the End-time.

The fourth relevant passage, used in the period between
Passover (15 Nisan) and Pentecost (6 Sivan), is *Jer*. 9.23-24,
which warns men not to glory in their wisdom, power or riches
/28/.

Not only was the Exodus the central model for redemption /29/,
but it would appear that the Messiah was expected to come at
Passover, a tradition recorded in the Palestinian and Jerusalem
targums and also found among the Samaritans in the *Memar
Marqa* /30/.

The 'Binding of Isaac', the 'beloved son' (*Gen*. 22.2 LXX),
as the type of the costly depth of God's love (cf. *John* 3.16)
and the expiatory sacrifice *par excellence* for sin (cf.

John 1.29), was held to have taken place on 14 Nisan when the
lambs were offered (*Jubilees* 18 /31/; cf. *John* 1.29; 13.1;
19.36; also 19.14, 31, 42). Both the Isaac-typology motifs of
costly love and expiatory sacrifice are seen in *1 John* 4.9, 16;
1 Cor. 15.3 ff.; *Rom.* 5.8, 10; 8.3, 32 /32/.

Thus the way was paved for, among other things, the
presentation of Jesus as the totally dependent and righteous
remnant of one of Israel in its calling as Son of God, the
perfect symbol of God's sovereignty and ownership (which is
the meaning of the Image of God /33/), and hence the true man
as the Last Adam (*1 Cor.* 15.45; *Rom.* 5.12 ff.). In him is to
be seen the God-given wisdom, power and wellbeing that mark
the true man.

The Wisdom Model

Wisdom, as part of the OT model for the true man, stands
for at least two complementary values, namely, the content of
God's will and obedience to that will. The concern of wisdom
with justice as the content of God's will is seen in Solomon's
request in *1 Kings* 3.9 for 'an understanding mind to govern thy
people, that I may discern between god and evil'. In the
corresponding passage in *2 Chron.* 1.10 he prays, 'Give me wisdom
and knowledge to go out and come in before this people, for who
can rule this thy people that is so great?'

The connection between wisdom and obedience to God is seen
in the parallelism of *Job* 28.28: 'And he said to man "Behold,
the fear of the Lord, that is wisdom: and to depart from evil
is understanding".' *Yir'ah*, 'fear' or 'reverence', means above
all, as Gerhard von Rad has pointed out, 'man's knowledge about
his dependence on God, especially his obligation to obedience
in respect of the divine will' /34/. Hence we can see the
groundwork for the confession in *1 Cor.* 1.23-24 that 'Christ
Crucified' is God's Wisdom.

But personified (and perhaps semi-hypostatized) Wisdom
was viewed in the later stages of the OT as created by Yahweh
'at the beginning of his work' (*Prov.* 8.22), and as being God's
agent of creation (explicitly in *Prov.* 8.27, 30; *Wisd.* 7.22;
8.5-6; implicitly in *Pss.* 104.24; 136.5; *Prov.* 3.19).

The creation, fashioned by Wisdom, reflects God's glory
and wisdom, and it sings a paean of praise to God which man

neither hears nor perceives (cf. *Isa*. 6.3 and *Ps*. 19; this is
picked up in *1 Cor*. 1.21 /35/). That man by himself can know
little or nothing of God's wisdom by searching the creation is
made plain by a number of passages (e.g. *Isa*. 40.28; *Job* 5.9;
11.7 f.; 25.2 f., 14; 36.26; *Sir*. 43.31 f.).

This is unlike the Greek or Stoic concepts of wisdom, where
wisdom comes through man's rational powers, whether rationally
intuited as in Plato, empirically built up as in Aristotle, or
rationally perceived from the cosmic order as in Stoicism /36/.
It is also unlike the Gnostic concept that wisdom is about
man's true origins.

On OT-Jewish lines, wisdom or knowledge was viewed as
basically concerned with that which was moral and interpersonal,
one's relationship with God and one's fellow men. Whereas in
the Greek view it was man's product or finding, in the
OT-Jewish view it was neither man's creation nor finding, but
rather God's gift, which included the demand for the obedience
of righteousness.

In Jewish intertestamental literature we find Wisdom
spoken of as having come and dwelt in Israel as Torah (*Sir*.
24.8-10; *Bar*. 4.1) in a form that man could 'hear'. This
equating of Wisdom with Torah is further shown when the Jewish
phrase, 'the yoke of Torah', is spoken of by Sirach as 'the
yoke of Wisdom' (*Sir*. 51.26). Thus Wisdom had come to mean not
only dependence on God expressed through obedience to his will,
but also the sum total of God's will and ways. In line with
this Wisdom is mentioned as being God's 'glory' and 'image'
(*Wisd*. 7.25-26).

IV. The Presentation of the Humanity
of Jesus and the Christians /37/

Now we are ready to see how Paul, Mark and Matthew present
Jesus as God's true man in terms of wisdom, power and wellbeing,
and the Christians as called to enter into the same pattern.

Paul

In Paul /38/ we find the following model.

(a) Man is intended to be, as the obedient and dependent
Son of God, the visible Image of God's ownership, sovereignty,

peace and good order, exercising the vice-regency under God
over the creation.

Although man *is* the image of God (*1 Cor*. 11.1) /39/, he
fails to fulfil his function through disobeying and not
depending on God, with the result that chaos increases (*Rom*.
1.27: he, turning from God, falls into ἀσχημοσύνη, 'dis-order-
liness'), and the creation has been subjected to futility (*Rom*.
8.19-22).

(b) Jesus, as the dependent and obedient Son of God (*Rom*.
1.3, etc.) is the properly functioning Image of God (*2 Cor*. 4.4;
Rom. 8.29), the 'firstfruits' (*1 Cor*. 15.20) and 'Eschatological
Adam' who has become the life-making Spirit (*1 Cor*. 15.45) of
our new humanity (see καινὴ κτίσις, 'new creature/creation',
2 Cor. 5.17; *Gal*. 6.15).

(c) Christians are to be conformed to the Image of Christ
(*Rom*. 8.29; *1 Cor*. 15.49; *2 Cor*. 3.18; cf. *1 Cor*. 3.21-23). We
are to be confirmed bodily, growing in the spiritual body as
we put to death the mortal body (*Rom*. 6.12; 8.13; *1 Cor*. 9.27;
2 Cor. 4.10; etc.) in the Body of Christ (*1 Cor*. 12.27; etc.).
We are to do this by suffering together with Christ in order
that we may also be glorified together with him (*1 Cor*. 12.26
in connection with 'Body of Christ'; *2 Cor*. 7.3; *Rom*.8.17-19
in connection with 'Sonship', with 'Body in 8.23-24, and with
'Image' in 8.29). The model for this suffering as applied to
Jesus and the Christians is the Binding of Isaac /40/. The
model for the glorification is that of the End-time Adam /41/.

We, as yet-to-be-perfected, adopted Sons of God, even now
are 'walking in newness of life' (*Rom*. 6.4c) by the Spirit of
adoptive Sonship (υἱοθεσία) whereby we are enabled to cry, in
dependence and growing obedience, 'Abba, Father' (*Gal*. 4.6;
Rom. 8.15; these are surely echoing the Jesus-tradition as
found in *Mark* 14.36).

Our perfection as Christians will be when we are glorified
together, with the glory being revealed in/to/for (εἰς) us
(*Rom*. 8.18; cf. *1 Cor*. 15.43 ff.). We shall be revealed to the
Creation as the (perfected) Sons of God (*Rom*. 8.19), that is,
when our body is redeemed (*Rom* 8.23) /42/ at the End-time
resurrection of the body (which is still future in Paul: *Rom*.
6.5b; *1 Cor*. 6.14; 15.49-58 /43/), so that we shall stand forth
as perfectly conformed to the Image of Christ, the Last Adam

(*1 Cor.* 15.49; *Rom.* 8.29). Then the Creation, delivered from
the bondage of corruption, will enter into the freedom of the
glory of the children of God (*Rom.* 8.21), that is, into God's
peace, his good order.

A slightly alternative form of expressing this End-time
consummation is that Christ must reign until all things have
been subjected to him by God, and the last enemy, namely, death,
having been abolished, the Son shall also be subjected to the
Father that God may be totally supreme in every way (*1 Cor.*
15.24-28, 50-58). The correlation of these two models lies
in the Pauline equation in which Christ = The Body = The Church
(cf. *1 Cor.* 11.24-29).

This Pauline 'salvation model' is couched in terms of the
fulfilment of God's purpose for man and the creation in and
through history, with the consummation only at the End.

Paul (like at least Mark, Matthew, John and Hebrews) views
Gen. 1-2 as basically concerned with God's abiding goal and
purpose for man and the creation which have been his intention
from the beginning /44/.

To this end Paul presents Jesus and the Christians in
terms of God's wisdom and power (in Isaac typology) and
wellbeing (in Adam typology), as is to be seen most clearly in
1 Corinthians as summarized below.

I CORINTHIANS: WISDOM, POWER AND WELLBEING

1 Cor.1.26: (Jer.9.23)	WISDOM (wisdom sought by Greeks - 1.22)	POWER (signs sought by Jews - 1.22)	WELLBEING
GOD'S MAN: Jesus	Christ crucified, 1.24 'foolishness'	Christ crucified, 1.24 'weakness'	15.3-5: Christ *dead* as *Isaac bound*: 'Low despised, *things that are not*', 1.28 (cf. Rom. 4.17) 15.20 ff.: Christ *raised* as the *Last Adam, the lifemaking Spirit* (1.30)
MEN: Pre-Christian, 1.26:	not wise	not powerful	not wellborn
God's primary gifts of Ministry, 12.28, 29	First, *Apostles,* who *proclaim,* by word and life-style, Christ crucified, *God's Wisdom,* i.e. his	Second, *Prophets,* who, by *building up* the Body of Christ, the Temple of the Spirit, show forth the authentic *power of God,* which is our only	Third /45/, *Teachers* who, by *teaching* the *faith believed* that is according to the Scriptures, keep us anchored to a stabilized understanding of God's work in Christ, which is the source of our new *wellbeing* now and in the future, which we have through

1 Cor.1.26: (Jer.9.23)	WISDOM (wisdom sought by Greeks - 1.22)	POWER (signs sought by Jews - 1.22)	WELLBEING
Abiding gifts of Spirit for Christians, 13.13	Love (chapt. 13)	Hope (chapt. 14) 14.25: God is among you	Faith (chapt. 15) Isaac bound/ Adam raised
The Christian's God-given:	Present (which is the greatest as love)	Future (which is yet to be perfected)	Past (begun when he was incorporated into God's past action in Christ through faith at baptism)

For Paul not only is Jesus the normative man, but he is also placed alongside 'one God, the Father' (1 Cor. 8.6a) as the 'one Lord, Jesus Christ, through whom are all things and we through him' (1 Cor. 8.6b), in a re-writing of the First Commandment /47/. We would suggest that Paul intends this to refer to Jesus as the agent of the renewed creation, the καινὴ κτίσις of Gal. 6.15 and 2 Cor. 5.17, which comes through the Last Adam as the life-making Spirit (1 Cor. 15.45), not as the agent of the primal creation /48/, but the shift to the latter would be the next step when Christ was proclaimed as pre-existent ontologically. For Paul Jesus is the cosmic ruler who must reign until all things have been subjected to him by God (1 Cor. 15.24-28), but he reigns only by virtue of what God has done and is doing in and through him, so that Jesus' dependence is carefully maintained.

We shall conclude our treatment of Paul by noting a passage in which Paul sets the example of the apostles over against that of the Corinthians, 1 Cor. 4.10:

'We are fools for Christ's sake, but you are
    wise in Christ.   - Wisdom
We are weak, but you are strong.   - Power
You are held in honour, but we in disrepute'. - Wellbeing

As Paul says in 4.7, all they have received is a gift, and
the whole of 4.8-13 is cast in the same three motifs, as are
many other passages and sections in the letter.

Mark

In Mark we find the three-part paradigm explicitly in
6.2-3: 'What is the wisdom (σοφία) given to him? What mighty
works (δυνάμεις are wrought by his hands! Is not this the
carpenter, the son of Mary ...?' Here are the themes of wise,
powerful and wellborn, introduced by the question: 'From where
have these things come to this one?' (6.2: πόθεν τούτω ταῦτα;).
The believer's answer is that God is the source of all three /48/,
and Mark structures his gospel accordingly.

Jesus as the one whose *wellbeing* is from God is seen at
his baptism (1.11): 'Thou art my son, the beloved; in thee I
am well pleased'. Jesus as the *wise one* whose words supersede
the Torah as written, is seen at the Transfiguration (9.7:
'This is my son, the beloved; hear him!'). Mark 9.8 emphasizes
Jesus being suddenly alone with the disciples; Moses and
Elijah, representing the Law and the Prophets, are gone. This
matches 13.31: 'Heaven and earth shall pass away, but my words
shall not pass away'. It is further reinforced by Mark's
synagogue lectionary nexus at the transfiguration, which
includes *Gen.* 41 /49/ in which the need for one who is discreet
and wise (*Gen.* 41.33) is met by Pharaoh's confession that there
is no one to match Joseph in discretion and wisdom (*Gen.* 41.39).

The third motif, *power*, takes us to the heart of Mark's
major purposes, for he is combatting a misunderstanding (or
misappropriation) of Jesus and the life in Christ couched in
terms of seeing Jesus as a figure of wonderworking power /50/.
John speaks of 'the stronger one' (ὁ ἰσχυότερος) who is coming
after him (*Mark* 1.7). Jesus speaks of the need to bind 'the
strong one' (ὁ ἰσχυρός) before that one's house can be
plundered (3.27). In the story of the epileptic child (which
is written against *Gen.* 3 /51/), the father says that the
disciples were not 'strong enough' (ἴσχυσαν) to cast out the
unclean spirit (*Mark* 9.18). The father appeals to Jesus to
help 'if you are able' (εἴ τι δύνη) and Jesus replies that 'all
things are possible to the one who believes' (πάντα δυνατὰ τῷ
πιστεύοντι) 9.23. The disciples then ask, 'Why were we not
able (οὐκ ἠδυνήθημεν) to cast this one out?' (9.28), and Jesus
replies, 'This kind in no way is able (δύναται) to come out

except in prayer' (9.29). Jesus has said that it is not 'those
who are strong' (οὐ ἰσχύοντες) who need a physician (2.17).
Not only has he told the disciples after he first speaks of
the necessity of the passion that 'whosoever would save his
life shall lose it' (8.35), but when, after the incident of
the rich man, the disciples ask, 'Who then can be saved?'
(10.26), Jesus' reply is, 'With men it is impossible (ἀδύνατον)
but not with God; for all things are possible (πάντα δυνατά)
with God' (10.27). When Peter calls attention to the withering
of the fig tree (which brackets the proleptic plundering of the
Temple for the sake of the Gentiles), Jesus tells the disciples,
'Have faith in God!' (11.22) and says 'Whatever you ask in
prayer, believe that you receive it, and you will' (11.24 /52/).
Thus Jesus in Mark is the strong one precisely when he casts
himself wholly on God in prayer in Gethsemane: 'Abba, Father,
all things are possible (πάντα δυνατά) to thee, ... but not
what I will but what thou wilt' (14.36). This is immediately
followed by Jesus' words to Simon: 'Were you not strong enough
(ἴσχυσας) to watch one hour?' (14.37). And at the cross,
when the veil is rent in two (15.38) /53/, it is the
representative of Roman might, a centurion, who might be
expected to hail Caesar as 'God's Son', who instead, seeing how
Jesus gave up his spirit, confesses to the whole world, 'Truly,
this man was God's Son' (15.39) /54/. This he says of the
one who 'is not able' (οὐ δύναται) to save himself' (15.31).

Thus, as the man who lives in total dependence on God,
Jesus is presented as truly wellborn at his baptism (1.11),
wise at transfiguration (9.7-8), and powerful in the passion
(Gethsemane, 14.36, and the cross, 15.38-39)`, and all of
these are presented as the work and gifts of the Father (6.2-3).

   The disciples. Let us now briefly indicate how the
disciples' humanity is related to that of Jesus. As noted some
years ago by Eduard Schweizer /55/, the three major statements
by Jesus of the necessity of the passion (8.31; 9.31; 10.32-34;
a fourth is 14.41, spoken as the disciples fearfully follow
Jesus to Jerusalem and the passion) are misunderstood by the
disciples each time (8.32 f.; 9.32-34; 10.35-37), and therefore
each time Jesus calls the disciples to follow him into his
suffering (8.34 ff.; 9.35 ff.; 10.38 ff.), and this call to
follow is expressed in terms of wellbeing, wisdom, and power,
respectively, as we shall show.

   In 8.34b-38 Jesus says to the individual, '... let him deny
himself .... For whoever would save his life (ψυχή) will lose

it and whoever loses his life for my sake and the gospel's will
save it. For what does it profit a man, to gain the whole
world and forfeit his life? For what can a man give in
return for his life? For whoever is shamed of me ..., of him
will the Son of Man also be ashamed, when he comes in the
glory of his Father, ...' We see the wellborn motif in the
notes of 'deny himself', 'lose his life ... save it', 'forfeit
his life', 'ashamed' and 'glory'. The note of riches is struck
by the words 'profit', 'gain the whole world' and 'what can a
man give'. Thus this section calls the disciples into the
true *wellbeing* of dependence on God in following Jesus.

In 9.35-37 the disciples, who have been discussing who was
the greatest of them (9.34), are told by Jesus, 'If any one
would be first, he must be last of all and servant of all'
(9.35). Then taking a child, putting him in their midst
(i.e. in the midst of the Church), and taking him in his
arms /56/, he says, 'Whoever receives one such child in my
name receives me, and whoever receives me, receives not me,
but him who sent me'. Here, without using the word 'love', is
the call to *love* of the brethren, which is *wisdom*, and this
passage is allusively reminiscent of the abiding relationship
of love with the Father which we saw in *John* 16.10 (and its
related footnote) in section I above.

In 10.32 Jesus has spoken of being delivered to the
Gentiles, and when the sons of Zebedee ask to be on his left
hand and right hand /57/ in his glory (10.37), he asks them,
'Are you able (δύνασθε) to drink the cup that I drink, or to be
baptized with the baptism with which I am baptized?' (10.38).
They reply, 'We are able' (δυνάμεθα). Subsequently Jesus says
to all of them, 'You know that those who are supposed to rule
over the Gentiles lord it over (κατακυριεύουσιν) them and their
great ones exercise authority over (κατεξουσιάζουσιν) them. But
it shall not be so among you; but whoever would be greatest
among you must be your servant, and whoever would be first
among you must be slave of all. For the son of man also came
not to be served but to serve, and to give his life as a ransom
for many' (10.42-45). Here we have the motif of *power*. The
elements of 'servant' (δοῦλος) and 'among you' are also found
in 9.35-37, and we would suggest that the overlap is due
probably to wisdom and power being related themes, as we saw
in section I.

Finally, let us look at *Mark* 10.17-31 which combines all
three motifs in terms of discipleship. The rich man, a would-be

disciple who kneels to Jesus as he goes in the way (10.17), i.e.
the way to the cross, keeps the commandments but falters at the
necessity of giving his all to the poor (10.21-22); here is
the *wisdom* motif. The *power* aspect follows in the discussion
about who *is able* to be saved (10.26-27), and the motif of
riches and wellbeing completes the section in terms of the
disciples having forsaken all and being promised a hundredfold
return (10.28-30) of houses and lands (riches) and brothers,
sisters, mothers and children (wellbeing /58/).

Matthew

    Matthew ties Jesus as the true Adam, the one in whom we
are becoming human, more explicitly than Mark to scripture and
scriptural types by re-writing Gen. 5.1 ('The Book of the
generations of Adam') as 'The Book of the generations of Jesus,
Christ, Son of David, Son of Abraham' (1.1). As the Christ he
embodies justice, God's power; as Son of David he shows mercy,
God's wisdom; as Son of Abraham he is by faith God's wellborn
man. When we pray the Lord's Prayer we enter into this same
humanity (as can be seen below).

    We shall now show some background for the following
connections:

a. Christ - Justice - Power - Deed (the passion to resurrection
    sequence);

b. Son of David - Mercy - Wisdom - Will (and also connected
    with the Temple);

c. Son of Abraham - Faith - Wellbeing - Word.

    a. 'Christ crucified' (= 'Power of God' in *1 Cor.* 1.23 f.
/59/) - cf. *Matt.* 12.18.21, citing *Isa.* 42.1-4, and including:
'Behold, my servant ..., I will put my spirit upon him [i.e.
anoint him as the Christ] and he shall proclaim justice to the
Gentiles; ... he will not wrangle or cry aloud ... he will not
break a bruised reed ... until he brings *justice to completion*'
(εἰς νῖκος: literally, 'to victory', an idiom meaning 'to
completion', 'totally').

    b. *'Son of David'*. *'Have mercy!'* is addressed to Jesus
five times, four of them linked with 'son of David': 9.27;
15.22; 20.30, 31; the fifth is 17.15. In 12.3-7 *David's* taking
the shewbread from the *Temple* at Nob is linked with the citing
of *Hos.* 6.6: 'I desire *mercy* and not sacrifice', which is also
cited in 9.13 (the only two times it occurs in the NT).

Matt. 2.6 (concerning the Davidic King of Israel in the
story of the Magi) cites *Micah* 5.2, but instead of 'who shall
rule my people Israel' as in the MT and the LXX, it is 'who
shall *shepherd* my people Israel', using ποιμάνειν.

Matt. 5.23 f., concerning bringing one's gift to the
altar (of the Temple - i.e. a sacrifice) requires that one
first be reconciled to one's brother, in this case asking the
brother for forgiveness. Thus Matthew explicates the depth of
the meaning of *Hos.* 6.6.

'Son of David' as connected with *persevering will* can be
seen in the 'Song of David', especially *2 Sam.* 22.22 f.:

For I have kept the ways of Yahweh,
  And have not wickedly departed from my God.
For all his judgments were before me:
  And as for his statutes, I did not depart from them.

That 'Son of David' is to be associated with *the three
middle beatitudes,* 'hunger and thirst for *righteousness*',
'*merciful*', '*pure* in heart' (*Matt.* 5.6-8), may also be seen in
the 'Song of David', *2 Sam.* 22.25-27a:

Therefore has Yahweh recompensed me according to my
  righteousness, according to my cleanness in his sight.
With the *merciful* /60/ thou dost show thyself merciful,
  with the blameless man thou doest show thyself
  blameless;
With the *pure* thou dost show thyself pure ....

c. *'Son of Abraham'*. Abraham in Jewish tradition was
viewed as the following /61/:

(a)   the Rock (πέτρα) God looked for on which to found
      the world (cf. *Matt.* 16.18: Peter's *faith* - 'You
      are Petros, and upon this rock (πέτρα) I will build
      my church'),

(b)   the great exemplar of faith,

(c)   the one who by faith acquired both worlds (i.e. this
      one and the next,

(d)   one who was ready to die for the hallowing of the
      Name, and

(e) a proselyte and maker of proselytes (based on *Gen.*
     12.1, 5).

With the foregoing background in mind, we are ready to
indicate in tabular form some of the major elements in Matthew
which are concerned with Jesus as the normative man of wisdom,
power and wellbeing in his teaching and in his actions, and his
disciples after him.

Gen. 5.1:   The Book of the generations of *Adam*

Matt. 1.1:   The Book of the generations of *Jesus,*

		Christ,	*Son of David,*	*Son of Abraham*
23.23	*Depths of Torah (Mic.* 6.8, read at or near Passover)	Justice	Mercy	Faith /62/
4.1-11	*Temptations* (based on *Deut.* 6-8)	4.8-10 Deed (wor-shipping and serving God)	4.5-7 (Temple) Will/Testing	4.2-4 Word /62/
5.3-11	*Beatitudes*	5.9-11 peacemakers - sons of God /63/,	5.6-8 righteousness	5.3-5 poor in spirit - theirs is *Kingdom of heaven* (future world)
		persecuted,	merciful,	mourn (repent-ance for sin /64/)
		persecuted.	pure in heart	meek - inherit the *earth* (present world).
5.13-7.11	Main body of *Sermon on Mount*	5.13-26 Works; peacemaking	5.27-6.18 Lust of heart; Temple and mercy; Righteousness.	6.19-7.11 Seek Father's Kingdom; Judge not others; Ask Father for good gifts.

	Christ,	Son of David,	Son of Abraham
6.9-13 *Lord's Prayer*	Will be done Bring not to the Test /65/, but deliver us	Kingdom come Forgive as we forgive	Hallowed be Name Give daily bread /66/
The True Man's:	POWER	WISDOM	WELLBEING

In connection with Jesus and the power motif, we may note that Matthew removes the δύναμις that goes forth from Jesus in *Mark* 5.30 to heal the haemorrhaging woman (cp. *Matt.* 9.21-22) and also the δύναμις from the form of *Deut.* 6.5 (the Shema) cited in *Mark* 12.30 (cp. *Matt.* 22.37). That is, in Matthew no grounds are left for Jesus or anyone else having strength in and of themselves.

Let us now look further at how Matthew presents Jesus as the true man, in effect the Torah incarnate, for this will show us how the whole gospel is structured in the same way that we have seen in the table above. It will also show us how Matthew relates the disciples' humanity to that of Jesus so as to maintain Jesus as both exemplar and yet the unique one /67/.

The paradigm of word, testing of the will, and deed is to be found in Jesus' three answers (*Matt.* 4.4, 7, 10) from *Deuteronomy* (8.3; 6.16; 6.13) to the temptations of the devil. Man shall live by the Word of God, not by bread alone (this is wellbeing through faith); he shall not put God to the test (but rather God shall test his will, a question of wisdom), and he shall worship and serve God alone (here is the element of power). Word, testing, deed, seen above all as faith, mercy and justice, respectively, denote the three major divisions of the remainder of the gospel after the prologue of *Matt.* 1.1-4.16.

The onset of these divisions is indicated by the phrase ἀπὸ τότε, 'from then'. Matthew uses ἀπό 113 times and τότε 90 times, but only three times does he use the phrase ἀπὸ τότε. The first occurrence of the phrase is in 4.17: 'From then Jesus began to preach....' Here is the *Word* of God. The second use of it is in 16.21: 'From then Jesus began to show that he *must* suffer'. Here is the *willing* of the Word. The third and last

time is in 26.16: 'From then Judas sought opportunity to betray
him'. Here is the beginning of the *deed*.

Where each division closes is indicated by Jesus
descending (καταβαίνειν) from a specified height. If the first
temptation took place at ground level (4.3 f.), then Jesus
descends (singular aorist participle) from the higher height of
the mountain at the end of the Sermon on the Mount (8.1). If
the second temptation is raised to the pinnacle of the temple
(4.5-7), then, after casting the die at the Transfiguration,
Jesus and the disciples are said to be descending (plural
present indicative participle) from an ever greater height, a
high mountain (17.1). But, as can be seen from the table
below, this will/wisdom aspect overlaps; as we might expect,
with the deed/power motif (cf. 26.36-46; 27.42. If the third
temptation occurs on a very high mountain (4.8-10), then Jesus'
(and the Father's?) surrogate, the ἄγγελος κυρίου, the angel of
the Lord, is said to descend (singular aorist participle) at
the end of the whole passion - entombment - resurrection
sequence from the only place that is higher: from heaven itself
(28.2). Thus the Word (of faith, that gives wellbeing) and
Deed (of justice, done by God's power alone) are from Jesus
alone, that is, he is the one Teacher (23.8) who has given the
Word of God in its depth of grace and demand (*Matt*. 5-7) and
the one Guide (23.10) who has gone in the Way of Torah, the
way of total justice (26.16-28.6). The disciples are joined
to him in his Sonship as they go with him in the way, willing
the word into deed by willing mercy, God's wisdom.

Thus Matthew may be outlined briefly overall as follows:

1.1-4.16   THE PROLOGUE

                Jesus = God's Man = Son of God = Israel

4.17-28.15   THE DRAMA

                Jesus as God's Man, the Son of God, is
                God's Wisdom/Torah in:

                WORD   4.17-8.1

                Testing of will   16.21-17.9 (initial
                                             casting of
                                             die)
                                  -27.50 (final act
                                             of will)

	DEED	26.16-28.2
28.16-20	THE SENDING	

Jesus as the Christ, the Son of Man, God
with us, sends the disciples forth into
mission.

The correlation of the details of the temptation and the
main portion of the gospel may be presented as follows:

The Temptation Narrative (*Matt.* 4.1-11) and its Themes

Temptations	Height at which they occur	Jesus' answer	Theme:
1. 4.3-4	Ground level ('these stones')	Man not to live by bread alone but by Word of God	WORD
2. 4.5-7	Pinnacle of the Temple	Not to tempt God	Tempting - Testing
3. 4.8-10	Very high mountain	Worship and serve God alone	DEED
End 4.11	Unspecified	*Angels came* and *ministered* to Jesus	

The Drama (*Matt.* 4.17-28.2) and its Themes

Onset: 'From then...'	Completion: Jesus 'descends'	Height from which he descends	Event completed at descent	Theme
1'. 4.17 Jesus began to preach	8.1	'the mountain' (5.1; 8.1)	Sermon on the Mount	WORD
2'a. 16.21 Jesus began to show that he must suffer	17.9	'high mountain' (17.1)	Transfiguration	Willing of WORD leading to DEED

Onset: 'From then...'	Completion: Jesus 'descends'	Height from which he descends	Event completed at descent	Theme
3'a. 26.16 Judas sought to betray him				
(2'b	(26.36-46, no 'descent')	Gethsemane (Mount of Olives)	(Triple agony: 'Thy will be done' [v.42; cf. vv.39, 44; 6.10])	(Tempting before DEED of Cross)
2'c	27.42	'the cross'	Jewish leaders: 'come down now'	Tempting to leave DEED incomplete
3'b.	28.2	'from heaven'	Angel of LORD came, aiding Jesus' followers	DEED now fulfilled

Thus we can see that Matthew's concern to present Jesus as God's true man, the remnant of one of Israel, the Son of God, in terms of wisdom (mercy), power (justice) and wellbeing (faith) has been the controlling aim in the structuring of his whole gospel (as it has been before him in *Mark*), and that he has carefully related the disciples to the same pattern, a relating that includes maintaining the Markan materials which we examined in this regard even if with modifications.

As Lord of the disciples he is Emmanuel, God with us (1.23), the Shekinah (18.20; cp. *Pirqe Aboth* iii. 2), and he has been given all authority in the creation (28.18). Thus again we encounter the tension between presenting Jesus as God's true man because truly dependent, and Jesus as the all-sufficient Lord of the Church and the Creation.

Conclusion

We have seen a pervasive and perhaps even increasingly
intensified use of the three-parameter model for man involving
wisdom, power and wellbeing extending from at least the eighth
century BC down through the era of the New Testament.

In the NT writings we have examined we have seen how
thoroughly this model has been used to undergird the witness
to the humanity of Jesus and the disciples.

With regard to the NT, we have noted the stress on the
wisdom element being ἀγάπη, 'love' (Paul and John), or ἔλεος,
'mercy' (Matthew), and the power element being a dying to self,
a building up of others (Mark, Matthew, 1 Corinthians), with
the wellbeing element being used to undercut any claims of the
'self-made man', be they education, race, riches, culture or
the like (e.g. *Matt*.3.9; *1 Cor*. 1.26; 4.8-13).

Finally, it needs to be said that the present paper is no
more than an 'interim report', for there is probably much more
data than the author has yet discerned in the materials of the
Apocrypha, Pseudepigrapha, the Qumran sect, rabbinic sources,
etc. (not to mention those he has probably overlooked in the
OT and NT writings). But it is the author's hope that what
has been presented is enough to convince all those working
with the well-springs of the Judaeo-Christian heritage that
here is a model for man that needs to be recognized, reckoned
with, and sought for in whatever primary materials they may be
working with.

NOTES:

/1/   Dr. Henry McKeating of the Theology Department, Nottingham
University, in a letter to the author has kindly pointed to the
need for definitions, and he has helped to sharpen the criteria
by which passages were identified for inclusion in the subsequent
list, although any weaknesses that remain are the author's.
Since this paper was delivered, there has appeared a largely
complementary study by W. Wuellner, 'Ursprung und Verwendung
der σοφός-, δυνατός-, εὐγενής- Formel in I Kor 1,26' in *Donum
Gentilicium* ed. by E. Bammel, C.K. Barrett and W.D. Davies
(Oxford, 1978), pp.165-183.

/2/   An earlier version of this section on background passages
was presented to the biennial conference of the (Indian)
Society for Biblical Studies at Bombay in January 1977.
/3/   That the king is viewed as a figure of *power* comes out
very clearly in such a passage as *1 Esd*. 4.1-12. See item 20
below.
/4/   The next section, *Ezek*. 28.11-19, also against the prince
of Tyre, makes explicit use of the Adamic model in the garden
of Eden, while the present section appears to use it implicitly.
/5/   Dr. Gerhard Wehmeier, my former colleague at the United
Theological College, Bangalore, India, has noted regarding
Ezek. 28.4 with its progressions from *hokmāh* and *tᵉbunāh*
('wisdom' and 'understanding') to *hayil* (usually rendered
'wealth' in this context) to *zāhāb wakesep* ('gold and silver'),
that the usual meaning of *hayil*, namely 'power', would be
interesting as it would then yield the sequence wisdom - power -
riches. However, 28.5, where *hayil* occurs twice more, with its
mention of wisdom in trading, makes 'wealth' the more likely
meaning. But in *Ezek*. 28.4f. LXX *hayil is* translated by
δύναμις.
/6/   Dr. McKeating in his letter pointed out the uncertain
meaning of this verb. The LXX renders this part of the verse as
'to be ready to go with the Lord thy God'. As far as I have
detected, *Mic*. 6.8 is the only OT passage with precisely this
combination. Apart from *Matt*. 23.23 (see below), it also
appears to be picked up in *1QS* 8.1, where, along with truth and
righteousness, these motifs are used to define the character of
the twelve men and three priests who constitute the community's
council.
/7/   *1 Esdras* 3.1-12 is the prologue to the story; 4.33-41 is
the epilogue; 3.1-5.3, plus 1.21-22 and 5.4-6, are the only new
materials in the book, the rest being drawn from *2 Chronicles*,
Ezra, and a small portion of *Nehemiah*. See O. Eissfeldt, *The
Old Testament: An Introduction* (Osford, 1965), p.574.
/8/   The wisdom sayings of Tobit are 4.13-19 (the present
section) and 12.6-10. See Eissfeldt, *op. cit.*, p.584.
/9/   This is within *Bar*. 3.9-37, a wisdom homily based on
Jer. 9.23 according to H. St. John Thackeray, *The Septuagint
and Jewish Worship* (London, 1921), pp. 95-100. There are other
elements within 3.9-37 which could be classed as
'rightmindedness', power and wellbeing, but they do not clearly
progress through the three parameters in sequence.
/10/   The translations of the *1QS* passages are those of
G. Vermes, *The Dead Sea Scrolls in English* (Harmondsworth,
revised 1968). The present author has yet to search either the

Dead Sea Scrolls or the Pseudepigrapha for further passages
which may reflect the wise - powerful - wellborn parameters.
/11/ This benediction concludes the Community Rule. On it see
A.R.C. Leaney, *The Rule of Qumran and its Meaning* (London, 1966),
p. 236.
/12/ This passage is given by Leaney, *op. cit.*, p.234, who is
translating the pointed text as given by A.M. Habermann,
Megilloth Midbar Yehuda [The Scrolls from the Judean Desert],
2nd ed. (Tel-Aviv, 1959). Vermes does not give the passage.
/13/ ἡλικία in the sense of age of strength or vigour is
found in *2 Macc*. 5.24; 7.27 and *1 Enoch* 106.1. Philo,
de Abrahamo 195 speaks of Abraham's begetting Isaac 'not in
years of vigour but in old age', μη καθ' ἡλικίαν ἀλλ' ἐν γήρᾳ.
/14/ Compare *Mark* 12.29-30, which uses ἐξ, 'out of', in all
four parts. It seems not unreasonable that Luke understood
Deut. 6.5 in the fashion that we have suggested (see passage
No. 2 above) and has modified the four-member form accordingly
by shifting the preposition in the last three members and
letting the 'heart' stand for the whole person.
/15/ The sign of God's love for Jesus is the latter's return
to the Father, *John* 14.20 ff.; 16.17 ff. See also passages
concerning the abiding relationship of love, *John* 3.35; 5.20;
10.17; 14.21, 23, 31; 15.9; 16.27. See also the love-commandment
in 13.34 and 15.12.
/16/ This passage was detected by Mr. Max S. Liddle, a
postgraduate student at the United Theological College,
Bangalore, India.
/17/ See note 19 below.
/18/ The data are presented in H.M. Riley, *Christian
Initiation* (Washington, D.C., 1974), to which my attention
was called by Mr. Liddle.
/19/ This is a further observation by Mr. Liddle. The
connection of νεανίσκοι with Christian initiation in *1 John*
strengthens the arguments of Scroggs and Groff that the
νεανίσκος of *Mark* 14.51 and 16.5 is a baptismal candidate
(R. Scroggs and K.I. Groff, 'Baptism in Mark: Dying and Rising
with Christ', *JBL*. 92 (1973), pp. 531-548). The further
association of νεανίσκος with strength reinforces the
likelihood that the νεανίσκος fleeing naked in *Mark* 14.51 is
forsaking his human strength in fulfilment of *Amos* 2.16: '...
he that is courageous among the mighty shall flee away naked
in that day, says Yahweh'. (Further confirmation for Scroggs'
and Groff's arguments is that *Mark* 16.1-8, in which the young
man is seated, clothed, on the right hand in the tomb,
proclaiming the resurrection, is written against the Jewish

lectionary background of *Exod*. 14-15, the great baptismal type
of the crossing of the Red Sea and Moses' song of triumph.
See C.T. Ruddick, Jr. 'Behold, I Send My Messenger', *JBL*. 88
(1969), pp. 381-417, who also shows that the other great
baptismal type, namely, the Flood narrative, lies behind
Jesus' baptism in Mark).

    Furthermore, in *Matt*. 19.20, 22, the rich, law-observing,
would-be disciple is called a νεανίσκος and the subsequent
discussion concerns who is powerful enough to be saved, with
this being possible only with God (*Matt*. 19.25-26). In fact,
we find here in terms of becoming a disciple the three elements
of wisdom ('keep the commandments', 19.19-22), power (19.23-26),
and riches ('We have forsaken all ...; what shall we have
therefore?', with the hundred-fold inheritance, 19.27-29).
Matt. 19.16-30 is simply a re-working of *Mark* 10.17-31, so
that the three-parameter pattern in connection with a would-be
disciple is already there in Mark. However, Matthew has
shifted the νεανίσκος motif to here from Mark's baptismal
context. Matthew deletes some Markan baptismal materials
(such as those in Jesus' response to the sons of Zebedee
(*Mark* 10.38-39; cp. *Matt*. 20.22-23), plus the νεανίσκος episodes,
Mark 14.51; 16.5. If one also recognizes that baptism in the
Triune Name in *Matt*. 28.19 is a later insertion (as indicated,
among other things, by Eusebius' pre-Nicaea testimony), then it
can be seen why νεανίσκος, apparently used in *Mark*, *Matthew*,
1 John and perhaps *Luke* 7.14 as a quasi-technical term for a new
convert, would occur in *Matthew* in a context which concerns
becoming a disciple, but without any baptismal connections.
/20/ In the LXX σοφὸς ἀρχιτέκτων, 'wise masterbuilder', occurs
only in *Isa*. 3.3, where it replaces the 'skilful magician' of
the MT (ἀρχιτέκτων is used also in *Sir*. 38.27 and *2 Macc*. 2.29).
In *1 Cor* 3.10-17 Paul is also likening himself to Bezalel, the
builder of the tabernacle. The verb ἀρχιτεκτόνειν, 'to
masterbuild', is applied to Bezalel in *Exod*. 31.4 and 35.2;
the only other occurrence of the verb applies it to Oholiab,
Bezalel's assistant, in *Exod*. 38.23 (37.21 LXX). The 'gold,
silver, precious stones, wood' of *1 Cor* 3.12 is based on *Exod*.
35.32 (see 31.4-5). God's 'spirit of wisdom', πνεῦμα σοφίας,
has been imparted to Bezalel, *Exod*. 35.21; 31.3. *Exod*. 35
was read in synagogue on about the second Sabbath in Nisan in
the second year of the Tishri cycle of the triennial lectionary
and hence falls within the time scheme of *1 Corinthians*,
Passover (*1 Cor*. 5.6-8) to Pentecost (*1 Cor*. 16.8). For solid
evidence concerning the lectionary (and Mark's use of it) see
Ruddick, *art. cit*., referred to in note 19 above.

/21/ See note 9 above.
/22/ Oxford, 1897; photomechanical reprint, Graz, Austria, 1954.
/23/ The three-fold pattern may well have ancient Near Eastern antecedents. That it has its close parallel in at least part of present-day Hinduism can be seen from the following. *The Hindu* (a Madras newspaper), on 27th November, 1976, p. 16, reported a discourse by Sri T.S. Balakrishna in Sai Kala Mantap, Madras, entitled 'Three Distinct Ailments of Mankind', the opening portion of which is given below (italics added):

> Three distinctive ailments usually afflict mankind in
> general. Posession of *wealth* makes one feel superior.
> By opening his purse, he thinks he can get anything
> done and forces others to be at his beck and call.
> Likewise a person occupying a unique position, more so
> an *official status* and confident that *his acts* have
> the backing of innumerable followers, may not hesitate
> to indulge in any *rash act*. The third is *intellectual
> arrogance* when a person by virtue of his study of
> texts, starts decrying all others, claiming he is
> more intelligent than all others. These men are
> oblivious to the fact that they are after all mortals.

/24/ An earlier form of this section was part of the author's paper delivered at the biennial conference of the (Indian) Society of Biblical Studies, Secunderabad, India, in January, 1975, and subsequently published as 'Jesus as the Wisdom of God: The Normative Man of History Moving to the Cosmic Christ', *Indian Journal of Theology* 24 (1975), pp.108-125.
/25/ In this Sabbath lectionary the Pentateuch was read once in three years. It could be begun either on the first Sabbath in Nisan (the Nisan cycle) or on the first Sabbath in Tishri falling after the Feast of Tabernacles (the Tishri cycle). For what is to the present author an undeniable demonstration that this lectionary existed in the first century AD in both the Nisan and Tishri cycles, and that Mark is structured on it, see Ruddick's article referred to in note 19 above. For data which suggest that the final redaction of the Pentateuch was for lectionary purposes see Aileen Guilding, *The Fourth Gospel and Jewish Worship* (Oxford, 1960), pp. 24-44, who argues that the origins of the triennial cycle go back to about 400 BC. For a bibliography of materials dealing with Jewish lectionary usage see J.C. Kirby, *Ephesians, Baptism and Pentecost* (London, 1968), pp. 192-196, and Jacob J. Petuchowski, ed., *Contributions to the Scientific Study of Jewish Liturgy* (New York, 1970), pp. xx-xxi.

/26/ *Mic*. 6.3 ff. was the reading from the Prophets read with
the ancient Torah reading for Passover, *Lev*. 23.4-8 (*b. Pes.* 76b).
Subsequently both of these were transferred to the
'ecclesiastical' New Year, 1 Nisan. *Gen* . 1.1-2.3 and *Exod*.
11.1-12.28 were read in the triennial lectionary on the first
Sabbath in Nisan in the first and second years respectively
of the triennial cycle begun in Nisan.
/27/ John J. Collins, 'The Son of Man and the Saints of the
Most High in the Book of Daniel', *JBL*. 93 (1974), pp. 50-66,
argues that *Dan*. 7 concerns primarily the angelic hosts but
includes the faithful Jews as well. However, Maurice Casey,
'The Corporate Interpretation of "One like a Son of Man" (Dan
VII 13) at the Time of Jesus', *NT*. 18 (1976), pp. 167-180, has
demonstrated that the corporate interpretation applied to Israel
was current 'from the time of the composition of the book of
Daniel onwards' (p.179).
/28/ Of the four Torah readings with which *Jer*. 9.23-24 was
read, three (*Lev*. 4.1-6.11 in 2nd year, Tishri cycle; *Num*.
14.11-45, 2nd year, Nisan cycle; *Deut*. 4.a5-6.3, 3rd year,
Tishri cycle) fell in Iyyar, the second month, and the fourth
(*Deut*. 8.1-9.29, 3rd year, Tishri cycle) fell at the beginning
of Sivan. All four fall within the time span covered by
1 Corinthians, namely Passover (*1 Cor*. 5.7 f.) to Pentecost
(*1 Cor*. 16.8).
/29/ David Daube, *The Exodus Pattern in the Bible* (London, 1963).
/30/ John Bowman, *The Gospel of Mark* (Leiden, 1965), p.52.
These sources speak of there being four especially significant
Passovers: at the first God created the world (*Gen*. 1), at
the second God made the Covenant with Abraham 'between the
pieces' (*Gen*. 15), the third was the Exodus out of Egypt
(*Exod*. 11.1-12.28), and on the fourth Messiah will come.
/31/ Geza Vermes, *Scripture and Tradition in Judaism* (Leiden,
1951), p.215. In later Jewish tradition the birth, binding
and death of Isaac were all dated on 15 Nisan, Passover itself;
see H.J. Schoeps, Paul (London, 1961), p.147, n.2.
/32/ In addition to the works by Vermes (pp. 193-226) and
Schoeps (pp. 126 ff., especially pp. 141-149) referred to in
the previous note, see especially N.A. Dahl, 'The Atonement -
An Adequate Reward for the Akedah? (Rom. 8:32)', in E.E. Ellis
and M. Wilcox, edd., *Neotestamentica et Semitica* (Edinburgh,
1969), pp. 15-19, and above all the thorough and judicious
article by R.J. Daly, 'The Soteriological Significance of the
Sacrifice of Isaac', *CBQ*. 39 (1977), pp. 45-75. NT references
to the Akedah he takes to be certain are *Heb*. 11.17-20; *Jas*.
2.21-23; *Rom*. 8.32; as probable he takes *John* 3.16; *Mark* 1.11

and parallels and 9.7 and parallels; *1 Cor.* 15.4; *Rom.* 4.16-25;
and as possible he takes on various grounds *Luke* 22.19b (a
passage we would delete from the text); *John* 1.29; 19.14;
Matt. 12.18; *Mark* 12.6; *1 Cor.* 11.24; *Gal.* 1.4; 2.20; *Eph.* 5.2,
25; *1 Tim.* 2.6; *Tit.* 2.14; *1 Pet.* 1.19-20.

/33/   In the Priestly narrative (*Gen.* 1.26-27) man in his
physical stature (perhaps his upright stature) *is* the image of
God. What the image *means* is that man belongs to God (*Gen.*
9.6), owing God perfect obedience and submission, and man
functions as the peripatetic and ubiquitous symbol of God's
sovereign ownership of everything on which the image shines
(cf. *Rom.* 8.18-30). Hillel the Elder (died *ca.* 10 BC) told
his disciples he was going to bathe as a pious deed. When
asked why it was pious, he replied that, like those appointed
to wash and polish the images of kings set up in theatres and
circuses, he was going to wash and polish God's image (*Lev. R.*,
Behar, xxxiv.3, quoted in C.G. Montefiore and H. Lowe, *A
Rabbinic Anthology* (1938; reprinted Greenwich, Conn. n.d.),
pp. 455 f.; cf. *Mark* 12.16-17 and pars.). On ṣelem, 'image',
in the Priestly narrative see the following. P. Humbert,
Etudes sur le recit de paradis et de la chute dans la Geneses
(Neuchatel, 1940), pp. 153 ff. P. Humbert, 'Trois notes sur
Geneses 1', in *Interpretations* ed. by N.A. Dahl and A.S.
Kapelrud (Oslo, 1955), pp. 85-96. P. van Imschoot, *Theologie
de l'Ancien Testament,* Tome II (Tournai, Belgium, 1956),
pp. 8-10.

/34/   G. von Rad, *Wisdom in Israel* (London, 1973), p. 243.

/35/   As demonstrated by G. von Rad, 'Some Aspects of the Old
Testament World-View', in *The Problem of the Hexateuch and
Other Essays* (Edinburgh, 1966), pp. 144-166, especially
pp. 165 f.

/36/   Paul picks up the Stoic concept in *Rom.* 1.20-21 as part
of his argument for subsuming all Gentiles under sin.

/37/   Much of the material for this section is drawn from the
author's article referred to in n. 24 above.

/38/   We assume Paul to be the author only of *Romans, 1 and 2
Corinthians, Galatians* and *Philemon.* For some of the reasons
why, see James M. Gibbs, 'The Bible in the Church: A Radical
View', *Bangalore Theological Forum* 6/1 (January-June, 1974),
pp. 2-4.

/39/   As shown above in n. 33, the image *is* man in his
physical form; it *means* that man belongs to God and is under his
authority (which is the point in *1 Cor.* 11.1), and its
function is to show forth God's sovereign ownership over
everything on which it shines.

/40/ The present writer believes it likely that Paul's frequent references to the Christians as ἀγαπητοί, 'beloved', is intended at least in part to call them to their task of suffering as 'little Isaacs' in Jesus, the 'Big Isaac', as *Gen.* 22, the binding of Isaac, speaks of Isaac as ἀγαπητός (*Gen.* 22.2, LXX).

/41/ The Isaac-bound (I)/Adam (A) typologies occur together several times: *1 Cor.* 15.3-19 (I), 20-49 (A); *Rom.* 5.8-11 (I), 12 ff. (A); 8.3, 32 (I), 18-30 (A).

/42/ Note the plural 'our' and the singular 'body'. Probably 'body' is singular to retain the link to the 'body of Christ' and the 'image of his Son' (*Rom.* 8.29).

/43/ Although for Paul Christians have died with Christ in baptism (*Rom.* 6.2-4, 6-8), their resurrection is future (6.5) and at present they are 'living as though from the dead', ὡσεὶ ἐκ νεκρῶν ζῶντας (6.13).

/44/ For Paul the locus of God's redemptive work in Christ is in man himself and not over the cosmic powers as such, as shown by Clinton D. Morrison, *The Powers That Be* (SBT 29; London, 1960), especially pp. 114-129. This becomes even more clear when *Colossians* and *Ephesians* are taken as deutero-Pauline. What has been changed is not the situation we face but rather our capacity for facing it.

/45/ Paul's relating of apostles to love and *1 Cor.* 13, of prophets to hope and *1 Cor.* 14, and of teachers to faith and *1 Cor.* 15, was first fully seen by one of my former students, the Reverend Roger Gayler. He was correcting Stephen S. Smalley, 'Spiritual Gifts and 1 Corinthians 12-16', *JBL.* 87 (1968), pp. 427-433. Smalley demonstrated the connection of apostles, prophets and teachers to chapters 13, 14 and 15 respectively, but, failing to note that the list of *1 Cor.* 13.13 is in chiastic order against chapters 13-15, he proceeded to connect apostles to love, prophets to faith and teachers to hope. Mr. Gayler further pointed out that the theme of Christian faith is prominent in 15.2, 11, 14 and 17 (where πίστις or πιστεύειν occur), but not in chapter 14.

/46/ That for Paul Christ = Wisdom = Torah as the embodiment of God's love may be seen in such passages as *1 Cor.* 9.21 ('as being not lawless before God but enlawed of Christ') and *2 Cor.* 3.1 ff. with its Pentecost/Sinai parallels (3.3: 'you are an epistle of Christ, ... written ... with the Spirit of the living God ... on tables which are hearts of flesh'). On love (of the neighbour) as the fulfilling of the whole law (which is Christ's) see *Gal.* 5.14, 23; 6.2; *Rom.* 13.8-10. For indications that Galatians is correlated to the Feast of

Pentecost, with its themes of the giving of Torah on Sinai
(which is now replaced by the 'law of Christ', *Gal*. 6.2), the
making of proselytes and the Abrahamic covenant of promise,
see the present author's review of John Bligh, *Galatians:
A Discussion of St. Paul's Epistle,* in *The Month,* 2nd n. s.,
Vol. 1 (1970), pp. 374-376. In view of such passages as given
above we are unconvinced that 'wisdom christology' is not to
be found in Paul, as is argued by A. van Roon, 'The Relation
Between Christ and the Wisdom of God According to Paul', *NT* 16
(1974), pp. 207-239.

/47/ *1 Cor*. 6.1-8.6a appears to follow the Decalogue from
Commandments X to I, and 8.6b-10.32 then reverses the order
from I to X. A summary of the structure is given in the
present author's 'The Bible in the Church', *BTF*. 6/1, p. 18,
n. 15 (see n. 38 above) and the details are to appear in the
BTF. in an article entitled 'Chiastic Structures as an Aid to
Understanding Paul's Letters to the Corinthians.

/48/ This matches Jesus' rejection of the adjective ἀγαθός,
'good', in *Mark* 10.18.

/49/ Ruddick, *art. cit.*, p. 410 (see n. 25 above).

/50/ The NT evidence is that those who promoted this view were
at least dominantly Jewish Christians. Recognizing that 'signs'
refer to acts of power, we may note that 'Jews demand signs and
Greeks seek wisdom' (*1 Cor*. 1.22), and it is Pharisees *(Mark
8.11),* Pharisees **and** scribes (*Matt*. 12.28), Pharisees and
Sadducees (*Matt*. 16.1) or Herod (*Luke* 23.8) who seek a sign
from Jesus. When Paul 'boasts' of what he has endured
physically, it is explicitly as a Hebrew of the seed of Abraham
over against his opponents, who are of the same stock (*2 Cor*.
11.22-29), whereas his 'boasting' about his revelation (*2 Cor*.
12.1-7) fits the 'Greeks seek wisdom' of *1 Cor*. 1.22.
Confirmation of this last point lies in the fact that *2 Cor*.
12.1-7 is balanced chiastically against the 'Jewish' power-type
of 11.22-29 (cf. the forthcoming article referred to in n. 47
above).

/51/ Ruddick, *art. cit.*, pp. 394-395. Note that this is the
only explicitly *permanent* cure in the gospel (*Mark* 9.25).

/52/ *Mark* 11.25 on forgiveness is an interpolation from
Matthew as demonstrated by H.F.D. Sparks, 'The Doctrine of the
Divine Fatherhood in the Gospels', in *Studies in the Gospels*
edited by D.E. Nineham (Oxford, 1955), pp. 244-245, and
accepted by H.W. Montefiore, 'God as Father in the Synoptic
Gospels', *NTS*. 3 (1956-57), p. 33.

/53/ Σχύζευν, 'to rend', and σχύσμα, 'a rent', occur only in
1.10; 2.21 and 15.38. In 1.10 the heavens are rent, a theme of

access to God; in 2.21 a piece of new cloth on an old garment
causes a rent, a theme of loss; thus in 15.38 we have both the
access of the Gentiles to God and the loss of the Shekinah
from the Jerusalem temple. A third theme in 15.38 is God's
counter-charge of blasphemy against the Jewish authorities by
the total rending of the veil in two pieces, matching the
high Priest's tearing of his clothes as a sign of hearing
blasphemy (14.63-64).

/54/ On the centurion's confession see C.H. Dodd's words cited
by R.H. Lightfoot, *The Gospel Message of St. Mark* (Oxford, 1952),
p. 58, note.

/55/ E. Schweizer, 'Mark's Contribution to the Quest of the
Historical Jesus', *NTS*. 10 (1963-64), p. 428.

/56/ Jesus takes the child in his arms as the Good Shepherd
of *Isa*. 40.11, alluded to by the larger context of the
modified quotation of *Isa*. 40.3 in *Mark* 1.3; cf. the other
shepherd motifs of *Mark* 6.34 and 14.37, plus 16.7. For the
major Markan themes alluded to in the combined quotation of
Mal. 3.1 and *Isa*. 40.3 in *Mark* 1.2-3, see James M. Gibbs,
'Mark 1,1-15, Matthew 1,1-4,16, Luke 1,1-4,30, John 1,1-51:
The Gospel Prologues and their Function', *Studia Evangelica*
VI ed. by E.A. Livingstone (Berlin, 1973), pp. 176-177.

/57/ The only occurrences of 'right hand' and 'left hand' in
Mark are here (10.37, 40) and 15.27, the two thieves crucified
on his right hand and left. Thus Mark designates the cross
as the glory, and this cross-reference also reinforces our
claim that *Mark* 10.37 ff. is, like Jesus' crucifixion, about
power.

/58/ Although a disciple may have left his father (10.29), he
does not receive a father one hundredfold, for he has only one
Father, God.

/59/ Since in *1 Cor*. 1.23 f. 'Christ crucified' is both God's
Power and his Wisdom, we need to show why the link of Christ
and Justice is with *Power* and the link of Son of David and
Mercy is with *Wisdom* rather than the reverse. The answer lies
in discerning the three-fold man-forming ministry envisaged by
Paul, the author of Ephesians, and Matthew.

    In 1 Corinthians we have seen the following connections:
Apostles proclaim the *Wisdom* of God, which is *Love*.
Prophets build up the Church by the *Power* of God, which
is our *Hope*.
Teachers maintain the members of Christ in *Wellbeing*,
which comes by *Faith*.

    By 'apostles' Paul means himself and others as (itinerant)
church-founders, as shown by A.T. Hanson, *The Pioneer Ministry*

(London, 1961). 'Prophet' refers to the local preachers or
pastors, as is obvious from the contents of 1 Cor. 14.

   Whereas in 1 Cor. 3.11 Jesus Christ is the only possible
'foundation', in Ephesians, a deutero-Pauline letter, he has
become the 'chief cornerstone', (Eph. 2.20), and the 'foundation'
has now become the 'apostles and prophets' (2.20) as the
founding generation who gave the mystery of the gospel to
which the church is now to hold fast (3.5). Thus in Ephesians
the present ministers of the church are 'evangelists' (i.e.
Church-founders), 'pastors' (i.e. equivalent to Paul's prophets),
and 'teachers' (4.11), with the terms 'apostles and prophets'
being reserved for the prior founding generation.

   When we turn to Matthew, 'justice' parallels Paul's 'hope',
i.e. a concern for how things will turn out, which is dependent
upon the 'power' of God; Matthew's 'mercy' corresponds to
Paul's 'love', the 'wisdom' of God, i.e. his abiding will, and
'faith' is the same term in both Matthew and Paul, and is
concerned with the basis for 'wellbeing' that God alone can
give.

   In Luke 11.49 we find the probably more original form of
a Q-saying: '... the Wisdom of God said, "I will send to them
prophets and apostles ...."' Matthew presents Jesus himself
as the Wisdom (or Torah) of God, so that the saying is placed on
Jesus' lips in Matt. 23.34 as follows: "I am sending to you
prophets and wise ones and scribes ....' When we note that
Paul, the apostle, speaks of himself as a 'wise one' (σοθός)
teaching 'wisdom' (1 Cor. 3.10; cf. 26 f.), we can see that
Matthew's 'wise ones' (σοφοὶ) stand in the position of Paul's
apostles in Matthew's redacting of the Q-saying. In Matt.
13.52 the 'scribe of the Kingdom' brings out of his treasure
(i.e. the scriptures) 'things old and things new', so that
Matthew's Christian 'scribes' correspond to Paul's and
Ephesians' 'teachers'. The order of 'prophets and wise ones
and, scribes' (Matt. 23.34) corresponds to the order 'Justice
and mercy and faith' as the deep things of Torah (Matt. 23.23),
this latter triad being apparently based on Mic. 6.8.

   Thus we may summarize the three forms of the three-fold
ministry as follows:

Matthew:	Prophets - Justice	Wise Ones - Mercy	Scribes - Faith
Paul:	Prophets - Hope	Apostles - Love	Teachers - Faith
Ephesians:	Pastors - Hope	Evangelists - Love	Teachers - Faith
All Three:	Power	Wisdom	Wellbeing

   It is on the basis of the apparent Matthaean connection
of prophets with justice and of wise ones with mercy, taken
along with the Pauline parallels, that the connection of 'Christ'

is made with 'power' and that 'Son of David' is connected with
'wisdom'. Jesus is crucified in Matthew both as the Davidic
'King of the Jews' (*Matt.* 27.11, 29, 37, 42) and as the one
'who is being called Christ' (*Matt.* 27.17, 22; cf. 26.68).
Thus as the crucified one he embodies both God's wisdom and
his power, as in *1 Cor.* 1.23 f., but he is openly proclaimed
to be the Christ in glory after the passion-entombment-
resurrection-exaltation event (*Matt.* 8.29; 16.20; 17.9) as the
fourteenth generation of *Matt.* 1.16 f. On the other hand, as
'Son of David' he has been confessed openly all through the
ministry by all kinds of people: by Gentiles, namely, the Magi
(2.1-12) and the Canaanite woman (15.21-26), by the blind
(9.27-31; 20.29-34), by a crowd of Jews (21.8 f.) and by
children in the temple (21.15), i.e. by all men of good will.
Only Pharisees (12.23 f.) and the chief priests and scribes
(21.15 f.; cf. 27.20) refuse to do so and try to prevent others
from doing so. This material is a further indication of the
distinction that Matthew makes between the titles 'Christ' and
'Son of David', and it strengthens our case for associating
'Christ' with 'justice' and 'power' on the one hand and 'Son
of David' with 'mercy' and 'wisdom' on the other hand.

/60/ *Ḥesed*, taken as 'merciful', in AV and RV, but as 'loyal'
in RSV. The LXX has ὅσιος, 'pious, devout, pleasing to God'.
/61/ See the entries under 'Abraham' in the index of G.F.
Moore, *Judaism*, Vol. 2 (Cambridge, Mass., 1946), p. 399.
/62/ 'These stones', λίθοι τούτοι, occurs only in 3.9 ('God
can rear up children to Abraham from these stones') and 4.3
('Change these stones to bread.' - cf. stone and bread in
connection with father in 7.9).
/63/ *Matt.* 27.54: Jesus is called 'Son of God' on the cross as
he makes peace.
/64/ *Matt.* 3.6-9; 5.4; 9.15; 11.18: these passages connect
John, weeping, fasting, mourning for sin and repentance.
/65/ The End-time Test which no man can stand in his own
strength.
/66/ Cp. 'daily bread' of the Lord's Prayer to the 'bread' of
the first temptation and also the 'stone' and 'bread' of 7.9
(concerning a father's gift and the Father's gifts).
/67/ See the present writer's article on Gospel prologues
(note 56 above), pp. 179-181, from which most of what follows
is drawn; also the article, 'The Son of God as the Torah
Incarnate in Matthew', *Studia Evangelica* IV edited by F.L. Cross
(Berlin, 1968), pp. 38-46. For further evidence that in Q Jesus
and John are the last messengers of Wisdom, while in Matthew
Jesus himself is Wisdom, see M. Jack Suggs, *Wisdom, Christology,
and Law in Matthew's Gospel* (Cambridge, Mass., 1970).

Christology, Prophecy and Scripture

Rev. S.G. Hall,
King's College,
London.

1. *Christology begins with Christ crucified and risen according
to the scriptures.*

Historically speaking, it is difficult to go further back in
the documentation of christology than 1 Cor. 15:3-4. It is not
the earliest writing we have from Paul, but it *is* early; and such
earlier passages as are relevant (e.g. 1 Thes. 1:9-10; Gal.3:1)
confirm that what Paul says here truly summarizes his message.   In
1 Cor. 15:1-4 he solemnly asserts the content of the good news
which he proclaimed to the Corinthians and which they received,
and which he says he received as tradition himself. The key
statement is: "That Christ died for our sins according to the
scriptures, that he was buried, and that he rose (or, was raised)
on the third day according to the scriptures" (15:3-4).

We can easily verify that this does summarize Paul's initial
Gospel from other texts: 1 Cor.2:2 "I determined to know nothing
among you except Jesus as Christ, and him crucified"; Gal.3:1
"Galatians ... before whose eyes Jesus Christ was portrayed
crucified" (the context shows it was initial preaching); 1 Thes.
1:9-10 "what entrance we had among you, and how you turned from the
the idols to serve the true and living God, and to await his son
from heaven, whom he raised from the dead, Jesus who is delivering
us from the coming wrath"; Rom. 1:1-4 "the gospel of God, which he
promised before through the prophets in holy scriptures,
concerning his son, who was born of the seed of David according to
the flesh, who was designated God's son by a might act according
to the holy spirit by the resurrection of the dead, Jesus Christ
our Lord". Some other elements are present, but the message is
the same: the crucified and resurrected Messiah. And in 1 Cor.
15 and Rom. 1, it is according to scriptures.

Now the point of this opening section is twofold. First, it
is to point out that no exposition of Christology is likely to

prosper unless it keeps firm hold upon this earliest core, i.e.
the dying and rising of Messiah according to the scriptures. Nor,
for that matter, is any attack on Christology which singles out,
for example, the fragility of historical evidence or the platonist
character of later expositions of *communicatio idiomatum* in the
incarnate, capable of deeply disturbing Christological faith; it
misses the mark. Secondly, the purpose is to draw attention to a
neglected feature of the pauline summary, "according to the
scriptures", which is spelled out more fully in Rom. 1:2 as "which
he promised beforehand through his prophets in holy scriptures".
In this sense, if in no other, faith in Christ is prophetic. It
belongs to the prophets. This deserves expanding.

New Testament writers begin the process which developed
increasingly in the Fathers, of hunting up Old Testament texts
which are "fulfilled" in Jesus and God's dispensation for the
Church. I need hardly illustrate the way in which even Paul
himself can pull a verse out of context (1 Cor. 9:9 applies the
law against muzzling a threshing ox to the question of clergy
stipends), and Matthew's practice is notorious. But that is a
superficial way of looking at it. One attractive treatment of
this exegesis is that of C.F.D. Moule /1/, who suggests that the
artificial amd superficial attempts to find fulfilment should be
seen as attesting the general faith in fulfilment, even where the
exegesis itself cannot be accepted. But this suggestion depends
on establishing the general conviction at some other level. There
are some obvious passages, and the material assembled by C.H. Dodd
in his splendid study *According to the Scriptures* remains
important /2/. However, though a number of specific passages
about the suffering servant, prophet, or son of man can be
identified and their use explored in such a way that one can see
a "substructure" for New Testament theology in favourite Old
Testament passages, there is a shortage of texts relating to the
resurrection after three days (Hos. 6:2 and Jonah seem too
superficial and unconvincing). I would look rather to the
fundamental appeal of Paul to Abraham, whom he sees as the
prototype of faith.

First, Romans 4. He is arguing that men are justified by
faith and not by the law, and he appeals to Abraham: "For what
says the scripture? 'But Abraham believed God and it was credited
to him as righteousness'" (4:3). He explains how this faith
related to Abraham's state of uncircumcised lawlessness, and
concludes that the promised blessing on Abraham's seed belongs not
to law-keepers but to believers, who are his real children (4:16-
17). Then in a final passage (a text we must look at), he

assimilates Abraham's faith to that of believers in Christ, and
the chapter ends: "But it was not written because of him alone
that 'it was credited to him', but also because of us, to whom it
is going to reckoned, us who believe in the one who raised Jesus
our Lord from the dead, him who died because of our transgressions
and was raised because of our justification" (4:23-5). *There* is
the basic pattern of faith: faith in God who raised up the Jesus
who died for our sins. Abraham has this kind of faith, because he
believed in the promise of God even though it was contrary to the
testimony of the senses; where breeding children was concerned,
Abraham and Sarah were both virtually dead (4:19). But Abraham
believed the promise that he would be father of many nations,
displaying faith in "God who quickens the dead and calls into
being things that are not" (4:16-17).

This kind of exegesis reduces some of the common attempts to
find explanations of κατὰ τὰς γραφάς in specific texts (Dan. 7 or
Is. 53) to the level of the superficial and artificial. It is to
a fundamental relation of God to those whom he calls and saves, a
God who creates and recreates those who trust him as Abraham did,
that Paul appeals. If modern Christians wish to meet their Jewish
and Muslim brothers on common ground, they might start
interpreting their gospel here, and not in Old Testament proof-
texts (as the early church did) or magisterial claims to miraculous
authority. The same argument is elaborated more fully but less
precisely in Gal. 3; but there a further element is present, which
needs exposition. There the context is an appeal to the gift of
the Spirit at the readers' first conversion: "You stupid Galatians,
who bewitched you, when before your eyes Jesus Christ was
portrayed crucified? This only I want to learn from you: Was it
from works of the law that you received the Spirit, or from the
hearing of faith? Are you so stupid? Having begun in Spirit, are
you now finishing in flesh?" (3:1-3). So the presence of the
Spirit attests the fulfilment of the promise to Abraham, who
believed and was thereby justified: Christ's death absorbed the
curse of the law "so that the blessing of Abraham might reach the
gentiles in Jesus Christ, in order that we might receive the
promise of the Spirit through faith" (3:14). So the Spirit in whom
they are baptized constitutes them the one Seed of Abraham,
belonging to Christ, heirs of the promise (3:16, 26-9). They enjoy
special status as sons: "And (showing) that you are sons, God sent
out the spirit of his son into your hearts crying *Abba*" (4:6). So
the confession of faith in God as Father is the evidence that the
believer shares the justification of Abraham, and it was a
significant part of his initial response to the preaching of Christ
crucified. Further, it is described in terms of God giving the

Spirit: "he who supplies you with the spirit and performs mighty acts in you" (3:5). This Spirit-gift we shall now explore.

2. *The essential New Testament faith is Spirit-inspired and in that sense prophetic.*

At first sight there are three ways in which the Spirit functions in New Testament theologies. First, there are miraculous gifts, including healings, prophesying, speaking with tongues, of which the disorderly assemblies rebuked at Corinth and the Pentecost scene in Acts 2 are examples. Secondly, there are ethical gifts, of which the love of 1 Cor. 13 and the list of virtues constituting the "harvest of the Spirit" in Gal. 5:22 are clear instances. We could include here the important passages in Rom. 8, which illustrate the conflicting mentalities of flesh and spirit and their final goal in destruction or eternal life (the conforming of the body to Christ). Thirdly, there are passages emphasizing the theological or confessional content of the Spirit's gifts. This is the Christologically relevant part.

First, the Spirit gives the confession of God in Christ. "God sent forth the Spirit of his Son into our hearts crying Abba" (Gal. 4:6). "Those who are led by the Spirit of God are all sons of God. For you did not receive a spirit of slavery again so as to fear, but you received a spirit of adoption by which we cry Abba, Father" (Rom. 8:14-15). Whatever else is involved, the gift of the Spirit in Acts has the same central feature: "We hear them telling in our own languages the magnificences of God" (Acts 2:11); "The believers from the circumcision who were with Peter were amazed that the gift of the holy Spirit had been poured out on the gentiles too; for they heard them speaking in tongues and magnifying God" (10:45-6). So the content of Spirit-filled utterance is primarily addressing God as Father, in union with his Son, or setting out the greatness of his works (as the contexts show in Acts, this is primarily the works of God in the mission, death and resurrection of Jesus).

So far, this is quite in keeping with a fundamental point of G.W.H. Lampe /3/ who argues that believers share Jesus' relation to God as his Father. God as Spirit creates man for progressive union and reconciliation with himself, Spirit of God united to Spirit of Man. Lampe bases his Christology on the perfect quality of that union in the historic Jesus, which he believes can be verified, for instance, from the "singular absence of penitence" which marks his relation to God /4/. So Lampe sees the most

important advance in Pauline theology as the identifying of the
Spirit of God with the Spirit of Christ; which means not only that
this relation is historically imparted through Jesus, but much
more: "The union of God and man in Jesus is re-enacted in every
believer; he shares in the sonship of Jesus, and... the
characteristic 'harvest' of the life of sonship consists of the
remodelling of his human spirit so as to reproduce some of the
human qualities of Jesus..." /5/. The effect of Lampe's stance is
to make the "in Christ" element of the New Testament writers
theocentric: in Christ, i.e. with the same spiritual relation to
God as Christ has, we glorify God in word and deed, as his Spirit
progressively fulfils itself in us. Even the parousia of Christ
at the end of time is demythologized as the consummation of the
Spirit's activity in making mankind as a whole Christlike /6/.
This approach is in marked contrast to C.F.D. Moule, who
consistently argues that the inclusive personality of the
glorified Christ, in whom believers exist as members of a body or
bricks in a temple "means, in effect, that Paul was led to
conceive of Christ as any theist conceives of God: personal,
indeed, but transcending the individual category" /7/. I believe
that Lampe under-estimates the Christological content of the
Spirit-given confession in Paul and the New Testament generally.

One famous but controversial passage in Paul shows a direct
and simple correlation between the Spirit-gift and elementary high
christology: "As to spiritual things, brothers, I do not want you
to be ignorant. You know that when you were gentiles you were
seduced to dumb idols by whatever means you were led. Therefore
I inform you that no one speaking in God's Spirit says "Jesus is
anathema", and no one can say "Jesus is Lord" except in holy
Spirit" (1 Cor. 12:1-3). The basic point of this text is to
contrast the idolatry and Christ-rejection of heathen and apostate
with the confession of true faith which is characteristic of every
believer. It is widely held that Paul is here dealing with an
obscure manifestation, charismatics who in the congregation come
out with the "*Anathema Jesous*" exclamation. But Paul's reply is
then pointless and obscure, since reference to the heathen past
and the assertion that "no one can say *Kyrios Jesous* except in
holy Spirit" are both irrelevant. Worse, it separates the passage
from the rest of the chapter, and from the fairly coherent
treatment in chapters 12-14 of the problems of presumptuous
charismatics. The problems are not significantly eased by the
suggestion that the anathema has been uttered by Christians on
trial who after apostatizing claim to have been inspired in
accordance with Christ's promise, nor by W.C. van Unnik's
proposal to interpret *Anathema Jesous* in terms of recognizing in

Christ only the earthly, fleshly side, in which he dies under the curse of Deuteronomy 27:26 /8/.

The function of 1 Cor. 12 is to argue that possession of what are considered higher gifts of knowledge and wisdom does not mark an exclusive possession of the Spirit: "The eye cannot say to the hand, I have no need of you" (12:21); "In one Spirit we were all baptized into one body, whether Jews or Greeks, whether slaves or free, and all were given one Spirit to drink" (12:13). Given this theme, the natural interpretation of 12:1-3 is to lay all the weight upon "no-one can say *Kyrios Jesous* except in the Holy Spirit": *all* confessing believers possess the Spirit. The gentiles, led by demons, and those who curse Christ, alone do not belong to the Spirit of God. This interpretation has the merit of helping to solve another exegetical crux, in 12:8, where "faith" is included in the list of spiritual gifts, and it is often supposed that it is some special capacity to remove mountains quite different from the normal sense of faith in Paul: "To one is given through the Spirit a word of wisdom, and to another a word of knowledge according to the same Spirit, to the next faith, in the same Spirit...". The problem vanishes once we accept that Paul's main point is that the hearing of faith which can only respond to the most eloquent and brilliant preaching with the simplest confession (presumably *Kyrios Jesous*) is just as much a spiritual gift as the preaching itself.

Other Pauline texts attest that confessing Jesus as Lord is basic to faith and conversion: "If you confess with your mouth Jesus as Lord, and believe in your heart that God raised him from the dead, you shall be saved" (Rom. 10:9). The parallelism associates *Kyrios Jesous* with the resurrection, and thus with the summary of the Gospel in 1 Cor. 15:3-4 with which we began. But more significantly it shows how the confession of God's work made by faith (and thus made "in the Spirit" and "in Christ") includes a Christological confession. It says, "*Jesus* is Lord, *God* raised him". So in Rom. 1:1-4 "The gospel of *God*... concerning his *Son*... Jesus Christ our *Lord*"; 1 Cor. 8:5-6 "For even if there are alleged gods either in heaven or on earth, as there are many gods and many lords, yet to us there is one God the Father, from whom are all things and we for him, and one Lord Jesus Christ, through whom are all things and we through him"; 1 Thes. 1:9-10 "you turned from the idols to serve a living and true *God*, and to wait for his *Son* from heaven, whom he raised from the dead"; perhaps most succinctly, Phil. 2:11 "that every tongue may confess 'Jesus Christ is Lord' to the glory of God the Father". The raising of Jesus means that God is now glorified in the proclamation of Jesus

as sovereign. So though there certainly are passages, such as the
two "Abba" passages in Paul, and the account of the Spirit's
function in Rom. 8:9-11, where the Spirit unites believers to
Christ in receiving from and confessing God the Father, these must
not be allowed to obscure the Christ-directed wording of both
preaching and believing.

This view-point can be substantiated in the rest of the New
Testament. In Acts, the argument of the preachers is regularly
"That Jesus is the Christ" (9:22; 19:28). It is precisely when
Peter gets to announcing to Cornelius that Jesus was the appointed
judge of quick and dead, and that the prophets testified that
every believer would receive forgiveness through his name, that
the Spirit fell on the assembled company and they were baptized
"in the name of Jesus Christ" (10:42-8). Lampe himself writes:
"According to the wider implications of Luke's own theology, the
newness of the Christian experience of the Spirit of God consists,
not in the possession of special charismata, but in the fact that
it is derived from the exalted Lord and Christ, and that it comes
as the power and inspiration to witness to his Lordship and
Messiahship" /9/.

It has often been remarked that Luke's Gospel is peculiar in
its emphasis on the gift of the Spirit in the opening chapters,
which is difficult to reconcile with developed Christian thinking.
But on inspection this proves false. The Spirit is certainly
present, in Zechariah, Elizabeth, Symeon and Anna. But they all
make essentially Christological confessions: "Elizabeth was filled
with holy Spirit, and cried with a loud voice and said, 'Blessed
are you among women, and blessed is the fruit of your womb. How
does it come about that the mother of my Lord should come to me?'
(1:42-3). "Zechariah was filled with holy Spirit and prophesied
saying: 'Blessed be the Lord the God of Israel, because he has
visited and paid ransom for his people, and has raised up (ἔγειρεν)
a horn of salvation for us in the house of his servant David'"
(1:67-9; the subject is of course Jesus, not John who was
manifestly not of the house of David). Spirit-inspired, Symeon
holds Jesus in his arms to declare that he has seen God's promised
salvation (2:27-32). Anna the prophetess, at prayer in the Temple
as ever, stands up at that moment and acknowledges God "and she
spoke of him (i.e. Jesus) to all those who were awaiting the
redemption of Jerusalem" (2:36-8). Even John the Baptist, filled
with Holy Spirit from the womb (1:16), demonstrates the fact by
leaping for joy at the presence of the newly conceived Jesus (1:41)
(1:41). And, of course, the very conception of the Messiah is due

to the inspiration of Mary by the Spirit (1:35) and her "spirit" rejoices in the salvation God brings through her (1:47).

Apart from Luke 1:16 John the Baptist is not said to be filled with Holy Spirit. Perhaps this is because the early Christians are aware that it is a term which distinguishes Christian baptism from that of John (Acts 18:24-19:7). But there is no doubt that John is a prophet (Mark 1:6) and more than a prophet (Matthew 11:9). John's function is limited, in the New Testament texts, to bearing witness to Jesus (Mark 1:7 par.; John 1:6-8; 1:19-34; 3:22-36). Indeed his testimony includes the vision of his atoning death: "Behold the lamb of God who takes away away the world's sin" (1:29), and of his function as receiver and giver of Holy Spirit: "I did not know him, but the one who sent me to baptize with water, he told me, 'The one on whom you see the Spirit descending and staying on him, he is the baptizer with Holy Spirit'. And I have seen and am witness that he is the son of God" (1:33-4).

Broadly speaking, I hope to have shown that at least one important strand in the New Testament sees the recognizing of God in Christ as a spirit-given vision, faith or confession. Even if spiritual gifts or spiritual influence may have other effects, this is the chief one. Most of the charismatic gifts in 1 Cor. 12 have this quality; and the moral harvest of Gal. 5:22 and elsewhere is certainly compatible with it. While I would reject Lampe's attempt to see the harvest as a modelling of the believer on the moral and spiritual character of Jesus in general /10/, it is certainly possible to undertake an *imitatio Christi* and to relate a Christological prophetic charisma to it when we see the imitation as primarily an imitation of his dying, a following of the crucified, as Lampe perceives. That is what Rom. 8:1-30 is mostly about: in the Spirit, the faithful are assimilated to the sufferings and final glory of Christ. But that does not contradict the Christ-centredness of the work of the Spirit; to acknowledge Jesus as Lord is done not only with the lips but in the heart, and to be like him is the life of the true slave of Christ.

3. *Insofar as Jesus is Spirit-filled and a prophet, he shares the church's christological perspective.*

In the opening of Mark, Holy Spirit is referred to three times: John says the Stronger than he will baptize with Holy Spirit (1:8); the Spirit descends on Jesus after John baptizes him, while he is proclaimed God's Son (1:10-11); and the Spirit takes him into the desert for testing by Satan (1:12-13). The first

reference is christologically neutral. One cannot here detect what
it is to be baptized with Holy Spirit. But when Jesus receives the
baptism, he receives the Messianic designation "You are my Son",
and some would see in the further title ἀγαπητός ("beloved" or
"unique") an allusion to the suffering destiny of one like Isaac or
like the suffering prophet of Isaiah 53; and the words "in whom I
am pleased" indicate his final vindication. Whatever the words
could have meant in Jesus' time, I have little doubt that such
thoughts were near the mind of the evangelist who wrote them.
Similarly, though it is Q and not Mark who recounts the "testing of
God's Son" by the three temptations, it is reasonable to see in
what follows an extension of this concept. As with the believer
afterwards, the gift of the Spirit exposes Jesus to trial and
suffering.

Generally speaking, it is true that Mark says little about
the gift of the Spirit in the works and words of Jesus. Austin
Farrer in his *Study of Mark* attempted to show that the Spirit-
baptism is fundamental for all that Mark wrote. Every miracle,
every parable, every teaching and suffering, is an expression of
this first endowment. I do not think that Farrer has ever been
proved wrong. But the Spirit is not even mentioned in the
confession scene at Caesarea Philippi (8:27-9:1), where the
sufferings of the Son of Man are first clearly and openly predicted.
Mark does not, as Matthew does (16:17-19), see Peter's words as
inspired. But the "must" (δεῖ) of Mark 8:31 is an appeal to
scripture. In Mark, at the moment of his arrest, Jesus says, "Let
the scriptures be fulfilled" (14:49). There is also a clear
moment of prophecy before the High Priest: when asked if he is the
Christ, the Son of the Blessed, he replies, "I am, and you shall
see the son of man seated at the right hand of Power and coming
with the clouds of heaven". Almost at once he is hooded and
tormented with blows and cries of "Prophesy!" (14:61-5). Thus his
most important self-confession is regarded as a prophecy by those
who heard it. It is also, as we can see, framed in the language
and ancient prophecy (Ps. 110/109; Dn. 7:12).

It is in Luke, and before him perhaps in Q, that the
prophetic and spirit-filled character of Jesus' primary mission
is expressed. There is a famous passage, which is usually read in
Matthew 11:25-7, but may be more originally expressed in Luke 10:
21-2: "In that hour Jesus rejoiced in the holy Spirit and said,
'I praise you, Father, Lord of heaven and earth, because you have
hidden these things from wise and understanding men and have
revealed them to babes; yes, Father, because that was pleasing in
your eyes. All things have been delivered to me by my Father, and

none knows who the Son is except the Father, and who the Father is
except the Son and he to whom the Son wishes to reveal him'".
Luke adds two verses of blessing on the eyes of the disciples, who
now see what many prophets wanted to see and could not (Luke 10:
23-4 = Matthew 13:16-17). My point is only this, that in Luke and
perhaps Q the highest instance of Christological statement is
regarded as an utterance in the Spirit. And seeing and hearing
what the disciples see and hear is a God-given revelation already
set out in advance in the prophetic writings. For Luke at least,
the prophetic principle applies in the ministry of Jesus even as
in the events urrounding his birth.

We should not hastily assume that this Q passage represents a
developed and necessarily late Christology. Harnack's
interpretation of it, in terms of a universalisable conception of
sonship and fatherhood is not altogether to be despised. But
neither is the possibility that Jesus himself did speak in
prophetic vein as the mouthpiece of God, and thus claim in it a
unique authority as "son" without exclusive Logos-type claims.
After all, Montanus later said in an ecstasy, "I am God almighty",
and his disciples understood him in the terms he intended. And
when John wrote Rev. 22:16, "I am the root and the offspring of
David, the bright and morning star", no one thought he was the
messiah: he was prophesying. This Q passage and several similar
passages from the fourth gospel are discussed by J.A.T. Robinson
/12/. He shows how much even of the Johannine material makes sense
from this perspective, even if it is not how the evangelist sees
his traditional material. But this may not be the best approach to
the Q sayings. If we concentrate on the quasi-Johannine language
of the Son who reveals the Father, and try to expound it in terms
of prophetic inspiration, no Christological conclusion follows.
There is all the difference in the world between confessing God in
Christ and confessing a God who inspires Christ. In the works of
the lapidary epigram of Malchion the prosecutor of Paul of Samosata,
"Participation and substance are not alike". The Q saying omits
all the cardinal terms of the Pauline summary - Christ, the death
for sins, the resurrection, the scriptures. It may (like the
Johannine revelation theology) take on great Christological depth
when attached to the mystery of the passion, as it is when embedded
in the Gospel framework. But in itself it shows nothing, since it
fails to identify the Son and revealer as the crucified.

If there is a significant continuity between the inspiration
of Jesus and that of the Church, it must lie in something
corresponding to the core from which we began: he believed in
Christ crucified, whom God raised up the third day. At a

superficial level, of course, the evangelists attribute this belief
to him. The sufferings and resurrection on the third day are in
Mark 8:31 par., and elsewhere, and the death for sins in Mark 10:
45/Matthew 20:28 and Mark 14:24 par., though suppressed by Luke in
both cases. That John has these themes, with an omniscient Christ
who dies for many, is clear (12:23-33; 13:3). Neither of these is
specifically an inspired or prophetic utterance. But John 12:
23-33, which has striking resemblances to the Caesarea Philippi
traditions in the Synoptics, is associated with the troubling of
Jesus' soul (12:27) and a heavenly voice resembling thunder or
angel (12:28-9). These are prophetic phenomena. The death of
Jesus and the Spirit are often associated in John, as in 1:29-33;
4:19-25; 6:63; 7:37-9; 14:25-6; 16:7-15; 19:30; 20:20-22. All this
material, like that from the Synoptics, needs closer exploration
than we can now make. But perhaps we have 'indicated *prima facie*
that Jesus shared the christological/prophetic perspective of the
later church.

     There remains the theme of prophecy to be considered, and this
in two respects. First, because Jesus concretely sees his own
death as continuous with the sufferings of the prophets of the
past. And secondly, because the prophets of the past declare the
sufferings of Jesus.

     First, the prophetic destiny. If Jesus predicted his own
death, it is less likely to have been in terms of accurate
prediction of the circumstances (Mark 8:31 par.) than in terms of
the general destiny of prophets. "Happy are you when men hate you,
and when they set you apart and reproach you and reject your name
as evil for the sake of the son of man.. for just so did their
fathers to the prophets" (Luke 6:23 Q); "See, I expel demons today
and tomorrow, and the third day I am perfected; but I must travel
today and tomorrow and the next day, because it is not possible
for a prophet to perish outside Jerusalem" (luke 13:32-3).
Jerusalem stones and kills prophets (13:34-5 Q), and its leaders
fulfil the destiny of those who have slain all the prophets from
Abel to Zacharias (Luke 11:50 Q). For that saying Jesus quotes the
authority of the Wisdom of God, speaking in the third person in
prophetic style (11:49; Matthew otherwise). The passage ends with
a summarizing glance at the law-keepers who shut the door of
knowledge, and at the plot against Jesus' life, so that even here
he dies for declaring the destiny of prophets and because, as a
prophet, he champions those outside the law (11:52-3). I know that
the *order* of Luke 11:45-54 is redactional. But it is possible that,
as often, Luke has hit on the true historical formula. To see
death at the hands of the law-possessors as the prophet's destiny,

and, therefore as Jesus' destiny, comes from the Wisdom of God, who is not distinguishable from his Spirit. There can be little doubt that the parable of the vineyard and the repeated messengers (Mark 12:1-12), similarly culminating in an attempt to apprehend Jesus, has the prophetic destiny in mind.

Secondly, the prophets of the past declare the sufferings of Jesus. The evidence for this in Jesus' own teaching is difficult to assemble with assurance. Some passages are apparently schematic and late summaries (Luke 24:46; John 5:39). But there can be little doubt that he related the resurrection in general (and thus for himself) to the God of Abraham (Mark 12:18-27 par.). He also sees his own betrayal and arrest (predicted prophetically, like the desertion of his followers) as a fulfilment. But it takes a little faith to accept the view that the necessity of his death (Mark 8:31) flows from a substructure of prophetic reading, as Dodd and Hoskyns, among others, would tell us. Others may be able to help with this point. For the moment, I am advancing to another.

But I hope to have indicated at least the possibility that Jesus viewed his destiny of death and resurrection from the same perspective as the Church, i.e. inspired by the Spirit and in continuity with the prophets of old.

4.   *The prophetic vision of God in Christ is the faith of the Old Testament prophets also.*

The general point which I have made is that Christology is based on a declaration of the death and exaltation of Jesus, which is itself a spirit-given and in that sense a prophetic confession, but which is also prophetic in that it belongs to the prophets of old. Now I want to emphasize that for the basic christological confession the two forms of prophecy are one, and to suggest that Christology cannot survive except on an Old Testament base.

It is quite obvious that, though the Church asserted that Christ died for our sins and was raised according to the Scriptures, this claim could not extend to the casual reading and study of the whole text. Not until there was a more consolidated system of doctrine, and an elaborate exegetical method (as in Origen), could the total system be brought into play. The elaborations of Hebrews and Barnabas are examples of the growth of pseudo-scientific exegesis to take in new and unexpected texts. The primitive exposition had to be *selective*, i.e. to take certain basic motifs and deploy them for the interpretation of the

prophetic message as a whole. Without these basic motifs, i.e.
without the Spirit-given resurrection faith, the Old Testament
cannot be understood. As Paul explains with more vividness than
clarity, the reading of Moses in the synagogue brings no
illumination, just as the people at the foot of the Mount were not
able to look on the unveiled face of Moses. Moses, however, could
look on the Lord and participate in the Lord's glory.
Correspondingly, the heart set free by the Spirit of the Lord
looks on the Lord's glory and becomes glorious like him through
the influence of the Lord's Spirit (2 Cor. 3:4-18). So the
Christian believer is in the same relation to the Lord as Moses,
looking with unveiled face on *Kyrios*. Paul goes on (4:1-15) to
argue that his own ministry of this gospel is rejected by some,
not because he is himself deceitful, but because the hearts of the
unbelievers have been "veiled"; he himself lives out the suffering
of Jesus, "having the same Spirit of faith, as it is written: 'I
believed, therefore I spoke'" (4:13). He knows that "he who
raised the Lord Jesus from the dead will raise us also with Jesus".
Here as elsewhere the basic kerygma is used to get *more* basic
kerygma out of the ancient text, which thus comes to represent a
covenant, not of writing, but of Spirit. So the actual process of
reading the scripture truly is a prophetic function, in the sense
that it requires the illumination that the Spirit of the Lord
gives. *Exegesis is a matter of inspiration.*

     The primitive Christian interpretation of the Old Testament
texts is not the only one possible. It can be contrasted with
that of the Qumran sect, or of rabbinic and traditional Judaism,
with that of later Christian and Muslim readings of it, and with
the bewildering variety of modern critical interpretations. On
the last point, it would be true to say that the diversity and
uncertainty in detail are greater now than they have ever been.
What we do know is that the Old Testament material has been worked
over time and again, with shifts of emphasis and sometimes flat
contradictions at the time of rewriting between the material
edited and the editor. There is also new writing inspired by
earlier, late prophets inspired by earlier, late law codes
interpreting earlier, wisdom books and psalms interpreting law
books and histories. It is one of the merits of recent
interpreters of the later Jewish traditions that they see this as
a continuous process, so that the Qumran, apocryphal and rabbinic
writers are simply extending the ancient process of midrash,
whether by argumentative pesher, haggadic expansion or other
illustrative material /13/. Now it is clear that Paul and the New
Testament writers are themselves heirs of the same general
tradition. Whether their work is true or not will depend on

whether there is a divine Spirit who speaks alike in the prophets
and scribes of the old text and in the good news of the apostles of
Jesus and in Jesus himself. That means, at least, that its truth
depends on whether the concept of a Messiah who dies for our sins
truly is according to the scriptures. If that is not true, then
there is no point in asking whether the Messiah is Jesus. The
question can certainly be relevantly discussed in terms of the
character of the God of Abraham: Is he a God who promises life
through death? Similarly, the God of Moses: Is he a God who
finally reveals himself face to face to those who turn to him?
One would probably not be able to avoid a central *paschal* theme:
Is the God of the Passover a God who personally delivers his chosen
from bondage in every generation? This has profound ramifications
for the significance of the death of Christ and for baptismal and
eucharistic thought. But Christology will collapse, and should
collapse, unless the sort of continuity can be verified. But even
when it is said, and even if the Christian midrash can be seen as
organically continuous with the development of the Old Testament,
and even if it can be seen as spiritually continuous with it in
intellectual terms so as to be an appropriate interpretation of it,
that does not in itself verify the Gospel. There is a least a
plausible spiritual continuity between Jewish orthodoxy or Islam
and the Old Testament, as well. The Gospel can only be verified
if in the case of Jesus the plausibility is actually fulfilled by
God himself, i.e. if God raised him from the dead and made him
both Lord and Christ. Then and only then is the confession Spirit-
inspired, a prophetic word from the true God, when it says "Jesus
Christ is Lord, to the glory of God the Father". Plainly, we could
start a whole new discussion about the meaning and verifiability of
the words "God raised Jesus from the dead, and made him both Lord
and Christ". But it remains true that without it Christology has
no beginning and no meaning.

NOTES

/1/   C.F.D. Moule, *The origin of Christology*, Cambridge (1977),
127-34.
/2/   C.H. Dodd, *According to the Scriptures*, London (1952).
/3/   G.W.H. Lampe, *God as Spirit: The Bampton Lectures 1976*,
Oxford (1977).
/4/   Op.cit., 111.
/5/   Op. cit., 79.
/6/   Op. cit., 168-171.
/7/   *The origin of Christology*, pp. 95 etc.

/8/   W.C. van Unnik, Jesus Anathema or Kyrios (1 Cor. 12,3),
*Christ and Spirit in the New Testament: Studies in honour of
C.F.D. Moule,* Cambridge (1973), 113-26.
/9/   *God as Spirit,* 69.
/10/   *God as Spirit,* 78f.; cf. 103f.
/11/   London (1951).
/12/   The use of the Fourth Gospel for Christology today, in *Christ
and Spirit in the New Testament: Studies in honour of C.F.D. Moule,*
Cambridge (1973), 61-78.
/13/   For example, Rene Bloch, Midrash, in *Supplement au
Dictionnaire de la Bible V,* 1263-81; G. Vermes, *Scripture and
tradition in Judaism,* Leiden (1961).

Studia Biblica 1978: III, 173-197

Hymn and Christology *

Prof. Dr. Martin Hengel,
University of Tübingen.

The liturgical form of worship in the early missionary churches is one of the many puzzling problems in the New Testament. As Hans Lietzmann, certainly an expert on this matter, remarked, there are "so many questions and so many unsolved problems" /1/. He offered the following plausible explanation: "There is little or no information about liturgy in the early writers; probably this was because such matters seemed too self-evident to need recording. Nor would Paul have discussed any of these if disorders had not arisen in Corinth causing him to issue exhortations and to give directions" /2/. What Paul states in *1 Cor.* 14 concerning the order of public worship will have to satisfy us for the time being.

I

Let us start by taking a look at the New Testament. In *1 Cor.* 14:26, Paul describes the order of public worship as follows: "What then, brethren? When you come together, each one has a hymn (ἕκαστος ψαλμὸν ἔχει), a lesson, a revelation, a tongue, or an interpretation. Let all things be done for edification". This listing reflects the many ways in which the gifts of the Spirit are at work in the divine service. It should be noted in particular that Paul places the hymn first in the list. Apparently, it had special significance for him in the worshipping community. Perhaps the service opened with a hymn /3/. It is also no accident that Paul uses the Greek word "ψαλμός" here (a word that could be misunderstood by the Greek reader) and not " ὕμνος ", or even "παιάν". To the Greek, ψαλμός meant lyre music. In the Septuagint, this word is used in the psalm headings to render the Hebrew "mizmor". In Hellenistic Judaism, it therefore acquired the special meaning of "religious song". The use of a new word by the translator of the Septuagint was certainly not

unintentional since the Jewish psalm differed considerably
from the traditional Greek "hymn to the gods"; the Greek hymn
had a strict metre dependent upon accented and unaccented
syllables. Paul assumes that the word "ψαλμός" would be
understood in its non-Greek and therefore its Jewish
connotation. This, at the same time, indicates the tradition
of the missionary churches with regard to their religious
hymnal poetry which was inspired by the Spirit.

From the context, it can also be seen that the sung
"ψαλμός" was not the memorized Old Testament "psalm", but
rather a *new* song given by the Spirit. It is, of course, clear
that this song was rendered in such a way that it could be
understood by all members of the community. It may well have
been memorized to facilitate community singing. The songs
were intended for the edification of the worshipping community
and, therefore, were not the glossollalic songs with which Paul
and the Corinthians were also familiar /4/. Next to instruction
and revelation, the hymn constituted a fundamental part of the
inspired Service of the Word in the Pauline missionary churches.

II

This picture is confirmed by two deutero-pauline
references, *Col*. 3:16-17 and *Eph*. 5:19-20. The *Col*. 3 passage
states:

> "Let the word of Christ dwell in you richly;|in all
> wisdom teach and admonish one another|with spiritual
> psalms and hymns and songs in the state of grace,|
> singing in your hearts to God. | And whatever you do,
> in word or deed,|do everything in the name of the
> Lord Jesus,|giving thanks to God the Father through him".

In *Eph*. 5:18-20, we read:

> "... but be filled with the spirit, addressing one another
> in psalms and hymns and spiritual songs,|singing and
> psalmodying to the Lord with all your heart,|always and
> for everything giving thanks|in the name of our Lord
> Jesus Christ to God the Father".

The Ephesians text is clearly dependent on the Colossians
text and, as such, constitutes the first commentary to this
text. We accept the punctuation of Westcott-Hort and Lightfoot

rather than that of the Nestle text and the Revised Standard
Version. ψαλμοῖς ὕμνοις ᾠδαῖς πνευματικαῖς should be understood
as referring to the preceding participles διδάσκοντες and
νουθετοῦντες. The author of Ephesians understood the text in
this way since he combined both participles in the one word
λαλοῦντες. In our opinion, the argument that liturgical
singing could hardly have served to teach and admonish is
unconvincing. It is precisely the hymn texts in the epistles
that have a teaching character and serve the paranesis. We
should not, however, allow ourselves to be sidetracked by this
problem. Our exegesis, in any case, should begin with λόγος
τοῦ Χριστοῦ since the meaning of the rest of the text is
derived from this phrase. In the assemblies for worship, the
word of Christ is to be a "testimony" to the events of
salvation as revealed in the life and work of Christ. This
"word" should govern everything else. It is striking that in
the New Testament the phrase "word of Christ" is used only
here. The author apparently wants to emphasize the
christological character of the "word" proclaimed in the
service. It is to "dwell in you richly" (and this means, at
the same time, always new) and "in all wisdom".

For the author, the word of Christ is concretely expressed
in public worship through the variety of songs which serve both
to teach and to admonish the worshipping community. The
various charismatic hymnists and singers are to edify the
assembly with their songs. Examples of songs that were
understood as "word of Christ" can be found in the New
Testament epistles, particularly in *Colossians* and *Ephesians*.

The three consecutive words ψαλμοί, ὕμνοι and ᾠδαί reflect
the abundance of terms, but they should not be understood as
characterizations for various *types* of songs. They are the
three most important terms used in the Septuagint to describe
a religious song /5/. As such, the terms are interchangeable.
It, however, is no accident that ψαλμός, the most important
term, is given first mention.

The adjective πνευματικός, following the three nouns,
demonstrates that the song in the service of worship is inspired
by the Spirit. The songs are gifts of the πνεῦμα; they are not
"human precepts and doctrines" (*Col.* 2:22), but rather "word
of Christ".

The last part of the sentence "sing in your hearts to God"

indicates that the previously mentioned song of worship is a
singing from the heart *in praise of God*. This means that the
Spirit, who gives this song, does not move only the lips but
first of all the heart, the innermost part of man. The
assembly permits the word of Christ to dwell among it when it
sings psalms of Christ which teach and admonish by recounting
in song Christ's act of salvation. In doing so, it gives glory
to God the Father of Jesus Christ. The conclusion of the
Philippian hymn "to the glory of God the Father" (*Phil*. 2:11)
is then completely consistent /6/. For the author of *Colossians*
as well as all other New Testament authors, the unity between
God and his Christ is obvious, in spite of all references to
Christ's subordination.

Our understanding is confirmed by the interpretation of
our text given in *Eph*. 5:18-19. Here, the simple imperative
"be filled with the Spirit" /7/, a command emphasizing that
the hymn in Christian worship is a gift of the Spirit, replaces
the demand "Let the word of Christ dwell in you richly...".
Teaching and admonishing have been combined in "addressing one
another"; but singing, ἄδοντες is supplemented by ψάλλοντες.
ψάλλειν does not mean lyre-playing, but rather psalmody, a form
of singing characteristic for Jewish tradition. Since the
number of syllables was not fixed in the verse line of the
psalm, no melody could be composed. A melodious introduction
and conclusion were permitted for each verse; a monotone was
prescribed for the remaining middle part of the verse. This
psalm form lent itself to a variety of possibilities; it could
be used either for short acclamatory litanies or for extensive
hymnological texts.

The "to God" (τῷ θεῷ) found in *Col*. 3:16 is replaced in
Eph. 5:19 by "to the Lord" (τῷ κυρίῳ). It most certainly ought
to be interpreted christologically. The shift in terminology
confirms the observation that the "hymn to Christ", as found in
the New Testament, is used more often in early Christian
worship than is the "hymn to God". This is certainly no mere
accident; the hymn to Christ was not only a special feature of
Christian cultic celebration distinguishing it from synagogue
worship, but also an expression of the fact that God reveals
his salvation only through his Son /8/.

Let us summarize what has been said up to this point.

The liturgical song was important for the public worship of
the early Christian missionary churches and constituted an
integral part of this worship.

This song was not only traditional singing but, just as often,
spontaneous poetry. It was not a human creation, but solely
the work of the Holy Spirit.

The content of this liturgical song was determined by the act
of salvation brought about in Christ, i.e., it was predominantly
a hymn to Christ.

In terms of *form*, it was a "psalm", i.e., the strict metre
found in Greek religious hymns was absent. The song was
derived from Old Testament and Jewish song tradition. In terms
of *musical presentation,* it resembled the psalmody found inside
this tradition.

III

The most detailed description of a "service of worship" in
the New Testament, chapters 4 and 5 of *Revelation,* uniquely
combines and interweaves hymns to God and to Christ. This,
however, is the heavenly worship before the throne of God and
not an earthly service. According to Jewish and Christian
tradition, the heavenly cult and worship are the very centre
of the world and of history. Therefore, one cannot simply
assume that these liturgical texts were taken from the worship
service of the community. Instead they were formulated by the
seer himself in the light of his work /9/. At the same time,
however, it is entirely possible that the author of the
Apocalypse indirectly refers to the liturgical practices of
his community. In spite of his Christian independence, the
author is apparently also strongly influenced by the apocalyptic
descriptions of the heavenly temple and cult. Such descriptions
first appeared in *Isaiah* 6 and *Ezekiel* 1 and continued through
the *hekhalot*-literature of Jewish mysticism and its hymns.

The account of the appearance of Christ in *Rev.* 5
represents the climax of this development. As the "slain"
sacrificial lamb, he alone is worthy to receive from God's hand
the mysterious sealed scroll of future judgement. With this
act, he, the crucified κύριος, is installed as God's
eschatological representative and entrusted with the execution
of God's plan for salvation and judgement. As a sign of the

authority granted him, the four living creatures and the
twenty-four elders fall down before him and worship him by
singing a *new song*. This setting, as well as the emphasis of
the singing and the "new song", lend a unique significance to
this first hymn to the Christ of the New Era. The hymn begins
with an acclamatory "Worthy art thou" (ἄξιος εἶ) which
introduces the new messianic ruler as the one delegated by God.

> "Worthy are thou to take the scroll
>   and to open its seals,
> for thou wast slain and by thy blood
>   didst ransom men for God
> from every tribe and tongue and
>   people and nation,
> and hast made them a kingdom and
>   priests to our God,
> and they shall reign on earth" (*Rev.* 6:9b-10)

This hymnic description of the saving act of Christ and
its consequences is followed by a further intensification of
the choir of all heavenly beings. The ἄξιος-doxology attributes
to the "slain" lamb seven predicates which had previously been
reserved only for God. In other words, the adoration received
by Christ is in no way inferior to the praise and worship
belonging only to God.

The heavenly worship reaches its climax in the second
doxology. The scene is now "opened up". Every "creature in
heaven and on earth and under the earth and in the sea and all
therein" join in a choir praising God *and* his Son:

> "To him who sits upon the throne and to the Lamb be
> blessing and honour and glory and might for ever and
> ever"! (*Rev.* 5:13).

It should be noted that the description of the heavenly
cult presented in *Revelation* 4-5 introduces the course of the
eschatological events. The *new song*, the scene with the sealed
scroll, and the sudden appearance of the "lamb" truly represent
a *new beginning*. In contrast to the eternal liturgy with the
trishagion before the throne of God, it represents a break, for
the beginning of the unparalleled eschatological events is
portrayed in Chapters 5 and following. In contrast with all
the other hymn texts of the Apocalyptist's work, he introduces
the first hymn to Christ as ᾠδὴ καινή, a new song. In doing

so, he sets this scene apart in an unusual way. The "new
song" is a fixed concept in the biblical psalms. The "old
song" is no longer adequate because God has performed new and
marvellous things. In Deutero-Isaiah, the song is an
eschatological doxology initiated by the new things God will
reveal:

> "'... new things I now declare;
> before they spring forth
>   I tell you of them'.
> Sing to the Lord a new song
>   his praise from the end of the earth"!
>   (*Is.* 42:9b-10a)

In *Revelation*, the motif is found only in 14:3, and here
it is a hymn sung by the angelic hosts before the Lamb and
the redeemed 144,000 on Mount Zion. This "new song" can only
be understood by members of the redeemed community. This,
however, means that the author intentionally relates the "new
song" to Christ and his redeemed congregation. The
christological hymn is a "new song" because it describes the
eschatological renewal of creation by the God-appointed
Messiah. Its theme in *Rev.* 5:9, therefore, is similar to that
of most New Testament hymns to Christ. It deals, first of all,
with the *death of Jesus* by encompassing his significance for
universal salvation. Chapter 5 considered as a whole, also
deals with the glorification and/or exaltation of Jesus which
causes all heavenly powers and creatures to pay homage to him
and also with his equal status to God in his sharing the throne
with him.

IV

Both chapters 4 and 5 of *Revelation* describe the heavenly
worship service. This description, therefore, could be
characterized as a "prologue in heaven" to the eschatological
events mentioned in chapters 6ff. This "prologue", however,
already anticipates the completion of God's rule mentioned in
the concluding doxology of *Rev.* 5:13. The seer's description
of this event in his vision of the "open door" to heaven is
typical for New Testament songs to Christ. The eschatological
era, therefore, is anticipated. Anonymous, spirit-filled poets
summarized the true heavenly drama seen by the seer "through
the Spirit". Here are a few examples:

"Therefore God has highly exalted him∣and bestowed on
him the name∣which is above every name,∣that at the name
of Jesus∣every knee should bow,∣in heaven and on earth
and under earth,∣and every tongue confess∣that Jesus
Christ is Lord,∣to the glory of God the Father".
(*Phil.* 2:9-11).

"... He was manifested in the flesh,
    vindicated in the Spirit,
    seen by angels,
    preached among the nations,
    believed on in the world,
    taken up in glory". (*1 Tim.* 3:16).

"He reflects the glory of God and bears the very stamp
of his nature,∣upholding the universe by his word of
power. ∣ When he had made purification for sins,∣he sat
down at the right hand of the Majesty on high".
(*Heb.* 1:3).

It would be helpful to take a look at the continuation of
this last hymn fragment. The author of Hebrews clearly reverts
to prose in v.4. The influence of the preceding hymn to Christ
is still evident /10/: Christ "having become as much superior to
angels as the name he has obtained is more excellent than
theirs" (*Heb.* 1:4). *Hebrews* is certainly unique in this
regard; the author is not content just to quote the hymn to
Christ and to seeing the consequences of the position of the
exalted Christ. He goes even further and points out the unique
position of Christ in the heavenly realm and in relation to all
creatures, including the angels, by quoting additional texts
from Old Testament "hymns" /11/. These six hymn texts include
Ps. 110:1, the most important christological text in the Old
Testament. The author had already alluded to it in the hymn
cited (1:3). In conformity with early Christian understanding,
he states here the same thing described in the "prologue in
heaven" of *Rev.* 4 and 5.

"For to what angels has he ever said
    'Sit at my right hand
    till I make thy enemies a stool for thy feet'?"
(*Heb.* 1:13).

It is remarkable how Old Testament psalms, to a certain
extent, are automatically understood as hymns to Christ in

Heb. 1. This type of interpretation is continued in ch. 2, where *Ps.* 8, a wisdom psalm, is quoted in verses 6-8 /12/. In its Old Testament context, the psalm referred to man.

> "What is man that thou art mindful
>   of him,
> or the son of man, that thou carest
>   for him?
> Thou didst make him for a little
>   while lower than the angels
> Thou has crowned him with glory
>   and honour,
> putting everything in subjection
>   under his feet".   (Ps. 8:5-7, *[LXX]*).

The christological interpretation brings this psalm text closer to the "prologue in heaven" of *Rev.* 5 since "everything" here refers to all creation. There is nothing which God did not put in subjection to him, even though we "do not yet see everything in subjection to him". Jesus, however, "who for a little while was made lower than the angels" was "crowned with glory and honour because of the suffering of death". If we disregard the notion of pre-existence which the author of Hebrews reads into the text of *Ps.* 8, we find the same christological pattern for the interpretation of this psalm in *Heb.* 2 as in the songs of *Rev.* 5. Parallels with the hymn in *Phil.* 2:9-11 are also obvious. There are three main points of comparison:

1.   Christ's sacrificial death is the reason for his
      exaltation.

2.   The reference in *Ps.* 8:7 to crowning with "glory" and
      "honour" is reflected in the repetition of "honour" and
      "glory" in both doxologies of *Rev.* 5:12 and 5:13 as well
      as in the bestowing "of the name which is above every name"
      of *Phil.* 2:9b.

3.   The subjection of all creation mentioned in *Ps.* 8:7 is
      reflected in *Rev.* 5:13 by the homage of all creatures
      before God and the Lamb, and in *Phil.* 2:11 by the equally
      important universal confession of all created beings
      before the κύριος.

Apparently, what we have here is an extremely old christological formula which is expressed in various ways. It is found in the interpretation of Old Testament psalms, in the apocalyptic vision of the heavenly worship to the glorification of the slain Messiah, and in the hymn to Christ. It appears in different periods of time, at different places, and in different contexts in tradition history.

V

It should be obvious by now that our main problem - the hymn to Christ in the early Christian worship service and its significance for the development of christology - cannot be understood if we do not consider those Old Testament texts which decisively influenced the development of christological thought; that is the "Christ-psalms", in addition to the "hymns to Christ" and the "hymn fragments" in the New Testament epistles and *Revelation*. The following three hymn fragments clearly reflect this influence:

1 Peter 3:18-22:

> "For Christ also died for sins once for all, | the righteous for the unrighteous, | that he might bring us to God, | being put to death in the flesh | but made alive in the spirit; | ... who has gone into heaven and is *at the right hand of God,* with angels, authorities, and powers *subject* to him.

Eph. 1:20-22:

> "... when he raised him from the dead and made him sit *at his right hand* ... | and he put *all things under his feet* | and has made him the head over all things ..."

Rom. 8:34:

> "... It is Christ Jesus, who died, | yes, who was raised from the dead, | who is *at the right hand of God,* | who indeed intercedes for us ..."

All these texts refer to the death and/or raising of Christ and his exaltation *at the right hand of God:* The motif can be traced back to the Christ-psalm, *Ps.* 110. It is the only Old Testament passage referring to enthronement at the

right hand of God. No other Old Testament text has been so
influential on the development of christology. On the other
hand, however, it should be noted that the fragments from
Ephesians and *1 Peter* that refer to *Ps*. 110:1 do not answer
all our questions. The formula "he has put all things under
his feet" in *Eph*. 1:22 is a quotation taken from a second
Christ-psalm, *Ps*. 8:7. We are already familiar with this
psalm from *Heb*. 2:7. The allusion is certainly more than
accidental. The connection between both psalms, from which
the early Christian interpreter drew the two different "titles"
of κύριος and υἱὸς ἀνθρώπου is intentional. This is also true
for the first fragment mentioned here. *Ps*. 110 is quoted in
1 Peter 3:22: "the right hand of God"; the formula "angels,
authorities, and powers subject to him" is dependent on *Ps*. 8:7:
"putting everything in subjection"; the verb ὑποτάσσειν is used
in both cases (*1 Peter* 3:22; *Ps*. 8:7). The special effect of
Ps. 8 is considerably less important with regard to the
enthronement at the right hand of God than *Ps*. 110. Primitive
Christianity understood the enthronement in the light of the
resurrected and exalted Christ, who then shared God's throne.
This understanding is found in almost all the important New
Testament texts.

The earliest reference by Paul in *Rom*. 8:34 reflects the
most interesting aspect of the tradition history. This
formula was clearly taken over from a hymn fragment since the
Pauline formulation "is at the right hand of God" appears word
for word in a hymnological context in *1 Peter* 3:22. Compared
to the quotation from *Ps*. 110:1, this Pauline version is
already a polished secondary form with a long tradition
history. Paul refers to the exalted Christ sitting at the
"right hand of God" only in this one passage, and here in a
fixed liturgical formulation that presupposes familiarity on
the part of those to whom the epistle was addressed.

The concluding line of *Rom*. 8:34 "who indeed intercedes
for us" which follows the enthronement "on the right hand of
God" is another helpful passage in Paul. ἐντυγχάνειν was used
in the Hellenistic world to mean 'beseech', 'pray', or even
'intercede'. The only other place we find it used in this way
is in *Heb*. 7:24-25 where the 'eternal' priesthood of Christ
is described in the words of *Ps*. 110:4; "but he holds his
priesthood permanently, because he continues for ever.
Consequently he is able for all time to save those who draw
near to God through him, since he always lives to make

intercession for them" /14/. The relationship of *Rom*. 8:34 to
Heb. 7:25b is obvious, even the formulation is similar. This
gives reason to assume that the tradition of the exalted
Christ as High Priest, which is developed in Hebrews in such a
unique way, was based on the hymn fragment already used by
Paul. It is therefore not difficult to uncover the origin of
the tradition. If *Rom*. 8:34c "who is at the right hand of God"
can be traced back to *Ps*. 110:1, the priestly intercession of
the exalted Christ in 8:34 might best be attributed to *Ps*. 110:4.
We are familiar with this passage from Hebrews: "Thou art a
priest for ever after the order of Melchizedek" (7:17). If
this is, in fact, the case, it would mean that *Rom*. 8:34 is
an early witness to the strong influence of *Ps*. 110 on the
development of a relatively old "hymn to Christ".

     The high priest motif had not been dealt with to any
great extent in interpretations of Psalm 110 until *Hebrews*.
It is very possible that another concept, namely the κύριος,
was much more important at that time. Next to the title
χριστός, κύριος was the title used most frequently by Paul.
A basically uncritical criticism committed an historical "fall
of man" when it attempted to attribute *this* title to the
alleged Hellenistic mystery cults. The title was accorded an
important place in a relatively early hymn to Christ; we have
only to look at the second verse of the hymn in Philippians
where "the name which is above every name", the designation
for God, κύριος, representing the *Tetragrammaton* was applied to
the crucified and exalted Christ. This interpretation of the
Christ-psalm, *Ps*. 110, goes back to an earlier period, however,
namely to the very beginnings of the primitive church.

     When the primitive church in Jerusalem, guided by the
power of the Spirit, began to interpret its overwhelming
experience of Jesus' resurrection theologically, it must have
quickly seen the importance of this psalm which was so unique
even in the Old Testament. The early effect can be seen by
its twofold use in the Markan synoptic tradition /15/. It is
entirely possible that Jesus alluded to it in his authoritative
statement before the High Priest /16/. Be this as it may, the
experience that Jesus was the crucified Messiah whom God raised
from the dead, and that he was the expected Son of Man, quickly
developed into the assurance that God had enthroned this Jesus,
the former *rabbi* as *adonay* at his right hand in accordance
with *Ps*. 110:1. This statement was so startling and so
revolutionary that, compared with the other statements in the

Psalms, the priesthood or pre-existence in *Ps*. 110:3 retreated
temporarily into the background. This then would explain why
the allusions concentrated on the first verse and why it later
proved to have such a strong influence on the hymns to Christ.
Through this Lord, the worshipping community was able to enter
the heavenly sanctuary /17/ with its inspired prayers and
songs, just as we find described in *Rev*. 5:8. His sitting at
the right hand of God created a permanent analogy between the
worship before the throne of God and that of the troubled
earthly community. As Lord, the community could call upon him
in the prayer *maranatha* to return as quickly as possible /18/.
This prayer was more than just a request for the immediate
parousia; it was also an expression of the close relationship
which Jesus' disciples had with their Lord who had been
elevated to share God's throne; an expression of the earliest
spirit-filled enthusiasm of the primitive church.

VI

On the basis of what has been said up to now, it can be
seen that the hymn to Christ strongly influenced the worship
of the primitive church and the development of christology.
This hymn type described Christ's saving act, particularly his
death and its soteriological implications, and, in the later
development of tradition, his pre-existence, mediation of
creation, and incarnation. Unfortunately, we do not have time
here for a detailed discussion of the understanding of
pre-existence. The main emphasis in each individual song may
be different. The hymn in *1 Peter* 2:21-25 is completely based
on *Is*. 53. It concentrates on the death of Jesus and the
salvation brought about by his death. The hymn in *Col*. 1:15-20
stresses the universal mediation of creation (vv.15-17) and the
reconciliation of "all things, whether on earth or in heaven"
(v.20) effected by Jesus' death. The prologue in the Gospel of
John refers particularly to the pre-existence of Jesus with
God and the incarnation of the *Logos*. In spite of the
differences in the individual motifs, most of the hymns and
hymn fragments have one theme in common: The contradiction and,
at the same time, the inner relationship between the death of
Jesus and his exaltation as described in the visionary
"prologue in heaven" of *Rev*. 5. Enthronement, authorization
of the resurrected Christ and, at the same time, the homage of
the divine and wordly powers, i.e., all of creation, belong to
this exaltation complex.

Two arguments could be raised to this theory. The number of
definitely identified hymns to Christ is not very large, and
the attempt to identify this type of hymn fragments in the
various New Testament epistles has not always been very
convincing /19/. The difference between hymnological prose
and the early Christian psalms, the metre of which often
cannot be established, is sometimes extremely difficult to
demonstrate. The New Testament epistles, however, are prose
texts. It is remarkable enough when the poetically constructed
texts can be identified. Eduard Norden /20/ presented formal
criteria for identifying poetic texts that have been generally
accepted. Next to the *parallelismus membrorum,* mention should
be made of the pronominal beginning, the use of descriptive
participles, the relative clauses, and the causal connection
with διά, ὅτι, ἵνα (corresponding to the $k\bar{\imath}$ of the psalms).
Sometimes a doxology is placed at the end. The secondary
additions are often difficult to discern. The eliminative
process becomes more hypothetical as more text is eliminated.
Differentiation between more detailed acclamations (e.g.,
1 Cor. 8:6) and the confessional formulae such as those found
in *Rom*. 1:3ff; 4:25; or *2 Cor*. 13:4 is not an easy task. These
formulae themselves could be fragments or verses taken from a
larger hymn unit. In spite of all the differences, some
agreement has been reached concerning the most important hymn
texts. In his history of the literature of the Primitive Church
(Geschichte der urchristlichen Literatur, Berlin-New York 1975),
Vielhauer lists six accepted texts in addition to the puzzling
fragment in *Eph*. 5:14, the Johannine prologue, and the hymns to
Christ found in *Revelation*. He also lists seven other
fragments that he considers to be "less certain". Deichgräber,
who is the most careful methodologically, gives five hymns of
Christ and four "smaller fragments". Wengst investigated a
total of nine New Testament texts, including the Johannine
prologue. The four hymn fragments from the nativity canticles
of *Luke* should also be mentioned. In contrast to this fairly
cautious observation, Schille maintains that he discovered more
than 30 New Testament hymn texts. His tendency to exaggerate
has more or less discredited the search for hymn texts in the
New Testament. By and large, there are a dozen christological
texts originating within a 50 to 60 year period (40-100 AD)
that are extremely important for our understanding of the early
development of christology (the Johannine prologue is included
in these texts, but *Revelation* is not). References to
composition of songs can be found in Pliny, the Letters of
Ignatius, and the *Odes of Solomon*. Afterwards however, the

references seem to stop. Justin's order of public worship does
not indicate any familiarity with the singing of extemporaneous
hymns; the order of worship is completely adapted to the service
of the word in the synagogue and includes the reading of
biblical texts and prayers. The difference between this later
order of public worship and the free activity of the Spirit in
the early period is considerable. The fact that second century
Christian gnosticism adopted the composition of hymns and,
according to the examples in the Naassene Hymn and the
fragments from Valentinus, used strict anapestic metre may be
a few reasons for this difference. In the writings of
Valentinus, Basilides, and Marcion, the hymns appear with the
names of the lyricists, i.e., a designation of the "intellectual"
property. The metre and the designation of the lyricist can be
considered an index for the "acute Hellenization of Christianity"
by gnosticism /21/.

From the period of the Pauline mission until Ignatius, the
liturgical song to Christ clearly exerted a strong influence on
the development of christological thought. Several questions
should be asked in this regard which will help us to understand
the problem better.

1.   Is it so impossible that the liturgical song to Christ was
     influential for a whole series of christological
     statements for which no song fragments can be established?
     We attempted to illustrate this sort of influence with
     Ps.110 and, to a lesser extent, with *Ps*. 8. Certainly
     these psalms were not "new songs" but rather Old Testament
     "Christ-psalms".

2.   Another question then immediately arises: Are the Old
     Testament "Christ-psalms" that were so influential for
     the development of christology directly related to the
     development of the hymns to Christ of early Christian
     worship or, compared with Old Testament-Jewish psalmody,
     are they basically a new form?

3.   This then brings us to our real problem. Can the
     development of the hymns to Christ be traced back beyond
     the Pauline epistles to that "silent" period between 30
     and 50 AD where the real and decisive christological
     development occurred?

4.   This, at the same time, raises questions for the history
     of religion: Is the early Christian hymn a product of
     the syncretically influenced enthusiasm of the Hellenistic
     missionary churches? If so, are its closest parallels
     to be found in the hymns of the mystery religions or the
     more "oriental" songs of the philosophic-gnostic circles
     such as those found in sections of the Corpus
     Hermeticum/22/? Can one assume, as German research often
     has, that the songs in early Christian texts were
     originally gnostic songs taken over with only a few minor
     changes?

5.   Concerning this thesis, it could be argued that "official"
     Pharisaic Judaism was not familiar with the singing of
     hymns in its synagogue worship, if we exclude the
     recitation of certain canonical psalms, such as the Hallel,
     on festival day. The religious hymns, the so-called
     piyyutim, were first introduced into synagogue worship
     between the fifth and sixth centuries and were not
     immediately accepted /23/.

                              VII

     The difference between the Pharisaic influence on the
synagogue service in Palestine and the reports that we have
of the Pauline assemblies in *1 Cor.* 14 even led such an
eminent scholar as Walter Bauer to assert that the worship of
the gentile Christian missionary churches was not only
superficially related to the synagogue celebrations but also
much more closely to the model of the mystery celebrations or
the hermetic-gnostic conventicles with their hymns, acclamations
and enthusiastic-ecstatic language /24/. This thesis, however,
must be emphatically rejected. It may well be true that the
usage of institutionalized psalmody in Palestine was confined
particularly to the temple and its great Levitical choirs, and
that Pharisaic synagogue worship was only familiar with
prayers, reading of biblical texts, and sermons. This Pharisaic
order of worship, however, was in no case the only form of
worship, even for Palestine. In addition to the hymns of the
nativity narratives of *Luke* and the *Psalms of Solomon*, the
Qumran texts attest to the abundance of religious hymns,
particularly for Jewish Palestine, which were sung during the
worship service in Qumran /25/. The refusal of the rabbinic
synagogue to accept hymns may well be related to the exclusion
of heretics. The Jewish diaspora was more free. According to

Philo, hymnody was extremely important. His statement
concerning the celebrations of the Jewish Therapeutae in Egypt,
which Eusebius then interpreted as Christian cultic celebrations,
reminds us very much of the worship of the primitive church.

Unquestionably, the "ψαλμός" of 1 Cor. 14:26 and the
"ψαλμοί" of Col. 3:16 and Eph. 5:19 stand in the tradition of
Old Testament-Jewish psalms. Only someone who was familiar
with the tradition could describe the liturgical song in this
way. The assumptions that the inspired early Christian hymn
has its closest parallels in the inspiration of Hellenistic
mysticism is not convincing. Certainly since Homer and Hesiod,
the Greeks almost fully accepted the idea of divine inspiration
of the poet. There, however, are also analogous understandings
in Judaism which are just as highly developed. One only has
to recall the well-known psalm passage "O Lord, open thou my
lips, and my mouth shall show forth thy praise" /26/. In the
"Last Words" of David in 2 Sam. 23:1-3, David himself confesses
that the spirit of God speaks through him:

> "The oracle of David, the son of Jesse,
> (the oracle of the man who was raised on high,
> the anointed of the God of Jacob,
> the sweet psalmist of Israel).
> The Spirit of the Lord speaks by me
> his word is upon my tongue". (vss. 1-2).

For ancient Judaism, David was not only a king but, as a
psalmist, also a great prophet inspired by the Spirit. Philo
quotes the psalms more than any other Old Testament text except
the Pentateuch. Next to Isaiah, primitive Christianity most
frequently quoted the psalter. This understanding is reflected
in a David text in the Psalms Scroll from Qumran Cave 11:

> "And the Lord gave him a discerning and enlightened spirit.
> And he wrote 3,600 psalms; ... And all the songs that he
> spoke were 446, and songs for making music over the
> stricken, 4. And the total was 4,050. All these he
> spoke through prophecy bnbw°h, which was given him from
> before the Most High". (vv. 3-11) /27/.

The idea that the song of praise to God was inspired is
just as strongly anchored in ancient Judaism as in the
Hellenistic world. The idea was more pronounced there, where
an awareness of the unique eschatological relationship between
the earthly world and the heavenly world was present.

VIII

Such an awareness was present in the first post-Easter
community; the primitive church in Jerusalem was fundamentally
influenced by this relationship. The appearance of the
resurrected Christ and the experience of the Spirit re-formed
its consciousness, and the worship service of the early
congregation became the spontaneous work of the Spirit. This
Spirit inspired the Christian prophets to admonitions,
"revelations", visions, and also to *glossolalia*. The
ecstatic-enthusiastic form of worship was certainly not a new
development in the gentile Christian missionary churches; it
goes back to the very beginnings of the church. The element
of enthusiasm distinguishes early Christian worship from the
order of worship in the synagogue cult. The congregation was
directly connected with the heavenly sanctuary through their
resurrected and exalted Lord, and the Lord himself was truly
present in their midst through the Spirit. God's rule was no
longer expected in the indefinite future, it was already
beginning here and now. If Jesus was the "first raised from
the dead" (*1 Cor.* 15:20), the Spirit was his "first fruits".
This unique eschatological-messianic self-consciousness of the
first community departed from the traditional forms and
conventions of worship and created something new. The picture
of the primitive community portrayed by Luke in *Acts* 2 to 5 is
neither exaggerated nor too idealistic. If anything, it is too
colourless and modest. The Early Christians were certain that
the Spirit of the prophets, which had withdrawn from Israel
with Ezra, was with them, more powerful than ever before.
The Spirit not only instructs the community, as it had the
Teacher of Righteousness, "to interpret all the words of his
servants, the prophets" (*1QpHab* 2:8f) /28/, but it also made
prophets of the members of the Jesus community. Just as in the
Old Testament, the activity of the Spirit included praise of
God's acts in song as well as prophecy and vision. A new
and inspired hymnody developed out of this tradition.

The Old Testament hymns were chanted and sung in a new way.
Naturally the "messianic" psalms and those psalms which could
be interpreted as messianic were included. In *Ps.* 2 (quoted
also in the Testimonies from Qumran), God adopts the Messiah
as his Son. In *Ps.* 8 (closely related to *Ps.* 110 and in a
certain way its "shadow") refers to the eschatological
exaltation of the Son of Man and the subjection of all powers
to him. *Ps.* 22 describes both the suffering of the Messiah
and his wonderful resurrection; *Ps.* 45, his exaltation and
divine status; *Ps.* 69, his suffering; *Ps.* 89, his inauguration
as "first born". The *hallel*-psalm, *Ps.* 118, is also important;
it is the last psalm that Jesus sang with his disciples before

the passion, and it is the psalm containing the description of
the stone rejected by the builders that became the head of the
corner (v.22) and the vision of the triumphant return of Christ
which portrays Jesus' destiny in a very specific way. The
liturgical use of *Ps*. 118:26 must go back to the earliest
community: the *hosanna* appears in all four Gospels in connection
with the entrance into Jerusalem, in the eucharistic liturgy of
the *Didache* (10:6), and in Hegesippus' account of the martyrdom
of Jacob /29/.

Luke gives us no information about the hymn in Christian
worship. Only one mention is made of singing: that of Paul and
Silas singing hymns and praying in prison at Philippi. We,
however, do have an account from the earliest community which
gives us a little more information: *Acts* 2:46b-47a "... breaking
bread in their homes, they partook of food with glad (ἐν
ἀγαλλιάσει) and generous hearts, praising God and having favour
with all the people". The comment that the celebrative meal
took place "ἐν ἀγαλλιάσει" (i.e., "in eschatological praise")
should be noted here. The most frequent use of the verb
ἀγαλλιᾶσθαι and the noun ἀγαλλίασις in the Septuagint is in
the psalms. Concerning New Testament usage, R. Bultmann says:
"God's help is consistently the object of the ἀγαλλιᾶσθαι, it is
joyful and thankful praise ... This praise refers to the
eschatological saving act of God" /30/. Ἀγαλλιᾶσθαι appears
in a special way as the anticipation of the joy of the redeemed
in the Kingdom of God, as described in *Rev*. 19:7, the last hymn
praising the beginning of God's rule and the "marriage of the
Lamb". When Christ is made manifest, you shall "rejoice with
unutterable and exalted joy" (*1 Peter* 1:8).

How could the "ἀγαλλίασις" in remembrance of the crucified
and exalted Lord and in the hope of his immediate return better
be expressed in the community meal than in a hymn to Christ,
whether as a messianic song from the psalter now understood as
being fulfilled, or as a new song inspired by the Spirit? The
main point here is that these "new songs" were songs of
thanksgiving and praise; primitive Christianity no longer made
use of the psalms of lament. Even the remembrances of Christ's
death do not conclude with laments; instead, they end with the
praise of victory, as in *Ps*. 22 /31/. From the very beginning,
the "remembrance" of Jesus' death and his saving act "for us"
as well as the orientation toward the exalted Christ and his
expected return in the near future were constitutive parts of the
early celebrative meal. The calls of *"maranatha"* or *"hosanna"*

apparently had their established place here; *hosanna* was
quickly transformed from a short bidding prayer into an
acclamation of praise. Is it not possible that the new hymns
to the death of Christ and his exaltation were also understood
as signs of the ἀγαλλίασις and as a remembrance of the activity
and destiny of Christ in narrative form?

IX

Let us summarize under four heads our results:

1.   The hymn to Christ developed out of the earliest worship
of the post-Easter community, i.e., it is as old as the
community itself. The "messianic psalms", which were
discovered anew after Easter and sung, formed the starting
point; new poetry was then added. The influence of the
messianic psalms, particularly *Pss*. 110 and 8, on the new
"song to Christ" can be clearly demonstrated. The song to
Christ which was considered the work of the new prophetic
Spirit of the eschatological era was independent over against
the other manifestations of the Spirit (i.e., prayer, prophetic
admonition, interpretation of scriptures, and the
re-presentation of the Jesus tradition) in the earliest
worship of the primitive church. As a part of the community's
praise to God, it was accorded a special place among these
various forms of praise. The "song to Christ" recounted the
work, being, and destiny of the crucified and exalted Lord.
The narrative and/or descriptive character was more pronounced
in them than in the hymns to God. The hymns to God and Christ
might be considered the "fruits" of the earliest post-Easter
enthusiasm. Their external form, however, comes from Judaism
and was taken from Jewish psalmody.

2.   The "song to Christ" originally expressed the
eschatological joy of the Lord's Supper, the ἀγαλλίασις of
Acts 2:46. Such joy can be understood as anticipation of the
expected fulfillment brought about by the return of the Son of
Man. From the very beginning, however, the community's
relationship to its exalted Lord after the appearance of the
resurrected Christ was never just orientated towards the
future but also related to the present. On the one hand, the
retrospective remembrance of the master, his person and his
passion, remained alive. On the other, the community was
certain that "their Lord" had been exalted to the right hand
of God and that he was also present in their midst through the

Spirit. Precisely because it believed that God's rule had
already begun with the resurrection of Jesus, it was natural
that the relationship to the exalted Christ was immediate and
related to this world. The resurrected Christ had not simply
"disappeared"; one knew where he was. He had not become a
"deus otiosus". The hymns to Christ taken from the Old
Testament psalter (*Pss*. 2, 8, 45, 110, 118), as well as the
new songs, offered a glimpse of God's heavenly sanctuary and
of the glorified Son of Man. The primitive church stood within
a Jewish-apocalyptic exaltation tradition, parallels for which
can be found in the fragments from *11 Q Melch*., the "Book of
Parables" in Ethiopian *Enoch,* and the *Metatron* Speculation of
3 Enoch. The "prologue in heaven" of *Revelation* reflects an
early Christian pattern that has its roots in Palestine. The
earthly worship, therefore, was closely connected to the
heavenly worship; *glossolalia* was probably understood as
"speaking with the tongues of angels" (*1 Cor*. 13:1). The
priestly intercession of the exalted Christ at the right hand
of God (Romans 8:34) corresponds to the *glossolalic*
intercession of the Spirit uttered in the assembly "with sighs
too deep for words" (*Rom*. 8:26 f). At the same time, the
heavenly praise of God and his Christ, as portrayed in
Revelation, corresponds to the inspired "sacrifice of praise"
as "fruit of the lips" (*Heb*. 13:15) in the hymns to God and
Christ during the earthly service.

3.   The hymn to Christ has more of an instructional character
than the early Christian prayers or hymns to God. Its influence
on the development of christology therefore, was stronger since
the passion of Christ, his glorification, and the subjection of
all powers were continually "narrated" and "proclaimed" anew.
It is difficult to separate narration and proclamation in early
Christianity. A little later, other functions such as
pre-existence before creation, mediation of creation, and
incarnation, were attributed to the exalted Christ in the hymn,
certainly as a consequence of the "name which is above every
name" granted to Christ in *Phil*. 2:9. This stage of development
had already been attained by the time of the Pauline mission,
i.e., the middle of the 40s. As a result, God's eschatological
"representative", because of the dignity of the revelation
manifested in him, also became his protological "representative".
God's word and activity in the eschatological era and before
time constitutes a unit, for the sake of God's truth. Neither
a gnostic nor a Samaritian myth (a myth of God incarnate) was
involved here. Rather, we see one last necessary stage of
Christian thought. The Christian community went "all out" here.

There was nothing else it could do; historically and
theologically, it also had the right. The effect of this
historical model of thought was later expressed by the Rabbis:
"And in this way you see how God works; all that he loves (more)
is put before everything else" (*Sifre Dt.* §37). Why should
the "beloved Son" not become the "first-born of all creation"
(*Col.* 1:15)? The wisdom tradition stemming from *Prov.* 8 and
Sir. 24 plays a major role in the transmission of this idea.
The hymn to Christ, then, served as a vital medium for the
continuing development of christological thought, beginning
with the messianic psalms and terminating in the Johannine
prologue. We still find traces of it in Ignatius and, in a
certain way, in the writings of Pliny, a Roman gentile. Pliny's
striking excerpt from an interrogation under torture: *carmenque
Christo quasi deo dicere secum invicem* ("when they sang in
alternate verses a hymn to Christ as to a god" /33/), was a
final stage of development, both christologically and
liturgically.

4.   In case my remarks have seemed too daring, I would like to
read a quotation from the distinguished Old Testament scholar
G. von Rad. In his book *Weisheit in Israel* von Rad states /34/:
"There was a kind of knowledge for Israel which, although
perhaps strange for us, could only be expressed in the form of
a hymn" /35/. This was particularly true - *mutatis mutandis* -
for early Christianity. The Spirit demanded that something new,
daring, and majestic be expressed in the "new song" of the
hymn to Christ, something which went beyond the possibilities
of expression provided by the sermon, interpretation of
scriptures, and even prosaic confessional formulas. Human
language has too little trust in God because it is so "earth
bound". Just as in ancient Israel with David and the prophets,
as well as with the Greeks, the Spirit attempted to say things
in poetic form which were not yet "ready" to be expressed *in
prose;* things which could be described only in the form of
narrative praise. Why should this not also be the case for
early Christianity, the strongest spirit-inspired movement in
the ancient world? Certainly Jesus did not write any hymns,
but his sayings, metaphors, *logoi,* and, perhaps even to some
extent, his parables were presented in poetic form. This is
why they were so easily understood by the listener. The same
is also basically true for the liturgical song to Christ.
Compared with the interpretations of the scribes or the
long-drawn-out sermons, the song text could be quickly
memorized, and the refrain completely or partly sung by the

community. A unity, therefore, was established between the
praising ἀγαλλίασις community and the spirit-filled διδασκαλία
community. In this way, the unity between the earthly community
and the heavenly community was made manifest. Paul was
certainly thinking of this power of praise to God to form
κοινωνία when, near the end of *Romans,* he admonishes: "May the
God of steadfastness and encouragement grant you to live in
such harmony with one another, in accord with Christ Jesus,
that together you may *with one voice* glorify the God and
Father of our Lord Jesus Christ". (*Rom.* 15:5-6).

From the very beginning, christology, the essence of early
Christian theology, developed in close relationship with the
inspired "song to Christ". Nowhere in early Christianity is
the relationship between praise to God and the development of
a theological concept as clear as with the development of
christological thought.

NOTES

*A lecture which was delivered also at Tantur near Jerusalem and
in German at Göttingen. It builds the basic framework of a
detailed investigation on which the author is working at the
present time.

/1/   H. Lietzmann, *Geschichte der Alten Kirche*[4], vol. I,
Berlin 1961, p.150 (my translation).
/2/   *loc.cit.*
/3/   A. Schlatter, *Paulus, der Bote Jesu*[4], Stuttgart 1969,
p.383.
/4/   Compare *1 Cor.* 14:15; see also *Test.Job* ch. 48-52.
/5/   In the Septuagint one can also find the sparingly used
term ᾆσμα which is absent from early Christian literature.
/6/   O. Hofius, *Der Christushymnus Phil 2,6-11,* WUNT 17,
Tübingen 1976, p. 8f.54f.65f, has proven beyond a doubt that
the closing doxology in *Phil.* 2:11 is an important and original
part of the hymn.
/7/   The preceding warning "Do not give way to drunkenness ..."
could be connected with the rejection of the dionysic θίασοι
and the drinking customs of heathen religious societies.
/8/   R. Deichgräber, *Gotteshymnus und Christushymnus in der
frühen Christenheit,* SUNT 5, Göttingen 1967, p. 60f.207f.
/9/   See K.-P. Jörns, *Das hymnische Evangelium,* SNT 5,
Gütersloh 1971, p. 178ff.

/10/   O. Hofius, *op.cit.* (note 6), p.80.
/11/   *Ps.* 2:7; *Deut.* 32:43; *Ps.* 104:4; 45:7f; 102:26ff; 110:1,
following the Septuagint.
/12/   The christological interpretation of *Ps.* 8 is without
doubt connected with the "Son of Man" in v. 5b. E. Grässer's
sentence (Beobachtungen zum Menschensohn in Hebr 2,6, in:
Jesus und der Menschensohn. Für Anton Vögtle, 1975, p. 412f)
that "the author of the Hebrews read and interpreted *Ps.* 8
which was in early Christianity seldom (!?) christologically
interpreted not in a messianic, but in an eschatological
perspective" (my translation) is just as misleading as the
assumption that the author here is referring to the gnostic
ἄνθρωπος- and συγγένεια doctrine. Messiah and Son of Man are
not opposites! Pre-Christian gnosticism should be ignored, for
it is a product of the imagination of several theologians and
historians.
/13/   The connection of the christological interpretation of
the enthronement at the right hand of God derived from *Ps.* 110:1
and the submission of the universe from *Ps.* 8:7 is also found
in a hymnic creed in Polyc. *ad Phil.* 2:1f. For the further
early Christian influence of *Ps.* 8:7 compare *Phil* 3:21; Justin,
Apol 40:1 and, in altered form, Athenag. *Suppl.* 18:2.
/14/   Christ the High Priest as intercessor and helper is also
to be found in *1 Clem* 36 in a liturgically formed text.
Towards the end is a quotation from *Ps.* 110:1. *1 Clem* is not,
as G.L. Cockerill (*JBL* 97, 1978, p.437-440) assumes, directly
dependent upon *Heb.* 7. There is an earlier High-Priest
tradition common to both.
/15/   *Mk.* 12:36 = *Mt.* 22:44; *1 Cor.* 15: 25-27.
/16/   For the connection between 'Son of Man' and 'seated at
the right hand of God' see *Mk.* 14:62 = *Mt.* 26:64; *Lk.* 22:69;
compare *Acts* 7:55; *Ep.Barn.* 12:10f; Hegesippus (Euseb *H.E.*
2,23,13). See also D.M. Hay, *Glory at the Right Hand; Psalm
110 in Early Christianity,* SBL Mon. Ser. 18, 1973, p. 108f.
/17/   Compare *Heb.* 4: 16; *Rom.* 5:2; *Eph.* 2:18; 3:12; *Heb.*10:19.
22.
/18/   *1 Cor.* 16:22; *Rev.* 22:20; *Did.* 10:6.
/19/   G. Schille (*Frühchristliche Hymnen,* Berlin 1965) offers
a deterrent example for an early Christian "Panhymnology".
/20/   *Agnostos Theos*[4], 1956, p. 177ff. 201ff. 240ff. 250ff.
Cf. J. Kroll, *Die christliche Hymnodik bis zu Klemens von
Alexandreia,* reprint Darmstadt,[2]1968, p.8ff.
/21/   For the hymns of the heretics see J. Kroll, *op.cit.*
p.82ff. *Muratori* line 82ff tells that the Marcionites used a
novus psalmorum liber (see A.v. Harnack, *Marcion,* reprint

Darmstadt 1960, p.175; compare also J. Kroll, *op.cit.* 38:
"The orthodox circles considered these hymns to be too modern
and too worldly and intending to prevent once and for all the
poisoning of the congregation with the heretical spirit they
forbade in their circles all extra-biblical hymns", (my
translation).
/22/ Compare e.g. *CH* 1:31; 5:10ff; 13:17-21. To the last
hymn see the excellent analysis of G. Zuntz, *Opuscula selecta,*
Manchester 1972, p. 150-177.
/23/ I. Elbogen, *Der jüdische Gottesdienst in seiner
geschichtlichen Entwicklung*[4], reprint, Hildesheim 1962, p. 502ff.
208 ff. It should be noted that scripture-reading and prayer
were delivered in an elevated style. See further J. Heinemann,
Prayer in the Talmud, Studia Judaica IX, 1977, p.139ff. For
research history see R.S. Sarason, Modern Study of Jewish
Liturgy, in: W.S. Green (ed.), *Approaches to Ancient Judaism:
Theory and Practice,* Brown Judaic Studies 1, Missoula, Montana
1978, p.97-172.
/24/ W. Bauer, Der Wortgottesdienst der ältesten Christen, in:
Aufsätze und kleine Schriften, Tübingen 1967, p. 155-209, esp.
171ff.
/25/ See E. Werner, Musical Aspects of the Dead Sea Scrolls,
The Musical Quarterly 43 (1957), p. 21-37; H. Haag, Das
liturgische Leben der Qumrangemeinde, *Archiv für
Liturgiewissenschaft* 10 (1967), p. 78-109; Sh. Talmon, The
Emergence of institutionalized Prayer in Israel in the Light
of the Qumran Literature, in: *Qumrân. Sa piété, sa théologie et
son milieu,* BEThL XLVI 1978, p. 265-284 (esp. 274ff).
/26/ *Ps.* 51:17, compare *Ps.* 40:4; *1QH* 9:10; 11:4: "Thou
puttest a song of praise into my mouth".
/27/ J.A. Sanders, *The Psalms Scroll of Qumrân Cave 11,*
DJD IV, 1965, p. 91f: *11QPs*[a]*DavComp.*
/28/ See O. Betz, *Offenbarung und Schriftforschung in der
Qumransekte,* WUNT 6, Tübingen 1960, p. 76f.
/29/ Euseb, *HE* 2, 23, 14.
/30/ *ThWNT* I, p. 19 (my translation).
/31/ See H. Gese, Psalm 22 und das Neue Testament. Der älteste
Bericht vom Tode Jesu und die Entstehung des Herrenmahles, in:
*Vom Sinai zum Zion. Alttestamentliche Beiträge zur biblischen
Theologie,* BEvTh 64, 1974, p. 180-201.
/32/ See M. Hengel, *Der Sohn Gottes*[2], Tübingen 1977, p. 104ff.
/33/ Plinius Minor, *Ep.* 10, 96, 7.
/34/ G. von Rad, *Weisheit in Israel,* Neukirchen-Vlyn 1970,
p. 71 (my translation).
/35/ *op.cit.* p.71 (my translation).

Centre and Periphery in the Thought of Paul

C.J.A. Hickling,
King's College, London

The difficulties involved in understanding and describing Pauline thought as a coherent entity have long been at least implicitly recognized, and it is now usual to concede that his activity as a theologian was not systematic /1/. The observation sometimes leads - as indeed it must, if it is assumed that the deficiency or absence of system is only superficial - to the recognition of a need to discover an underlying principle of coherence: among recent writers, one may instance H. Ridderbos /2/ and E.P. Sanders /3/ (widely different as their approaches are), the latter using the metaphor of a 'centre of [Paul's] thinking'. The question of the correct identification of this is, he says, 'among the most difficult in Pauline studies' /4/.

The purpose of the present essay is, first, to underline and illustrate the difficulty of this search for a 'centre', which may be greater than has yet been allowed. Attention was drawn some time ago to the 'elasticity of mind' and 'flexibility' which Paul displayed in the exercise of his theological 'opportunism' /5/, and recent studies have given us new reasons for considering the extent of this adaptability. 'Interpretation has come to focus not so much upon a supposed internal consistency in Pauline thought as upon his resilience and his ability to explore the possible contours of the Christian religious life in different historical contexts' /6/. The need to correct misapprehensions current in any one of the churches he founded - while at the same time retaining his own good standing with its members - may have led Paul to modify, at least in emphasis and perhaps even in content, what he had already said elsewhere (or even to the same community) /7/. Within the somewhat shifting picture of Paul's theological stances that emerges, what stable centre - if any - is to be identified? It would be too much to say that survival was his only concern - the survival, that is, both of his relationship with his converts, repeatedly threatened as it was, and of his credibility as a representative of the beliefs of 'the churches of God' (1 Cor 11:16). Nevertheless, the question remains. Where so much appears to be in some measure adventitious, what is unconditioned and, as it were, non-negotiable?

In what follows, three areas of Pauline thought will be taken as samples. In each case, it is possible to juxtapose statements which are in some degree of disharmony with each other or even mutually contradictory. It will be suggested - as the second, and very tentative, concern of this essay - that a 'centre' may be found, not in a single theological proposition, but in an aspect of Paul's experience of being Christian.

First: Paul gives varied answers to the question how one should view the history of Israel (in a fairly exact sense, i.e. the history of God's people since Abraham). Three accounts can be distinguished. Gal 3 and 4 provide an almost unreservedly negative assessment: the whole experience of Israel was a parenthesis /8/ in a divine purpose which, in the promise to Abraham, already fore-saw the successful evangelization of the Gentiles /9/. The state-ment (3:7) that Abraham's sons are those who believe (i.e., manifestly, in Jesus) already implies a serious depreciation of historic Israel. 3:23 - 4:2 uses images of unwelcome, enforced restraint to express the whole significance of the period stretching from Sinai to the coming of Jesus /10/. For one who had once been 'a Hebrew of the Hebrews, a very Pharisee as far as Law is concerned' (Phil 3:5) /11/, this amounts to an extraordinarily radical relativizing of the whole of the Jewish past since Abraham. Here, at least, it must be said that Paul rejects 'salvation history' as that term is commonly understood /12/.

When we compare with this the most closely corresponding passages in Rom 1-8 - not with a view to establishing a synthesis with with an open mind /13/ - we find that Israelite history after Abraham is passed over in almost complete silence. Its 'parenthetical' character is indeed concealed, and the somewhat self-conscious equating of Jew and Gentile in relation both to justifying grace (3:30) and to Abraham's paternity (4:11f) gives an impression that τὸ περισσὸν τοῦ Ἰουδαίου (3:1) is receiving here the respect it was denied in Galatians. But the impression is superficial /14/. Faith without circumcision justifies and renders one a child of Abraham, circumcision without faith does neither: all the distinctiveness of the Jew, save only the name itself, is overlooked. Similarly, in 5:12-21 the history of the human race is sketched as having been under the dominion of sin and death from Adam's transgression onwards. Not only is there no room left for a 'salvation history' for Jews, but the reverse is

implied: the only feature distinguishing Israel in history since
Abraham is that sin, already present in the world when Moses came,
was from his time onwards provided - in the case of Israel alone,
we are surely to understand - with a gauge by which to be measured
and accounted (vv. 13f). Yet, as has just been claimed for 4:11f,
the failure to ascribe saving value to the events at the Red Sea
and Sinai is concealed by Paul's silence and - we may perhaps add -
his tact.

In Rom 9-11 a different assessment emerges (its restriction
to these chapters, apart from the possibility that 3:2b should be
considered here, may be significant) /15/. Rom 9:4, like 3:2b and
1 Cor 10:1ff, ascribes positive value to the events of the Exodus
and the giving of the Law at Sinai. Here there can be no doubt
that Israel's post-Abrahamic past had included a real 'saving
history' not only of revelation but also of redemption /16/. Moreover, it would be a mistake to assume from the relative proportions
of the text of the Pauline corpus devoted to this positive assessment and to the negative one just described, that the former is
'peripheral', a *captatio benevolentiae* for 'theologically' Jewish-
Christian consumption, while the latter represents Paul's true
belief. We must not forget the adventitious element in the
processes by which some of Paul's letters survived, nor the
essentially occasional nature of much of their content. The few
passages quoted to illustrate a positive assessment of Israel's
past may be more representative than the extant letters allow us to
think.

We may turn to a necessarily brief consideration of the closely
related (and voluminously discussed) topic of Paul's view of the
Law. Here, the difference between Galatians and Romans seems to be
clearer /17/. In the earlier letter Paul's attitude is almost
unreservedly hostile. 3:19 goes as far as possible towards
dissociating the Law altogether from any divine origin /18/. In
4:1-11 acceptance of its (here, mainly calendrical) rules by the
baptized is asserted to be tantamount to repudiation of baptism
/19/. Law is that to which a man must die if he is to be alive to
God (2:19). In terms of Paul's overarching framework of thought,
the absolute contrast between the old order of things and the new,
this is to place the Law firmly on the side of the old. It is
hardly an exaggeration to say, with J.W. Drane, that 'Paul's
statements on the Law in Galatians can ... be called blatantly
Gnostic' /20/.

Rom 1-8 exhibits, in general, the same contrast between ἐξ
ἔργων νόμου and ἐκ πίστεως as Galatians, though we can perhaps

observe Paul softening the impact of this contrast: is this part
of the function of the difficult phrases διὰ νόμου πίστεως (3:27),
and ὁ... νόμος Πνεύματος τῆς ζωῆς (8:2) /21/? Unambiguously, in
any case, he is concerned to avert the suspicion that he opposes
the Law - the reverse, he claims, is the case (3:31). The Law is
holy (7:12), and fulfilment of what it desiderates is the purpose
of Jesus' mission (8:4). But it is only when we move beyond the
argument of 1-8 that we meet the full width of the spectrum of
attitudes Paul displays, for at 13:8-10 he virtually returns, and
with some emphasis, to a straightforwardly Jewish understanding:
to fulfil the Law is the proper goal of behaviour /22/, and what
matters is the correct interpretation of the Law, namely - for Paul
(as, in a celebrated dictum, for Hillel) /23/ - its reduction /24/
to the love commandment.

What, then, are we to make of these dissonances in Paul's view
of Israelite history since Abraham, and of the Law, whose provision
was the most outstanding single incident in that history?

In the latter case - Paul's view of the Law - a partial
synthesis has become familiar. Law, in itself the expression of
God's will for human moral achievement, encountered a situation
already irretrievably marred, but for the later irruption of grace,
by sin. A fatal contamination occurred. The Law ἠσθένει διὰ τῆς
σαρκός, and the ideally good became, through its contact with what
it was intended to regulate, not the support and directive for human
aspiration but its enemy. Will this solution serve? If the teaching
of Galatians is as radical as Drane and H. Hübner have suggested,
one may be doubtful. But this account of the matter may at least
point us towards a somewhat different approach to the question of
a 'centre'. It may be that the same entity - the Law - is seen in
a totally different light, and is held to function in totally
different ways, according to the religious standpoint from which
it is regarded.

The inconsistencies to be detected within what Paul says about
Israelite history may be interpreted in a similar manner; and in
both cases one may fruitfully apply a comment of Sanders made in a
different context. The account of the plight of human nature given
in Romans 7 is not, he says, an independent analysis of the human
condition, but 'describes, rather, the pre-Christian or non-Christian
life *as seen from the perspective of faith*' /25/. In the same way,
Paul looks back at the past of Israel, and at that Law which was so
widely regarded as the most outstanding feature of that past, from
the standpoint of his personal understanding - and in some degree,
perhaps, of his experience - of what it means to be Christian. And

this necessarily implied a fundamental ambiguity. For the almost
simultaneous awareness of continuity and of discontinuity with the
past which renders so complex the question of 'salvation history'
in Paul is most vividly seen when he is writing autobiographically.
Thus at Phil 3:7f Paul speaks as one who stands at the frontier
between past and future and turns his back decisively on the old
order; yet the passage is introduced (vv.2f) by the contrast
κατατομή/περιτομή, which affirms his membership of a true Israel
standing in total distinction from a false one /26/. This last
point is indeed crucial for this whole issue. When Israel's past
is seen to be continuous with the empirical Judaism from whose
rejection of the apostolic preaching Paul had himself suffered
physically as well as in other ways (2 Cor 11:24, Rom 9:2), it is
judged to be something that is almost the reverse of a 'saving'
history. When, however, that past is viewed as providing the antecedent history of the Christian community (note the οἱ πατέρες ἡμῶν
of 1 Cor 10:1, addressed as the phrase is to a group predominantly
if not exclusively Gentile), a different assessment is made.

Does this not render possible a first attempt to locate a
'centre' in Paul's thought? It is the necessity to interpret the
past from the standpoint of the present, when the present means
standing at a frontier between the old order and the new, vividly
and experientially aware of the life-denying power of everything
that precedes initiation into Christ, yet also knowing that 'everything is from God' (2 Cor 5:18) and that God's fidelity to his
promises is his most essential attribute (cf 2 Cor 1:20). One
might almost say that the 'centre' lies in christology in the
precise sense of Christ's relation to God: Christ relativizes all
that went before him, yet he is the Son of the God who created all
things and called not only Abraham but also Israel and Moses.

From Paul's views of the (Israelite) past, we may turn more
briefly to his evaluation of the present in its relation to the
eschatological future, the second of the main areas selected for
consideration in this essay. Here, inconsistencies are must less
visible. A simple and, no doubt, traditional scheme pointed to the
manifest activity of the Spirit as being an anticipation as well as
a guarantee of the rest of God's eschatological gifts, which were
reserved until the parousia. For the most part, the variations to
be found in Paul's references to present and future time are
variations only of emphasis. Nevertheless, some questions may be
raised.

First, did Paul himself originally believe that Christians have

already experienced all the resurrection there is? Was it from him
that the Corinthian Christians had learned their exhaustively
realized (or 'collapsed') /27/ eschatology? /28/. 2 Cor 5:16, it
has been held, speaks of Paul's conversion as an eschatological
event, and the following verse, with its allusion to 'a decisive
realization in the present [Vergegenwärtigung] of what it is elsewhere only permissible to hope for from the new [i.e. still future]
aeon', shows Paul to be - here, at least - fully at one with the
'enthusiasts' of Corinth /29/. Certainly the tenses of 5:17
support this interpretation /30/. However, the anarthrous καινά
of this text leaves open how much of the eschatological promise
still remains unfulfilled, and it seems extremely hard to think
that, either here or at any point, Paul could have included
resurrection within that part of the Last Things that is already
accessible to Christians.

     Secondly, if in both 1 Cor 15 /31/ and Rom 8 /32/ Paul
deliberately emphasized the reservation of the resurrection of
Christians until the Last Day, was he motivated in doing so, at
least in part, by concern to keep the beliefs of the Gentile or
partly Gentile churches in line with those of the first Jewish-
Christian communities, strongly futurist as the latter are likely
to have been in their eschatology? If so, there may be something
a little adventitious in the stress laid on the future in both
chapters. The tension which is so often said to exist in Paul's
thought between the 'now' and the 'not yet' may - in part - be
linked with a tension between what he had felt in his own experience
and what he knew to be the orthodoxy of the first churches. 2 Cor
6:2b springs to mind as a particularly unambiguous declaration of
the reality of salvation in the present: Paul selects, and applies
to the Corinthians' situation as well as to his own, phrases which
in their original Isaianic context emphatically referred to the
present (or rather, indeed, to a recent past). It is especially
striking that, in using this quotation, Paul was drawing into
present reference a word - σωτηρία - which elsewhere (most clearly
at Rom 13:11, but also in the great majority of his uses of σώζω)
signifies the future deliverance of the Last Day. No doubt there
is a real tension, or perhaps oscillation, in Paul's thought between
a predominantly futurist and a predominantly realized eschatology;
but, despite the marked leaning towards the former in the highly
personal statement at Phil 3:12-14, one may suspect that, in the
last analysis, it is God's gifts available in the present that
were supremely important to him /33/.

     Thirdly, this present availability of some of the eschato-
logical gifts is asserted in some passages /34/ which use the

language of revelation. It is true that in 1 Cor 15 and Rom 8
Paul expounds the content of the received gospel in terms of its
traditional chronological structure, with its distancing of the
future from present experience. Is it, however, possible that the
importance of the present becomes predominant when Paul's basic
thought is of the gospel as in process of being proclaimed - when,
that is, he thinks of the message with which he had been entrusted
as itself part of God's saving and essentially eschatological work?
2 Cor 4:6 seems particularly significant in this respect. In
immediate connection with the preaching of the Christian message
/35/, Paul here states that God is making possible knowledge of
God's glory within human experience in the present (there is a
clear contrast in emphasis, perhaps in content, with 1 Cor 13:12).

In this second main area of Paul's teaching, then, we find
further evidence of diversity, of a 'phenomenon of oscillation'
/36/. As in the previous case, we may suggest that a 'centre' is
to be found in the perception of the same reality from different
standpoints. As pastor - and perhaps specifically as one whose
'care of all the churches' included a certain anxiety that
individual communities should retain the traditional stance of hope
and expectation - Paul observed the 'frontier' between the old order
and the new as part of a chronologically spaced series of stages
which would not be complete until the parousia. But as an apostle,
that is, as one entrusted with the preaching of the gospel, he knew
that he himself belonged altogether to the new order and spoke
authoritatively from within it. It was perhaps in the proclamation
of the gospel that he especially experienced eschatology as *sich
realisierende* /37/ (cf 2 Cor 2:15f, where a decisive and irrevers-
ible judgement is seen to be going on in the two opposite responses
that are made to the preaching; and it is no accident that several
statements in which high claims are made for the present experience
of Christians are found within the opening chapters of 2 Corinthians, preoccupied as they are with the defence and explication
of the calling of the apostle as evangelist).

Lastly, the status and function of Christ during his pre-
existence are the subject of one extended passage and some brief
references, while in one place it is possible that no room is left
for his pre-existence at all. Once again, diversity of emphasis is
undeniable, and it might be held legitimate to claim actual
inconsistency.

The meaning of ὁρισθέντος Υἱοῦ θεοῦ in Rom 1:3f, the last of
the passages just alluded to, is not clear. The thought may be

that the resurrection 'declared' /38/ openly a status Jesus had
enjoyed from all eternity /39/ (γενομένου in v.3 would therefore
indicate his coming, as it were from elsewhere, into historical
visibility). Other views have been argued, however /40/, and the
ambiguity of the wording Paul has adopted is its most puzzling
feature. It must be conceded, at the least, that if Christ's pre-
existence was indeed a firm belief in Paul's mind, he must have
thought it either not very vulnerable to critical questioning (which
is, perhaps, a possibility) or not very important: for he presumably
left himself open to as wide a variety of interpretations in his own
day as in ours. Whether he composed this short passage about Jesus'
status or merely endorsed it as it came to him from the tradition
(with or without glosses), Paul could scarcely have laid less
emphasis on Jesus' pre-existence than he does here.

At the opposite extreme, 1 Cor 8:6 (which is also possibly
derived from already formulated wording) /41/ presents the pre-
existent Christ as mediating - by implication, at least - God's
activity in the creation of the universe. It is true that, as in
Rom 1:3f, there is no temporal reference, and the intention is to
affirm Jesus's status rather than his eternal existence - or rather,
to attribute to him (however paradoxically, in juxtaposing the two
parallel statements about him and about God) the divine attributes
of uniqueness and of responsibility for the coming into being of
all things, but not explicitly that of having existed for ever.
This is however obviously implied in δι' οὗ τὰ πάντα, and, even if
emphasis is hardly placed on this particular point (it is Christ's
uniqueness as Κύριος that immediately concerned Paul), the estimate
of Christ's status and function before history began is very high.

Phil 2:6-11 stands in contrast to both these utterances to the
extent that a story, even if in the most rudimentary sense of the
word, is narrated about Jesus before he entered human history /42/.
Not only did the Christ of this hymn exist before his descent into
the world, but it was in this pre-existent state that the all-
important decision for self-abasement was made. But Phil 2:6-11
may also offer a more serious contrast with 1 Cor 8:6. The opening
words of the hymn, enigmatic as they are, are silent about any
involvement of their subject with God's work in creation, and it is
a little difficult to see how, preoccupied as they are with a
relationship (actual, potential, or abjured) between Christ and God,
they effectively leave room for a concept of co-operation in making
the universe. Perhaps it would be wrong to exaggerate the significance of this. But what of the dramatic climax at vv. 10f? The
supreme moment of the recompense given to Jesus for his costly self-
humiliation in obedience is that he receives the homage of the whole

created order. This is the highest indication of the new 'level'
of glory that has now been granted, one which excels what was his
from the beginning; for God αὐτον ὑπερύψωσεν, and the bestowal of
the divine Name itself indicates - we are surely to understand
/43/ - a higher dignity even than the possession of the μορφὴ θεοῦ.
It would be difficult to think that those who first recited this
hymn (if such it is) believed that the 'heavenly, earthly and sub-
terranean things' owed their very existence to the hymn's subject
in the first place. It is true that the initial state of this
divine figure whom the hymn identifies as Christ has often been
regarded as Adamic in some sense, and the Adam of Gen 1:28 is told
to exercise lordship over the rest of creation; but nothing of this
last thought appears in Phil 2:6-11. Rather, the obeisance made by
heaven and earth to the Christ of the hymn, and the acknowledgement
of his sovereignty by 'every tongue', are - within the thought-
structure of this passage - the free response of the cosmic
witnesses on observing the conferment upon him of the highest
conceivable honour. At this point, we are perhaps entitled to
speak, not only of variation in emphasis, but of inconsistency.

The remaining allusions to Christ's pre-existence (e.g. 2 Cor
8:9 and the employment of the *Sendungsformel* at Gal 4:6, Rom 8:3)
are few and brief /44/, cohering better with Phil 2:6-11 than with
1 Cor 8:6 but not excluding the claims of the latter. What might
be meant, then, for a search for a 'centre' in Paul's thought
about the status and function of Christ before his entry into
human history? It must be admitted that such a search might be
futile. If anything lies at the 'periphery' of Paul's concerns -
by which only a relative distance from more vital interests need,
and should, be understood - this part of his teaching might be a
likely candidate. Jesus' work in salvation preoccupies his
attention, and the 'pre-temporal past' of Jesus has as little
bearing on that work as his historical 'past' /45/; it would hardly
be surprising, then, if Paul were found to tolerate, even to over-
look, inconsistencies within different formulations of belief about
Christ as he was before the creation of the world (especially if
these formulations were taken over from others, as is widely held
at least in the case of Rom 1:3f and Phil 2:6-11) /46/.

Nevertheless, the following may be tentatively put forward as
a common standpoint from which Paul elected to make use, in varying
contexts most of which bear in some way on the conduct of Christians,
of the statements we have been considering. It is, once again, the
concept of a decisive turning-point in time - of the *Aeonenwende* -
that dominates his thought. In Rom 1:3f, whatever may have been
true of the transcendentally remote or of the immediate past, it is

the declaration of Christ's glory as now known that matters - a
declaration, moreover, of which the recipients are those brought
within the sphere of the new order. Again, while Christ is the
agent through whom the created order came into existence, it is
stated in the same breath that Christians, too, owe their existence
as such to him. The call to a future glory with Christ that is
implied in ἡμεῖς δι' αὐτοῦ lays as much stress on the redemptive
work of Christ in the new order as it does on his place in creation.
It hardly needs to be said that the second half of the narrative of
the 'Christ-hymn' in Phil 2 is the *raison d'être* of the whole, and
lays the fullest possible stress on the new dignity of Christ
acknowledged in the new order. And if 2 Cor 8:9 appears to speak,
as far as Christ is concerned, principally of a contrast between
former glory and subsequent abasement, a third stage of augmented
glory in which Christians participate with Christ is obviously
implied. In whatever way Paul looks back to what is now past in
the history of Jesus, it is his new status and function, the glory
of the new age and the bestowal of this glory on 'many brethren',
that consistently forms the focus of his conviction /47/.

     With this, we may return to E.P. Sanders' own answer to the
question of a 'centre' in Paul's thought (a question which he
formulates, as we have already noted, with aims somewhat different
from those of this essay). 'There appear', he says, '... to be
two readily identifiable and primary convictions which governed
Paul's Christian life: (1) that Jesus Christ is Lord, that in him
God has provided for the salvation of all who believe ..., and that
he will soon return to bring all things to an end; (2) that he,
Paul, was called to be the apostle to the Gentiles' /48/. In the
light of our own discussion, a rider may be offered to these closely
linked statements. God has already brought about in Christ a
decisive and final *transformation of time*. Christ's being acknowledged as Lord, and God's offer of salvation through him, signalize
- and themselves belong to - a new era in time, and so does the
apostle's work in communicating these things. But in Paul's
imagination this *Aeonenwende* always bore the predominantly dualistic
colour provided by the world-view of apocalyptic. It was 'out of
darkness' that the light had shone (2 Cor 4:6). Paul apprehended
both God's invasive grace in Christ and his own call, inseparable
as these events were for him, in terms of a stark and almost
completely unqualified breach between the old and the new, between
what had preceded Christ's manifestation to Israel and to himself
and what was resulting from it /49/.

     Here, surely, is the centre of Paul's thought, and indeed of

his religion: not simply, or even principally, in the content of
his assertions about God and Jesus and his own calling, but in the
sense of fundamental and paradoxical contrast, as of one standing
at a cosmic frontier, with which this content was perceived /50/.
To this sense of contrast we may trace most of the varied attitudes
he displayed towards Judaism, and also - if more tentatively - the
tolerance of diversity in the ways in which Christ himself was
imagined in the 'pre-temporal' past. In a different way, the
experiential awareness that the decisive transformation of time
had already occurred was in some tension with a more cerebral
recognition that an authoritative, because traditional, long-term
scheme of time's evolution reserved the visible transformation for
a still future End /51/.

    Finally, we must note that, at what are perhaps the most
brilliant points of his response to experience, Paul's knowledge
of the redemption and consecration of suffering (2 Cor 4:7-18,
6:4-10) enabled him to transcend the contrast between the old and
the new. The words he claimed to have heard in ecstasy, 'power is
fully realized (τελεῖται) in weakness' (2 Cor 12:9), point to a
supreme reconciliation of opposites. ἀσθένεια is elsewhere, with
its cognates, a word frequently characteristic of the state of
affairs under the old order apart from Christ, or as it still
persists temporarily alongside the new order in Christ. Here,
ἀσθένεια with all that it implies - both Christ's crucifixion (cf
2 Cor 13:4), and the apostle's participation in his suffering /52/ -
are seen to be the locus of God's fullest revelation of himself.

NOTES

/1/   It is thus somewhat startling to re-read Schweitzer's
declaration that Paul 'proceeds with a logical consistency, which
in its simplicity and clearness compels assent as a piece of
thinking', *The Mysticism of Paul the Apostle*, London, [2] 1953, p.139.
/2/   *Paul: An Outline of his Theology*, Grand Rapids, 1975 (ET of
Paulus: Ontwerp van zijn theologie, Kampen, 1966), pp.13-43.
Ridderbos formulates his question as 'where the entrance is to be
sought into the imposing edifice of Paul's theology', and in general
his view presupposes a far greater degree of coherence than is
assumed in the present study. He also works with a fully traditional Pauline 'canon' which seems to include the Pastorals,
whereas the present essay excludes, in common with a widely agreed
consensus, 2 Thessalonians, Colossians, and Ephesians, as well as
the Pastorals.
/3/   *Paul and Palestinian Judaism. A Comparison of Patterns of*

Religion, London, 1977, pp.431-442.
/4/   *Ibid.*, p.433.
/5/   The phrases are those of H. Chadwick, 'All Things to All Men',
NTS 1, 1954-5, pp. 264, 275.
/6/   W.G. Doty, *Letters in Primitive Christianity*, Philadelphia,
1973, p.37.
/7/   Thus J.W. Drane finds a considerable modification in 1
Corinthians of the positions adopted in Galatians, and accounts
for this by claiming that the teaching of Galatians had been
illegitimately extended in the interval between the two letters
(which Drane dates in this order); cf the summary of his reconstruction, *Paul: Libertine or Legalist?*, London, 1975, p.124. Much
earlier, J.C. Hurd offered an account of *The Origin of 1 Corinthians*
(London, 1965) which exhibits an almost complete *volte-face* by Paul
on several matters when dealing with the same community.
/8/   So F.F. Bruce, *Paul, Apostle of the Free Spirit*, Exeter,
1977, p.190.
/9/   This is surely the significance of προευηγγελίσατο taking up
the previous προϊδοῦσα ὅτι ἐκ πίστεως δικαιοῖ τὰ ἔθνη ὁ θεός of
Gal 3:8; cf. F. Mussner, *Der Galaterbrief* (Herders theologischer
Kommentar zum Neuen Testament, IX), Freiburg im Breisgau, 1974,
ad. loc.
/10/   Cf H. Ridderbos, *op. cit.*, pp. 147f.
/11/   The first phrase may be significant in this context, for D.
Georgi has claimed that the term Ἑβραῖος was used to emphasize
the distinctiveness of the Jews with particular reference to their
corporate history (*Die Gegner des Paulus*, Neukirchen-Vluyn, 1964,
p.55). In any case, pride in Jewish national history seems to have
been characteristic of Hellenistic Judaism: cf H. Hegermann, 'Das
hellenistische Judentum', in J. Leipoldt and W. Grundmann, edd.,
Umwelt des Urchristentums, I, Berlin, 1966, pp. 318-322, M. Hengel,
Judaism and Hellenism, I, London, 1974, pp. 92-100 (the assumption
that Paul's intellectual roots lay in Hellenistic Judaism still
seems sound: cf, e.g., S. Sandmel's comparison of Paul with Philo,
The Genius of Paul, New York, 1958, pp. 46-53). These considerations make Paul's assessment of the history of Israel particularly
striking. - It is tantalizing that we can make so little, with
any degree of precision, of the phrase κατὰ νόμον Φαρισαῖος. This
use (the earliest extant, S. Sandmel, *op. cit.* p.14) of the word
Φαρισαῖος comes from a period for which our knowledge of the
Pharisees is now widely acknowledged to be almost non-existent.
/12/   E. Käsemann speaks of 'dialectic and paradox' in Paul's
attitude to salvation history ('Justification and Salvation
History', in.*Perspectives on Paul*, London, 1971, pp. 66ff), but
this over-schematizes his view. F. Mussner's excursus '"Heilsgeschichte" oder γραφή' *op. cit.*, pp. 334-341, vigorously denies

that, in Gal 3 and 4, Paul thinks in any sense in a *heilsgeschicht-lich* manner.
/13/ As is the only method of interpreting Paul that should be adopted; cf H. Hübner, *Das Gesetz bei Paulus. Ein Beitrag zum Werden der paulinischen Theologie* (FRLANT, 119), Göttingen, 1978, pp.13ff.
/14/ Cf E. Käsemann, *An die Römer* (Handbuch zum neuen Testament, 8a), Tübingen, 1974, pp.109f.
/15/ It is not the intention of this essay to enter into the question of the racial and religious origins of those addressed in Romans. We have learned, since J. Munck (cf. *Paul and the Salvation of Mankind*, London, 1959, especially pp. 87ff - on the 'Judaizing Gentile Christians' identified behind Galatians - and, e.g., pp.206ff), to recognize that Jewish Christians were not necessarily the only ones interested in the Old Testament and its claims for Israel. What is clear is that the Roman Christians had been rendered suspicious of Paul as an alleged antinomian (3:8); chapters 9-11 read well - especially in the light of their opening verses - as an apologia directed to those who thought that the Pauline teaching damned historical Israel without qualification (as indeed it had on at least one occasion, 1 Thess 2:16).
/16/ Cf. C.K. Barrett, *From First Adam to Last*, London, 1962, pp. 49f. Barrett describes εἰς τὸν Μωϋσῆν ἐβαπτίσαντο as an 'honorific reference to Moses', but the implication is surely wider - this was a real saving event as well as being a 'type' of Christian baptism.
/17/ For detailed discussions see the works of J.W. Drane and H. Hübner already mentioned.
/18/ Even if δι' ἀγγέλων does not indicate (or at least hint) that the angels are the source of the giving of the Law, the double mediation - through the angels and also through Moses - interposes the maximum distance between God and the reception of the Law; cf F. Mussner, *op. cit.*, *ad loc.*, H. Hübner, *op. cit.*, p.28. Bultmann thought that at Gal 3:19 Paul was 'appropriating the Gnostic proposition that ... [the Law] was given by subordinate angelic powers', *Theology of the New Testament*, I, London, 1952, p.174.
/19/ Such is surely the force of v.9, if γνόντες θεόν ... γνωσθέντες ὑπὸ θεοῦ may be rendered 'having *once* known God ... having *once* been acknowledged by God'. ἐπιστρέφετε κτλ and ... δουλεῦσαι θέλετε are very severe statements, as in v.11.
/20/ J.W. Drane, *op. cit.*, p.112. 2 Cor 3:7-11 also presents a drastic, though measured, criticism of the Law; of my 'The Sequence of Thought in II Corinthians, Chapter Three', NTS 21 1974-5, pp. 387f.
/21/ Cf E. Lohse, 'ὁ νόμος τοῦ Πνεύματος τῆς ζωῆς. Exegetische Anmerkungen zu Röm 8,2', in H.D. Betz and L. Schottroff, edd., *Neues Testament und christliche Existenz*, Festschrift for H. Braun,

Tübingen, 1973, pp. 279-287, where νόμος in this verse is taken to
refer to the Torah seen in a positive sense. - Or is Paul, in both
these phrases, creating deliberately paradoxical expressions in
order, by a kind of irony, to make the contrast between law and
faith as sharp as possible? I am grateful to my colleague Canon
J.L. Houlden for this and other suggestions about the content of
this paper .

/22/ Cf H. Hübner, *op. cit.*, p.76. The almost casual and - in
the light of Romans and Galatians as a whole - startling reference
to τήρησις ἐντολῶν θεοῦ at 1 Cor 7:19 must also be mentioned here;
cf J.W. Drane, *op. cit.*, p.65.

/23/ Tractate Shabbath, 31a; the 'golden rule' is not, of course,
identical with the 'love commandment', but the thought is
comparable in identifying one precept as summarizing the whole Law;
cf J. Jeremias, 'Paulus als Hillelit', in E.E. Ellis and M. Wilcox,
edd., *Neotestamentica et Semitica* (Festschrift for M. Black),
Edinburgh, 1969, p.90.

/24/ The word is Hübner's, *op. cit.*, p.78.

/25/ *Op. cit.*, p.443 (italics mine).

/26/ Cf P. Richardson, *Israel in the Apostolic Church* (SNTS
Monograph Series, 10), Cambridge, 1969, pp.115-7. Gal.1:10-16 is
somewhat similar in its unreserved rejection of Paul's Jewish past
followed by quotations of the call-narrative of Jeremiah and of the
'Servant's' acknowledgement of his mission at v.15, showing that
Paul saw his own call as prefigured in the history of Israel's
prophetic tradition.

/27/ The phrase is that of J.H. Schütz, *Paul and the Anatomy of
Apostolic Authority* (SNTS Monograph Series, 26), Cambridge, 1975,
p.90.

/28/ So J. Héring, 'Saint Paul a-t-il enseigné deux résurrections?',
Revue d'Histoire et de Philosophie Religieuse, XII, 1932, quoted
by J.C. Hurd, *op. cit.*, p.285. It is tempting, but cannot, perhaps,
be more than that, to think that the second corrector of P[46],
Vaticanus, and 1739, with other witnesses - a not unimpressive
arr`ay - might retain the original intention of Paul at 1 Cor 6:14
(ἐξήγειρεν for ἐξεγερεῖ).

/29/ P. Stuhlmacher, 'Erwägungen zum ontologischen Charakter der
καινὴ κτίσις bei Paulus', Evangelische Theologie, 27, 1967, pp.6,
8, 22.

/30/ Moreover, Rom 14:7-9 may lend some support to the view that
Paul sometimes thought of Christians as already enjoying the kind
of life that follows resurrection. It is to this life that ἔζησεν
refers, in antithesis to ἀπέθανεν, in the case of Jesus, in v.9.
Hence, when the same verb is used - again in antithesis to forms of
ἀποθνήσκειν in the preceding verses, this time referring to the
triumphant aspect of the present life of believers, it is natural

to think that, in some sense, the latter is being thought of as
the life characteristic of resurrection: there is, again, a hint
of the 'collapsed eschatology' in relation to the resurrection
which has been attributed to the Corinthian Christians; cf also
Rom 6:10f.

/31/ Cf the discussion in J.H. Schütz, *op. cit.*, pp.84-113.

/32/ As discussed, in terms of Pauline redaction of traditional
material, by P. von der Osten-Sacken, *Römer 8 als Beispiel
paulinischer soteriologie* (FRLANT, 112), Göttingen, 1975. Both
1 Cor 15 and Rom 8 are commented on from the point of view of
Paul's correction of over-realized eschatology in the brief
excursus 'Paulus und der Enthusiasmus' in U. Luz, *Das Geschichtsverständnis des Paulus* (Beiträge zur evangelische Theologie, 49),
München, 1968, pp. 384-6.

/33/ 2 Cor 5:8 and Phil 1:21-3 notwithstanding, since in neither
case is the preferred future the Last Day itself; in any case, the
densely compressed phrase τὸ ζῆν Χριστός in itself indicates a very
high evaluation of the present.

/34/ Notably Rom 1:17f, 3:21, 2 Cor 4:6.

/35/ As the preceding context makes clear, whether or not the
verse alludes to Paul's conversion experience.

/36/ This phrase is used in connection with the smaller-scale
diversity within 1 Cor 7 by H. Chadwick, *art. cit.*, p. 265.

/37/ Cf E. Güttgemanns, *Der Leidende Apostel und sein Herr* (FRLANT,
90), Göttingen, 1966, pp. 318-322.

/38/ So Bauer-Arndt-Gingrich, s.v. ὁρίζω in this verse.

/39/ So H. Ridderbos, *op. cit.*, p. 68.

/40/ E.g. F. Hahn, *The Titles of Jesus in Christology*, London,
1969, p. 249.

/41/ Cf K. Wengst, *Christologische Formeln und Lieder des
Urchristentums* (Studien zum Neuen Testament, 7), Gütersloh, 1972,
p. 140.

/42/ There seems little to be said for the view that the opening
lines of the hymn allude to the historical life of Jesus; cf. R.P.
Martin, *Carmen Christi: Phil ii 5-11 in Recent Interpretation and
in the Setting of Early Christian Worship* (SNTS Monograph Series
4), Cambridge, 1967, pp. 63-6.

/43/ Cf R.P. Martin, *op. cit.*, pp. 235-247. Martin is hesitant
about the question whether the 'last state' of the Christ of the
hymn is higher than the first or simply very high indeed, but seems
to allow the former as at least as likely and perhaps having
slightly the greater plausibility. J. Gnilka is more confident
that the former interpretation is correct: *Der Philipperbrief*
(Herders theologischer Kommentar zum Neuen Testament, X/3), Freiburg
in Breisgau, 1968, p. 125.

/44/ Some 14 passages from letters considered Pauline for the purposes of the present essay are discussed by R.G. Hamerton-Kelly, *Pre-existence, Wisdom, and the Son of Man. A Study of the Idea of Pre-existence in the New Testament* (SNTS Monograph Series, 21), Cambridge, 1973, pp. 103-168, but many of these are not in an immediate sense statements about Christ's pre-existence.

/45/ That is, of course, the events which would constitute his biography up to the Last Supper, and to which Paul, despite his knowledge of at least a tradition of the sayings of Jesus, does not allude at all (*pace* G.N. Stanton, *Jesus of Nazareth in New Testament Preaching*, SNTS Monograph Series, 27, Cambridge, 1974, pp. 86-116).

/46/ Cf R.G. Hamerton-Kelly, *op. cit.*, pp. 192-195.

/47/ This is only partly true of Phil 2:6-11, from which soteriology is notoriously absent.

/48/ *Op. cit.*, pp. 441f.

/51/ F.F. Bruce, *op. cit.*, pp. 75f, 123, has been the most recent writer to suggest that Paul's thought was greatly influenced by his 'conversion experience', and the dramatic and total transition from darkness to light involved in that experience may well have contributed to this essentially imaginative feature of his theological thought in general (for which such terms as 'dialectic' seem both too imprecise and too cerebral).

/50/ With some temerity, then, one may suggest that the justification of the ungodly is - not, indeed, a *Nebenkrater*, but - the expression in one highly important thought-context of a deeper principle arising from the 'centre' as here tentatively defined. The antitheses folly-wisdom (1 Cor 1:27, 2 Cor 12:9f), 'my righteousness' - i.e. 'righteousness' aspired to on a basis of Law-observance - as opposed to 'righteousness of God' (so formulated at Phil 3:9), and - most profound of all - non-existence as opposed to existence (1 Cor 1:28b, Rom 4:17b) and death as opposed to life, all rest on the same basic antithesis of the absence of God from the human situation and his presence in it as the free giver of what is essentially discontinuous with all that had gone before. The doctrine of grace, in other words, is in Paul the root of nearly everything else, and is closely related to the understanding of time which it has been part of the concern of this essay to elucidate.

/51/ It should perhaps be said that the three areas of Pauline thought selected as samples were not chosen for any reasons of symmetry or of position within a possible 'structure' - the latter term in any case suggests a model which is inappropriate - but simply as evincing diversity in a particularly obvious way. It is hoped to apply a similar scrutiny to other parts of Paul's writings in a more extended study.

/52/ As expounded, with particularly far-reaching and profound observations, by E. Güttgemanns, *op. cit.*, pp. 112-124, 165-170.

Studia Biblica 1978: III, 215-223

Paul's Reading of Isaiah

Rev. C.J.A. Hickling,
King's College,
University of London.

The New Testament writers as a whole quote considerably more often from Isaiah than from most other books in the Old Testament apart from the Pentateuch: quotations from Isaiah represent about 15% of all quotations from the Old Testament in the New /1/. Paul, however, seems to have had a particular predilection for Isaiah: in his case, some 26% of the Old Testament quotations are from that book /2/ - or rather, they are taken from a very small number of chapters in it /3/. It is the purpose of this paper to ask why Paul was so interested in relatively short sections of the text of Isaiah /4/, or - as we should presumably say - in a relatively small number of columns in the scroll (or scrolls) of this book, which we may envisage him as carrying about during his travels, like the Ethiopian eunuch /5/.

First, a number of passages in *Isa.* 40-55 seem to have attracted his attention (it can hardly be more than coincidence that a considerably higher rate of dependence corresponds rather closely with what has become an almost universally accepted division of the Isaianic corpus) /6/. Within this section of the book, the part of the text most used is 49-51: there is a longer gap (approximately the equivalent of four columns and part of a fifth) /7/ between 51:1 and 52:5 than between any of the verses quoted from 49-51 /8/, which may therefore engage our attention as having yielded the first of two clusters of quotations. Here, a conjecture lies ready to hand. It has been claimed, for example by Cerfaux /9/ and Kerrigan /10/, that Paul saw himself as fulfilling the prophecies about the Servant in *Isa.* 40-55. Perhaps this is to go too far, not least since Paul had no reason to read what critical scholarship has named the 'Servant Songs' as isolated in any way from their context. But the prophecy in *Isa.* 49.6 that God's servant would receive a commission to evangelize the

Gentiles - even though Paul does not make use of this verse in
any of the letters that survive /11/ - might naturally endue
the passage which it concludes with particular personal
significance. Thus it is in relation to his own mission that
he uses 49:1 and 4. His attention having been once drawn
to the text at this point, however, he may have read and
re-read its wider context, so that passages came to mind in
a variety of situations. Thus 49:8 is quoted in a section of
paraenesis; 50:8ff contributed to the formulation of the
rhetorical climax of *Romans* 8 at 8:33f; 49:13 is probably
alluded to at *2 Cor*. 7:6 /12/: and - considerably more
doubtfully - 49:18 may have contributed to the citation of
45:23 at *Rom*. 14:11 the opening formula ζῶ ἐγώ /13/.

A second group of quotations within *Isa*. 40-55 follows
almost immediately on the first, and falls within chapters
52-55. Here the seven quotations (five of them from
Romans) /14/ are more widely spread and include two substantial
'gaps' (about 1.8 columns between 53:1 and 54:1, and about 1.4
between 54:16 and 55:10, on the basis of the rough computation
used earlier). It is harder in this case than in the previous
one to propose one passage which initially led Paul to notice
adjacent ones, but one may tentatively suggest that 52:7,
standing as it does in a passage which concludes with a
reference to the Gentiles, struck him as having a personal
application to himself (rather as was suggested in the case of
49:1-6). His own use of this text at *Rom*. 10:15 applies,
indeed, to Christian evangelists in general. His eye having
first alighted on the words concerning the εὐαγγελιζόμενος ἀγαθά,
he then noticed and remembered other passages which were in
varying degrees adjacent, and these appear in a variety of
contexts, ranging from the almost casual use of 52:5 at *Rom*. 2:24
to the skilful employment of 54:1 as the climax of the midrash
on Abraham's two sons at *Gal*. 4:27 /15/.

Next, we may turn to Isa. 28 and 29, where a different
reason may be proposed for Paul's initial interest. Both these
chapters, Lindars claims, were at an early stage of Christian
history 'drawn into the apologetic of response' /16/, that is,
into the service of a theory which accounted for Jewish obduracy
in the face of the apostolic preaching by asserting that so it
had been divinely ordained. Not all of Lindars' arguments
are equally convincing /17/, but he is surely right in saying
that the use of the article in *Rom*. 9:32 (τῷ λίθῳ τοῦ
προσκόμματος) 'very strongly gives the impression that he

expects his readers to be familiar ... already' with this stone
/18/. On this showing, the Isaiah text was already part of a
τόπος of theodicy known to the Roman Christians because already
current in 'anti-Jewish' apologetic. Here, therefore, Paul
may either - if Lindars' view about 28 and 29 as a whole is
correct - have read and re-read chapters already selected by
the church as having particular Christian significance
(something like this may account for Paul's extensive use of
Isaiah in general); or - more cautiously - the stone
testimonium of 28:16 may have led him to these chapters, in
which he then found much else that was of interest to him.
29:16, with its reference to the potter, should perhaps be
left out of account, since it has been shown that 'the link
between ... creation and the image of the potter is ... very
widespread in Judaism' /19/, and Paul may not have been
explicitly alluding to the reference in this chapter. 29:10,
however, is in a different category. It is a surprising text
for Paul to have used in its context in *Rom.* 11: possibly the
link with *Isa.* 6:10 that is afforded by the idea of the
closing of eyes indicates that, like the stone testimonium,
it belonged in pre-Pauline apologetic /20/. If not, its
occurrence may be an indication that the whole of these two
chapters was familiar to him. 29:14 is used in a theologically
comparable way at *I Cor.* 1:19f, though here it is the
recalcitrance of (largely Gentile) Corinthian devotees of
'wisdom' that is in view, not that of the Jews. Earlier in
this pair of chapters, 28:11ff supplies a text - again, a
rather surprising one of not altogether straightforward
application /21/ - for Paul's criticism of glossolalia. Once
again, he seems to have become sufficiently familiar with a
limited section of Isaiah to find there material which proved
useful in somewhat diverse situations /22/.

     The three groups of chapters considered so far yield by
far the largest clusters of quotations or allusions. We may,
however, note that one smaller cluster exhibits the phenomenon
already observed of passages adjacent in their original context
but used by Paul in widely varied situations. From 9-11, while
neglecting the Messianic prophecy at 9:5f ('Paul nowhere
offers a scriptural proof for Jesus' Messiahship' /23/), he
takes for application as far apart in Romans as 9:27f and 15:12
the remnant text of 10:22 and the 'root of Jesse' prophecy at
11:10; and one may add what is at least the strong
likelihood that 9:2 (LXX) /24/ has influenced the wording of
the quotation of *Gen* 1:3 at *2 Cor* 4:6 /25/: the future

indicative of prophecy, φῶς λάμψει in Isaiah is exactly
reproduced, and contrasts to some extent with the subjunctive
in the γενηθήτω φῶς of Genesis. Here, if one poses again the
question asked of earlier groups of quotations, it might be
thought that either of the passages illustrating the Gentile
mission (as *Isa.* 9:2 does in context) might first have attracted
Paul's attention /26/.

If there is any substance in the case here presented,
interesting questions might be raised about the way in which
other first-century readers of the prophets, or indeed of the
biblical texts generally, approached the private reading which
seems to be implied (for the phenomena do not seem to be
explicable on the basis of liturgical use: even if it were
possible to show that some of these passages occurred as
haftaroth for festivals, the continuous reading which seems
to be presupposed goes far beyond the limits of a haftarah /27/).
The author of Hebrews seems to have used adjacent passages in
Isaiah in a manner comparable with what has been investigated
here, and he, too, appears to have made a particularly
extensive use - though by rather remote allusion, it is
claimed, rather than by quotation - of *Isa.* 40-55 /28/. At all
events, it seems that the creative influence widely
acknowledged to have been exercised by the Old Testament on
the beginnings of Christian thought arose at least in some
cases through a continuous reflective reading of extended
passages, as well as through the more frequently studied
applied exegesis of discrete texts with which we are familiar
mainly through the Qumran documents /29/.

NOTES

/1/   The figures given by H.M. Shires, *Finding the Old
Testament in the New*, Philadelphia, 1974, pp.72-74, are
'1,604 N.T. passages that are directly dependent upon the
O.T.', 248 of these citations being from Isaiah.
/2/   i.e. 25 out of a total of 93 (E.E. Ellis, *Paul's Use of
the Old Testament*, Edinburgh, 1957, p.11). It is clear that
comparison of these figures with those of Shires can only be
a rough indication, since there is a considerable margin of
uncertainty in identifying what are true quotations, and Ellis
and Shires were working on independent principles in this
respect; while W. Dittmar, *Vetus Testamentum in Novo*, Göttingen,
1903, pp.171-237, had included some somewhat doubtful supposed

allusions to arrive at a total - if both Colossians and
Ephesians are omitted from the count - of 43 passages used by
Paul.
/3/   Dittmar's list (see the previous note) indicates the
following chapters of Isaiah as the sources of passages used
by Paul (again, omitting Colossians and Ephesians): the
chapter or chapters in Isaiah are given first in each case,
followed by the number of passages used:- 1-27: 8; 28,29:5;
40-45: 7; 49-55: 15; 59:2; 64,65: 6. The most dense 'clusters'
are:- 28,29: 5; 49:6; 52.5-53.1:4 (all in Romans); 65:5.
/4/   This book, as is generally recognized, Paul knew in Greek,
(whether or not he also referred to the Hebrew text, cf. A.T.
Hanson, *Studies in Paul's Technique and Theology,* London, 1974,
pp.196-200). No attempt is here made to enter into the vexed
problem of the text of Paul's Greek bible, which in more than
one third of his quotations varies from the present text of
the LXX (P. Vielhauer, 'Paulus und das Alte Testament', p.35,
in L. Abramowski and J.F.G. Goeters, edd., *Studien zur
Geschichte und Theologie der Reformation* - Festschrift for
E. Bizer - Neukirchen-Vluyn, 1969, pp.33-62); in any case,
Isaiah has a more complicated textual history in Greek than any
other OT book as a result of its exceptionally heavy use in the
NT, cf. J.W. Wevers, 'Septuaginta-Forschungen', *Theologische
Rundschau,* NF, 22 (1954), II, 'Die LXX als Übersetzungsurkunde',
pp.171-190, here p.178.
/5/   H. Ulonska, in his unpublished dissertation *Die Funktion
der alttestamentlichen Zitate und Anspielungen in die
paulinischen Briefen,* Münster, 1963, pp.27, 64, according to
Hanson, *op. cit.,* p.198, doubts whether Paul could have
carried about a copy of the Greek Old Testament as he
travelled. The scroll (or scrolls, see next note) of Isaiah,
and no doubt of any other single book of the Old Testament, would,
however, be easily portable, as is shown by the measurements of
1QIs^a (Hebrew) and those conjectured by F.G. Kenyon for a
standard scroll in Greek (respectively, 24 feet long and
26.2 cm high and 32-35 feet long and 9 or 10 inches high,
forming, when rolled up, a cylinder about one or one and a
half inches in diameter: see M. Burrows, ed., *The Dead Sea
Scrolls of St. Mark's Monastery,* I, New Haven, 1950, pp.xiv,
xvii, and F.G. Kenyon, *Books and Readers in Ancient Greece and
Rome,* Oxford, second edition, 1951, pp.66f). Cf., in any case,
2 Tim. 4:13, where Timothy is evidently to bring a number of
rolls with him, including some written on parchment.
/6/   Kenyon's observation that 'a roll of about 32-35 feet
would hold, in a medium-sized hand, one of the longer books of

the New Testament ... or a book of Thucydides, but no more'
(*op. cit.*, p.64) prompts the question whether early copies of
the Greek Isaiah must not, sometimes at least, have
occupied more than one scroll (all surviving early copies are
of course in codex form, cf. Ziegler's list of witnesses to
the text in his edition of Isaiah in the Göttingen LXX (1967),
pp.7-11). I am grateful to Mr. T.S. Pattie, of the British
Library, for calculations based both on biblical codices and
on classical scrolls from which he deduces 'that an Isaiah
with wide margins and large letters would need two rolls of
10 metres; a neat but not cramped Isaiah would need a roll of
12 or 13 metres; and a cramped Isaiah in tiny letters could
be written on a roll 8 or 9 metres long'. This leaves open the
possibility that a good copy of Isaiah may have had our
chapters 40-66 as a second volume.

/7/   This very rough guess is based on Kenyon's estimate of
25-45 lines to a column and 18-25 letters to a line (*op. cit.*
p.59).

/8/   The longest gap - 49:23 - 50:8 - would, on the basis
indicated in the previous note, amount to a little less than
two columns.

/9/   Cf. *Recueil Lucien Cerfaux*, II, (= Bibliotheca
Ephemeridum Theologicarum Lovaniensium VI - VII), Gembloux,
1954, pp.446-454.

/10/ Cf. A. Kerrigan, 'Echoes of Themes from the Servant Songs
in Pauline Theology', in *Studiorum Paulinorum Congressus
Internationalis Catholica 1961* (= Analecta Biblica 17-18), II,
Rome, 1963, pp.217-228.

/11/ The omission is repaired at *Acts* 13:47.

/12/ Somewhat surprisingly, this is the only passage in the
LXX in which ταπεινός and παρακαλῶ occur in a manner similar
to their use by Paul here; *Isa.*54:11 is much less close.

/13/ Cf. Dittmar, *op. cit.*, *ad loc*, and C. Smits, *Oud-
Testamentische citaten in het Niewe Testament*, (Collectanea
Franciscana Neerlandica, dl 8), 's-Hertogenbosch, 1952-63,
p.498, though the formula ζῶ ἐγώ is frequent in Ezekiel and
occurs some five times elsewhere in the Greek bible.
49:23 is cited by Dittmar among the passages given at *1 Cor.*
14:25, but is perhaps too remote a parallel to count.

/14/ And of these, three are from *Rom.*9-11. It causes no
surprise, in view of the nature of the argument in Romans in
general and in *Rom.*9-11 in particular, that a high proportion
of Paul's O.T. quotations (42 according to Shires, *op.cit.* p.53)
are found in Romans, and that 33 quotations or allusions to the
O.T., 12 of them from Isaiah, are found in *Rom.*9-11 according
to Dittmar (*op. cit.*, p.189-201).

/15/   *Isa.* 54:1 is, in fact, by no means an obvious proof-text
for the assertion that not Jews but Christians are the
children of the heavenly Jerusalem; in particular, the emphasis
on the large number (πολλὰ) of the barren woman's offspring
does not fit into the train of thought, for Paul had made no
allusion (though he might have done) to the vast number of
the progeny promised to Abraham through Isaac (e.g. *Gen* 17:16).
Is it possible that (as F.F. Bruce has conjectured, 'Galatian
Problems, 5: Galatians and Christian Origins', *BJRL*, 55, 1972-3,
p.269), Paul *began* with the Isaiah text as vindicating the
claims of Christians on the basis of the manifest statistical
success of the Gentile mission (cf *Rom.* 15:18f, which suggests
a substantial success in terms of numbers)? The opening words
εὐφράνθητι, στεῖρα ἡ οὐ τίκτουσα would then - especially since
Abraham was already in Paul's mind - naturally suggest Sarah,
introduced as she is at the beginning of *Gen.* 16 by the
statement that οὐκ ἔτικτεν αὐτῷ (sc. Abraham; less immediately,
εὐφράνθητι might also evoke the references to Sarah's laughter,
albeit sardonic, at 18:12ff). In a sense, the strange (and,
to a Jew, scandalously paradoxical) midrash at *Gal.* 4:21-6 may
be read as a Christian answer to the riddle propounded in
Isa. 54:1 for those who do not see its historical allusion.
/16/   B. Lindars, *New Testament Apologetic*, London, 1961,
p.175; cf. p. 164, note 1, where attention is drawn to the
unusual number of quotations, mainly in Paul, taken from
these chapters.
/17/   The use of the 'stone testimonium' (*Isa.* 28:16) at
1 Peter 2:6 does not necessarily tell us anything about pre-
Pauline exegesis: indeed, if the epistle is regarded as in
some way related to the Pauline corpus, one might be less
cautious. Lindars' evidence may be applicable only to Paul's
own 'apologetic'.
/18/   *op. cit.* p.177.
/19/   U. Luz, *Das Geschichtsverständnis des Paulus*, Beiträge
zur evangelische Theologie, 49, München, 1968, p.238.
/20/   Cf. B. Lindars, *op.cit.*, p.164.
/21/   Few commentators seem to note that God's miraculous
speech - so Paul would surely read the text - is addressed
τῷ λαῷ τούτῳ, and that it is awkward to think that this was
necessarily *unbelieving* Israel; moreover as J.P.M. Sweet notes
('A Sign for Unbelievers: Paul's Attitude to Glossolalia',
N.T.S. 13, 1966-7, p.243), the οὐδ᾽ οὕτως of Paul's rather
curious reproduction of Isaiah is significant: the miraculous
communication ought to have succeeded, yet did not. May not
the thought be: in view of this failure, and also of the fact

that God's purpose cannot fail, 'tongues' cannot be a sign to
believers ('Israel')? The only alternative is that they are a
sign to unbelievers. But such is the disorder in the *practice*,
in Corinth, of a gift which is in itself good that its true
function, as indicated by scripture, is frustrated (*1 Cor.*14:23).
It is surely not necessary, with J.D.G. Dunn (*Jesus and the
Spirit*, London, 1975, pp.230f), to assume a polemical intention
in the assertion that glossolalia is a sign to unbelievers.

/22/ Though a unifying theme, namely God's prevenience both
in grace and in judgement, may be detected in all these
passages.

/23/ P. Vielhauer, *art. cit.*, p.42.

/24/ According to the verse numeration adopted in the
Göttingen edition (ed. J. Ziegler, see note 5.)

/25/ So H. Windisch, Meyer-Kommentar, 1924, ad loc., and
C. Smits, *op. cit.*, p. 441.

/26/ In view of the likelihood that Paul knew these chapters
well, one may raise the question whether a reminiscence of
Isa 10:12 lies behind *2 Cor* 10:5. In each case, the thought is
of destruction brought upon what exalts itself or is exalted,
and the ὕψωμα of the Pauline phrase may recall Isaiah's ὕψος:
the former noun is neither common nor an obvious one in this
context. Moreover, the metaphor is military in both cases.

/27/ The haftaroth set out in the *Jewish Encyclopaedia* (VI,
p.136) are mostly of about the length of one chapter in our
bibles; interestingly, one of the exceptions is *Isa* 49:14-51:4,
appointed for the Sabbath named *'ekeb* (in the annual cycle).
However, there is room only for conjecture - which has, indeed,
not been lacking - about the haftaroth in use in the first
century: it is most unlikely that the haftaroth of the
Palestinian (or Galilean) triennial cycle of lections - as
opposed to the sedarim themselves - are much earlier than the
sixth or seventh century (so B.Z. Wacholder, Prolegomena to
J. Mann, *The Bible as Read and Preached in the Old Synagogue*,
I, 1940, reprinted New York, 1971, pp. XXIX-XLII, and
J.J. Petuchowski, ed., *Contributions to the Scientific Study
of Jewish Liturgy*, New York, 1970, pp. XIX-XXI). From the
point of view of this study, therefore, it must remain only
an intriguing coincidence - short of some form of other
evidence - that 'almost half of the "triennial" haftaroth were
taken from the Book of Isaiah, and some two-thirds from
chapters 40 to 66' (Wacholder, *op. cit.*, p. XXXII), and that
in the same cycle selections from *Isa* 40-61 were read for the
three 'sabbaths of consolation' following the 9th Ab (Jewish
Encyclopaedia, *loc. cit.*).

/28/ I am grateful to Dr. Paul Ellingworth for these
suggestions, the detail of which is set out in his unpublished
doctoral thesis (Aberdeen, 1977) 'The Old Testament in Hebrews:
exegesis, method and hermeneutics', especially the 'excursus on
the use of *Isa* 40-66 in Heb.' It seems unlikely that
examination of the use of the Hebrew Bible by the Rabbis would
yield any comparable findings, though a partial parallel may
exist in the predilection allegedly shown by Rav (Abba Arika)
for Sirach, cf. Y.S. Zuri, *Rav*, Jerusalem, 1925, pp.357-8 (in
Hebrew: I am grateful to Mr. H. Maccoby of Leo Baeck College
for this and related information).
/29/ This paper is a shortened version of one given to
Professor P.R. Ackroyd's Old Testament seminar at King's
College, London.

The Sufferings in 1 Peter and "Missionary Apocalyptic"

Rev. John Holdsworth,
The Vicarage,
Abercraf,
Swansea SA9 1TJ,
Wales.

The problem of the sufferings in 1 Peter has occupied critical scholarship for some time. The problem has been whether, and to what degree, the πειρασμοῦ (1:6,4:12) have historical reference. The further problem has been to date them accurately enough to be able to support a particular hypothesis about authorship - the main eventual concern of most critics. Within this critical framework, the possibility of the sufferings having an eschatological reference more usually associated with the apocalyptic writings has been largely neglected.

1 Peter does not contain the usual apocalyptic designations of suffering; θλῖψις and διωγμός /1/. Ardnt and Gingrich ascribe to the term which is used πειρασμός (and cognate verb πειράζω) a more ethical sense of trial /2/, which though appropriate for some occurrences of the words /3/, and possibly for 1 Peter, seems to obscure their sense elsewhere in the N.T. The ethical description is difficult, for example, at Acts 20:19, Paul's description of the work of the Jews within the context of a summary of the advance of the Gospel, and also at Jas.1:12 a beatitude about the reward (στέφανος τῆς ζωῆς) for ὅς ὑπομένει, an echo of Dan.12:12. This is very close to the traditional use of θλῖψις at e.g. Jn.16:33 and διωγμός at e.g. Matt.5:10ff. There is evidence of a relationship between the three terms as follows:

1. The Lucan version of the parable of the sower interprets the seed which falls on the rock as producing those who hear with joy but fall away ἐν καιρῷ πειρασμοῦ (Lk.8:13). The Matthean parallel has the hearers scandalised γενομένης θλίψεως ἢ διωγμού (Matt.13:21).

2. Rev.2:10 has πειράζω in parallel with θλῖψις apparently alluding to Dan.1:12,14.

3. Rev.3:10 uses πειρασμός in a context where θλῖψις would have been expected.

The relationship between πειρασμός and θλῖψις seems best expressed at 1 Thess.3:4f. Here πειρασμός is a symptom of θλῖψις. In this passage πειρασμός is associated with apocalyptic imagery by virtue of being caused by ὁ πειράζων. We should also note:

(i) That πειρασμος is the work of ὁ διάβολος at Lk.4:13, who in the Matthean parallel is called ὁ διάβολος Matt.4:5,8, ὁ πειράζων 4:3, and (Σατανᾶς) 4:10 (cf. ὁ Σατανᾶς Mk.1:12.)

(ii) That in the Matthean form of the Lord's Prayer, the petition not to be led into πειρασμός is a parallel to that to be kept ἀπὸ τοῦ πονηροῦ where the definite article may be titular (Matt.6:13).

(iii) That in the eschatologically ethical passage 1 Cor.7, ὁ Σατανᾶς is the subject of πειράζω in v.5.

It would seem that πειρασμός can have apocalyptic associations inasmuch as the origin of πειρασμος is more important than its nature. Thus it contributes to the theodicy which is characteristic of apocalyptic. Two other occurrences are interesting in this connection. First, at Lk.20:40,46 (parr.) where πειρασμός is used suggestively in a historicised account of Jesus' suffering, with a historicised command for 'the future Church', and second at 2 Peter 2:9 where πειρασμός occurs in a theodicy/vindication situation. The use in 1 Peter is entirely consistent with this interpretation. There the subject of the testing is ὁ διάβολος (5:8). Hence we have no need to regard the πειρασμού as part of a physical or legal assault. We can rather regard them as interpretative, part of 1 Peter's theodicy and a possible accompaniment to apocalyptic in terms of mission rationale.

This would perhaps be unremarkable were it not for the incidence in 1 Peter of a combination of apocalyptic language, ideas, imagery, and to some extent form which is unusual in the

N.T. outside the recognised Synoptic Apocalypses and the Book
of Revelation. In a paper of this length it would clearly be
impossible to fully substantiate this claim though a more
widely illustrated argument could be presented with little
difficulty.

We may note the occurrence of the verbs ἀποκαλύπτω (1:5,12;
5:1) and φανερόω (1:20; 5:4) as well as the definite form
ἀποκάλυψις (1:7,13). Throughout 1 Peter there is an atmosphere
of imminence about the end and a stress on the end as
foreshadowing judgement which is typical of apocalyptic, as is
the theme of persecution and the vindication of the righteous.

Ecclesiologically we may note that the basic idiom is
that of the New Temple, an idiom which has its roots in Ezek.,
universalised in Second Isaiah, and whose implicit apocalyptic
theme is made explicit in Zech.9-14 /4/. This theme has its
ultimate employment in the N.T. Apocalypse /5/. We may note
also the recent attempt to trace a connection between the
ministry described at 1 Peter 5:1-5 and that of Qumran, with
particular reference to the figure of the מְבַקֵּר and also the
singular attitude taken to election both in terms of the
Christian community, and of Christ.

Eschatologically there are several occurrences of
apocalyptic vocabulary, some of which are N.T. *hapax legomena*.
In particular, attention could be drawn to:

λυπέω *(1:6)* to grieve

λυπέω in the passive as here is relatively rare, but two
passages evidence this form used to describe the awareness of
the community awaiting vindication in apocalyptic terms.

(i)   Jn.16:20 (fut. passive) contrasts the grieving
       with eventual joy, in a passage expressing the
       difference between "Christians" and the world
       using apocalyptic vocabulary.

(ii)   En.102:5 introduces the aorist pass. of λυπέω
       into a theodicy vindication situation "Grieve not
       .... wait for the day of judgement of
       sinners."

δοκιμάζω *(1:7)* to test

Two occurrences of this verb are particular interesting.

(i)   1 Cor.3:13. This passage describes the ongoing
       work and rationale of the early community and
       includes a description of testing by fire with
       consequent revelation on the apocalyptic Day of
       the Lord.

(ii)   Shepherd of Hermas Hv.4:3:4. Here it is used in
       connection with the explanation of the visage of
       the Beast and its partly golden colour "For as the
       gold is tested by the fire and made useful so ye also
       (that dwell in it) are being tested in yourselves."
       Those that abide are purified by the fire and "so ye
       also shall cast away all sorrow and tribulation and
       shall be useful for the building of the tower."
       This is part of the symbolism of "the mighty
       tribulation which is coming."

κολαφίζω *(2:20)*

κολαφίζω, an uncommon verb which in 1 Peter describes the lot to
be expected from the σκολιοί, is almost exclusively Christian.
It describes the blows suffered by Christ at his trial (Matt.
26:67; Mk.14:65) and is used by Paul to describe Christian
witness (1 Cor.4:11). The only other N.T. reference is notable
in that it attributes the "beating" to Satan (2 Cor.12:7). It
seems that here is an example of the identity of Christ's
experience, and that of Christians, which has no need of an
historical *a priori*.

μακροθυμία *(3:20)*

     This word, predicated of God, often expresses the awareness
of the pregnancy of the present time pending apocalyptic action
in terms of judgement.

(i)   Rom.2:4. μακροθυμία leads to repentance pending
       the Day of Wrath.

(ii)   Rom.9:22. God desires to show his wrath but has
       μακροθυμία

(iii) 2 Pet. 3:15. This attribute of God is predicated
       of Christ in an apocalyptic setting.

(iv)   Ig. Eph. 11:7 expresses the typical usage.   "These
       are the last times.   Henceforth let us have reverence;
       let us fear the long-suffering of God lest it turn
       into a judgement against us."   (cf. 1 Pet.4:7).

Since 3:20 tells us that the present time (or the present
theology) corresponds to when God had μακροθυμιά in the case of
Noah we can safely assume that the awareness of the present time
was in similar apocalyptic terms to those above.   (It would be
interesting to pursue the use of the Noah pericope in the
Synoptic Apocalypses here),

and πύρωσις *(4:12)*

Briefly also we may note that the Christological and
Theological titles of 1 Peter: e.g. ἀμνός and ποίμηω all have
apocalyptic parallels /8/.   We may also consider the incidence
of other apocalyptic elements such as the (possible) pseudonymity,
the allusion to Βαβυλών, and the preaching to the dead.

Formally, if we consider 1 Peter to be a letter, then the
(uneasy) epistolary framework and the parenetic sections could be
compared with apocalyptic parallels.   If we consider it to be
a liturgy of some kind, then we shall acknowledge that the
prayer, hymn and recurring doxology forms are all, in other
contexts, vehicles of apocalyptic thought.

Recent commentators have been more reticent in accepting
that 1 Peter does contain apocalyptic imagery, ideas, vocabulary,
etc. than have their predecessors.   Moffat's commentary /9/
includes many references to e.g. 1 Enoch and 4 Esdras, whilst
that of F.W. Beare /10/ contains only one reference to each of
these works.   The older commentators who acknowledged the
references sought to explain them.   Moffat does so by reference
to the traditions with which Peter the apostle was familiar;
Goodspeed /11/ by designating it as a world-affirming rejoinder
to the N.T. Apocalypse.

We must acknowledge that 1 Peter is *not* an apocalypse as
such.   Many obviously essential elements of apocalyptic are
missing from it.   Goodspeed's theory is not convincing.   An
answer to a specific apocalypse would surely contain more overt
reference to it and the designation of the addressees as aliens
and exiles is hardly world-affirming.

However there lies within this problem the possibility of
answer to a number of current N.T. concerns. The prevailing
view is that apocalypses are (or were) produced when a clash
occurs between the powers of this world and the faithful -
to assure them of vindication in a specific *political* situation.
The apocalypses which would be universally acknowledged as
such certainly have this background. In 1 Peter (and not
exclusively there) we see the basic elements of a missionary
theology which sees a constant, ongoing and necessary disjuntion
and struggle between powers antipathetic to the Gospel, and
the Gospel itself, which needs no necessary background of
political action. The language of what we might call "political
apocalyptic" is congenial to this missionary theology and the
main purpose of political apocalyptic viz. to produce a theodicy
is also appropriate to the ongoing mission situation in which it
provides a kind of theodicy or mission rationale in terms of the
universality of God, and his, in fact, having a purpose for his
people within history.

If we wanted to widen our appreciation of the scope of what
we might call "missionary apocalyptic", the apocalyptic which
accompanies the Church's theology of mission and by virtue of
which set-backs and advances are described in apocalyptic terms
we might stray into two other areas.

(i)   In the Epistles generally there are descriptions of
      mission in terms of a continuing battle with
      antipathetic powers, e.g. in Col. the missionary
      advance is described in terms of transference (of
      people) from the dominion of darkness into light
      (1:13), the disarming of the powers (2:15), and
      death to the στοιχεῖα τοῦ κόσμου (2:20).

(ii) In the Gospels the story of the mission of the
      Church is transposed on occasion on to the story
      of the historical Jesus so that Jesus is made to
      both experience and foretell the fortunes of the
      Church. The Synoptic Apocalypses are examples of
      such foretelling. The combination of apocalyptic and
      mission and the consequent combination of Jesus' and
      the Church's "history" is most obvious in Matt.
      whose missionary discourse is peculiarly apocalyptic.
      Bornkamm's study of the "Stilling of the Storm in
      Matthew" has shown how the Church's mission seen in
      apocalyptic terms is made part of the history of
      Jesus, and how at least one theology current in the

early Church connected discipleship and mission
and viewed the Church's relation to the world as
one of a small boat on a sea struck by an apocalyptic
storm.

One characteristic of this missionary apocalyptic is its
association with sharing the sufferings of Christ (continuing
his θλῖψις Col. 1:24). In this regard I want to return to
1 Pet. to consider briefly the other term used there for
suffering, παθήματα (1:11,4:13,5:1).

This word is seldom used in the N.T. other than to
describe the sufferings of Christ. When the sufferings are
not predicated of Christ the context is such as to require an
identification between the sufferings of believers and those
of Christ (2 Cor.1:5f.). In fact this seems to be the special
function of the word. Continuing in or sharing in the
sufferings of Christ is almost a synonym for pursuing an
early Christian vocation. παθήματα is used with apocalyptic
language in connection with vocation and mission: with θλῖψις
at Col.1:24, and with διωγμός at 2 Tim.3:11.

Perhaps these observations might provide some avenue
through the impasse which the study of 1 Peter seems to have
reached, as well as possibly illuminating the meaning of the
author at 4:16 ".... if one suffers *as a Christian* let him not
be ashamed, but under that name let him glorify God."

NOTES

/1/ θλῖψις cf. Rev.2:10; Jn.16:33; Matt.24:9,21,29 διωγμός
cf. Matt.13:21; Mk.4:17; 2 Thess.1:4; Acts 8:1; 13:50 etc.
/2/ πειρασμός "temptation, enticement to sin."
     πειράζω "to discover what kind of person someone is."
W. Bauer, *A Greek-English Lexicon of the New Testament and
other Early Christian Literature* (trans. W.F. Ardnt and F.W.
Gingrich) Chicago 1973[14].
/3/ e.g. πειρασμός 1 Tim.6:9; πειραζω Gal.6:1.
/4/ *vide* R.J. McKelvey, *The New Temple*, Oxford, 1969 *passim*.
/5/ Rev.21.
/6/ Nauck "Probleme des Frühchristlichen Amtsverstandnisses
(1 Peter 5:2f.)" *ZNW* 48 1957 pp.200-220 cited by J.H. Elliott
"Ministry and Church Order in the New Testament: A Traditio-
Historical Analysis" *CBQ* 32 1970 pp.367-391 p.372.

/7/   *vide* J.H. Elliott, *The Elect and the Holy* (Supp.to Novum
Testamentum Vol. XII) Leiden 1966.
/8/   ἀμνός cf. Rev.14, En.89 ff.   The parallels are with
community awareness rather than vindicating leadership.   ποίμην
cf. Zech.13:7-9; Κτύστης cf. En.94:9ff.; II Macc.7:23.
/9/   J. Moffatt, *The General Epistles,* London, 1928.
/10/   F.W. Beare, *The First Epistle of Peter,* Oxford, 1970[3].
/11/   E.J. Goodspeed, *New Solution of New Testament Problems,*
Chicago, 1927, p.31.

Romans 8:19 — On Pauline Belief and Creation

Dr. Günther Kehnscherper
Ordinary Professor of Practical Theology,
University of Greifswald,
35 Stellingstrasse,
22 Greifswald,
Germany (DDR).

It was in 1953 that in a theological broadcast the assertion was made by G. Bornkamm that "the created universe as a whole will take part in the salvation which is to come, because the universe as a whole participates in the curse under which man is lost". Being part of Creation, Nature, too, participates in the certitude of salvation. Christian hope thus cannot be confined to the future existence of mankind.

At that time R. Bultmann rejected such assertions about the future as unbecoming "mythological speculation" /1/. Ten years later R. Bultmann was sharply criticized and finally proved wrong by H. Wenz /2/. The intricate nexus between mankind and the whole created universe on their way to salvation cannot be denied. Ever since that time the exegesis of Rom.8, especially of vs. 18-23 and 28-30, has been stimulating theological discussions up to the writings of J. Moltmann /3/. With a view to the longing on the part of the created universe he asks for a new way of Christian thinking, in which the salvation in Jesus Christ and Christian hope for salvation is extended to the universe. He wishes that the believers, too, regard the history of the universe as considered with the history of salvation.

For H.H. Jenssen and H.G. Fritzsche theological thinking that starts from Jesus Christ ranks Nature among the created universe. Only by the salvation in Jesus Christ is a theology of Nature made possible, which is to be understood as the "Christian word to Nature" /4/. Nature is the object of theological interpretation, not the background of the history of salvation of mankind. The congregation to which salvation

is promised and which is set free by the Spirit, represents the
glory of God's salvation in the universe. Therefore, the hope
of the created universe is not only the expectation of the
salvation that is to come, it becomes the focus of attention
of the congregation at present. With Paul δόξα is not a
future stage of salvation. On the contrary, it can be
experienced already at present /5/. This process has been
going on ever since God was perceived to work salvation through
Jesus Christ. That means, according to all the papers and
commentaries quoted above, that the present state of Nature,
which we are bound to call unfortunate and full of suffering,
is to come to an end. God will not surrender his creation to
the perdition brought about by man.

Not yet fully realized are P. Tillich's rich ideas on
Rom.8, above all those that aim at actualizing the
eschatological dimension /6/. Since the Catholic theologian
H.K. Gieraths /7/ has published a thorough study of the
exegesis of Rom. 8:19-28, that uses patristic, medieval and
modern commentaries, this paper is devoted to a number of
recent German and English publications.

                                   I

Horst Balz (cf. note 1) has led the way in the German-
speaking world. He shows the "waiting with eager expectation"
on the part of the created universe to be the particular case
in the New Testament. But the expectation of the ἀποκάλυψις
of God's sons is without parallel too. Rom. 8:19 does not
expect the epiphany of *Christ* as described in 1 Cor. 1:7 or
2 Thess. 1:7, but the relevation of *Christians*. It is true,
we could have expected an expression of the hope on the part
of the created universe for the coming day of judgement
(2 Petr, 3:13) or hints at the ἀποκατάστασις πάντων (Acts 3:21).
But Paul seems to stress a special kind of nexus between the
created universe and the congregation to which salvation is
promised, the 'Heilsgemeinde'.

No mention is made of a special kind of salvation that is
meant for the created universe. The created universe waits with
eager expectation to take part in the full verification of the
present spiritual reality of the salvation of God's sons.

The difficult parenthesis οὐχ ἐκοῦσα may mean that

frustration came upon the created universe as a doom. Man
subjected it, he is the stimulus, and it is by his fault that
the created universe was subjected to frustration. In the
form of an interpreting parenthesis Paul hints at man's guilt
in this context of frustration. H. Balz /8/ and W.D. Stacey
(cf. note 22) see its context within the history of religions,
in Jewish statements on the creation and fall.

Helpful in this respect is Henning Paulsen /9/, who
understands the hope for salvation in Rom. 8 as a corrective
of the present and a condition for the liberation from the
powers of ἁμαρτία and σάρξ.

In Rom. 5:12 - 8:39 the reality of salvation itself and
its significance for the believer's existence is dealt with.
This point is made conclusive and impressive by the contrast to
the previous way of being /10/.

There is no need to enter into a discussion of the well-
known commentaries by Heinrich Schlier, Ernst Käsemann,
O. Kuss and W. Barclay with their useful contributions to
Rom. 8. Nor need I discuss Ernst Fuchs. Mention should be
made, however, of W.G. Kümmel's detailed investigation entitled
"Römer 7 und das Bild des Menschen im NT". (Munchen 1974), of
the Catholic theologian A. Vögtle's fundamental contribution
"Das Neue Testament und die Zukunft des Kosmos. Kommentare
und Beiträge zum Alten und Neuen Testament" (1970), and of
Peter von der Osten-Sacken's "Römer 8 als Beispiel
paulinischer Soteriologie" (Göttingen 1975). Emphasis is
laid on the fact that in no other place does Paul deal with
the certitude of salvation so fundamentally and with a similar
combination of reflective and doxological statements.

There is universal consensus among modern commentators
that this text occupies a unique place among the letters of
Paul, not as a declination from his basic ideas, but as a
climax. Paul interprets Christ and his salvation among men
and in a world that after Christ belongs without
qualification not to itself but to God.

Furthermore, it should be stated that the theology of
creation is no topic of its own in the New Testament. With
Paul statements on this topic, if made the object of theological
reflection as in Rom. 8, are always to be found in a
christological and soteriological context.

The hermeneutic canon for the reception of the Jewish Old
Testament traditions on Creation is formed by the saving work
of God through Jesus Christ, i.e. christology. With H.H. Jenssen
we should speak of a christology of Creation as far as Paul is
concerned rather than of a theology of Creation.

Rom. 8:19-23 is not a marginal note, but the climax of
Pauline soteriology. It aims at interpreting and actualizing
existing traditions about Creation. The reality and experience
of salvation, if combined with the eschatological dimension,
show the universe take God's creation and make it a place to
verify one's belief in (cf. Eph. 2:10). These statements come
close to what is said about the nexus between Salvation and
Creation in vol. I cf. K.H. Schelkle's "Theologie des Neuen
Testaments. Bd.I: Schöpfung. Welt-Zeit-Mensch" (Düsseldorf 1968).

As for myself, I learned from Peter von der Osten-Sacken's
monograph that Paul could understand the presence of salvation
only by speaking of the future at the same time. On the other
hand, Paul speaks of the future for the sake of the believers'
present. Christians' life under the conditions of this
existence and of this aeon is for him the most prominent
theme of eschatology and Rom. 8:18-39 is a model of this.
Salvation is already a reality, if God has acted with Christ.
Should Nature, which suffers by and from Man, be totally
excluded from it?

II.

In English literature special emphasis was laid in recent
years on Rom. 8:28 (see E.C. Blackmann, J.P. Wilson,
E.H. Daniell, M. Black, K. Grayston, A.R.C. Leaney and
H.G. Wood /11/).

The question of the created universe and its longing for
and participation in, salvation has been dealt with by such
outstanding theologians as T. Fahy /12/, F.R.M. Hitchcock /13/,
E. Hill /14/, E. Lewish /15/, B.M. Metzger /16/, C.C. Oke /17/,
G. Philip /18/, D.M. Stanley /19/, J. Swetnam /20/ and
R.C. Tannehill /21/. I cannot, however, set out their ideas
here. W.D. Stacey seems to be representative. Unlike the
older commentators, e.g. Schlatter and Tholuck, he understands
by κτίσις "the whole created order - man, bird, beast, field,
forest, everything ..." Because of Man they all are subject

to suffering. The total cosmos of Jewish apocalyptic is
concerned here, the totality of the created universe that faces
God at a certain time and in a certain historical situation.
In this connexion the following thorough investigations should
be mentioned: J.G. Gager, "Functional Diversity in Paul's use
of End-Time Language", *JBL* 89 (1970) 325-337, and J.G. Gibbs,
"Creation and Redemption. A Study in Pauline Theology",*Suppl.
Nov. Test.* 26, Leiden 1971.

With a view to homiletics it is important to say that
E. Lewis (cf. note 15) speaks of Rom. 8 as a fundamental piece
of Paul's philosophy. Especially today this new view of the
world will have to be in the centre of our preaching. Similar
ideas are to be found with C.C. Oke (cf. note 17), who
attributes to suffering Nature a special hope for salvation.

Valuable are the historical parallels in apocalyptic and
rabbinic sources which are quoted by W.D. Davies /23/ in order
to prove Paul's statements on man's responsibility for the
frustration and sufferings of the created universe. Paul thus
conforms with established Jewish tradition, he "is clearly
reflecting current Rabbinic speculation upon creation" /24/.

III.

A totally new situation has arisen in recent years, above
all for practical theology. The fundamental statements of
Rom. 8:19-23 are increasingly becoming the biblical starting-
point for diverse systems of theology of Nature. Systematic
theologians and scientists find perspectives for a new theology
of Creation by linking it up with the problems of New Testament
soteriology. H.G. Fritzsche, G. Altner, K.M. Meyer-Abich,
A.M.I. Müller and W. Pannenberg are among the best-known
authors /25/.

Being part of the created universe, Nature, too, takes part
in the history of salvation. But how does salvation take place
and who confers it? Are there any special forms of
participation on the part of the created universe? How much
depends here on the "sons of God"? Answers to these questions
are expected in our sermons by the churches and congregations,
and by Christian scientists as well. Homiletics must come in
here.

As far as theological literature up to 1970 is concerned, the interpretation of Nature seems to be theologically superfluous and forgotten, with no problems left. Our churches and our sermons had to do without a well-grounded tradition of theological concern for Nature and without a responsible interpretation of the phenomena of suffering Nature.

In a situation where a "practical theology of Nature" is to be created (and demanded by homiletics), Rom. 8:19 acquires special significance.

The first push came from Christian scientists. Reg Bird characterizes the problem as follows: "Genetic manipulation means that scientists have developed a method which allows the production of new species of microbes" /26/. The development may be useful, but it is not without risk for the scientists and the population as a whole. Maybe a new abuse of much-vexed Nature is imminent?

Out of the many statements on this subject I will quote only J.K. Dutton, of Great Britain, who, dealing with the problem of genetic experiments upon men, expresses the view that such experiments should on no account be allowed, because the consequences of the manipulation with transformed or artificial genes are mostly unknown. It is possible that vital regulating and functional systems of Nature are being destroyed /27/. The Church and Society Department of the World Council of Churches at Geneva, which has so far concentrated its activities on reducing the dangers of atomic explosions and the dangers caused by nuclear radiation, has now turned to the dangers of the "biologization of the cosmos". The future of the biosphere is in danger. Therefore the Council demands a halt in experiments in gene manipulation.

There are many more grave ecological problems which scientists, farmers, economists etc. are challenged to solve in Christian responsibility: Is there a form of exploitation of Nature in which the reality of God appears also in economic reality /28/? A committee led by Gert von Wahlert (German Federal Republic) is concerned with the economy of the seas, a field much larger than that of fishery. Another field is that of biological agriculture, i.e. the avoidance of artificial manure and fertilizers. For these investigations large sums are provided by the Evangelical Church in Germany (Fed.Rep.), until businesses and states have realized their responsibility /29/.

In the GDR the use of increased nitrogen adhesion via microbes in place of mineral manure is being tested.

Support for tropical forestry is another field of exemplary ministry of the churches, arising from a theology of Nature. After enormous damage caused by aridity in consequence of clear felling have occurred, a 2,000-mile strip of forests is to be set up in the Sahel zone of Central Africa. In 1965 these territories, today famine-stricken, still exported 15,000 tons of high quality foodstuffs. Then the forests were felled, although specialists were unanimous in predicting disastrous consequences of any disturbance of an ecological equilibrium that has grown up over thousands of years. Ecological breakdowns in these territories are not only of regional importance but are likely to have global consequences.

Is the Church to come in to help only after the event as in former times, or is it to detect, change and remedy such culpable activities of Man?

A similar abyss of human guilt in face of Nature has been shown up during the discussions on the limits of growth in the Club of Rome. Has theology taught our churches, clergymen and congregations to show up new ways in Christian responsibility in discussions on questions such as those raised by Dennis Meadows and his colleagues? In our days, more than ever, Christian theology must stimulate new forms of behaviour to Creation /30/.

IV.

New Testament work has not been in vain. It is gratifying to see important publications on human responsibility for Nature and Cosmos which proceed from the soteriological statements of Rom. 8 and which are consciously founded on the results reached by New Testament theology /31/.

A modern theology of Nature explains the sufferings caused by estrangement and speaks of the end of these sufferings in terms of natural christology.

A theology of Nature speaks of what man has been guilty of doing.

A theology of Nature speaks of what God has done, is doing now and will do in Jesus Christ.

A theology of Nature speaks of what man must not do, i.e. offend Nature, which is temporarily entrusted to him as the last thing but one, by glorifying it, deifying it or destroying it as an object of exploitation.

A theology of Nature speaks of what man has to do. "Having been given perception of Jesus Christ, man has to perceive within himself as well as around himself Nature, which is entrusted to him; he has to cultivate it in his behaviour and attitude .." /32/. H. Dembowski sums up: "On account of a right perception of God and man and nature through Jesus Christ, man is expected rightly to perceive God and man and nature too."

In pastoral ministry a new understanding of Creation and Salvation helps us to arrive at a theology of gratefulness.

Besides, can we in our pastoral ministry neglect the fact that in the ecological and economic crises of many countries there is an element of divine retribution, which is mentioned in Rom. 1:18? We have no right to exclude from this retribution economic injustice, which in its turn is the source of many other kinds of injustice. Maybe Judgement is taking place in the course of political and economic events? At any rate, the saving purpose of God includes the responsibility of 'God's sons' for the economic and ecological problems in Nature. There is no denying this biblical fact. With united efforts we will have to work out the meaning of taking Salvation seriously with respect to Nature. The answer will be different in each case and difference of opinion is likely to occur, but that such an answer must be arrived at is beyond any doubt: it is a consequence of Christian obedience of faith.

Christian belief in Creation, according to Rom. 8:19, is therefore by no means a theoretical view of the world. We believe not in Creation, but in the Creator. It is for that reason that we believe, too, that Nature is part of Creation, which is the object of the saving work of God through Jesus Christ. He who believes that takes a different view of the world and is granted really new hope.

NOTES

/1/   Horst R. Balz, *Heilsvertrauen und Welterfahrung.
Strukturen der paulinischen Eschatologie nach Romer 8, 18-39*,
Munchen 1971 11.
/2/   H. Wenz, *Die Ankunft unseres Herrn am Ende der Welt.   Zur
Überwindung des Individualismus und des bloßen Aktualismus in
der Eschatologie R. Bultmanns und H. Brauns*, (Arbeiten zur
Theologie I 21) 1965, 48 ff.
/3/   J. Moltmann, *Theologie der Hoffnung*, (BEvTh 38) 1966[5] 30,
60.
/4/   H.-H. Jenssen, "Zu Problemen der Naturpredigt", *Evang.
Pfarrerblatt*, Berlin, 1964 183 f.; Hans-Georg Fritzsche,
Lehrbuch der Dogmatik II, Berlin 1967 314,321; Helmut
Fritzsche, "Historische und aktuelle Aspekte zum Verhältnis des
Christentums zur Naturwissenschaft", *Die Zeichen der Zeit*,
Berlin 11-12/1977 401-416.
/5/   G. Kittel, *ThW* II 253,39 ff.
/6/   P. Tillich, *Systematische Theologie*, Band II Stuttgart,
1958 50; Band III 1966 107 u.458 f.
/7/   H.K. Gieraths, *Knechtschaft und Freiheit der Schopfung*,
Diss. Bonn 1950.
/8/   H. Balz, *Heilsvertrauen* 41 ff.
/9/   H. Paulsen, *Uberlieferung und Auslegung in Romer 8*,
Neukirchen 1974.
/10/   Cf. H. Paulsen, *Uberlieferung* 18 u.20.
/11/   For the theses of the authors and the sources look at
H. Balz, *Heilsvertrauen* 103-115, 132 ff.
/12/   T. Fahy, "Romans 8:16-25", *Irish Theological Quarterly*
23, 1956 178-81.
/13/   F.R.M. Hitchcock,"'Every creature', not 'all creation'
in Romans 8:22", *Exp.* VIII 11 (1916) 372-383.
/14/   E. Hill, "The Construction of three Passages from St.
Paul", CBQ 23 (1961) 296-301.
/15/   E. Lewis, "A Christian Theodicy. An Exposition of Romans
8:18-39", *Interpretation* 11 (1957) 405-420.
/16/   B.M. Metzger, *Index to Periodical Literature on the
Apostle Paul*, Leiden 1960.
/17/   C.C. Oke, "Suggestion with Regard to Romans 8:23",
Interpretation 11 (1957) 455-460.
/18/   G. Philip, "Creation Waiting for Redemption, an Expository
Study of Romans 8:19-22", *ExTimes* 5(1893/94) 315 ff., 415 ff.,
501.
/19/   D.M. Stanley, *Christ's Resurrection in Pauline
Soteriology.*   Rome 1963[2].

/20/   J. Swetnam, "On Romans 8:23 and the "Expectation of
Sonship", *Biblica* 48(1967) 102-108.
/21/   R.C. Tannehill, *Dying and Rising with Christ. A Study in
Pauline Theology*, (BZNW 32) Berlin, 1966.
/22/   W.D. Stacey, "Paul's Certainties II: God's Purpose in
Creation-Romans 8:22-23", *ExTimes* 69(1958) 179-181, esp. 179.
/23/   W.D. Davies, *Paul and Rabbinic Judaism. Some Rabbinic
Elements in Pauline Theology*, London, 1955 1962[2].
/24/   **W.D.** Davies, *Paul* 38; cf. C.H. Dodd, *The Bible and the
Greeks*, 1935 106; dt., *The Epistle of Paul to the Romans*,
London 1960[14]; dt., *Das Gesetz der Freiheit*, Munchen 1960.
/25/   H.-G. Fritzsche, *Lehrbuch der Dogmatik*, Bd.II, Berlin 1967;
Band III, Berlin 1975 (Anthropologie und Christologie);
G. Altner, *Zwischen Natur und Menschengeschichte,
Anthropologische, biologische, ethische Perspektiven fur eine
neue Schöpfungstheologie*, München 1975; K.M. Meyer-Abich, "Zum
Begriff einer Praktischen Theologie der Natur" in: *EvTh* 1/1977,
Munchen 3-20; A.M.K. Müller - W. Pannenberg, *Erwägungen zu
einer Theologie der Natur*, Gutersloh 1970; H. Dembowski, "Ansatz
und Umrisse einer Theologie der Natur" in: *EvTh* 1/1977 33-49;
J. Hubner, "Schöpfungsglaube und Theologie der Natur" in:
EvTh 1/1977 49-68.
/26/   *New Scientist*, 12.June 1975.
/27/   J.K. Dutton, "Kontrolle der Genmanipulation" in:
Wissenschaftliche Welt, London und Berlin (dtsch.Ausgabe) 3/19766
25f.
/28/   K.M. Meyer-Abich, *Zum Begriff* 19.
/29/   G.v. Wahlert, in: *LM* (Luth. Monatshefte/Hamburg) 8/1975
430.
/30/   The Church of Scotland has a project for the study of
Religion, Society and Technology. Prof. J. Whyte of the
Practical Theology Department of St. Andrews University in
Glasgow does research work on the questions of ecology.
Here is the Bibliography of Theology and the Environment:
I.G. Barber (ed.), *Western Man and Environmental Ethics*,
Addison-Wesley 1973; Charles Birch, "Creation, Theology and
Human Survival" in: *Ecumenical Review*, Vol.XXXVIII, 1ff.;
John Black, "The Dominion of Man: The Search for Ecological
Responsibility" in: *EUP* 1970; T.S. Derr, *Ecology and Human Need*,
Westminster Press, Philadelphia 1975; dt., *Ecology of Human
Liberation*, WSF 1973; H. Montefiore (ed.), *Man and Nature*, Collins
1975; John Passmore, *Man's Responsibility for Nature*, Duckworth
1977; L. White, "Historical Roots of our Ecological Crisis" in:
Science 1976 155 ff and 1203 ff.

/31/ G. Altner, *Schopfung am Abgrund. Die Theologie vor der Umweltfrage,* 1974; M. Schloemann, *Wachstumstod und Eschatologie. Die Herausforderung christlicher Theologie durch die Umweltkrise,* 1973; W.D. Marsch, "Christliche Zukunftshoffnung und rationale Zukunftsplanung", in: *Futurum* 3/1973 235-50; M. Scheler, *Die Stellung des Menschen im Kosmos,* 1966[7]; H.G. Fritzsche, *Die Perspektive des Menschen. Naturphilosophische Aspekte zur theologischen Anthropologie,* Hamburg 1969; K.M. Meyer-Abich, "Das Harren der Natur. Eine Praktische Theologie der Natur als Aufgabe" in: *Ev.Komm.* Stuttgart 8/1975 487 ff.; Gerhard Kehnscherper, "Max Plancks Forderung an Theologie und Kirche", in: *Wiss.Zschr.d.Univ. Greifswald* X.Jg. 3/1961 243-252; W. Wickler, *Die Biologie der Zehn Gebote,* München 1972[3]; O. Jensen, *Unter dem Zwang des Wachstums. Ökologie und Religion,* München 1977; K. Meyer zu Uptrup, *Spiel der Schopfung,* Gütersloh 1975, "ku-Praxis" 4; cf. Günther Kehnscherper *ThLZ* 9/1977 694-697.
/32/ H. Dembowski, *Ansatz* 46f.

The Blood-stained Horseman: Revelation 19.11-13

Sophie Laws,
The Theological Department,
King's College,
Strand,
London WC2.

It is a truism that the book of Revelation is a book full
of images. Luther's comment on it, in his 1522 Preface, is
well known: "My spirit cannot accommodate itself to this book";
he could not regard it as prophetic or apostolic since it
dealt so exclusively in "visions and dreams". Some of these
images are glorious, and have been the inspiration of Christian
art and poetry; others, however, repel: images of martyrs who
call impatiently for vengeance (6;9f); of horses wading in
blood up to their bridles (14;20); of men gnawing their tongues
in unrelievable pain (15;20); and of a bridegroom riding to his
bride in a bloodstained garment.

It is this last image which I propose to examine: that
of the rider on the white horse, with bloodstained garment, in
Rev. 19;11-13. Two preliminary issues must be settled; first,
the text of v.13. There are numerous variant ways of
describing the way in which the rider's garment is stained,
the majority of them participial constructions from the verbs
ῥαίνω and ῥαντίζω and their compounds, serving to describe the
garment as "sprinkled" with blood. I would, however, adopt
with B.M. Metzger the reading βεβαμμένον as "both the best
supported ... and most likely to provoke change" /1/; the
rider's garment is "dipped" in blood. Secondly, this rider
on the ὕππος λευκός is manifestly not the same as the rider of
6;2, though they share some of the same characteristics: both
are crowned, and both go forth to conquer. This second rider
is clearly, from the preliminary summons to the marriage of
the lamb (vv.7,9) and from his names (vv.13,16), a figure of
Christ, and to the overall picture of vv.7-16 two Old Testament
passages have obviously contributed: the description of the
royal bridegroom, who goes both to marriage and to conquest
in Ps.45; and of the vintager, the executor of wrath, of
Is.63;1-6.

This is, then, an image of Christ, and an image of Christ
as a bloodstained rider is a startling and harsh one.
Commentators therefore set about, in the best traditions of
detective fiction, to ask, "Whose blood"? One traditional
answer to the question of the blood with which Christ is stained
is that it is his own. Those who follow him in v.14 wear
white garments, because they have "washed their robes and
made them white in the blood of the lamb" (7;14); but their
leader still carries the marks of the blood by which he gained
the victory (12;11). This interpretation would be consistent
with the way the author introduces reference to the Cross into
his other images of Christ: the "one like a son of man" of
1;12 says, "I died, and behold I am alive for evermore" (v.18);
and the lamb of 5;6 stands "as though it had been slain". I
suspect that this interpretation lies beyond the ῥαίνω / ῥαντίζω
variants on the text, the language of sprinkling being
evocative of sacrifice, as in Ex.24;6-8 (cf. 1 Peter 1;2,19).
Leon Morris, in his *Tyndale New Testament Commentary*, is quite
clear that this is the right interpretation: "... it is more
than difficult to hold that he [John] writes of blood without
a thought of the blood shed on the cross" /2/.

R.H. Charles, however, in his *I.C.C.* commentary, is
equally clear that it is the wrong interpretation: "... the
idea that the blood on His Vesture is His own ... cannot be
entertained"; we have here "not the Slain One, but the Slayer"
/3/. Certainly, this image of Christ comes in the context not
of the statement of the redemptive act by which the final
purpose of God is inaugurated (cf. 5;1-10) but of the final
triumph and judgement by which it is completed (19;1f). For
Charles, the bloodstains are understood in relation to the
image of the executor of wrath of v.15: the blood is that of
his enemies; not the nations of vv.15,18 who are yet to be
smitten, but the alliance of kings (for Charles, Parthian
kings) who have been drawn up for battle in 17;12-14 and may
thus be deemed now to have been defeated. G.B. Caird agrees
that the blood is part of the picture of the execution of
wrath, but disagrees as to the manner of that execution. For
him the blood is that of the martyrs, for it is through their
suffering that God works out his judgement: the winepress is
trodden *outside* the Great City, not within it (14;20), and
Babylon who is given the cup of wrath in 16;19 is subsequently
shown as the harlot drunk with the blood of the saints (17;6)
/4/.

I wonder, though, if it is right to assume that the image of 19;15, of treading the winepress, is anticipated in the language of v.13. Verse 15 draws on Is.63;1-3, the picture of the vintager who has trodden the winepress alone. It may be stressed that this is an *image* of Yahweh's execution of wrath upon the nations, not a description of it. The vintager's garments are stained red, and this is a natural element of the image; they may be seen to be red with αἷμα, but it is το αἷμα τῆς σταυυλῆς, "the blood of the grape", a familiar idiom (e.g. Deut. 32;14; Ecclus. 39;26) /5/. There is another figure in the Old Testament whose garments are similarly soaked: the young lion Judah of Gen. 49;1-12, who "washes his garments in wine and his vesture in the blood of grapes" (v.11).

My suggestion is that this figure also contributes to John's vision of the horseman. (He is, incidentally, also a rider, "binding his foal to the vine", as are neither the vintager nor, in the LXX, the royal bridegroom; but this is not a point to be pressed). I make the suggestion on several grounds. John has already drawn on this passage of Genesis, in 5;5. There the seer was told of the lion of the tribe of Judah, and sees instead a lamb (v.6). Here in 19;7,9 the marriage of the lamb is announced to him, but in vv.11f he sees instead the new figure of the rider. The identity of lamb and rider would not, however, be left to be deduced, for the rider indicates his character as the lamb by wearing the garment of the lion, Judah, in which guise he was first introduced. Then, the Judah passage of Gen.49 was understood messianically /6/. The image of the vintager of Is.63, certainly evoked in v.15, is an image of Yahweh. It is characteristic of John's presentation of Christ that he takes messianic images and associates with them the language of God: thus the "one like a son of man" of 1;12 identifies himself in v.17f as "the first and the last and the living one" (cf. Is.41;4, 44;6, 48;12; Ex.3;14 [LXX]; and within Revelation itself, 1;8 and 4;8f); and the lion of 5;5 is the lamb "with seven eyes" (v.6, cf. Zech. 4;10). This association of the language of the Messiah and the language of God would come the more readily when images of the two have a similar content. Both Yahweh and the Messiah are variously seen stained with "the blood of the grape"; this is a powerful image (the more so when the phrase is used as it would be here in the Revelation, and presumably also in 14;20, in abbreviated form), but it is still an image. (There appears, in fact, to be some tradition of an association of Gen.49;10-11 with Is.63;1-6 in

Jewish exegesis, though it is not clear how early it is
established /7/. The association of the passages would have
a particular impact in the context of John's christology, but
it may be that when the author makes it he is drawing on a
tradition of reading these passages in which each might evoke
the other).

To conclude, then, my very tentative suggestion is this:
when John introduces the figure of the horseman in his
"bloodstained" garment, the image of the lion, Judah, the one
who "washes his ... vesture in the blood of grapes" is in his
mind - or in his vision. As one piece of the total mosaic of
the passage 19;7-16 it serves a double function. It evokes
the earlier vision of the lamb, and it leads on to the notion
of the "winepress of the wrath of God". As a linking image
it serves John's purpose of presenting Jesus as the Messiah and
as, to some extent, in the role of God.

NOTES

/1/ B.M. Metzger, *A Textual Commentary on the Greek New
Testament* (London; New York, 1971), p.763.
/2/ L. Morris, *Revelation* (Leicester, 1969), p.230.
/3/ R.H. Charles, *The Revelation of St. John* (Edinburgh, 1920),
Vol. II, p.133.
/4/ G.B. Caird, *The Revelation of St. John the Divine* (London,
1966), pp.244-246.
/5/ It may be noted that the confusion of the image of Is.63
by the echo of v.3, "their juice/blood (נצחם) is sprinkled
on my garments" in v.6, "I poured out their juice/blood on the
earth", is absent from the LXX in which the former clause
does not appear.
/6/ A demonstration that this was so in the first century is
found in G. Vermes's citation of *4QP Bless.* in *The Dead Sea
Scrolls: Qumran in Perspective* (London, 1977), p.69, and,
though less explicitly, in *Test. Jud.* 1.6.
/7/ References may be found in J. Bowker, *The Targums and
Rabbinic Literature* (Cambridge, 1969), p.290f.

'Spirit' in Pauline Usage: 1 Corinthians 5.5

S.D. MacArthur,
University of Glasgow.

In order to try to determine the meaning of πνεῦμα in
I Corinthians 5;5b in a brief communication, the necessary
exegetical preliminaries would appear to be to indicate the
most probable grammatical arrangement of verses 3-5 and to
discuss the meaning of 5a.

It is natural to connect the prepositional phrase σὺν τῇ
δυνάμει τοῦ κυρίου ἡμῶν Ἰησοῦ (verse 4b) with the genitive
participle συναχθέντων, and then to attach the prepositional
phrase ἐν τῷ ὀνόματι τοῦ κυρίου Ἰησοῦ (4a) to the immediately
preceeding accusative participle τόν...κατεργασάμενον /1/,
which is the object of κέκρικα (cf. verses 12f) /2/. Verses 3-5
may then be translated as follows: "I for my part, being absent
in body, but present in spirit, have already judged as one who
is present the person who did such a thing in the name of the
Lord Jesus, when you and my spirit are gathered together with
the power of our Lord Jesus, to hand over such a person to
Satan for the destruction of the flesh, that the πενῦμα may be
saved on the day of the Lord". The main idea in verses 3 and 4
is that Paul associates himself closely with the Corinthinans
when they come together to judge this gross sinner; he will
really be present with them then /3/. Verse 5 tells what their
collective judgement entails.

Many scholars maintain that verses 3-5 concern the sinner's
excommunication /4/. Verse 5a expresses the fact that having
been exiled from the church this person will be *ipso facto*
under the power of Satan, the God of this world (2 Cor. 4;4: cf.
Col. 1;13). This is doubtful; since it is not Paul's view that
people within the church are necessarily out of Satan's reach
(cf. 2 Cor. 12;7: 1 Thess. 2;18), it is not clear that he
would equate excommunication with being given over into Satan's
power. Furthermore, the phrase "for the destruction of the
flesh", no matter how it is taken, tells against this

interpretation. If this phrase refers to illness and/or death, these take place within the church (cf. 11;30); if it refers to the destruction of fleshly lusts, "these would, presumably, be strengthened rather than destroyed by sending him back to the world" /5/. If Job 2;6, παραδιδωμί σου αὐτόν, has influenced Paul's phrasing here, this would make it even more likely that he envisages a special subjection of this person to Satan. The language of 5;5a thus suggests something other than excommunication /6/.

It has been suggested that Satan will function here in his traditional role of accuser /7/, but Paul does not elsewhere allude to this function of Satan, and Romans 8;31 ff. suggest that Paul may not have been inclined to think of Satan in this way; it is also not clear how accusations of Satan result in the destruction of the flesh. It is equally unlikely that Satan appears in our verse as temptor; the man has already committed fornication; it seems senseless for the church to hand him over to Satan for further temptation to sin. For similar reasons, Satan does not function here as adversary of the gospel.

It follows that Satan is seen as one who brings on physical woe. 1 Corinthians 11;29 f. state that those who partake of the Eucharist unworthily, eating and drinking judgement (κρίμα) upon themselves, become ill and even die. This suggests that the judgement passed in our verse against unworthy Christian living would have the same sort of results /8/. Primitive Christian literature associates the devil with the infliction of physical suffering (Acts 10;38), death (Heb. 2;14) /9/, and physical suffering unto death (Ig. Rom. 5;3).

We have determined that Satan is seen here as one who inflicts physical woe; it might seem to follow that we should allow 'flesh' a purely physical referent. It has been argued that Satan cannot be an agent for the destruction of the flesh in the ethical sense of the term, because Satan would then be envisioned as working against his own interests /10/. However, the "thorn" in the flesh given to Paul by an angel of Satan (2 Cor. 12;7) has the effect not only of causing physical discomfort but also of countering a tendency toward pride; here Satan would seem to be working against his own interests. An ethical referent for "flesh" in our verse thus cannot be ruled out, although the physical referent seems paramount.

Ὄλεθρος τῆς σαρκός can incorporate the notion of the "utter

defeat of the sinful flesh"; Philo speaks of the utter defeat
of wisdom (ὀλέθρῳ φρονήσεως, *Deus imm. sit* 166), of
righteousness and every virtue (*Conf. ling.* 86), and of the
mind (*Som.* ii. 179). In our verse ὄλεθρος must also
incorporate the meaning of physical suffering or death or
physical suffering unto death. Philo often uses ὄλεθρος to
designate physical death (e.g. *Spec. leg.* i;160; iii;147; iv;127)
/11/. Every employment of the term in the Septuagint (where it
occurs more than twenty times) specifically designates or, rarely,
clearly incorporates the notion of actual physical death.
Ὄλεθρος can be used too of physical suffering, but it seems
to have this particular signification only in contexts which
relate to the woes of the wicked in the last days and eternity
(1 Thess. 5;3: 2 Thess. 1;9: 4 Macc. 10;15, τον αἰώνιον τὃυ
τυράννου ὄλεθρον; cf. 1 Tim. 6;9). Our verse views the
destruction of the flesh as taking place before this (Paul
elsewhere only alludes to activity of Satan previous to the
eschaton, 7;5: 2 Cor. 2;11: 4;4: 11;14: 12;7: 1 Thess. 2;18:
2 Thess. 2;9: cf. Eph. 2;2). It may be noted that the notion
of eternal ὄλεθρος as physical suffering, being the opposite
of eternal life, is not very different from the notion of
death.

Thus it appears probable that 1 Corinthians 5;5a refers
to the death of the malefactor at the instigation of Satan.
This may not be sudden death; it may be a slow death which
involves physical suffering. Since ὄλεθρος is used on occasion
to suggest unspecified sorts of woe (e.g. Philo *Gai.* 91: Satan's
ὄλεθρος is unspecified in Ig. Eph. 13;1), it may just be that
Paul contemplates only sickness and torment for this sinner,
but it is certainly much more likely that 1 Corinthians 5;5a
spells his death /12/.

We now turn to consider the meaning of πνεῦμα in 5b.
Scholars have understood it in various ways. It has been seen
as the divine power imparted to this particular believer which
"ought no longer to be left in his possession, but must be
rescued by his death, in order that it may form part of the
perfection and wholeness of the body of Christ at the Last Day"
/13/. Although it may be said in favour of this view that it
fits the context, viz. Paul's predominant concern for the state
of the whole church, and that elsewhere in Paul where πνεῦμα is
contrasted with "flesh" the Holy Spirit is meant (except perhaps
Col. 2;5), it does not seem acceptable for two reasons: it is
hard to conceive of the divine Spirit being saved or rescued,

and individual salvation is predicated in 3;15, where Paul also
is mainly concerned with the state of the whole church.

Eduard Schweizer maintains that πνεῦμα is the imparted
divine πνεῦμα insofar as it creates a new I. "The πνεῦμα of
the sinner which is to be delivered is the I given to him by God,
a portion of God's Spirit, though the whole of the new man of
the believer is represented therein" /14/. Schweizer's
interpretation does not seem to be open to the objection that
Paul could hardly contemplate the salvation of the imparted
divine Spirit. Yet it is far from obvious that Paul does or
would use πνεῦμα to represent the specifically Christian person.
Elsewhere in his epistles Paul distinguishes the imparted
divine Spirit from the human person it indwells /15/.

J. Cambier holds that πνεῦμα here is a qualitative religious
term which characterizes the whole human person /16/. It may be
urged against this interpretation that πνεῦμα elsewhere in Paul
always seems to represent an external influence on or an
internal aspect of but never the human person *as* such.

Some scholars consider that πνεῦμα represents "the
essential, inward self" /17/ or "the higher faculty" /18/. One
may object to this that Paul nowhere else singles out this
human spirit for salvation /19/. Other scholars consider that
πνεῦμα represents the human spirit regenerated by the apportioned
divine Spirit /20/. Against this it may be said that Paul
nowhere countenances such a confluence of πνεύματα.

Another possibility is that Paul may not have intended
πνεῦμα to designate anything definite. Πνεῦμα may be emotively
loaded and connotative of, say, "whatever is true, whatever is
honorable" and such like (Phil. 4;8) in contrast to what
"flesh" calls to mind /21/. This is unlikely; although Paul
appears aggravated in our chapter, verses 3-5 seem to
constitute on the contrary a careful and solemn statement of
just what must be done to this fornicator. At any rate, the
Corinthians, like readers until the present day, would not have
understood the term πνεῦμα in this loose sense but in a
particular precise way.

Thus it would appear that none of the interpretations of
πνεῦμα which have been put forward thus far are satisfactory.
Against some, rather weighty objections can be levelled,
whereas with regard to others, only indecisive doubts arise.

There is another way we can understand πνεῦμα in our verse
which seems perhaps less doubtful than any other. Πνεῦμα can
represent the condemned person insofar as he will exist after
his death in the realm of the dead (cf. πνεῦμα in 1 En. 22 and
possibly the Greek of Sir. 9;9 /22/) wherein or from whence
(cf. πνεῦμα in Luke 24;37, 39: ruah in B. Berakhoth 18B) he will
be called to judgement. Verse 5b does not concern the manner
of the duration of his eternal life. It relates rather what
will be the mode of being in which he faces judgement and finds
approbation on the day of the Lord (cf. 1;8: 3;13: 4;3).

One thing that may be said in favour of this interpretation
is that Paul would probably not have employed any term other
than πνεῦμα to represent this fornicator as one who is in or
from the realm of the dead at the Last Judgement. He could
conceivably have used ψυχή for this (cf. e.g. 1 En. 102;11:
103;7), but ψυχή in Paul characteristically refers to the
whole living person on earth /23/. Πνεῦμα has no such
characteristic meaning in Paul. In our letter Paul has already
made reference to the Holy Spirit (2;4 et. al.),the spirit of
the world (2;12a), the human spirit as self-understanding (2;11a),
and probably (4;21) disposition and (5;3 f.) the vehicle of a
person's invisible presence through space and time. What
characterizes πνεῦμα in Pauline usage, then, is precisely its
variegated employment. Paul could perhaps have written
ὁ νεκρός or ὁ καθεύδων instead of τό πνεῦμα, but by doing so
he would have dissipated the contrasting chiastic effect of
our verse, viz. Satan-destruction-flesh; spirit-salvation-Lord.
Paul might also have felt that νεκρός was too final but καθεύδων
too innocuous a word with which to depict the situation of this
saveable great sinner. Thus it does not appear that the
interpretation of πνεῦμα in verse 5b being suggested here
can be called into question on the grounds of Pauline
linguistic usage.

It is a semantic axiom that "the correct meaning of any
term is that which contributes least to the total context" /24/.
Another advantage of this interpretation over others is that
it does not necessitate any supplementary speculations about
a supposed anthropological significance of the Holy Spirit
(contrast e.g. Schweitzer) or soteriological significance of
the human spirit (contrast e.g. Héring). It understands
I Corinthians 5;5b as a straightforward statement which does
not require any special reflection on our part or on the
Corinthians' part in order for it to be properly understood.

On this interpretation, the verse says simply: the dead person
will be saved on the day of the Lord /25/.

In conclusion, I have argued that, no matter how we
understand verse 5b, 5a probably contemplates the death of the
fornicator. 5b lays it down that he will also be saved at the
Last Judgement /26/. I have suggested that πνεῦμα represents
this person insofar as he at that time exists in or comes out
of the realm of the dead. I have further suggested that
because this interpretation is so simple and straightforward,
and accords with Pauline linguistic usage, it seems more
plausible than the other conceivable interpretations that have
been offered.

NOTES

/1/   This seems preferable to loading both prepositional
phrases pleonastically on to συναχθέντων or linking ἐν τῶ ὀνομ.
κτλ. with the far-away infinitive παραδοῦναι. The idea is that
the miscreant has not lived worthily of the name with which he
was justified (cf. 6;11; 2 Thess. 1;12). There is no warrant
for attaching ἐν τῶ ὀνόμ. κτλ. with the less proximate κέκρικα
since elsewhere in Paul not judgement but Christian living
(Col. 3;17) is connected with the name of Jesus. Cf. in favour
of the construction adopted here, J.P. Murphy-O'Connor, O.P.,
'I Corinthians, V, 3-5', *Revue biblique* xciv (1977), pp.239f.
/2/   Παραδοῦναι is dependent on συναχθέντων; cf. 7.25b.
/3/   'The obvious meaning of the passage is, not that Paul
though absent agrees with their verdict, but that his spirit
is gathered together with them in its formulation,' E. Best,
One Body in Christ, (London, 1955), p.59.
/4/   E.g. Calvin, *The First Epistle of Paul the Apostle to the
Corinthians,* (Edinburgh, 1960), p.108.
/5/   G.G. Findlay, *The Expositor's Greek Testament* ii, (London,
1900), p.809. The idea that life in the world of the unredeemed
would produce in this exile a longing for life in the church of
the redeemed is an arbitrary and unlikely supposition.
/6/   Cf. F.F. Bruce, *I and II Corinthians,* (London, 1971), p.55:
'the language implies a severer sentence than excommunication'.
/7/   A.C. Thiselton, 'The Meaning of *Sarx* in I Corinthians 5.5',
S.J.T. xxvi (1973), pp.213, 224f.
/8/   'Was 5,5 die Gemeinde, das bewirkt 11,30 der Einzelne
selbst', E. Sokolowski, *Die Begriffe Geist und Leben bei Paulus,*
(Göttingen, 1903), p.129 n.1.

/9/   'The prince or angel of death is here identified with the
devil - that is, Satan. It is not easy to parallel this
outright identification, but it is not inconsonant with the
general teaching of the New Testament', Bruce, *The Epistle to
the Hebrews,* (Grand Rapids, 1964), p.49; cf. John 8.44; cf. also
B. Baba Bathra 16a, where the fact that God specially cautions
Satan to spare Job's life (Job 2.7b) proves to Resh Lakish that
he is the angel of death.
/10/ P. Bachmann, *Der erste Brief des Paulus an die Korinther,*[2]
(Leipzig, 1910), p.211.
/11/ Occasionally in his allegorical exegesis Philo adds to a
Scriptural reference to physical death a reference to an
ethical sort of ὄλεθρος; for example, the destruction of Abel
represents the destruction of the teaching devoted to God
(ὀλέθρω του φιλοθέου δόγματος Ἄβελ, *Det. pot. ins.* 103).
This suggests that when Philo uses ὄλεθρος of an ethical sort
of death or utter defeat, the idea of real physical death is
not far from his mind.
/12/ Tertullian *De pud.* xiv. 16 holds that 5.2 also refers to
his death: 'pro quo lugerent? Vtique pro mortuo'. The LXX
phrase cited by Paul (with a change in the verb from the
singular to the plural) in 13b refers to death specifically
in Deut. 17;7: 21;21: 22;21,24: 24;7 (it includes death in 19;19).
/13/ H. von Campenhausen, *Ecclesiastical Authority and Spiritual
Power in the Church of the First Three Centuries,* (London, 1967),
p.134 n.50, following G. Bornkamm.
/14/ *T.D.N.T.* vi, p.435.
/15/ It is arbitrary to assume that when Paul says, 'the grace
of (our) Lord be with your πνεῦμα' (e.g. Gal. 6;18), he intends
to say quite the same thing as when he says, 'the grace of (our)
Lord be with you' (e.g. 1 Cor. 16;23), unless there are other
grounds on which we may make this assumption.
/16/ 'La chair et l'esprit en I Cor. V, 5', *N.T.S.* xv (1968-1969),
pp.221, 223f., 228.
/17/ C.K. Barrett, *A Commentary on the First Epistle to the
Corinthians,* New York, 1965), p.126.
/18/ C.T. Craig, *The Interpreter's Bible* x, (Nashville, 1953),
p.62.
/19/ Origen (ed. C. Jenkins, *J.T.S.* ix (1908), p.364) and
Chrysostom (*P.G.* lxi, p.124) opine strangely that Paul speaks
of the salvation of the higher part of the person to indicate
that the whole person will be saved; quite the opposite
conclusion would be apt to be drawn.
/20/ E.g. J. Héring, *The First Epistle of Saint Paul to the
Corinthians,* (London, 1962), p.36.

/21/ Cf. Thiselton, art. cit.

/22/ The Hebrew of Sir. 9.9d, ובדמים תטה אל־שחת (I Levi, *The Hebrew Text of the Book of Ecclesiasticus*, (Leiden, 1969), p.13), 'and in your blood you incline unto a pit', clearly refers to the adulterer's (9a-c) punishment of death by stoning (Lev. 20;10: Deut. 22;22), which entailed being pushed into a pit (M. Sanhedrin vi. 4). This becomes in the Greek translation, καὶ τῷ πνεύματί σου ὀλίσθῃς εἰς ἀπώλειαν, which may be translated, 'and in your spirit you slide into destruction', ἀπώλεια representing not loss of life (as e.g. in Jos. *Vita* 272) but the place of the suffering of the wicked dead (as in the LXX of Job 26;6: Prov. 15;11 and in Rev. 17;8,11: cf. also the construction, ὤλισθον ἐς Ἅδου, *Epigr. Gr.* 587 line 1), and πνεῦμα the mode of survival of persons in the netherworld (cf. Jos. *Ant.* xviii 14, punishment of evil ψυχαί under the earth after death).

/23/ A possible exception is in the phrase ἐκ ψυχῆς, Col. 3;23: Eph. 6;6, but this may mean 'with the whole self' and not with only part thereof as in ὀφθαλμοδουλία.

/24/ E.A. Nida, cited by Thiselton, 'Semantics and New Testament Interpretation', *New Testament Interpretation*, ed. I.H. Marshall, (Exeter, 1977), p.84.

/25/ It can be objected against this interpretation that πνεῦμα when it refers to deceased persons always carries a qualifying genitive. Thus we might expect Paul to have written, 'his spirit will be saved'. As it happens, this is a primary objection also to understanding 'the spirits' in 1 Pet. 3;19 as deceased human persons. R.T. France, for example, argues as follows: 'but in none of these cases is πνεῦμα used absolutely: it is always qualified by "of the dead", "of the righteous", etc. If τά πνευματα here meant "men who have died", it would be a unique absolute use in this sense. This does not exclude the possibility entirely, but it casts strong doubt on it', 'Exegesis in Practice: Two Samples', ibid., p.269. If, apart from this possible objection, the interpretation of πνεῦμα in I Corinthians 5.5b being suggested here appears plausible, then we may want to reconsider the currently prevalent interpretation of 'the spirits' in 1 Pet. 3;19, which sees them as the apostate angels of Gen. 6;2, 4 rather than deceased human sinners who perished in the flood. It may be that the New Testament affords two examples of πνεῦμα used absolutely to represent the deceased in the realm of the dead.

/26/ Paul does not say how nor if his being put to death in itself enhances his salvation. It may be that he is simply saved after not because of his death; that is, ἵνα may be consecutive rather than final here; cf. C.F.D. Moule, *An Idiom-Book of New Testament Greek,*[2] (Cambridge, 1971), p.144.

Studia Biblica 1978: III, 257-263

Early Christian Exegesis of the Apocalypse

T.W. Mackay,
Brigham Young University,
Provo,
Utah 84602,
U.S.A.

The Apocalypse of John is a perplexing and enigmatic composition which scarcely made the New Testament canon. It is indeed a strange book, but it is even stranger, more bizarre, as described in the multifarious commentaries of subsequent centuries. Curiously, it is not among Greek writers, but rather in the Latin west - especially North Africa - that we discover a developed exegetical tradition of the Apocalypse. From the North African writers, Tyconius and Primasius, the tradition then passed to several others, principally to the Venerable Bede and from him to the Carolingian Renaissance.

One of the curious phenomena of Biblical exegesis is the shift from a fundamentally literal interpretation in the earlier writers to an increasingly complex and elaborate "allegorical" approach. While some writers and movements in the second and third centuries exhibit allegorical tendencies, it is more particularly the Fathers and Doctors of the fourth and fifth centuries who establish the Christian tradition for subsequent writers /1/. As to the interpretation of the Apocalypse of John,the clear demarcation is positioned in the early fourth century, after which time the remnants of literal interpretation are either eroded from the tradition or at least diluted. It is primarily from the Donatist Tyconius that the main thrust of allegorizing and de-eschatologizing the Apocalypse arises. The interpreters become preoccupied with the Church and its triumph; after all, has it not survived the persecutions of pagan Rome?

One cause of the transformation in the exegetical tradition has, however, a distinct significance which must not be ignored.

I refer to Christianity becoming part of the political
propaganda of the fourth century /2/. It focused upon the
traditions of the cultural heritage while stressing a
world-wide culture-polarization by fusing into the noble
abstraction *Romania* or *Romanitas* all that was good, lofty,
worthy of allegiance or pertained to civilization. The
opposite, of course, was *Barbaria* - desolation, uncivilized
and economically undeveloped rabble. Under the Roman emperor,
the *restitutor orbis,* the Christians sensed and proclaimed
the inception of the millennial kingdom. Perhaps this is why
Tyconius takes the three and half years to be 350 years at
which time the Antichrist is overcome; that is to say, in its
union with Rome, the Church is now the Church Triumphant /3/!

As an illustration of the changing perspective and mode
of interpretation, the various identifications of the Two
Witnesses are always identified as Elijah (Elias) and Enoch /4/.
This is true both in "orthodox" and "heretical" writers as well
as in various apocalyptic and apocryphal texts. Even
Victorinus, who suggests that instead of Enoch the companion of
Elijah is to be Jeremiah and not Elisha or Moses as *multi
putant*, still considers them to be two actual prophets in the
last days /5/. Tyconius, on the other hand, identifies them
as the two testaments which the Church possesses and which,
therefore, give it power as it preaches throughout the world /6/.
This interpretation is echoed by the subsequent commentators.

Another example, which also relates to the two Prophets,
pertains to the temple at Jerusalem. While the Old Testament
prophets look to the time when the temple would stand in
resplendent glory, Christian writers, especially those
involved in the multi-faceted allegorical exegesis, found it
a source of severe embarrassment. In an article entitled
"Christian Envy of the Temple" /7/, Hugh W. Nibley points out
that the Church possesses no adequate substitute for the
Temple, and that in yearning for its return, Christians have
from time to time attempted to revive in the Church practices
peculiar to the Temple. This conviction of the uniqueness of
the Temple has produced a persistent fear or hope that the
Temple might be restored, thus seriously challenging "the
official Christian position, that Church and Temple cannot
coexist and hence [that] the latter has been abolished
forever . . .." /8/. Consequently, commentators regularly
equate the Church and the Temple, and thus they dismiss
summarily a restoration of the Temple. However, as is

nervously admitted, John's description of the Temple in
Apocalypse 11, can only be of a literal Temple at Jerusalem /9/.
Is this, in fact, the Temple which was destroyed in A.D. 70,
or some other Temple? Inasmuch as this is placed at the
eschaton, the literal interpretation would take this to be
the prophetic vision of a Temple which was not yet constructed
when John had his vision. Needless to say, such a position was
not popular in normative Christian exegesis.

As a corollary to the Temple, we may mention the gathering
or restoration of the twelve tribes of Israel. It is, of course,
to the 144,000 that I refer. The commentators readily cite
the solution, stated by Tyconius in the *Liber Regularum* and
reiterated by Augustine in *De Doctrina Christiana,* that the
number signifies the entire Church or the whole body of Saints
/10/. Even Tertullian states how "the figurative interpretation
is spiritually applicable to Christ and His Church and . . .
relates to what is promised in heaven not on earth" /11/. This
is already a far step from Paul in Romans 11:17-27, speaking
of the natural and wild olive branches and alluding to the
future of Israel. From Irenaeus on, the standard explanation
for the occurrence of Mannasseh in place of Dan in the list
of the twelve tribes is because the Antichrist was to procede
forth from Dan /12/. Now, Augustine does accept the fact that
a portion of the Jewish people adhere to the gospel and that
some of the "carnal seed of Israel" were blessed while others
"belonged to the apostasy" (or *discessio*) /13/. In this
statement Augustine summarizes the doctrinal and exegetical
arrogance of normative Christianity: the Church is now the
body of Christ, the Temple, the means of salvation, and as
such has absorbed to itself the blessings of Abraham, Isaac
and Jacob. Also the *discessio* or apostasy predicted by
Paul /14/ is minimized by Augustine and his associates to
desertion from the Church not the perversion of it as described
by the earliest writers. By such interpretation the Antichrist
does *not* reign supreme but is cast out of the Church (Apoc. 12:9).
This is the effect of fourth century propaganda: the doctrine
of the two ways lying open to individuals *and* to the church
now becomes the Way of the Church versus the Way of
Antichrist - *Romanitas* and *Barbaria* in different garb. This
view championed the institutions, the hierarchy, the
organization of the *ecclesia* as Rome was doing in the *imperium.*
[The parallel to our own society should be obvious].

A final example of the conflict between early Christian
literalism and the later normative allegorical tradition may
be seen in the position taken with regard to the millennium.
Jerome condescendingly relates that Papias "promulgated the
Jewish tradition of a millennium, and he is followed by
Irenaeus, Apollinarius and the others, who say that after
the resurrection the Lord will reign in the flesh with the
saints" /15/. Augustine, in the *De Civitate Dei*, scathingly
condemns chiliasm and a literal resurrection /16/. Eusebius,
too, gives further evidence of the shift from the early
Christian belief in a literal millennium following a physical
resurrection to the de-eschatologized use of the word millennium
to describe the perpetual heavenly kingdom of Christ /17/.
Curiously, however, times of crises, as seen in the *Historia
Francorum* by Gregory of Tours and as sensed by people living
around the year A.D. 1000, have dramatically renewed belief
in or at least speculation about, a literal end and a literal
millennium.

The Church in the fourth century by allying itself with
its former persecutor, the Roman state, also becomes entrapped
by the concomitant political propaganda, including Constantine's
purported attempt to legislate the millennium. What the
schoolmen had done to Homer and the other great writers of
Classical antiquity, the Christian schoolmen now did to the
Bible. In order to absorb the Bible into their *Romanitas*,
they interpreted the Bible with the same moralizing,
allegorizing approach as was used by their pagan counterparts.
For western Christianity, Tyconius' articulation of the
allegorical approach in his *Liber Regularum*, together with
Augustine's stamp of approval, helped to encourage a
de-eschatologized, allegorical exegesis. It is certainly
indisputible that his *Commentary on the Apocalypse* became the
primary point of departure for the most significant and
influential commentators prior to the Carolingian Renaissance.
Then, especially through Bede, this tradition was perpetuated
in the Carolingian Age.

At times the study of intellectual history can itself
produce a barrier to the very item being studied. In the case
of Christianity, we tenaciously cling, and with good reason,
to what has been preserved. Nevertheless, it is disquieting
to realize that all too frequently our understanding of
primitive Christianity is perceived through the eyes of the
fourth-century Church /18/. While we may dismiss as "gnostic"

or "heretical" or "schismatic", various movements and the
literature by them (although it must be avowed that
Roman Christianity systematically and relentlessly destroyed
or obscured "heretical" literature), still, in very fact, the
Christian exegetical tradition of the Apocalypse has for its
mainspring the work of the Donatist, Tyconius, although his
work and that of his contemporaries is not in harmony with
earliest Christianity.

As Eusebius states in the commencement of *Ecclesiastical
History,* we look back at the apostles as though over a deep
abyss /19/. While our view of Church history assumes the
perpetuation and growth of the Church, there is disquieting
evidence, such as the transformation of scriptural exegesis,
which gives us cause for concern /20/. Primitive Christianity
was a tender and ephemeral entity which by all admissions did
not survive the second century. As Vielhauer has said, "the
union of prophecy and Apocalyptic, . . . finds expression . . .
most impressively in the author of the Apocalypse of John . . ..
Later Apocalyptic and prophecy again fall apart . . . . By the
end of the first century prophecy has lost its original
significance . . . . In a church which was building more and
more on the hierarchical offices and the normative tradition,
it soon had no place; as such, it was suspected of being
Gnostic, and about the middle of the second century was forced
into heresy by an orthodoxy which was in process of
consolidating itself. It flourished occasionally on the edge
of the church, in Elchasai at the beginning of the second
century and in Montanus at its end . . ." /21/. After the
demise of the Primitive Church came "Operation Salvage" and
an exegesis inimical to the eschatological and apocalyptic
perspective of early Christianity.

As we approach the turn of the century, we are bemused by
the sudden concern on the part of some who have been heir to
the normative Christian tradition that perhaps, just perhaps,
pristine Christian literalism may have been far more accurate
than we could care to believe.

NOTES

/1/   I refer to the exegetical tradition in the West. See
Beryl Smalley, *The Study of the Bible in the Middle Ages* (Notre
Dame, 1964), especially pp.1-36; cf. Claudio Leonardi, "Il
Venerabile Beda e la Cultura del Secolo VIII," *I Problemi
dell'Occidente nel Secolo VIII* ('Settimane di Studio del
Centro italiano di studi sull'alto medioevo', vol. 20),
pp.603-58; Henri de Lubac, *Exégèse Médiévale. Les Quatre
Sens de l'Écriture* (2 vols. in 4 parts; Paris, 1959-64);
Gerald Bonner, *Saint Bede in the Tradition of Western
Apocalyptic Commentary* (Jarrow Lecture, 1966).
/2/   Hugh Nibley, "The Unsolved Loyalty Problem: Our Western
Heritage", *Western Political Quarterly,* vol. 5 (1953), pp.
631-57.
/3/   Tyconius *Liber Regularum,* ed. F. Burkitt, "Texts and
Studies", vol. 3, pt. 1 (1896), p.61 (lines 4, 7), p.64 (lines
25-28).
/4/   Tertullian *De Anima,* L, 5 *(C.C.L.,* Vol. 2, 856 (lines
33-35)); Hippolytus *De Christo et Antichristo,* XLIII in Migne,
Patr. Gr., Vol. 10, col. 761A; Prosper of Aquitaine *Chronicon*
in *M.G.H.,* Auct. Ant., Vol. 9, p.493. This tradition continues
in the iconography of the illuminated Beatus manuscripts as on
the Gerona Cathedral MS., fol. 164[R] *Isti sunt due olibe et due
candelaba (sic)* with the names Elias and Enoc; also fol. 166[R]
*Antichristus ciuitatem Ihrslm [= Ierusalem] subuertit . . .
Eliam et Enoc occident (sic). [Sancti Beati a Liebana in
Apocalypsin Codex Gerundensis* (in facsimile with 1 vol.
prolegomena by Jaime Marqués Casanovas, Caesar E. Dubler, and
Wilhelm Neuss; Olten and Lausanne: Urs Graf-Verlag, 1962).
Cf. Joseph S. Considine, "The Two Witnesses: Apoc. 11:3-13",
Catholic Biblical Quarterly, vol. 8 (1946), pp.377-92.
/5/   *C.S.E.L.,* vol. 49, p.98.
/6/   Lo Bue, Francesco and Willis, G. G., eds., *The Turin
Fragments of Tyconius' Commentary on Revelation* (Cambridge,
1963), p.143, lines 2-4; cf. Caesarius (ed. G. Morin;
Maredsous, 1942), vol. 2, p. 239, lines 2-3; Primasius in
Pat. Lat., vol. 68, col. 866C and 867A; Beatus (ed. Sanders;
Rome, 1930), V, 11, 2a and 4b (p.445).
/7/   H. Nibley, "Christian Envy of the Temple", *The Jewish
Quarterly Review,* vol. 50, (1959-60), p.98.
/8/   *Ibid.,* p.69.
/9/   E.B. Allo, *Saint Jean, L'Apocalypse* (Paris, 1921), p. 129.
cf. J. Massyngberde Ford, *Revelation,* "Anchor Bible"; (Garden
City, 1975), p.171.

/10/ Tyconius *Liber Regularum*, p.60 (lines 5, 6); Augustine
De Doctrina Christiana, III, 35, 51 (*C.C.L.*, vol. 32, p.111
[lines 33-35]).
/11/ Tertullian *Adv. Marcionem*, III, 24, 2 (C.C.L., vol. 1,
p.542 [lines 12-18]).
/12/ Irenaeus *Adv. Haereses*, V, 30, 2 in Migne, *Pat. Gr.*,
vol. 7, col. 1205; cf. Primasius in *Pat. Lat.*, vol. 68, col.
867D.
/13/ Augustine *De Ciu. Dei*, XX, 19 (*C.C.L.* vol. 48, p. 730
[line 10]) uses *refuga* as in the Old Latin text; n.b. Pelagius'
exposition on 2 Thess. (ed. J. Armitage Robinson, "Texts and
Studies", vol. 9, pt. 2, p.443); *nisi antichristus uenerit,
non ueniet Christus. quod qutem 'discessio' hic dicit, alibi
eum 'refuga[m]' appellauit in Latinis exemplaribus: utrumque
autem ita intellegendum est, quod nisi uenerit refuga
[ueritatis], siue sui principatus desertor, siue discessio
gentium a regno Romano, sicut in Danihelo per bestiae imaginem
dicit.* See also the Editio Maior of the New Testament by
Wordsworth, White *et al.*, vol. 2, p. 563.
/14/ Acts 20:29-30; cf. Eusebius (quoting Hegesippus)
Hist. Eccl., III, 32, 7-8; see also 2 Thess. 2:1-12.
/15/ Jerome *De Vir. III.*, 18.
/16/ Augustine *De Ciu. Dei*, XX, 7.
/17/ Eusebius *Hist. Eccl.*, III, 39.
/18/ See for example Smalley, p. 140; n.b. H. Nibley, "Passing
of the Primitive Church", Church History, vol. 30 (1961),
pp. 131-54.
/19/ Eusebius *Hist. Eccl*, I, 3.
/20/ H. Nibley, "Evangelium Quadraginta Dierum", *Vigiliae
Christianae,* vol. 20 (1966), pp. 1-24.
/21/ P. Vielhauer in E. Hennecke and W. Schneemelcher's
New Testament Apocrypha, vol. 2 (trsl. R. McL. Wilson;
Philadelphia, 1965; rp. 1976), pp. 606-607.

A Reconsideration of the Origins of a Christian Initiation Rite in the Age of the New Testament

Rev. M.J. Moreton,
Lecturer in Theology,
University of Exeter,
St. Mary Steps Rectory,
Matford Road,
Exeter EX2 4PE.

The purpose of this paper is to try to place the question of the origins of a Christian initiation rite within fresh perspectives. Two books on baptism in the New Testament have recently been re-published in England - Professor Cullmann's and Dr. Beasley-Murray's /1/. These, however, in spite of their detailed and informative exegesis are in the end, at least to me, unbelievable. It is this that prompts me to suggest a fresh approach to the question.

Let me start with the situation in Mark-Matthew. Here there are two points which can be made at once upon which there will be little disagreement. The first is that for them John's baptizing is marked off fundamentally from Jesus's baptizing. They belong to different orders of baptizing. John's baptism is a baptism in water upon repentance. Mark, though not Matthew, adds εἰς ἄφεσιν ἁμαρτιῶν, "with a view to gaining the remission of sins by God in the world to come". Jesus's baptism by contrast is not a baptism in water but in holy spirit /and fire/. This suggests that in the eyes of the evangelists the boundary between this present world and the world to come has been or is being dissolved. When Jesus ascends from the water, the spirit of God descends upon him. The age of restoration and of resurrection has begun with him. Mark-Matthew thus distinguish between John's baptizing and Jesus's baptizing in content.

The second point which will hardly be disputed follows from this. The distinction is not only in content but also in form. Jesus, unlike John, did not baptize in water - or such is the view of Mark-Matthew. There are indeed two passages in Mark in

which the evangelist is able to use βαπτίζειν in what is a
non-technical sense from a Christian point of view. The first
is in 7;4 where, mentioning the tradition of the elders, he
refers to the "baptizing" of what is brought from the market
place. Later, Christian scribes in the Egyptian tradition
felt there to be a incongruity in this statement, and so
eliminated from Mark's text what was for them a sacramental
term, replacing βαπτίζειν with ῥαντίζειν. The second passage
is in 10;38f where βαπτίζειν and its substantive are used in a
figurative sense in parallel with the drinking of the cup -
the cup, that is to say, of suffering: "Are ye able to drink
the cup that I drink? or to be baptized with the baptism that
I am baptized with"? In this case as early as Matthew
βαπτίζειν was felt to be ambiguous, for he omitted the clause
about baptism from Mark's parallelism.

In Mark-Matthew we do not of course simply have the
reporting of what happened in the days of Jesus. They see the
days of the Church as belonging to the same era as the days
of Jesus. This era did not for them begin with the
resurrection of Jesus. It is traced back proleptically to the
earliest epiphany of Jesus - in Mark to his baptism, in
Matthew to the genealogy. The Church then did not baptize in
water when in its view Jesus did not do so. The mainly Jewish
adherents of the Church were *ipso facto* undergoing a baptism
in holy spirit and fire /2/. And when it was a question of
receiving non-Jewish converts, as in the case of the Gentile
centurion and of the Syrophoenician woman, they were to be
received on the basis of faith.

The impact of all this upon us would be greater were it
not for the *crux interpretum* of Mt. 28:19b: "baptizing them
into the name of the Father, and of the Son, and of the Holy
Ghost". Here the MS. evidence, beginning in the fourth century,
is unanimous. It must be admitted that only the most compelling
reasons should lead us to go against such evidence. Such
reasons are not furnished simply by the fact that Justin,
Tertullian and Eusebius can paraphrase or allude to the
paragraph without repeating the whole phrase in 19b /3/. The
problem is constituted by the fact that the formula finds the
reader - or to be more precise the reader in the Matthaean
Church - totally unprepared for this development. On the
basis of Mt.1;1 - 28;19a,19b comes as a complete surprise,
and is manifestly a reversal of Matthaean practice. Outside
the Matthaean Church, however, an initiation rite appears to

have been gaining ground; and such a rite had become general
practice by the middle of the second century. It is that
development, rather than Matthew's text, which enables us to
understand the formula in 19b - a formula, incidentally, that
agrees with the declaratory baptismal formula that is
characteristic of the East. But before we can make further
headway with the problem of 19b, we need to know more about
the circumstances of the transmission of the text of the
Gospels in the earliest stages. In what circumstances could a
catholicising formula come to prevail?

When we turn to Paul we find, I venture to think, the same
attitude that we find in Mark-Matthew. To Paul's mind conversion
to Christ and reception into the Church were on the basis of
faith. For him the proper and truly the sufficient response to
the kerygma was in principle faith. Now just as Mt.28;19b is
a *crux interpretum,* so for Paul is 1 Cor. 1;14-17: "I thank
God that I baptized none of you ... For Christ sent me not to
baptize, but to preach the gospel". It is very difficult to
resist the conclusion that here Paul expresses a depreciatory
view of baptism, although many of us might try to get round
it somehow. Thus, Paul was perhaps too busy preaching or
thinking about the kerygma to have time to baptize. Or perhaps
he regarded baptism as but the corollary of faith, and that
it could be safely left to those whose thoughts and
responsibilities did not lie on the same level as those of an
apostle. Alternatively, it might be argued that Paul refrained
from baptism only in Corinth after first encountering
rivalries and disorders there. But such a suggestion
disregards the force of Paul's antithesis: Christ sent me not
to baptize but to evangelize.

But let us suppose that Paul meant what he appears to
mean - that he took a low view of baptism, and actually came
to disapprove of it in practice. It can hardly be questioned
that he disapproved of baptism for the dead, although he was
prepared to exploit it in an *ad hominem* argument about the
resurrection of the body. Did he deep down really approve of
baptism for the living? In his eagerness to censure his
opponents in Corinth, he came near to repudiating baptism
altogether, when perhaps Sosthenes at his elbow or some other
amanuensis reminded him that he had baptized Crispus and
Gaius, and furthermore Stephanas and his company. Perhaps
baptism was *their* practice in Corinth, and in the past he had
gone as far as he could to meet them on this point, but

subsequently had second thoughts and gave up the practice.

But what was their practice? In Galatia the practice of
his opponents included circumcision as well as baptism (Gal.
5;2-12). It looks therefore as though Paul's opponents
generally assumed that some form of proselyte baptism was
de rigueur when it came to admitting former pagans into the
Church. They can hardly be blamed out of hand. His Galatian
opponents can perhaps only be criticized on the grounds on
which Paul in fact criticizes them, namely, that circumcision
is so wholly identified with Judaism that it cannot but be
seen as entailing the obligation to keep the whole Law. Of
course he did not object to the *tertium quid* in proselyte
baptism, namely, the performance of good works in commutation
of sacrifice, and in fact he commends it for example in
Rom.12;1. The immersion bath, however, may have seemed to have
a somewhat neutral character. In itself there might be
something to be said for it, as his own practice at first in
Corinth suggested. But its significance would inevitably be
coloured by the context in which it took place. If it went
along with circumcision, as it apparently did in Galatia,
then it were better not done at all. Thus there was a serious
difference between Paul and his opponents over baptism - a
difference which may reflect the difference over proselyte
baptism that existed within Judaism. 1 Cor.1;14-17 then
seems to be the key to Paul's attitude to baptism because it
clearly reveals his own practice.

In the light of this text and its implications, can we
arrive at a satisfactory interpretation of what Paul says
elsewhere about baptism? In the first place, in 1 Cor.10;1ff
he makes use of an illustration not of his own devising, for
the passage of Israel through the Red Sea was already
understood as a precedent for proselyte baptism. He himself
of course extends the illustration in order to relate the
spiritual meat and drink in the wilderness to the eucharist.
But he rests this argument on their premises, in order to
enjoin upon them his conclusions. The fathers had the types
of the Christian mysteries, yet perished in the wilderness.
Let his opponents who have the antitypes beware lest by similar
presumption they also perish. It is *their* attitude to baptism
and the eucharist that is in question. They presume too much.
For himself, although he regards the tradition of the
eucharist as "from the Lord", he never says as much about
baptism.

His basic position is stated in Gal.3;26: "Ye are all sons
of God, through faith, in Christ Jesus", whether they were by
descent Jews or Gentiles. Can then the following verse be
taken in a discriminatory sense? "As many of you as were
baptized into Christ" - though not all had been - "did put on
Christ": a simile which must be drawn from the putting on of
clothes after the immersion bath of the proselyte. Paul uses
the verbs in the second person plural, as though he is speaking
about them, excluding himself and others. He does not concede
that baptism is of general obligation. It formed no part, for
example, of his own conversion.

In Romans however he is in a less combative frame of mind.
Here, with more graciousness, he classes himself with his
readers. Thus in the highly and rightly so valued passage in
Rom.6;3ff, he speaks in the first person plural. He again uses
ὅσοι, but tactfully places himself with those whom he is
addressing: "all we who were baptized". But he builds into what
he has to say about baptism his fundamental kerygma. Baptism,
that is to say, is to be related not to the flesh, to
circumcision, but to the flesh of Christ, to the word of the
cross, not to the Law but to the Gospel. Thus Paul, I suggest,
standing aloof for his part from an initiation rite,
nevertheless invested *their* practice with *his* teaching.   *Their*
baptism is construed with *his* gospel. This bringing together
of burial in the water of baptism with the burial of Christ
eventually became normative in Christian teaching, although
of course it required the formation of the Pauline corpus and
its publication to give the idea currency. It eventually
finds expression in the baptistery of the third century
house-church in distant Dura-Europos, where the mural of the
tomb of Christ adjoins the font. It is embodied in the
juxtaposition of the baptistery with the Anastasis in
Jerusalem in the fourth century. Thereafter it passed into the
catholic tradition everywhere /4/.

Mark-Matthew and, deep down, Paul seem to be agreed that
faith is the proper and sufficient response to the kerygma.
This view presupposes that, for all their polemic against
Pharisaism and Judaism generally, the Church inherited from
Judaism an ethos of faith and morality which enabled the
Church to assimilate conversions from paganism. But the more
Christianity was exposed to the pagan world, the more acute
became the problem of the conditions upon which pagan converts
might be received. Paul, in spite of his deepest convictions

could not turn away from this problem. His compounding of
their baptism with *his* gospel reveals his recognition of it.
Belief required a moral basis, and this called for an
initiation discipline of some kind. The trends towards such
a discipline are illustrated in all their complexity in the
Johannine documents and in Luke-Acts.

Let us take the Johannine documents first. In the opening
historical section in Jn.1;19-34, whether we accept the text as
it stands or adopt a theory of supplementation under the
influence of the synoptic tradition, a distinction is drawn,
as in the synoptic tradition, between the witness of John in
baptizing and the appearance of Jesus as endowed with the
Spirit. As in Mark-Matthew, this distinction would lead us to
expect that Jesus did not himself baptize, as the correction
in Jn.4;1f shows. Indeed it lends some support to the
conjectural emendation of 3;5 by the omission of the words
ὕδατος καί. Thus in the encounter of Jesus with both John and
Nicodemus we are presented with the dichotomy of flesh and
spirit. In contrast with all this, 3;22ff embodies a
tradition of Jesus baptizing. It is tempting to accept this
as historical, if only because it is not really up the
Evangelist's street. We have already seen that Mark-Matthew
abandoned this tradition. Its absence from Luke suggests
that he did not know about it, for it would have suited his
parallel treatment of John and Jesus. If in the end it
survived in the Fourth Gospel, in spite of its disparity with
the σάρξ-πνεῦμα antithesis, it is probable that vested
interests in Johannine circles wanted it kept in. That is
to say, baptizing was going on somewhere.

In this same line of tradition stands the Siloam story.
We seem to have here a concession to the flesh; for the man's
sight is restored by anointing and washing, although after an
interval of time the confession of belief follows. In a
rudimentary way Jn.9;1-7, with anointing preceding washing,
seems to be at the beginning of a line of development that
surfaces next, outside the New Testament, in *Didascalia
Apostolorum*. All this however is at variance with the Bethsaida
story, where the word of Jesus is placed in contrast with the
healing properties of the pool, and the cripple is healed
without washing and without regard to belief.

And what are we to make of χρῖσμα in 1 John 2;20,27?
Attempts to insist upon the figurative use of this term are

counter-balanced by the fact that a literal interpretation is
equally possible and no less satisfactory. It is similarly no
less possible that χρῖσμα is pre-supposed by the reference to
the πνεῦμα in 1 Jn.5;6-8, along with water and blood, meaning
the mysteries of baptism and the eucharist. If this is so,
then we have a further illustration here of the Syrian
initiation structure. Moreover, the formula in the uncial
text of Jn.3;5, γεννηθῇ ἐξ ὕδατος καὶ πνεύματος, is clearly
related to this situation in 1 John, although in that case it
is a formula which is taken up in the Roman baptismal tradition.

Thus the Fourth Gospel, which seems never to have been
finally revised and co-ordinated, together with 1 John,
reveals complex and conflicting tendencies in regard to
initiation. A contemplative view of Christ and the world
does not seem yet to have been fully reconciled with the
development of practice.

Even more diverse than the evidence of the Johannine
documents is the evidence of Luke-Acts. Here of course one
must constantly bear in mind that Luke's interest in an
initiation rite is subordinate to his main apologetic thesis.
This indeed gives to his evidence its special value, since
he has not sought to systematize it, but is content to present
it as he found it in his sources. Thus he accepts the
treatment in Q and Mark in regard to the baptism of John and
Jesus. In Acts he cites a case of conversion without making
any mention of baptism - the case of Sergius Paulus; and two
cases of conversion where only baptism in water is mentioned -
the case of the Ethiopian eunuch and of the jailor at Philippi.
He describes another case - that of Cornelius - in which the
Spirit is given prior to baptism; and the same pattern seems
to be found in the first account of Paul's conversion. In
both these last cases, it will be noticed, the evidence again
concurs with the old Syrian initiation structure. In two
other cases he associates the gift of the Spirit with the
laying on of hands after baptism - those of the apostles Peter
and John in Samaria, and of Paul in Ephesus. Finally, in the
D text of Acts 2;38f, 8;12ff, and 19;5f, there is an approach
to a basic common structure in initiation: repentance or
belief, baptism for the forgiveness of sin, and the gift of
the Spirit by the laying on of hands. This no doubt represents
the structure and meaning of initiation where the D text
originated. Unless, then, Luke is writing with great freedom,
it is probably true that the variety of accounts results from

the variety of practice represented in his sources. Accordingly
in Luke's time, between the fall of Jerusalem and the first
citation of Luke-Acts, namely in Justin, initiation rites of one
kind or another were developing predominantly in the course of
the Gentile mission.

This variety of initiation practice in the Johannine
documents and Luke-Acts derives from a catchment area of
indeterminate extent. It is by contrast in local documents
that we first encounter a baptismal rite as taken for granted
without qualification. I refer to Ephesians, 1 Peter and Titus.
The 'one baptism' of Eph.4;5 is evidently applicable to Jews
and Gentiles alike, to whom the epistle is addressed. In
1 Peter not only is baptism taken for granted, but a further
stage of definition is apparent. The play on the paschal
character of the Christian life suggests that baptism took
place, at least ideally, at Easter. The description of an
initiation rite in Tit.3;5 as "a bath of regeneration and
renewal by the Holy Ghost" - a formula similar to that in
Jn.3;5 - discloses an environment that is Hellenistic rather
than Jewish. And although it tells us little or nothing of
the structure of the rite, it is a distant development from
the state of affairs in Mark-Matthew where the Messianic
confession was not attended by the baptismal bath.

If finally Ephesians, 1 Peter and Titus convincingly
represent baptism as a local requirement, the longer ending
of Mark yokes baptism with belief as necessary for salvation
as a universal requirement: "Go ye into all the world, and
preach the gospel to the whole creation. He that believeth
and is baptized will be saved". And it is perhaps on such a
view that Mt.28;19 is to be understood, and on such a view
that 19b has been formulated - in vivid contrast with the
apostolic mission in Mt.10 which was local in extent, with
the announcement of the nearness of the Kingdom and the
injunction to heal and to exorcize as its main content.

May I summarize this presentation of the evidence? (i) It
is conceivable, on the basis of Jn.3;22ff, that Jesus baptized,
at least at first, following John. (ii) Such a tradition,
however, is entirely absent from Mark-Matthew. Their
congregations, within Judaism, were constituted not by an
initiation rite, but by the Law and the prophets and by faith -
faith being the sole stipulation in the case of the reception
of Gentile adherents. (iii) Paul likewise strove to organize

Christian congregations on the principle of faith. But his
situation was not quite that of Mark-Matthew. He was dealing
with a Judaism that was more open and more exposed to the
Gentile world, in which definition of the position of adherents
to Christ in the face of paganism was sought by carrying over
the requirements of proselyte baptism. Paul, though rejecting
circumcision, was prepared to tolerate baptism, but only by
investing its meaning with his own gospel. (iv) The need for
a rite of transition from paganism to Christianity is apparent
in the varied sources of the Johannine documents and of Luke-
Acts. But variety of practice was characteristic of this
period, and no single form of initiation prevailed or could
claim originality. (v) Other late New Testament documents show
a baptismal rite to be essential for entry into the Christian
Church. 1 Peter infuses the rite with paschal associations.
Titus reveals the impact upon the initiatory rite of Greek
concepts. The longer ending of Mark supposes baptism to be
a universal requirement; and to this stage of development the
formulation of Mt.28;19b perhaps belongs.

      Thus there seems to be a gap between what was conceivably
the practice of Jesus himself and the adoption of an
initiatory rite in the developing practice of the Church. At
an early date circumcision was prised out of this practice; but
the rite was enriched with unction and the imposition of hands,
in order to give expression to the range of belief in Christ.
The gospel in its manifold significance was built into the
Church's initiation rite. The evidence for all this is
fragmentary and widely dispersed over a century of development.
The attempt, so widespread in recent scholarship, to isolate
the bath as including the whole significance of Christian
initiation seems to be arbitrary, and to misrepresent the
complexity of development by which the Church emerged as a
self-conscious entity. Here in initiation, no more than in
Christology, authenticity cannot be identified with some
extrapolated moment of primitive simplicity. In the flux of
development of belief and practice no such moment can be shown
to have existed. What we have got in the age of the New
Testament is not at some point a primitive, stable form of
initiation, but a lengthy development which has to be seen in
its wholeness.

      A couple of generations later Tertullian provides us in
De Baptismo with the only complete account of initiation in
the pre-Nicene period. The rite on which he comments is a

traditional rite. In his controversy with Marcionites he
assumes that it goes back to the time of Marcion /5/. It is a
rite which seems to underlie what Justin has to say on this
subject /6/, and which seems to have its counterpart in the
eddies of main-stream catholicism - the Gospel of Truth, what
Irenaeus has to say about the Marcosians, and the Gospel of
Philip /7/. It is improbable that these sources supplied
catholicism with its complex rite. It is more likely that
catholic and gnostic Christians alike inherited a tradition
that derived from the earlier decades, witnessed fragmentarily
by the documents of the New Testament. The one new element at
this stage, apparent however at least from the time of
Ignatius, is the association of the initiation rite not only
with Christological development, but with the development of
orders within the Church /8/.

    I am very conscious that this interpretation of the
evidence, as I have outlined it, runs against the view that
"There are two sacraments ordained of Christ our Lord in the
Gospel, that is to say, Baptism, and the Supper of the Lord" /9/;
and equally that it offends against the view that baptism, like
all other sacraments, rests on "an immediate institution by
Christ" /10/. I shall not be so rash as to propose a solution
of the problem thus raised in a closing paragraph. But I will
conclude with two points which must surely figure in any
solution. First, the Church of the age of the New Testament
itself attributed the institution of baptism to the risen Lord:
"Go ... make disciples ... baptize ... teach ... and lo, I am
with you always even unto the end of the age". And secondly,
in the final state of the Fourth Gospel baptism no less than
the eucharist was understood to derive its authority from the
Crucified, whose side was pierced after death: "And straightway
there came out blood and water".

NOTES

/1/   O. Cullmann, *Baptism in the New Testament*, ET SCM, 1950;
1978.
       G.R. Beasley-Murray, *Baptism in the New Testament*,
Macmillan, 1962; Paternoster 1978.
/2/   Thus in Mk.3;29: Mt.12;31f, blasphemy against the holy
spirit is the unforgivable sin. Is the idea of baptism in fire
preserved in the obscure saying in Lk.12;49?

/3/   Justin, *Dial*.39:   Tertullian, *Adv.Marc.*, iv.43 end:
F.C. Conybeare's article, "The Eusebian form of the text of
Matt.28;19", originally published in *ZNW*, 1901, was summarized
in a subsequent article, "Three early doctrinal modifications
of the text of the Gospels", published in *The Hibbert Journal*,
vol. 1, 1902-3. pp.102-8.
/4/   It is perhaps alluded to by Tertullian, *De Bap*.11:
*quia nec mors nostra dissolvi posset nisi domini passione nec
vita restitui sine resurrectione ipsius.*   It is explicit, for
example, in Cyril of Jerusalem, *Myst. Cat.* 2: text, 4, 6-8, and
in John Chrysostom, *Bap.Instr.*, Stav.7;22; PK.1;12; 2;8-11.
/5/   *Adv.Marc.*, ed. E. Evans, i.14.3.
/6/   *1 Apol.* 61,65;   *Dial*.39,87.
/7/   Gospel of Truth, 35;5 - 37;3.   Irenaeus, *Adv.haer* I xxi.
3-4.   Gospel of Philip lxviii.
/8/   Ignatius, *Smyrn*. viii.
/9/   Articles of Religion of the Church of England (1562), xxv.
The same standpoint is found in the Revised Catechism (1962),
para. 38: "Christ in the Gospel has appointed two sacraments
for his Church, as needed by all for fulness of life, Baptism,
and Holy Communion".
/10/   Bernard Leeming, *Principles of Sacramental Theology*,
2nd ed. 1960, Principle XII.   "In the mind of the Council
[of Trent], the 'institution' would seem to mean not any 'mediate'
institution, but an institution made immediately by Christ
himself" (p.398).   Vatican II, however, adopted a different
approach, and in the Constitution of the Sacred Liturgy
(4 December 1963) used language that was more sensitive to the
problems of historical evidence.

The Problem of Suffering and Ethics in the New Testament

Rev. J. Nissen,
Institut for Ny Testamente,
Aarhus Universitet,
Hovedbygningen, 8000 Aarhus C.
DENMARK.

Introduction

Modern scholarship has devoted an increasing amount of attention to the ethical dimension of the New Testament. At the same time there is a growing interest in the sociology of religion. But in spite of this, most scholars have not been particularly careful to ask about the social background and significance of the biblical texts. It is often overlooked that the theologies of the New Testament writers have to be related to the communities for whom they wrote. In other words, it has to be asked: What was the cultural, religious and socio-economic setting for the different writings?

In this paper, I am not going to discuss these problems in general. Rather I should like to concentrate upon the relationship between suffering and ethics, or more precisely, between suffering and the ethos of the early communities. In this respect the distinction, made by L.E. Keck, between ethics and ethos is helpful: "That ethos is not ethics should be clear enough, for ethics is the systematic reflection on the nature of the good and the right, whereas ethos refers to the lifestyle of a group or a society" /1/.

There is a demand for analyzing the contextual nature of New Testament theology; the texts reflect the belief and praxis of the first communities. Therefore all biblical theology is a *theology of experience* (Erfahrungstheologie).

It is useful to study how the first Christians used *their* traditions (esp. the Old Testament) to interpret *their own*

experiences. They did not receive the traditions in a passive
way, but reinterpreted them into new situations. As a whole
the New Testament reflects, how communities received and
interpreted traditions about Jesus and made them applicable
to a new context /2/.

The central fact in the Christian tradition is that Jesus
was crucified, and the first Christians were shocked by this
fact of suffering and death /3/. It is not a mere coincidence
that the passion narratives have so many references to the
Old Testament. In the light of previous experiences of
suffering they tried to explain *this* experience of defeat /4/.

Below I shall indicate how this issue was dealt with by
two authors who wrote for two distinct communities, and I shall
argue that the actual life of these communities has influenced
the way in which the cross of Jesus was described.

The Gospel of Mark

In *Mark* there is a tension between the concept of "gospel"
and that of "suffering" /5/. On the one hand *Mark* stresses
how Jesus conquered demons and healed the sick. In other
words: "He has done all things well ..." (7:37) thereby
eliminating the sufferings of human beings.

On the other hand Jesus is portrayed as one who was going
to suffer and to die. In *Mark* the passion narrative has a very
prominent position. And the second part of the gospel is
introduced by an extended section of discipleship (8:27-10:52).

This dialectic relationship between the healing Jesus and
the suffering Jesus has been interpreted in quite different
ways. According to Vielhauer it is the purpose of *Mark* to
demonstrate Jesus as Son of God adopted at the baptism,
presented at the transfiguration and enthroned at his death.
The whole gospel could be described as a sort of liturgy of
enthronement /6/.

According to another view this approach is too schematic.
The role of Jesus as the *Suffering* Servant is ignored. "In
the proportion of *Mark's* theology suffering and death loom very
large" /7/.

It may even be that *Mark* intended to correct a one-sided belief in Jesus as miraculous healer. In that case the situation in the Markan community could be compared with that of the Corinthian community. This interpretation is supported by passages as 15:31-32, where his adverseries challenge Jesus by saying: "He saved others, but cannot save himself" /8/.

In the gospel of Mark ethics is defined by the author's "concentration upon Jesus' divine presence with men as one who serves them and suffers and dies for them. Consequently, the ethic here is not articulated in terms of obedience to the love command, but in terms of following Jesus as his disciples: serving, suffering and giving oneself as he served, suffered and gave himself (8:34; 9:35; 10,21,29-31, 32-45)" /9/. It is, however, a striking fact that the disciples are *not* ready to follow their master in his humiliation and suffering.

They did not pass the crucial test: they rejected the idea of a suffering messiah (8:33), left their master and denied him; and he died in total isolation /10/. The uniqueness of the role of Jesus is stressed by all the synoptic gospels by using the greek verb πασχω only in the sayings of Jesus relating to His own person /11/.

Some scholars have argued - in my opinion correctly - that the gospel of Mark could be labelled a "martyr"-gospel. The aim of the author would then be to strengthen the Christians of his day to face persecution in the knowledge that Jesus himself suffered /12/. There are good grounds for supposing this, when we look at ch.13, esp. v.7-20. The signs referred to in these verses are normally considered in Jewish Apocalyptic to be the signposts of the end. The author of *Mark* has remoulded the tradition and *contextualised* it in relation to the mission and presence of the community (esp. v.9-11). The situation of the community is marked by persecution, suffering and ambiguity /13/.

There is a similarity between the fate of Jesus and that of his followers. Jesus posed a threat to the religio-political power-structure of his time /14/. It was impossible that He should co-exist peacefully with the religious and political authorities of his time. In a similar way the community had to face the tribulation and persecution (13:7-9) and it could only hope for deliverance by the appearance of the Son of Man (13:26) /15/. Or to quote Kee: "The community is already

living in a proleptic way the life of kingdom of God, and
through its message, its witness of life and its charismatic
powers, it is calling the world to join it in obedient, joyful
anticipation of the kingdom's consummation" /16/.

For the readers of Mark's gospel persecution was a
reality. In spite of this they had a hope. Experience had
shown that the Lord was not far away, and could uphold and
strengthen his threatened people. "The declaration that Jesus
is a Son of God comes at the moment of his greatest and
apparent defeat. The resurrection, when it comes, will be
the proclamation of a victory, that has already been won" /17/.

Not only christology and ethics, but also eschatology and
ethics are intertwined. This does not, however, mean, that
Mark is uninterested in the welfare of the world or that there
is a call to retreat from the world and its problems /18/.
Rather, *Mark* is showing a community which has its own norms
and standards different from that of the world. The community
is a fellowship with a counter-culture or a counter-ethos,
the community of the new age, for whom there is a hope in the
midst of suffering /19/.

1 Peter

The situation in *1 Peter* is not unlike that of *Mark*. If
the ethical implications of eschatology are basic to the
understanding of *Mark,* the same holds good for *1 Peter*. Both
writings are probably reflections of Roman theology and speak
to Christians who may at any time be called to face the reality
of persecution /20/.

But even more than *Mark* the first epistle of Peter
focuses on the idea of *imitatio Christi* as the basis of
Christian living. According to several scholars the author of
this letter has abandoned the Pauline concept of salvation
through faith. Sanders, for instance, suggests, that it was
turned into salvation through works. The Pauline "for your
sake" has now become to mean that Christ died as an example
of proper behaviour. Furthermore he argues that it is
particularly interesting to see how the long *Haustafel* in
1 Peter 2:13-3:7 is employed. It is related to the principle
of *imitatio·Christi,* suffering as Christ suffered, cf. 2:21.
And the author lays emphasis on the submission side of the

Haustafel /21/. A similar position has been taken by U. Luz
who argues that whereas Paul did not legitimate and explain
his own pains by referring to the resurrection and coming
glory of Christ, the author of *1 Peter* did /22/. Finally
S. Schulz together with many other German scholars considers
1 Peter to represent "early Catholicism", i.e. degeneration
from the early more correct insights of the Pauline gospel /23/.

In my opinion this is a position which cannot be
convincingly maintained. The concept of conformity to or
participation in the servanthood of Christ is also essential
to other parts of the New Testament. In agreement with Paul
the author of *1 Peter* emphasizes the uniqueness of Christ's
suffering. "The writer's plea", comments J.N.D. Kelly, "is
not that slaves should attempt to reproduce all the particular
details of Christ's passion which he is recapitulating. That
is in any case excluded since "he suffered for you", "bore our
sins", etc. Rather it is that they should expect to have to
suffer, and suffer without having in any way earned it, and
that they should be ready to exhibit the same uncomplaining
acceptance" /24/.

Surely, formulations such as "he suffered for you" cannot
support the idea of reproduction of a pattern. The suffering
of Christ is not only an example to follow, it is also the
reason and motivation for following him. The person who
follows in his steps (4:1) does know the distance to him.
Jesus suffered innocently. He did not revile again when he
was reviled, he suffered, but he did not make threats (2:23).
The same attitude is required from Christians (3:19 and cf. 2:22
with 3:11). However, the context and application of the
tradition indicates, that the necessity of Christian suffering
is not deduced from the suffering of Christ. It is the other
way round. The suffering of Christ is made present in a
situation where the community is suffering. It is related to
a concrete reality of experience /25/.

In this respect it is helpful to make a distinction
between a slavish imitation and one that is creative. The
difference is that the latter, according to the personality
concerned, produces ever new patterns that have a genuine
individual stamp within a genuine likeness. The following of
Jesus does not mean becoming a Jesus oneself, and it does not
refer to an exact copying of the historical life of Jesus /26/.

So, in *1 Peter* there is a difference between the suffering
of Christ which is redemptive and that of the believers which
is not. Suffering is part of the existence of the faithful
in a world which has gone away from God. The suffering to
which Christ is calling the community is suffering for doing
right (2:20; 3:17) or suffering as being a Christian (4:16) /27/.
1 Peter does not insist on suffering as such, rather it is
directed towards undeserved suffering (4:19), doing well while
suffering (2:20; 3:17), suffering for the sake of
righteousness (3:14). In short, suffering for the sake of
others /28/.

One striking fact of *1 Peter* is that Christians, and
especially slaves should accept innocent suffering without
complaint as Jesus did (2:20; 3:14-18; 4:12-16). This could
very easily be interpreted as support for maintaining the
status quo. But there are good reasons for following Yoder in
his more balanced view, that "the *Haustafeln* do not consecrate
the existing order when they call for the acceptance of
subordination by the subordinate person; far more they
relativize and undercut this order by then immediately turning
the imperative around" /29/.

The aim of *1 Peter* is neither to teach withdrawal from
the structures of this world, nor to proclaim a specific order
of society, but to proclaim the kingdom of Christ /30/. In a
context which is dealing with the socio-political reality
Christ is not attested as the ruling one, but as the suffering
and crucified one (2:21-25). It would be wrong to identify
the sufferings of Christ with passivity or apathy. Emphasis
is laid on welldoing, even suffering in welldoing, but this
does not mean conformism, but responsible and critical attitude
to the environment (the world) /31/.

1 Peter is a letter of *hope* written in order to encourage
perseverance in the face of suffering. At this point there
are similarities not only to the gospel of Mark /32/, but also
to Romans 8 /33/. R. Russell characterizes the situation as
follows: "... the experience of real suffering necessitated
the appeal to realized eschatology as a basis of hope" /34/.
There is an invitation to "joy in suffering" (cf. 1:6). This
should not be misinterpreted as a glorification of suffering.
To talk about joy in midst of suffering is another way of
saying, that the love of God is a contradiction of all
suffering. It witnesses to God's presence in suffering and
provides redemption for suffering through the cross of Jesus /35/.

Conclusion

In this short paper it has been pointed out that there is an obvious concern for suffering in two communities of early Christianity. But the same concern could be found in other writings reflecting the life of other communities. Here it would take up too much space to show how the experience of the first communities first and foremost was the experience of suffering and persecutions, caused by the confrontation with Jews and Gentiles (Romans). Persecution for the faith is not independent of social ethics. There are indications to show that "the "cross" of Jesus was a political punishment; and when Christians are made to suffer by government it is usually because of the practical import of their faith, and the doubt they cast upon the ruler's claim to be "Benefactor"" /36/.

An examination of other texts would probably reveal that it is in the context of despair and hopelessness that hope is born. However, such a survey of the different writings point to the *variety* of articulations of Christian experience. In this connexion the function of the spirit should not be overlooked /37/.

Each community existed within its own social and cultural tradition and was called upon to make the intention of Jesus relevant to its own context. There were different ways in which the once-and-for-all Christ event was imagined by those who had experienced it in their own life and that of the community /38/.

It is in this process of re-enacting the Christ-event /39/ that the spirit has a specific function. The presence of the spirit is marked by love and by resistance to demonic powers, the fruit of pain, suffering and disaster. Or to quote a black theologian: It is the spirit, who "is calling beside us, who hears and expresses our speechless groans, who empowers and guides us to continue in the fellowship of Christ' suffering. This spirituality in suffering becomes light and hope in the struggle for a new world in which dwells God's justice and peace" /40/.

In contemporary theology there is a need to develop a theology of suffering /41/. It has been the aim of this paper to argue that in this respect we could learn a great deal from the experiences of the early communities.

NOTES

/1/   L.E. Keck, On the Ethos of Early Christians, in: *JAAR* 42 (1974),pp.435-452,   p.440.
      See also J.G. Gager, *Kingdom and Community. The Social World of Early Christianity*, 1975 and G. Theissen, *Soziologie der Jesusbewegung*, 1977.
/2/   Cf. K. Berger, *Exegese des Neuen Testaments*, Heidelberg 1977.
/3/   Cf. J. Ferguson, *The Place of Suffering*, Cambridge and London 1972, p.80.
/4/   Cf. G. Gerstenberger and W. Schrage, Leiden, Stuttgart 1977, p.121f.
/5/   Cf. J.L. Houlden, *Patterns of Faith*, Fortress 1977, p.37.
/6/   Cf. P. Vielhauer, Erwägungen zur Christologie des Markusevangelium, in: E. Dinkler (ed.): *Zeit und Geschichte* (Festschr. R. Bultmann), Tubingen 1964, p.155-169.
/7/   Cf. Houlden, *Patterns of Faith*, p.38.
/8/   For a fuller discussion of this see H.-R. Weber, *Kreuz*, Stuttgart 1975, p.164-174.
      Mark's critical attitude to miracles does not mean that he rejected them totally. Wonders and miracles were part of the life of the first Christians, and Mark himself interpreted the passion as a miracle. It is the *same* person, who served by healing and served by suffering.
/9/   Quoted from V.P. Furnish, *The Love Command in the New Testament*, SCM 1972, p.74.
/10/ Cf. U. Luz, Theologia Crucis als Mitte der Theologie im Neuen Testament, in: *Evang. Theologie* 34 (1974), p.116-141 (p.133).
/11/ Cf. M. Vellanickal, Suffering in the Life and Teaching of Jesus, in *Jeevadhara* no.20 (1974), p.144-45.
/12/ See Ferguson, *The Place of Suffering*, p.81.
/13/ Cf. K. Berger, *Exegese des Neuen Testaments*, p.210. Berger connects this concept with that of the "Messiasgeheimnis", and asks how the true Christians can be recognized: "Nur die Leser des Mk.Ev. wissen es. Für alle Aussenstehenden aber gilt, dass man ihn erst am Ende auf den Wolken des Himmels erkennen wird. Dem Leiden der Gemeinde und des Christus entspricht die Verborgenheit seines Messiastums".
/14/ Cf. S. Kappen, The Man Jesus: Rupture and Communion. Reflections on the Gospel according to Mark, in: *Religion and Society* 23 (1976), p.66-76, esp. p.72-4.
/15/ Cf. H.C. Kee, *Community of the New Age, Studies in Mark's Gospel*, SCM 1977, p.150f.

/16/ Kee, *ibid*. p.174-5.

/17/ S. Neill, *Jesus Through Many Eyes*, Fortress 1976, p.86.

/18/ So J.T. Sanders, *Ethics in the New Testament*, SCM 1975, p.33.

/19/ Cf. Kee, *Community of the New Age*. For the concept of a counter-church see also F. Herzog, *Liberation Theology. Liberation in the Light of the Fourth Gospel*, New York 1972 (esp. Part 4: The Liberation Church, the Counter-Church, Joh 13:1-17:26). A similar view is expressed in H. Gollwitzer, Zum Problem der Gewalt in der christlichen Ethik, in: *Forderungen der Umkehr*, München 1976, p.126-148 and C.E. Braaten, *Christ and Counter-Christ. Apocalyptic Themes in Theology and Culture*, Fortress 1972.

/20/ Cf. Neill, *Jesus Through Many Eyes*, p.89.

/21/ Sanders, *Ethics in the New Testament*, p.83, n.35.

/22/ U. Luz, *Theologia Crucis*, p.129: "Die eigene Existenz der Christen wird, weil sie Leiden, vom Kreuz her nicht kritisch hinterfragt, sondern bestätigt: Leiden is Chance, die eigene Sünden loszuwerden (4,1) in die Fusstapfen Christi zu treten und, ohne zu rebellieren, gerecht zu leiden (2,21) und damit eine Chance zur Rettung derer der Gottlose und Sünder kaum teilhaftig wird (4,18). Der Weg zur einer Tugendlehre des Leidens ist nicht gross, wohl aber die Distanz zu Paulus".

/23/ S. Schulz, *Die Mitte der Schrift*, 1976, p.275-6.

/24/ J.N.D. Kelly, *A Commentary on the Epistle of Peter and Jude*, A.and C. Black 1969, p.120.

/25/ Cf. Gerstenberger and Schrage, Leiden, p.160.

/26/ Cf. J.G. Davies, *Christians, Politics and Violent Revolution*, SCM 1976, p.146.

/27/ Cf. Ferguson, *The Place of Suffering*, p.93.

/28/ Cf. The important contribution by E. Schillebeeckx, *Christus und die Christen*, Herder 1977, p.212ff.

/29/ J.H. Yoder, *The Politics of Jesus*, Eerdmans 1972, p.181. See the discussion in the whole Chapt. on "Revolutionary Subordination", p.163-192.

/30/ Cf. K. Phillips, *Kirche in der Gesellschaft nach dem ersten Petrusbrief*, Gutersloh 1971, p.27 and 49.

/31/ Cf. H. Millauer, *Leiden als Gnade, Eine traditionsgeschichtliche Untersuchung zur Leidenstheologie des ersten Petrusbriefes*, Bern 1976. See also two articles from his teacher, L. Goppelt, Prinzipien neutestamentlicher Sozialethik nach dem 1. Petrusbrief, in: *Neues Testament und Geschichte* (Cullmann-Festschr. Zurich 1972, p.285-296) and: Jesus und die "Haustafel"-Tradition, in: *Orientierung an Jesus* (Festschr. für J. Schmid), Freiburg 1973, p.93-106. His recent

commentary on 1 Peter (*Der erste Petrusbrief*, Gütersloh 1978)
was not available to me. For the relationship to the synoptic
tradition, esp. Matth 5:38-48, see L. Schottroff,
Gewaltverzicht und Feindesliebe in der urchristlichen
Jesustradition, in: *Jesus Christus in Historie und Theologie*,
Festhschr. für H. Conzelmann, Tübingen 1975, p.197-221. Here
it is argued, that "Feindesliebe ist Appell zu einer
missionarischen Haltung gegenüber den Verfolgern" (p.215).
/32/ J. Schattenmann (in: The little Apocalypse of the
Synoptics and the First Epistle of Peter, *Theology Today* 11
(1954), p.193-8) thinks, that 1 Peter is a commentary on
Mark 13.
/33/ In *Romans* 8 the problem is why Christians who have the
spirit must suffer in the world. In Paul's thinking the
sufferings do not call into question the glory and the hope.
On the contrary the sufferings are the "Sitz im Leben" of the
future glory. Paul's starting point is the experiences of
weakness and suffering and he interprets these experiences as
the context of salvation. See A.M. Aagaard, Præstetjeneste.
En tolkning af Rom 8,18-30, in: *Tema og tolkninger*, Aarhus 1976,
p.146-157. For the significance of Romans 8 for Paul's thought
on suffering and hope see also J.D.G. Dunn, *Jesus and the
Spirit*, SCM 1975, esp. p.326ff.
/34/ R. Russell, Eschatology and Ethics in 1 Peter, in:
The Evangelical Quarterly 47 (1975), pp.78-84, p.80.
/35/ Cf. E. Otto and T. Schramm, *Fest und Freude*, Stuttgart
1977, p.162, where it also is stated: "Freude im Leiden als
Ausdruck christlicher Glaubensexistenz bedeutet schon jetzt
Anteil an jener endgültigen Freude, die aufstrahlt, wenn Gott
alle Tränen abwischen wird, und der Tod nicht mehr ist und
kein Leid (Offb 21,4)".
/36/ Cf. Yoder, *The Politics of Jesus*, p.128.
/37/ For *Luke-Acts* see for instance S. Brown, *Apostasy and
Perseverance in the Theology of Luke*, Rome 1969. For the
gospel of John see among others Gerstenberger and Schrage,
Leiden, p.181. (On the significance of the exclusion from the
synagogue, see J.L. Martyn, *History and Theology in the Fourth
Gospel*, New York 1968).
/38/ Cf. J. Navone, *Communicating Christ*, St. Paul
Publications 1976, p.28.32.
/39/ Cf. Navone (The Chapter: Christ's command to re-enact,
p.34ff). Concerning the relationship between theology
(pneumatology) and experiences see also the important article
by G. Sauter, Wie kann Theologie aus Erfahrungen entstehen? in:
Theologie im Entstehen, hrsg. L. Vischer, München 1976, p.99-118.

/40/ Ph. Potter, One Obedience to the Whole Gospel, in:
International Review of Mission 29 (1977), p.354-65 (p.364-5).
/41/ Important contributions have already been published, e.g.
J. Moltmann, *Der gekreuzigte Gott,* München 1972, E.
Schillebeeckx, *Christus und die Christen* (quoted earlier in
this paper), K. Koyama, *No Handle on the Cross,* Orbis Books
1977, D. Sölle, *Leiden,* Stuttgart 1973 and J.H. Cone, *God of
the Oppressed,* SPCK 1977 (Seabury Press 1975).

Paul's Last Captivity

Jerome D. Quinn,
Professor of New Testament,
The Saint Paul Seminary,
2260 Summit Avenue,
St. Paul, Minn. 55105,
U.S.A.

The historical reconstructions of the events that climaxed
in the final imprisonment and execution of the apostle, Paul,
are still as debatable as ever /1/. The historian's
difficulties are rooted in the first-century sources, in the
authentic correspondence that Paul certainly dispatched during
one or another imprisonment in the first Christian generation,
as well as in the second generation documents that recalled the
deeds and words of the apostle.

A preliminary sketch of the historian's problem can be drawn
from a comparison of the data transmitted by the *ipsissima vox*
of the historical Paul with the data about Paul adduced by the
author of *I Clement*. From authentic Pauline correspondence we
glimpse the "alarums and excursions" in the career of a man often
imprisoned, often in mortal peril. There are glimpses of the
plans of a man who often changed his plans. From those
documents emerge the names of cities and places that he had
visited and still others that he planned to visit, including
Rome and Spain. But even a relative chronology for this
correspondence is vexed, not least among the very documents
that could conceivably have come from the end of Paul's life.
Indeed, no one has broached the way to a historical demonstration
that a given letter came from the eve of the apostle's death.
Even in chains Paul resolutely wrote about the ways of God with
man rather than about the ways in which men were bringing him
to execution. The historian (whose tastes are admittedly highly
specialized) has no option but to take Paul as he wrote and to
admit frankly (if not cheerfully) that from the primary sources
he can recover practically no hard data, chronological or
geographical, about the last days of the apostle.

If Paul spoke thus himself, how was he remembered in the
second Christian generation? No later than 96 A.D., *I Clement,*
whose author certainly had read some of the Pauline
correspondence of the previous generation, recalled a Paul,
harassed and hated, stoned and exiled, in prison seven times
(to be exact!); a Paul who (he hints) had been to Spain; who
was finally driven to earth "by jealousy and strife" and who
gave his final witness unto death "before the rulers" in
Rome /2/. *I Clement* is a real letter to an actual congregation.
To that extent it resembles the authentic Pauline letters to
churches. Its author was no less pastorally and theologically
oriented than Paul; so again the historian is hardly less
frustrated as he attempts to disengage hard facts from a
document that was not especially exercised about the details
of the last imprisonment of Paul. The Roman church was
certainly convinced, at the end of the second Christian
generation, that Paul had been legally executed in that city.
Furthermore, they are not likely to have fabricated the
observation that internecine Christian hatreds precipitated
that tragedy.

Sometime after the actual Pauline letters were dispatched
and most probably (in my judgement) before *I Clement,* two other
bodies of documentation were addressed to the Christian believers
of the second generation. Both compositions professed to recall
and to sketch the life, mission, and teaching of Paul.

One work appeared in two complementary volumes or rolls
containing a massive theologico-historical narrative which we
title *Luke-Acts.* That work concluded with a long survey of the
Pauline apostolate, ending abruptly with Paul under house arrest
in Rome, "for two years". The author, writing in the second
Christian generation, certainly knew more of the apostle's
life. Thus he represents Paul as convinced that he would
never again see the Ephesian Christians (Acts 20:25,38) and
that he would certainly "stand before Caesar" in Rome (Acts 27:
24). Several chapters of his work detailed the legal process
that Paul went through in Palestine; yet there is not a word
about the climactic and critical trial, the Roman one. In
other respects too the sketch of Paul is curiously fragmentary.
The reader of Acts would never infer that the historical Paul
had projected a mission to Spain, that he had ever written a
single letter.

There is still another composition from the second
generation that deals with Paul, a little collection of three

letters dubbed the *Pastoral Epistles* (= *PE* hereafter) /3/. They
profess to emanate from Paul himself. Their vocabulary and
style, conspicuously different from other Pauline correspondence,
bespeak a common origin. I suspect that behind them lie short
notes from the historical Paul and his staff, perhaps an
original "letter of introduction" behind *Titus*, a more personal
and urgent letter behind *II Tim*. These materials were expanded
and rewritten after Paul's death to include, for instance, the
names of opponents and enemies. That was not characteristic
of the actual Pauline letters, as it was not characteristic of
I Clement or Ignatius. Indeed, the latter actually explained
in his letter to the Smyrnaeans (5.3), "Now I have not thought
right to put into writing their unbelieving names; but would
that I might not even remember them, until they repent
concerning the passion, which is our resurrection". I submit
that the PE as we now have them were written as a unit, as an
"unreal" correspondence divided into three letters (as
distinguished from an actual or real correspondence of
individual letters separately dispatched and later collected
by others). In this respect the *PE* resemble that volume or
roll (*biblion*) of seven "unreal" letters which introduce
Revelation (*Rev* 1:11). The order within that collection has
been dictated by the route that a putative letter-carrier would
actually take in delivering them to the churches of Asia Minor
(W. Ramsay). I suggest that the PE were written to give the
reader among other things an oblique glimpse of Paul's last
journey and imprisonment.

The PE, as they appeared in the original volume of "unreal"
correspondence, were in the order *Titus-I Timothy-II Timothy* /4/.
That is the order in which they appear in their earliest citation
as a group, in the Muratorian fragment. The way in which the
letters are composed also argues for this order. The expansive
(66-word) introduction to *Titus* (1:1-4) appropriately introduces
a thirteen chapter collection. To put such an introduction
before the three brief chapters of *Titus* alone would be like
building the west portal of York minster in front of a village
church. Moreover the themes which *Titus* introduces briefly are
expanded and reorchestrated in *I Tim*. Further, the two
"letters" to Timothy are deliberately juxtaposed, to be read
in tandem. The abrupt conclusion of *I Timothy* (with no personal
greetings) argues for this, as does the textual history of
I Tim 6:21. Even the second-century manner of citation suggests
that these two letters were read as a unit /5/. Finally,
II Timothy read as Paul's last will and testament, appropriately

concludes such a correspondence; *Titus* read in last place is
an anticlimax.

In this little volume, as in *Acts*, the author intended to
vindicate and exalt the Pauline mission, to ensure the
continuation of the Pauline *kerygma* and *didache* in the decades
following his execution. The reader was meant to "overhear"
the absent apostle as he continued to direct the mission and
teaching of two men who shared his apostolic task, who were
thus "two witnesses" to his work and words, who were his lawful
children and thus his heirs.

It was Dibelius who asserted that "the so-called Pastoral
Letters ... cannot be used as sources for Paul's life and
teaching", adding later, "it has been established that in
trying to understand Paul, we have to disregard the Pastoral
Letters" /6/. That drastic judgement followed upon the heady
realization that the *PE* were probably not from the historical
Paul in the same sense that *Galatians* and *Romans* were. So the
PE were to be disregarded and ignored by the historian in
search of what Paul was actually like, much as one might safely
ignore the beard and long hair left on the barber shop floor
by the freshly shaved and crewcut collegian. But that
straitened concept of authentic sources for an individual's
history presupposes that in the end only a man's self-
description of his views and his activities really belongs to
his biography. However, the impact of a man's life and ideas
and work and even of his death upon his contemporaries also
belongs to his history; nor need all "contemporaries" die in
the same year as the person who has directly or indirectly
influenced them. The *PE* attempt to transmit and preserve
something of Paul's impact on the believers whom he evangelized.
They were written at least as early as *Luke-Acts,* and that
would mean the eighties of the first Christian century. It has
often been noted that the *PE* link Paul with places known
otherwise in the NT only from *Acts* (thus Pisidian Antioch,
Iconium, Lystra, Crete, Miletus). It has not been noted that
the *PE* resemble Acts also in their exaltation of Paul's
teaching without ever quoting his correspondence (at most a
Pauline phrase or tag of three words running appears a few
times). Pauline letter collections were surely in circulation
by the time of *I Clement* which cited not only Paul's life but
actually quoted his letters, a practice that Ignatius, Polycarp,
et al. carried into the second century. But that would make
it quite reasonable to infer that the *PE* were written *before*

such collections were assembled. Again *PE* resemble Acts in
their silence about a Spanish mission for the apostle. Late
second century reconstructions of Paul's career, such as the
juicy, imaginative farrago called the *Acts of Peter* as well as
the Muratorian fragment (apparently basing their notices on
Rom 15 and *I Clement*) have no qualms about dispatching Paul
to Spain after the Roman imprisonment narrated in the Lukan
Acts. Did the author of *PE* simply choose not to include this
trip? or was he unaware of it? or did such a trip ever occur?
The testimony of *I Clement* makes it likely that a Pauline
mission in the western reaches of the Empire was somehow known
in the second Christian generation. If a report was in
circulation, it is improbable that an author who had picked up
information about what happened to Paul in the Asian hinterland
around 50 A.D. was simply unaware of a dramatic journey to the
western boundary of the Roman world in the mid-sixties. Most
probably, *PE* chose not to advert to the mission in so many
words - perhaps because the author intended only to sketch the
last months of Paul's apostolate, not to write a history of all
that had occurred in the five years or more since the Roman
imprisonment described in *Acts*. The author had, as we shall
see, good reasons for not wanting to rehearse all the details
of those months and the epistolary genre dispensed him from
that unpleasant task.

This volume of "unreal" correspondence opens with Paul
free and somewhere in the eastern Mediterraenean, *en route* from
Crete (*Titus* 1:5), dispatching and recalling members of the
entourage with which he travelled, including the Titus to whom
this "letter" is addressed, (*Titus* 3:12-13,15). Paul is
projecting a stay in Actium/Nicopolis in north-west Greece
during the winter ahead. The reader is meant to understand
that this correspondence began no earlier than late spring or
early summer and that the general direction of Paul's journey
had been from south-east to north-west.

The next "epistle", *I Timothy*, presumes a continuing
movement in this same direction. Paul, still *en route*, now
urges a second co-worker, Timothy, to stay on in Ephesus while
the apostle continues on his way into Macedonia (*I Tim* 1:3).
The apostle does not say "I *left* you in Ephesus" as he said of
Titus, "I *left* you in Crete" (*Titus* 1:5; cf. also *II Tim* 4:13,20).
The chaotic Greek of the sentence avoids saying that Paul was
actually in that city. Even the judgement on Hymenaeus and
Alexander (*I Tim* 1:19-20) seems to have been done *a longe* (as

once the Corinthian scandal has been dealt with). Still, Paul
is represented as fully intending to join Timothy at an early
date, perhaps before winter (cf. *I Tim* 3:14; 4:13).

   With *II Timothy* an abrupt, dramatic change of scene and
atmosphere has occurred. The apostle, previously free and quite
without premonition of danger, now writes from Rome as a
prisoner in desperate straits, in Munck's phrase, "a caged
eagle". There is no question of his going to Timothy. Timothy
must come to him. The final "epistle" in this little volume
has the characteristics of a last will and testament /7/. It
is the written and authentic instrument by which the revered
patriarch and father transmitted the divinely bestowed
inheritance to his legitimate children. The testament was
meant to ensure the responsible use of goods and powers on the
part of the heirs who are in turn to share them, to guard them,
and to transmit them to still other descendants. In the Jewish
handling of this genre, the testator foresees and prophesies
the trials and perils that will beset this transmission. Both
the epistolary and testamentary form signal the crucial
importance for the *PE* of the life, work, and teaching of Paul.
If in *Luke-Acts* the apostles and Paul were the heirs of Jesus'
testament, now in *PE* Titus and Timothy are heirs of Paul's
testament and must ensure the transmission of the goods and
powers that Jesus had bestowed on his apostle (cf. *I Tim* 1:12 with
II Tim 2:1-2).

   It was characteristic of the genre of "unreal" letters to
include data meant to satisfy curiosity about the life of the
putative author. Here in *II Timothy* these data are rather
more plentiful than in the two preceding letters, though they
still come in isolated flashes, like strobe lights, which give
the reader a glimpse of an otherwise unknown Onesiphorus
seeking out and comforting the imprisoned apostle and then
being himself overtaken by sudden death (*II Tim* 1:16-18).
Other figures are recalled, like snatches of a nightmare -
Phygelus, Hermogenes, Philetus and again Hymenaeus (*II Tim* 1:15;
2:17). In the final chapter of *II Timothy* (4:9-21) the
biographical light steadies somewhat and the reader catches a
glimpse of the apostle's decimated staff. Demas had deserted
him. Paul himself had sent Crescens north to Gaul and Titus
east to Dalmatia. Tychicus has been sent as courier with this
dispatch to Timothy, whose place he apparently is to take in
Ephesus. The *PE* at this juncture envision only Luke out of the
apostle's entourage as still remaining with Paul. Hence the

instructions aim to reconstitute the apostle's staff by
summoning Timothy and Mark (to replace Demas and Tychicus).
Apparently Titus and Crescens can be expected to return. In
any case, Timothy is asked to bring a familiar cape, papyrus
rolls, and the notebooks that the apostle had deliberately left
at Carpus' house in Troas (II Tim 4:13).

The name of that city, which was on the main navigational
route from Asia Minor to Rome /8/, suggests that Timothy and
Mark will come to Paul by the route that the apostle had been
on not long before, as he moved northward from Crete, putting
in perhaps at Miletus as his party moved toward Macedonia.
The reader may be meant to infer that it was from Miletus that
Timothy went with visible regret (II Tim 1:4) to Ephesus. In
any case, another member of Paul's entourage, Trophimus, fell ill
there and Paul had had to leave him behind (II Tim 4:20). His
mention of the fact is already a hint to Timothy and Mark, as
they come to Paul, to route themselves through Miletus to
visit and bring news about Trophimus. Similarly Paul's note
that Erastus stayed in Corinth implies not only that he had been
part of Paul's entourage up to that point, but also that Timothy
would be sailing the same route and ought to visit that
influential public accountant's home on his way /9/.

But why were Paul's belongings, his winter clothes and
library, in Troas? In that Roman colony of perhaps 30,000
people he had seeded the faith in the preceding decade
(II Cor 2:12: cf Acts 16:8;20;5-12). On this reconstruction
he had put in there again as he and his party made their way
toward Macedonia. A fellow Christian and Roman, named Carpus
(note the accent on the penult), had extended hospitality to
the apostle. The very mention of that city's name reminded
Paul of something more that had happened to him there and so
he warned Timothy to beware of an Alexander who (to distinguish
him from the person of that name in I Timothy) is identified
as "the coppersmith". It may be no accident that a guild of
coppersmiths has been documented from the inscriptions of Troas
/10/. This man had fiercely attacked the preaching and
teaching of the Pauline entourage (τοῖς ἡμετέροις λόγοις:
II Tim 4:15) and posed criminal charges against Paul as an
individual (πολλά μοι κακὰ ἐνεδείξατο: II Tim 4:14) /11/. I
suggest that this is the moment when "all (the Christians) in
Asia abandoned me, including Phygelus and Hermogenes" (II Tim
1:15), a moment to which this letter returns when it adds,
after the description of the coppersmith's attack, "at my first

defense, no one stood by me but all left me in the lurch".
(*II Tim* 4:16). The reader is to infer that the members of
Paul's own entourage were legally incapable of vindicating him,
and that those believers who could have done so, particularly
two key witnesses who were natives of this area, were
conspicuously absent /12/.

Was the coppersmith a Jewish Christian, carried away
perhaps by nationalistic enthusiasm in those first heady
months after May in 66 A.D. (Josephus, *JW* 2.284) when the
Jewish revolt raced like a firestorm over Palestine? Was he
convinced that Paul's apostolate to the pagans had made him a
renegade from and traitor to the cause of his own people and
their land? Did this Alexander take advantage of the rising
tensions and deep suspicions that had been unleashed by the
Palestinian rebellion to denounce Paul as a seditionary and
the disciple of a seditionary whom the Romans had executed a
generation before? *I Clement* remembered Paul (among others) as
precipitated into his final contest by jealousy, hatred, and
strife *among Christians* /13/. Still, the precise nature of
the capital charges eludes us and the epistolary form that the
author of *PE* chose made it unnecessary to go into details that
would perpetuate accusations that he was convinced were
groundless. It is conceivable that accusations which would
not have stood up in a Roman court in 61 A.D. would be taken
seriously, even against a Roman citizen, after the Jewish revolt
erupted. Under arrest the apostle was remanded to Rome. His
co-workers must have followed him there (except for Erastus who
stayed at Corinth).

The Paul of *II Timothy* (4:16) has no sooner recalled
standing abandoned in the *prima actio* at Troas, than he offers
a prayer for the forgiveness of the deserters. There follows
the apostle's assertion that the risen Jesus stood by him and
empowered him to bring the Christian proclamation to completion
and to make it possible for "all the pagans ($\pi\alpha\nu\tau\alpha$ $\tau\alpha$ $\dot{\epsilon}\vartheta\nu\eta$)"
to believe. The Lord pulled his apostle out of "the lion's
jaws" (*II Tim* 4:17). Here, I suggest, is an appeal to the
history of the former Roman imprisonment described in Acts
(as in *II Tim* 3:11 there was an appeal to the former
persecutions at Antioch, Iconium, and Lystra). Paul had
learned from his own past experience how the Lord used even the
imperial courts for bringing the gospel to unbelievers, in fact
emphatically "to *all* the gentiles". This may be a covert
allusion to the Spanish mission, following on the apostle's

previous Roman trial. One recalls *I Clement's* note that he was
"sent into exile" (i.e. banished from the city) and taught "the
whole world" (5.7). He who previously had to "stand before
Caesar" (*Acts* 27:24) had also experienced the Lord's rescue.
But this new imprisonment and trial will issue in the final
rescue, for now "the Lord will deliver me from every vicious
charge and he will save me for his kingdom in heaven" (*II Tim*
4:18).

Like *Titus, II Timothy* closes with a reference to the
coming winter but now with the foreboding that the apostle will
not see another spring. The final epistolary greeting gives
the reader a glimpse of the Roman congregation around Paul.
The names of four of them remind one of the four and more
witnessing signatures attached to a Roman will /14/. Perhaps
another hint at the testamentary genre is thus provided.

So the *PE* drop the curtain on Paul's final journey, arrest,
and captivity. Is their reconstruction of the apostle's last
days credible? Are their data apt to be authentic? There is
no question that Eusebius thought so. He has Paul immediately
after the two-year Roman house-arrest reported in *Acts* enter
"again into the ministry of the proclamation" (cf. *Titus* 1:3).
It was precisely to the *PE*, not to *Acts,* that he turned for his
sketch of Paul's last days /15/. Still earlier, the Muratorian
obliquely implied in its crabbed way that the story of Paul's
death was to be found not in *Acts* but in the *PE*.   The instincts
behind that choice were sound. On such a reconstruction of
Paul's last days, the *PE* supply what the other Paulines do not.
The events alluded to in *PE* were on the whole never intended to
fit *inside* the chronological schema presupposed by the authentic
Paulines. Moreover they were never intended to fit inside
the chronology of *Acts*. It is difficult enough to align the
chronology of *Acts* with that of the authentic Paulines. The
PE really cannot be telescoped back into the Paulines or *Acts*
without rewriting all the documents /16/. On the reconstruction
submitted here both the *PE* and *Acts* are secondary sources that
have assembled and transmitted some historical data about the
last days of Paul, perhaps twenty years after his death. The
PE complement the narrative of *Acts* without contradicting it.
They are obviously aware of certain traditions that are in
Acts. They are at pains to safeguard the prediction of *Acts* 20
while straining over what must have been an inescapable fact,
that Paul had been arrested for the last time at Troas in
Asia Minor, not far from Ephesus. The genre of the "unreal"

letter has dispensed the narrator from rehearsing or explaining
the betrayal, the charges, the capital sentence on a Roman
citizen after due process of Roman law, the still lively shame
of a criminal's execution. The epistolary witness now, of a
"Timothy" and a "Titus", is to gain Paul's acquittal and free
him for the second Christian generation, though none had been
able to save him in the first.

NOTES

/1/   See, most recently, S. Dockx, *Chronologies néotestamentaires*
... (Gembloux: Duculot, 1976), Wolfgang Metzger, *Die letzte
Reise des Apostels Paulus* (Stuttgart: Calwer, 1976), and
S. de Lestapis, *L'enigme des pastorales de Saint Paul* (Paris:
Gabalda, 1976) as well as the reviews in *NRTh* 99 (1977) 276-277;
Bib 58 (1977) 461-462; *CBQ* 40 (1978) 128-130; *Rev Sc Rel* 195
(1978) 45-46.
/2/   A short communication to this Congress on some of the
observations submitted here, has appeared as a critical note
entitled, "Seven Times He Wore Chains" in *JBL* 97 (1978) 574-576.
/3/   The documentation for some of the positions on the
following pages will be marshalled in the commentary being
prepared for volume 35 of the Doubleday Anchor Bible, *I and II
Timothy and Titus*.
/4/   For the documentation, see my article, "The Last Volume
of Luke", *Perspectives on Luke-Acts* (C.H. Talbert, ed.;
Danville, VA: Association of Baptist Professors of Religion, 1978).
/5/   Irenaeus, *Adversus Haereses* 3, 3, 3 (Harvey 2.10).
/6/   M. Dibelius, *Paul* (London: Longmans, 1953) 6-7.
/7/   See the article cited in n.4 for further materials.
/8/   See J.M. Cook, *The Troad* (Oxford: Clarendon, 1973), esp.
6, 16-40, 198-204, 383-391, and C.J. Hemer "Alexandria Troas"
Tyndale Bulletin 26 (1975) 79-112.
/9/   On the latest form of the Erastus inscription, see
J.H. Kent, *Corinth: The Inscriptions* (Princeton, N.J.:
American School of Classical Studies at Athens, 1966) volume
VIII, part III, pp. 21-22 and # 232 with plate 21. See A.J.
Malherbe, *Social Aspects of Early Christianity* (Baton Rouge, LA:
Louisiana State, 1977) 72-74, 80, and the literature cited
there for the sociological implications of the Pauline notices
concerning Erastus.
/10/   *CIG* ii.3639 with the corrections on p.1130; the original
editors submitted that it was no earlier than the second

Christian century.   See J.M. Cook, as cited in n.8, pp.67, n.3,
201, 390-391.   On the Pauline mission and the guilds to which
his "middle-class" listeners could have belonged, see
Malherbe, cited in n.9, pp. 86-91.

/11/   Cf. *Titus* 2:10; 3:2; *I Tim* 1:16, noting the juridical
connotations of this verb.

/12/   The name, Phygelus, is rare and appears to be documented
only in Western Asia Minor: *CIG* ii.3027; G. Dittenberger,
Sylloge, 599[16] for a Samian Phygelus.

/13/   See the article cited in n.4 above (n.39).

/14/   See for examples the papyri cited in A.S. Hunt and
C.C. Edgar, *Select Papyri* (LCL; Cambridge, Mass.; Harvard,
1932) i. 248, 252 and cf. 238, 254.

/15/   *HE* 2.22; the Eusebian reconstruction from *PE* of the
last days of Paul differs somewhat from that submitted in
this paper.

/16/   See the studies and reviews cited in n.1 above.

Paul's Theological Difficulties with the Law

Heikki Räisänen
Professor of New Testament Interpretation,
Kalliotie 10 B7,
04400 Jarvenpaa,
FINLAND.

I. The Problem

It is often thought that all the problems of the early
Christians vis-a-vis the Torah were solved by Paul - not only
because of his powerful practical activity, but first and
foremost thanks to his clear, cogent and penetrating theological
thought on the issues /1/. The position that Paul was a
coherent, although not systematic, thinker is said to need
little defence today /2/, and at least one prominent scholar
claims that the Apostle belongs with the great figures in the
history of the philosophy of religion /3/. No wonder that
this patron saint of Christian thought /4/ figures largely as
an undisputed authority both in debates among Christians
concerning the self-understanding of Christian faith and in
discussions of Christianity's relation to other traditions,
especially to Judaism.

In this paper I wish to argue that Paul's thought is the
real problem, rather than being the obvious solution to
theological problems concerning the law. Paul had vast
difficulties with the law, not on the existential level in
his pre-Christian life, as older generations of interpreters
used to think, but as a Christian, on the theoretical
theological level. As a consequence Paul's interpreters face
challenging hermeneutical problems, the wrestling with which
is likely to affect deeply one's view of the nature of one's
Christian tradition.

In antiquity, Porphyry made the comment that Paul displays
the ignorant person's habit of constantly contradicting himself,
and that he is feverish in mind and weak in his reasoning /5/.

Coming from a decided opponent of the Christians this opinion
is, of course, biased /6/; yet one wonders whether Porphyry
would not at this point have won the approval of some of Paul's
Jewish-Christian opponents. Even Paul's followers have never
been able to agree on what he really meant. It is perhaps
understandable that Marcion and his orthodox opponents reached
quite different conclusions /7/. But what is one to make of
the fact that still in our time scholars like, for example,
Cranfield and Kasemann, can propose diametrally opposed views
of the relation of law and gospel in Paul's thought? Where
one interpreter says that gospel and law are essentially
one /8/, the other maintains that they are quite undialectically
opposed /9/. The observation that both scholars have had
recourse to some rather obvious harmonizing operations, as will
be indicated later on, does not lessen the problem.

If one is not happy with extreme statements which explain
away half of the material, what is one to do? Unless one
takes refuge in the secure realm of dialectic and paradox -
a step seldom taken by Christian scholars when they interpret
contradictions in, say, the Dead Sea Scrolls or in the Koran -
one is left with a few options in coming to grips with the
tensions in Paul's thought on the law. I will name four.

1. One can try to trace a development in Paul's view of
the law from the earlier letters to *Romans*, as has been
recently done in a stimulating way by John Drane /10/. I
do not find this approach convincing, however. Drane is only
able to construct the development from the 'libertine' *Epistle
to the Galatians* through the 'legalist' *I Corinthians* to the
mature synthesis of *Romans* by way of a very early dating of
Galatians, which is puzzling in view of the striking
similarities between *Galatians* and *Romans*; and there seems to
be no place at all in this picture for *I Thessalonians*.
Besides, several of the contradictions in Paul's thought are
already seen in *Galatians*, and most are still there in
Romans /11/. The different outlook of different letters seems
to be accounted for by different situations; in *Galatians* Paul
makes a fierce attack, whereas he has to be on the defence in
Romans /12/. This is not to deny that Paul's thought developed
during his missionary activity. It is only that I do not
detect any straightforward development from one extant letter
to another /13/. Whatever development there was in Paul's
theology of the law, must have taken place before he wrote
Galatians (see below, section 6).

2. Even though the violent solution of J.C. O'Neill, who
attributes large parts of Romans and Galatians to later
editors, has little to commend itself, his approach does shed
some light on the problem /14/. O'Neill arrives at his unlikely
conclusions because he starts from the assumption that in order
to have been able to exert such an influence on his
contemporaries, Paul must have been - in John Locke's phrase -
'a coherent, argumentative, pertinent writer' /15/, and such
a writer is not disclosed by his analysis of *Romans* and
Galatians.   The basic assumption is questionable. It is by
no means clear that Paul's influence should have been due above
all to the logic of his thought, rather than to the spell of
his person or to the massive effort of his missionary activity.
But even if O'Neill's method is arbitrary, several of his
observations concerning obscurities and contradictions are
acute.

3. The situation is reflected in an interesting way in
some remarks from one of Paul's most ardent admirers. Hans
Conzelmann enumerates a number of contradictions in Paul's
teaching on the law. He then states bluntly that, taken
literally, this teaching would be quite incomprehensible and
would lead to absurd conclusions /16/. Conzelmann elevates
himself above the offence by denying in good existentialist
fashion that the ideas of Paul should be 'objectified'. Paul's
teaching on the law cannot be taken at face value. It is
nothing but a theological *Interpretament*, demonstrating what
Nicht-Evangelium is /17/. The impression that this is too
easy a way out is confirmed, when one reads further. Paul's
'arguments are complicated, but it must be asked whether their
complexity is not appropriate. The gospel is not complicated,
but my position is; it is therefore difficult to understand it
in terms of thought'. Here a theological virtue is made out of
historical necessity. Obviously, what is complicated is not
necessarily 'my' position in the light of the gospel, but
rather *Paul's* situation as a theological thinker in a very
particular social and historical situation. If there really
are self-contradictions and other problematic points at the
very core of Paul's theology, ought not this to lead to a
reassessment of the role of this theology in Christian thinking,
not least in its relation to other traditions /18/?

4. The fourth option alongside the developmental,
source-critical and existentialist ones is simply to acknowledge
the existence of tensions and contradictions without

amelioration. One would then have to try and find an
explanation, probably of an historical and even psychological
nature, to this phenomenon. Here the names of William Wrede /19/,
Johannes Weiss /20/, and James Parkes /21/ can be mentioned.
This is the working hypothesis to which I have been led when
trying to find my way through the jungle of Pauline studies.
Whether it is of any use can, of course, only be judged in
connection with comprehensive textual analyses; yet I hope that
a sketch of some central aspects may not be without interest.

It may be felt that the criticisms which follow are not
quite fair to Paul, and are partly anachronistic, formulated
from the perspective of a later age. This may indeed be true
(at least for point 8 below). Let me therefore emphasize that
the motivating force behind the questioning is, for better or
worse, a theological one. It is because of the constant use
of and appeal to Paul's thought by later generations (including
our own) that it has seemed unavoidable to subject the reasoning
of the Apostle to a more rigorous scrutiny than would have
been reasonable under different circumstances.

II. The basic anomalies in Paul's thought on the law

Space will not allow more than a quick enumeration of some
of the anomalies in Paul's theology of the law. No doubt the
weight of these differs from case to case. Some are probably
trivial, others essential. Perhaps some are only seeming
contradictions, but to my mind most are incapable of
harmonization.

1. The concept of law oscillates between the Torah and
something else /22/.

2. The law is discussed as an undivided whole, yet it is
often practically reduced to a moral law /23/.

3. The law has been abrogated; nevertheless its 'just
requirement' (*Rom.* 8.4) is still in force and is met by
Christians (see below, section 3).

4. Nobody can fulfil the law, and yet its requirements
are fulfilled even by some non-Christian Gentiles (see below,
section 4).

5. The power of sin in the world is ascribed to Adam's fall on one hand (*Rom.* 5) and to the law on the other (*Rom.* 7).

6. The law was given 'for life' (*Rom.* 7.10), yet it lacked even theoretically the life-giving power (*Rom.* 8.3, *Gal.* 3.21) /24/.

7. The law was only a temporary addition to God's 'testament' (*Gal.* 3.15ff.), yet a dramatic act on God's part was needed to liberate men from its curse (*Gal.* 3.13) /25/.

These apories are immanent within Paul's own thought. One can add a few more difficulties, where Paul's premisses, rather than his logic, seem to be at fault.

8. Paul's interpretation of the Old Testament in support of his position is arbitrary /26/.

9. The statement that the law (and only the law as opposed, say, to the apostolic paraenesis) calls forth and multiplies sin, is problematic, to say the least /27/.

10. Why should one have to fulfil the *whole* law in order to avoid the curse? Why is the possibility of repentance and forgiveness excluded /28/?

III. Is the law abrogated in Christ?

Paul has two sets of statements concerning the validity of the law for Christians. According to one set the law has been abrogated once and for all. According to the other the law is still in force, and what it requires is charismatically fulfilled by Christians.

The first line of thought is quite obvious in *Gal.* 2.15-21, 3.15-25, and *Rom.* 7.1-6. The Christian has died to the law through the law. The law was added later in order to be in force until the coming of the promised seed or the age of faith. Before faith we were under the law, guarded and held in check by this stern schoolmaster, yet after the coming of faith we are no longer under the pedagogue. In view of such clear statements the burden of proof lies heavily upon those who wish to contend that, for Paul, law and gospel are one /29/, or even that Paul was 'an enthusiastic teacher and defender of the law' /30/. The breakdown of such interpretations can

be observed in Cranfield's efforts to evade the obvious
conclusion. Following Calvin he claims that even in *Gal.* 3
Paul is only speaking of 'bare law', 'the law as seen apart
from Christ' rather than 'the law in the fullness and
wholeness of its true character' /31/. Legalism, rather than
the law itself, is abrogated. One can only wonder: 'What
exactly happened at Sinai according to this interpretation'?
Was only the narrow legalistic interpretation of the law given
by the angels? It is clear that Cranfield's thought is
directed by a rigid *Systemzwang*, the guiding principle being
the statement 'God's word in Scripture is one' /32/. The
result is a simplification of Paul's theology.

As the notion of the termination of the law cannot be
explained away from *Gal.* 3 and *Rom.* 7, the never-ceasing
controversy about the meaning of *Rom.* 10.4 seems immaterial.
In whatever way one interprets *that* passage, the notion of
the end of the law (in the sense of termination) *is* there in
Paul's thought. So is the notion of the fulfilment of the
law, though. Paul's theology does include a line of thought
which could be summed up by saying that Christ is the goal of
the law, whether or not that thought is expressed in *Rom.* 10.4.
The law itself, rightly understood, predicts Christ and points
to him (e.g. *Gal.* 4.21, *Rom.* 3.21b). I take it, however, that
τέλος means 'end', in the sense of termination, in *Rom.* 10.4,
in the light of the polemical context (both v.3 and v.5), as
well as in view of the parallel passage in *II Cor.* 3 (note
the mention of the τέλος of the fading splendour in v.13,
which cannot possibly mean its 'goal'). That the law is
spoken of in a much more positive way a few verses before
(*Rom.* 9.31) is another matter and only shows the elasticity of
Paul's thought; in 10.1 a new start is made, and in this
passage Paul speaks of the law in polemical terms.

So much, then, for the abrogation of the law. On the
other hand, there are clear statements to the effect that the
law is still relevant and that its requirements are to be
fulfilled. In *Gal.* 5.14 and *Rom.* 13.8-10 the essence of
Christian conduct is defined in terms of fulfilment of the
law /33/. Paul can without hesitation speak of the law in a
quite positive way as the norm of conduct. Again, in *Rom.* 8.4
it is stated that the purpose of the sending of God's son was
that what the law justly requires should be fulfilled in the
life of Christians walking according to the Spirit. Whether
Rom. 3.31 also belongs here is not clear.

These texts are not at all adequately dealt with by those
who find only the idea of the abrogation of the law in
Paul /34/.   Käsemann, for instance, advances a 'redaction-
critical' interpretation.   *Rom*. 8.4 and 13.8-10 represent
Jewish-Christian tradition, occasionally taken up and quietly
reinterpreted by Paul /35/.   Now Paul does undoubtedly cite a
fragment of tradition in *Rom*. 8.3f., even though v.4 may well
be reformulated by the Apostle himself.   The verse cannot,
however, be just an undigested piece of tradition.   The talk
of 'us' and of 'walking according to the Spirit' at the end
of v.4 is so closely connected with the line of thought in the
sequel that the verse must necessarily reflect Paul's own
intentions /36/.   In addition, it corresponds in content to the
notion of charismatic fulfilment of the law as the fruit of
the Spirit, clearly expressed in *Gal*. 5.

It is often conceded that Paul does occasionally speak of
the law as if it were still in force, yet this is considered
as a harmless slip, due to Paul's inability to abandon
completely his earlier Jewish mode of thought /37/.   But
Rom. 8.4 does not look like an occasional lapse.   It is an
emphatic statement, made in a passage where the nature of the
law is the explicit subject-matter of a thorough discussion,
and intimately woven into the context that follows.   Such a
statement must be heard as the voice of Paul, however
embarrassing this may appear to our more systematic minds.   I
am unable to harmonize the two sets of statements.   The common
explanation that Paul rejects the law as a way of salvation
but retains it as an expression of God's will in ethical regard
only restates the problem in different words.   Johannes Weiss
saw indeed clearly that Paul has two contradictory lines of
thought, both equally true and irrefutable to him,
comprehensible as deposits of two different epochs of his
life /38/.   We will later be in the position to see that it is
perhaps after all not the conservative line that is the more
disturbing element.

Recently the idea has gained considerable support that
Paul presupposes a change in the status and nature of the law
after the Christ-event.   In Christ the Torah has been converted
from 'the law of sin and death' to the 'law of faith' or 'the
law of the Spirit of life'.   Instead of being abrogated the
law has been liberated from its perverted state as a law of
works; in its new spiritual quality it is valid for the
Christian /39/.   Yet even so the question would remain, if only

a perversion of the true law was effected on Sinai (unless one
assumes a development in Paul's thought from *Galatians* to
Romans). This interpretation hinges, of course, on the
exegesis of *Rom*. 3.27 and 8.2, where νόμος is taken to refer
literally to the Mosaic law. In my view, this interpretation
is to be rejected, and the well-established understanding of
νόμος πίστεως and ὁ νόμος τοῦ πνεύματος τῆς ζωῆς as
metaphorical usage to be preferred. The most important point
is that the νόμος is conceived of either as the effective
means of the exclusion of boasting (3.27) or even as the
subject of man's liberation (8.2). Paul is speaking of what
the νόμος has *achieved*, not of what has happened *to* it.
Therefore, this attempt to bridge the gap between negative and
positive statements about the law fails /40/.

IV. Can the law be fulfilled?

     Let us turn to another problem - the question whether or
not the law can be fulfilled.

     In important passages Paul places a heavy emphasis on the
fact that nobody is able to fulfil the law *in its totality*.
Those commentators are certainly right who assume that this
thought is presupposed in *Gal*. 3.10-12 /41/. This is borne out
by *Rom*. 1.18-3.20; the same thought is reflected in *Gal*. 5.3
and probably 6.13. This thought is important for Paul's
contention that no one can be saved by works of law.

     What was indicated in *Gal*. 3 is developed by Paul in
Rom. 1.18-3.20. In 1.18-2.29 Paul purports to give an empirical
demonstration for the thesis that both Greek and Jew are under
sin·(3.9).

     A reader coming to Romans from Galatians will be somewhat
surprised by the nature of the argument. In Galatians Paul
had implied how necessary it is for those under the law to
fulfil the *whole* law. One should expect him to show in Romans
that the law is never fulfilled in its totality, however
seriously you try; everybody falls short of perfection and is
doomed to remain under the curse. That was to be the line of
thought of Augustine and Luther, but Paul does not proceed so.
He starts, in accordance with a strong Jewish tradition, by
branding the whole Gentile world as a mass of homosexual
idolators, full of wickedness, depravity, lust, viciousness,

murder, etc. (1.18-32). Moving on to the Jews, he then sets
forth a series of the gravest possible accusations, on the
basis of which even the Jew is shown to be a transgressor of
the law (2.17-24). Instead of saying that even the best fall
short, Paul claims: you are all thieves, adulterers, and
temple-robbers.

Logically, of course, Paul has only shown that circumcision
is of no avail to a Jew who is guilty of grave transgressions
of the law /42/. Yet he himself thinks he has by this argument
proved that both Greeks and Jews are 'under sin' (3.9) - a
blatant non sequitur /43/.

The real difficulty for Paul's main thesis, however, is
posed by verses 2.14-15, 26-27. Here he states that even
some Gentiles fulfil what the law requires. There can be no
question here of Gentile Christians /44/, still less of an
imaginary hypothesis /45/. Paul is speaking of real Gentiles,
using them as weapons in his attack against the Jews: you
transgress the law that you have; these do not have it, and
yet there are those among them who do all that is required by
it /46/! These verses are most revealing. Inadvertently Paul
can speak in a quite positive fashion of Gentiles fulfilling the
law, because he does not at the moment reflect on the plight
of Gentiles (but rather on that of the Jews). A few moments
earlier he did theorize about the Gentiles, and then the
picture was quite different (1.18-32). *Phil*. 3.6 shows that in
another context Paul can well admit that it is possible for a
Jew as well to fulfil the law.

These observations indicate that there is something
strained and artificial in Paul's theory that nobody can fulfil
the law; artificial, that is, from Paul's own point of view
(rather than ours) /47/. We can, as it were, catch a glimpse
of Paul the man, whose feelings and instincts do not wholly
follow the thoughts of Paul the theologian. The man shows
through, when the self-imposed theological control relaxes.
The explanation is that Paul the theologian is somehow pushed
to develop his thought in a preordained direction, backwards as
it were. He simply *has* to come to the conclusion that the law
cannot be fulfilled, in order to be able to contend that Christ
did not die in vain (*Gal*. 2.21). It can only be the firmness
of the preconceived conviction that prevented Paul from seeing
the weakness of his 'empirical' argument.

A comparable phenomenon may be observed in *Rom*. 7.14-25,
where Paul is speaking of the non-Christian under the law.
Man apart from Christ cannot do anything that is good; his
moral effort is a total failure. Notwithstanding the venerable
tradition of an existentialist interpretation of this
passage /48/ one has to insist that Paul does indeed describe
a moral conflict inside of man. According to the Bultmannian
interpretation the meaning of the passage is rather that man
desires life, but his striving for life brings about death,
however perfect his life may be. To arrive at this
interpretation, however, one has to twist the meaning of all
the central words in the passage /49/. I find this
interpretation another ingenious specimen of the kind of
harmonizing one cannot avoid, if one wants to construct a
consistent Pauline theology of the law. In reality, Paul seems
to have taken up a popular *topos* of Greek ethical tradition,
starting with Euripides /50/, analogies to which can be found
in the theology of Qumran /51/. Paul has made this
traditional material serve his 'apology of the law', which to
be sure turns out to be a demonstration of the weakness of the
law.

Both in *Rom*. 1.18-32, 2.17-24, and 7.14-25 Paul takes an
empirical observation of everyday life, or an ethical
commonplace of popular tradition, as his point of departure.
This he then exaggerates to the extreme and makes it the basis
of a sweeping generalization. In *Rom*. 1-2 the observation is:
'many live in grave sins'; the conclusion: 'all are under sin'.
In *Rom*. 7 Paul moves from the empirically known common
phenomenon of moral conflict and moral failure to the
conclusion that man is 'sold under sin' and 'is not able to do
good at all'. In the first instance Paul is following
Hellenistic-Jewish, in the latter popular Greek models. In
both cases, the conclusions reached are bluntly contradicted by
the mention of Gentiles fulfilling the law (*Rom*. 2). Paul just
had to arrive at as negative a description of humanity apart
from Christ as possible.

That Paul works backwards in his theology of the law is,
of course, well known, and the case has recently been forcefully
argued by E.P. Sanders /52/. Yet it is surprising how seldom
one sees anything problematic in this process, which is felt
to underline all the more the supreme glory of the gospel.
Even Sanders can in the end speak of Paul's penetrating
analysis of the human predicament /53/. Yet one can hardly have

it both ways. It is certainly no common experience that a
penetrating analysis of anything (except for a mathematical
problem!) should follow, when the analyst has a rigidly fixed
point of departure and a predetermined goal. Paul may have
made acute individual observations about man, but the overall
argument in *Rom.* 1-3 and in *Rom.* 7.14ff. is far from
penetrating. This is conveniently shown by the comments of
some interpreters, when they try to rescue the reasoning of
the Apostle. C.K. Barrett notes on the charges against the
Jews in *Rom.* 2.17ff. that 'Paul's argument is lost if he is
compelled to rely on comparatively unusual events, and it
is simply not true that the average Jewish missionary acted in
this way' /54/. Consequently, Barrett presents a metaphorical
interpretation of Paul's accusations which is ingenious rather
than convincing; in fact, Paul's argument is lost. Again, on
Rom. 7 we have the eloquent testimony of Käsemann. He attacks
fiercely the idea that Paul should speak in this passage of a
moral conflict; were that the case (and that is what most
commentators still think), then Paul 'works with the wrong
tools and constructs a bad theology, or rather no theology at
all but a psychology oriented toward the ethical problem'.
This would, according to Käsemann, amount to a nonsensical
'psychology of sin' that remains even beneath the level of
Qumran, and one would have to oppose the Apostle energetically
in the name of man /55/. I for myself would find the passage
more profound had Paul really designed it as a description of
the Christian. But this kind of psychological penetration was
left to Augustine and Luther, who in the light of their very
different experiences read into Paul's text something which
was not there /56/.

     At this juncture one may hazard the guess that Paul's
theory of the law as the cause of sin owes its origin to an
analogous generalization of an everyday experience. The
starting point seems to be, as *Rom.* 7.7ff. shows, the
experience of the 'forbidden fruit'. From the experience that
prohibitions often invite transgression Paul has moved on to
the sweeping statement that this is always the case as
regards the law (but *only* as regards the *law*) and that this
is even the very purpose of the law. Apart from general
considerations, the artificiality of this line of thought is
seen in *Rom.* 5.12ff., where the dominion of sin in the world
is ascribed to the fall of Adam rather than to the law, and the
law is introduced as an afterthought in a way that raises more
problems than it solves /57/. I find it hard to agree with

those who value this negative assessment of the law as a
contribution of theological genius /58/. I cannot help seeing
it as another instance of an artificial theorizing, the result
of which is dictated by a priori considerations: Christ is the
only way to salvation; therefore the law cannot be one;
therefore another purpose must be found for the law, and a
negative one at that.

V. *The fulfilment of the moral law by the Christians*

It is time to return to the question of the fulfilment of
the law. There is one exception to the general inability: the
Christians do fulfil the law charismatically, as a fruit of
the Spirit (*Gal.* 5.22ff., *Rom.* 8.4, 13.8ff.) /59/. In this
regard the Christians are different from all other people.
Paul emphasizes in Galatians the difference in regard to Jews
by claiming that 'under the law' works of flesh emerge (5.18ff.),
whereas in the life of Christians fruit of the Spirit is
produced. According to Galatians 'Christians live on a new
level of existence,and so their actions will automatically
follow from this new kind of experience' /60/. The
difference between the letter and the Spirit can therefore be,
as it were, empirically verified in the lives of men.

It is easy enough to see how problematic and unfair such
an assertion is. In demonstrating that (Gentiles and) Jews do
not fulfil the law, Paul makes use of denigration and
caricature /61/. In asserting that Christians do fulfil
the law in the Spirit (and be it only the moral law), he
gives rein to wishful thinking, or at least makes another
sweeping generalization, this time to the optimistic direction.
He has, indeed, different standards for Jews and Christians
respectively.

Again, there is something strangely artificial in Paul's
theory. At bottom, Paul the man does *not* think that a
Christian is guided by the Spirit quite as automatically as
Paul the theologian implies in Galatians. Leaving aside the
clear case of the Corinthian correspondence, this fact is
likewise born out by *I Thessalonians*. This letter, besides
not showing any interest in problems of the law, does not
contain any one-sided ethic of the Spirit. Paul obliged his
Gentile converts to lead a decent life according to normal
Jewish standards and did not shun away from giving clear

precepts about this (*I Thess.* 4.1-2). Behind the paraenesis
of ch.4 lies the perception that there are certain, not very
serious but nevertheless real, defects in the conduct of the
Thessalonians, which are to be removed /62/. It is, therefore,
clear that Paul did *not* base 'all his ethics on the Spirit' /63/.
The ostensible avoidance of almost any concrete norms in
Galatians seems to be the exception and not the rule, a
somewhat artificial product of a particular situation. In a
certain sense it is paralleled by the likewise strained
contention that it is impossible to fulfil the law outside
the Christian community.

VI. Conclusion

Why, then, did Paul the theologian proclaim with great
pathos things which Paul the man was not quite able to digest?
The answer can here only be hinted at: somehow this must have
been due to the controversies in which Paul became engaged.
Probably only gradually did Paul develop those radical thoughts
for which he is famous. At first he presumably adopted roughly
the opinions of the Hellenist group in Jerusalem (whatever
precisely those opinions were /64/!). His concern was
probably only that Gentile converts need not take on themselves
the burden of what is often called the ceremonial law. The
question of the law was in itself more or less an adiaphoron /65/.
It was his stern Jewish-Christian opponents who eventually made
this practically oriented approach impossible. They were able
to make a strong *heilsgeschichtlich* case for the view that the
law must be seen as an indivisible whole, which one can only
either accept as a whole or abandon. Faced with this
alternative and sensing the force of the opponents' claim, Paul
was *driven* to argue for a total abrogation of the law. He was
able to bring himself to defend this position vigorously on
the theoretical level, yet without the undivided support of
his heart. To prove his case he needed arguments, the more the
better. So he was also driven to a constant quest of evidence
for the failure and inadequacy of the law; here almost anything
would qualify. This somewhat chaotic social and psychological
situation, which is still reflected in Romans, seems to account
for the antinomies in Paul's thought: why the law is both
abrogated and also in force, why it cannot and yet can be
fulfilled, and so on. For similar polemical reasons he also
came to claim in such an extravagant fashion that what is not
possible to achieve under the law is produced spontaneously by

the Spirit in the life of Christians. This contrast was
something required by his overall contention, and in the heat
of the struggle Paul was, unconsciously no doubt, led to make
the facts fit the argument.

        This reconstruction is, of course, no more than a
hypothesis, and one which needs much further elaboration and
clarification. In an embryonic form it can be found in
Wrede's book on Paul /66/. Whether or not there is any truth
to it, one thing seems clear: Paul the theologian is a less
coherent and less convincing thinker than is commonly assumed.
By way of intuition Paul seems to have arrived at profound
insights, but he did not succeed in giving any clear
theoretical account of them /67/. His was a very vivid mind
and a very sharp intellect; of that there is no doubt. But
he was too much under the influence of the overwhelming
experience of the Spirit, which was so characteristic of the
life of the new Christian communities, to be able to give room
for calm reflection. He sensed too strongly the experience
of liberation (for example from fear, *Rom.* 8.15) and renewal
to be able to tackle impartially the problems of relating the
new experience to the sacred tradition of the past. No wonder
his followers interpreted him one-sidedly, in one way or
another. What else could they have done?

        Indeed, it seems to me that almost any early Christian
conception of the law is more consistent, more intelligible and
more arguable than Paul's - whether you take *Matthew* or *Luke,*
Hebrews or *James,* Marcion or Justin /68/. Surely this would
apply also to the theology of Paul's Judaizing opponents, if
only their arguments were known to us. Even though I have my
roots in a church alleged to be the most Lutheran in the
world, it seems to be impossible to make Paul's theology *the*
norm with which one can measure everything else in the world of
early Christianity /69/ (not to speak of Judaism!).

        However much sympathy we may have with the man and his
achievement, the theological difficulties of Paul with the law
become at the end inevitably our theological difficulties with
Paul. The current emphasis in Pauline studies on the
theological achievement of the Apostle is one-sided, especially
when it is coupled with extreme antipathy to psychological
considerations. Very serious thought should be given to the
fact that at the very heart of the process that led to the
separation of Christianity from Judaism lies a massive begging

of the soteriological question (as Christ is the only true
answer, all other answers must *a priori* be wrong), coupled
with confused polemical argument, rather than any balanced
discussion of the Torah /70/. Here a tremendous hermeneutical
challenge faces Christian theology /71/.

NOTES

/1/   E.g. E. Lohse, *Grundriss der neutestamentlichen Theologie*
(1974), pp.145,161.
/2/   E.P. Sanders, *Paul and Palestinian Judaism* (1977), p.518,
with reference to Bultmann, Conzelmann, Bornkamm, Käsemann,
Whiteley, Kümmel, and A. Schweitzer.
/3/   B. Gerhardsson, '1 Kor. 13. Om Paulus och hans rabbinska
bakgrund'. *Svensk Exegetisk Årsbok* 39 (1974), p.121.
/4/   Cf. M. Grant, *Saint Paul* (1976), p.4. Grant, to be sure,
allows for ambiguities and 'flagrant self-contradictions' in
Paul's thought.
/5/   In Macarius Magnes, *Apocriticus*, III 30, 34. See
A. Harnack, *Kritik des Neuen Testaments von einem griechischen
Philosophen des 3. Jahrhunderts* (1911), pp.58-61, 64-67.
/6/   But see Harnack's comments, *op.cit.*, pp.133-4.
/7/   Cf. M. Wiles, *The Divine Apostle* (1967), p.50.
/8/   C.E.B. Cranfield, 'St. Paul and the Law', *SJT* 17 (1964),
p.68.
/9/   E. Käsemann, *An die Römer* (1974³), p.272.
/10/ J.W. Drane, *Paul: Libertine or Legalist?* (1975). For
earlier development theories see Sanders, *op.cit.*, p.432 n.9,
and H. Hübner, *Das Gesetz bei Paulus* (1978), pp.9-15. Hübner's
book, which appeared during the congress, merits careful
consideration. For some criticisms see the following footnote.
/11/ Both points are denied by Hübner, *op.cit.*, who finds a
clear development from Galatians to Romans. Galatians portrays
Christ as the end (termination) of the Mosaic law; in Romans,
however, Christ is only the end of the misuse of the law (p.129).
I can here only refer to Hübner's interpretation of a few key
passages. <u>1</u>. Hübner denies that *Gal.* 5.14 refers to the Torah
(thus removing a major inconsistency from Galatians) and
consequently that *Gal.* 5.14 and *Rom.* 13.8-10 are real
parallels (thus maintaining the difference between the two
letters). See on this below, n.33. <u>2</u>. He claims that *Gal.*
3.19b and *Rom.* 5.20a do not contain the same idea. The former
speaks of the law as provoking transgressions; the latter only
means that offences are recognized as conscious transgressions

of the law (pp.73-4). But, in view of the parallel statement
concerning the abundance of grace in v.20b, *Rom*. 5.20a must
surely refer to concrete increase of sin, just as *Gal*. 3.19 does.
Rom. 5.20b cannot mean that men become more and more conscious
of grace! 3. Hübner thinks that the 'law of faith' *Rom*. 3.27
and the 'law of the Spirit of life' *Rom*. 8.2 refer to the
Torah. See below, the end of section 3.

/12/ Cf. already E. Grafe, *Die paulinische Lehre vom Gesetz*
(1884), pp.22-25.

/13/ That Paul's *formulation* and *explication* of his thought
developed is beyond doubt.

/14/ *The Recovery of Paul's Letter to the Galatians* (1972);
Paul's Letter to the Romans (1975).

/15/ *Galatians*, p.8; *Romans*, p.16.

/16/ *Grundriss der Theologie des Neuen Testaments* (1968[2]),
pp.248,251. Readers of the ET (*An Outline of the Theology of
the New Testament*, 1969), pp.225,227-8, are likely to miss the
point. The ET, p.227, even speaks of 'the Pauline doctrine
of *sin*', where the German has *Gesetz*.

/17/ *Op.cit*., p.251

/18/ Contrast the somewhat cavalier dismissal of H.J. Schoeps's
approach by Conzelmann, *op.cit*., pp.180-1.

/19/ *Paulus* (1904), pp.48-9.

/20/ *Das Urchristentum* (1917), p.427.

/21/ *Jesus, Paul and the Jews* (1936), pp.128-9.

/22/ See the discussion of *Gal*. 3-4 in U.Luz, *Das Geschichtsverständnis des Paulus* (1968), p.153. He demonstrates 'ein
merkwurdiges Schwanken des Gesetzesbegriffes bei Paulus'.

/23/ See the description of the problem concerning *Gal*. 5.14
in H. Hübner, 'Das ganze und das eine Gesetz', *Kerygma und
Dogma* 21 (1975), pp.241-2. On Hübner's own solution see below,
n.33.

/24/ Cf. already A. Ritschl, *Die christliche Lehre von der
Rechtfertigung und Versöhnung*, II (1882[2]), p.254.

/25/ Cf. Drane, *Paul*, p.6.

/26/ P. Vielhauer claims that 'Paulus ... auch gemessen an
der zeitgenössischen jüdischen Exegese den alttestamentlichen
Texten Gewalt antut. Die rabbinische Exegese verfährt, wenn
auch unhistorisch, so doch streng methodisch ... Die
paulinische Exegese ist durch keine Methode reguliert, Paulus
wechselt und mischt die Methoden nach Belieben'. 'Paulus und
das Alte Testament', *Studien zur Geschichte und Theologie der
Reformation* (Festschrift E. Bizer, 1969), p.51. Differently
S. Sandmel, *The Genius of Paul* (1958), pp.25-6: Paul is neither
more nor less arbitrary than the rabbis, Philo, or the Church
Fathers.

/27/   The standard Jewish reaction is quite justified.   One may
compare Origen's difficulties with *Rom.* 5.20: Wiles, *op.cit.*,
p.52.   See also the comments of A. Jülicher, 'Der Brief an die
Römer', *Die Schriften des Neuen Testaments*, II (1907), p.274.
/28/   This question was raised by C.G. Montefiore, *Judaism and
St. Paul* (1914), p.75.   It is brilliantly discussed by Sanders,
op.cit., (n.2 above).
/29/   Cranfield, *art.cit.*, see n.8 above.
/30/   M. Barth, 'Die Stellung des Paulus zu Gesetz und Ordnung',
Evangelische Theologie 33 (1973), p.517.
/31/   Cranfield, *art.cit.*, pp.62-3.
/32/   *Art.cit.*, p.68.
/33/   Hübner, *art.cit.* (n.23), p.246, denies that ὁ πᾶς νόμος
Gal. 5.14 refers to the Mosaic law; Paul has only the Christian
'law' of love in mind.   Only in *Rom.* 13.8-10 does Paul, in
Hubner's view, sum up the Torah in the commandment of love.
Hubner thinks that in *Rom.* 13 Paul no longer has the *totality*
of the law in mind (as he had in *Gal.* 5.14).   But is not
precisely the totality of the Mosaic law hinted at in v.9:
'and any other commandment there may be'?   *Gal.* 5.14 and *Rom.*
13.8-10 seem to be perfect parallels.
/34/   Sandmel, *Genius*, does not even mention them in his book.
/35/   Käsemann, *op.cit.*, pp.209f., 348f.
/36/   Cf. P. von der Osten-Sacken, *Romer 8 als Beispiel
paulinischer Soteriologie* (1975), p.145.
/37/   E.g. L.H. Marshall, *The Challenge of New Testament Ethics*
(1947), p.231.
/38/   Weiss, *Urchristentum,* p.427.
/39/   E.g. E. Lohse, 'ὁ νόμος τοῦ πνεύματος τῆς ζωῆς', *Neues
Testament und christliche Existenz* (Festschrift H. Braun, 1973),
pp.279-287; von der Osten-Sacken, *op.cit.*, pp.245-6; Hübner,
Gesetz, pp.118ff.
/40/   See my article 'Das "Gesetz des Glaubens" (Rom. 3.27) und
das "Gesetz des Geistes" (Rom. 8.2)', *NTS* 26 (1979-80),
pp.101-17.
/41/   E.g. A. Oepke, *Der Brief des Paulus an die Galater*
(1960[2]), p.72; Luz, *Geschichtsverständnis,* p.149; Hübner,
'Das ganze ... Gesetz' (n.23), p.244.
/42/   Cf. below, n.54.
/43/   To be sure, 'sin' is spoken of as an enslaving power in
3.9; to be 'under sin' certainly implies more than just doing
sinful acts.   But there is no clear-cut distinction between the
two conceptions, as is shown *i.a.* by the parallelism between
'trespass' and 'sin' in 5.20.   The sinful acts demonstrate that
men are under the power of sin; were the acts not demonstrable,

Paul could not have made his 'charge' (3.9).

/44/ So Augustine and still e.g. M. Barth, *art.cit.* (n.30),
p.521 n.62. Against this interpretation cf. G. Bornkamm,
Studien zu Antike und Christentum (1963), p.109.

/45/ So e.g. Andrea van Dülmen, *Die Theologie des Gesetzes bei
Paulus* (1968), pp.77,82.

/46/ I cannot agree with those who find the point of these
verses in the idea that God is justified in condemning the
Gentiles, too; so e.g. Bornkamm, *op.cit.*, pp.98f., 110. At
least this idea is totally absent in vv.26-27, where it becomes
clear that Paul is not speaking of Gentiles for their own sake,
but only in order to attack the Jews.

/47/ Cf. C.H. Dodd, *The Epistle of Paul to the Romans* (1932),
p.37: 'For the purposes of his general argument he takes the
extreme view that no one ... does or can obey the law; but in
concrete cases he allows that in some measure at least the good
pagan (and of course the good Jew, as he implies in ii.28) can
do the right thing'. See also O'Neill, *Romans*, p.48.

/48/ The classical statement is that of R. Bultmann, 'Römer 7
und die Anthropologie des Paulus', *Imago Dei* (Festschrift
G. Krüger, 1932), pp.53-62. In a slightly modified form it is
maintained, among others, by Käsemann, *op.cit.*, pp.192f., 195.

/49/ See the critique of P. Althaus, *Paulus und Luther über
den Menschen* (1963[4]), pp.47-9; cf. also W. Schrage, *Die
konkreten Einzelgebote in der paulinischen Paranese* (1961),
pp.195f. According to Althaus the 'total artificiality' of
Bultmann's interpretation is seen in the fact 'dass sie alle
wesentlichen Begriffe von Röm. 7 im klaren Widerspruch zum
Kontext und zum sonstigen paulinischen Sprachgebrauch umdenken
muss'. Althaus lists the words 'good', 'evil', 'want', ποιεῖν,
πράσσειν, καλεργάζεσθαι, and (for 7.7f.) ἐπιθυμία. Even
Käsemann, *op. cit.*, p.194, admits that Bultmann's
interpretation of κατεργάζεσθαι as 'bring about' cannot be
upheld. How he nevertheless manages essentially to agree with
Bultmann, is something of a mystery to me.

/50/ H. Hommel, 'Das 7. Kapitel des Römerbriefs im Licht
antiker Ueberlieferung', *Theologia Viatorum* 8 (1961/62),
pp.90-116.

/51/ H. Braun, 'Römer 7,7-25 und das Selbstverstandnis der
Qumran-Frommen', *ZTK* 56 (1959), pp.1-18.

/52/ *Paul and Palestinian Judaism*, pp.442ff.

/53/ *Op.cit.*, p.509. Is this really compatible with his
observations that Paul's 'description of the human plight
varies, remaining constant only in the assertion of its
universality' (p.474) and that 'Rom. 7 is a somewhat tortured

explanation of the law and its purpose' in the light of 'the
conviction that God has provided for universal salvation in
Christ' (p.475)?

/54/ *The Epistle to the Romans* (1957), p.56.

/55/ Käsemann, *op.cit.*, p.193.

/56/ See K. Stendahl, 'The Apostle Paul and the Introspective
Conscience of the West', *HTR* 56 (1963), pp.199-215; Althaus,
op.cit., (n.44).

/57/ See G. Strecker, 'Befreiung und Rechtfertigung',
Rechtfertigung (Festschrift E. Käsemann, 1976), p.499.

/58/ So Irene Beck, 'Altes und neues Gesetz', *Münchener
Theologische Zeitschrift* 15 (1964), p.129.

/59/ This should not be explained away, as does Cranfield,
art.cit., p.66; *Romans*, I (1975), p.384. Correctly e.g.
F.F. Bruce, 'Paul and the Law of Moses', *BJRL* 57 (1975), p.275.

/60/ Drane, *Paul*, p.53.

/61/ Sandmel, *Genius*, p.29, notes that Paul's description is
here 'grotesque and vicious'. Among the few Christian exegetes
who have admitted that this is so is P. von der Osten-Sacken,
'Das paulinische Verständnis des Gesetzes im Spannungsfeld
von Eschatologie und Geschichte', *Evangelische Theologie* 37
(1977), pp.564f.

/62/ E. Best, *The First and Second Epistles to the
Thessalonians* (1972), pp.156-7, 160.

/63/ So Jülicher, 'Römer', p.276.

/64/ A thorough discussion of the problem of the Hellenists
is found in M. Hengel, 'Zwischen Jesus und Paulus', *ZTK* 72
(1975), pp.151-206.

/65/ This, of course, implied a critical or selective attitude
toward the law from the start, but no hostility. One recalls
the Alexandrian allegorists, mildly (!) criticized by Philo
in *De migr. Abr.* 89ff., who had given up outward observance of
the Torah. Were they in some sense the precursors of Stephen
and/or Paul?

/66/ Wrede, *Paulus*, pp.72ff., 84. Cf. also Strecker, *art.cit.*
(n.57), pp.480f.

/67/ Cf. the judgement of Parkes, *op.cit.*, (n.21), p.128:
'The letter to the Romans comes as near being a theological
treatise as anything which Paul wrote - and causes one to give
thanks that he wrote no other, for the abiding genius of Paul
lies in his mysticism and his practical teaching, not in
systematic theology. His purpose is to establish the central
position of the Cross and Atonement in relation to both Jewish
and Gentile experience. The result is both artificial and
unsatisfactory'.

/68/ Of course, each of these conceptions is fraught with some
problems of its own.
/69/ Against S. Schulz, *Die Mitte der Schrift* (1976).
/70/ Sanders, *op.cit.*, p.552, puts the matter succinctly:
'In short, this is what Paul finds wrong in Judaism: it is
not Christianity'.
/71/ A step in the right direction is, in my view, the
concluding chapter in Rosemary R. Ruether, *Faith and Fratricide*
(1974).

POSTSCRIPT

Since this paper was delivered, the following articles by the
author, related to the present subject, have appeared:

'Das "Gesetz des Glaubens" (*Rom.* 3.27) und das "Gesetz des
Geistes" (*Rom.* 8.2)', *NTS* 26 (1979-80), pp. 101-17.

'Zum Gebrauch von *epithymia* und *epithymein* bei Paulus',
StudTheol 33 (1979), pp. 85-99.

'Legalism and Salvation by the Law. Paul's Portrayal of the
Jewish Religion as a Historical and Theological Problem', in:
S. Pedersen (ed.), *Pauline Literature and Theology* (1980).

Les Titres Néotestamentaires du Christ dans la Liturgie Gnostique de Médînet Mâdi

Julien Ries,
Président,
Institut Orientaliste,
1348 Louvain-la-Neuve,
BELGIUM.

La découverte récente d'une *Vita* de Mani conservee dans un
codex grec d'Oxyrhynchos daté paléographiquement du Vème
siècle, nous apporte une précieuse documentation complémentaire
aux nombreux renseignements déjà fournis par la bibliotheque
manichéenne trouvée à Médînet Mâdi en 1930 /1/. Grâce au
Kephalaion 1 du Fayoum ainsi qu'à la *Vita* du *Codex* de Cologne,
nous voyons plus clairement comment Mani a conçu et présenté
sa mission. Le *Codex* cite notamment le début de l'*Evangile* de
Mani : "Moi Mani, apôtre de Jésus-Christ par la volonté de Dieu
le Père de la vérité, duquel moi aussi je suis né" /2/.
Augustin nous a conservé l'*incipit* de l'*Epistola Fundamenti* :
"*Manichaeus apostolus Jesu Christi, providentia Dei Patris*" /3/.
Le *Kephalaion 1* du Fayoum nous a gardé, chaque fois présenté
en douze articles, un double résumé des doctrines de Mani :
d'une part, la mission gnostique, d'autre part, les mystères
dualistes, deux volets d'un symbole de foi de l'Eglise
manichéenne /4/. A la lumière de ces textes, s'éclairent
davantage le début et la perspective de l'oeuvre du Prophète de
Babylone. Formé dans la communauté elkhasaite depuis l'âge de
quatre ans, Mani reçut le 1er avril 228, la visite du messager
du Royaume de la Lumière. Douze ans plus tard, le 19 avril 240,
le même messager appelé le Paraclet Vivant est venu révéler
à Mani, âgé de vingt-quatre ans, les mystères cachés aux
générations antérieures. Le jeune Prophète est chargé de
continuer l'oeuvre de Jesus qui avait annoncé la venue du
Paraclet.

Cette documentation rend possible une étude plus
approfondie de la christologie de l'Eglise manicheenne.
Pareille recherche présente un grand intérêt. En premier lieu,

elle nous fait découvrir certaines structures essentielles de la
doctrine du Prophète babylonien. Ensuite elle donne un nouvel
éclairage à la littérature patristique de la controverse
antimanichéenne. Enfin, elle nous fait saisir pourquoi et
comment, le manichéisme s'est présenté comme l'Eglise gnostique
par excellence, annoncée par Jésus et fondée par Mani le
Paraclet. Notre propos va se contenter de mettre en évidence
quelques titres néotestamentaires de Jésus dans la liturgie
gnostique de Médînet Mâdi.

I. *Les trois figures de Jésus dans l'économie manichéenne du
    salut*

   1. *Jésus la Splendeur*

       La première figure de Jésus, longuement décrite au
       Kephalaion 16, est celle de Jésus la Splendeur, cinquième
       Grandeur lumineuse du Royaume /5/. Dans la lutte contre
       la Ténèbre, le Père de la Grandeur charge Jésus la
       Splendeur de la quatrième mission de reconquête. Selon
       le *K.16,* 54, 4-5, au cours de cette opération Jésus
       transmet le message libérateur à Adam et Eve qui
       viennent d'être créés. Hypostasiant ce message en vue
       d'en faire une institution de salut, Jésus la Splendeur
       forme la Grande Pensée et la Gnose avec ses deux
       diadoques, *Tôchme-Sôtme,* Appel-Ecoute. Ainsi, il met
       en route la cinquième étape de reconquête de la lumière,
       l'ultime mission qui prend place au début du troisième
       moment du temps médian. Jésus la Splendeur est un Etre
       transcendant et cosmique, vie et salut des hommes,
       créateur de la Gnose (*Saune*). A la suite de son oeuvre
       et durant le troisième moment du temps médian se
       succèderont les messagers gnostiques dont la lignée va
       de Sethel fils d'Adam jusqu'à Mani le Paraclet promis par
       Jésus lors de sa venue dans un corps apparent /6/.

   2. *Jesus Patibilis*

       La deuxième figure de Jésus porte plusieurs noms. Dans
       le *Contra Faustum* (XX,2) Augustin parle de la doctrine
       trinitaire enseignée par Fauste. Il lui fait dire que
       par l'effusion de l'Esprit, la terre a conçu et enfanté
       *Jesum patibilem qui est vita ac salus hominum, omni
       suspensus ex ligno.* Nous retrouvons un texte analogue

dans le *Contra Secundinum* où le correspondant d'Augustin
parle du Sauveur "crucifié dans le monde entier et en
toute âme" (2-3). Ce Jésus est constitué par l'ensemble
des parcelles lumineuses prisonnières de la matière.
Les *Kephalaia* coptes l'appellent "Croix de la Lumière".
Le *Kephalaion 85* fait une longue dissertation sur cette
"Croix de la Lumière", âme du monde en vue du respect
de laquelle le Maître a imposé le sceau des mains /7/.

3. *Jésus le Christ*

Un troisième personnage vient recouvrir les deux autres.
A leur dimension mythique il ajoute une dimension
historique : c'est Jésus-Christ, venu en ce monde au
milieu du peuple juif. Au *Kephalaion 1*, qui introduit
sa catéchèse, Mani met en évidence le rôle salvifique
de ce Jésus, personnage historique. Dans l'éventail
des douze événements majeurs du salut constituant les
articles du credo manichéen de la mission gnostique, le
Prophète reprend huit traits de la vie de Jésus depuis
sa venue jusqu'à son ascension /8/. Cette dimension
historique et cette figure de Jésus fils du Père, forment
la pierre d'angle de la mission de Mani. En effet,
Jésus venu au milieu des Juifs mais dans un corps
spirituel, a fondé l'Église qui malgré les efforts de
Paul et de deux justes - probablement Marcion et
Bardesane - est remontée dans le pays de la lumière,
laissant la terre sans fruit. C'est l'heure de Mani.
Le Prophète n'hésite pas à utiliser *Joa*, 16, 8-11 pour
présenter sa mission comme une restauration de l'Église
de Jésus et comme l'oeuvre du Paraclet annoncé par le
Sauveur /9/.

II. *Jésus est Lumière*

1. *L'influence néotestamentaire*

L'*Eucologe* de Médînet Mâdi comporte notamment un
recueil de trente-cinq hymnes groupés entre les hymnes
de Bêma et les hymnes d'Héraclide /10/. A ces hymnes
numerotés par le rédacteur du manuscrit copte, il faut
ajouter deux hymnes christologiques insérés plus loin
dans le recueil /11/. Après avoir pris connaissance du
contenu du recueil et en l'absence de titre, Allberry

l'a intitulé *Psalms to Jesus*. En effet, Jésus y occupe
la place centrale, celle de Sauveur de l'âme. Dans
ce recueil liturgique, la silhouette de Jésus est
esquissée au moyen de nombreux traits néotestamentaires.

Jésus est la lumière des croyants. L'hymne *Ps.M252*, 61-63,
s'adresse à "Jésus lumière des croyants" qui révèle sa
merveilleuse image et sa splendeur immaculée : "Tu es
la résurrection de la mort; tu es la vraie lumière des
croyants". Dans nos textes l'expression "vraie lumière"
de *Joa*, 1,9 se retrouve fréquemment sur les lèvres du
fidèle qui répète à Jésus: "Tu es ma lumière" /13/.
Notons que l'utilisation du mot grec *eikôn*, image,
permet au rédacteur copte d'exprimer sans difficulté le
docétisme manichéen pour lequel le corps de Jésus est
un corps apparent, pour lequel aussi le personnage de
Mani est la réplique visible du Paraclet.

Jésus est la lumière du monde. Dans l'hymne *Ps.M.*
p.120-121, une prière litanique dans laquelle alternent
les invocations et le répons, les appels à Jésus
s'inspirent en partie des évènements relatés dans les
Évangiles chrétiens:naissance d'une femme, crucifixion,
ascension. Nous y trouvons aussi des doctrines
néotestamentaires telles que la présence du Père dans le
Fils ainsi que l'exclusion de la chair et du sang du
royaume des cieux. Le rédacteur écrit notamment :
"J'entends que tu as dit : Je suis la lumière du monde"
(*Ps.M.*p.121,19). La citation copte est identique
à *Joa*, 8, 12 d'un manuscrit, rédigé lui aussi en
copte A2 et provenant de la région d'Assiout /14/.

Le répons de l'hymne *Ps.M 247*, 55, 17-18 réunit deux
thèmes, celui de la lumière et celui de la vie :
"Viens à moi, ô Christ qui es vie, viens à moi, lumière
du jour". L'union de ces deux thèmes est johannique :
Joa, 1, 4. Dölger a d'ailleurs fait remarquer que les
thèmes *phôs* et *zôè* passaient très régulièrement de la
liturgie chrétienne antique à la liturgie païenne /15/.
Par ailleurs, l'expression "lumière du jour" est une
allusion au soleil. Le *K.65*, 162, 32-33 parle du soleil
qui procède du Père qui est Lumière. Par ailleurs,
adaptant dans un sens gnostique *Joa*, 8, 42, le *K.65*,
163, 19 montre le soleil qui procède du Père et vient
dans le monde. Ces textes sont les témoins d'une

d'une utilisation subtile de passages néotestamentaires
dans les speculations manicheennes sur la lumière.

Le thème de la guidance par Jésus-Lumière que nous
trouvons notamment en *Joa*, 8, 12, entre plusieurs fois
dans la formulation de la prière manichéenne. L'hymne
Ps.M.246, 54, 6-10 exhorte l'âme en butte aux
difficultés suscitées par les ténèbres et lui fait
proclamer : "Viens a moi, Lumière, mon guide ... Lève-toi
tu as un Sauveur, ta défense c'est le Christ".
La réponse de Jésus ne se fait pas attendre : "Je suis
partout, je porte les cieux, je suis le fondement, je
porte la terre, je suis la lumière qui éclaire et donne
la joie aux âmes, je suis la vie du monde. (*Ps.M.246*,
54, 25-28).   Un développement analogue se rencontre
dans l'hymne *Ps.M.248*, 56, 21-27, adressée au Seigneur
Jésus le Sauveur des âmes : "Viens mon Seigneur Jésus,
le Sauveur des âmes qui me sauve de l'ivresse et de
l'erreur du monde. Ta lumière éclaire devant moi comme
la lumière d'une lampe". Il s'agit bien du thème de
Joa, 8, 12 : celui qui suit Jésus ne marche pas dans
les ténèbres mais dans la lumière. Le theme se retrouve,
dans un autre contexte dans l'hymne *Ps.M.250*, 59, 1, 20
et 21 où Jésus le Monogène est présenté comme la
résurrection de celui qui est mort dans l'Eglise. Il
est la Lumière. Dans un geste salvifique, il tend la
main droite à l'âme en détresse.

2. *Titulature néotestamentaire et figures mythiques de*
   Jésus-Lumière

Notre brève analyse de textes liturgiques manichéens mis
en parallèle avec certains passages johanniques, vient
de nous montrer que le recueil christologique de
Médinet Mâdi souligne, au moyen de nombreux traits
néotestamentaires, la figure de Jésus-Lumière. Par
contre, c'est dans les hymnes de Bêma que nous trouvons
Jésus la Splendeur, ce personnage cosmique du Royaume
de la Lumière, chargé de révéler à Adam le message
gnostique. Célébrée le jour du nouvel an gnostique, la
solennité de Bêma était à la fois le grand jour du
pardon des péchés, le mémorial de la Passion de Mani et
la célébration du triomphe de la Gnose /16/. En
présentant le Bêma comme la nouvelle alliance, cette
liturgie s'attache tout particulièrement à l'action

cosmique de Jésus qui, en collaboration avec l'Homme
Primordial, ramène dans le Royaume les étincelles
lumineuses prisonnières de la matière. Les hymnes de
Bêma soulignent l'action de la voie céleste lumineuse,
du soleil libérateur, de la lumière divine, du combat
permanent entre la Lumière et la Ténèbre /17/. Dans
ces textes, la figure de Jésus la Splendeur ne se
présente pas sous des traits néotestamentaires, mais elle
se trouve sous l'influence de la théologie solaire dont
nous avons de larges extraits dans les *Kephalaia 65, 66*
et *67*. Cette théologie solaire manichéenne nous semble
tributaire notamment de certaines doctrines égyptiennes
ainsi que du culte de Mithra.

À côté du personnage mythique divin qui porte le nom
de Jésus la Splendeur, il y a *Jesus Patibilis*, la Croix
de la Lumière, l'âme du monde constituée par l'ensemble
des parcelles lumineuses arrachées au Royaume de la
Lumière, lors du combat primordial. La liturgie de
Médînet Mâdi parle plusieurs fois, de façon explicite
de la Croix de la Lumière /18/. Un passage de la
liturgie des pélerins nous semble particulièrement
éclairant (*Ps.M.*p.159-160). Dans sa prière, l'élu en
marche sur la route missionnaire de la Gnose, demande
à Dieu de mettre en lui un esprit droit et un coeur
saint, puis il ajoute : "Le coeur saint est le Christ;
s'il ressuscite (s'il grandit) en nous, nous ressuscitons
(nous grandissons) en lui" (*Ps.M.*p.159, 23-25). Le
rédacteur va continuer à jouer sur l'ambiguïté du verbe
copte *tôoun* (*tôn* en A^2) qui peut signifier monter ou se
lever mais qui peut aussi avoir le sens de
ressusciter. Apres une allusion à la résurrection
(ascension) de Jésus, le redacteur specule sur la Croix
de la Lumière: "Jésus est ressuscité (monté); il est
ressuscité (monté) en trois jours. La Croix de la
Lumière ressuscité (monté) en trois puissances: le
Soleil, la lune, l'Homme parfait. Ces trois puissances
constituent l'Église du macrocosme. Jésus, la Vierge
et le *Nous* qui est au milieu d'eux , voilà l'Église du
microcosme. Le royaume des cieux, voyez, il est en nous,
voyez, il est hors de nous. Si nous croyons en lui,
nous vivrons éternellement" (*Ps.M.*p.-60, 16-22).

Sur la base du thème néotestamentaire de la résurrection,
ce texte se livre a une spéculation sur la Croix de la
Lumière en corrélation avec la résurrection de Jésus, ce

qui permet de faire une véritable présentation de
Jesus Patibilis. En tant que lumière en provenance du
Royaume d'en haut, *Jesus Patibilis* est un Être céleste
d'essence lumineuse, consubstantiel à l'essence du
Royaume, indispensable pour la formation de l'Eglise
du macrocosme. En tant que lumière prisonnière liée à
la matière, ce *Jesus Patibilis* est immanent au monde
auquel il donne la vie en vue de réaliser le salut de
l'homme et du cosmos. Cosmogonie et sotériologie sont
liées indissolublement. Dans ce contexte la doctrine
néotestamentaire ne sert pas à présenter la titulature
de Jésus mais elle sous-tend l'esquisse de *Jesus
Patibilis* qui n'est pas une figure biblique mais qui
rappelle le *Salvator salvandus* de certaines religions
orientales et particulièrement le *Bodhisattva* bouddhiste.

III. *Jésus le Sauveur*

1. *La sotériologie*

Dans la religion de Mani, la sotériologie est vraiment
centrale puisque tout est fonction de la libération de
la lumière. C'est au cours du deuxième temps que se
réalise le salut qui, en trois étapes, aboutira à la
séparation totale de la Lumière et de la Ténèbre. La
première étape est la lutte de l'Homme Primordial. La
deuxième étape englobe la création du cosmos jusqu'à
la formation d'Adam. La cosmogonie prépare la
sotériologie. Le troisième moment du salut commence au
réveil d'Adam illuminé par Jésus la Splendeur et se
terminera par le grand feu eschatologique. Cette
troisième étape du deuxième temps se caractérise par la
succession des messagers du Royaume. En effet, dès que
Jésus la Splendeur, Sauveur transcendant et cosmique a
mis en place *Tôchme-Sôtme*, les deux diadoques Appel-
Ecoute, l'histoire du salut devient visible grâce aux
messagers et prophètes : Sethel, Enosch, Henoch,
Abraham, Zarathustra, le Bouddha, Jésus et Mani.

Le salut est un événement cosmique car il s'agit de
libérer toute la lumière. Il est aussi un événement
individuel puisqu'il faut libérer l'âme, étincelle
divine retenue prisonnière dans la matière. Les textes
liturgiques de Médînet Mâdi concentrent leur attention

sur cet aspect individuel. Chaque gnostique doit
adhérer aux mystères dualistes et dès lors vivre dans
un choix permanent : ainsi, il est fils de lumière.
Par sa chute dans la matière, la partie inférieure de
l'âme ou *psukhê* est blessée. Engagée moins profondément,
le *noûs* ou partie supérieure de l'homme s'éveille sous
l'effet du message gnostique. Aussitôt, il prend
conscience de sa situation tragique. Les textes
liturgiques de Médînet Mâdi soulignent spécialement
l'amnésie de l'âme à la suite de l'oubli de son origine
divine. Le message dualiste va tenir lieu de mémoire.

L'hymne *Ps.M.248*, 56-58 montre clairement les trois
étapes du réveil. Le message gnostique commence par
projetter sa clarté sur l'âme qui saisit progressivement
la vision dualiste du cosmos. Cette lumière provoque le
recul de l'amnésie; l'âme commence à sortir de
l'indifférence et de la torpeur. Enfin l'âme découvre
son origine divine. C'est le moment où naît l'angoisse.
C'est aussi le début de la *katharsis* que tout gnostique
doit opérer en lui-même. Rassemblant toute la substance
spirituelle présente en lui, il se libère de la
contrainte de son corps et, comme l'*arhat* bouddhiste qui
en cette vie déjà atteint le *nirvâna*, l'élu manichéen
dégagé de la matière, finit par tourner en roue libre :
il est devenu un élu parfait.

2. *Jésus est Sauveur*

Jésus intervient d'abord dans le réveil de l'âme, puis
dans la réalisation progressive du salut. Le recueil
christologique de l'*Hymnaire* nous a gardé quarante et
une invocations aux Sauveurs dont trente-neuf sont
directement adressées à Jésus. Vingt-six fois, Jésus
est invoqué comme *Sôtèr* /19/. L'âme appelle Jésus à son
aide dans le combat contre l'angoisse et contre la
matière. Nos hymnes désignent Jésus le Sauveur encore
par un autre vocable : *Perefsôte*, le Sauveur ou *Parefsôte*,
mon Sauveur. Le sens de cette construction substantive
copte, typiquement dualiste, est clair : "celui qui tire
dehors". En effet, le Sauveur arrache l'âme à la prison
de la matière. Dans nos textes, Jésus reçoit une série
de qualifications relatives à ses activités de Sauveur.
Nous allons nous y arrêter quelque peu.

Jésus est Seigneur, *Djais* dans nos textes coptes
subakhmimiques de l'*Eucologe*. Notons que le mot grec
kurios n'est jamais utilisé dans le Nouveau Testament
sahidique alors que le mot *sôtèr* s'y trouve
régulièrement /20/. Ce fait explique probablement
l'absence du vocable *kurios* dans la liturgie de Médînet
Mâdi. En cela, nous aurions une confirmation de
l'influence des textes néotestamentaires coptes sur la
rédaction du recueil christologique manichéen. Dans ce
dernier, le titre *Djais*, Seigneur, apparaît cent et sept
fois, dont neuf fois seulement comme titre de Mani. Dans
tous les autres cas, *Djais*, le Seigneur, est Jésus.
Trente-quatre fois Jésus le Sauveur est appelé *Christos*,
trois fois avec une référence directe à un texte
néotestamentaire /21/. *Christos* n'est jamais un titre
donné à Mani. A ce sujet, un passage de l'*Eucologe*
trace bien la perspective du rédacteur. En effet, dans
l'hymne *Ps.M.266*, 83, 2, Mani est appelé "fils du Christ".

Jésus le Sauveur est Dieu : *Noute*. Au début du xxe
siècle, la découverte des textes de Tourfan avait
attiré l'attention sur le problème de Jésus dans le
manichéisme /22/. La fréquence de *Yishô* dans les
textes d'Asie Centrale avait fait comprendre que les
éléments christologiques ne constituaient pas une
concession tardive de l'Eglise de Mani aux nécessités
de la propagande en terre chrétienne. Les documents de
Médînet Mâdi et la *Vita* du *Codex* de Cologne confirment
ces conclusions. Ainsi, l'hymne *Ps.M.*122, 9, contient
une véritable profession de foi en la divinité de Jésus :
"Je te reconnais Dieu, la terre te reconnaît homme".
Cette profession de foi est bien dans la ligne de *Joa*,
6, 69. En *Ps.M.244*, 51, 16, le gnostique fidèle
proclame : "Ils ont oublié Dieu qui est venu et s'est
lui-même livré à la mort pour eux". Jésus est aussi
appelé le Dieu saint. Cette expression du *Ps.M.262*, 76,
31, inspirée par *Lc*, 4, 34 et *Joa*, 6, 69, est peut-être
un emprunt direct à la liturgie chrétienne. L'idée de
filiation divine de Jésus ne se retrouve pas moins de
seize fois dans nos hymnes, d'ailleurs régulièrement
exprimée en des formulations proches de textes
néotestamentaires /23/. Ainsi Jésus est "Fils bien-aimé
du Dieu de vérité", une formule liturgique fréquente dans
les doxologies finales de l'*Hymnaire* /24/. Par une
citation explicite de *Joa*, 14, 10, l'hymne *Ps.M.121,*25

souligne l'intimité entre Jésus et son Père : "J'entends
ceci : Tu es dans ton Père et ton Père est caché en Toi,
mon Seigneur". Ces textes nous montrent que le
rédacteur manichéen n'a pas hésité à recourir au
Nouveau Testament en vue de parler de Jésus comme Dieu et
comme fils de Dieu.

Si la liturgie gnostique insiste sur la présentation de
Jésus comme Dieu, Seigneur et Fils de Dieu, elle
s'arrête cependant aussi au role de Jésus Sauveur
décrit comme époux de l'âme. À la base de la doctrine
du salut individuel nous trouvons l'anthropologie
manichéenne de l'âme formée du couple *noûs-psukhê*. Le
noûs est l'élément sauveur moins engagé dans la matière
et facile à réveiller; la *psukhê* est la partie vraiment
prisonnière de la matière, l'élément à sauver mais dont
le réveil n'est pas une oeuvre aisée. Le salut de l'âme
se réalise en une sorte d'eschatologie individuelle qui
lui fait retrouver sa pureté première, la détache du
corps de péché et l'amène graduellement à redevenir
cette étincelle divine libre qui, au moment de la mort,
rejoindra le Royaume de la Lumière. Ce processus
quotidien de la libération progressive se fait grâce à
la présence de Jésus, l'époux de l'âme. Ce titre
d'époux, plus d'une fois utilisé par la prière
liturgique et dans des contextes différents, nous permet
de voir que le thème évangélique de l'époux est vraiment
entré dans le vocabulaire manichéen.

Le développement du thème se fait notamment à l'aide du
symbolisme de la chambre nuptiale dans laquelle Jésus
recoit l'âme sauvée comme un époux recoit l'épouse :
"Jésus le Christ, reçois-moi dans tes chambres nuptiales,
toi mon Sauveur" (*Ps.M.263*, 79, 19-20). Dans cet
hymne malheureusement mal conservé, plusieurs détails
nous orientent vers des passages néotestamentaires.
Ainsi, en 79, 29-30 où il est question de l'époux qui
purifie l'âme par des eaux pleines de grâce, nous avons
une reminiscence de *Eph.*, 5, 26. Les versets 80, 12-13,
assez mutilés, font allusion à l'huile de la pureté
apportée par l'époux ce qui nous fait penser à la
parabole des vierges de *Mt*, 25, 1-13. L'âme proclame sa
libération en se considérant dès à présent, en une vision
eschatalogique anticipée, comme "une sainte épouse dans
les chambres nuptiales de la Lumière" (*Ps.M.264*, 81,

13-14). Comme en *Mt,9*, 15 qui parle de la joie des
disciples en présence de l'époux, l'hymne *Ps.M.*177,
29-30 implore: "Place-moi dans tes chambres nuptiales,
afin que je chante avec ceux qui te chantent ô Christ
...". Il n'est dès lors pas étonnant de rencontrer des
allusions à la robe nuptiale et au festin des noces.
C'est le cas en *Ps.M.261*, 76, 10-12 où nous avons le
thème de *Mt,22*, 10-11 sur le festin des noces.

Une imagerie importante de la symbolique manichéenne du
salut obtenu avec l'aide de Jesus, est empruntée à
l'allégorie néotestamentaire du bon pasteur. Ainsi, le
thème du gardiennage et de l'agneau sous-tend tout le
developpement de l'hymne *Ps.M.251*, 60-61. Nous y
voyons l'âme se réfugier sous la houlette du gardien :
"Je suis ton agneau, tu es mon bon pasteur. Tu es venu
à mon secours et tu m'as sauvé des loups destructeurs"
(60, 26-27 = *Joa*, 10, 11-14). Ailleurs se trouvent des
emprunts à la parabole de la brebis perdue. Ainsi, au
moment du réveil dans la prison de la matière, l'âme
angoissée se tourne vers Jésus le Christ et se
présente en ces termes : "Moi aussi, je suis du nombre de
tes cent brebis que ton Père a mis entre tes mains afin
que tu les fasses paître" (*Ps.M.273*, 93, 4-6). Ce
texte nous fait bien voir le travail du redacteur
gnostique qui utilise simultanément la brebis perdue de
Mt, 18, 12 et le bon pasteur de *Joa*, 10, 27-29. La
symbolique évangélique du gardiennage se retrouve en de
nombreux endroits de notre recueil christologique où il
est question de la voix du pasteur, des pâturages, des
brebis sans pasteur ainsi que des loups destructeurs /25/.
Dans une recherche ultérieure il serait intéressant de
voir si le rédacteur manichéen a travaillé directement
sur des textes néotestamentaires ou s'il a simplement
utilisé des textes liturgiques déjà constitués à l'aide
d'emprunts au N.T.

IV. *Jésus est Juge*

Le titre de juge décerné à Jésus et le thème du jugement se
rencontrent fréquemment dans deux collections d'hymnes de
l'*Eucologe*, le recueil christologique et le recueil de Béma.

1. *Le recueil christologique*

La religion dualiste de Mani préconise un salut cosmique
consistant dans la libération de toutes les parcelles
lumineuses enchaînées à la matière ténébreuse lors du
gigantesque combat entre la Lumière et la Ténèbre. Au
terme de ce salut qui a débuté avec la mission de l'Homme
Primordial se situe le grand feu eschatologique.
A l'intérieur du salut du macrocosme, se réalise le salut
du microcosme : la libération de chaque âme et son
retour dans le Royaume après la dissolution du corps.
La prière liturgique se préoccupe essentiellement de ce
salut de l'âme et dans ce contexte, elle s'adresse à
Jesus chargé de juger chaque homme au moment de la mort.
Dans cette fonction, Jésus reçoit le titre de *Kritès*,
employé dix-sept fois dans notre recueil. Comme en
2 Tim., *6-8* et en *Rom.*, *2*, *5-6*, le redacteur manichéen
insiste sur l'impartialite de ce juge. "Il existe un
juge au-delà de la dissolution du corps et il n'y a
personne qui soit capable de se cacher devant lui quand
il recherche les actions d'un chacun et récompense selon
les mérites" (*Ps.M.242*, 49, 14-16). Ce texte fait
penser à une liturgie funéraire. En effet, dans ce
premier hymne du recueil christologique, le rédacteur
continue sa réflexion en énumérant la foi du fidèle,
ses souffrances, les persécutions endurées, pour finir
par présenter au juge les aumônes, les prières et le
zèle d'une vie entière (49, 17-22). Puis à l'élu fidèle
la liturgie révèle l'identité du juge: "Un voleur a été
sauvé sur la croix parce qu'il t'a reconnu (confessé).
Tu as oublié tous les péchés qu'il avait commis; tu
t'es souvenu du bien" (*Ps.M.242*, 49, 23-25). Ici le
texte de *Lc.*23, 40-43 est mis à contribution pour
insister sur l'importance de la gnose en vue du
jugement. Ailleurs, la liturgie parle de la vérité
(*Ps.M.247*, 56, 6). Ainsi justice et gnose marchent de
pair. La liturgie rejoint la loi fondamentale de la
vie manichéenne qui se résume en un mot : *dikaiosunè* /26/.
Ce juge est aussi un Dieu fort que l'âme invoque à l'heure
de l'angoisse et à l'heure du jugement /27/. Nos
textes liturgiques réconfortent les disciples de Mani,
sans cesse persecutés et par ailleurs, obligés de mener
une vie austère de jeûne, de prière, d'aumône,
d'abstinence et de continence. Aussi proclament-ils
avec enthousiasme que Jésus est la résurrection de

celui qui meurt dans l'Église /28/.

2. *Les hymnes de Bema*

L'analyse des vingt-trois hymnes de Bêma actuellement
publiés, permet de saisir les trois significations de
cette fête majeure que l'Église de Mani célébrait
chaque année fin février ou debut mars, au terme d'un
jeûne rigoureux de vingt-six jours /29/. Aux origines,
jour annuel du grand pardon institue par Mani lui-même,
la fête de Bêma devint rapidement le mémorial de la
Passion du Prophète puis la solennité annuelle de la
Gnose. Dans la pensée du Prophète, ses disciples
doivent se grouper, les bras chargés des jeûnes, des
aumônes et des prières de l'année. Jusqu'à la fin du
temps du mélange, le Bêma se dressera comme signe visible
du triomphe du Bien sur le Mal et cela jusqu'au moment
où Jésus lui-même viendra s'y asseoir afin de juger
les nations /30/.

Les hymnes de Bêma montrent la présence simultanée de
Jésus et de Mani au milieu de l'assemblée en prière.
Cependant, dans le rôle de juge, Jésus occupe la
première place. Sans repentir, il n'y a point de
pardon des fautes. Or, la repentance est elle-même un
don de Jésus qui fait signe en secret et dit:
"Repentez-vous afin que je puisse vous pardonner vos
péchés" /31/. Le rôle de Jésus est un rôle de *Kritès*.
Si Mani est mystérieusement présent grâce au symbolisme
de la grande icône dressée au sommet de l'estrade à
cinq degrés, Jésus est proche de chaque fidèle puisqu'il
a proclamé dans sa prédication "Je suis près de vous
comme le vêtement de votre corps" (*Ps.M.239*, 39, 24).
Par ailleurs, en vue de montrer que le Bêma est bien
le trône de Jésus le Juge, le rédacteur cite Paul :
"Paul le glorieux rend témoignage en disant à ce sujet :
Au Bêma du Christ il n'y a acception de personne" /32/.
En la personne de Jésus, *Bêma* et *Kritès* sont liés car
il s'agit de séparer les deux races. Ainsi la
rémission des péchés au jour de Bêma est une anticipation
et une annonce du jugement de la fin du deuxième temps.
La liturgie de Bêma présente Mani dans le rôle de
Sauveur, *Perefsôte*, qui comme un médecin, se penche
sur l'humanité blessée. Son diagnostic est sûr. Il
connaît la blessure de chacun. Par ailleurs, a toute

maladie il apporte le remède. Ses *Écritures* constituent
sa trousse médicale. Son message continue le message
de Jésus. Dernier révélateur de la Gnose, il est le
sceau des messagers du salut.

CONCLUSIONS

Au terme de cette recherche limitée à quelques titres
néotestamentaires de Jésus dans la liturgie manichéenne de
Médînet Mâdi, il est possible d'aboutir à plusieurs conclusions.

Dans sa présentation des trois figures de Jésus, la
religion de Mani utilise comme élément essentiel le thème de la
lumière. Pour décrire la figure de *Jésus Messager du Royaume*
venu au milieu des Juifs, les hymnes christologiques de Médînet
Mâdi empruntent sans hésiter les traits néotestamentaires
johanniques de Jésus lumière du monde, lumière des croyants,
lumière qui fait vivre. Par contre, *Jésus Patibilis*, l'âme
lumineuse du monde, se situe dans un contexte cosmique avec,
cependant, l'utilisation du thème évangélique de la resurrection.
Quant à la figure de *Jésus Splenditenens*, éveilleur d'Adam et
createur de la Gnose, c'est ailleurs qu'il faut chercher les
influences. Les *Kephalaia* de Médînet Mâdi - des documents de
catéchèse manichéenne - nous orientent vers les théologies
solaires, notamment égyptienne et mithraïque.

Le manichéisme est essentiellement une religion de salut.
Dans cette sotériologie gnostique fondée sur un dualisme
radical, Jésus occupe des fonctions capitales. Si les
Kephalaia parlent davantage de Jésus la Splendeur qui est a
l'origine du salut et de *Jésus Patibilis*, l'âme du monde à
sauver ou *Salvator salvandus*, par contre, la prière liturgique
s'adresse de manière très familière à Jésus Sauveur et cela
en vue d'obtenir d'abord le réveil de l'âme prisonnière,
ensuite le secours divin sur la route du salut. Ainsi, le
recueil christologique connaît surtout Jésus comme *Sôtèr* et il
le présente sous les vocables néotestamentaires de Seigneur,
Christ, Dieu, Epoux, Pasteur. Manifestement, le rôle de Jésus
dans le salut de fidèle est vu comme essentiel. Mani est le
Fils de Jésus et son Messager. Cependant, la christologie de
ces hymnes reste sous-tendue par le dualisme gnostique.

Sans hésiter, la liturgie de Médînet Mâdi attribue un rôle
spécifique à chacun des deux Sauveurs : Jésus et Mani. Dans
les hymnes christologiques, Jésus est le Juge impartial, *Kritēs*,

qui rend à chacun selon ses actes. La liturgie de Bèma garde à
Jésus ce rôle de *Kritēs*, notamment dans le contexte du pardon
des péchés. Les deux recueils liturgiques donnent à l'action
du Juge une teinte nettement paulinienne. Par ailleurs, la
célébration de Bêma ne manque pas d'insister sur les fonctions
eschatologiques de Mani, Sauveur des âmes. Cependant
l'intervention de ce Sauveur n'est pas celle d'un Juge mais
celle du Médecin par excellence de l'humanité blessée. Il s'agit
bien de la perspective que nous retrouvons dans de nombreux
textes : Mani se présente comme l'Envoyé de Jésus.

NOTES

/1/   A. Henrichs - L. Koenen, Ein griechischer Mani-Codex, dans
Zeitschrift fur Papyrologie und Epigraphik, 5, Bonn, 1970,
97-216. A. Henrichs - L. Koenen, Der Kolner Mani-Codex
(P. Colon. inv. nr. 4780) dans *Zeit. Papyr. Epig*, 19, Bonn,
1975, 1-85. C.R.C. Allberry, *A Manichaean Psalm-Book, Part II*,
Stuttgart, 1938. H.J. Polotsky, *Manichaische Homelien*,
Stuttgart, 1934. H. Ibscher - C. Schmidt, *Kephalaia I*,
Stuttgart, 1940. A. Böhlig, *Kephalaia II*, Stuttgart, 1966.
Dans notre étude nous designons le *Psalm-book* par les mots
Hymnaire ou *Eucologe*.
/2/   *Zeit. Papyr. Epig.*, 19, Bonn, 1975, 67.
/3/   *Cont. Ep. Fundamenti*, V.
/4/   J. Ries, Un double symbole de foi gnostique dans le
Kephalaion un de Médînet Mâdi, dans *Nag Hammadi Studies*, IX,
Leiden, 1978, 139-148.
/5/   *Kephalaion 16*, 49, 29-35; 50, 1-4; 53, 18-32; 54, 1-32;
55, 1-11.
/6/   *Kephalaion 1*, 12, 10-34; 13, 1-35; 14, 1-18.
/7/   *Kephalaion 85*, 208-213.
/8/   *Kephalaion 1*, 12, 21-34; 13, 1-10.
/9/   *Kephalaion 1*, 14, 4b-10.
/10/   C.R.C. Allberry, *A manichaean Psalm-Book, Part II*,
Stuttgart, 1938, p.49-97.
/11/   *Psalm-Book*, p.116-117; 120-124.
/12/   En vue de simplifier nos citations, nous utiliserons les
sigles suivants : Ps.M = A Manichaean Psalm-Book; K = Kephalaia;
Hom = Homelien. Les chiffres qui suivent le sigle désignent
respectivement le numéro, la page, la ligne des textes dans
l'édition princeps quand les pièces des recueils sont numérotées.
En l'absence de numérotation dans les recueils, les chiffres
indiquent respectivement la page et la ligne dans l'édition
princeps.

/13/ Ps.M.268, 85, 23; Ps.M.269, 87, 16 et 17; Ps.M.271, 89, 27.

/14/ S.M. Thompson, The Gospel of St. John, Londres, 1924.

/15/ Fr. J. Dölger, Sol salutis, Gebet und Gesang im christlichen Altertum, Munster, 1925.

/16/ C.R.C. Allberry, A Manichaean Psalmbook, 1-47.

/17/ Voir notamment Ps.M.227, 22, 4-9; Ps.M.227, 21, 26; Ps.M.228, 23, 14; Ps.M.233, 30, 28; Ps.M.234, 32, 19; Ps.M.240, 41, 1; Ps.M.241, 42, 7.

/18/ Ps.M.257, 61, 3-6; Ps.M.268, 86, 23-30; Ps.M. p.159-160.

/19/ Voir notamment Ps.M.243, 50, 15; Ps.M.248, 56, 15; Ps.M.248, 57, 15; Ps.M.252, 62, 10; Ps.M.254, 64, 32; Ps.M.255, 66, 3, 9.

/20/ Voir L. Th. Lefort, Concordance du Nouveau Testament Sahidique, I, Les mots d'origine grecque, Louvain, 1950.

/21/ Ps.M.245, 53, 23. Ps.M.247, 55, 17. Ps.M.260, 75, 7.

/22/ E. Waldschmit et W. Lentz, Die Stellung Jesu im Manichaismus, Berlin, 1926.

/23/ Ainsi Ps.M.250, 59, 29-30 = Mt, 14, 33; Ps.M.242, 49, 29-30 = Mt, 3, 17 et Rom; 3, 4. Ps.M.251, 60, 8 et 17 = Lc, 8, 28. Ps.M.265, 82, 30 = Joa, 5, 26.

/24/ Tois exemples : Ps.M.248, 57, 31-32; Ps.M.260, 75, 7-8; Ps.M.252, 62, 31.

/25/ Ps.M.252, 62, 27; Ps.M.276, 96, 15-16; Ps.M.246, 54, 16; Ps.M.253, 63, 11-12; Ps.M.251, 60, 27; Ps.M.252, 61, 25.

/26/ J. Ries, Commandements de la justice et vie missionnaire dans l'Eglise de Mani, dans Gnosis and Gnosticism, Leiden, 1977, 93-106.

/27/ Ps.M.255, 65, 29, 30-31 = Apoc. 18,8.

/28/ Ps.M.250, 59, 17-18 = Joa, 11, 25 et Ps.M.255, 67, 14-15 = Apoc. 1, 17-18.

/29/ C.R.C. Allberry, A Manichaean Psalm-Book, 1-47. Sur la fête de Bêma, on peut voir C.R.C. Allberry, Das Manichaische Bema-Fest dans Zeitschrift fur die Neutestamentliche Wissenschaft, 37, Berlin, 1938, 2-10. H.Ch. Puech, Les fêtes et les solennités, le Bêma, dans Histoire des Religions, 2 Paris, 1972, p.625-628. J. Ries, La fête de Bêma dans l'Eglise de Mani, dans Revue des études augustiniennes, 22, Paris, 1976, 218-233.

/30/ Ps.M.229, 25, 22-26; Ps.M.227, 20, 31 et 21, 1.

/31/ Ps.M.239, 39, 19-22; Ps.M.236, 34, 21-24.

/32/ Ps.M.222, 7, 15-25 = Rom., 14, 10.

Studia Biblica 1978: III, 337-343

What about 1 John?

Stephen S. Smalley,
Precentor,
Coventry Cathedral,
35 Morningside,
COVENTRY CV5 6PD.

The usual scholarly view of John's first letter is that it was written as an orthodox attack on docetic error, both doctrinal and ethical. Westcott's comment is typical: 'the false teaching with which (John) deals is Docetic and specifically Cerinthian' /1/. And this is the understanding of the purpose of *1 John* followed by Dodd, Bultmann, Kümmel and others /2/, all of whom regard this work as in some sense a piece of anti-'gnostic' polemic /3/.

I want to suggest that the situation addressed in *1 John* was by no means so straightforward; and that docetism, while an integral part of the total scene, was not the only heresy which exercised the writer's mind. To outline my proposals with any coherence means that I must first make some brief allusion to my conclusions - which cannot here be argued - about the intention of the Fourth Gospel, and the relationship between the Johannine Gospel and letters /4/.

I see John's Gospel as a pastorally-motivated document, written as an attempt to reconcile two conflicting groups of Christians within the Johannine Church: ex-Jews, who regarded Jesus as less than God; and ex-pagans (or ex-Jews, influenced by Hellenism), who thought of him as less than man. The fourth evangelist is not concerned with 'orthodoxy' and 'heresy' as such (his theology is too diverse for that) /5/; but he *is* anxious to present his readers with a perfectly balanced christology, holding in tension the twin affirmations that Jesus is both one with God and one with man /6/. Just here, in the problems which may well have beset the Johannine community, we can perhaps discover the reason for John's distinctive view

of the person of Christ, and his equally typical emphasis on
love and unity among the brethren /7/.

1 JOHN

Given this approach to the Fourth Gospel, what (we may ask)
about *1 John*? I regard the Gospel and letters of John, *pace*
Dodd /8/, as deriving from the same spiritual and intellectual
milieu - that of the Johannine church itself - if not from the
same hand(s) /9/. This impression is strengthened, to my mind,
by the situation which seems to have developed from the Gospel
to the letters. For it appears that by the time the letters
were written (say, the late 80s or early 90s /10/), the climate
had changed markedly. The heretical 'tendencies' which the
fourth evangelist was trying to counteract had crystallised
into recognisable errors; and the divisions which he had sought
to resolve had become more defined. As a result of this we are
confronted in *1 John* with an orthodox attack on *two* heresies,
not one.

Admittedly, when descriptions of actual heretical doctrine
occur in this letter they *seem* to be overtly anti-docetic; for
example, *1 Jn*.4:2 ('By this you know the Spirit of God: every
spirit which confesses that Jesus Christ has come in the flesh
is of God'). But there is nothing to suggest that docetism is
the *only* heresy under attack, or that all theological statements
in *1 John* must be interpreted exclusively in an anti-docetic
light.

Notice first that some christological allusions in this
document are manifestly 'high', rather than 'low'. Thus the
theology of 4:17, for example, which draws attention to the
perfect union existing between Jesus and the Father, as the
archetype of the Christian's communion with God, can scarcely
be regarded as a potential asset in the battle against docetic
inclinations /11/! Secondly, many descriptions of the person
of Christ in 1 John are, to say the least, ambivalent in their
purport. Instances of this phenomenon occur in 2:22f. and 5:1,
where references to belief in 'Jesus as the Christ', and to
denial of that belief, *could* involve a stress on either the
Lord's divinity or his humanity /12/.

If this second suggestion be accepted, it is then possible
to argue that the explicit indications of an heretical presence
among the readers of *1 John* may refer to the extreme of

docetism *or* to its exact opposite of adoptionism. This is true,
for example, when the writer mentions the 'antichrist' (2:18),
those who 'mislead' (2:26), false prophecy (4:1), false teaching
(2:27), 'error' as opposed to 'truth' (4:6), and failure to
'know' or 'see' God in Christ (3:1; *cf*. verse 6).

TWO HERESIES?

An exhaustive study of *1 John* from the point of view of
its possible ambivalence, where heresy is concerned, yields the
following results.

1. *Presumed anti-docetic references*

    (a) 2:3-5 (gnosis, if true, is morally practical).

    (b) 2:15-17; 3:13; 4:4-6; 5:4,19 (the 'world' viewed in
         dualist terms, in order to find common ground with
         the docetic heretics).

    (c) 3:19f., 24 (*cf*. 2:20f.) (true gnosis is the knowledge
         of God [in Christ] by the Spirit).

2. *Clear anti-docetic references*

    (a) 1:1-3; 2:6,8; 4:2f,9,17 (the life/flesh of Jesus
         are both real).

    (b) 1:7b-10; 2:2,12; 3:5,8,16; 4:10 (the death of Jesus
         is real, in answer to the real sin of man).

3. *Clear anti-adoptionist references*

    (a) 2:1, 13f., 20, 28, 29; 3:2,3,5,7 (Jesus is sinless
         [δίκαιος], pre-existent, holy and pure; he will come
         in glory at the end).

    (b) 3:23 (4:3?) (we are to believe in this Jesus).

    (c) 1:5-7a; 5:14f. (thus we can walk in the light, and pray
         effectively through him).

4. *References which could be to either heresy*

    (a) 2:22f.; 5:1a (Jesus is the Christ, *or* the Christ is
         Jesus).

(b)   2:25; 3:14; 5:11f., 13 (there is life in Christ).

(c)   3:8; 4:9, 14f.; 5:5 (but see verse 6), 20 (Jesus is
      Son of God).

(d)   3:24; 4:13 (we have the real presence of Jesus in the
      Spirit).

(e)   4:17b (the Christian is to Christ, as Christ is to
      God) /13/.

(f)   5:6-10 (the threefold witness - of the Spirit,
      together with the baptism and death of Jesus - to
      the reality of the incarnation) /14/.

From this survey it is possible to claim that roughly half
the allusions to the presence of heresy among the readers of
1 John are either ambivalent (perhaps deliberately so, given the
situation in the Johannine church as postulated earlier), or
deliberately anti-adoptionist. Moreover, if the references
which I have interpreted as anti-adoptionist had been intended
as anti-docetic, would not the writer have made this clearer?
Thus the statement in 4:2, for example, 'Jesus Christ has come
in the flesh', is not necessarily synonymous with the
announcement at 5:20a, 'the Son of God has come'. The latter
can equally be taken to mean, 'the Jesus who came in the flesh
is not only Messiah /15/ (that may be an anti-adoptionist
note!), but also Son of God; and such is his status that he
gives us what God gives - that is, eternal life /16/.

CONCLUSION

I suggest on this basis that what we find in 1 John is a
church split not two ways (orthodox and docetic /17/), but
three. In addition to an orthodox group, with its balanced
christology and 'catholic' outlook, I detect a Hellenistic,
gnostically-inclined group (possibly associated with the
teaching of Cerinthus), with an heretical, docetic christology;
and also a Jewish group (possibly inclined towards Ebionism /18/),
with an heretical, adoptionist christology. I propose that it
was to this complex situation /19/, in which the doctrinal lines
had hardened, that the writer of 1 John addressed his first
letter, and then 2 and 3 John /20/.

NOTES

/1/   B.F. Westcott, *The Epistles of St. John: the Greek text,
with notes and essays* (London, 1883), p.xxxiv.
/2/   C.H. Dodd, *The Johannine Epistles* (London, 1946),
pp.xvi-xxi, esp. xx; R.K. Bultmann, *Die drei Johannesbriefe*
(Göttingen, 1967), pp.43-5, *et passim*; W.G. Kümmel, *Introduction
to the New Testament* (ET London, 1975[2]), pp.440-2. But see
R. Schnackenburg, *Die Johannesbriefe* (Freiburg im Breisgau,
1965[3]), pp.15-23, esp. 19f.; also J.C. O'Neill, *The Puzzle of
1 John: a new examination of origins* (London, 1966), pp.46-8
(the teaching under attack is not docetic heresy, but assault
on the Christian faith as such - the refusal to acknowledge
that Jesus is Messiah). See further on this interpretation
G.W.H. Lampe, '"Grievous Wolves" (Acts 20:29)', in B. Lindars
and S.S. Smalley (edd.), *Christ and Spirit in the New
Testament: studies in honour of Charles Francis Digby Moule*
(Cambridge, 1973), pp.261f.
/3/   But those who opt for this view do not always agree about
the precise nature of the 'gnostic' error refuted. *Cf.* D.
Guthrie, *New Testament Introduction* (London, 1970[3]), pp.870f.
(*1 Jn.* belongs to the 'pre-gnostic' stage; similarly R. Law,
The Tests of Life: a study of the First Epistle of St. John,
Edinburgh, 1909, pp.25-38, esp. 37f.); against W.G. Kümmel,
op. cit., p.442 (the writer of *1 Jn.* is resisting a 'developed
form' of gnosticism).
/4/   See further S.S. Smalley, *John: Evangelist and Interpreter*
(Exeter, 1978), esp. pp.138-48.
/5/   *Cf.* S.S. Smalley, 'Diversity and Development in John',
NTS 17 (1970-1), pp.276-92, esp. 278-85.
/6/   *Jn.* 10: 30; 14: 28b, *et al.*
/7/   *Jn.* 13: 34; 17: 11, *et al. Cf.* E. Schweizer, 'The
Concept of the Church in the Gospel and Epistles of St. John',
in A.J.B. Higgins (ed.), *New Testament Essays: studies in
memory of Thomas Walter Manson, 1893-1958* (Manchester, 1959),
pp.230-45.
/8/   C.H. Dodd, 'The First Epistle of John and the Fourth
Gospel', *BJRL* 21 (1937), pp.129-56; also *The Johannine Epistles,*
pp.xlvii-lvi.
/9/   Certainly the Gospel and letters of John are closer
together than either of these to the Apocalypse; although even
there it is possible to detect subtle but real affinities. On
the latter point see S.S. Smalley, 'John and the Apocalypse',
Orita (Ibadan Journal of Religious Studies) 2 (1968), pp.29-42.

/10/   This dating is not unreasonable if the Fourth Gospel may
be assigned to a period c. AD 85; so S.S. Smalley, *John:
Evangelist and Interpreter*, pp.82-4. But see J.A.T. Robinson,
Redating the New Testament (London ,1976), pp.254-311 (the
letters and the final version of the Gospel of John - in that
order - were all written before AD 70).

/11/   The obscurity of this verse, to which the MS variations
bear testimony, does not affect its basically elevated
christological content. *Cf.* the exegesis of C.H. Dodd, *The
Johannine Epistles*, pp.119f.

/12/   See further the table below. Equally, the reference in
such passages need not be to *either* extreme; it could be to
the standard confession, expected from any believer, of the
Christhood of Jesus. It is noteworthy that in 2:22b and 23a
the antichrist is not characterised as 'he who denies that
Jesus is the Christ (so 2:22a), but merely as 'he who denies the
Son' (*bis*). Similarly, and consequently, the true Christian is
described in 2:23b as 'he who confesses the Son'. See further
note 16, below.

/13/   *Cf. Jn.* 14:10, and note 11 above. The identity of Jesus
and God seems to be in mind in this passage, rather than the
distinction between God and Jesus in terms of the Son's humanity.

/14/   With *1 Jn.* 5:8, *cf.* 4:2b. However, the ultimate
attestation here is God's, and this is to the (divine) Sonship
of Jesus (*cf.* verses 10-12). Note that in John's Gospel the
baptism of Jesus revealed that he was God's Son (*Jn.* 1:32-4),
and his death was a manifestation of his true kingship (19:19-22,
30). See further on this passage J.L. Houlden, *A Commentary
on the Johannine Epistles* (London, 1973), pp.125-32.

/15/   Note the 'high' christological description in *1 Jn.* 5:
20b, 'God's Son Jesus *Christ*'.

/16/   *Cf. 1 Jn.* 5:20b, c. Similarly, the confession required
of the believer at 4:3 is (according to the best witnesses)
simply an open confession of 'Jesus', rather than (as in 4:2)
an acknowledgement of 'Jesus who has come in the *flesh*'. As
Mrs. Judith M. Lieu, of Birmingham University, has pointed out
to me, the Greek of 4:2 (using the accusative and a participle
with ὁμολογεῖν, rather than an accusative and infinitive - as
when Polycarp quotes this verse in *Phil.* 7 - or a ὅτι clause)
is in any case unusual. As it stands, 4:2 could be taken as a
straightforward description of Jesus, rather than as the heart
of a confession *about* him. Note also that some verses in *1 Jn.*
appear to refer to *both* postulated heresies 'in parallel', one
in each half of the verse. *Cf.* 3:5 - 'he appeared to take away
sins' (anti-docetic); 'in him there is no sin' (anti-adoptionist).

/17/ *Cf.* J.L. Houlden, *op. cit.*, pp.1-20.
/18/ *Contra* B.F. Westcott, *op. cit.*, p.xxxiv. On Ebionism
(the evidence for which is conflicting) see J. Daniélou, *A
History of Early Christian Doctrine before the Council of Nicea,
vol.1: The Theology of Jewish Christianity* (ET London, 1964),
pp.55-64. Confusingly, but - in the light of the thesis
advanced in this article - perhaps significantly, Cerinthus
himself was in the end identified with the Ebionite position!
See further J.A.T. Robinson, 'The Destination and Purpose of
the Johannine Epistles', in *id., Twelve New Testament Studies*
(London, 1962), pp.134-6, and the literature there cited. As
Dr. Robinson reminds us, however, we need not assume that
Judaism and gnosticism belong to different worlds (*ibid.*, p.136).
/19/ If the writer of *1 Jn.* were speaking to a situation in
which *two* heresies were abroad, this would account not only
for his balanced christology, but also for his stress on love
and unity (3:11-18; 4:7-21, *et al.*). *Cf.* the approach of the
fourth evangelist, outlined above. This might also account for
the more theocentric character of *1 Jn.*, compared with the
Fourth Gospel. Possibly the later writer was less willing to
lay himself open to christological misunderstanding!
/20/ By the time of *2 Jn.*, docetism seems to have gained the
upper hand over adoptionist heresy (see verse 7); and when
3 Jn. appeared, the final schism between orthodoxy and (docetic)
heresy had evidently taken place (see verses 9f.) - although the
drift from the Johannine church (on *either* heretical count?)
had apparently begun earlier (see *1 Jn.* 2:19). Against the view
that the writer of *1 Jn.* was addressing specific readers, see
W.G. Kümmel, *op. cit.*, p. 437 (the 'entirety of Christianity'
is in view).

Stephen in Lucan Perspective

Graham Stanton,
University of London,
King's College,
Strand,
London WC2R 2LS

Of the many puzzling passages in *Acts*, chapters 6 and 7
have good claims to be considered as the most enigmatic. They
have teased scholars for a very long time. Not surprisingly,
it was F.C. Baur who, in 1829, made the first significant
attempt to grapple with the historical and theological problems
raised by these chapters /1/. Baur was well aware of the
difficulties posed by *Acts* 1-5, but he had no doubts about the
historicity of the speeches and felt that with Stephen and the
Hellenists Luke was at last on firm historical ground.

In this paper I shall say very little about the origin of
the speech in chapter 7 and I shall not attempt to offer a
historical reconstruction of Stephen's teaching. I want to
explore a further point made by Baur. Baur claimed that there
are two kinds of apologetic speech in *Acts*, one of which
believes that Christianity is to be reconciled with the Jews
(Peter's speeches) and the other doubts whether the Jews can
be converted (Stephen's speech). I wish to argue that Baur
set scholarly study of these chapters on the wrong track by
insisting that Stephen's speech was *unlike* the other speeches;
on the other hand, Baur's observation that parts of *Acts* do
reflect apologetic vis à vis Judaism is correct.

Since Baur's day scholars have pondered over the Hellenists,
the seven, Stephen's opponents, the nature of the OT textual
traditions on which the speech has drawn, the so-called trial,
the reference to the Son of Man, and the extent to which Luke
has used sources in these two chapters. But even though
opinion has been deeply divided on all these issues, scholars
have drawn a whole series of bold conclusions about Stephen's
place in the development of early Christianity. A few scholars

have suggested that Stephen was a solitary figure among early
Christian leaders /2/. Much more frequently, Stephen has been
linked with a particular group in the early church. He has
been associated with parts of *Matthew* /3/, with some of the
material behind *Mark* /4/ with Q /5/, and with the Fourth
Gospels /6/. Many scholars have seen Stephen as the precursor
of Paul /7/; some have seen him as closely related to the
opponents with whom Paul is disputing in *II Corinthians* /8/.
Others have linked Stephen with the *Epistle to the Hebrews* /9/.
But that is not the end of the matter. Stephen, it has been
suggested, was sympathetic to Samaritan views /10/. It has
even been argued that the speech in *ch*. 7 stems originally from
James, and represents Jewish Christian theology in Jerusalem /11/.
One is tempted to say in desperation; will the real Stephen
please stand up /12/!

In almost all of these discussions two important
preliminary questions have rarely been asked and even more
rarely been faced squarely: what does Luke understand the
teaching of Stephen to have been and how are these two chapters
to be related to Luke's own emphases in his two volumes? All
too often either the speech in *ch*. 7 has not been studied
alongside the other speeches in *Acts*, or 7.2-50 has been
separated from *ch*. 6, or both!   M. Simon quoted approvingly
W.L. Knox's view that the first step towards understanding
Stephen's message is to separate the speech from the story as
a whole /13/. In his important article on the Hellenists, the
seven and Stephen, M. Hengel concentrates on chapter 6 and
makes very little use of the speech /14/. In the first two
editions of his book, *Die Missionsreden der Apostelgeschichte*
U. Wilckens completely by-passed Stephen's speech /15/, as did
E. Schweizer in his influential and perceptive article on the
structure of the speeches in Acts /16/. E. Haenchen seems to
have been very uneasy about *ch*. 7: in his commentary he argued
that Luke had used a non-polemical, edifying Palestinian homily
into which he inserted a small handful of verses. However, in
a short discussion of more recent scholarly work which was
added to later editions of the commentary, Haenchen conceded in
passing that he thought that the speech was rather more
important for Luke's theology than he had believed earlier /17/.
In this respect, at least, Haenchen was on the right track,
though he was unable to follow this path very far.

I wish to challenge the frequent assumption that many
problems melt away if the narratives about Stephen are separated

from the speech. The speech in *ch.* 7 is much longer than any
of the other speeches in Acts: it is as long as the major
speeches in chapters 2 and 13 put together. It takes up one
twentieth of Luke's second volume and it must have been
included by him for quite definite reasons. Stephen's speech
may seem to some modern readers to be a rather tedious recital
of OT history, but from Luke's point of view it is a most
important part of his work.

Acts 7 is a 'set-piece' speech comparable with the 'set-
piece' speeches in *chs.* 2, 3, 4, 10, 13, 14, 17. Since Luke
relates his speeches most carefully to their contexts, he is
likely to have done so here. Although there are good grounds
for supposing that in *ch.* 7, as well as in the other speeches,
Luke has made use of traditional material, here, as elsewhere,
the speech reflects Luke's own style and theological
emphases /18/. However extensive Luke's source or sources may
have been, he has covered his tracks with such great skill that
it is entirely in order to look at the Stephen material, as it
were, in Lucan perspective.

*

The accusations made against Stephen in 6.11, 13f. are
often said to be dealt with inadequately or only in part in the
speech /19/. As far as I am aware, few if any writers have
asked about *Luke's* intentions in listing the accusations in
6.11 and 13f. Does Luke intend his readers to take these
verses as an *accurate* report of what Stephen said? In verse 11
we are told that Stephen's opponents secretly instigated
(ὑπέβαλον) men to state that they had heard his blasphemous
words against Moses and God. And in v.13 Stephen's accusers
are said explicitly to have been *false* witnesses. Surely Luke
intends the reader to understand that these accusations are
unfair! Surely the *false* witnesses do not give an accurate
account of the teaching of Stephen!

This is confirmed by the way Luke presents accusations
elsewhere in *Luke-Acts*. The accusations brought against the
apostles in the early chapters and especially those brought
against Jesus and Paul either have no truth in them at all, or
else they need to be modified very considerably. Luke usually
presents accusations of opponents in direct speech and rebuts
or modifies them strongly with a speech.

At *Luke* 23.2ff. three accusations are made against Jesus
before Pilate: 'We found this man perverting our nation, and
forbidding us to give tribute to Caesar, and saying that he
himself is Christ a king.' The reader of the earlier chapters
of Luke's Gospel knows well that these accusations are not
entirely fair or accurate.

In Athens Paul is accused of presenting 'new teaching'
(*Acts* 17.9); the speech which follows shows that Paul's
teaching is not entirely *new*. In the later chapters in *Acts*
Paul is frequently wrongly accused and the reader is left in
no doubt that the accusations which are being made are false.
Acts 21 is especially important. Paul is told by James and the
elders that Jews 'who have believed' have heard that Paul
teaches Jews among the Gentiles to forsake Moses. A few
verses later we are told that Jews from Asia accuse Paul of
teaching men everywhere 'against the people and the law and
this place; moreover he also brought Greeks into the temple,
and he has defiled this holy place.' (21.28) The accusations
made here against Paul are strikingly similar to the accusations
made against Stephen. The verbal agreement is impressive and
suggests that Luke's own hand can be discerned:
compare *Acts* 6.13; ὁ ἄνθρωπος οὗτος οὐ παύεται λαλῶν ῥήματα
κατὰ τοῦ τόπου τοῦ ἁγίου (τούτου s.v.l.)καὶ τοῦ νόμου with
Acts 21.28; οὗτός ἐστιν ὁ ἄνθρωπος ὁ κατὰ τοῦ λαοῦ καὶ τοῦ
νόμου καὶ τοῦ τόπου τούτου πάντας πανταχῇ διδάσκων ... καὶ
κεκοίνωκεν τὸν ἅγιον τόπον τοῦτον. The reader of *Acts* 21 is
left in no doubt at all that these accusations against Paul are
quite unwarranted.

These parallels suggest that in *Acts* 6 Luke considers that
the accusations against Stephen are mischievous - and indeed
that is the tone of the narrative. On the one hand Stephen
speaks τῇ σοφίᾳ καὶ τῷ πνεύματι (6.10), while his opponents
instigate men secretly to bring accusations against him; the
opponents are false witnesses, Stephen (as 22.20 makes explicit)
is the true witness.

So the attentive reader of *Luke-Acts* expects that these
accusations against Stephen will be shown to be false or at
least misleading. And that is what I take the speech to be
doing, at least in part /19/.

                                 *

Did Stephen attack Moses and the law, as his accusers alleged? Of course not. In his reply Stephen places Moses on a pedestal and devotes half of the speech to him. Verse 37 refers to the prophet like Moses whom God would raise up - Luke's readers will not miss the Christological allusion, as this has been prepared for at 3.22.

Moses, Stephen insists (in v.38), received the law (λόγια ζῶντα) to give to God's people - to us (ἡμῖν) says Stephen, carefully including himself. A number of manuscripts (including Χ and B) read ὑμῖν, but in view of the references in verses 38 and 39 to οἱ πατέρες ἡμῶν this reading is almost certainly an example of the frequent scribal confusion between ἡμῖν and ὑμῖν which were pronounced alike /20/.

As we shall see a little later, Luke aligns Stephen carefully *with* Moses: Stephen, like Moses, the prophets, Jesus (and Paul) is rejected by part of Israel. So the accusation that Stephen spoke blasphemous words against Moses (6.11) is plainly ridiculous. Stephen returns to the law in the final words of the speech: the law was delivered by angels, but it was not kept. So how can Stephen be said by his opponents to have spoken against the law (6.13)? How could he have said that Jesus would change the customs delivered by Moses (6.14) when he emphasised that it was his opponents (and, by implication, not he himself) who had failed to keep the law? So much for the accusations concerning the law. In Luke's view neither Stephen nor Paul rejected the law: at 25.8 Paul rebuts the similar accusations which have been made against him.

But what about the other accusation made against Stephen? Did he speak κατὰ τοῦ τόπου τοῦ ἁγίου (6.13)? Did Stephen say that Jesus would destroy the temple (καταλύσει τὸν τόπον τοῦτον 6.14) /21/? This is a very much more difficult question than Stephen's (and Luke's) attitude to the law. I have suggested that accusations in *ch*. 6 are intended by Luke to be seen by his readers as mischievous, as indeed the speech shows the accusation about the law to have been. How, then, is the reply in the speech to the accusation about the temple to be interpreted? Is this accusation simply conceded to be correct? It is not impossible that the speech accepts that one of the accusations is valid but that the other is invalid /22/, but this would not be consistent with Luke's methods elsewhere.

Nearly all exegetes accept that in the speech Stephen
attacks the temple, even though elsewhere in Luke's two volumes
the temple is frequently placed in a favourable light and there
is hardly a trace of a negative attitude. As soon as we look
at *Acts* 6 and 7 in Lucan perspective, Stephen's attitude to the
temple becomes a particularly difficult question.

There would seem to be three possible explanations: (i)
Luke has retained without modification a source which contains
a very different attitude to the temple to his own; (ii) Luke's
own attitude is not quite as consistently positive as I have
just indicated; (iii) the final verses of Stephen's speech
should not be construed as a full-scale assault on the temple
and an acceptance of the accusation of 6.13f.

The first possibility is undoubtedly an attractive
solution and it cannot easily be ruled out. However, as we
shall see, so much of *Acts* 6 and 7 can be seen as thoroughly
Lucan that it would be surprising if Luke had failed to alter
such a discordant note.

The second explanation has been set out by J.C. O'Neill.
He suggests that in Luke-Acts there are several hints that the
Temple is to be destroyed and that piety centred on the temple
will fail. 'Paul is arrested and accused of profaning the
Temple at the very moment when he is paying particular
attention to its purificatory requirements. (21.21ff.) Just as
God had told him to go to the Gentiles as he was praying in the
Temple, so he is arrested and begins his fateful journey to
Rome when he is about to complete the days of purification. It
seems that God himself is driving Christians out of the Temple,
and showing that they cannot confine themselves to its
limitations' /23/. But this is surely over-subtle. In the
final chapters in Acts Luke takes pains to emphasise that Paul
did` not attack the temple or the law. At 25.8 Paul roundly
declares that he has not committed any offence against either
the law of the Jews or the Temple or Caesar. In the next
chapter Paul tells Agrippa that he was seized by the Jews *in
the temple* (26.21) and in the final chapter Paul explains to
the leaders of the Jews in Rome that he had done nothing
against the people or the customs of the fathers (28.17,19).
Luke's presentation of Paul's attitude is so consistent that
O'Neill's own question is pertinent: 'If Luke was content to
show the church slowly discovering what God really meant about
the Temple, why did he bother to construct an elaborate

foretelling of this and insert it so early' /24/? O'Neill's
own resolution of the difficulty is drastic: in the section 6.8-
8.3 the four references to Jesus are insecurely anchored and
were Christian interpretative additions to a source in which
Stephen was not a Christian. But the more strongly Lucan
redaction of a source (or sources) is appealed to, the more
difficult it becomes to understand why Luke has placed an
attack on the temple *at this point* in his narrative.

Even though the third solution runs counter to the usual
exegesis of 7.44-50, it must be considered carefully. I wish
to suggest tentatively that Luke's intention has frequently
been misunderstood: in Luke's eyes at least, Stephen did not
reject totally the temple and the law. The speech is intended
by Luke (whatever the original intention of any earlier
tradition may have been) to show that *both* accusations against
Stephen were misrepresentations. However, the speech is not
just intended to provide a reply to the accusations; as we
shall see, the main theme is a counter charge which runs through
the whole speech, steadily becoming more prominent as the
speech proceeds to the climax of vv.51-53.

At the end of the speech Stephen rounds on his accusers,
and, not surprisingly, arouses their fierce opposition. Two
related criticisms are made by Stephen: his accusers have
resisted God's Holy Spirit (ἀεὶ τῳ Πνεύματι τῷ Ἁγίῳ ἀντιπίπτετε)
and disobeyed God's law; the betrayal and killing of Jesus was
all of a piece with the persecution and killing of the prophets.
We shall return to the latter of these two themes later.

Stephen's insistence on the disobedience of part of Israel
is, in effect, a summary of the argument of the two sections of
the speech which immediately precede the climax of vv.51-53.
These two sections are strikingly similar. Both conclude with
an explicit citation of Scripture (7.42f. and 49f.) which is
very closely related in each case to the immediately preceding
narrative. In both cases the Scripture citation merely
underlines the charge which precedes it. Verse 50, οὐχὶ ἡ χείρ
μου ἐποίησεν ταῦτα πάντα; not only marks the climax and the key
to vv. 44-50, but the work of God's hands (v.49f.) is set in
stark contrast to the work of men's hands (v.48) and to the
delight of those who rejected Moses and rejoiced in the works
of their own hands (v.41) and who worshipped the figures which
they made (v.43).

These two sections, then, are constructed in the same way
and are so closely related to one another that we expect to
find that they are making a similar point. In the first
section (7.39ff.), those who disobeyed and rejected Moses not
only offered a sacrifice to an idol and delighted in the work of
their own hands: they disobeyed God, with the result that God's
promise to Abraham that his posterity would *worship* him in the
promised land could not be fulfilled (cf. verse 7 and verse 42).
Amos 5.25ff. is not cited from the LXX to argue *against*
sacrifices: the point is rather that in the wilderness period
Israel offered sacrifices to idols rather than *to God;* idols
which they made were *worshipped* (προσκυνεῖν is added to the LXX
citation) rather than God.

The second of these two related sections (44-50) also
insists that God does not dwell in objects made with hands
(ἀλλ' οὐχ ὁ ῞Υψιστος ἐν χειροποιήτοις κατοικεῖ). The argument
of this section turns on v.50, the final clause in the citation
from *Isaiah* 61.1-2: οὐχὶ ἡ χείρ μου ἐποίησεν ταῦτα πάντα; the
work of *God's* hands is contrasted strongly with the work of
men's hands (cf. v.49f. with v.48). Lake and Cadbury note
that *Is.* 66.1 is also used in *Barnabas* 16.2, but they fail to
observe that *Barnabas* does not include the next verse in *Is.*66,
the verse to which I have just referred as crucial to Stephen's
argument (v.50) /25/. *Isaiah* 66.1 is cited in Barnabas as
part of an extremely vigorous anti-temple polemic which is
completely different in its argument and in its tone from
Acts 7 /26/. *Acts* 7.44-50 is not an attack on the temple, as
so many exegetes have assumed. There is no implication that
in building the temple Solomon was disobedient. The point is
rather that ὁ ῞Υψιστος (the term chosen is surely significant
here) does not *dwell* ἐν χειροποιήτοις (v.48) for his hand has
made heaven and earth. In the light of the related preceding
section the implication would seem to be not that the temple
was a ghastly mistake (any more than sacrifices were) but that
in supposing that ὁ ῞Υψιστος dwells ἐν χειροποιήτοις he has not
been truly *worshipped* and has been spurned. The argument of
the passage is then picked up immediately in verse 51b, ὑμεῖς
ἀεὶ τῷ Πνεύματι τῷ ῾Αγίῳ ἀντιπίπτετε, ὡς οἱ πατέρες ὑμῶν καὶ
ὑμεῖς.

This exegesis is advanced tentatively. Not all of the
difficulties of these verses have been solved. Some may well
have arisen as a result of Luke's inadequate redaction of a
source. In particular, it is not easy to see why the period of

the σκηνὴ τοῦ μαρτυρίου is apparently compared so unfavourably
with the period of the temple. But on the interpretation just
offered the speech does confirm (as we expect from Luke's
methods elsewhere) that the accusations against Stephen were
mischievous. An attack on false worship rather than on the
temple as such is more consistent with Luke's attitude
throughout his two volumes. As we shall see shortly, Luke
links Stephen and Paul so very closely that he is unlikely to
have assumed that they had a radically different attitude to
the temple, especially when he shows very clearly that they
shared a similar attitude to the law.

*

In vv.51-53, which form the climax of the speech, the
accusations against Stephen are not forgotten, but Stephen's
counter-charge is much more prominent. The ire of Stephen's
opponents is not roused by a repudiation of the temple,
(contra E. Haenchen and many other exegetes) but by his attack
on the stubbornness of part of God's people who even persecuted
some of the prophets and killed those who announced the advent
of the δίκαιος. But this is not a theme which emerges for
the first time at the conclusion of the speech, for it holds
the whole speech together.

In the light of the accusation that Stephen spoke
'blasphemous words against Moses and God' (6.11) and 'words
against this holy place and the law' (6.13) the fact that
Abraham is Stephen's starting point is significant. Abraham
is referred to as 'our father': Stephen insists that he and
his opponents share Abraham as their father. This is more than
captatio benevolentiae. One of the features of the speech is
the repeated use of 'our father' or 'our fathers' to refer to
Israel's leaders of old. This happens thirteen times in the
speech, making the switch at the climax in verses 51 and 52
to 'your fathers' especially striking /27/. Stephen aligns
himself with part of Israel, but not with the whole of Israel.

The phrase 'our fathers' is also used at 3.13 (Peter's
speech), 5.30 (Peter and the apostles), 13.17 and 32 (Paul),
15.10 (Peter), 22.14 (Paul, quoting Ananias), and 26.6 (Paul)/28/.
In Paul's final statement, which comes as the climax to the
whole book, there is an equally dramatic switch from 'our
fathers', the usual phrase to which the reader has become
accustomed, to 'your fathers' (28.25): Luke makes Paul and

Stephen speak with the same voice.

I take the central point of vv.2-8 to be God's two-fold
promise of the land: in verse 5, in spite of the fact that
Abraham did not have a child, and in verse 7, in spite of
Israel's enslavement in Egypt /29/.

The short summary of the Joseph traditions is simply a
linking section. Why should Luke not summarise the story of
God's people, for it was his story too? It is noteworthy that
in Paul's speech in the synagogue in Pisidian Antioch, where
there is another sketch of the history of Israel, the
patriachal period is covered in one verse, 13.17. So Luke
devotes these few verses to Joseph: there is no need to search
for any deeper significance /30/.

Verse 17 is especially important: here Luke reminds the
reader most carefully of God's promise of the land to Abraham.
And since it is through Moses that God fulfilled his promise,
Moses is placed on a pedestal and approximately half of the
speech is devoted to him. Since Moses is treated so thoroughly
here, it comes as no surprise to find that he is not even
mentioned by name in Paul's historical sketch in chapter 13.

The major theme of the whole speech, the 'rejection' theme,
emerges explicitly at verse 25. As the following verses make
clear, Moses is rejected by his own brethren, 'the sons of
Israel'. In verses 35, 37 and 38 Moses is referred to with
touches of Lucan rhetorical artistry: and this is precisely
the point at which the argument of the speech begins to gather
momentum: τοῦτον τὸν Μωυσῆν ... οὗτός ἐστιν ὁ Μωυσῆς ... οὗτός
ἐστιν ὁ γενόμενος. The importance of Moses could hardly have
been underlined more firmly: he is portrayed as a prophet, sent
by God to his people, but rejected. The lengthy part of the
speech devoted to Moses is directly related to Stephen's final
denunciations of his opponents in verses 51-53.

The first half of the speech is not a tedious recital of
OT history which shows 'no purpose whatsoever' /31/, but part
and parcel of the argument. The speech as a whole is concerned
with the contrast between, on the one hand, Abraham, Joseph
(God was with him, verse 9), Jesus the δίκαιος, Stephen himself,
(and, later, Paul) and, on the other hand, that section of
Israel which rejected Moses, the prophets, Jesus, Stephen (and,
later, Paul). But it is not just God's messengers who have been

rejected; it is God himself who has been opposed (v.51b). God
promised Abraham that his posterity would possess the land and
worship God in the land (v.7). God fulfilled his promise
through Moses, but part of Israel did not truly worship God
either in the wilderness period or later when the temple was
built. Stephen's accusers oppose the Holy Spirit, but in stark
contrast Stephen himself, full of the Holy Spirit, gazes into
heaven and sees the glory of God and Jesus standing at the
right hand of God (v.55). In short, God faithfully fulfils
his promises, but part of his people consistently fails to
serve and to worship him; Israel is split into two: some reject
(later in Acts it is clear that this is the vast majority, in
spite of Luke's accounts of mass conversions of Jews), some
accept.

Peter's speech in chapter three is concerned with similar
themes. Peter, like Stephen, stresses that he and his hearers
share the God of their Father Abraham. Both speeches stress
that Jesus the δίκαιος, whose coming was foretold by the
prophets, was rejected and killed. In chapter three those who
reject the prophet like Moses will be rejected or destroyed
utterly *from the people* (3.23). It is not a question of God
rejecting the *whole* of Israel, but of a split within Israel,
precisely as in ch.7. These two speeches are not unalike, in
spite of obvious differences: both are full of Lucan emphases.

*

I turn, finally, to the relationship of the Stephen
material to the rest of *Luke-Acts*. I have stressed that the
speech and the accusations must not be separated. I have also
suggested that the speech should be studied alongside the other
speeches in *Acts*. Luke's selection of material in the speeches
is not haphazard: some points mentioned in the speeches in
chapters 2, 3 and 4 are developed much more fully in ch.7.
Some of the OT material given in detail in ch.7 is not repeated
in ch.13. It is clear that whether or not Luke has drawn on
earlier sources or traditions, the speeches have been
constructed with great skill.

But it is possible to go further than this. *Acts* 6 and 7
form an integral part of one of Luke's main themes. The
prophets sent by God to his people were rejected and killed,
as Luke emphasises not only in Stephen's speech but also at
Luke 11.49ff, using Q material. Jesus, Stephen and Paul were

all rejected - mischievous charges were brought against them.
The reader is left in no doubt of their innocence. They did
not pervert or mislead God's people, they did not *reject* the
law and the temple root and branch. As we have seen, it is
striking just how similar are the accusations made against
Jesus, Stephen and Paul - surely we catch here an echo of
Jewish attacks on Christianity in Luke's own day which Luke is
most anxious to rebut. In his two volumes Luke is concerned
to stress that Christianity should be seen in Roman eyes as
harmless. It is also clear (and this point has been noted much
less frequently) that Luke has pondered deeply on Israel's
rejection of the Gospel and on the main lines of Jewish
apologetic and polemic.

Luke also emphasises that God's cause triumphs in spite of
Jewish rejection. Jesus is denied and killed, but God raises
him from the dead. Stephen is rejected and killed, but God
triumphs. The Stephen material comes at a most important point
in Luke's story of the triumphant spread of the Christian
movement. The persecution which arose following the death of
Stephen leads directly to the next stage in Luke's story, 8.4
to 11.18, as 8.1, 8.4 and 9.31 make clear. The section of
Acts which then follows, 11.19 to 15.35, is also linked
directly to the Stephen material by Luke's careful note in 11.19.

The reader of *Acts* discovers that Gamaliel the Pharisee
was correct: this plan or undertaking of the followers of Jesus
is not of men, for it did not fail - it is of God, and could
not be overthrown. Finally, Paul is similarly wrongly accused
and rejected: the reader knows full well that he will suffer a
similar fate to Jesus and Stephen. But in spite of rejection
by the Jews the Christian cause will continue to triumph.

In this article I have attempted to relate the accusations
against Stephen in ch.6 to the speech in ch.7. I have argued
that these two chapters do not fit awkwardly into Luke's
overall argument, for it is possible to see Stephen in Lucan
perspective. I have taken a further step more tentatively and
have suggested that the usual account of Stephen's attitude to
the temple is mistaken, for even this is not out of line with
Luke's own attitude. Whether my exegesis of vv.44-50 is
plausible or not, it is clear that the main theme of the speech
is thoroughly Lucan: the story of God's people is a story of
God who fulfils his promises to his people; even though part of
his people has constantly rejected God and his messengers, God's
cause triumphs ultimately.

The main reason for the inclusion of the Stephen material
in Luke's two volumes has been expounded along two very
different lines. Some have argued that Luke intends to stress
that God's people must always be on the march and must pull up
their stakes as Abraham did and leave national particularism
behind. This is often taken to be the point of the opening
verses of the speech /31/. But Abram's journey into Egypt,
which would have been grist to this mill, is passed over in
silence. And there is no attempt to hide the fact that God's
promise to Abraham that his people would possess the land *was*
fulfilled - indeed fulfilment of the promise is stressed /32/.

Nor is the Stephen material given such prominence by Luke
because he wants to stress that Stephen's death marks the final
rejection of Israel and the turning to the Gentiles. Stephen's
death leads to persecution, but the Hellenists do not move out
immediately into Gentile territory. Even at 11.19, after the
whole Cornelius episode and the Gentiles' Pentecost, the
Hellenists, except for a minority, are speaking to Jews only.

I have tried to consider *Acts* 6 and 7 as part of Luke's
overall purpose in his two volumes. I do not wish to suggest
that nothing can usefully be said about the historical Stephen
and his teaching. But before we can even begin to consider
Stephen's place in early Christianity and the relationship of
his theological views to Paul's, we must learn to look at the
Stephen material in Lucan perspective. For Luke, Stephen's
death is important because it marks the first involvement of
Paul with the Christian movement - and Luke reminds his readers
of this at 22.20. But for Luke the even more important point
is that Stephen and Paul shared the fate of Jesus; neither
Jesus, nor Stephen, nor Paul ever intended to alienate Israel.
Luke's Stephen is the precursor of Luke's Paul.

NOTES

/1/   See W.G. Kümmel, *The New Testament: the History of the
Investigation of its Problems*. (E.Tr. London, 1973), pp.127 ff.
and the references given there; see also M. Hengel, "Zwischen
Jesus und Paulus: Die 'Hellenisten', die Sieben und Stephanus
(Apg. 6,1-15; 7,54-8,3)", *ZThK* 72 (1975), pp.151-206 again
with references.

/2/   M. Simon, *St. Stephen and the Hellenists in the Primitive
Church* (London, 1958); M.H. Scharlemann, *Stephen: A Singular
Saint,* (Rome, 1968). In the second edition of his *The Theology
of Acts in its Historical Setting* (London, 1970) J.C. O'Neill
suggests that Stephen was not a Christian; the references to
Jesus in 6.8 - 8.3 are taken as later additions (probably by
Luke himself) to the source. (pp. 87ff).
/3/   E.P. Blair, *Jesus in the Gospel of Matthew,* (New York,
1960).
/4/   R. Scroggs, "The Earliest Hellenistic Christianity" in
Religions in Antiquity: Essays in Memory of E.R. Goodenough
ed. J. Neusner (Leiden, 1968), pp. 176-206.
/5/   T. Boman, *Die Jesus-Überlieferung im Lichte der neueren
Volkskunde* (Göttingen, 1967), pp. 112ff. Mr. R. Piper (one of
my research students) is investigating the relationship between
Stephen and Q in his forthcoming dissertation on wisdom
traditions in Q.
/6/   O. Cullmann, *The Johannine Circle* (E.Tr. London, 1976).
/7/   See especially M. Hengel, *art. cit.* Hengel concludes
thus: "Sie (die Hellenisten) allein kann man im vollen   Sinne
des Wortes die 'vorpaulinische hellenistische Gemeinde' nennen".
/8/   G. Friedrich, "Die Gegner des Paulus im II Korintherbrief",
Abraham unser Vater ed. O. Betz, M. Hengel, P. Schmidt, (Leiden,
1963), pp. 181-215.
/9/   W. Manson, *The Epistle to the Hebrews* (London, 1951),
chapter II.
/10/   A. Spiro, "Stephen's Samaritan Background", in J. Munck,
The Acts of the Apostles (New York, 1967), pp. 285-300;
M.H. Scharlemann, *Stephen: A Singular Saint* (Rome, 1968),
pp. 36-51. See also R. Pummer, "The Samaritan Pentateuch and
the New Testament" *NTS* 22 (1975-6), pp. 441-3; E. Richard,
"Acts 7: An Investigation of the Samaritan Evidence", *CBQ* 39
(1977), pp. 190-208; R.J. Coggins, "The Samaritans and Acts"
forthcoming in *NTS*.
/11/   H.J. Schoeps, *Theologie und Geschichte des
Judenchristentums,* (Tübingen, 1949).
/12/   For a brief history of research on *Acts* 6 and 7, see
J. Kilgallen, *The Stephen Speech: A Literary and Redactional
Study of Acts 7.2-53.* (Rome, 1976), pp. 3-26. In addition
to the literature cited by Kilgallen, see G. Stemberger, 'Die
Stephanusrede (Apg 7) und die jüdische Tradition' in ed.
A. Fuchs, *Jesus in der Verkündigung der Kirche* (Freistadt, 1976),
pp. 154-174. R. Pesch, *Die Vision des Stephanus* (Stuttgart,
1966); W.D. Davies, *The Gospel of the Land* (Berkeley and London,
1974), pp. 267ff.; E. Grässer, "Acta-Forschung seit 1960", *ThR*

41 (1976) pp. 141-194, 259-90.

/13/ M. Simon, *Stephen*, p. 3f., quoting W.L. Knox, *Acts*, pp. 23f and 72.

/14/ M. Hengel, 'Zwischen Jesus und Paulus'.

/15/ U. Wilckens, *Die Missionsreden der Apostelgeschichte* (Neukirchen-Vluyn, 1961 and 1962). Prof. S.G. Wilson has kindly pointed out to me that in the third edition, 1974, (to which I have not had access) Wilckens does include a discussion of Stephen's speech.

/16/ E. Schweizer, 'Concerning the Speeches in Acts' in *Studies in Luke-Acts*, ed. L.E. Keck and J.L. Martyn (London, 1968), pp. 208-216.

/17/ E. Haenchen, *The Acts of the Apostles* (Oxford, 1971), E. Tr. of the 14th German edition (1965), p. 128.

/18/ See especially J. Kilgallen's appendix, 'Some Literary Traits in the speech of Stephen', *The Stephen Speech, op. cit.*, pp. 121-163. Kilgallen fails to refer to stylistic traits which many scholars have taken as *not* typically Lucan.

/19/ Compare Lake and Cadbury's opening comment on the speech in *Beginnings of Christianity* Vol. IV (London, 1933), p. 69: 'This is not a rebuttal of the charges brought against him'.

/20/ See also below, p. 353 where attention is drawn to the importance of the switch in verses 51 and 52 from 'our father' or 'our fathers' (used 13 times in the speech) to 'your fathers'.

/21/ The accusation in 6.11 that Stephen spoke blasphemous words against *God* may also refer to the temple.

/22/ Cf. B.S. Easton, *Early Christianity* (London, 1955), pp. 115-118; also Lake and Cadbury, *Beginnings of Christianity*, Vol. IV, p. 69.

/23/ J.C. O'Neill, *The Theology of Acts, op. cit.* p. 81.

/24/ *Ibid.*, p. 88.

/25/ *Beginnings of Christianity*, Vol. IV, p. 81f.

/26/ Lake and Cadbury note that both OT passages (*Amos* 5.25 ff. and *Is.* 66.1) are quoted by Justin, *Dialogue* 22 and suggest possible use of testimony books. However, (as Haenchen also notes) this is unlikely as the two passages are not cited by Justin in succession and Justin gives the exact source of both quotations. Justin does not include *Is.* 66.2, which clinches the argument in *Acts* 7; *Amos* 5 is used by Justin to make a rather different point.

/27/ 7.38 may possibly be an exception, as ὑμῶν is read by some manuscripts. ἡμῶν, however, fits the context more naturally but could readily have been replaced by ὑμῶν, as the two words were pronounced alike.

/28/ At 3.25 some manuscripts read 'your fathers', but if the
switch from the first person plural to the second person plural
at 28.25 is intentional, the original reading may have been
ἡμῶν (contra B.M. Metzger, A Textual Commentary).
/29/ See N.A. Dahl, 'The Story of Abraham in Luke-Acts' in
Studies in Luke-Acts, op. cit., pp. 142ff.
/30/ J. Kilgallen, op. cit., pp. 46-63 and p. 97, suggests
that Joseph is portrayed as a forerunner of Christ. But if Luke
had intended to use the Joseph traditions typologically surely
this would have been done more explicitly. As H. Conzelmann
notes in his commentary, the sufferings of Joseph are almost
passed over.
/31/ M. Dibelius, Studies in the Acts of the Apostles (London,
1956), p. 168 f.; W. Manson, The Epistle to the Hebrews (London,
1951) chapter II. W.D. Davies, The Gospel and the Land
(Berkeley and London, 1974), pp. 267 ff.
/32/ See J.C. O'Neill, The Theology of Acts, op. cit., p. 80.

St. Paul and Panaetius

R.G. Tanner,
The University of Newcastle,
New South Wales 2308,
AUSTRALIA.

In a master theme study offered in 1973 /1/ I argued, as
against the positions of Sevenster /2/ and Spanneut /3/, that
many passages in St. Paul's epistles suggest that their author
was familiar with Stoic physical theory. Further reflexion
confirms my view that Sevenster's valuable comparison between
the doctrines of Seneca and Paul suffers from its preoccupation
with extracting from the Roman philosopher what he thinks about
issues central to Pauline Christianity and its failure to
examine what remarks about Stoicism of Seneca's day we could
extract from the Pauline writings. Against Spanneut one must
say that though one cannot but agree that une espèce d'osmose /4/
is a very potent way of spreading scientific information, then
as now, one also finds in Paul too much acquaintance with an
elaborated system for a person innocent of systematic studies.

It might well be argued that as *Acts* 9,30 and 12,25 when
taken together indicate that Saul spent four years in Tarsus we
may conclude that he occupied the years AD 37-41 in preparing
himself for missionary work among Gentiles. Such a preparation
would almost certainly have involved study of pagan philosophy.
If so the instruction most readily available in Tarsus was
likely to be Stoic, for the city produced many leaders of that
school. Zeno of Tarsus ruled the Stoic school in Athens after
Chrysippus died in 206 BC, and his pupils included two
subsequent successors to his office, Diogenes of Seleucia and
Antipater of Tarsus, both of whom taught the reforming 'Middle'
Stoic Panaetius of Rhodes and also Boethus of Sidon. Amongst
their pupils at Athens was also Archedemus of Tarsus, who
founded the Stoic school in Babylon, while another prominent
Stoic from Tarsus in a later generation was Athenodorus who
taught Augustus. In the second century AD Tarsus was still a
centre for philosophical teaching, for the Sceptic Herodotus

who taught Sextus Empiricus had classes there. There is thus
some reason to recognise the possibility that Paul obtained
instruction in Greek dogmatic philosophy, particularly Stoicism,
whilst in Tarsus. Indeed, Rudolph Bultmann in 1910 saw evidence
of Stoic-Cynic diatribe in the style of the Pauline epistles /5/.
Today we might attribute this to Stoic impact on the Jewish
thought of the school of Gamaliel rather than to St. Paul's
putative Greek education, but the fact remains that St. Paul can
be shown to exhibit concepts familiar to contemporary Stoics.
Consequently the position taken in this paper is not necessarily
vitiated by the lack of specific intention by Paul to assimilate
his thought to the Stoa. It will be sufficient to show rather
the interpretation a Stoic reader would place upon the text of
the Epistles, and how far such an understanding would dispose
the reader to interpret the Christian Gospel as consonant with
contemporary Stoicism.

        Granting this enquiry is useful, why should we pick on the
Stoicism of Panaetius? We cannot ignore the observation of
Rist: "Although Panaetius was very influential in his day, and
influenced many others, notably Cicero, his period of great
influence was short. The Stoics of the Imperial Age, though
familiar with his work, tend to prefer older authorities.
Hence we find ourselves in the position of having only a quite
small number of texts where the actual name of Panaetius occurs.
Yet apart from a few special cases, it is only these texts which
can be used to reconstruct his work" /6/. In the face of this,
why not seek for influence from Posidonius whose fragments are
more numerous, or seek parallels between Seneca and Paul on a
different basis from that employed by Sevenster?

I. PANAETIUS RECONSTRUCTED

        Basically it is my conviction that Panaetius was profoundly
innovative. Certainly his contemporary Boethus of Sidon who
shared Panaetius' disagreement with the doctrine of ἐκπύρωσις
had introduced a different epistemological chain from that of
Zeno /7/.

ZENO	Presentation	Assent	Comprehension	Knowledge
	φαντασία	συγκατάθεσις	κατάληψις	ἐπιστήμη
BOETHUS	Attention	Perception	Effort	Knowledge
	νοῦς	αἴσθησις	ὄρεξις	ἐπιστήμη

In this context νοῦς is employed as the sense found in νοῦν
προσέχειν - "pay attention". Given the problem of rebutting
Carneades' New Academy view that perception was not reliable
because of possible false preconception or faulty observation,
Boethus here appears to introduce *attention* and *effort* as a way
of ensuring reliability of impressions.

Did Panaetius also address himself to this difficulty? I
believe he does so in a passage usually quoted in relation to
εκπύρωσις - Stobaeus *Eclog.* I.20: "Panaetius considers (νομίζει)
the eternity of the universe to be more probable (πιθανώτερον)
and more agreeable to himself (μᾶλλον ἀρέσκουσαν ἑαυτῷ) than
conversion of all substances into fire" /8/.

We may regard νομίζει "I *own, admit, adknowledge* or
consider, as representing the same function as Boethus' νοῦς or
Zeno's φαντασία. But the derived noun is νόμισμα a current coin
(*LSJ,* II), and we find current coin in trade always produces
πίστις or trust in the perceiver or receiver. So the likely
second term from πιθανώτερον is πίστις (*LSJ,* I,1) trust or
belief. Now a coin is acceptable because the providence of man
creates it as a part of the social structure. Though ἀρέσκοντα
can mean placita or opinions, thus LSJ, IV, the usage is not
earlier than Plutarch, two centuries later. The more normal use
of the participle is LSJ, V, "gratifying" or "pleasing". So,
if the sentence is a quotation and not a paraphrase, the word
is likely to mean "gratifying". Now the receiving of coinage
does give pleasure; so if the currency metaphor is being
employed here, it is reasonable to say that pleasure is a
by-criterion of value reinforcing probability. Thus on this
view the Panaetian answer to Carneades is in two parts. First,
objects devised by the cosmic Providence will be designed to
be rightly perceived by the human intelligence, itself also
formed of rational πνευμα and so akin to that Providence.
Secondly, the sympathy of parts of the universe will mean that
any perception in harmony with the structure of the Universe
will be of its own nature spontaneously gratifying, and in
consequence will be shown to be a *right opinion,* rather than
knowledge. We might reasonably expect Panaetius to concede so
far to Carneades as to use the Platonic term for correct sense
impression unchecked by reference to the world of Forms -
ὀρθὴ δόξα.

The suggestion seems borne out by Sext Empiricus *Adv. Dogm.*
XI, 73 (van Straaten 69) "Panaetius says that some pleasure

(ἡδονὴν) is according to nature, some contrary to nature" /9/.
He is here discussing a view of Zeno that ἡδονή was an
irrational elation whilst χάρα was the corresponding rational
elation. Panaetius is conceding that Epicurus and other
philosophers can mean Stoic χάρα by their own term ἡδονή, and
that it is unjust to insist that they are praising the selfish
pleasure which alone the Stoic means when he uses ἡδονή. The
pleasure of right perception is of course rational because it
is in harmony with the sympathy of the cosmos. It may well
have been called ἡδονή or χάρα, but perhaps in the light of
Plato's Χάρις καὶ ἡδονή as a doublet in *Gorgias* 462e Panaetius
chose to call it χάρις, a more common word than χάρα. We can
now consider the underlying prior assumption of each chain.
Zeno clearly believed in some form of ἔννοιαι or general
notions existing in the mind, whilst Panaetius would have tended
to put πρόνοια in that situation in view of his major
philosophical work on Providence.

ZENO: General Notions: Presentation: Assent:
            Comprehension: Knowledge.

BOETHUS: Right Reason: Attention: Perception: Effort:
            Knowledge.

PANAETIUS: Providence: "Coins": Belief: Pleasure:
            Right Opinion:

     Now the feature of Panaetian metaphor which is most
significant is the choice of *coin* as the image of a generally
valid and acceptable impression. Coinage is something by
definition to be used - by being received it furnishes a
pleasure and a right opinion of its worth, but by being
expended rightly it wins a man popular favour and glory. Its
input affects a man's *attitude*, its *output* affects his
reputation.

     At this point we need our other highly significant passage
in Diogenes Laertius VII, 41 (van Straaten 63) "Panaetius and
Posidonius begin with the physics, as Phanias the friend of
Posidonius reports" /10/. This statement is in contrast with
the practices of Zeno, Chrysippus, Archidemus and Eudromus as
reported by Diogenes Laertius in the same chapter. They put
logic first, physics second, and ethics last. Now Panaetian
physics were novel to the Stoa in stressing the world's eternity
and denying ἐκπύρωσις, agreeing with Aristotle in practice, but
not exactly by a mere surrender to syncretism. The reason may

be that Panaetius' master Antipater wrote a treatise to justify Plato's view that only the *beautiful* was *good*. In *SVF* III,iii, 43 and 44 we find that Antipater held the universe finite and spherical, thereby being most apt to motion, and, unlike Boethus, he considered all the universe and the heavens were the substance of the deity. Now in *SVF* III,iii, 33 he shows us god is happy, imperishable and benevolent; therefore God is *good*. But if the universe is God's substance, then its name κόσμος (good order *and* decoration) implies *beauty*. So in being like God the universe expresses his goodness by its beauty alone - a point proved by identifying homomyns. On Platonic terms drawn from Phaedrus and Symposium, *Beauty* is the only ideal Form visible to our senses - therefore it is also the ideal Form the universe can express to our senses. If knowledge of *Goodness* must derive from physics or "nature", not logic, as Panaetius held, then to him it was vital that our universe be not merely beautiful, but, like God himself, benevolent. Thus Providence will express its truth and goodness in the beauty, fitness and order of the universe. Therefore the true perception of this will thus be always pleasurable, and thus such perfect goodness cannot perish by cyclic destruction, which thereby stands refuted.

In addition, if physics is the foundation of logic and ethics then these sciences should mirror the physical pneumatic pulsation of nature whose pneumatic τόνος is so vital to the existence of the objects of sense. If so, we might draw a cyclic diagram of the input and output processes of "coinage" as sensation to show double expanding rectilinear pulsations followed by contracting curvilinear ones, positing cosmic *right reason* as the energising power.

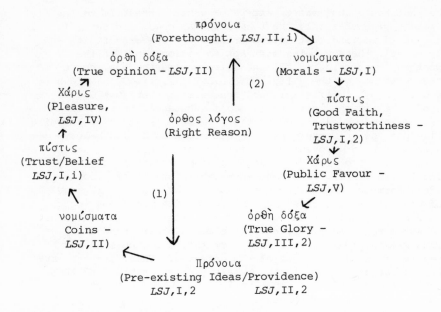

πρόνοια
(Forethought, *LSJ*,II,i)

ὀρθὴ δόξα
(True opinion - *LSJ*,II)

νομίσματα
(Morals - *LSJ*,I)

Χάρις
(Pleasure,
LSJ,IV)

(2)

ὀρθὸς λόγος
(Right Reason)

πίστις
(Good Faith,
Trustworthiness -
LSJ,I,2)

πίστις
(Trust/Belief
LSJ,I,i)

Χάρις
(Public Favour -
LSJ,V)

(1)

νομίσματα
Coins -
LSJ,II)

ὀρθὴ δόξα
(True Glory -
LSJ,III,2)

Πρόνοια
(Pre-existing Ideas/Providence)
LSJ,I,2   *LSJ*,II,2

The first impulse (1) causes a perception input process or
logic: the second expression (2) completes the cycle with a
matching process, behavioural output or ethics. Here the
familiar Stoic doctrine of meaningful amphibology of terms also
emerges. Accepted νομίσματα or *coins* issue in acceptable
ethics of "sterling worth". Accepted πίστις or *belief* issues
in acceptable *trustworthiness*. Χάρις likewise means at once
both *pleasure* received and *influence* exercised.

Finally δόξα is both one's acceptance of evidence (or
opinion) and a favourable view we impress on others - or *glory*;
whilst πρόνοια is both divine *providence* and individual
forethought. Aristotelian monistic definition is quite
inappropriate to these dynamic pulsating terms. Panaetius'
solution to the objection of the new Academy of Carneades is
that valid perceptions act like a coinage devised by the state,
being providentially ordained to seem valid, trustworthy and
pleasurable, and that once accepted perceptions are immediately
acted out and thus "put into circulation". A true impression
will seem probable and agreeable and the true opinion of it
is validated by its being expressed in behavioural response.

It is unfortunate that the violence in Athens between
Epicureans who favoured Mithradates and Stoics who favoured
Sulla /11/ led to a tendency by all other schools to denounce
all Epicureans after Sulla's victory. This doubtless caused
general neglect of Panaetius by those who saw him now as
sharing Epicurean ground in valuing some form of *kinetic
pleasure*. Of course at Panaetius' death the rivals of the
Stoa were the Academy. But 30 years later when Epicurus was
the foe, Panaetius' reputation suffered in his own school -
presumably because of his sensory criteria. None the less both
his personal influence on Rome and the impact of his Roman
experience on the philosopher's own thinking make his
logical-ethical cycle very interesting in Latin terminology.

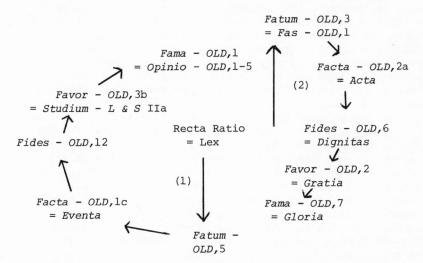

Such a cycle would be neat and memorable to Roman hearers,
but it equates *fatum* with πρόνοια as well as ἑιμαρμένη, thus
giving to Roman thinkers the notion of destiny as a force or
statute rather than a living cosmic being. The "F" cycle would
carry overtones. It cheapens the ordinary perceptions of
average men by the varied amphibolic possibilities of *opinio*
and by suggesting a pleasure in prejudice with the use of *favor*.
The alternate cycle is a fairer rendering - but less memorable.

It may well be argued that we have here a large argument
based on a single metaphor. However, *DL* VII, 92 (van Straaten
108) reminds us that Panaetius stated there were two virtues -

theoretical and *practical* /12/. In the *Offices,* where Cicero
follows Panaetius closely in much of Books I and II, he treats
the four cardinal virtues in a bi-partite manner - first the
understanding which right reason or moral choice (*lex*)
activates, then the *activity* so expressed. In this list
theoretical *sapientia* is expressed in practical *prudentia*,
theoretical *aequitas* in practical *benevolentia*, theoretical
fortitudo in practical *constantia*, and theoretical *verecundia*
in practical *decorum*. Now you may say that the distinction I
make is a false one, and that all eight can be both theoretical
and practical. Yet, if we view them educationally, this is not
so, and unless we use them to form character by training in
moral *profectus,* what is the point of this catalogue? In fact
the public school system used to exemplify Panaetian principles.
Subjects like Divinity, Geometry, Latin and Greek were taught
to train minds to exercise practical wisdom in high offices of
Church and state. Arnold's emphasis on placing the
administration of reward and punishment so much with his
prefects was designed to prepare fair minded rulers of India,
who would be benevolent administrators rather than whimsical
tyrants. Compulsory "rugger" and compulsory boxing and hard
conditions were planned to make men constant and resolute when
national interest or the cause of humanity demanded. The
discipline of chapel and study, the demand for total loyalty,
and the moral taboos against lying, thieving and vice were
designed to make men behave decently and honourably on all
occasions. The system had and has its successes and its
failures; but it rests to my mind on an unnoticed basis in
systematic Panaetian Stoicism. In this sense we find knowledge
- *prudence,* fairness - *benevolence,* fortitude - *constancy* and
modesty - *decency* are genuine input-*output* terms explaining
Platonic wisdom, justice, courage and temperance for Panaetian
readers.

Finally, come the fragments of the *de Virtutibus* which
Antoine de La Sale claims to quote from this lost Panaetian
work of Cicero.

The *Supplementum Ciceronianum* edited by Knoellinger
contains an extensive portion of this work which appears to
look to the text of the *de Virtutibus,* as Soederhjelm believed,
though Gustafsson held that they were French quotations from a
work of Seneca. Ancient testimony suggests that the lost
treatise followed Panaetius very closely. If we grant that
La Salade of Antoine de la Sale is a French treatise

incorporating frequent Ciceronian quotations, then Knoellinger is entitled to print the attempted Latin reconstruction of the likely quotations as he has done on pp. 77-91. Further, it is not improper to consider them possible Panaetian fragments, if, as some scholars insist, their tone is consistent with van Straaten's collection. In a very probable reconstruction among the fragments in the *Supplementum* virtues are compared to grains of seed /13/. This figure of speech is not elsewhere found in Cicero in relation to moral qualities. But like our assumed coinage metaphor, it is very Panaetian in stressing the inevitable *output* of every *input*; the doctrine that *perception*, if valid, will express itself in *action*. Curiously this doctrine became part of the liturgy of our 'Panaetian' public school system. Let us recall the end of term hymn

> Let thy Father - hand be shielding
> All who here shall meet no more,
> May your *seed time* past be yielding
> Year by year a richer store!

It seems that the Panaetius I seek to recover had, through Cicero, very deeply influenced the education system of England in the past two centuries. Furthermore, St. Paul could well have been exposed to Panaetian teachings in Tarsus or elsewhere. The question is whether there are such Panaetian elements specifically evident in the Epistles.

II. PANAETIAN OVERTONES IN PAUL

Already in the first Thessalonian Epistle one may see suggestions of a Panaetian perception cycle. The notion of faith and love as a breastplate and the hope of salvation as a helmet (5,8) suggests input terms also answering to the Stoic first primary impulse of self-preservation. On the other hand love belongs more to the outgoing cycle related to the second primary impulse of love for others. However, in *I Cor.* 9.1 charity or ἀγάπη is firmly declared superior to γνῶσις or knowledge, which suggests that ἀγάπη is to replace Zeno's ἐπιστήμη or Panaetius ὀρθὴ δόξα for a Stoic reader. Then, in the analysis of Chapter 13, the order Faith-Hope-Charity is set firmly. Now we set out the work of prevenient Grace in leading us to love God and supervenient Grace leading us to love our neighbour. To the Jew fear of the Lord had been the beginning of wisdom; for the Christian it is love of the Lord.

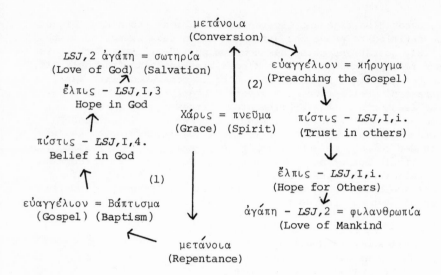

μετάνοια
(Conversion)

LSJ,2 ἀγάπη = σωτηρία
(Love of God) (Salvation)

εὐαγγέλιον = κήρυγμα
(2) (Preaching the Gospel)

ἔλπις - LSJ,I,3
Hope in God

Χάρις = πνεῦμα
(Grace) (Spirit)

πίστις - LSJ,I,i.
(Trust in others)

πίστις - LSJ,I,4.
Belief in God

(1)

ἔλπις - LSJ,I,i.
(Hope for Others)

εὐαγγέλιον = Βάπτισμα
(Gospel) (Baptism)

ἀγάπη - LSJ,2 = φιλανθρωπία
(Love of Mankind

μετάνοια
(Repentance)

Just as each successive Panaetian perception carried into
action made the next response to the same data firmer, likewise
the Pauline translation of initial repentance into love for
others would deepen the next response to prevenient grace and
enrich understanding of the Gospel. The statement "we see now
in a mirror by conjecture, then face to face" /14/, suggests
the shadow portion of Plato's line D in contract to A where one
beholds the Forms /15/, but also the Panaetian view that the
beauty of the world reflects the goodness of God.

Considerable significance in Paul's treatment of the
resurrection becomes evident in I Cor. 15.36-38 with the
metaphor of seed. "That which thou sowest, thou sowest not the
body that shall be, but bare grain of wheat or some other
grain; but God giveth it a body as it hath pleased him, and to
every seed its own body". This seems to be the metaphor of
Cicero de Virtutibus which we have suggested to be Panaetian.
Whilst it is the metaphor also of the myths of Osiris or
Demeter, it is open for us to apply to natural science which
was Panaetius' starting point an argument he evidently used in
relation to ethics and logic to link perceptions and behaviour.
The remark in V.56 - ἡ δε δύναμις τῆς ἀμαρτίας ὁ νόμος "the
field of force/dynamism of sin is the Law" can refer to Stoic
natural law as well. Further, like Stoic ἀμάρτημα, this "sin"
is pneumatic irregularity. Then the rest of the sentence reads:

τῷ δὲ θεῷ χάρις τῷ διδόντι ἡμῖν τὸ νῖκος - *thanks* To God giving
us the *victory* - i.e. χάρις in the other sense of *Grace* which
puts us into the salvation-cycle instead, with regular pulse.

When we turn to the Roman Epistle we are offered a brief
passage in I.19-20 very comparable with Cicero *de Officiis* I, 4,
11-14 (van Straaten 98) despite its brevity /16/. A long
discussion follows about Law and judgement which is directed
at Judaising Christians. On the other hand the Stoic tendency
to employ the one word in a double sense may also suggest that
the Stoic view of Law discussed by Panaetius in *de Providentia*
and *de Magistratibus* might also seem under review by implication
for a gentile Stoic reader.

In St. Paul's sense Panaetius would agree that "Law
killeth" in reference to wider ranges of code than the Jewish
law. Without Spirit (πνεῦμα) or Right Reason the letter kills.
But if the experience shocks a man enough, punishment might
bring his hegemonic parts more in tune with the cosmic
pulsations of the universal Stoic pneuma, thus beginning a
reformative process of repentance in Paul's sense which may
admit pneumatic Grace and salvation /17/.

Of great interest in the *Epistle to the Romans* is the
approval expressed for the apparatus of the Roman State in
13,1-7. The Christian is to be subject to the State for its
officers are ordained by God, and he who stands up against
magistrates has rebelled against the decree of God, and those
who resist will receive judgement. "Rulers are a fear (φόβος)
to bad acts, not good ones. If you do good, you will have
praise from the magistrate who is God's paymaster to you for
good. If you do ill be afraid, he does not wear the sword for
nothing. He is God's paymaster, the avenger for public
opinion against the man doing evil. Therefore must one be
subject, not because of public opinion but because of sense of
duty. So pay taxes, for men exacting for this purpose are
public servants of God. So pay to all of them your dues,
tribute to whom tribute is owed, excise to whom due excise,
fear to whom fear, honour to whom honour is owed". This may
well have seemed a paraphrase or summary of Panaetius
de Magistratibus in which the Providential role of government
was discussed. We may wonder if this passage and the
redefinition of the Kingdom of God as not meat and drink, but
justice, peace and joy, are designed for similar political ends.
The expectation of the Parousia and the kingdom in Thessalonians

and Corinthians might well have caused some gentiles to suspect
an attempt to set up a rival state. On this view 14,17 can be
viewed as repudiating any miraculous "loaf and fishes"
Christian donations aimed at public support, like those offered
by Nero a few years earlier. By AD 57 with a visit to Rome
and Spain in view Paul is careful to dissociate himself from
the Cynic-Stoic opposition to hierarchy and Empire and the
alleged conspiracy of Caecina Paetus the Stoic against Claudius
in AD 42. Hence the Panaetian political flavour is added to
Panaetian epistemology and ethics in this Epistle.

III. CONCLUSION

Panaetius was not the only Greek thinker to influence Paul.
Apart from Cynic and Stoic influences, it is likely that
Antrochus of Askalon may have engaged his attention. The main
aim of this paper is to show areas where the apostle of the
Gentiles may be held to have derived inspiration from the
intellectual heritage of his converts, and where certainly
converts of Stoic training would be liable to understand him in
this sense, whatever his own intentions.

NOTES

/1/   St. Paul and Stoic Physics.
/2/   J.P. Sevenster, *Paul and Seneca*, Brill, 1961.
/3/   M. Spanneut, *Le Stoicisme des Peres de l'Eglise*, Le Seuil,
1957.
/4/   Spanneut, *op.cit.*, pp.75-6.
/5/   R. Bultmann, *Der Stil der Paulinische Predigt und die
Kynisch-Stoische Diatribe*, Göttingen, 1910.
/6/   J.M. Rist, *Stoic Philosophy*, CUP, 1969, p.173.
/7/   Appendix 1(a).
/8/   Appendix 1(b).
/9/   Appendix 1(c).
/10/   Appendix 1(d).
/11/   Ernst Badian, *Rome, Athens et Mithradates, Assimulation
et Resistance a la Culture Greco-Romaine: Les Belles Lettres*,
Paris 1976, pp.501-522. Badian does not however draw out the
later impact on philosophy.
/12/   Appendix 1(e).
/13/   Appendix 1(f).
/14/   1 Cor. 1, 13, 12.
/15/   Plato, *Rep.*, 509 D 6-8. cf. R.G. Tanner, Διάνοια and
Plato's Cave, *CQ XX*,1970, pp.81-91.
/16/   Appendix 1(g).
/17/   See Appendix 2(a)-(d) for comparative epistemological
chains.

APPENDIX

1(a) Diocles Magnes apud Diog. Laërt. VII 54. ὁ μὲν γὰρ Βόηθος
      κριτήρια πλείονα ἀπολείπει, νοῦν καὶ αἴσθησιν καὶ
      ὄρεξιν καὶ ἐπιστήμην.

1(b) Stobaeus, *Eclog.* I, 20; ed. C. Wachsmuth–O. Hense, I, 171;
      v. L. 69; F. 25. Παναίτιος πιθανωτέρας εἶναι νομίζει καὶ
      μᾶλλον ἀρεσκουσαν αὐτῷ τὴν ἀιδιότητα τοῦ κόσμου ἢ τὴν τῶν
      ὅλων εἰς πῦρ μεταβολήν.

1(c) Sextus Empiricus, *Adv. Dogm.* XI, 73: Παναίτιος δε τινα
      μεν κατα φύσιν ὑπάρχειν (ἡδονήν), τινα δε παρα φύσιν.

1(d) Ποσειδώνιος ἀπο τῶν φυσικῶν ἄρχονται, καθά φησι φανίας ὁ
      Ποσειδωνίου γνώριμος ἐν τῷ πρώτῳ τῶν Ποσειδωνείων σχολῶν.

1(e) *D.L.* VII, 92: Παναίτιος μὲν οὖν δύο φησιν ἀρετάς,
      θεωρητικην καὶ πρακτικήν.

1(f) Octo sunt res *efficientes laudabiles principes et rem
      publicam gubernantes. Quae res quasi semina virtutis
      proficiscuntur ex animo iusto et sano boni ac diligentis
      principis et conciliant animos civium.* Nam ex bono animo
      proficiscuntur bonae voluntates et ex bonis voluntatibus
      nascuntur bonae actiones, propter quas res publicas
      administrantes a civibus amantur.

1(g) Principio generi animantium omni est a natura tributum, ut
      se, vitam, corpusque tueatur, declinetque ea, quae
      nocitura videantur, quaeque ad vivendum sint necessaria,
      anquirat, et paret, ut pastum, ut latibula, ut alia
      ejusdem generis. Commune item animantium omnium est
      conjunctionis appetitus, procreandi causa, et cura
      quaedam eorum, quae procreata sunt. Sed inter hominem
      et beluam hoc maxime interest, quod haec tantum, quantum
      sensu movetur, ad id solum, quod adest, quodque praesens
      est, se accommodat, paullulum admodium sentiens
      praeteritum, aut futurum. Homo autem, quod rationis est
      particeps, per quam consequentia cernit, causas rerum
      videt, earumque progressus, et quasi antecessiones non
      ignorat, similitudines comparat, et rubus praesentibus
      adjungit atque annectit futuras: facile totius vitae
      cursum videt, ad eamque degendam praeparat res
      necessarias. Eademque natura vi rationis hominem

conciliat homini et ad orationis, et ad vitae societatem:
ingeneratque in primis praecipuum quendam amorem in eos,
qui procreati sunt: impellitque, ut hominum coetus, et
celebrationes, esse, et a se obiri velit: ob easque
causas studeat parare ea, quae suppeditent et ad cultum,
et ad victum: nec sibi soli, sed conjugi, liberis,
ceterisque, quos caros habeat, tuerique debeat. Quae
cura exsuscitat etiam animos, et majores ad rem gerendam
facit. Inprimisque hominis est propria veri inquisitio,
atque investigatio. Itaque cum sumus necessariis
negotiis curisque vacui, tum avemus aliquid videre,
audire, addiscere: cognitionemque rerum aut occultarum
aut admirabilium ad beate vivendum necessariam ducimus.
ex quo intelligitur, quod verum, simplex, sincerumque
sit, id esse naturae hominis aptissimum. Huic veri
vivendi cupiditati adjuncta est appetitio quaedam
principatus, ut nemini parere animus bene a natura
informatus velit, nisi praecipienti, aut docenti, aut
utilitatis causa, juste et legitime imperanti: ex quo
animi magnitudo exsistit, humanarumque rerum contemtio.
Nec vero illa parva vis naturae est rationisque, quod
unum hoc animal sentit, quod sit ordo; quid sit, quod
deceat; in factis dictisque qui modus. itaque eorum
ipsorum, quae adspectu sentiuntur, nullum aliud animal
pulchritudinem, venustatem, convenientiam partium sentit.
quam similitudinem natura ratioque ab oculis ad animum
transferens, multo etiam magis pulchritudinem, constantiam,
ordinem in consiliis factisque conservandum putat:
cavetque, ne quid indecore, effaeminateve faciat: tum in
omnibus et opinionibus, et factis, ne quid libidimose aut
faciat aut cogitet. quibus ex rebus conflatur et
efficitur id, quod quaerimus, honestum: quod etiam si
nobilitatum non sit, tamen honestum sit: quodque vere
dicimus, etiam, si a nullo laudetur, natura esse laudabile.

2(a)   Zeno: ἔννοιαι: φαντασία:

       General Notions: Presentation:

       συγκατάθεσις: κατάληψις:

       Assent: Comprehension:

2(b)   Boethus: ὀρθὸς λόγος: νοῦς: αἴσθησις:

                    Right Reason: Attention: Perception:

                    ορεξις: ἐπιστήμη:

                    Effort: Knowledge:

2(c)   Panaetius: πρόνοια: νομίσματα: πίστις:

                    Providence: Coins: Belief:

                    χάρις: ὀρθὴ δόξα:

                    Gratification: Right Reason:

2(d)   Paul: μετάνοια: Βάπτισμα: πιστις:

                    Repentance: Baptism: Faith:

                    ἔλπις: ἀγάπη:

                    Hope: Love:

St. Paul's View of Militia and Contemporary Social Values

R.G. Tanner,
The University of Newcastle,
New South Wales,
AUSTRALIA.

The Apostle of the Gentiles wrote to his Greek-speaking converts of the new Churches in language appropriate to the cultural background of his readers. Elsewhere I have considered Paul's use of some Stoic concepts to interpret his ideas to Greeks or Romans of some education who wished to see their new faith in terms of their Classical intellectual heritage /1/. Now it is appropriate to review the usage in the Epistles of expressions related to the preoccupations and social structure of the early Empire.

Essentially the Augustan Army was the pneumatic spirit which in Stoic terms was holding the inert body of the Empire in unity and tension /2/. From their Romanized background the first gentile Christians not unnaturally retained a great respect for the military system and the Imperial structure of that age. Two important values were stressed from the days of Claudius to those of Trajan. First was the old doctrine which had served so mischievously in the field of warfare in the first century B.C., that of total obedience to one's general or *fides* which derived from the bond of the military oath or *sacramentum* which tied the soldier to his commander in virtue of the latter's *imperium*. Secondly, a view which had developed from the increasing use of Italian allied troops to replace Roman conscripts in the Eastern Wars of the second century B.C., the opinion that it was particularly glorious to win victories *citra Romanum sanguinem* - "without shedding Roman blood" - by the use of allied auxiliary units without calling on the reserve force of Roman legionaries. Evidence for this is readily to hand from Tacitus, *Agricola* 35, and Richmond and Ogilvie's plate V (from Trajan's column) in their edition of that text. The notion of Christianity as a faith from which

apostasy is a deed as shameful as military desertion was thus
a natural opinion. Further there seems to be an accompanying
view evident in Paul and equally in Ignatius of Antioch that
one's body was an expendable "auxiliary" whose death might win
a martyr's crown of glory analogous to the military *corona aurea*
for the believer's "legionary" soul /3/.

Quite a number of distinctive "military" passages occur in
the Pauline Epistles. It is my view that Paul used as his
illustrations from pagan daily life current events very fresh
and contemporary in his mind at the time of writing, and that
some may therefore offer contributory evidence for dating of
the epistles.

Let us look first at the Thessalonian Letters of AD 51-52.

1 Thess. 5,2-10. The point of this passage is that the
Christian must be alert like soldiers in a gatehouse or on
excubiae. They must not get drunk and fall asleep, but they
must wear the breastplate of faith and love and the helmet of
the hope of salvation whilst on duty. The Lord, like the
Legatus, may make a surprise night inspection.

2 Thess. 1,8 compares the coming of the Lord in judgement with
an imperial punitive expedition against rebel tribes such as
that of Corbulo in Frisia in AD 47. The more probable model
is the attempt of Meherdates to secure the throne of Parthia
with Roman support in the same year. The converts of Paul are
similarly to be counted worthy of the kingdom for which they
suffer, and like Meherdates' followers expect him to punish
those who oppress them with similar oppression; Christians may
look for this from the Lord who will similarly be revealed as
present in person with his Legates (angels) /4/ of his forces
(δυνάμεις), punishing those who do not recognise him by burning
their towns and villages.

2 Thess. 2 is political rather than military, prompted by
Caligula's insane administration and his attempt to have his
own statue installed in the Holy of Holies by a Roman army under
his legate Petronius. "Unless the defection comes first and
the man of lawlessness stands revealed, the son of destruction,
the one opposing and setting himself above every god that is
acknowledged and every object of awe (σέβασμα/σεβαστός) so far
that he set himself upon the temple of God, declaring that he
himself was God". These shocking events of course occurred

whilst Paul was probably studying at Tarsus in AD 37-41 /5/.

2 Thess. 3, 6-12 concerns the need for legionary-like discipline
and manual work. Paul had ἐξουσία (*potestas*) like a Legate of
a legion, but he worked to set an example of disciplined
behaviour and manual work.

The Corinthian Epistles written from Ephesus between
AD 52 and 55 are next to be examined. The first extract is
not military but relates to the Isthmian Games which were
restored to Corinth by the Romans after the City was rebuilt
in 46 BC and which were held every two years. Paul probably
saw them during his stay in AD 51-52.

1 Cor. 9,24-7 Paul trains his body like a contestant for the
footrace in the stadium or like a boxer, who do so merely for a
perishable crown (at first wild parsley or celery, but pine in
this period), whilst the Christian seeks an everlasting crown.

1 Cor. 16,13 returns to the guard duty metaphor: "Stay awake,
stand fast in the faith *(fides),* behave like men (with *virtus),*
be strong *(fortes estote);* let all things be done among you
with charity (ἀγάπη replacing *obsequium)*".

2 Cor. 6,7-9 may refer to a legionary soldier's role standing in
a battle line. "By means of the weapons of justice on our
right and left sides, by glory and dishonour, through fame and
infamy. We are deceivers yet sincere, as unknown yet well-known,
as dying and behold we live, as being chastised yet not slain".
Here are portrayed the vicissitudes of a soldier subjected to
the kind of warfare and ambush current on the Rhine and Danube
frontiers.

2 Cor. 10,3-6. "Walking in the flesh we do not practice our
militia after the flesh, for the weapons of our *militia* are
not fleshly but powerful through God for the overthrow of
fortresses, and we are destroying ambushes and every high
position raised up against the knowledge of God, and taking
captive in war every resolve to bring it to subjection to
Christ, and we hold ourselves in readiness to punish every
insubordination, as soon as our obedience is fulfilled". Here
we have a picture of conquest and pacification of a frontier
district as a figure of Christian effort.

Rom. 13,1-8 is an interesting defence of civil obedience
to the Roman authority, which is declared God-ordained, and

Paul insists that all civil disobedience is disobedience against
God. This skirts round the problem of the divinity of the
Emperor: Paul as a Jew and a Roman did not have to burn incense
to God the Father on the altar of Rome and Augustus. Perhaps
later Christians might properly have avoided persecution by
burning it on the precedent of Naaman the Syrian in the house
of Rimmon. Verse 12 urges Christian to shun works of darkness,
putting on the armour of light.

The captivity epistles are of doubtful date and
provenance to many scholars. Such implications as one can
find suggest a Roman origin, certainly for Colossians. There
2, 13-15 seems to compare our redemption to the rescue of a
beleaguered force by a victor in a Roman civil war. Declared
public enemies, such legionaries were under death sentence,
but their leader's victory had wiped out their alleged
disloyalty by giving him the power to force Senate and People
to annul the decrees against them, i.e. in Jesus' case, through
his cross. Finally, he openly had shown that men with
government and power had been stripped, and he had led them
in his triumph. The decking of the city with triumphal
ornaments for Nero because of Corbulo's victories in AD 60 or
perhaps for those claimed by Paetus in AD 62 could well have
been seen by Paul in Rome, but no such sight could be seen
elsewhere.

Apart from the mention by Paul of Epaphroditus as his
"fellow-soldier"(Philippians 2,25), there is little other
military reference in the "captivity" epistles, but there is
much concern with Roman social life. The precepts for Christian
family life in *Col.* 3,18-4,1 are very much those of the
Institutes of Gaius, maintaining *patria potestas* in the Lord
over wives, children and slaves /6/. In *Gal.* 4,1-7 Christians
are bought by Jesus from servitude to the Law in order that he
may duly manumit them, whereby as *liberti* they take his *nomen*
and become entitled to rank for inheritance like sons. In
Eph. 2,11-19 the gentile converts are no more foreigners but
fellow citizens with the Saints - the Claudian policy of
extending Roman citizenship to reliable provincials /7/ from
which Paul's own father may have benefited under Augustus seems
to be used as the model. On the other hand 6,10-17 returns to
the military figure of defending a town under siege, which may
or may not be a topical reference to Paetus' disastrous
capitulation at Rhandeia in AD 62 /8/. So Christians will do
better than the legionaries had done in the defence or Rhandeia,

as the shield of faith will ward off the burning arrows from
the catapults of the besiegers. As in *1 Thess.* the helmet is
of salvation, but the breastplate is now of justice rather than
love and faith, the shoes are the gospel of peace and the girdle
is truth. Unlike the men there on guard duty in peace time,
our soldier repelling besiegers has the sword of the spirit.

Phil. 1,21-3 appears to reject the Stoic doctrine of
suicide as an option open to the wise. "For me life is Christ
and to die is gain. If I live in the flesh, this is a result
of my work, and I do not know which I shall choose, for I
am gripped by two simultaneous drives, having the desire to
pack up and be with Christ, which is much the better; yet to
abide in the flesh is most necessary for your sake".

Phil. 2,5-8 compares Christ to a punished Roman slave. He
takes the form of a slave, humbling himself till death - a
slave's crucifixion. His exaltation by God is in proportion to
his self-emptying.

The Pastoral Epistles contain similar interesting points
/9/. *1 Tim.* 2,12-15 urges female subordination on Jewish
grounds, but with a praise of wifely silence enough to delight
the Elder Cato! In *2 Tim.* 2,3-5 we find another exhortation
to be a good soldier of Christ, followed by the reminder that
athletes who break the rules are not crowned. In *Titus* 2,15 to
3,2 Christians are to be reminded to accept the civil
authorities, to obey them, and to keep the peace. The little
Epistle to Philemon is ambivalent. Whilst Paul sends home
Philemon's runaway slave Onesimus, he does not merely ask him
to remit the customary penalty, but may imply that he expects
one Christian to manumit another who happens to be his slave.
This is contrary to the earlier teaching that, whilst there is
neither bond nor free in Christ, slaves should obey their
masters as wives obey their husbands. Perhaps if the Epistle
is Pauline and if its author had lived longer he might have
questioned the institution of slavery, but this is speculation.
Certainly his admirer Ignatius of Antioch defended slavery /10/.

These instances we have examined indicate the extent to
which Paul sought to present and illustrate his Gospel in terms
of the contemporary gentile social structure of the Roman
world.

NOTES

/1/   In a paper in this collection entitled 'Saint Paul and Panaetius'.
/2/   S. Sambursky, *Physics of the Stoics*, p.4.
/3/   Paul, *1 Cor.* 4,10-13. Cf. Ignatius, *Ep. to the Romans* IV,1.
/4/   ἄγγελος = *nuntius: legatus* is equivalent in some cases *(O.L.D. 1)*. So *angel* or *nuntius* is treated as a full synonym for *legatus* by Stoic amphiboly.
/5/   R.G. Tanner, 'Saint Paul and Panaetius'. (See note 1).
/6/   Gaius, *Institutes* I, 9-20.
/7/   Tacitus, *Ann.* XI,24.
/8/   Dio. LXII, 21,2.
/9/   There is an unpalatable possibility that *1 Tim.* 6,12 may draw its imagery from a successful gladiator winning manumission from the arena.
/10/   Ignatius, *Ep. to Polycarp*, IV,3.

The Revelation of God's Righteousness in Romans 1:17

D.H. van Daalen,
17 Primrose Crescent,
Harrington,
Workington, Cumbria,
CA14 5PP.

Δικαιοσύνη γὰρ θεοῦ ἐν αὐτῷ ἀποκαλύπτεται, 'in it is revealed the righteousness of God'. A simple phrase, it seems, yet it has given rise to a great deal of controversy. Traditionally the interpretation has mainly followed two lines. Most Catholic interpreters have followed Augustine's observations in *De spiritu et littera*. Writing as he did in view of the Pelagian controversy, and thinking in Latin, he could not take *iustitia dei* in this and a number of other passages in the sense of one of God's perfections. However, it had not escaped his notice that in the Old Testament the righteousness of God is used sometimes parallel with his salvation. God's salvation, without question, is the salvation worked by God, and it seemed obvious to Augustine that God's righteousness must be interpreted similarly as a righteousness worked by God /1/. *Iustitia dei* then is a righteousness bestowed by God by which a man is made *iustus*. And, incidentally, God is a *iudex iustus* when he rewards those *iusti*.

Protestant interpreters have been influenced similarly by Luther. 'It is only in the Gospel', Luther says, 'that the righteousness of God is revealed, that is to say, who is righteous, and how one becomes righteous before God, sc. only through faith, by which one believes God's word' /2/. In his translation of this verse he renders accordingly, *die Gerechtigkeit die vor Gott gilt*, 'the righteousness that counts before God', that is to say, the righteousness of faith; however, as faith is God's gift, Luther too was thinking in terms of a God-given righteousness, and he quotes Augustine with approval /3/. He too, it should be noted, thought in Latin and was engaged in a controversy about justification.

Not all interpreters have been so careful as Augustine and
Luther in regarding God as the sole author of δικαιοσύνη θεοῦ,
but the majority have followed them in taking it in an
anthropological sense. That is one point on which such very
different modern interpreters as Althaus, Cranfield, Lagrange,
Michel, O'Neill and countless others are agreed, however much
they may disagree otherwise /4/.

However, others take a different view /5/, and it must be
said that theirs seems the more natural one. On the face of it
δικαιοσύνη θεοῦ seems to refer to that δικαιοσύνη by which God
himself is δίκαιος. When Paul wrote the controversies in which
Augustine and Luther were engaged lay still in a distant and
unknown future. Moreover, he did not think in Latin: his
languages were Hebrew and Greek.

In Hebrew the words in question are those from the root
ṢDQ: the substantive nouns s^edaqa and $sedeq$ and the adjective
ṣaddīq. In the OT, the expression ṣidqat YHWH actually occurs
only once /6/, the plural sidqōt (or $s^edaqōt$) YHWH four
times /7/, sidqat ʾēl or ṣidqat ʾelohīm not at all; but there
are numerous instances where s^edaqa and ṣedeq, used either
absolutely or with suffix, clearly refer to YHWH's s^edaqa/ṣedeq.
In some cases the reference is to a s^edaqa granted by God to
his people or to specific people, usually in the sense that he
intervenes to save them /8/, but occasionally in the sense of
a gift of s^edaqa bestowed upon them /9/. There are also a few
passages where the reference is to the s^edaqa which YHWH demands
/10/. In the great majority, however, of cases where s^edaqa or
ṣedeq is used with reference to YHWH the word wants to say
something about what YHWH is like. His s^edaqa means that he is
ṣaddīq.

What does that mean? Words of the root ṢDQ are quite
frequent. The verb is comparatively rare; it occurs 41 times,
but the adjective is used 206 times, s^edaqa 157 and ṣedeq 119
times, a total of 523 times /11/. Traditionally, owing to the
translations δικαιοσύνη and iustitia, these words have been
connected with 'justice' or 'righteousness', but in most cases
that is extremely unsatisfactory, and Leenhardt has a point
when he speaks of la sottise de traduire ce mot par 'justice'
/12/. It is, in fact, extremely difficult to think of a Latin
or an English word that would cover satisfactorily all the
passages where the words occur, and it is not surprising that
there is a host of literature on the subject /13/. Within the

limited time available we will make only a few points.

1. SDQ does not refer to any abstract ideal of justice /14/.
It is often used with reference either to YHWH's actions or to
human conduct, and it should not come as a surprise that the
verb with which it is connected more frequently than with any
other is ^cSH, 'to do' /15/.

2. The Greek and Latin translations were probably affected
by the fact that $\d{s}^edaqa$ is used frequently in close connexion
with $mi\check{s}p\bar{a}t$, and even when that is not the case it is often
used in a forensic context. We must add, however, that there
is not one instance where $\d{s}^edaqa$ is used with reference to
punishment: there was evidently no such thing as a retributive
$\d{s}^edaqa$ /16/. Whenever it is used in a forensic context it
refers to the protection of the poor, the weak and the
innocent /17/, not to the punishment of the guilty.

3. The manner in which $\d{s}^edaqa/\d{s}edeq$ is used parallel
with words of the roots $^{\circ}MN$, YSR, $Y\check{S}^c$, and $\d{H}SD$, suggests that
it refers to someone who is on the one hand faithful and
reliable, on the other hand kind and merciful, and ready to
help. When used of YHWH the reference is frequently to his
faithfulness to his Covenant and therefore to his people, or
to his kindness towards them and his readiness to come to their
aid. $\d{S}^edaqa/\d{s}edeq$ is evidently used to say that YHWH is a God
of salvation.

4. Correspondingly, human $\d{s}^edaqa$ is people's conduct in
relation to YHWH and his Covenant, and indicates such conduct
as is pleasing to YHWH /18/.

5. It would therefore be true to say that $\d{s}^edaqa/\d{s}edeq$ is
a *Verhältnisbegriff* /19/; it refers to the relationship between
YHWH and his people.

6. Even so, these words do want to say something about
YHWH himself: $\d{s}edeq$ is what YHWH is like /20/. It can
therefore be said that YHWH is *saddīq*.

That is the probably unreflected but real context within
which Paul's thinking on δικαιοσύνη θεοῦ would move. It may
be objected that he wrote and presumably thought in Greek /21/.
That is true, but his thinking was affected profoundly by the
Hebrew OT. Moreover, there is ample evidence that his Greek

was moulded by his knowledge of the LXX, where δικαιοσύνη
would be found in the same contexts as $s^e daqa/sedeq$ and would
therefore suggest the same associations /22/. Finally, the
word δικαιοσύνη itself was much less narrow in its application
than iustitia /23/, and it could even be argued that
retribution was no part of it /24/.

It therefore seems likely that by δικαιοσύνη θεοῦ Paul
meant something similar to what is meant by OT writers when they
use $s^e daqa/sedeq$ with reference to YHWH, and that would mean
first and foremost that δικαιοσύνη by which God himself is
δίκαιος. It would be difficult to give a definition of
δικαιοσύνη but it clearly refers to God in his actions, in his
relationship with and fidelity to his people, and, as God is
true, to what he is really like. That, I submit, is supported
by the word ἀποκαλύπτεται. Surely, revelation as Paul
understood it, is not a matter of the disclosure of certain
truths: revelation is this that God reveals himself.

That is also borne out by the end of the first part of
this letter, especially chapter 3:26: πρὸς τὴν ἔνδειξιν τῆς
δικαιοσύνης αὐτοῦ ἐν τῷ νῦν καιρῷ, εἰς το εἶναι αὐτὸν δίκαιον
καὶ δικαιοῦντα τὸν ἐκ πίστεως Ἰησοῦ. The last part of the
verse is awkward if we take καὶ in a copulative sense, as most
translators do. Cranfield has suggested that it should be
taken advertially, and interprets, '"that God might be
righteous even in justifying", i.e. that he might justify
righteously without compromising his own righteousness' /25/.
That, however, would mean operating with an abstract definition
of righteousness unsupported by what we have found so far. The
suggestion that καὶ should be taken adverbially is an excellent
one, but then in a slightly different sense, for which there is
ample evidence in Greek usage: 'to show his "righteousness" in
the present time, to the effect that he (himself) is "righteous"
even to the extent of justifying him who depends on the faith
of Jesus'. Paul was not operating with an abstract notion of
justice and trying to demonstrate how God could be just and
merciful at the same time, for there was no such contrast
between $s^e daqa$ and hesed. The idea that God's justice demanded
the damnation of the sinner whilst his mercy pleaded for his
salvation, so that the divine wisdom had to find a solution
that could satisfy both, would simply not have occurred to him.

In the Gospel δικαιοσύνη θεοῦ is revealed. That does not
mean that it demonstrates that, or how, God conforms to some

extraneous notion of righteousness. God does not have to prove
or explain himself. The Gospel simply tells us what God has
done and thereby reveals what he is really like. Any definition
of δικαιοσύνη θεοῦ will therefore have to be derived from the
Gospel itself.

However important the question of the theodicy may be, in
the final resort God needs no justification: it is we who are
in need of justification /26/. That is emphasised by the
ἀποκάλυψις ὀργῆς θεοῦ ἀπ' οὐρανοῦ in 1:18-3:20. There is
nothing surprising about the ὀργη θεοῦ; what is surprising is
the justification of the sinner, and δικαιοσύνη θεοῦ is
revealed precisely in the Gospel of justification.

The present tense ἀποκαλύπτεται shows that by the Gospel
Paul simply means the message of God's work in Christ as it is
preached. The proclamation of the Gospel is the means by which
God reveals himself. That is why it is the power of God for
salvation /27/.

Here is where Augustinian and Lutheran interpretations
find a certain relative justification. This is the δικαιοσύνη
θεοῦ, that he justifies the sinner /28/, that is to say, claims
him for his own /29/, and sanctifies him /30/, so that he
becomes ṣaddĩq, δίκαιος /31/.

NOTES

/1/   Aurelius Augustinus, De spiritu et littera, xi.
/2/   Joh. Ficker (ed.), Anfänge reformatorischer
Bibelauslegung, I. Luthers Vorlesung über den Römerbrief
1515/1516, Leipzig, ²1923, p.14.
/3/   loc.cit.
/4/   P. Althaus, Paulus und Luther über den Menschen,
Gütersloh, ²1951; C.E.B. Cranfield, A critical and exegetical
Commentary on the Epistle to the Romans (ICC), Edinburgh, 1975,
I. pp.92ff.; M.J. Lagrange, Saint Paul, Epitre aux Romains
(Et. Bibl.), Paris, ⁴1931, pp.19f; O. Michel, Der Brief an die
Römer (Meyer), Göttingen, ¹²1963, pp.58f; J.C. O'Neill, Paul's
Letter to the Romans (Pelican), Harmondsworth, 1975, pp.38f.
/5/   C.H. Dodd, The Epistle of Paul to the Romans (Moffatt),
London, 1932, pp.9ff; A.F.N. Lekkerkerker, De Brief van Paulus
aan de Romeinen, Nijkerk, 1962, I, pp.47ff; cf. also W.G.
Kümmel, Die Theologie des Neuen Testaments nach seinen
Hauptzeugen, Göttingen, 1969, p.175.

/6/   Deut. 33:21.
/7/   Jud 5:11; 1 Sa. 12;7; Mic. 6:5; Ps. 103:1.
/8/   Is. 33:5; 51:5; 54:17; Ps. 48:10; 24:5, etc.
/9/   Ps. 72:1; 51:5, &c; cf. Klaus Koch, SDQ im Alten
Testament, Diss. Heidelberg, 1953, pp.30ff.
/10/ Ps. 119: 142 etc.
/11/ Figures after Klaus Koch in E. Jenni & C. Westermann,
Theologisches Handwörterbuch zum Alten Testament (THAT),
Munich, 1976, II, col.511.
/12/ F.J. Leenhardt, L'épître de Saint Paul aux Romains (CNT)
Neuchâtel, 1957, p.13; Eng. tr. The Epistle to the Romans,
London, 1961, p.50.
/13/ The most important listed in Cranfield, Romans, pp. 92f;
and in Koch's article in THAT, II, col. 507ff.
/14/ Gerhard von Rad, Theologie des Alten Testaments, I,
Munich, [5]1966, pp. 386ff; Eng. tr. Old Testament Theology
Edinburgh, 1962, pp.370ff.
/15/ Koch, SDQ im A.T., p.3.
/16/ Von Rad op.cit., p.389, Eng. tr. p.377.
/17/ Koch, THAT, II, col.518.
/18/ Cf. Pss. 11:7; 24:16.
/19/ W. Eichrodt, Theologie des Alten Testaments, I, Leipzig,
1933, p.121ff; Eng. tr. Theology of the Old Testament, London,
1960, pp.239ff (where other literature is quoted); cf. Von Rad,
l.c.; id. Das erste Buch Mose (ATD), Göttingen, 1952, p.156;
Eng.tr. Genesis London, 1972, p.185.
/20/ Cf. the use of sedeq in Pss. 50; 97.
/21/ Cf. D.H. van Daalen, '"Faith" according to Paul', in
The Expository Times, vol. lxxxvii, Edinburgh, 1975, pp. 83ff.
/22/ Most commentators recognise this but seem to hesitate to
draw the consequences; thus, for instance, Cranfield points to
the connexion with sedeq but still operates with a formal
interpretation of righteousness, op.cit. pp.94, 312; Dodd,
op.cit. pp.9ff, is more consistent.
/23/ Cf. Leenhardt, loc.cit.; also D.H. van Daalen, 'Paul's
doctrine of justification and its Old Testament roots', in
Studia Evangelica, VI (TU 112), Berlin, 1973, pp. 556ff.
/24/ Plato, Politeia, I.ix.335e.
/25/ Cranfield, op.cit. p.213.
/26/ Cf. Günther Bornkamm, Das Ende des Gesetzes, Munich,
[5]1966, pp.196ff.
/27/ Cf. Karl Barth, Kurze Erklärung des Römerbriefes, Munich
1956, pp.22ff.; Eng.tr. A shorter Commentary on Romans, London
1959, pp.21f.
/28/ Rom. 3:21-26; 8.1, etc.

/29/ Van Daalen, Paul's doctrine of justification, pp.561ff.
/30/ *Romans* 6-8; of Calvin's comment: *sequitur ergo sine regeneratione neminem posse induere ipsius iustitiam,* Ioannis Calvini *in Novum Testamentum Commentarii,* ed. Tholuck, Berlin, 1834, Vol.V, p.xiii.
/31/ Cf. what was said above about human $s^e daqa$.

Studia Biblica 1978: III, 391-402

Pluralism and Mission in the New Testament

Rev. Dr. John J. Vincent,
Urban Theology Unit,
210 Abbeyfield Road,
Sheffield, S4 7AZ.

"Pluralism" I take to mean "A lot of different things
going on", and thus "a lot of different basic ideas informing
action". The Concise Oxford Dictionary offers "(Philos.)
system that recognises more than one ultimate principle", as
against "monism".

In 'this sense, pluralism is not especially a characteristic
of our contemporary time. Nor yet is pluralism necessarily a
feature of secular rather than religious societies /1/. A
"pluralistic" society is one in which a multitude of things -
values, world-views, presuppositions, lifestyles, and so on -
exist side by side. These things may be religious or
non-religious: in most cases they are a mixture of both.

The opposite of a pluralistic time is a monolithic or
monochrome time. Settled societies, in which state, economics
and religion are able to impose a single, unified view, are
monochrome. Such might be thought to be, at least comparatively,
mediaeval or Victorian England. Such a monochrome view has
contributed to what we call "the establishment".

The New Testament was written in a fairly riotously
pluralistic time.

Judaism itself was marked by basically irreconcilable
world-views within itself. Even war and conflict did not
produce a monochrome society. The Sadducees co-operating with
the Roman occupation army, the high priests seeking their own
succession, the Pharisees preserving faithfulness to a
developed law, the Essenes and Qumran sectarians seeking a new
righteousness in primitive monasticism, the Zealots securing
liberation by violence, the Ch'sithim awaiting in faith the

coming one.

This confused picture must have been even more complex at
the time. Within Pharisaism there was the rise of Rabbinicism
and the Schools of Hillel and Shammai. Within Palestine itself,
regional, cultural and social differences separated all but
completely Galilee, Jerusalem, Samaria, the Decapolis, and so
on. The Judaism of Jesus' day was a richly pluralistic
phenomenon /2/. One game for New Testament scholarship is to
attempt to place our own Christian heroes somewhere within it.

But then *our own heroes*. Where exactly did Jesus stand?
Where did his disciples stand, and did they all stand in the
same place: or was it, as appears, a pluralistic alliance of
convenience from the beginning? Where did the first Galilean
disciples and their associates stand? Where did the first
followers of the Way in Jerusalem stand /3/? Where did the
first believers in more Greek influenced parts of Palestine
stand? Or diaspora Jews? Or proselytic Jewish converts?

So: did the pluralism of Judaism merely become a *wider*
pluralism, or was it now a unity? In what sense did commitment
to Jesus produce primarily a *unity* or primarily a greater
diversity?

The initial reaction is obviously, "well, *unity*". "Unity"
is the prime fruit of Christian commitment in the New Testament.
But the matter is far less clear. E.F. Scott's arguments
concerning theological "varieties" in New Testament faith are
persuasive /4/. F.C. Grant writes:

(The diversity) is not limited to choice of language, as
if the New Testament writers all meant the same thing
but selected different words for saying it. The
diversity involves some of the basic ideas of New
Testament theology; the religious attitude, ethos, and
approach of quite different groups; and also a variety
in practice, in organization, and in types of religious
activity, which the studies of the past generation have
made so clearly evident that no fair-minded student can
ignore them. Unless he is obsessed by a preconceived
theory, ecclesiastical or other, he will be compelled
to reckon with this genuine and far-reaching diversity
in the religion of the New Testament /5/.

Commenting on this, John Knox writes:

> As a matter of fact, we can be sure that the religion
> of the early church was even more diversified than the
> religion of the New Testament, because the New Testament
> represents a selection from among documents in the
> interest of unity, and documents representing certain
> extremes have been excluded. Moreover, it is likely
> that some strains in primitive Christianity were not
> significant enough to produce documents at all or for
> some other reason did not do so. Both Grant and Scott
> would insist as strongly upon the unity of early
> Christianity as upon its variety. But the real nature
> of this unity cannot be seen until the diversity is
> fully taken into account; nor, indeed, can its strength
> be truly estimated. For it was a unity strong enough
> not only to tolerate a wide variety of belief and
> practice, but also, to bear the strains of deep division
> between important leaders and large groups of
> Christians /6/.

Further, Knox sees not the development towards consensus, but
rather "the persistent, and often deepening, character of the
diversities among the early communities". James Dunn says
"there was no one christology in first century Christianity
but a diversity of Christologies" /7/ - and similarly with
kerygma, confessional formulae, the use of the Old Testament,
and concepts of ministry, worship, sacraments and the Spirit.

Most of the decisive elements in early Christian faith,
therefore, must be seen as *optional* ways of describing a central
reality. They are temporary, culturally determined
approximations, written in the language and thought forms
and under the presuppositions of limited, specific
geographical, ethnic, social and political groups.

Let us look briefly at Paul before turning to the Gospels.

The evidence of Paul in his letters is that the pluralism
developed even further as the Christian mission proceeded.

1. The faith itself became formed and was formulated in
the context of decisively influential but extremely varied
mores, cultures and semantic worlds. This is the implication
of the fact that we have letters from one leading figure

addressed to diverse geographical, cultural and religious
groups; together with the fact that we have only one side of
the debate in each case.

2. "Special doctrines" - e.g. justification by faith in
Romans, or salvation apart from "law" in *Galatians,* or Wisdom
Christology in certain texts /8/ developed out of *missional,
strategic,* or *opportunist,* rather than doctrinal, much less
theoretical or "abstract-truth" considerations. That is, the
question with Paul was, given this situation, or given this
existing world-view or mental formulation or semantic mind-set,
how can the central Christ commitment and mystery be both
expressed and also developed?

3. *Controversy* occurs out of missional considerations.
It is out of the situation of *threat* that the mind of Paul -
like other minds - developed. As C.K. Barrett writes,

> The controversies in which he was engaged helped to make
> him the man he was, and it was in debate that some of his
> most characteristic, and most important, doctrines were
> hammered out. It is for example doubtful whether we
> should have had in the form in which we know it his
> doctrine of justification by faith had it not been
> threatened before it was formulated by the judaizing
> movement. It is doubtful whether he would have thought
> through (though presumably he would have continued to
> practise) his own conception of apostleship if he had
> not been confronted by false apostles. It is doubtful
> whether his Christology would have developed as it did
> if he had not encountered gnostic and other attempts,
> mostly well-meaning but not for that reason adequate,
> to locate the figure of Jesus in history and the universe
> /9/.

4. The central Christ reference seems to have remained
comparatively simple. Jesus was the one "appointed": he had
been killed on the cross and had been raised up again and now
is Lord. That is to say, the central "message" did not relate
to any of the specific doctrinal *implications,* all of which
were developed in mission situations, and adapted to them.
There was a central core of agreed *commitment,* separate from
how that commitment might be described. I am not inclined to
use any of the actual *words* of Paul to indicate this basic
commitment. "Faith", "belief", "in Christ", "justification",

etc. all seem to point to a basic commitment which is
indicated by the phrases or words, but which is not contained
in them - though it might have become controlled by them in
time.

5. The mission of the early church, visible in Paul's
letters, was precisely to take this basic Christian message,
manifest in signs and in a new community, to any available
area. That area itself then to a considerable extent determined
the shape of Christian obedience and lifestyle appropriate
within its own context. This is surely what was happening at
Corinth, and we must remember that we only have one side of
the correspondence.

Thus, the Pauline corpus is a witness not only to a
widely pluralistic scene in the early church, to which Paul
was writing, but also to widely pluralistic, opportunist,
adaptory and ("doctrinally") mutually exclusive formulations
by Paul himself.

We now turn to *the Gospels*.

As redaction-criticism proceeds, it is expected that it
will be easier to isolate, or at least imagine, the situations
in which the Gospel writers worked, and the situations to
which they addressed themselves. We will thus be in a better
position to understand the pluralistic scene, as Christian
disciples in widely differing situations seek to follow the
Lord as presented to them.

But the situation is extremely complicated. The assurance
with which some scholars speak of certain situations or
groupings has to be set beside the equally certain but
opposite conclusions of others. The contemporary development
of Gospel studies necessitates making guesses out of an
ever-increasing number of possibilities in terms of situations,
cultural or social milieus, religions and groups, which can be
assumed to have been within the early church.

Thus, we are faced with an ever-growing pluralism of
possible situations. A tentative listing might illustrate the
point, based on the attributions Markan scholars have made
over the last few decades concerning the origin of sayings in
Mark:

A. Possible elements in the writer's situation

1. His own purpose, private to him.

2. His confirmation of the Church for which he writes.

3. His polemic against the Church for which he writes.

4. His writing assuming non-Christians (Jew or Gentile) read him.

5. His writing to keep the former Jews in the Church committed.

6. His writing to keep the former Gentiles in the Church committed.

B. Possible elements in the tradition situation

7. A tradition dear to the Roman Church.

8. A tradition dear to the Galilean Church.

9. A tradition dear to the Antiochene Church.

10. A tradition dear to the Hellenistic-Judaic Christians.

11. A tradition dear to the conservative-Judaic Christians.

C. Possible elements from the disciples' situation

12. A tradition derived from Peter, or other individual disciples.

13. A tradition derived from the twelve together.

14. A tradition derived from other disciples, not of the twelve.

D. Possible elements in the Jesus's lifetime situation

15. A statement made by Jesus.

16. A Jesus statement immediately misunderstood and thus altered.

17. A Jesus statement misunderstood but nevertheless handed on.

18. A Jesus statement misheard but nevertheless handed on.

19. A statement which emerged from discussion upon his words.

E. Possible elements in a variety of situations

20. A statement correctly heard and handed on, but then by
content or implications modified as different disciples
or churches used the statement to mean particular things,
in preaching, liturgy, controversy, defence or catechesis.

The latter point could be elaborated almost *ad infinitum*.

Two comments must be added, even to this formidable but
obviously incomplete list.

First, none of the four basic situations is known to us.
It is not a question of proceeding from an agreed history of
the early church and then reviewing Mark or the disciples or
the Jesus-situation in the light of it. All "histories" of the
early church are hypothetical, and there are so many
constructions of the evidence that it is unlikely that we shall
ever come to the position where we can speak with confidence
of the various elements named in "B" above, much less be agreed
concerning the *theological* history implied by them.
Redaction-criticism, again, has exposed the complicated
nature of "A", and the conflicting opinions of redaction
critics indicate that both the gospel writer's situation and
also his intention are two more unknowns. A future study will
be concerned with what can be said about the disciples'
situation. Obviously, the situation in Jesus' lifetime is
unknown. So that a basic problem is how to deal simultaneously
with four unknowns - "A", "B", "C" and "D".

Secondly, it must be observed that any given text or
passage may bring into play any number of factors named, in
indefinitely multiplying combinations. Thus, a text might be
the writer's own purpose (1), polemical against his church (3),
which while mainly Gentile has to take account of Jews (5), the
text being based on a tradition dear to the Galilean church (8),
derived from anonymous persons (14), based on a statement of
Jesus more or less correctly handed on, though not understood
(17), modified by its regular use by certain groups of
Christians (11), in defence against Romans (or Jews, or other
Christians) (20). And, of course, all this could have been
done because Mark, or his church, or the tradition, believed
the statement to be a present statement of the reigning Christ,
as well as (or rather than) a word of the earthly Jesus.

Recent Markan studies illustrate the dilemmas.

Gerd Theissen, Etienne Trocme /10/, Johannes Schreiber /11/
and Howard Clark Kee (who seems not to know the others) suggest
certain situations out of which Mark was writing. For example,
Kee writes:

> In his portrait of Jesus, Mark speaks to and from a
> community which is influenced *both* by the Jewish-Hasidic-
> Essene-apocalyptic tradition, with its belief in cosmic
> conflict about to be resolved by divine intervention and
> the vindication of the faithful elect, *and* the Cynic-Stoic
> style of gaining adherents by itinerant preaching, healing
> and exorcisms from village to village, existing on the
> hospitality that the local tradition offered /12/.

Etienne Trocmé adds that Mark is much more apt for travelling
missionaries than for settled believers. I myself argue that
Mark exposes the possibility open to his contemporaries of a
dynamic, changing, action-related relationship to disciples,
and thus to Jesus /13/.

Thus, the message of Jesus has been "adapted", we may
imagine, both at the points of writing, and at many points of
application. Actually, I believe that Mark was himself very
inconsistent, in terms of both history and theology /14/.
Is the reason for this that Mark was not *able* to impose a
consistent understanding on the pluralistic material before
him? Or was he *unwilling* to adapt consistently the diverse
material to the felt needs of any one group; but wished to
open up the opportunity for groups to identify with *elements*
in the Jesus story? Is Mark left "wide open" so that people
in widely varied contexts can find something? If this is *not*
so, then Mark remains usable only by apocalyptic and missionary
groups.

When we turn to the other Gospels, the situations
addressed indicate a further pluralism and a greater variety
of situations. Luke seems to be designed for a settled,
Hellenistic community, in which Jesus is the Spirit-inspired
healer, teacher and saviour of all people; though the community
itself might have been divided into rich and poor, free and
slave, rulers and ruled. Matthew seems to adapt the Christ
mystery for a Jewish-Christian community reliving the Exodus
and establishing a new Torah; but the situation "at the bottom"

might have been that of a deprived slave-group seeking its own
social and cultural survival by claiming an Exodus covenant as
compensation - such as the first Exodus Israelites in Egypt.

I have suggested elsewhere /15/ that there are ways in
which the pluralistic elements in contemporary Christianity
can find points of identity and identification with various
pluralistic elements in New Testament Christianity. Indeed,
the plurality of the *four* Gospels constitute in themselves
a special *missional* opportunity and invitation. Just as the
message in the Gospels varied in accordance with the background,
the writer, and the situation addressed, so the message of
Christianity itself varies. Perhaps only Gospel Halls, Inner
City Christians and Radicals need Mark, and suburban Christians
can be allowed Luke, and the establishment can stay with
Matthew. The predilection of Anglicans for John is a
sociological mystery. Indeed, our work in the Urban Theology
Unit is forcing us to the conclusion that there seem to be
many kinds of Christianity. One kind is imposed from the top.
But there are completely different kinds of Christianity
actually working at the bottom. The same seems to have been
true in the Pauline churches, and probably within churches out
of which or to which Gospels were written.

The mission of the earliest Christians took place in a
pluralistic time. Moreover, we must add, the pluralistic
potential of the Christian message was itself the seed of
pluralistic versions. A pluralistic time provides special
opportunities for mission. In a monochrome time, only one
version of Christianity seems possible. Then, to become a
Christian is to become someone who accepts the dominant
assumptions and mores of society, for which a version of
Christianity provides a chaplaincy. In a pluralistic time,
many versions of Christianity become possible. Then, to
become a Christian is to become someone who assimilates to one
of an infinite variety of forms and versions of Christian
existence and commitment. Each form and version remains
authentic to certain essential parts of the Christian core of
faith, yet reflects, embodies, and prophesies within one or
more specific, limited but life-supporting areas or mores of
the pluralistic culture. Mission becomes the infinite
multiplication of aspects of the Christ-mystery as they reflect
within and bring judgement on the pluralistic areas.

The unique opportunities for mission afforded by pluralism
can be missed or avoided. In the New Testament itself, there

is already evident a growth towards what has charitably been
called "early Catholicism". In fact, what seems to have
happened is that there was a constant tension between the
necessity to hold to a central commitment to Christ on the
one hand, and an assumption that such a central commitment to
Christ had to be visible in a mutually agreed or imposed canon
of accepted scripture, creed of accepted beliefs, and church
order. Out of a fundamental charismatic pluralism, the
outlines of a monochrome Christendom were beginning to be
enforced. And the mission itself was ceasing to be an
over-the-wall sharing of person to person in a pluralistic
world.

Two conclusions follow.

First: no-one within the Christian family can have
everything at once. In the New Testament, a basic commitment
to Christ is constrained, empowered and driven forward within
basically irreconcilable contexts. Each disciple seeks his
commitment within the limitations and possibilities of his
own special situation. On the basis of this, he "theologises".
In the Urban Theology Unit, we have ceased to speak of "Gospel"
and talk of "bits" of Gospel. We ask, "What bits of your
situation come alive in the light of what Gospel bits" /16/?
We are working at a "Worker's Mark's Gospel" at present which
will set contemporary stories beside Gospel stories, and
attempt to get a "debate" going between the two.

How wide can the Pluralism be? Our second conclusion must
be that we do not yet know. It is at this point that the
question of the central Christ-mystery has to be raised, but
in a new way. The central Christ-mystery in the earliest
Church was that Jesus was Christ, in life, death and
resurrection. But that statement - the apostolic kerygma
(Dodd, Bultmann, creeds) - did not in fact prove to be an
adequate means whereby the Christian faith could be commended
or lived by within the pluralistic situations of New Testament
times. Indeed, in the end, the kerygma proved not to be the
central Christ-mystery, which became expressed in other ways.
The kerygma proved to be itself the means whereby central
questions within some cultural contexts were avoided. The
kerygma itself was capable of such wide adaptations to
pluralistic situations as to become within them not a decisive
divider, but a mere affirming chaplaincy which could be
assimilated without any conversion taking place - as when the

dead-and-rising god became merely one more Greek god-hero.

We can scarcely avoid at least one conclusion regarding the situation facing Christian commitment in our time. If the received basic norms of faith do not prove themselves adequate to project people into courageous, joyful, self-giving and radically alternative faith-life, then inevitably there will be a "return" to the Gospels or the early chapters of *Acts* in a new way, as at least an alternative to the emerging New Testament consensus orthodoxy. Thus, people in our time seeking alternative Christ-images discover a radical, alternative, Jesus, teaching reversals, calling to new lifestyles, creating new community, setting up paradoxes, calling people to leave all, creating disciple groups. Inevitably, as in the New Testament, once a new "key" has been sensed or discovered within a new socio-cultural situation, by a new group of people, then other versions or "orthodoxies" come into question. For the new "key" could prove to be the Christ-mystery itself. At least, it will produce new scholars using a new tool to come to the New Testament pluralism of "keys". A new canon emerges, and a new test of orthodoxy. And if the "radical" picture was the true one, then *some* versions of culture-affirming Christianity were already "heretical" in New Testament times.

NOTES

/1/   Robin Gill, *Social Context of Theology* (London & Oxford: Mowbrays, 1975), pp.120-122, seems to identify the occurrence of pluralism with that of secularisation. He writes, "It must seem strange that sectarianism can still flourish in an apparently pluralist society" (p.122), where he means "an apparently secular society". David Martin, "The Secularisation Question", *Theology* LXXVI, 1973, p.86 argues that "our religion is less pluralistic than it was in Victorian times", but bases this on the claim that "a deistic, moralistic religion-in-general" prevails, which he thinks denies the description "secular".

/2/   Cf. many works, esp. recently Martin Hengel, *Judaism and Hellenism*, 2 Vols. (London: SCM Press, 1974).

/3/   Cf. Gerd Theissen, *The First Followers of Jesus* (London: SCM Press, 1978).

/4/   E.F. Scott, *The Varieties of New Testament Religion* (New York: Charles Soibno's Sons, 1943).

/5/   F.C. Grant, *An Introduction to New Testament Thought* (New York & Nashville: Abingdon, 1950), p.30.

/6/   John Knox, *The Early Church and the Coming Great Church* (New York & Nashville: Abingdon, 1955), p.23.

/7/   J.D.G. Dunn, *Unity and Diversity in the New Testament* (London: SCM Press, 1977), p.226.

/8/   Cf. J.D.G. Dunn, "Christ and Wisdom: the Origin of Incarnational Christology", *Congress Papers*.

/9/   C.K. Barrett, "Pauline Controversies in the Post-Pauline Period", NTS 20 (1974) 3, 229-45, p.229.

/10/   Etienne Trocmé, *The Formation of the Gospel according to Mark* (London: SPCK) 1975.

/11/   Johannes Schreiber, *Theologie des Vertrauens* (Hamburg: Furche-Verlag, 1967).

/12/   Howard C. Kee, *Community of the New Age* (London: SCM Press, 1977), p.105.

/13/   *Disciple and Lord,* Basel University Dissertation, 1960/1975.

/14/   Cf. M.E. Glasswell, "St. Mark's Attitude to the Relationship between History and the Gospel", *Studia Biblica 1978: II. Papers on The Gospels* (Sheffield: JSOT Press, 1980) pp.115-127.

/15/   John J. Vincent, *Alternative Church* (Belfast: Christian Journals, 1975), pp.140-6.

/16/   Cf. *Stirrings: Essays Christian and Radical,* ed. John J. Vincent (London: Epworth Press, 1976). Also my essay, "Doing Theology", in *Agenda for Prophets,* ed. Rex Ambler and David Haslam (London: Bowerdean Press, 1980), pp.123-134

A pre-Marcan Dating for the Didache: Further Thoughts of a Liturgist

Joan Hazelden Walker,
Swinton Dene,
Duns,
Berwickshire, Scotland.

The discovery of the *Didache* in 1873 has been acclaimed in many a eulogy, in many a language and by many a scholar. And rightly so. Yet I do not believe anyone to have observed in recent years that this document was to provide at the right moment in time a *note comique* in Christian textual scholarship. One can almost swear that a benign genie with an unlimited wealth of extravaganza materialises upon the open page at the first movement of the pen, and that an attendant fairy-tale godmother transforms the cautious pedant into a Cyrano de Bergerac. For how else can one explain the unending fascination expressed in such an abundance of words for a work written in so few? Or why those, like myself, stray from our chosen pastures time and again? Or, indeed why the bibliography exceeds any reasonable expectation?

In 1963 I read a paper, subsequently published /1/, entitled, "An argument from the Chinese for the Antiochene origin of the *Didache*". In actuality this was not as outrageous as its title might suggest, because there is irrefutable evidence that the first two documents which belong to the initial decade of the coming of Christianity to China, have not only a substantial portion of the *Didache,* but also reveal a marked preference for Matthaean material in the Chinese life of Christ. Of course one is fully aware that the time span between the documents is something in the nature of six hundred years. But the gospel spread slowly along the caravan trail of the silk route which terminated in Antioch. For the Chinese, Antun, as they called it, was the furthermost boundary, the capital of the west, the seat of the Roman emperor /2/. I concluded from the evidence that /3/ "however vague the details, the fact remains that this eastern branch of Christianity

emanated from Antioch in the first century. It would have
brought with it such written records as were then available in
the mother church. .What was more natural than its conservative
use of these, even though more and, no doubt better, written
documents became increasingly available. It is not surprising,
therefore, that the earliest documents from China are so
indebted to a version of St. Matthew's gospel and to the
Two-Way method of the *Didache*".

   One's enthusiasm is frequently tempered over the years. I
would no longer stand four square on a certain Antiochene home
for the *Didache*, but I remain unshaken in my belief in its
Palestinian/Syrian origin in spite of all the arguments *vis à
vis* Egypt. This time, with even greater *panache*, I am prepared
to postulate that the Christian elements in this document are
pre-Pauline, thus denying the arguments for an Egyptian origin
on the basis of its ignorance of the works of Paul. However, I
appreciate that just as this document went from Antioch
eastwards at a very early date, so too, it could have gone
southwards, and that its original home may well have been in
Jerusalem or thereabouts.

   However outrageous my pre-Pauline hunch may appear in this
instance, it has at least a considerable weight of evidence
which comes from the painstaking research of several scholars
during the past decades, in particular, those deeply concerned
with the primitive liturgy of Judaeo-Christianity and its
demonstrable affinities with the Qumran rituals. Jean-Paul
Audet /4/ had certainly paved the way for further investigation
into the first years of the Christian communities and given
hope to those of us liturgists who felt in our bones that this
document was pre-Marcan. Anton Vööbus in his *Liturgical
Traditions in the Didache* /5/ time and again, came to
conclusions which he seems unable to believe. His meticulous
text studies produce evidence which leads him to see this
document 'within the precincts of the primitive Christianity
in Palestine' /6/, yet, in the final analysis, he hesitates,
afraid of his own daring! *Mirabile dictu,* that benign genie
appears again! After I had prepared this paper I received from
Jean Magne of Paris two offprints /7/ with the encouraging,
"Pre-Marcan? YES!" and thus further ammunition for my audacity.

   Contrary to the opinion of James Kleist /8/ the *Didache*
is "... the result of one well-considered plan". Granted that
it blends together materials new and old and the hands of

varying redactors can be delineated, the major proportion of
the Greek text of the Jerusalem codex presents itself as a
church manual. It is the earliest of the church orders, a
recognisable forerunner of the long line of medieval *ordines*.
Its contents have a logical sequence - the preparation of a
candidate, baptismal rituals, fasting, daily prayer and weekly
observance, the eucharist, the full spectrum of ministry - all
rounded off with a little apocalypse, and this final warning
note so clearly proclaiming that "in terms of the old religions,
Christianity has no sacral space, no sacral time and no sacral
staff to perform the rites" /9/. Every section of the manual
has its concluding key passages which lead naturally into what
follows, thus betraying the catechetical nature of the document
and the recording of the spoken word. The whole is *didache* not
kerugma, as later ordinals are instructions of "what, when and
how" /10/. The writer asks the catechist to make constant
reference to the gospel and such quotations as he himself gives,
that is in quote, are economical in the extreme. The gospel he
supposes is written, not oral; perhaps the original Aramaic
Matthew /11/ to which Papias makes reference /12/.

Concerning chapters 1-6 much has been written; they are
rooted in pagan and Jewish catechetical method; they have
affinities with the *Manual of Discipline* of Qumran; they have
been adapted for Christian use by teacher(s), apostles, with
key phrases from an early gospel; they were widely disseminated -
from the upper reaches of the Nile to the lands of China. Such
observations have been clearly stated and need no further
comment. The concluding chapter of this section leads naturally
into baptismal rituals. Kleist believed that the paraphrased
version of the decree of the Council of Jerusalem set the
terminus ad quem around the year 60 thus allowing for some ten
years' time lag /13/. Audet sees ch. 6,2-3 as the first of the
four 'tu' passages /14/, rubristic interpolations made at an
early stage; hence a dating prior to 50 is not impossible.

The rituals of baptism are primitive. The candidate having
received the true way, the illumination, is baptised after a
two-day fast by triple immersion into the *Name* of the Lord.
There is little doubt that the trinitarian formula is a
redaction, possibly made some hundred and fifty years later /15/.
The full implications of this concept of *Name* is discussed
further on. Suffice to state now that the spoken *Name* is the
reality, so that he who is illuminated (he who has followed the
Way of Life (Light)), who has experienced *metanoia* (and note

well that there is no mention of confession and forgiveness of
sins) is received back into the godhead from which he came /16/.
The key word "fast" brings the catechist to the rubristic
requirement of the weekly observance of Wednesdays and Fridays
in contradistinction to the Mondays and Thursdays of the
hypocrites, and this admonition suggests the further instruction
to say three times daily the "our Father". I drew attention
to these rubrics as long ago as 1959 /17/; my hypotheses was
used by Massey Shepherd in 1960 /18/. It was re-examined last
summer by Paul Bradshaw at the sixth congress of *Societas
Liturgica*. I had written that both observances were closely
linked with catechetical instruction on the passion and posed
the theory that they were pre-Marcan and possibly Antiochene
in origin. It was as yet too soon to assimilate the importance
of the Qumran documents for early liturgy, nor indeed has many
of the far-reaching studies been published.   Annie Jaubert has
done much to acquaint us with the calendrial practices of the
events of the passion in the light of a sacerdotal calendar /19/,
she has now pointed to a weekly fasting observance in Qumran
circles other than those of Mondays and Thursdays cited by the
Didache as a Jewish custom /20/. Jean Daniélou /21/ and
J. van Godouever /22/ have provided more and more details on
Jewish, especially sectarian, traditions; all of which
underline the primitive nature of the *Didache* and its very
early dating.

The prayer rituals lead naturally into chapters 9-10;
chapters which have occasioned every shade of opinion, ancient
and modern. In my study on the earliest Roman Liturgy, I
accepted the assertion of Vööbus /23/ that these prayers were
eucharistic, a Christian *qidduš* stemming from the first years
of Christianity and of Palestinian/Syrian origin. I remained
puzzled by the omission of some sort of institution narrative
but took refuge in the notion of diversity of practice. Yet I
still clung to some concept of the reality of the spoken word.
However, after a further twelve months of reflection I have
turned again to the use of the *Name* in the *Didache* rituals.
The sacred formula in the mouth of a master or priest, the
disclosure of his name by deity to adherents were all part
and parcel of an age-long belief in the reality of the spoken
word and name to which both Jews and pagans were heirs.   The
examination of the concept *Name* by Vööbus /24/ seemed to me to
be more fundamental than he indicated. Time and again I
returned to Luke's record of the Emmaus incident which I
believed held the key (hence my joy on receiving Jean Magne's

writings). Did the omission of the institution narrative lie,
not with any question of *arcani disciplina* nor with any
hypothesis of eucharist *versus agape* but the certainty of the
presence of the risen Christ in the cup and loaf through this
concept of *Name*. Certainly the *Didache* bears witness to this
concept in both the baptismal formula (possibly twice) and in
the eucharistic prayers. Luke's record of the Emmaus incident
most certainly suggests this.

Jean Magne examines the texts of three incidents: the
garden of Eden, Emmaus and the *Didache* rituals of chapters 9-10
(he adds the earliest gospel account of the miracle of the
loaves recorded by *Mark* 8,1-10 as additional weighting) /25/.
His conclusions are very pertinent. He discovers what he calls
a sacrament of *gnosis*, seen in Christian terms in eucharistic
action:

Gen. 3,6-7	*Luke* 24,30-1
Eve took the fruit, gave it to her husband, they ate it	Jesus took bread, pronounced the blessing, broke it and gave it to his disciples
and their eyes were opened and they knew they were naked	and their eyes were opened and they knew (recognised) Jesus

Hence the eucharistic bread is seen as opening the eyes and
conveying sacramentally *gnosis*, knowledge, hence the first
stages of the Christianisation of this concept in the *Didache*
prayers:

We give thanks (eucharistise) (1) over the cup for the vine
                                    of David

                               (2) over the bread for (life)
                                    and *gnosis*

                               (3) at the conclusion for
                                    gnosis (faith and
                                    immortality)

and all THROUGH JESUS YOUR
SERVANT

I had already come to the conclusion before reading Magne
that the *Didache* was not just pre-Marcan but pre-Pauline, for
Paul in *I Corinthians,* as the evangelists in their accounts of

the miracle of the loaves, the last supper and the Emmaus
incident, represent a sophisticated development. I find the
hypothesis that they portray the Christian understanding and
adaptation of the fruit of paradise as the sacrament of
knowledge, a fascinating one, and look forward to the promised
study of Jean Magne /26/.

I believe it possible to demonstrate that Paul was aware
of the *Didache* rituals when he wrote *I Corinthians*. His
cup-bread sequence /27/ and his statement of unity in one bread
are all too close to be coincidental. Paul was writing to
those who had not come by way of Judaism and thus needed special
instruction to grasp a highly developed concept. For them the
eucharistic prayers in the *Didache* were inadequate. Paul
repeated the words of the institution which he claimed to have
received from the Lord. The Corinthians hearing these would
surely have drawn the obvious conclusion - Christ said and it
was - those who ate and drank unworthily were guilty of the
body and blood of Christ. What is more - and this indeed
betrays a later development - Paul made the connection between
the passover rituals, the last supper and the cross - a
connection completely wanting in the *Didache*.

Both Vööbus /28/ and Magne /29/ consider with meticulous
care the phrase in the *Didache* 9,4 which speaks of the *klasma*
(later *sperma*) scattered over the hills which when gathered in
become one mass, one bread. This famous metaphor, found in
the liturgical traditions of both east and west antedates,
in their opinion, any gospel account of the miracle of the
loaves and fishes. In origin it stems from the age-long myth
of the death and resurrection of nature, a reenactment of
dispersion and reassembly. Hence a drama unfolds which finds
expression in the myths of ancient Egypt and Greece where the
body of the deity is dismembered and then recomposed. The Jews
return again and again to the theme of dispersion and reassembly
and always in pastoral terms; the flock scattered over the hills
and the shepherd who accomplishes their ultimate herding.
Magne believes that the *Didache* prayer almost certainly in its
first edition, followed the pastoral motif. This interpretation
is the only one which makes sense of the construction of the
sentence and the venue of the dispersal. For sheep, not corn,
are scattered over the hills and mountains. Paul reinterprets
this notion in his cup-bread passage; for him the many become
as one loaf. The later editions of the *Didache* take first the
idea of seed-corn, which at harvest becomes bread and later on,

as broken bread, the eucharistic particle.

As Vööbus demonstrated the close ties with Judaism and the influence of sectarian Jewish customs upon the first Christian communities, so Magne has demonstrated the close parallels with the thought-patterns of later Christian gnostics. Yet Magne does not leave it here, but shews how at the very heart of Christian action, witness the *Didache* rituals, lie the origins of the gnostic movement from which, he believes, comes Christianity by way of Judaism.

On chapters 11-16 there is little need for comment. Recent scholarship cuts the ground away from those who produce traditional and apologetic arguments on categories of ministry. The terms of reference for those who serve are consistent with the accepted customs of the Graeco-Roman world; they are re-iterated later by both Paul and John. The return to the Sunday eucharist in chapter 14 has been hotly discussed. Assertions that it represents the true eucharistic celebration and others that it is a redaction are equally mistaken. The writer introduces the subject here with the identical rubric of chapters 9, 10, namely "give thanks". In this instance, however, he describes the three-fold rite which precedes public worship. *Metanoia* in this context is the ritual act comprising confession, reconciliation and almsgiving. It is thoroughly Jewish. Such a concept of *metanoia* is absent, as I noted, from the baptismal ritual where it is recognised implicitly as the illumination through the way of life.

In conclusion I maintain that the *Didache* stands self-revealed not only as pre-Marcan but pre-Pauline, a document which, as its title rightly states, is the teaching of Jesus through the twelve apostles. It is teaching expressed in those thought-patterns which were the heritage of both Jew and Gentile. This is the "new" theology, the new *gnosis* understood by those who lived in and around Jerusalem and the cities that lay within the Palestinian-Syrian borders where Paul was still a newcomer, a voice yet to be heard.

I said in the beginning of this paper that there is a magic around this document. Let us hope that its spell is eternal and its mystery insoluble!

NOTES

/1/   *Studia Patristica 8*, ed. F.L. Cross, Berlin 1966, 44-50.
/2/   "An argument from the Chinese", *loc.cit.*, 45f.
/3/   *Ibid.*, 47.
/4/   *Études bibliques: La Didaché: Instructions des apôtres*,
Paris 1958; "Affinités littéraires et doctrinaires du 'Manuel
de discipline'" in *Revue biblique* 59, 1952, 219ff., and 60,
1953, 45ff.
/5/   *Papers of the Estonian Theological Society in Exile*,
no. 16, Stockholm 1968.
/6/   *Ibid.*, 169
/7/   "KLASMA, SPERMA, POIMNION. Le voeu pour la
rassemblement de Didaché IX, 4" in *Mélanges d'histoire des
Religions offerts a Henri-Charles Puech*, Paris 1974, 197ff.:
"Le chant de la perle à la lumière des écrits de Nag Hammadi"
extract from *Cahiers du Cercle Ernest-Renan*, 100, 1977, 23ff.
/8/   *The Didache, the Epistle of Barnabas, the Epistle and
the Martyrdom of St. Polycarp, the Fragments of Papias, the
Epistle to Diognetus* in Ancient Christian Writers Series 6,
Westminster 1948, 4.
/9/   J. Hazelden Walker, "The Earliest Roman Liturgy: Sacred
Space - Sacred Time - Sacred People - Sacred Cult" in *Aufstieg
und Niedergang der Römischen Welt* (volume on *Religion* awaiting
publication).
/10/   S.J.P. van Dijk - J. Hazelden Walker, *The Origins of the
Modern Roman Liturgy. The Liturgy of the Papal Court and the
Franciscan Order in the Thirteenth Century*, London/Westminster
MD 1960, 26; see also by same authors: *The Ordinal of the
Papal Court from Innocent III to Boniface VIII and Related
Documents, Spicilegium Friburgense* 22, 1975.
/11/   In particular, Audet, *op.cit.*, 166ff., and 208ff.
/12/   Ed. Kleist, *op.cit.*, 118.
/13/   *Op.cit.*, 5.
/14/   *Op.cit.*, 105ff.
/15/   Vööbus, *op.cit.*, 21 and 29ff.
/16/   It is obvious to me that the full implications of the
Didache baptismal rituals and the expression *Name* need
considerable scrutiny in the light of the work of Jean Magne,
particularly in respect of his study on the *Song of the Pearl*.
/17/   "Terce, Sext and None. An Apostolic Custom"?. Paper
read at the Third International Patristic Conference, Oxford
1959; published in *Studia Patristica* 5, Berlin 1962, 206ff.
/18/   *The Paschal Liturgy and the Apocalypse*, London 1960.

/19/ *La date de la Cène, calendrier biblique et liturgie chrétienne*, Paris 1957.

/20/ 'Jésus et le calendrier Qumrân' in *New Testament Studies* 7, 1960, 1ff.

/21/ For the list of his extensive publications on Judaeo-Christianity see especially, his work in *The Christian Centuries*, vol. 1, ed. J. Daniélou and H. Marou, London 1964.

/22/ *Fêtes et Calendriers bibliques*, 3rd edition *with additions*, trans. from Eng., Paris 1967. See also J. Hazelden Walker, 'The Earliest Roman Liturgy' *loc.cit. under* "Sacred Time".

/23/ *Op.cit.*, 169

/24/ *Ibid.*, 113ff.

/25/ "Le chant de la perle", *loc.cit.*, 8; see also, 'KLASMA, SPERMA, POIMNION', *loc.cit.*, 208, note 1.

/26/ *L'Eucharistie. Des célébrations actuelles au fruit du paradis* in Origines chrétiennes 3 (in preparation).

/27/ 1 *Cor.* 10, 16f.

/28/ *Op.cit.*, 137ff.

/29/ 'KLASMA ...', *loc.cit.*

Postscript

Since giving this paper a new edition of the *Didache* has been published: *La doctrine des douze apôtres (Didache). Introduction, texte, traduction, notes, appendice et index*, ed. Willy Rordorf and André Tuilier in *Sources chrétiennes* 248, Paris 1978. See my review/article, 'Reflections on a new edition of the *Didache*' in the 1980 issue of *Vigiliae Christianae*.

Adam in Paul's Letter to the Romans

Rev. Dr. A.J.M. Wedderburn,
Lecturer in New Testament,
St. Mary's College,
St. Andrews,
Fife   KY16 9JU,
SCOTLAND.

This paper concentrates, not on that passage in *Romans* which deals explicitly with Adam, ch.5: 12-21, but on two other passages in which a number of scholars have seen an implicit reference to Adam, 1:18ff. and 7:7ff.. These have their relevance for 5:12-21, as we shall see, but it is on these two other passages that I propose to concentrate. In doing this I hope to raise some issues concerning, first, the more detailed question of how Paul uses the Old Testament and, secondly, more general questions of Paul's theology. That the first may be valuable is suggested by the fact that when E.E. Ellis discusses "the doctrine of the Fall" in his book, *Paul's Use of the Old Testament,* he confines his discussion to *Rom.*5:12-21 /1/. The value of the second may be indicated by Heinrich Schlier's brief excursus on "Adam in Paul" in his recent commentary on *Romans,* in which he completely ignores ch.7 despite his references to Adam in his commentary on this chapter (pp.223ff.) and only alludes in passing to 1:18ff. as illustrating how the gentiles sin "without the law" (p.182) /2/.

I

That the story of Adam lay in the background in *Rom.*1:18ff. was cogently argued by M.D. Hooker:

Of Adam it is supremely true that God manifested to him that which can be known of him (v.19); that from the creation onwards, God's attributes were clearly discernible to him in the things which had been made, and that he was thus without excuse (v.20). Adam, above and before all

men, knew God, but failed to honour him as God, and grew
vain in his thinking and allowed his heart to be darkened
(v.20). Adam's fall was the result of his desire to be
as God, to attain knowledge of good and evil (Gen.iii.5),
so that, claiming to be wise, he in fact became a fool
(v.21). Thus he not only failed to give glory to God but,
according to rabbinic tradition, himself lost the glory
of God which was reflected in his face (v.23). In
believing the serpent's lie that his action would not
lead to death (Gen.iii.4) he turned his back on the truth
of God, and he obeyed, and thus gave his allegiance to a
creature, the serpent, rather than to the Creator (v.25).
Adam, certainly, knew God's δικαίωμα ...; by eating the
forbidden fruit he not only broke that δικαίωμα, but also
consented with the action of Eve, who had already taken
the fruit (v.32) /3/.

This argument of Hooker's is very illuminating and it would be
very easy simply to endorse it and leave it at that; after all,
it is hardly surprising if, when he comes to consider how
God's judgement has come to rest upon man or how sin has taken
a grip on man, Paul finds his thoughts naturally turning to
the account of Adam's fall in *Gen*.3.

But at this point the actual wording of Paul's text sounds
two warning notes: (1) the Old Testament allusions to a fall in
this passage are to accounts, *not of Adam's fall, but of Israel's
fall into idolatry* /4/. Thus v.23 echoes *Ps*.106:20, "They
exchanged the glory of God for the image of an ox that eats
grass" (LXX *Ps*.105:20, ... ἠλλάξαντο τὴν δόξαν αὐτῶν ἐν
ὁμοιώματι μόσχου ...)' and *Jer*.2:11, "My people have changed
their glory (LXX ἠλλάξατο τὴν δόξαν αὐτοῦ) for that which does
not profit"; v.21 may already have alluded to *Jer*.2:5, "(your
fathers) went far from·me, and went after worthlessness, and
became worthless (LXX ἐματαιώθησαν)" /5/. In addition we may
note the language of the general prohibition of idolatry in
Deut.4:15-18, which may also be echoed here.

But before we make too much of this we should note that,
as J. Jervell points out /6/, Jewish tradition frequently
associated Adam's fall and the sin of the golden calf. In
some traditions the Exodus and the giving of the law were
viewed as a new creation; Moses regains the position lost by
Adam /7/, and Israel at Sinai are glorious beings and like
angels /8/. But they behaved like Adam and so lost their

immortality; as Adam brought death into the world so did the
golden calf /9/. Indeed in some circles a sort of doctrine of
hereditary sin seems to have sprung up around the tradition of
the golden calf /10/. In *Mekilta* Tractate Bešallaḥ 7 (ed.
Lauterbach I pp.248f.) R. Akiba and R. Pappias use *Ps*.106:20
to interpret *Gen*.3:22, "the man is become as one of us", in
such a way as to deny that this means that man has become
angelic; "it only means that God put before him two ways, the
way of life and the way of death, and he chose for himself the
way of death" /11/.

       This may all be seen as a development of that sort of
reflection on man, particularly Jewish man, which blends
together creation and law-giving; as early as *Sirach* we find
a blending of the creation described in 17:1 with the giving
of the law in 17:11-13 /12/. Some such idea of the continuity
of Adam with Israel after the giving of the law seems to be
implicit in *Rom*.5:14; with the giving of the law through Moses
men resume sinning in the way Adam sinned. Whereas Ben Sira was
not writing historically, Paul is, after a fashion, and this
creates problems for him /13/.

       But was Adam's sin idolatry in Paul's eyes? Hooker
initially states that "According to Paul's account here the sin
into which man originally falls is that of idolatry", but
subsequently she seems to tone down her assertions: Adam was
guilty of serving the creature rather than the Creator and it
is "from this confusion ... that idolatry springs" (she does
not say here that it actually was idolatry). Again

       In listening to the voice of the serpent, Adam has not
       only failed to exercise his rightful dominion over
       creation, but by placing himself in subservience to a
       creature, *has opened up the way to idolatry* /14/.

But if listening to the serpent and placing himself in
subservience to it is not idolatry, when else did Adam commit
it? Moreover, Hooker's hesitation here is perhaps occasioned
by her recognition that "there is nothing in the Genesis
narrative itself to suggest that Adam was an idolater" /15/.

       She was perhaps right to be cautious at this point, since
there are aspects of this account of the "Rake's Progress" of
man's decline which are unexpected if *Gen*.3 has played a
determinative role in its formation. Adam in Genesis only

turns away from God after his sin and only then is he barred
from God's presence (*Gen.*3:8,23f.); in *Romans* man turns away
from God and only then does he fall into idolatry (1:21-5).
More seriously, the attempt to see in *Rom.*1 allusions to the
sexual seduction of Eve by the serpent as it is found in some
Jewish traditions stumbles against the fact that sexual
perversions are a further development of man's decline and
not its cause. If Genesis has influenced Romans at this point
it is more likely that it is *Gen.*6:1-4 with its account of the
unnatural union of the sons of God with the daughters of men
rather than the account of Eve's temptation /16/. In other
words the order of events is not quite what we would expect if
*Gen.*3 were *the* dominant influence upon this account;
consequently it is overstating the case when Hooker claims
that "Paul's account of man's wickedness has been deliberately
stated in terms of the Biblical narrative of Adam's fall"/17/.

This brings us to the second 'warning note' issued by the
text of *Rom.*1:18ff.: (2) the language of *Genesis* is echoed at
several points in this passage, but *the allusions are to ch.1,
not to ch.3*. Thus the words ἀπὸ κτίσεως κόσμου in 1:20 may
introduce an allusion to the creation story of *Gen.*1 /18/.
The order of created things named in 1:23 is similar to that
of *Gen.*1:20-5, although it must be granted that a number of
items are omitted from the list and man is placed first /19/.
The references to male and female in 1:26f. may allude to
*Gen.*1:27, "male and female he created them" /20/. Finally, the
insertion of the term εἰκών in 1:23 may refer to man's creation
κατ' εἰκόνα ἡμετέραν καὶ καθ' ὁμοίωσιν (*Gen.*1:26) /21/.

At this point it is necessary to digress slightly to
consider the likelihood and the implications of this last
allusion, since it is by no means either uncontroversial or
straightforward. C.K. Barrett, for instance, in his
commentary, sees the addition of the εἰκόνος to the ὁμοιώματι
as an example of hendiadys: the "reduplication emphasizes the
inferior, shadowy character of that which is substituted for
God" /22/. But is that all? Hooker argues that Paul, as
opposed to other New Testament writers, elsewhere uses εἰκών
in the sense of "image" or "likeness", so that meanings like
"idol" or "shadow" would be uncharacteristic;

Twice he refers the term to Christ, who is 'the image of
God'; once to man in an exposition of *Gen.*1:27; and four
times to the future glorified state of the Christian, who

is being changed into, or conformed to, the image of
Christ or of the Creator /23/.

We may further note how, when Paul uses εἰκών when he is
speaking of man, he often clearly seems to do so with an
implicit reference to the Genesis account of man's creation:
I Cor. 11:7, as Hooker notes, is based on *Gen*. 1.27, *I Cor*.
15:49 is in the context of his contrast of Adam and Christ,
and *Col*. 3:10, whether Pauline or not, speaks of our putting
on the new man who is being renewed κατ᾽ εἰκόνα τοῦ κτίσαντος
αὐτόν. Furthermore, as Hooker argues, the singular ἀνθρώπου ·
contrasts significantly with the following genitive plurals.

But here we find a surprising development in Hooker's
argument, for it seems to follow from what she has said that
(a) we should see here a reference to the creation of man in
Gen. 1:27, and (b) that we should not expect here a negative
sense of εἰκών, like "idol", or "shadow" as opposed to reality,
but rather a positive one, as elsewhere in Paul, where εἰκών
suggests a relationship of dignity. In other words, we should
expect here a rendering like "they exchanged the glory of the
immortal God for the likeness of his (God's) image, namely
mortal man (i.e. ἀνθρώπου in apposition to εἰκόνος), and for
the likeness of things that fly, of quadrupeds and creeping
things". Rather, she endorses Barrett's interpretation and
translates "for a likeness of (a) an image of corruptible man,
(b) various types of animals" /24/. In doing this she has
given εἰκών a sense that is significantly different from
Pauline usage elsewhere.

But here a further question arises: is Paul in 1:23
talking about a change in the object of man's worship or a
change in man's nature? *Ps*. 106:20 certainly seems to have had
the former in mind and this is what most commentators understand
Paul to have meant. But Jervell comments that the φθαρτὸς
ἄνθρωπος must be Adam and that Paul is speaking here of men
being copies of Adam /25/. Here then is yet a further
dimension to this verse, but certainly not the only one since
it is harder to imagine Paul saying that men are also copies
of birds, quadrupeds and creeping things. In other words
three ideas intermingle in this verse, rather uncomfortably we
may think:

(1) fallen man worships creatures, not his Creator (*cf*.
v.25);

(2)   fallen man includes among the objects of his worship
man who is God's image, not God himself;

(3)   fallen man is no longer in the image of God, but in
the image of Adam.

In other words there are a number of different levels or
dimensions to Paul's allusions to the Old Testament at this
point, superimposed the one upon the other, just as creation
and lawgiving, fall and idolatry mingle in Paul's language.

At this point we may note that Paul was certainly aware
that εἰκών could also mean "image" in the sense of "idol" and
that means, to put it paradoxically, that man for him both
was an image and could have one. Indeed, which one he had
affected which one he was, since the Old Testament and Paul
seem to have held that a man may in some way become like that
which he worships. That idea is implicit in *Jer*.2:5 to which
Paul may allude in 1:21: Israel "went after worthlessness, and
became worthless" /26/. Similarly a switch of worship back to
a proper object can effect a saving transformation: 'we all,
... beholding the glory of the Lord, are being changed into
his likeness (εἰκών) from one degree of glory to another'
(*II Cor*. 3:18). Worship of, and communion with, base things
debases man, and a similar concentration on worthy objects of
worship exalts him /27/. Thus it comes as no surprise that
for Paul men have not only changed their focus of worship, but
also thereby their very nature.

But did they thereby lose God's image and only regain it
through Christ? Paul says nothing explicit about this and
indeed may not be consistent with regard to it /28/. Certainly
(a) he nowhere expressly speaks of a restoration in Christ of
man's primal state; (b) in *I Cor*. 15:45-9 he takes the
creation of the first man as being only that of a living soul
and, despite his use of εἰκών in these verses, he speaks of
men now being in the image of mortal man, not of God /29/; yet
(c) in *I Cor*. 11:7 (male) man is God's image and glory. This
last statement is hard to reconcile with what Paul says
elsewhere about fallen man, notably in *Rom*. 3:23, and it may
be that this is yet another of the inconsistencies and
questionable arguments that beset this passage of
I Corinthians /30/. Here we have, I believe, one example of
Paul's lack of coherence and consistency, in short of a
systematic theology, a lack of which we shall shortly see yet

further evidence.

But, to return to *Rom*. 1:23, how are we to translate this
verse in the light of the different nuances of meaning that we
have uncovered? In his use together of the two senses of εἰκών,
Paul plays on an ambiguity of this word. Not that such a
word-play should surprise us from the writer who could so freely
play on the word κεφαλή in *I Cor*. 11:3f., saying that man both
had a head (literally) and was one (figuratively) in that he
had authority over woman. But, unlike *I Cor*. 11:3f., *Rom*. 1:23
is very hard to translate in such a way that the word-play and
the ambiguity remain; in English we are almost forced to opt
either for the one or the other, either for man as the image
or for the image as what man has; perhaps the nearest that we
can get to a satisfactory rendering is "they exchanged the
glory of the immortal God for the likeness of an image, mortal
man, and of birds and quadrupeds and creeping things", thus
at least leaving it open whose image mortal man is, God's or
man's, and whether the exchange is of natures or of objects of
worship. Playing on words certainly may make for obscurity of
argument, but was Paul's argument always as lucid as possible?
I Cor. 11:2-16 does not allow us to say that.

In conclusion we may therefore say that what we have in
Rom. 1:18ff. seems to be a synthetic description in which the
ideas of *Gen*. 3 have played a part, along with other Old
Testament passages describing Israel's fall into idolatry and
later experience of idolatry; these different materials have
been superimposed the one upon the other to produce a composite
narrative. This story is not timeless - compare the aorists of
vv.21ff. -, but it is not to be pinned down to any particular
point in the Old Testament story; the essence of Israel's
history and man's history as a history of turning ever further
away from God is summed up vividly in this account /31/.

                                II

We have not the time to go into the whole complex problem
of the other passage that we are considering, *Rom*. 7:7ff. /32/.
But it is necessary to note that Paul is here dealing with the
status and nature of the law, and in particular with the
question "Is the law sin?" (7:7). In the following verses he
reflects upon the experience of encounter with God's command.
But the controversial question is "Whose experience?" - that of

Paul, of the redeemed or the unredeemed, of Jews or gentiles?

But we are concerned with the influence of the story of
Adam on this passage and in particular on vv.7-13 which are
marked off from the following verses by the aorist verbs (the
same tense as used in the story told in 1:18ff.). A number of
exegetes see the story of Adam lying behind these verses; in
particular, E. Käsemann observes of them that "there is nothing
in our verses which does not fit Adam and all of it only fits
Adam" /33/. But again the verbal allusions to the Fall story
are hard to find: perhaps the sole candidate is the ἐξηπάτησεν
of v.11 and that allusion is none too obvious, being detectable
only with the help of *II Cor*. 11:3 and *I Tim*. 2:14 and the
references there to the serpent's deception of Eve. Yet now the
mythological serpent is replaced by the personified power of
sin in what may perhaps be described as a piece of
demythologizing, yet one which still uses figurative language.

The reference to Adam here becomes the more intelligible
when we consider some of the uses made of the Adam story in
Jewish exegesis:

(1) the commandment not to eat of the tree of the
knowledge of good and evil was viewed as a receiving of the
whole law *in nuce* /34/; this seems to lie behind *IV Ezra's*
comment that Adam transgressed God's statutes (pl.) /35/.
According to Targum Neofiti on *Gen*. 2:15 Adam was put in the
garden to "do service according to the Law and keep its
commandments" /36/. *bSanh*. 56b contains a discussion on the
number of commandments given to Adam: according to R. Judah
(mid 2nd. cent.) Adam was only forbidden to commit idolatry, but
the slightly earlier R. Judah b. Bathyra added blasphemy and
others added social laws. Another tradition depicts God as
proposing to give the law through Adam, but then reflecting
that if he had not managed to keep the six commandments given
to him he was not going to cope with 613 /37/.

(2) Adam's - and Eve's - disobedience was seen as a breach
of the tenth commandment which is quoted in 7:7: according to
bSabb. 145b-146a the serpent injected lust into Eve, and in
Apoc. Mos. 19:3 he pours upon the fruit of the tree "the poison
of his wickedness, which is lust" /38/.

(3) This "coveting" or "lusting" was seen as being at the
root of all disobedience to the law. The same passage of

Apoc. Mos. cited above describes "lust" as "the root and
beginning of every sin". The Letter of James 1:15 describes a
chain reaction in which "desire when it has conceived gives
birth to sin". In Philo *Decal.* 173 the tenth commandment is
said to prohibit desire, that "fount of injustices", from which
flow the most lawless deeds of all sorts; there is no escaping
it, since "like a flame in the forest, it spreads abroad and
consumes and destroys everything" /39/. According to the Amora
R. Yaqum "whoever transgresses, 'Thou shalt not covet', is as
though he has transgressed all the Ten Words" /40/. In *I Cor.*
10:6 Paul describes Israel in the wilderness as ἐπιθυμηταί
κακῶν /41/.

It is consistent with this that Paul in *Rom.* 5:14 classes
together Adam and those who have the law and distinguishes them
from those who lived between Adam and Moses; Adam possessed a
commandment and so his fall was a παράβασις, a transgression of
a concrete command of God.

At this point we may note in passing a recent and ingenious
interpretation of these verses by P. von der Osten-Sacken /42/;
his suggestion is that to desire not to covet or desire, because
it is in itself a form of desiring, is therefore a transgression
of the tenth commandment. This is ingenious, but perhaps too
ingenious. This desire would be, after all, akin to the
ζῆλος θεοῦ of *Rom.* 10:2, which is nothing sinful in itself, but
is misdirected. It is therefore preferable to see this
desiring prohibited by the tenth commandment as an evil sort
of desiring which lies behind all sinning.

Nor, again, is it surprising that Paul, seeking to show man
confronted by a command of God, should go back to the story of
man's beginning and his first encounter with God's command.
Adam lies behind the first person singular of these verses, as
the first to taste the bitter experience of an unaided
confrontation with God's demand, unaided, that is, by the
Spirit of God /43/. Here speaks "Adamitic man" /44/,
exemplified by his prototype, Adam. Thus the answer to the
question "Whose experience of encounter with the command of God
is depicted here?" is, as far as vv.7-13 are concerned, Adam
and after him all whom he represents; thus this would not be
the Jews alone, but would still apply particularly to them. The
reference to the period of existence without the law should not
therefore be understood to refer to a period of childish
innocence in the life of every man, or at least of every Jew,

like the time before becoming a *bar-miṣwah* at the age of
thirteen /45/, but rather as a reference to the myth of
mankind's primal innocence in the Garden of Eden, however
short-lived that period may have been /46/.

Hence it would be difficult if, after taking this line of
interpretation, we went on to interpret vv. 14ff. as applying,
in the first instance, to redeemed man or to Paul himself.
Despite the change indicated by the use of the present tense,
some continuity must be maintained between the 'I' of vv.7-13
and the 'I' of vv.14ff. /47/. But to pose the alternatives
here in terms of either redeemed or unredeemed perhaps distorts
the issue. For Paul the redeemed man yet has to struggle with
the unredeemed in himself; this emerges from a verse like
I Cor. 15:49, where, if we retain the future φορέσομεν which
seems to fit in better with the whole thrust of the passage,
we are confronted with an interesting problem when we ask whose
image Christians bear now; in the past that of the man of earth,
in the future that of the man of heaven, but what now? No
verse, it seems to me, highlights better the tension and the
transitional nature of the Christian's position in Paul's
thought. But Paul's point is to remind the Corinthians that
they still share the nature of Adam, they are still χοϊκοί,
and as they are, as flesh and blood, they are not ready for the
kingdom of God (*I Cor*. 15:50) /48/. If we look at *Rom*. 7:14ff.
in the light of this then it becomes clearer how our old
natures, our Adamic natures, still struggle on, even in
Christians; it becomes even clearer what a struggle this is if,
as we have suggested, Paul describes here the struggle of man
left to himself, confronted with the bare command of God, still
"sold under sin" (7:14) /49/; this may be something of an
unreal abstraction in the case of the redeemed, but Paul leaves
out of consideration at this point the question of the Spirit's
intervention and only introduces that in ch.8.

III

We have now looked somewhat cursorily at the evidence for
the impression made by the Adam story on these two passages.
It needs to be emphasized again that this influence is not
surprising; it would have been more surprising if Paul could
have spoken of man's present state and its causes and its
nature without reference to the wealth of highly suggestive
imagery contained in the Genesis narrative. It also needs to
be said that Paul would have been only too aware that Adam by

his very name stands for all men; just how aware he is of the
interchangeability of Adam and ἄνθρωπος is indicated in *I Cor.*
15:45b where, having referred to ὁ πρῶτος ἄνθρωπος Ἀδάμ
(Ἀδάμ as the proper name), he refers to Christ, not as
ὁ ἔσχατος ἀνθρωπος, but as ὁ ἔσχατος Ἀδάμ /50/.

But, if we now turn to *Rom.* 5:12-21, it might at first
sight seem that the allusive hints have been replaced by direct
assertions, and imaginative reflections on the condition of
mankind in general by a far more literalist use of the *Genesis*
narrative as the story of an individual man. The first
comparison would be true up to a point: yet it is not until
v.14 that the εἷς ἄνθρωπος of v.12 is named. But the second
comparison must be handled with greater caution since this
passage has been used by conservative scholars who wish to
maintain the literal truth of *Gen.* 1-3 /51/. In the first
place, whether or not these chapters were literally true is
probably not a question over which Paul would really have been
consciously exercised; like most of his contemporaries he could
simply assume it. But far more important is the question
whether the literal truth or otherwise really matters for Paul's
purposes. Certainly Adam is not for Paul just one individual
human being among others, any more than Christ is; like Christ,
he is, by virtue of his position in God's plan, representative
of other men and he blazes a trail for them to follow /52/.
But, unlike Christ, he is still, for Paul, chronologically the
first man, and this is also significant for Paul; he is not just
some timeless exemplar of a certain existential experience of
man with his God /53/. By insisting on the guilt of this man
Paul, along with his fellow Jews, insists on the universality
of sin: all men are in its clutches; from the first it has
dominated human history. The history of sin is co-terminous
with the history of mankind /54/. Moreover, and this is even
more significant for Paul in this context, this history of sin
and history of man is not made up of a series of isolated
individual lives or episodes, but of a complex interwoven
pattern of lives acting upon one another and events bringing
forth other events; from the first, one man's actions have of
necessity affected other men and his world. These insights may
of course be safeguarded by a literal interpretation of *Gen.1-3*,
but such a literal interpretation is not the only possible
safeguard for them. And if we take all these three passages of
Romans together it would be even more difficult to maintain
that the literal interpretation was central to Paul's purposes.

But if these two passages thus complement our understanding
of *Rom*. 5:12-21 there is one respect in which they do not.
In 5:13f. Paul deals with the question of the sense in which
those between Adam and Moses, *i.e.* those who did not have
express commandments from God, could be held to have sinned /55/;
his answer seems to be that they did - and what Jew, knowing
the events recorded in the Old Testament during that period,
from the murder of Abel to the stubborn obstinacy and cruel
oppression of Pharaoh, would want to maintain otherwise? That
they did sin is confirmed for Paul by the fact that they too
died; death reigned then too. It may be correct as an
exegesis of Paul to stress the distinction between plain
sinning and transgression (*cf*. *Rom*. 4:15), but in that case
the questions of the justice of a penalty being exacted from
those who sinned in ignorance and of the legitimacy of
describing this ignorant behaviour as sinning loom even larger
/56/. Yet strangely Paul makes no use of the argument of 1:18ff.,
that all men knew enough of God to be without excuse for their
neglect of him and their consequent sin, nor indeed of the idea
of 2:14f., that the gentiles have God's law written on their
hearts even if they do not have the written law of Moses /57/.
But he does not and his argument is the weaker for that; he
has raised the question how sin can be reckoned when there is
no law and his answer has simply been that sin was there /58/.

This seems to underline two things: first, that Paul, in
common with the rest of contemporary Judaism, had no one
systematic and coherent account of the origins of human sin.
Secondly, like his contemporaries he was content to use
different elements from the Jewish traditions at different
times in different ways, without resolving the tensions that
thus arose /59/. Interestingly he lets these tensions remain
even in a document which some have handled, wrongly in my
opinion, as a sort of dogmatic treatise, and one which
certainly offers a more sustained and connected argument than
we get elsewhere in his letters /60/. This in turn may suggest
that Paul was either not all that logical in his thinking or at
least not logical in the sense in which we understand the term.
But why should we not allow Paul to have his human weaknesses?
Although Paul's opponents may have said that "His letters are
weighty and powerful; ... as a speaker he is beneath contempt"
(*II Cor*. 10:10), is it after all so surprising to find his
written arguments also coming apart at the seams?

NOTES

/1/   Edinburgh, 1957, pp.58-60; he only sees in 1:23 a ref. to
Ps. 106:20 and in 7:11 a ref. to *Gen*. 3:13 which he does not
discuss further.

/2/   *Der Römerbrief, Herders Theol. Komm. zum NT* vi
(Freiburg/Basel/Wien, 1977), pp.179-89.

/3/   'Adam in Romans i', *NTS* vi (1959/60), pp.297-306, here
pp.300f..

/4/   J. Jervell, *Imago Dei: Gen.1,26f. im Spätjudentum, in
der Gnosis und in den paulinischen Briefen (FRLANT* NF lviii,
Göttingen, 1960), p.318, suggests that Paul's allusion to the
Ursünde of the Jews here is deliberate, in that he is turning
Jewish polemical material used against gentiles into a
polemic against Jews; but it would be wrong to restrict the
application of this passage to Jews or to argue that it
applies only to gentiles.

/5/   This could equally well be a ref. to II Kings 17:15
(LXX ἐπορεύθησαν ὀπίσω τῶν ματαίων καὶ ἐματαιώθησαν).

/6/   *Op.cit.*, pp.115., 321; for the parallels drawn between
Gen.1-3 and Sinai in rabbinic thought *cf.* J.B. Schaller,
*Gen.1.2 im antiken Judentum: Untersuchungen über Verwendung und
Deutung der Schöpfungsaussagen von Gen.1.2 im antiken Judentum*
(Diss. Göttingen, 1961), pp.147-50.

/7/   *Cf., e.g., Deut.R.*11:3 (Moses is greater than Adam);
Pes.R. 21:6; Ps-Philo, *Bib.Ant.* 12:1 (glory of Moses); also
Memar Marqah V.§4 (ed. Macdonald I p.128, II p.209).

/8/   *Exod.R.*32:1; *Lev.R.*11:3; *Num.R.*16:24; *Deut.R.*7:12 (Resh
Lakish, 3rd cent.); *Pesikta* 37a and parallels in
Strack-Billerbeck IV, p.940; but *cf.* R. Scroggs, *The Last Adam:
a Study in Pauline Anthropology* (Oxford, 1966), p.53, who
points out that "image" is a word rarely used in Jervell's
evidence.

/9/   *Mek.* Bahodeš 9 (ed. Lauterbach II, p.272); *Exod.R.*32:1,7;
*Lev.R.*11:3; *Num.R.*16:24; *Pes.R.*10:6; *cf.* Strack-Billerbeck IV,
p.941; *bMK* 15b speaks of the loss of God's image by sin in
general.

/10/ *bSanh*.102a; *jTaan.* 5(6) (tr. Schwab IV, p.184);
*Exod.R.*43:2; *Eccles.R.*9:11 §1; *Lam.R.*2:1 §3.

/11/ Lauterbach I, p.248n., explains that the suffix of מחנ֗י
is here treated as a third person singular; *cf.* Jervell,
op.cit., p.85, on the similar מ֗י֗נ֗י֗ה of Tg. Onk..

/12/ *Cf.* Jervell, *op.cit.*, pp.31-7.

/13/ *Cf.* U. Luz, *Das Geschichtsverständnis des Paulus (Beitr.
zur evang. Theol.* xlix, München, 1968), pp.193-211; see further
below.

/14/ *Loc.cit.*, p.301 (my italics). C.K. Barrett, *From First Adam to Last: a Study in Pauline Theology* (London, 1962), p.18, follows Hooker in identifying Adam's sin with idolatry, but without her qualifications.
/15/ *Loc.cit.*, p.302.
/16/ As Hooker in fact sees (*loc.cit.*, p.302).
/17/ *Loc.cit.*, p.301.
/18/ Hooker, *loc.cit.*, p.299; *cf.* Jervell, *op.cit.*, p.320.
/19/ Hooker, *loc.cit.*, p.300, following N. Hyldahl, 'A Reminiscence of the Old Testament at Romans i.23', *NTS* ii (1955/6), pp.285-8.
/20/ Jervell, *ibid.*; *cf.* O. Michel, *Der Brief an die Römer (KEK* IV, Göttingen, 1966⁴), p.68; but *cf.* also Jervell, *op.cit.*, p.305, where he sees a ref. in 1:26 to *Gen.* 3:6, 13.
/21/ Hooker, *loc.cit.*, p.297f., 303-6.
/22/ *A Commentary on the Epistle to the Romans (Black's NT Comms.*, London, 1957), p.38.
/23/ *Loc.cit.*, p.298.
/24/ *Loc.cit.*, p.304.
/25/ *Op.cit.*, p.323; *cf.* p.321 - in Jewish thought 'das Urbild oder erste Abbild ist Adam, εἰκών, während die Menschen, seine Nachkommen, "Abbilder", אדמות‎, ὁμοίωμα benannt werden'. (Evidence on pp.97,104f..) P. Schwanz, *Imago Dei als christologisch-anthropologisches Problem in der Geschichte der Alten Kirche von Paulus bis Clemens von Alexandrien* (Halle, 1970), p.55, argues that because of the following genitives the ref. must be to God's own glory, not to that possessed by men; yet he does not reckon with the possibility of Paul's playing on words here (*cf.* below).
/26/ *Cf. II Kings* 17:15.
/27/ Jervell, *op.cit.*, pp.321f., does not hesitate to draw the inference that by idolatry man becomes like the beasts, lacking knowledge of God and incapable of leading a moral life.
/28/ Jervell, *op.cit.*, p.313, comments that *Rom.* 1-3 is unusual in its use of the idea of the image of God in that it contains no reflection how and why man lost his likeness to God. Yet that he has lost it may be seen from his lack of God's glory (*Rom.*3:23) *if* glory and God's image are equated (*cf. I Cor.*11:7; also Jervell, *op.cit.*, pp.325-31). But F.-W. Eltester, *Eikon im Neuen Testament (BZNW* xxiii, Berlin, 1958), p.163, holds that in Jewish tradition, while man's glory might be lost in the Fall, the image of God was not (but *cf.* his findings on pp.125-7).
/29/ *Cf.* Jervell, *op.cit.*, pp.284-92; the absence of any ref. to *Gen.*1:26f. in *I Cor.* 15:45-9 may be due in part to Paul's

polemical stance and partly to his concentration on man's
physical nature, yet his silence about *Gen.* 1:26f. is a
weakness. E.F. Scott comments on *Eph.* 4:24 that in Christ
"man's true creation has only now taken effect" *(The Epistles
of Paul to the Colossians, to Philemon and to the Ephesians,
Moffatt NT Comms.*, London, 1930, pp.219f.), but to treat this
idea as typical of Paul might be a dangerous argument from
silence.

/30/ For man as God's image rather than in God's image *cf.
Wis.* 2:23; *Vit.Ad. et Ev.* 14:1f.; 37:3; *Apoc. Mos.* 10:3; 12:1;
33:5; 35:2; Phocylides 106. That *I Cor.* 11:7 is out of step
with Paul's view elsewhere is emphasized by Schwanz, *op.cit.*,
pp.19f., 54; *cf.* Jervell, *op.cit.*, pp.292-312. A further
complication is introduced by Schwanz's contention that for
Paul the created image of God in man is something quite
different from that bestowed in Christ *(op.cit.*, p.57); the
latter is identical with the indwelling Christ and so there
can be no question of this image being lost and regained. He
may be right in thinking that the two ideas came to Paul by
different routes, but the wisdom traditions of Hellenistic
Judaism were more likely to be Paul's immediate source for the
second concept than Gnosticism *(cf.* Jervell, *op.cit.*, p.296.)

/31/ Contrasted with these aorists is the present of 1:18,
parallel to that of 1:17; if at all possible it should be
treated as a true parallel *(cf.* G. Bornkamm, "The Revelation
of God's Wrath (Romans 1-3)" in *Early Christian Experience*,
London, 1969, pp.47-70, here pp.61-4; see also G. Herold,
*Zorn und Gerechtigkeit Gottes bei Paulus: eine Untersuchung
zu Röm. 1.16-18, Europäische Hochschulschriften* Reihe xxiii,
Theol. Bd. xiv, Bern/Frankfurt, 1973, pp.260ff., 302ff.).
But the history of sin may lie in the past while God's
judgement is revealed as judgement in the present; *pace* Herold,
op.cit., pp.312ff., God's wrath was there in the past, despite
his patience *(Rom.* 3:25f.), and took the form of giving men up
to their self-chosen ways; only in the light of the gospel is
this seen to be neither impotence nor unheeding lovelessness,
but God's judgement; God's refraining from intervention is
seen to be judgement when he intervenes to save and man's
former alienation is shown in its true light when God draws
near to reconcile.

/32/ Surveys of the different interpretations of these verses
may be found most recently in O. Kuss, *Der Römerbrief*
(Regensburg, 1963²), pp.462-85, K. Kertelge, "Exegetische
Überlegungen zum Verständnis der paulinischen Anthropologie
nach Römer 7", *ZNW* lxii (1971), pp.105-14, and J.D.G. Dunn,

'*Rom*. 7,14-25 in the Theology of Paul', *TZ* xxxi (1975),
pp.257-73. The particular value of Kuss's survey lies in its
questioning whether we are right to speak in terms of mutually
exclusive alternatives here.
/33/ *An die Römer (HNT* viiia, Tubingen, 1974[2]), p.186; *cf*.
Schlier, *op.cit*., pp.223ff.; but *cf*. E. Brandenburger, *Adam und
Christus: exegetisch-religionsgeschichtliche Untersuchung zu
Römer 5,12-21 (1. Kor. 15) (WMANT* vii, Neukirchen, 1962),
pp.215-17, especially p.216: the use of *Gen*. 3 does not mean
that we have here a direct ref. to the Fall or that "we are
to understand the ἐγώ as Adam or even as mankind incorporated
in him or the ἐντολή as the command given in Paradise. Rather
the Adam-event is here understood in a typical, exemplary
sense: as the 'Urgeschichte' of each (post-Mosaic) man set under
the law ...". But of nobody is it true in quite the same way
as it was true of Adam in the story, so that Käsemann's verdict
may stand.
/34/   *Cf*. Jervell, *op.cit*., p.325; Scroggs, *op.cit*., pp.33, 42f..
/35/   *IV Ezra* 7:11 (ed. B. Violet, *GCS* xviii, Leipzig, 1910,
pp.130f.: *constitutiones meas* - pl. also in Syr. and one
Arabic version; sing. in Eth., missing in one Arabic version
and Arm.).
/36/   Ed. A. Diez Macho (Madrid/Barcelona, 1968), p.501.
/37/   *Gen.R*.24:5 (Soncino tr. I, p.202 - attributed to
R.Judah also; in Strack-Billerbeck III, p.41, to R. Jehuda
b.Simon, *ca*. 320); the six commandments concern idolatry,
blasphemy, the authority of judges, shedding of blood,
unchastity and robbery (*Deut.R*.2:25; *cf*. *bSanh*. 56b; *Midr.Ps*.
1:10); seven commandments in *Gen.R*.16:5f.; *cf*. Strack-Billerbeck
III, p.37.
/38/   *Cf*. F. Büchsel in *TDNT* III, p.169; he also draws attention
to *IV Macc*. 2:6; *cf*. also *Aboth* 4:21.
/39/   *Cf*. also §§142, 150, 153.
/40/   *Pes.R*.21:17.
/41/   *Cf*. S. Lyonnet, "Tu ne convoiteras pas' (*Rom*.7:7)" in
Neotestamentica et Patristica (Festschr. O. Cullmann, *Suppl.
Nov.Test* vi, Leiden, 1962), pp.157-65, here pp.159f..
/42/   *Römer 8 als Beispiel paulinischer Soteriologie (FRLANT*
cxii, Göttingen, 1975), p.204.
/43/   That Paul is talking of man's unaided effort here may be
indicated by the αὐτός in the summary of 7:25 (whether or not
it is a gloss): it might be paraphrased "(I) left to myself/by
myself".
/44/   *Cf*. G. Bornkamm, 'Sin, Law and Death: an Exegetical Study
of Romans 7' in *op.cit*., pp.87-104, here p.94, and v.d.

Osten-Sacken, *op.cit.*,p.200. Although Adam's experience is
representative his experience is peculiarly his own.
/45/ So, *e.g.*, E. Best, *The Letter of Paul to the Romans*
(Cambridge Bible Comm on the NEB, Cambridge, 1967), pp.81f.;
criticized by Bornkamm, "Sin, Law and Death", pp.92f., 102 n.15.
It is doubtful how far Jews could be described as "without
the law" before they reached this age; *cf. Tos.* Ḥag. 1:2 in
C.G. Montefiore, H. Loewe, *A Rabbinic Anthology* (London, 1938,
repr. Meridian Books, n.d.), §1467; it is similarly doubtful
how far a child before this age could be said to be without
experience of sin: *ibid.* § 780 (*Tanḥ.* Berešit § 7 f. 10a)
suggests that sin was experienced from the age of ten and
§ 1370 (Tanna debe Eliyyahu p.13) that "a little child at
school" has to keep himself from sin.
/46/ So Schlier, *op.cit.*, p.224. *Cf. bSanh.* 38b; *Gen.R.*18:6;
*Exod.R.*32:1; *Cave of Treasures* 7a:1-2 (ed. Budge p.65);
6 hours; for *Jub.* it is longer - Adam is only brought into
Eden 40 days after his creation and Eve 80 (3:9), and they
remain there for 7 years. (*Pace* Kertelge, *loc.cit.*, p.108, v.9
does not allow us to interpret the past tenses of vv.7-13 as
referring simply to the old aeon when man was under the law).
/47/ *Cf.* Kuss, *op.cit.*, p.463.
/48/ *Cf.* further on Paul's argument with the Corinthians in
this ch. my article on "Body of Christ and Related Concepts
in 1 Corinthians", *SJT* xxiv (1971), pp.74-96, especially
pp.90-4.
/49/ *Pace* C.E.B. Cranfield *(The Epistle to the Romans, ICC,*
Edinburgh, 1975, I, pp.342-7), while the redeemed man *qua*
redeemed might perhaps be called σαρκινός, however inconsistent
that may imply that he is (*cf. I Cor.* 3:1), πεπράμενος ὑπὸ τὴν
ἀμαρτίαν is another matter.
/50/ *Cf.* Barrett, *First Adam* p.19; the same awareness seems
to lie behind the often-quoted *Syr.Bar.* 54:19.
/51/ *E.g.* J. Murray, Art. "Adam in the New Testament", *New
Bible Dict.* (London, 1962), p.14.
/52/ *Cf.* Barrett, *First Adam,* p.5; compare also the
interesting switch from sing. to pl. in *Sir.*17:1-3.
/53/ *Cf.* Luz, *op.cit.*, p.201: "Adam is for him not simply
the mythological personification of every man, but a historical
figure at the start of world-history".
/54/ *Cf.* Schlier, *op.cit.*, p.182; Luz, *op.cit.*, p.207: " 'Adam'
serves to show the dimensions of human sin from which Christ
redeems us, and thus the dimensions of salvation"; sin is
rather a *Tatschicksal* engulfing the whole world.

/55/   *Cf*. Brandenburger, *op.cit*., pp.180-205; also Luz, *op.cit*.,
pp.198-201.
/56/   Particularly is this true when (as Luz, *op.cit*., pp.202f.,
maintains) παράπτωμα as "die Sündentat als Geschichtsmacht"
existed prior to the law; *cf*. also Brandenburger, *op.cit*.,
pp.184-7.
/57/   *Cf*. G. Bornkamm, "Gesetz und Natur (Röm. 2:14-16)" in
Studien zu Antike und Urchristentum (Beitr. zur evang. Theol.
xxviii, München, 1963), pp.93-118, especially p.101: "So νόμος
refers to the one law of God which has been given to Jews and
gentiles, but in different ways".
/58/   So Brandenburger, *op.cit*., pp.203-5, sees that Paul's
answer implies that God's will is not only known in the form of
the law of Moses (or his command to Adam), and that Paul could
have supported his argument along the lines of 1:18ff.; he
does not do so because he here wishes to avoid treating the
law as more than something temporary.
/59/   As Jewish tradition also let the tension remain: *e.g*.
IV Ezra 3:21, *cor enim malignum baiolans* Adam transgressed -
whence did he then get this evil heart? It seems to be, not
the result of his sin, but its cause; was he then created
evil? We are not told. (*Pace* G.H. Box in (ed.) R.H. Charles,
The Apocrypha and Pseudepigrapha of the Old Testament II,
Oxford, 1913, p.563, *baiolans* is better translated 'bearing'
than 'clothing himself').
/60/   Similarly Brandenburger, *op.cit*., pp.205-14, points out
the impossibility of harmonizing 5:12-21 and 7:7-13: in the
former, before the law comes, one may both know and experience
sinning, but in the latter sin is 'dead' though not
non-existent (*cf*. p.215); in the former the law's coming
increases sin, in the latter it brings it to life.

The Martyrdom of Peter was Before the Fire in Rome

A.E. Wilhelm-Hooijbergh,
10 Petruslaan,
6564 AK H.Landstichting,
HOLLAND.

Although J.A.T. Robinson dates *2 Timothy* to AD 58 as the last of Paul's epistles, he remains convinced that Peter and Paul died after 64. Peter in 65, Paul in 66. Robinson suggests that Peter was one of the victims of the festivities Nero organized in his gardens to punish Christians, not so much for setting fire to the city as for their anti-social tendencies as Michael Grant translates Tacitus /1/.

Robinson dates these festivities later than Tacitus, who dates the fire in 64 from the 19th till the 31st of July and the festivities in the same year. Robinson however prefers the games the next year, the spring of 65, but Tacitus elaborately describes how in the spring of 65 there was a plot to kill Nero on the very day of the circus games for Ceres (12-19 April). Nero being fond of such games, the conspirators hoped that he would dare to leave his house and garden. The plot was disclosed and Nero, becoming increasingly frightened, redoubled his guard. Under these circumstances he was not likely to organize festivities in his gardens /2/.

But why does Robinson redate the fateful garden party? There is a gap to be filled between Peter's death and the succession of Linus, as bishop in 68. Already in the early centuries this was a problem. Peter and Paul must have died just before, in 68, as Eusebius accepts and Jerome affirms /3/.

Now Clemens Romanus in his first epistle to the Corinthians /4/ also alludes to the death of both. But Paul's death can be almost exactly dated, because we have more certainty about the dating of some events in his life. We may be sure, for instance, that he lived two years in Rome in a rented house, with a soldier in charge of him, perhaps for two

years /5/. And according to Clement he went to Spain (the
limits of the West) and "he gave testimony before the rulers,
and thus passed from the world and was taken up into the Holy
Place". His years in Rome were from 60-62 at the latest and
perhaps one year in Spain. Soon after that he must have been
beheaded, and Peter crucified a year before.

But what about the years between Peter's and Paul's
death and Linus becoming bishop in (probably) 68? As Dr. Brooks
recently /6/ acknowledged the authenticity of the *Epistula
Clementis*, I feel justified in basing my reply to the above
question on this document. This epistle was not yet known to
Eusebius, although he knew already something about the now
so-called *Pseudo-Clementines* /7/.

In this epistle of Clement to James, the *"episcopus
episcoporum"* we can read that Peter appointed Clement to be his
successor /8/. In this case Clement's episcopacy fills up the
years from the death of Peter till Linus. For what reason
Clement abdicated and gave his office to Linus we may only
guess. About Linus we know nothing, except that Paul mentions
him in *2 Tim*. 4.21. Was Clement's retreat the outcome of a
party struggle? Each of the apostles had a certain adherence.
Perhaps he hints at the troubles in the Roman church in his
Corinthian Letter /9/.

Peter was not crucified in Nero's garden, as Robinson
suggests. In Tacitus many Christians "were fastened on
crosses and, when daylight failed, were burned as lamps by
night"! Was Peter crucified upside down here? This is also
known in Syriac tradition /10/. Tradition about Peter's death
is quite different. In the *Quo vadis* legend /11/ he was a
victim of jealousy of high officials. Their wives and
concubines were converted, and they organised Peter's
crucifixion even without Nero's approval. When Nero heard it
he was very angry and said he would have punished Peter more
severely himself. Agrippa had commanded Peter to be crucified
on an accusation of godlessness.

Peter's death cannot be dated without dating Paul's.
Perhaps it is better, therefore, to try and fix the date of
Paul's death in relation to the fire of Rome. In Suetonius,
Tacitus and the *Acts of Paul* /12/ Christians were *punished*.
In Tacitus and the Acts they were "burned with fire".
Suetonius starts this chapter with the fire in Rome, but there
is no relation between this and the punishment of Christians.

In the *Acts of Paul* Nero locked up a number of soldiers, who
were converted by Paul and "commanded the soldiers of the
great king to be sought out, and set forth a decree to this
effect, that all that were found to be Christians and soldiers
of Christ should be slain". And among others Paul also
was brought, bound. When Caesar heard that Paul's king would
fight against the world with fire he commanded "all the
prisoners to be burned with fire, but Paul to be beheaded after
the law of the Romans".

The notice that *2 Tim.* was written in 58 is also of
interest for the dating of the death of Peter and Paul.
Finally, however, the most important source for dating the
death of Peter and Paul is the year in which Clement wrote
his first epistle to the Corinthians. This was before the
destruction of the temple in Jerusalem as has been established
in my article in the Heythrop Journal of July 1975, and in
Robinson's *Redating the N.T.* in 1976. Clement suggests that
Paul was killed soon after his arrival from Spain and Peter
died according to tradition about a year before Paul and also
βιαίως, - *vi*! as Clement writes in the Epistle to James /13/.
Their death could not have been but one or two years before
Clement wrote his epistle to the Corinthians.

NOTES

/1/   John A.T. Robinson, *Redating the New Testament,* SCM,
London, 1976.
       Tacitus: *The Annals of Imperial Rome,* Penguin, 1959.
/2/   *Ann.* xv. ch. 50-54, especially ch. 53.
/3/   Eusebius Eccl. III, 13: 80 - 12 = 68! cf. Rob. p. 147.
/4/   Ch. 5.
/5/   *Acts* 28:16, 30. Or merely just after he arrived in Rome?
/6/   Communication given at the Patristic Conference at
Oxford, September 1975, by the Rev. Dr. Edward C. Brooks.
/7/   Eusebius III, 38.   /8/ *Epistula Clementis* 2, 3.
/9/   Ch. 54, 2.
/10/   Robert Murray: *Symbols of Church and Kingdom, A Study in
Early Syriac Tradition,* Cambridge University Press, 1975, p.238.
/11/   M.R. James, *The apocryphal N.T.,* Clarendon Press, 1972,
pp.332-3. (*Acts of Peter* III, ch.33-36).
/12/   Suetonius, *Nero* ch.16. cf. ch.38; Tacitus *Ann.* XV, 44;
Acts of Paul, ed. James p.294-5.
/13/   *Epistula Clementis* 1, 5.

In 2 Tim. 1:17 the Greek and Latin Texts may have a Different Meaning

Dr. Ann E. Wilhelm-Hooijbergh,
10 Petruslaan,
6564 AK H Landstichting,
Holland.

"He (Onesiphorus) was not ashamed to visit a prisoner, but took pains to search me out when he came to Rome, and found me". This is the NEB translation of the T.V. (-Textum Vaticanum-) *sed cum Romam venisset, solicite me quaesivit et invenit.* This seems to be a rather free translation of the Greek text: ἀλλὰ γενόμενος ἐν ῾Ρώμῃ σπουδαίως ἐζήτησέν με καὶ εὗρεν. A translation from Greek into Latin, however, is impossible, because there is no participle of 'esse', nor is there any participle of the active perfects of other verbs, not even of a deponent. Therefore one has to translate using subordinate clauses. Now γενόμενος means "being (in the past)" and "having been". The present time would be γινόμενος. A very good text in which we may see the difference we find in the *Letter to Diognetus* /1/: ἀλλὰ ἀποστόλων γενόμενος μαθητης γίνομαι διδάσκαλος ἐθνῶν; "but having been a disciple of the apostles I am becoming a teacher of the heathen".

In Liddell & Scott we find s.v. γίγνομαι : ὁ γενομενός στρατηγός the ex-strategus and ἡ γενομενή γυνή the former wife.

Now the Latin translation of our text could have been also - and more literally: *sed cum Roma esset.* But it is also possible that in the earliest translation *Roma* was used and then it would mean "coming from Rome". This could not have been translated with *esse.* When we translate 'having been in Rome' Onesiphorus searched Paul in Caesarea. It is unusual for Paul to inform the reader from where he is writing. This would be an exception here, when Paul was in prison in Rome. He could have written "Onesiphorus being *here*" instead of in Rome.

Studia Biblica 1978 III

John A.T. Robinson in his interesting *Redating the New Testament* /2/ supports my own view that Paul was in prison in Caesarea. However, he still lets Onesiphorus search for him in Rome. But Paul wrote *Romans* early in 57, "shortly before setting off for Jerusalem" as Robinson writes on p.55 and now we are in the autumn of 58, that is one year and a half later. In view of this I doubt if Robinson's supposition, that Onesiphorus has not heard about Paul being in Caesarea and got his information in Rome, is logical. When we read *2 Tim.* 1,17 with "having been" in Rome we get this translation: "But having been in Rome he searched for me hastily (in Caesarea and hastily because he had to change boats for Ephesus) and found me etc." (That Paul wrote this epistle in Caesarea was my conclusion when I timed the date of Clement's first epistle to the Corinthians /3/). With this suggestion of "having been in Rome" I hope to support Robinson's dating: "written in Caesarea before Paul went to Rome!"

For γενόμενος = "having been" we will look at some other passages. There is apart from *2 Tim.* one passage that does not support my view apparently. In *Acts* 13,5 we meet καὶ γενόμενοι ἐν Σαλαμῖνι T.V.: *et cum venissent Salaminam*. NEB: "Arriving at Salamis". This is not exact, for they ought to have come into Salamis before they preached the word of God in more than one synagogue; "being" or "when they were" is more to the letter. But Paul assists me with his own words in *Acts* 19,21: Now in μετὰ τό γενέσθαι με ἐκεῖ δεῖ με καὶ ῾Ρώμην ἰδεῖν ἐκεῖ is the same as ἐν + dativ. (in Jerusalem). The T.V. has: *Postquam fuero ibi*. NEB :"After I have been there I must see Rome also". Γενομένην as "passed" we read in *Luke* 23,19: διά στάσιν τινὰ γενομένην ἐν τῃ πόλει T.V.: *propter seditionem quandam* factam *in civitate*. NEB: "for a rising that had taken place in the city".

For γένεσθαι εἰς = "to come to" there are far more examples. Some of them follow here. *Acts* 20,16: ἔσπευδεν γάρ τὴν ἡμέραν τῆς πεντηκοστῆς γενέσθαι εἰς ῾Ιεροσόλυμα. T.V. (freely): *festinabat enim ut diem Pentecostes faceret Hierosolymis*. NEB (freely): "he was eager to be in Jerusalem on the day of Pentecost".

Acts 21,17: γενομένων δὲ ἡμῶν εἰς ῾Ιεροσόλυμα T.V.: *Et cum venissemus Ierosolymam* without any difference in the Latin translation from γενόμενος ἐν ῾Ρώμῃ = cum venisset Romam. NEB (freely): "so we reached Jerusalem".

There are several verbs used in the N.T. for "to come to" all with εἰς; mostly all of them are translated by *venire* in the T.V.

With my translation of *2 Tim.* a few difficulties disappear: no second journey in Asia, with sufferings in Pisidian Antioch, Iconium and Lystra, N.B. in the same sequence as before /4/.

But still another question remains. In *2 Tim.* 4,20 Paul writes that he left Trophimus as a sick man in Miletus. And in *Acts* 21,29 Trophimus was seen with Paul in the city, which was the reason why Paul was captured. Trophimus was seen with Paul in the city. There and then?

In the T.V. we read only: *viderant enim* (the Jews *qui de Asia erant) Trophimum Ephesium in civitate cum ipso, quem aestimaverant quoniam in templum introduxisset Paulus.* *Viderant enim* is a very simple translation of ἦσαν γὰρ προεωρακότες Τρόφιμον which is an uncommon means of expression when one only means to say what the T.V. does. The NEB gives a better translation: "had seen previously", but leaves unsolved when this was. An exact translation may be: "for they were those who had seen previously the Ephesian Trophimus with him in the city". Of course we understand that the Asiatic instigators saw both, Paul and Trophimus, in Jerusalem now! But if Paul left Trophimus sick in Miletus this is not possible. Robinson supposes that Luke mixed up Trophimus and Tychicus (the twins Robinson says) coming both from Asia /5/. Indeed Tychicus was with Paul in Caesarea, because he was sent by Paul to Ephesus /6/. Both were in Paul's company coming from Macedonia. They waited for Luke *cum suis* in Troas. Luke could not have known the two of them very well, as he adds the provinces or cities where they come from /7/.

Another possibility is that "they had seen before" refers to another time, in Ephesus, where Paul was for at least two years or they spotted them in Jerusalem some other year. But this remains unsolved. Once more: the expression ἦσαν γὰρ προεωρακότες is very uncommon. It is also unlikely that Paul this time walked in Jerusalem with Trophimus or other converted heathen because he had to be very careful as is written in detail in *Acts* 21: 18-26. Alas we cannot use *2 Tim.* 4,20 as an argument!

Finally: the proof that *2 Tim.* was written in Caesarea is
also of interest for the dating of the year of Paul's and
Peter's deaths.

NOTES

/1/   *Epistle to Diognetus* XI,1.
/2/   SCM Press London, 1976, pp.75-76.
/3/   Robinson, p.334, n.106.
/4/   *2 Tim.* 3,11; *Acts* 13,50; 14,5. 19.
/5/   *Acts* 20,4: Ἀσιανοὶ δὲ Τύχικος καὶ Τρόφιμος. Some codices
have Ἐφέσιοι instead of Ἀσιανοὶ
/6/   *2 Tim.* 4,12.
/7/   *Acts* 20,4 and 21,29.

Philo and New Testament Christology

Dr. R. Williamson,
Senior Lecturer in New Testament Studies,
The University,
Leeds LS2 9JT.

The central problem of Christology for Christian theologians is the problem of relating the two kinds of language about Jesus of Nazareth felt to be necessary to describe Him adequately. M.F. Wiles /1/ refers to the language of Christology as involving, within the "whole story" it tells, "two stories"; "a human story" and "a mythological story" /2/. It would seem that language not normally used to describe human beings, but restricted in its full, proper and unqualified use to descriptions of God, is needed in the case of attempts to do justice in words to the significance of Jesus. The Chalcedonian fathers insisted that "our Lord Jesus Christ is one and the same Son, the same perfect in Godhead, the same perfect in manhood, truly God and truly man . . . . *homoousios* with the Father as to his Godhead and the same *homoousios* with us as to his manhood".

It may be that a clue to the meaning of the language of the second of the "two stories" about Jesus told by the New Testament writers (the first in the Chalcedonian definition) is to be found in what Philo of Alexandria wrote, and in particular in what he wrote about Moses. It is likely that Philo was struggling with the same problem of language in relation to Moses that New Testament and later theologians wrestled and wrestle with in the case of Jesus. A.W. Argyle /3/ has argued that "The influence of Philo of Alexandria on the history of Christology has been so important that Christians ought to know more about him than most Christians do". But it must not be thought that the usual references to Philo in works on Christology in the sections devoted to the Logos concept exhaust Philo's relevance. Philo's thought is important also because of the solution he found to that problem.

Like Philo (who belongs to the same period of history as
Jesus and the earliest Christianity), the writers of the New
Testament lived and moved in two worlds, the world of Judaism
and the world of Greece and Rome. Like Philo, the writers of
the New Testament were for the most part seeking to render
intelligible to readers whose language and thought world was
more Greek than oriental a faith which was Jewish and, as far
as Christianity was concerned, was associated in its origins
with the life and words of a Palestinian Jew. It is possible,
therefore, that the language Philo used to present Moses to
his Gentile readers contains at least some hints as to why the
New Testament writers said what they did about Jesus and what
it meant for them and their readers.

Wherever Moses is referred to in Philo's writings it is,
in the words of C. Spicq /4/, "avec d'exceptionels éloges".
The "best of kings, of lawgivers and of high priests" (*De vit.M.*
II.187) was for Philo "this greatest and most perfect of men"
(*ibid.*, I.1). The fact that Philo produced a biography of
Moses, the *De vita Mosis* I and II, is itself of interest.
J.W. Earp /5/ notes that "Philo makes comparatively little use
of Moses as a symbolical figure". The *De vita Mosis,* unlike
most of Philo's other works, deals with its subject without
the usual abundance of allegorical exegesis of the biblical
text. The story of Moses is told in a fairly straightforward,
biographical fashion. There is no suggestion that Moses was
not a real, historical person. Philo in fact begins his
biography by explaining that his purpose was to write the
life-story of his hero, describing "the man himself as he
really was" (*De vit.M.* I.2). Moses, for Philo, "was a human
being", like, *e.g.*, Socrates /6/. He is rarely, if ever,
dissolved into a symbol, as many of the other Old Testament
characters are.

With some additions to the biblical narrative, which have
parallels in Josephus, Philo tells the Pentateuchal story of
Moses' birth, infancy and education. He refers to his racial
affinities and gives an account of the discovery of the hidden
baby Moses by the daughter of the Egyptian Pharaoh. Philo's
account of Moses' education is highly idealised /7/. Philo
could even say that Moses' contemporaries were so amazed by
his adolescent self-control that they "considered earnestly
what the mind which dwelt in his body like an image in a shrine
could be, whether human or divine or a mixture of both, so
utterly unlike was it to the majority, soaring above them and

exalted to a greater height" (*De vit.M.* I.27).

    Frequent references are made to Moses' extraordinary moral
and spiritual qualities /8/. Philo nowhere allows his readers
to think of the possibility of sin or imperfection on the
part of Moses. Even his murder of the Egyptian is treated as
a narrative of "a righteous action" /9/. According to the
Quod Deus 156 Moses was the "friend of God" whose high priestly
prayers for the people were always heard because of his life
of perfect virtue. So lofty is the estimate of Moses to be
found in Philo's writings that one is driven to ask if Philo
thought of him as actually divine. This question Philo
himself asked. "Was not the joy of his partnership with the
Father and Maker of all magnified also by the honour of being
deemed to bear the same title?", he asks in the *De vit.M.* I.155.
He continues, "For he was named god and king of the whole
nation, and entered, we are told, into the darkness where God
was". In the *De somn*.II.189 the name θεός is said to be "a
prerogative assigned to the chief prophet, Moses, while he
was still in Egypt, where he is entitled the God of Pharaoh"/10/.
In the *Qu. in Ex.* II.49 he is called "the divine (and) holy
Moses" /11/.

    In the *De somn.* I.36 it is stated that on Sinai Moses
became incorporeal for forty days. But even more remarkable
is the way in which, in the *Qu. in Ex.* 46, Philo explains that
Moses experienced a "second birth better than the first". In
the case of this second birth, Philo says, Moses had no mother
"but only a father, who is (the Father) of all". In his new,
second existence, we are told, Moses differed from "the
earth-born first moulded man", since the new Moses had no
body. This "divine birth" of Moses, Philo suggests, "happened
to come about for him in accordance with the ever-virginal
nature of the hebdomad".

    There is also, at certain points in Philo's works, a
close association between Moses and the divine Logos. In the
De mut.nom. 11Off. Philo interprets the "Shepherd" of
Ps.23:1 as "the divine Word" which guides man's mind away from
the objects of sense. Since it is Moses who rescues man from
the bondage of the material the clear implication of this
passage is that, in a real sense, Moses is, or is an expression
of, the Logos. Philo does in fact, in the *De migr. Abr.* 23,
call Moses the Logos, "the Law-giving Word". He can even say,
in the *De vit.M.* I.155, that God "committed to Moses the

entire cosmos as a possession fit for God's heir" /12/.

When he describes Moses' death Philo not only tells how,
inspired by the divine Spirit, he foretold it beforehand and
how the whole nation mourned for a whole month (*De vit.M.* II.
291), but also how, when he was ready to leave "this mortal
life for immortality", God "resolved his two-fold nature of
soul and body into a single entity, transforming his whole
being into mind, pure as sunlight", so enabling him to
prophesy "to each tribe in particular the things which were
to be and hereafter must come to pass" (*ibid.*, 288). The
prophecy he made of his own death came at the very moment,
Philo tells us, "when he was already being exalted
(ἀναλαμβανόμενος) and stood at the very barrier, ready at the
signal to direct his upward flight to heaven" (*ibid.*, 291) /13/.

There is also a remarkable passage in the *De somn.* I.164ff.
which consists of a prayer addressed to Moses. Of it E.R.
Goodenough has written that the words are "not an address
to one who is dead and gone. Philo sees in Moses an active
and present power, and the prayer to Moses for guidance, light
and anointing, is precisely such a prayer as Christian mystics
have for centuries been addressing to Christ" /14/. The
prayer in question includes the words, "do thou thyself, O
sacred Guide, be our prompter and preside over our steps and
never tire of anointing our eyes, until conducting us to the
hidden light of hallowed words thou display to us the
fast-locked loveliness invisible to the uninitiate".

Yet Philo was absolutely sure that God could not become a
man. As F. Copleston remarks /15/, "it does not require much
thought to recognise that the Philonic philosophy could never
admit the Christian doctrine of the Incarnation - at least if
Philonism were to remain self-consistent - since it lays such
stress on the Divine Transcedence that direct "contact" with
matter is excluded". Again and again Philo insists, in the
words of Num.23:19, that God "is not as a man" /16/. In the
De op.m. 69 he states that "neither is God in human form, nor
is the human body Godlike" /17/.

Philo, then, while fully aware that Moses was a real,
human being, and deeply convinced that God could not become a
man, could, because of his acknowledgement of Moses' supreme
place as a revealer of the truth about God through the Torah,
speak, *e.g.*, about his second, divine, virginal birth, his

supernatural knowledge, his extraordinary, indeed perfect,
goodness, his identity or association with the Logos, his rôle
as the recipient of men's prayers, his possession of the cosmos,
his translation at death, and even of his divinity. Does this
help us to understand what led the early Christians, who
lived, like Philo, in a world where emperors could regard
themselves as divine and men like Apollonius of Tyana could
be reverenced as divine men, to think and speak and write about
Jesus as they did? Was it because they were convinced that
for them to tell the whole truth about God, especially for
Gentile hearers or readers, it was necessary to tell the story
of Jesus in a two-dimensional form, with "a human story" and
"a mythological story"? Is that, in part at least, why the
writers of the New Testament described Jesus as the Son of
God, as the image of God and the Word of God made incarnate?
Is that why they spoke of His virginal conception, His
Transfiguration, His exorcisms, His Resurrection? Is that
why they thought of Him as more than a charismatic, prophetic
figure, but as pre-existent, as the One through whom God made
the world, and as for ever alive to intercede with the Father
and to be present with His disciples? Does all this involve
the view, expressed in such statements as the Chalcedonian
definition, that there is a unity of substance between Jesus
and God? Or is it all commentary on the significance of the
human Jesus, an attempt to interpret and express adequately
His rôle as a special, indeed supreme, Revealer of God, just
as Philo could make statements about Moses' relationship to
God, similar to Christian statements about Jesus, without ever
allowing them to infringe the Jewishness of his belief in God
or his recognition of the genuine, unimpaired humanity of
Moses? Is it perhaps inevitable that whenever someone, be it
Moses or Jesus, is believed to be the agent of a special
revelation of God, a "mythological story" is added to a "human
story"? Is it this reason that mythological statements are
made and legendary accretions develop within the "human story",
in the case of Moses in Philo's writings, and in the case of
Jesus in the documents of the New Testament /18/?

NOTES

/1/   *Christ Faith and History* (C.U.P., 1972), ed. S.W. Sykes
and J.P. Clayton, Part I, I, 'Does Christology rest on a
mistake?', pp.3-12. See also Wiles' *The Remaking of Christian
Doctrine* (S.C.M., 1974), esp. Ch.3, 'The Person of Christ',
pp.41-60.

/2/   See among recent discussions of the allegedly
mythological character of some forms of Christological
language *The Myth of God Incarnate* (S.C.M., 1977), ed. J. Hick.
/3/   In his article, 'Philo, the Man and his Work' (*ExT*,
Vol. LXXXV, No.4, Jan., 1974), p.115. A good introduction to
Philo is E.R. Goodenough, *An Introduction to Philo Judaeus*
(Oxford, 1962). See also the same author's *By Light, Light*
(Yale U.P., 1935). Among many important works on Philo's
thought are H.A. Wolfson, *Philo*, I and II (Harvard U.P., 1948),
J. Drummond, *Philo Judaeus*, I and II (Williams and Norgate,
1888), É. Bréhier, *Les Idées Philosophiques et Religieuses de
Philon D'Alexandrie* (Paris, 1925), and P. Heinisch, *Der
Einfluss Philos auf die älteste christliche Exegese* (Münster,
1908).
/4/   *L'Épître aux Hébreux* (Paris, 1952), I, p.67.
/5/   In the 'Index of Names' to the Loeb edition of Philo's
works, Vol.X, p.386.
/6/   *De somn.*I.58.
/7/   *De vit.M* I.21ff.
/8/   For Philo's estimate of Moses as a prophet see, *e.g.*,
De Somn. II.189. On Moses' various virtues see, among many
other passages, *De op.m.*8, *Leg.All.* II.15 and III.140, *De virt.*
175 and 201, *De cher.*45, *De vit.M.* I.9 and 24, and II.29,
66 and 104, etc., etc.
/9/   *De vit.M.*I.44.
/10/   In this passage Philo is discussing Lev.16:17 and
concludes that the high priest, when he enters the Holy of
Holies, is neither wholly God nor man, "but one contiguous with
both extremes". To Aaron, then, the word θεός cannot be
applied, though to Moses it can.
/11/   See also *Hyp.*6.9 and *Qu. in Ex.*II.29.
/12/   Cf. *De mut.nom.*110ff. and its application of Ps.23 to
Moses. Goodenough, *By Light, Light*, p.201, decides that the
allegory is "definitely one of the saving activity of Moses".
Drummond, *op.cit.*, II, pp.191-2, sees in the passage a
portrayal of Moses as the Logos.
/13/   Cf. *De virt.*76.
/14/   See *By Light, Light*, Ch.VIII, 'The Mystic Moses",
pp.197-234.
/15/   *A History of Philosophy*, I, Greece and Rome (Burns Oates
and Washbourne, 1947), p.461.
/16/   See, *e.g.*, *De dec.*32 and *Quod Deus* 53.
/17/   Cf. *Quis rer.* 234 and 265, and *De virt.* 65. On the
general question of the possibility, or impossibility, within
Philo's thought of the idea of an incarnation of the Logos see

my *Philo and the Epistle to the Hebrews*   (Leiden, 1970), Ch.6, pp.142-159, 'Time, History and Eschatology'.

/18/ A full treatment of the subject, of which what appears is merely a brief excerpt, would require an examination of many more relevant passages in Philo's works. For a discussion of 'Moses in Philo and Hebrews' see my *Philo and the Epistle to the Hebrews*, pp.449-491.

The Myth of God's Mother Incarnate

Dr. R.E. Witt,
1 Oakwood Park Road,
Southgate,
London N14 6QB

A good long time ago, at the international Patristic
Congress in Oxford on September 9, 1971, I chose as my theme
"A Protestant View of the Catholic Mother of God". My
treatment of the subject was in line, naturally enough, with
all that had occupied my mind in writing the book, issued
four months earlier, under the title *Isis in the Graeco-Roman
World*. Seven years have passed. Interest in Mariology has
not abated. Yet writers on Christian doctrine have not given
heed to the conclusions reached in the book's last chapter
"The Great Forerunner". Today, therefore, I find it opportune
to look at the Mariological question once again, in the light
of some passages in the volume of essays published last year
under the editorship of John Hick as *The Myth of God Incarnate*.
In that book, to be sure, seven pillars of this country's
theological Establishment (to be referred to as "The Essayists")
are seen supporting views which have been swiftly condemned as
heretical. To me it does not matter much. What I think
important is that the team of Essayists should have shaken
complacency and have stirred belief into rethinking basic
assumptions. In the end the Essayists as professing Christians
must be adjudged victors or vanquished on their Christology and
therefore on their theory of the Incarnation.

Have they then fastened their attention hard enough on the
theology of Mother and Child? Have they pondered the mythology
of the non-Biblical *Theotokos*? Is the observed fact of
hyperdulia to the *Panagia* one of the historical necessities of
the Church, or not?

Bultmann in the Germany of the Second World War caused New
Testament scholarship the century's big shock by propounding
his theory of Demythologization. "Divest the Gospels of

mythological forms in order to uncover the meaning underlying
them". So Bultmann sought to interpret the gospel story,
according to current parlance, not in a cosmological but in an
anthropological, an existential sense. Surely, however, his
exegetical method is as old as the earliest Church Fathers.
For Clement and Origen, following Philo the Jew, had found that
the key to understanding scripture was allegory. Bultmann's
interpretation may differ from theirs as even more radical in
degree, but it is of just the same kind. When he emphasizes
his existential approach, let us recall what another theologian,
with the same outlook on truth as subjective, has to say about
the Incarnation. This for Kierkegaard is manifestly true
because of its irrationality. "The absurd is that the
eternal truth has come into being in time, that God has come
into being, has been born ... precisely like any other
individual human being".

     For Bultmann, as for the Essayist Wiles, the incarnational
doctrine can be separated from "the legends of the Virgin Birth".
Nevertheless, Bultmann with his eye on Chapter Six of the
Fourth Gospel confesses that the Jesus whose father and mother
are known must also be the pre-existent Son of God. Twentieth
century theologians need candour. If the God-Man was born
precisely like any other human being, then (to quote the words
of the Essayist Frances Young) he must have inherited "the
normal genetic links in human descent". What is more, he must
have come forth from a mother whose womanhood had undergone all
the physiological experiences that childbirth entails. In the
second century Origen in the *De Principiis* could write about
the Wisdom of God entering the womb of a woman. Today, when
science has immeasurably widened the study of human
reproduction and when babies can be conceived and born without
sexual intercourse through artificial insemination, ours is a
sex-sophisticated society. The incarnation means a unique and
supernatural birth through God's intervention in human history.
This doctrine the Essayists separate from what they call
Christianity. Wiles classifies it as one "of four basic
Christian myths". Nevertheless, in alliance on this issue
with two otherwise mutually antagonistic theologians, Pittinger
and Pannenberg, he concedes that it is datable. In other
words, a birth is established in time and place. According to
the Third Evangelist, Mary brought forth Jesus at Bethlehem in
the reign of Caesar Augustus. This we are expected to believe
as true. The political figures named are historically
authentic, not mythical.

What now of parthenogenesis? The Church's traditional
creed involves its acceptance as an event unparalleled in
history. To the Essayists here is obviously the great
stumbling block. So it would be to the *avant-garde* of the
Women's Liberation Movement. The possibility of pregnancy
through the agency of what Origen termed "Divine Wisdom"
would be loudly repudiated in that quarter. Instead, the
Nativity story would be interpreted, in the manner of the
Platonist Celsus and of our own latter-day William Blake,
as the truth about an unmarried girl whose virginity had been
lost. A mythical explanation would not avail.

Again, modern feminists would find the dogma of the
Immaculate Conception as little to their liking as it seems
to be to the Essayists. Equally, however, advanced thinkers
on sexual ethics would never tolerate the notion of sinfulness
in human mating. To them it would be no better than myth.
Yet both the Catholic Augustine and the Protestant Luther never
doubted that the Virgin Mary was born in sin.

From all that I have said so far, you will see what are
some of the problems as we consider with modern criteria the
humanity of the *Theotokos*. For the Essayist Cupitt *Theotokos*
is indeed a "blasphemous phrase". Why? Because like the term
Incarnate Lord it is an accretion in the latter history of
Christendom. In answer to his charge that it lacks the
authority of the canonical gospels, Catholic theologians of
the Eastern and Western Churches will contend that it is
implicit there; that therefore disbelief in the person of
Panagia-Theotokos is itself blasphemy; that Cupitt is guilty
of heresy. Heresy or not, his view may be described (in the
words of my lecture title) as *The Myth of God's Mother
Incarnate*.

Cupitt speaks as an *ultra*-Protestant. He is but following
the pattern of Luther, whose attitude towards what he
condemned as the cult of Mary, as I pointed out in 1971,
exemplified the deep yearning of the heart for the superhuman
presence of the Mother of God. Long before the Essayists of
1977, Luther had expressed his abhorrence of Mariolatry as
weakening the divinity of the Second Person of the Trinity.
We all know that herein still lies one of the hardest stumbling
blocks for those many professing Christians who as Protestants
stand outside the two great churches governed by their
respective Heads in Constantinople and Rome. But can

Protestantism find its way round the problem somehow?

The Essayists gloat over their historical perspicacity.
They ape Bultmann, whose dictum was that myth is the view of
the world that is out of date: "Das mythische Weltbild ...
einfach das Weltbild einer vergangenen Zeit". Starting out
from the New Testament they gaze into the Christian Era. The
period we label B.C. sweeping away endlessly they forget.
They might well look more carefully at it when discussing myth
and incarnation, and at one aspect in particular, i.e. the
pre-Christian mythology of Mother and Child.

Easily the most important incarnational theology before
the emergence of Christianity was that which developed in Egypt
about Isis and Horus. This was the theme of my book. Let us
note that in one sense the nativity of Horus the Child was
mythical and therefore timeless. Yet Horus had his yearly
birthday in the Egyptian calendar. In another way also he
appeared in time. For every new baby Pharaoh was his
incarnation. In the legend, a local habitation was given to
him. For Isis his Mother fled into the wild swamps of the
Nile Delta, to bring him forth in safety.

In the concluding book of the New Testament there is
embedded a remarkable apocalyptic myth. As Bousset suggested
a long time ago, the Vision of the Woman in *Revelation*
Chapter XII is linked with Egyptian mythology. The Woman whose
Son was born in the wild and who was afterwards *carried on
the stream* (ποταμοφόρητος) is portrayed in the manner of Isis.
Much ingenuity has been exerted in the effort to identify the
female figure either with Mary Mother of Jesus or with the early
Church. The evidence flatly contradicts such an interpretation.
Here, almost at the end of the canonical New Testament, we meet
one form of the Myth of God's Mother Incarnate.

Why is this included in our *Apocalypse*? I have no direct
answer to offer you now. As well ask why the Egyptian
background plays so important a part in the non-Canonical
Gospels. What can be stated with confidence concerning Egypt
is the following : it was there that the writing of early
Christian documents began. The Essayist Frances Young
pertinently cites some words of A.D. Nock: "Christian theology
and above all christology have [their roots] in Alexandria".
Hence we have to relate the writings which comprise the New
Testament to the environment where some of them at least were
produced. Alexandria cannot be bypassed.

In Egypt the Myth of God's Mother Incarnate was
immemorially old. Alexandria was pre-eminently the city of
Isis Theotokos. Small wonder that Christian writers, such as
the author of the *Apocalypse,* took good notice of it. If this
is so, then we have no need to search, as do the Essayists, for
latter-day perversions of gospel truth. Already in the
Hellenistic Jewish world of Egypt's capital, before any output
of Christian literature, the cult of Lady Isis, Lord Sarapis
and the Young Horus must have been thoroughly well known,
though the extent of the influence it exerted on the new
religion still remains for scholars to assess. One of the
Essayists cites words of W.L. Knox which are highly relevant
to my present purpose, about the personification of Wisdom
in the Bible as modelled on "the female figure of Isis with all
her attractions". This identification I have discussed,
pointing out how *Isis/Hagia Sophia* is represented by Philo of
Alexandria as Mother of the Divine Logos. Egyptian mythology
was useful to the hellenizing Jew. We are already treading
on the threshold of the new age in theology.

Enoch Powell, in his review of my *Isis* book, drew a
contrast between what seemed to him the characteristics of
Christianity and Isiacism. The one had an "historical origin",
whereas Isis "remained a shadowy being of indeterminate
origin, not embraceable except as a fable or an image". As I
reflect on the position of the B.V.M., the *Panagia-Theotokos,*
in non-Protestant Church doctrine, I wonder whether the
antithesis which Mr. Powell attempted to establish is really
valid.

For me the distinction between myth and history must be
clearcut. Christendom has always been faced with what the
First and Third Evangelists record as fact, the Birth at
Bethlehem. Its truth is canonical.

Nevertheless, within the primitive Church, literature was
in circulation which eventually had to be relegated to the
realm of mythology, books such as *Protevangelium of James*
and *Pseudo-Matthew*. On what grounds this was done it is not
my task to explain. Only one fact need concern us now. The
fictitious evangelists wrote fiction, for religious romance was
a most popular *genre* in those days. In apocryphal *Matthew*
idols bow down as Mary enters the Egyptian temple. In the
Arabic *Gospel of the Saviour's Infancy* she makes a mule return
to human shape, exactly as Isis changes the ass back into the

man Lucius in the novel by Apuleius. Apocryphal gospels, acts
and revelations were rife. Christian and Gnostic writers
competed for success. Later on, the bounds were set by the
establishment of the New Testament canon. But in the earliest
times works circulated in which the Myth of God's Mother
Incarnate was already gathering a strength which would endure
down the centuries.

Consider the iconography of *Panagia-Theotokos* and her
supremacy in the ecclesiastical arts. She was the inspiration
of men like Leonardo and Rafael. Pinturicchio (for an
Egyptianizing Pope, it may be added) dared to paint an
Isis-Mary as Queen of Heaven in the Sainted Room of the Vatican.
Mary's Roman basilicas - Maggiore, Sopra Minerva, Navicella -
dominate the previous haunts of Isis. Mary lies at the heart
of some of the greatest choruses of Lutheran Bach - the
Et Incarnatus and the *Omnes Generationes*. Catholics everywhere
keep her name on their lips. In Greece she holds sway as
Panagia and to her is sung the Hymn τῇ ὑπερμάχῳ Στρατηγῷ as
Salonica's champion protectress. I mention all these facts
to show that what Protestantism condemns as *hyperdulia,* as
myth that has cast a cloud over the Christmas birth, is itself
of the stuff of history.

What then? We are hearing much these days about the
reunion of Christendom. Make no mistake. It will never come
unless the churches can reach a Mariological compromise. This
is why I have spoken as I have. You might now read (or
re-read) my chapter "The Great Forerunner".

Studia Biblica 1978: III, 453-459   453

The Meaning of περὶ ἁμαρτίας in Romans 8.3

N.T. Wright,
Merton College,
Oxford,
ENGLAND.

The intention of this paper is to offer a new argument, based on the context, for taking περὶ ἁμαρτίας in *Romans* 8,3 to mean "as a sin-offering". Though many commentators accept this interpretation /1/, about as many again reject it /2/, and since neither see any contextual reasons why Paul should introduce the idea of the sin-offering here the case usually turns on the commentator's view of Paul's Septuagint allusions in general /3/.

Before we can proceed, however, we should note a third view which has been supported by a minority at various stages of the history of interpretation. This view takes the phrase καὶ περὶ ἁμαρτίας not with the preceding πέμψας but with κατέκρινεν, which follows it /4/. While it is true that "περὶ with the genitive to mean 'on the charge of' or 'on the grounds of' in a judicial setting is common in the New Testament" /5/, it appears to be straining the force of the καί to make it emphatic in this context, and by no means all the early commentators took the phrase in this sense /6/. In addition, it is one of the presuppositions of this view that neither of the regular options is really open: so if we can find a good reason for either in the context, the need for this alternative suggestion is greatly reduced.

We may therefore return to the main argument. The case for the general meaning ("to deal with sin") depends likewise on the assumption that there is no contextual reason why Paul should have referred to the sin-offering, and thus falls if such a reason is given. In addition, as Thornton has pointed out /7/, the general view "gives the isolated preposition περί a burden of meaning to carry in a way which is unprecedented in the New Testament, and unusual, if not unprecedented, elsewhere".

The way is therefore open for arguments, both old and new, on
behalf of the sacrificial interpretation.

   We must begin with the old (and strong) argument from the
LXX background. It is well known that חטאת is taken by the
LXX, rightly, to mean on some occasions "sin" and on other
occasions "sin-offering", in such a way that we could construct
a sliding scale of usage, from the meaning "sin" to the meaning
"sin-offering", in which nevertheless the meaning "sin" in the
phrase "for sin" would still have inescapably sacrificial
associations. At the "sin" end of the scale comes the phrase
περὶ τῆς ἁμαρτίας, which usually translates על-חטאת and
sometimes לחטאת , and which normally means "for sin", as in the
phrase περὶ τῆς ἁμαρτίας αὐτοῦ ἧς ἥμαρτεν /8/. Near this end
of the scale (though this is more difficult) comes ἁμαρτία by
itself. Though it may well mean "sin-offering", it might be
argued that the LXX translators here took חטאת to mean "sin",
identifying the sacrifice with the sin /9/.

   At the other end of the scale comes the phrase τὸ περὶ τῆς
ἁμαρτίας, which means simply "the sin-offering". This is
frequent and undisputed /10/. Our problem is the location on
the scale of περὶ ἁμαρτίας, the phrase we find in Rom.8,3. It
occurs 54 times in the LXX, of which no fewer than 44 stand
parallel to phrases such as εἰς ὁλοκαυτωμα, εἰς θυσιαν σωτηριου,
and the like /11/. περὶ ἁμαρτίας regularly translates לחטאת
or simply חטאת where εἰς ὁλοκαυτωμα translates לעלה or simply
עלה . This makes it clear that περὶ ἁμαρτίας, in the great
majority of cases, must mean "as a sin-offering", parallel to
"as a burnt-offering", etc. It is, in other words, simply the
anarthrous equivalent of το περὶ τῆς ἁμαρτίας. Of the
remaining ten occurrences, one is Isa.53,10, the only place
where περὶ ἁμαρτίας stands for אשם in the MT. It could
conceivably be argued that the other nine /12/ should be put
further down the scale, nearer to the meaning "for sin", but
even if this were so the phrase would still have strong and
unavoidable sacrificial associations. We may conclude that,
whereas περὶ τῆς ἁμαρτίας usually means 'for sin', and το περὶ
τῆς ἁμαρτίας means "the sin-offering", περὶ ἁμαρτίας should
usually be translated either "sin-offering" /13/ or "as a
sin-offering".

   The characteristic sentence in which περὶ ἁμαρτίας occurs
is well exemplified by Lev.9,2: λαβὲ σεαυτῷ μοσχάριον ἐκ βοῶν
περὶ ἁμαρτίας καὶ κριὸν εἰς ὁλοκάυτωμα. This form, with a verb

of sacrificing or taking for sacrifice, a direct object of the
creature to be sacrificed, followed by περὶ ἁμαρτίας, is
exactly parallel to Rom.8,3: ὁ θεὸς τὸν ἑαυτοῦ υἱὸν πέμψας ...
περὶ ἁμαρτίας. The LXX evidence therefore provides a strong
argument in favour of the translation: "God, sending his own
son ... as a sin-offering". Even if this were not accepted,
it could not be denied that at the very least the phrase
means "for sin" with all the overtones of the sacrifices of
Leviticus and Numbers.

        This argument, however, has only convinced about half the
commentators, while the other half reject it on the grounds
that the context provides no reasons why Paul should have
wished to speak specifically of the sin-offering here. It is
this view which we now wish to challenge.

        The context in which the sin-offering is to be used, as
laid down in Leviticus and Numbers, is not merely any sin. It
is particularly unwilling sins or sins of ignorance. This
emerges clearly in the use of the root שׁגג in the relevant
texts /14/, translated in the LXX by ἀκουσιαζεῖν /15/,ἀκούσιος
/16/, and ἀκουσίως /17/. The sin-offering covers sinful
actions which the sinner either did not know he was committing,
or did not know were sinful: in principle he wanted to keep
the law, but through ignorance, or against his will, he
failed /18/. The opposite of such unwilling sins is the sin
committed "with a high hand" /19/, for which there is no
sacrifice: the man responsible for such sins is to be "cut off
from among his people". This same division of sins into
"unwilling" and "deliberate", with the sin-offering as the
remedy for the first, is clearly reflected in later Judaism /20/,
and in one important passage in the New Testament. In Hebrews
10,26 the writer says that for the man who sins willingly
there is no further sin-offering, but rather the prospect of
judgement: Ἑκουσίως γὰρ ἁμαρτανόντων ἡμῶν μετὰ τὸ λαβεῖν τὴν
ἐπίγνωσιν τῆς ἀληθείας, οὐκέτι περὶ ἁμαρτιῶν ἀπολείπεται
θυσία, φοβερὰ δὲ τις ἐκδοχὴ κρίσεως ... κτλ. This evidence
from LXX, Mishnah and NT /21/ leads us to suspect that if Paul
used a phrase like περὶ ἁμαρτίας, the context might well refer
to sins committed unwillingly or in ignorance.

        This is precisely what we find in the context of Rom.8,3.
The first four verses of ch.8 show how God is doing "what the
law could not do", so as to deal with the problem described
in 7,14-25 /22/. Our argument, fortunately, does not depend

Studia Biblica 1978 III

on the decision as to whether 7,14-25 refers to pre-Christian man /23/ or Christian man /24/. In the context of the question about the law which gives 7,14-25 its structural outline, those verses describe a man who sins in a particular way, summed up in 7,15: ὃ γὰρ κατεργάζομαι οὐ γινώσκω. οὐ γὰρ ὃ θελω τõυτο πράσσω, ἀλλ᾽ ὃ μισῶ τõυτο ποιῶ. The sin described in these verses is precisely sin of ignorance, unwilling sin. The man who sins in this way delights in God's law (7,22), yet finds again and again that he fails to keep it. The remedy which the Old Testament offers for this very condition is the sin-offering, and when we meet, in the very passage where Paul is showing how God deals with the condition of 7,14-25, the phrase which elsewhere in the Greek Bible regularly means "as a sin-offering", there can no longer be any suggestion that the context does not support the sacrificial interpretation. Though Paul can view Christ's death in various other ways (in, for instance, *Rom*.3,24 ff., *1 Cor*.5,7) he here draws attention to that death seen in one way in particular, the way relevant for dealing with sin as it is committed in 7,14-25.

We have said that this view holds good whatever decision we make about the interpretation of 7,14-25. If these verses are taken to refer to pre-Christian man, the sin-offering will refer to the death of Christ as that death rescues man from unwilling sin committed before he became a Christian: this would need to be taken in the context of Paul's wider analysis of the predicament of man without Christ, in which other kinds of sin are also present, and also dealt with by the death of Christ /25/. It must be said, however, that our view appears to make more for those who see 7,14-25 as describing the Christian who still finds himself sinning despite his best intentions. This is not to minimize the difficulties of holding this view /26/. It is to say that the Christian in this position can see that his predicament does not ultimately matter, since God has dealt with it in the death of Christ. The Christian is in the position of the man in *Lev*.4, or *Num*.15. That is, he is a member of the people of God, desiring to live according to God's law. God does not require him now to be perfect: that would be to live again "under the law". Instead, God has made provision for the sin which he still commits. Nor is this antinomian in its implications, since it is precisely unwilling sin that is in question. The Christian, according to Paul, is not able to avoid sin totally, as though he were a gnostic perfectionist. He is, however, in contrast to man in Adam, man in the flesh, able to submit gladly to God's law /27/,

so that when he does sin it is against his deepest desires and
intentions. He still sins, but in a manner which Paul has
analysed as "ignorantly" and "unwillingly". Within the context
of this argument περὶ ἁμαρτίας, in its full meaning of 'as a
sin-offering', has an important role to play.

NOTES

/1/   E.g. F.F. Bruce, *The Epistle to the Romans*, London, 1963,
p.161: H.C.G. Moule, *The Epistle of Paul the Apostle to the
Romans*, Cambridge, 1879, p.139: C.J. Vaughan, *St. Paul's
Epistle to the Romans*, London, (6th edn.) 1885, p.149 f.: most
recently E. Käsemann, *An die Römer*, Tübingen, 1973, p.208. Cf.
too *TDNT* 8.383 f. (E. Schweizer) and 6.55 (E.H. Riesenfeld).
Among EVV this meaning is taken by RV, RSV mg., and NEB.
/2/   E.g. C.K. Barrett, *A Commentary on the Epistle to the
Romans*, London, 1957, p.156 (Barrett says the general sense
is "more probable"): C.E.B. Cranfield, *A Critical and
Exegetical Commentary on the Epistle to the Romans*, vol.1,
Edinburgh, 1975, p.382: O. Kuss, *Der Römerbrief*, Lieferung 2,
Regensburg, 1959, p.493 f.: M.-J. Lagrange, *Saint Paul:
Épître aux Romains*, Paris, 1950 (1st edn., 1916), p.193:
O. Michel, *Der Brief an die Römer*, Göttingen, 4th edn., 1966
(1st edn., 1955), p.190: W. Sanday and A.C. Headlam, *A Critical
and Exegetical Commentary on the Epistle to the Romans*, 5th
edn., Edinburgh, 1902 (1st edn., 1895), p.193. This general
sense is followed by AV, RV mg., RSV, NEB mg.
/3/   The omission of the phrase in 110 *pc* is clearly due to
homoioteleuton, though Jülicher regarded it as a gloss (*Die
Schriften des Neuen Testaments 2*, Göttingen, 3rd edn., 1917
(1st edn., 1907), ad loc.). The Jerusalem Bible appears to
treat the phrase as superfluous.
/4/   So Chrysostom, in *PG* 60.514: Theodoret of Cyrrhus, in
PG 82.129 A: 'Ambrosiaster' in *PL* 17.123 C: J.A. Bengel,
Gnomon Novi Testamenti, London, 1862 (reprint of 3rd edn.),
p.528: recently T.C.G. Thornton, "The Meaning of καὶ περὶ
ἁμαρτίας in Romans 8.3", *JTS* n.s. vol.22, 1971, pp.515 ff.
Cranfield (*loc.cit*) cites Calvin as taking this view, but
this is misleading, since while Calvin translated the last
clause of v.3 *etiam de peccato damnavit peccatum in carne,*
when expounding the text he clearly supported the sacrificial
meaning, taking περὶ ἁμαρτίας to represent אשם . See J. Calvin,
in *The Epistles of Paul the Apostle to the Romans and to the
Thessalonians*, tr. by R. Mackenzie, Edinburgh, 1961, pp.156,

159 f.: for the original, *Corpus Reformatorum* 77   (*Calvini Opera* 49), 137, 139 f.

/5/   Thornton, p.516: see *John* 8,46; 15,22; 16,8 f.: *Acts* 23,6; 24,21; 25,9. 20: *Jude* 15.

/6/   E.g. Origen, *PG* 14.1093 ff. This, coupled with the awareness of Gennadius of Constantinople and Photius of Constantinople that the phrase could be taken both ways (K. Staab, *Pauluskommentare aus der griechischen Kirche,* Münster, 1933, pp.375, 509), rules out any argument on the basis of early or Greek-speaking commentators. Perhaps Origen was more sensitive to the LXX background of the NT than Crysostom and other Antiochenes.

/7/   *Loc.cit.*

/8/   See *Lev.*4,3 (twice); 4,14. 28; 5,6 (twice); 5,7.9; 8,2; 8,14; 9,15; 10,16; 16,6. 11. 15. 27 (twice); *Num.*15,25.

/9/   See the various forms in *Ex.*29,14. 36; *Lev.*4,8. 20. 24. 25. 29. 32. 33. 34: 5,12; 6,17 (LXX/MT 6,10); 6,25 (LXX/MT 6,18); *Num.*6,14.

/10/   See *Lev.*5,8; 6,25 (LXX/MT 6,18); 6,30 (LXX/MT 6,23); 7,7; 9,7. 10. 22. 10,17. 19 (twice); 14,13 (twice). 19; 16,25: *Num.*29,11; *2 Macc.*2,11. Note also the variants τὸ περὶ ἀμαρτίας in *Num.*6,16; *Ezek.*42,13: and τὸ ὑπὲρ ἀμαρτίας, etc., in *Ezek.*40,39; 44,29; 45,22. 25; 46,20.

/11/   See *Lev.*5,7; 7,37; 9,2. 3; 12,6, 8; 14,22; 14,31; 15,15. 30; 16,3. 5; 23,19: *Num.*6,11; 7,16. 22. 28. 34. 40. 46. 52. 58. 64. 70. 76. 82. 87; 8,8. 12; 15,24; 28,15. 22; 29,5. 11. 16. 19. 22. 28. 31. 34. 38: *2 Kings* 12,17 (EVV 12,16): *2 Esdr.*8,35; *Ps.*39,7 (EVV 40,6; MT 40,7).

/12/   *Lev.*5,6. 11 (twice); 16,9: *Num.*15,27: *2 Esdr.*6,17; *2 Chr.*29,21: *Ezek.*43,21: *2 Macc.*12,43.

/13/   As in *Ps.*39,7; compare *Hebr.*10,6. 8.

/14/   שגא , *Lev.*5,18: *Num.*15,28: שגאה , *Lev.*4,2. 22. 27: 5,15. 18; 22,14: *Num.*15,24. 25 (twice). 26. 27. 28. 29: שגה , *Lev.*4,13: *Num.*15,22.

/15/   *Num.*15,28.

/16/   *Num.* 15,25 (twice). 26.

/17/   *Lev.*4,2. 13. 22. 27; 5,15: *Num.*15,24. 27. 28. 29.

/18/   Compare also *Lev.*5,18 (περὶ τῆς ἀγνοίας αὐτοῦ) and *Lev.*22,14 (κατὰ ἄγνοιαν). The particular meaning of the sin-offering is noted by Sanday and Headlam, *loc.cit.*, but they do not see it as relevant to *Rom.*8,3. Many commentators, failing to see the precise reference of this sacrifice, argue as though only a general sacrificial meaning could be implied if the phrase were taken to mean "sin-offering".

/19/ Cf., e.g., *Num*.15,30 f. (רמה ביד : LXX ἐν χειρὶ
ὑπερηφανύας). Compare Mishnah, *Ker*.1,2; 2,6; 3,2.
/20/ Cf. Mishnah: *Shab*.7,1; 11,6; *Sanh*.7,8; *Hor*.2,1-6;
and see the notes of H. Danby, *The Mishnah*, Oxford, 1933,
pp.111 n.3, 562 n.16.
/21/ Apart from those listed in n.5 above, the NT passages
in which περὶ ἁμαρτίας or its equivalents occur are: *Heb*.5,3;
10,6. 8. 18; 13,11: *1 Pet*.3,18; *1 John* 2,2; 4,10; *Gal*.1.4
should be added if the v.1 is to be read, but this is very
unlikely: see E. de W. Burton, *A Critical and Exegetical
Commentary on the Epistle to the Galatians*, Edinburgh, 1921,
p.lxxx, 13.
/22/ The thing 'which the law could not' is not the provision
of a sin-offering, nor the condemnation of sin, but the giving
of life: compare 7,10; 7,24 and 8,10-11.
/23/ See the commentary of E. Käsemann, pp.178, 184, 191 for
literature on this passage, especially the work of Kümmel and
Bultmann.
/24/ For this view, see A. Nygren, *Commentary on Romans*,
(ET of *Romarbrevet*, Stockholm, 1944), Philadelphia, 1949,
pp.265-303; Cranfield, *op.cit*., pp.330-370; J.D.G. Dunn,
"Romans 7.14-25 in the Theology of St. Paul", *TZ* 31, 1975,
pp.257-73; J.I. Packer, "The Wretched Man in Romans 7",
Studia Evangelica 2 (= *TU* 87), 1964, pp.621-627.
/25/ See *Rom*.1,18-3,20 with 3,21-26.
/26/ Particularly the description of v.14. It should be
noted, however, against the view of Kümmel, Bultmann and
others, that the problem described in these verses is not
"legalism", but sin.
/27/ See 8,6-8, with Cranfield, *op.cit*., pp.383 ff., and
K. Barth, *A Shorter Commentary on Romans* (ET of *Kurze Erklärung
des Römerbriefes*, Munich, 1956), London, 1959, pp.88 ff.

Christ and the Powers of Evil in Colossians

Rev. Roy Yates,
9 The Crescent,
Hipperholme,
Halifax, W. Yorks,
ENGLAND.

In the syncretistic philosophy that was propagated at Colossae the cosmic powers played an outstanding role, to the neglect of Christ. Paul's reply to the Colossian brethren in warning them against such speculation calls forth a unique development of Christian doctrine, especially in the field of Christology.

They are referred to collectively as 'principalities and powers' /1/, and as 'the elements of the world' /2/, and there is even a suggestion that there was a temptation to worship these angelic spirits /3/. In a world where the forces of tyranny were felt to be particularly strong, and men and women seemed to be overshadowed by a cosmic totalitarianism and a sense of fate, Paul uses the vocabulary of 'principalities and powers' to lay special emphasis on the pressures which are brought to bear on the individual by the various social, religious and political collectives in which his life is involved, with particular emphasis on the political life of man /4/. His message is that none of these powers or pressure groups can either come between the Christian and his Lord, or bring him to God /5/. In fact they are seen to be part of creation and therefore subject to Christ /6/, who by his cross and resurrection has shown them up for what they are /7/, and revealed their power to be counterfeit and hollow. The time of their final subjugation is in sight /8/, although for the present the conflict continues in the lives of Christians /9/.

Just as the 'principalities and powers' have their main point of reference in the corrupt pagan political institutions, so the 'elements of the world' have their main point of reference in the religious life of mankind outside Christ. In

Galatians /10/ and Colossians /11/ τὰ στοιχεῖα can mean either
elementary forms of religion, Jewish and Gentile, which have
been superseded by Christianity; or the elementary spirits
thought to be behind pre-Christian religion. Because of the
victory of Christ the elements are now seen to be 'weak and
beggarly' /12/, since the believer has died from the sphere of
their influence in his Baptism, and been raised with Christ to
be outside their control /13/. Once set free from this yoke
it would be ridiculous to return to bondage again by either
accepting the precepts of the Jewish Law /14/, or by
acknowledging the existence of anything other than illusion
behind the worship of paganism /15/.

     In Colossians the superiority and victory of Christ over
the powers is proclaimed by a number of daring metaphors, each
of which underlines the uniqueness of Christ and recalls the
Colossians to the significance of their Baptism.

     In Col.1:13 Paul uses the complete antithesis between
light and darkness /16/ to illustrate the contrast between their
former way of life, lived under the dominion of darkness, and
their present state of grace, in which they have redemption
and the forgiveness of their sins. Here 'darkness' is used
of that sinister sphere where the principalities and powers hold
sway /17/. The Colossians are assured that they have already
been translated out of this realm to the sphere of Christ's
influence, where the benefits of his victory and passion are
to be felt /18/. Paul associates this great transition with
the moment of Baptism, when the convert dies to his old way of
life, and obtains remission of sins.

     The significance of Baptism and the consequent dying and
rising with Christ is applied to the 'elements of the world'
in Col.2:8 and 2:20. It is in this section of the epistle
(2:6-3:4) that we learn most about the false teaching at
Colossae that caused so much distress to Paul. One of the
tenets of the heresy appears to have been that mere Baptism into
Christ was not enough for complete salvation, and that further
degrees of initiation were required. It seems that the
syncretists called their teaching 'philosophy' /19/, but Paul
characterises it as 'human tradition' /20/ and as 'empty
deceit' /21/. It entailed numerous regulations concerning food
and drink /22/, cultic observancies /23/, asceticism /24/, and
the worship of angels /25/. In this speculative system, which
has certain features in common with later Gnosticism, Christ

was given a place alongside the other angelic mediators. In
embracing this 'philosophy' the Colossians, who had been
delivered from the bondage of darkness, were now in danger of
falling into a worse state of bondage than before, and thereby
being robbed of their freedom in Christ. In particular there
was the danger of them lapsing into the legalistic practices of
Judaism, and thereby subjecting themselves unnecessarily to
the bondage and curse of the Law.

In this context, as in Galatians /26/, τα στοιχεĩα /27/
can mean either 'elementary teaching' of a rudimentary,
pre-Christian and even infantile kind, as preached by the
Colossian heretics; or the 'elemental spirits' which, according
to the false teaching, held sway over the world and were to be
placated by worship. The issue is not clear-cut, but a
reference to 'elemental spirits' seems to be called for by the
context, which also refers to the 'principalities and powers'
/28/ and the 'worship of angels' /29/, and draws a complete
contrast between Christ, the Pleroma of Divinity, and the
elemental spirits /30/.

It needs to be said that the Jewish Law of itself is not
evil /31/, but when misused it takes on certain of the
characteristics of the demonic, to become a stumbling block
rather than an aid to salvation. Christians are declared to
have passed from the influence of the Law and from the sphere
where the elemental spirits hold sway into the Kingdom of
Christ, where they have no power. This idea is underlined by
the Baptismal metaphors found in the context /32/, and
especially in Col.2:20, where the theme of dying and rising
with Christ is used with direct reference to the elements.
From now on Christians can live in the service of Christ with
immunity from their power and bondage. Once set free from
their yoke it would be a sign of spiritual retrogression to
return to the observance of the Law, and the consequent
placating of the elemental spirits, which are now shown up to
be 'weak and beggarly' /33/.

Paul's main attack on the position accorded to the
'principalities and powers' is to assert the superiority of
Christ by the two-fold right of creation and redemption. First
Christ is declared to be superior to the principalities and
powers because of his agency in their creation. The Christ-hymn
of Col.1:15-20 contains one of the most exalted statements of
the Person of Christ in the New Testament. W.D. Davies /34/

has suggested that speculation on the figure of Wisdom could
provide the background in which the thoughts expressed in the
hymn developed. Judaism had already ascribed to Wisdom a
pre-cosmic origin and a part in the creation of the world.
It was believed to be involved in both creation and redemption.
'The two-fold function is here transferred to Christ, who is
not only the agent in creation in a physical sense but also
the agent of the moral recreation of mankind' /35/. His
pre-existence is implied in such phrases as 'the first-born
of all creation' /36/, 'Before all things' /37/, and 'the
beginning, the first-born from the dead, that in everything he
might be pre-eminent' /38/. The title πρωτοτοκος πασησ κτισεως
/39/ in particular underlines his uniqueness by which he is
distinguished from all creation. As the firstborn he stands
over against creation as Lord /40/. He is not only infinitely
superior but different in kind from the host of lesser
mediators listed in Col.1:16, in whom the Colossians were
tempted to put their trust. They were all created 'in him' /41/,
'through him and for him' /42/ and 'in him all things hold
together' /43/. It is asserted that creation finds its goal
in Christ alone, and that the principalities and powers, as
created beings, are also subject to the Lordship of Christ.
How then can there be any possible grounds for worshipping or
placating such inferior beings when there is access to God
through Christ himself, who is the Pleroma of Divinity /44/?

Secondly the superiority of Christ over the principalities
and powers is revealed by his work of Redemption on the cross.
It is illustrated in dramatic terms in Col.2:14-15. This is a
difficult passage fraught with problems of grammar and
interpretation. Again in a Baptismal context the contrast is
drawn between what Christians were and what they now are in
Christ. He has wiped the slate clean to give them a fresh
start, cancelling the bondage of their past by his death. All
our sins are represented by a χειρόγραφον /45/, an 'IOU' with
all its legal demands /46/, which we were unable to discharge
ourselves, and the outcome of which would be judgement and
death. Christ himself has discharged this debt by his own
death. He has 'taken it out of the way', 'blotted it out' /47/,
and 'nailed it to the cross' /48/. For the sake of Christ God
has forgiven all our sins.

Paul now continues the message of Christ's triumph in 2:15
as he addresses it to the principalities and powers. The
interpretation of the verse depends on the subject of the

sentence, and on the force of the participle ἀπεκδυσάμενος. Grammatically there is no indication of a change of subject from v.13 to v.15, so it could be held that God is the subject of the whole section, but it is also possible to suppose a change of subject from God to Christ somewhere in v.14, and thus to take Christ as the subject of v.15 /49/. The Authorised Version translates ἀπεκδυσάμενος as 'spoiled', interpreting the participle as a middle with an active sense /50/. But it is questionable whether this verb could be so used in the middle voice /51/. In the active it means 'to undress', but here it is middle, and that normally means 'to undress oneself', or 'to divest oneself'. The question now faces us: of what did he divest himself? The Latin Fathers /52/ favoured the insertion of τὴν σάρκα or τὸ σῶμα. J.A.T. Robinson, following the R.V. margin, tries to revive this interpretation, arguing that, 'It is through the σάρξ that death and its forces have control over human nature. The dying Jesus, like a king, divests Himself of that flesh, the tool and medium of their power, and thereby exposes them to ridicule for their Pyrrhic victory' /53/. Linguistically there is more to be said for following the rendering of the Greek Fathers /54/, 'Having stripped off and put away the powers of evil'. J.B. Lightfoot /55/ thus comments, 'The powers of evil, which had clung like a Nessus robe about his humanity, were torn off and cast aside for ever'. The principalities and powers are thus exposed for what they are. They are held up to public ridicule /56/, and, deprived of their power, they are led as a victorious general displays his captives and trophies in a triumphal procession /57/. Their power and dominion is shown up to be counterfeit and hollow; a cosmic confidence trick which collapses like a house of cards when exposed. There is now no reason why the Colossians should continue to live as though they were still subject to them, and hide-bound by their rules and regulations. In fact when the Christian acknowledges the implications of the Lordship of Christ in relation to his own life /58/, and in relation to the cosmos /59/, he is released from allegiance to any other force or power and becomes free to live life in the service of Christ. This freedom of the Christian man is one of the unassailable results of Baptism into Christ and his Church.

These references from Colossians give us ample illustration of Paul's teaching on the powers of evil; and of how forces which of themselves are good, like the Law or the society life of man, can become so perverted by misuse that they

become an influence for evil rather than good. The
'principalities and powers' and the 'elements of the world'
are 'symbolic representatives of an aspect of human
existence' /60/ which, through the corruption of human sin,
appear to assume personal and demonic proportions. The
witness of Colossians is that these powers are a part of
God's creation and therefore subject to the Lordship of
Christ, who by his victorious death on the cross has exposed
their weakness, and shown that Christians need no longer live
under their fear or dominion.

NOTES

/1/   Col.1:16, 2:10, 2:14f.
/2/   Col.2:8, 2:10.
/3/   Col.2:18.
/4/   Rom.13:1ff; I Cor.2:6-8.
/5/   Rom.8:38f.
/6/   Col.1:16.
/7/   Col.2:20, 2:14f; Eph.1:21.
/8/   Eph.3:10; I Cor.15:24.
/9/   Eph.6:12.
/10/   Gal.4:3, 4:9.
/11/   Col.2:8, 2:20.
/12/   Gal.3:9.
/13/   Col.2:20, 3:1.
/14/   Gal.4:1-11.
/15/   Col.2:8, 2:20.
/16/   Cf. Lk.22:52; Jn.1:4f, 3:19ff, 8:12, 11:9f, 13:35f,
Acts 26:18; Eph.2:2; I Pet.2:9.
/17/   T.K. Abbott *The Epistles to the Ephesians and to the
Colossians*. (Edinburgh, 1897) p.98 'σκότος here is not to
be regarded as personified'.
/18/   F.F. Bruce *Commentary on the Epistles to the Ephesians
and the Colossians*. With E.K. Simpson. (London, 1957) p.189
'An example of truly realized eschatology'.
/19/   Col.2:8.
/20/   Col.2:8.
/21/   Col.2:8.
/22/   Col.2:16, 2:21.
/23/   Col.2:16.
/24/   Col.2:23.
/25/   Col.2:18.

/26/ Gal.4:3, 4:9.
/27/ Basically στοιχεῖα seems to mean 'the component parts of
a series', hence 'the letters of the alphabet', 'the elementary
ABC', 'elementary teaching', 'the elements of which the universe
is composed', and 'elemental spirits'. See G. Delling *TWNT*.
Vol.VIII pp.670-82 for the use of στοιχεῖα outside the N.T.;
and W.F. Arndt and F.W. Gingrich *A Greek-English Lexicon of
the New Testament and other Early Christian Literature*.
(Chicago, 1957) p.776 for its use in the N.T.
/28/ Col.2:9, 2:14f.
/29/ Col.2:18.
/30/ Cf. Col.1:19, 2:9. The Pleroma of Divinity is in
Christ in bodily form, and not in the ethereal elemental
spirits. It seems that 'Pleroma' was a word used in the
false teaching in a sense not unlike its later Gnostic meaning,
and that Paul adopts this catchword of theirs, infuses it
with his own high view of the Person of Christ, and uses it
to show the supreme and exalted position of Christ which was
being challenged by the heretical teaching.
/31/ C.E.B. Cranfield 'St. Paul and the Law'. *SJT* 17 (1964)
pp.63ff argues that in Gal.4:3 and 4:9 Paul is not referring
to the Law itself, but to the legalistic misuse of it. But
this does not alter the fact that there ought to be no reason
for a Gentile convert to observe its precepts.
/32/ Circumcision - 2:11, 2:13; Dying and rising with Christ -
2:12f, 2:20, 3:1ff; Cancellation of the bond ; 2:14.
/33/ Gal.3:9.
/34/ *Paul and Rabbinic Judaism*. (London, SPCK, 2nd Edn., 1955)
pp.150ff. Also C.F. Burney 'Christ as the ΑΡΧΗ of Creation'
JTS 27 (1926) 160-77.
/35/ W.D. Davies *op.cit.* p.152.
/36/ Col.1:15b.
/37/ Col.1:17a.
/38/ Col.1:18a.
/39/ N. Turner *Grammatical Insights into the New Testament*.
(Edinburgh, 1965) pp.122f. In the context of the hymn
πρωτότοκος is capable of two interpretations: i) to translate
as a time metaphor alluding to Christ's primacy over the
created world 'begotten before any created thing'; ii) to take
'first-born' in the sense of 'supreme', 'supreme over all
creation'. Both are appropriate to Christ. He is the first
in rank over all created things, and he was begotten before
all created things.
/40/ Col.1:16.
/41/ Col.1:16.

/42/ Col.1:16.

/43/ Col.1:17.

/44/ Col.1:19, 2:9.

/45/ A hand-written document of any kind, but used almost
exclusively of an autographed bond of obligation. Cf. Philemon
19. J.A.T. Robinson *The Body*. (London, 1952) p.43 n.1
describes it as 'our written agreement to keep the law, our
certificate of debt to it'.

/46/ The dative τοις δόγμασιν in 2:14 is a cause of difficulty.
J.A.T. Robinson *op.cit.* p.43 n.1 treats the dative as implied
in the action of the verb 'to subscribe to' (behind χειρόγραφον)
our subscription to the ordinances'. F.F. Bruce *op.cit.*
p.237 n.58 takes it as a dative of accompaniment, 'the bond,
decrees and all'.

/47/ 'Smeared out' or 'obliterated', as writing on wax was
smoothed away.

/48/ There seems to be no evidence for the alleged custom of
cancelling a bond by piercing it with a nail, or that the bond
was cancelled by crossing it out with the Greek letter Chi(X).
The metaphor is most probably a dramatic reference to the
forgiveness that resulted from Christ's death on the cross.

/49/ J.B. Lightfoot *Saint Paul's Epistles to the Colossians
and to Philemon*. (London, 2nd. Edn. 1876) p.185. N. Turner/
J.H. Moulton *A Grammar of New Testament Greek*. Vol.III
(Syntax), (Edinburgh, 1963) p.55.

/50/ F. Blass and A. Debrunner *A Greek Grammar of the New
Testament and other Early Christian Literature*. (Cambridge,
1961) 361:1.

/51/ C.F.D. Moule *The Epistles to the Colossians and to
Philemon*. (Cambridge, 1957) p.101.

/52/ See J.B. Lightfoot *op.cit.* p.190.

/53/ *op.cit.* p.41.

/54/ See J.B. Lightfoot *op.cit.* p.190. Also the rendering of
the R.V.

/55/ *op.cit.* p.190.

/56/ δειγματίζω - H. Schlier TWNT. Vol.II p.31 'to make a
public exhibition'. έν παρρησία - 'boldly' not 'publicly'.

/57/ θριαμβεύω - G. Delling TWNT. Vol.III pp.159f 'to triumph
over, to lead in a triumphal procession'.

/58/ Col.2:14.

/59/ Col.2:15.

/60/ G.B. Caird *Paul's Letters From Prison* (Oxford, 1976) p.46.